M000251931

# WRITER'S CHOICE

## GRAMMAR AND COMPOSITION

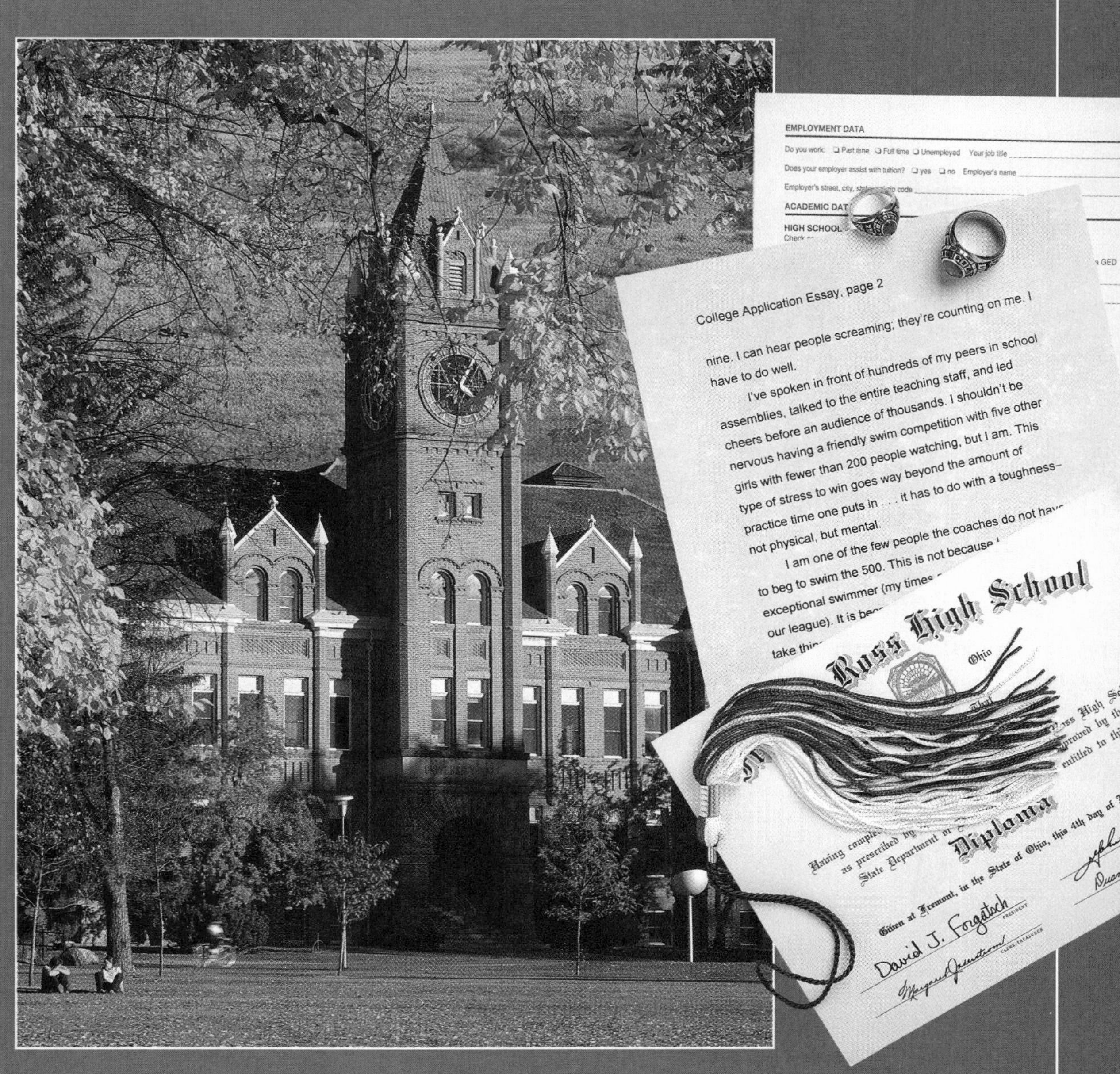
EMPLOYMENT DATA
Do you work: Part time Full time Unemployed Your job title
Does your employer assist with tuition? yes no Employer's name
ACADEMIC DATA
HIGH SCHOOL
GED
College Application Essay, page 2
nine. I can hear people screaming; they're counting on me. I
have to do well.
I've spoken in front of hundreds of my peers in school
assemblies, talked to the entire teaching staff, and led
cheers before an audience of thousands. I shouldn't be
nervous having a friendly swim competition with five other
girls with fewer than 200 people watching, but I am. This
type of stress to win goes way beyond the amount of
practice time one puts in . . . it has to do with a toughness–
not physical, but mental.
I am one of the few people the coaches do not have
to beg to swim the 500. This is not because
exceptional swimmer (my times
our league). It is
Ross High School
Ohio
Diploma
Given at Fremont, in the State of Ohio, this 4th day of
David J. Forgatch

## Student Advisory Board

# WRITER'S CHOICE

## GRAMMAR AND COMPOSITION

Andrew Wyeth, *Winter*, 1946


*Consulting Author for Composition*
**William Strong**

*Grammar Specialist*
**Mark Lester**

*Visual-Verbal Learning Specialists*
**Ligature, Inc.**



**GLENCOE**

McGraw-Hill

New York, New York  Columbus, Ohio  Mission Hills, California  Peoria, Illinois

## Consulting Author for Composition

**William Strong** is Professor of Secondary Education at Utah State University, Director of the Utah Writing Project, and a member of the National Writing Project Advisory Board. A nationally known authority in the teaching of composition, he is the author of many volumes, including, most recently, *Writing Incisively: Do-It-Yourself Prose* Surgery (McGraw-Hill, 1991).

As Consulting Author, Dr. Strong helped to develop the structure and content of Part 1: Composition. He reviewed and edited all Composition units. Dr. Strong also conceived and wrote Unit 8: Style Through Sentence Combining. He collaborated on *Sentence Combining Blackline Masters*, which accompanies *Writer's Choice*.

## Grammar Specialist

**Mark Lester** is Professor of English at Eastern Washington University. He formerly served as Chair of the Department of English as a Second Language, University of Hawaii. He is the author of *Grammar in the Classroom* (Macmillan, 1990) and of numerous professional books and articles.

As Grammar Specialist, Dr. Lester reviewed student's edition material from Part 2: Grammar, Usage, and Mechanics. He collaborated on *Grammar Reteaching Blackline Masters*, which accompanies *Writer's Choice*.

## Associate Consultant in Writing

**Bonnie S. Sunstein** is Associate Professor of English and Director of the Master of Arts in Teaching Program at Rivier College in Nashua, New Hampshire. Dr. Sunstein has taught extensively in New England in colleges and secondary schools, as well as in the New Hampshire Reading and Writing Program. She has published in the area of writing and teaching and is the coeditor of *Portfolio Portraits* (Heinemann, 1992) and the author of a forthcoming book about teachers and writing (Boynton/Cook).

As Associate Consultant in Writing, Dr. Sunstein established the theoretical framework for integrating writing portfolios into *Writer's Choice*.

## Contributing Writers

**Larry Beason** is Assistant Professor of English at Eastern Washington University. Dr. Beason is the writer of *Grammar Reteaching Blackline Masters*, which accompanies *Writer's Choice*.

**Willis L. Pitkin Jr.** is Professor of English at Utah State University. Dr. Pitkin is the writer of *Sentence Combining Blackline Masters*, which accompanies *Writer's Choice*.

## Visual-Verbal Learning Specialists

**Ligature, Inc.,** is an educational research and development company with offices in Chicago and Boston. Ligature is committed to developing educational materials that bring visual-verbal learning to the tradition of the written word.

As visual-verbal and curriculum specialists, Ligature collaborated on conceiving and implementing the pedagogy of *Writer's Choice*.

Cover, Tom Dietrich/
Tony Stone Images, (inset)
Aaron Haupt.



Printed in the United States of America.

Send all inquiries to:
Glencoe/McGraw-Hill
936 Eastwind Drive
Westerville, Ohio
43081

ISBN 0-02-635892-1
(Student Edition)
ISBN 0-02-635893-X
(Teacher's Wraparound Edition)

3 4 5 6 7 8 9 10 VH/MC 99 98 97 96

## Acknowledgments

Grateful acknowledgment is given authors, publishers, photographers, museums, and agents for permission to reprint the following copyrighted material. Every effort has been made to determine copyright owners. In the case of any omissions, the Publisher will be pleased to make suitable acknowledgments in future editions. Elements of Style (Third Edition), by William Strunk Jr. and E.B. White, Copyright ©1979, Macmillan Publishing Co., Inc. Earlier editions ©1959 and © copyright 1972 by Macmillan Publishing Co., Inc. Reprinted by permission of Macmillan Publishing Co. *Continued on page 870*

## Composition Advisers

The advisers reviewed Composition lesson prototypes. Their contributions were instrumental in the development of the Writing Process in Action lessons.

***Michael Angelotti***
*Head of Division of Teacher Education*
*College of Education*
*University of Oklahoma*

***Charles R. Duke***
*Dean of the College of Education and Human Services*
*Clarion University*

***Carol Booth Olson***
*Director*
*University of California, Irvine, Writing Project*

***Judith Summerfield***
*Associate Professor of English*
*Queens College, City University of New York*

***Denny Wolfe***
*Professor and Associate Dean*
*Darden College of Education*
*Old Dominion University*
*formerly Director, Tidewater Writing Project*

## Educational Reviewers

The reviewers read and commented upon manuscripts during the writing process. They also critiqued early drafts of graphic organizers and page layouts.

***Lenore Croudy***
*Flint Community School*
*Flint, Michigan*

***John A. Grant***
*St. Louis Public Schools*
*St. Louis, Missouri*

***Vicki Haker***
*Mead Junior High School*
*Mead, Washington*

***Frederick G. Johnson***
*Georgia Department of Education*
*Atlanta, Georgia*

***Sterling C. Jones Jr.***
*Detroit Public Schools*
*Detroit, Michigan*

***Barry Kincaid***
*Raytown School District*
*Kansas City, Missouri*

***Evelyn G. Lewis***
*Newark Public Schools*
*Newark, New Jersey*

***M. DeAnn Morris***
*Crescenta Valley High School*
*La Crescenta, California*

***Anita Moss***
*University of North Carolina*
*Charlotte, North Carolina*

***Ann S. O'Toole***
*Chesterfield County Schools*
*Richmond, Virginia*

***Suzanne Owens***
*Glendale High School*
*Glendale, California*

***Sally P. Pfeifer***
*Lewis and Clark High School*
*Spokane, Washington*

***Marie Rogers***
*Independence High School*
*Charlotte, North Carolina*

***Barbara Schubert***
*Santa Clara County Office of Education*
*San Jose, California*

***Ronnie Spilton***
*Chattahoochee High School*
*Alpharetta, Georgia*

***Robert Stolte***
*Huntington Beach High School*
*Huntington Beach, California*

## Student Advisory Board

The Student Advisory Board was formed in an effort to ensure student involvement in the development of Writer's Choice. The editors wish to thank members of the board for their enthusiasm and dedication to the project. The editors also wish to thank the many student writers whose models appear in this book.

Thanks are also due to Miami University of Ohio for help in the selection of models from student portfolios.

Contents

# Part 1 Composition

## UNIT 1 Personal Writing



**Grammar Link**

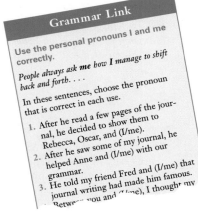

**Use the personal pronouns I and me correctly.**

*People always ask **me** how **I** manage to shift back and forth. . . .*

In these sentences, choose the pronoun that is correct in each use.

1. After he read a few pages of the journal, he decided to show them to Rebecca, Oscar, and (I/me).
2. After he saw some of my journal, he helped Anne and (I/me) with our grammar.
3. He told my friend Fred and (I/me) that journal writing had made him famous.

# UNIT 2 The Writing Process

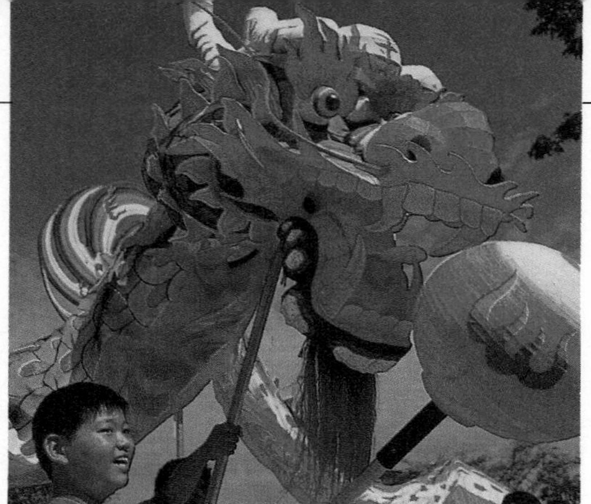

# UNIT 3 Descriptive Writing



### Grammar Link

**A pronoun must agree with its antecedent in number (singular or plural) and gender (masculine, feminine, or neuter).**

Use pronouns to replace key words and remind readers of ideas mentioned earlier.

*I did not remember a time when the* ***salt-lick*** *was as deserted as this. Always before* ***it*** *had been crowded with grantii, impala, kongoni, eland, waterbuck, and a dozen kinds of smaller animals.*

Write the following sentences adding an appropriate personal pronoun. Then underline the antecedent of that pronoun.

1. Many students decided to send ____ college applications to state colleges.
2. Teachers and guidance counselors

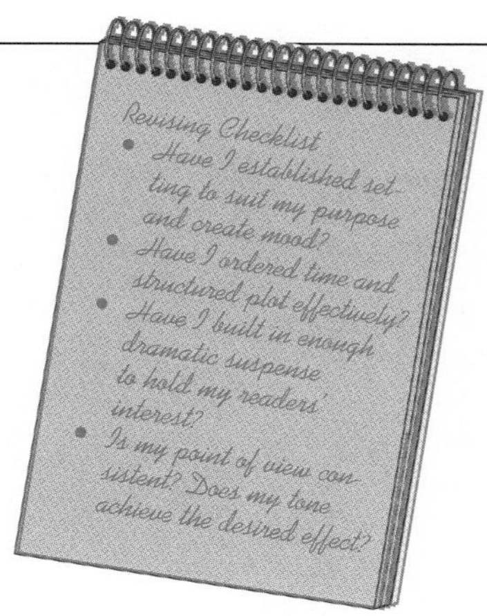
Revising Checklist
• Have I established setting to suit my purpose and create mood?
• Have I ordered time and structured plot effectively?
• Have I built in enough dramatic suspense to hold my readers' interest?
• Is my point of view consistent? Does my tone achieve the desired effect?

# UNIT 4 Narrative Writing

## UNIT 5 Expository Writing

**Expository Writing in the Real World**



Grammar Link

**Use simple sentences in the imperative to communicate instructions clearly.**

*Lift lid located on the left side of recorder. Press TIMER SET button.*

Rewrite each complex sentence as several simple sentences. Write imperative sentences when effective.

1. You should always read the manual before you try to operate any new

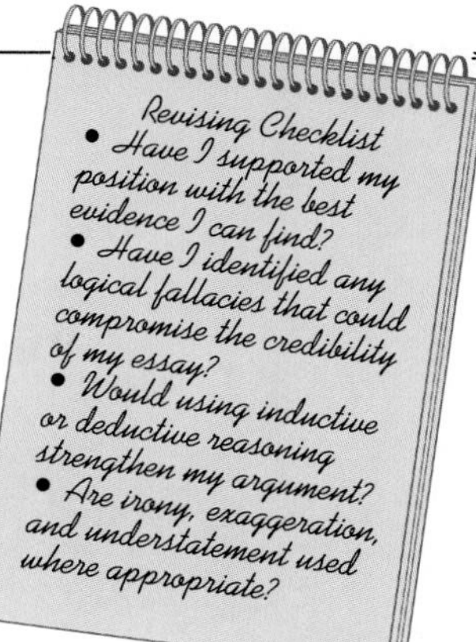
Revising Checklist
• Have I supported my position with the best evidence I can find?
• Have I identified any logical fallacies that could compromise the credibility of my essay?
• Would using inductive or deductive reasoning strengthen my argument?
• Are irony, exaggeration, and understatement used where appropriate?

UNIT 6

# Persuasive Writing

# UNIT 7 Research Paper Writing

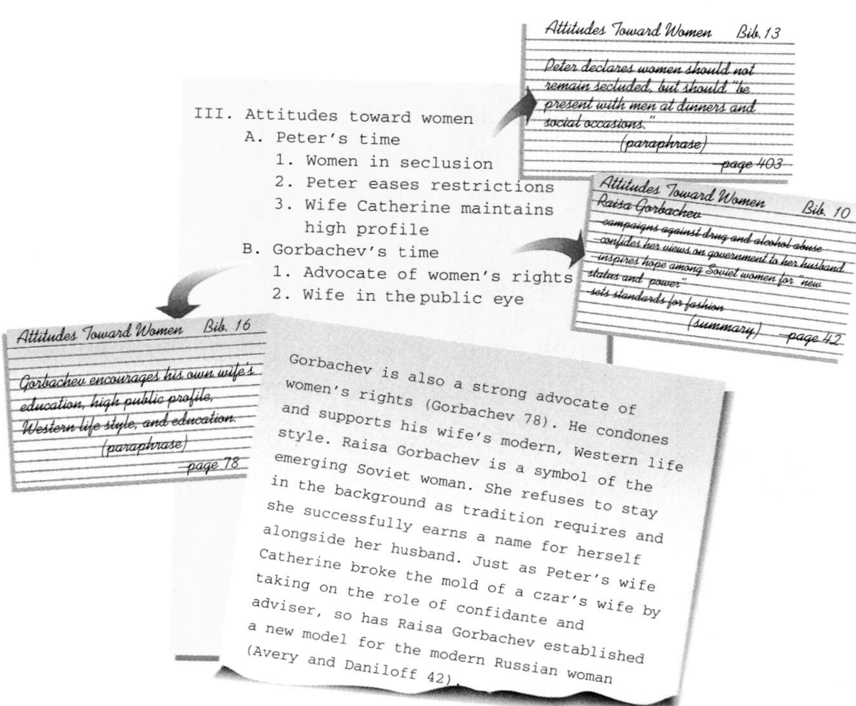

Attitudes Toward Women Bib. 13
Peter declares women should not remain secluded, but should "be present with men at dinners and social occasions."
(paraphrase)
page 403
III. Attitudes toward women
A. Peter's time
1. Women in seclusion
2. Peter eases restrictions
3. Wife Catherine maintains high profile
B. Gorbachev's time
1. Advocate of women's rights
2. Wife in the public eye
Attitudes Toward Women Bib. 10
Raisa Gorbachev
campaigns against drug and alcohol abuse
confides her views on government to her husband
inspires hope among Soviet women for "new status and power"
sets standards for fashion
(summary)
page 42
Attitudes Toward Women Bib. 16
Gorbachev encourages his own wife's education, high public profile, Western life style, and education.
(paraphrase)
page 78
Gorbachev is also a strong advocate of women's rights (Gorbachev 78). He condones and supports his wife's modern, Western life style. Raisa Gorbachev is a symbol of the emerging Soviet woman. She refuses to stay in the background as tradition requires and she successfully earns a name for herself alongside her husband. Just as Peter's wife Catherine broke the mold of a czar's wife by taking on the role of confidante and adviser, so has Raisa Gorbachev established a new model for the modern Russian woman (Avery and Daniloff 42).

UNIT 8

# Style Through Sentence Combining

**Skills and Applications**



**Exercise B: Exercise Matters**

**Directions** Combine each cluster of numbered items into one or more sentences. Combine clusters, if you wish.

**1.1** Regular exercise has many benefits.
**1.2** The benefits are physiological.
**1.3** These include reduced risk of heart disease.
**1.4** These include lowered blood pressure.
**1.5** These include lowered cholesterol levels.

**2.1** Particularly helpful are aerobic activities.
**2.2** They condition the heart to pump blood.
**2.3** The blood is oxygen-rich.
**2.4** They condition muscles to use oxygen.

**3.1** Many activities create a "training effect."
**3.2** These activities include jogging.
**3.3** These activities include swimming.
**3.4** These activities include cycling.
**3.5** These activities include aerobic dance.
**3.6** The "training effect" strengthens the heart.

**4.1** This training effect is developed over time.
**4.2** Exercise sessions last from fifteen to sixty minutes.
**4.3** Sessions occur from three to five days per week.

**5.1** The heart gradually becomes stronger.
**5.2** It actually pumps more blood per beat.
This decreases the heart rate while
decreases th

# UNIT 9 Troubleshooter

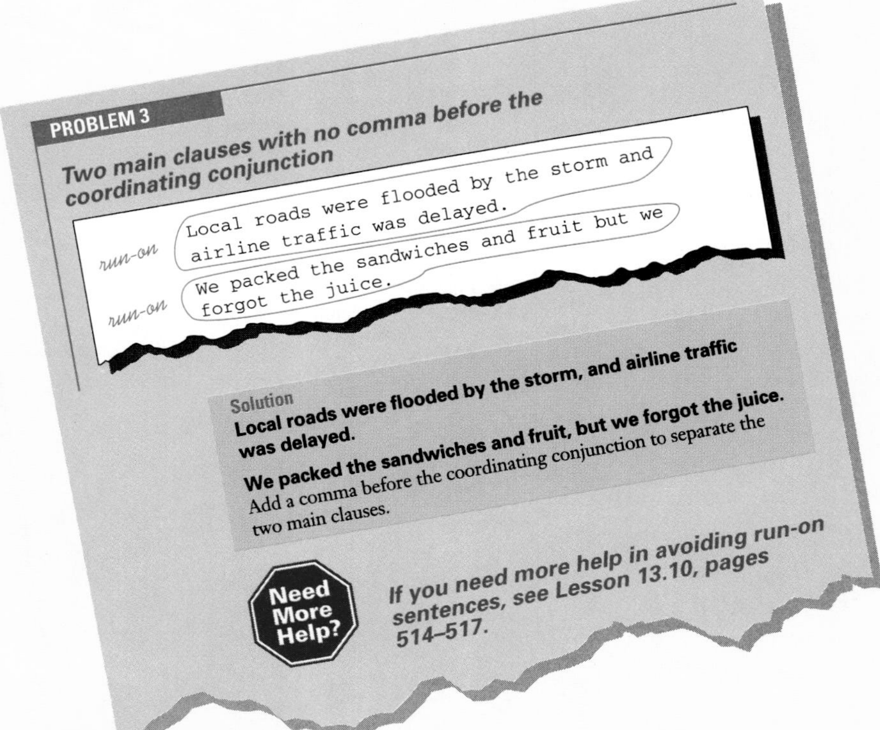

PROBLEM 3
Two main clauses with no comma before the coordinating conjunction
run-on
Local roads were flooded by the storm and airline traffic was delayed.
run-on
We packed the sandwiches and fruit but we forgot the juice.
Solution
Local roads were flooded by the storm, and airline traffic was delayed.
We packed the sandwiches and fruit, but we forgot the juice.
Add a comma before the coordinating conjunction to separate the two main clauses.
Need More Help?
If you need more help in avoiding run-on sentences, see Lesson 13.10, pages 514–517.

# Part 2 Grammar, Usage, and Mechanics

## UNIT 10 Parts of Speech 396



## UNIT 11 Parts of the Sentence 450

UNIT 12

## Phrases 476



UNIT 13

## Clauses and Sentence Structure 498



MAIN CLAUSE SUBORDINATE CLAUSE
Carousels look lively when they spin.
S V S V

MAIN CLAUSE
SUBORDINATE CLAUSE
Carousels that are spinning look lively.
S S V V

UNIT 14

## Diagraming Sentences 526

UNIT 15

# Verb Tenses, Voice, and Mood 536



UNIT 16

# Subject-Verb Agreement 564



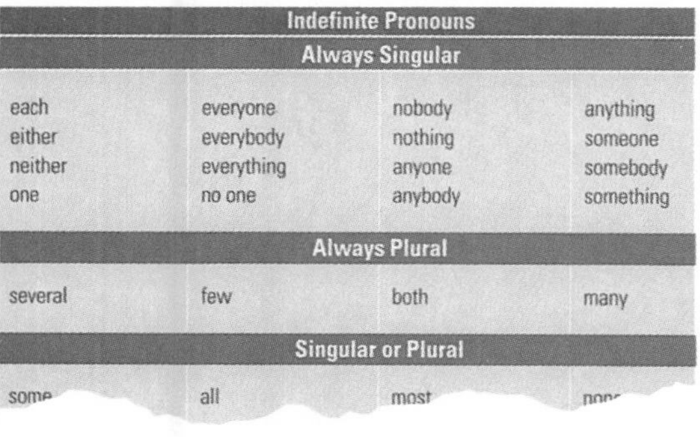

| Indefinite Pronouns | | | |
|---|---|---|---|
| **Always Singular** | | | |
| each<br>either<br>neither<br>one | everyone<br>everybody<br>everything<br>no one | nobody<br>nothing<br>anyone<br>anybody | anything<br>someone<br>somebody<br>something |
| **Always Plural** | | | |
| several | few | both | many |
| **Singular or Plural** | | | |
| some | all | most | non |

UNIT 17

## Using Pronouns Correctly 586



UNIT 18

## Using Modifiers Correctly 612

UNIT 19

## Usage Glossary

## UNIT 20 Capitalization 656



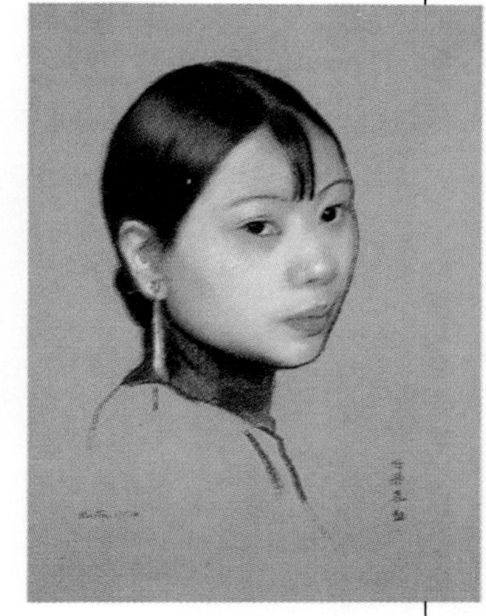

## UNIT 21 Punctuation, Abbreviations, and Numbers 674

# Part 3 Resources and Skills

Excuse me, could you direct me to the lift?
Do you mean the elevator?

## UNIT 22 The English Language 721

## UNIT 23 Library Resources 736

## UNIT 24 Using Dictionaries 744

# Literature Models

### Composition Models

Each literature selection is an extended example of the mode of writing taught in the unit.



### Skill Models

Excerpts from outstanding works of fiction and nonfiction exemplify specific writing skills.



### Language Models

Each Grammar Review uses excerpts to link grammar, usage, or mechanics to literature.

## Fine Art

Fine art—paintings, drawings, photos, and sculpture—is used to teach as well as to stimulate writing ideas.

# Case Studies: Writers at Work

Each case study focuses on a real writer working on a real-life writing project. Come on backstage!

**Li-Young Lee**

**Poet**
Memoirs, *A Poet Discovers His Life*
Page 4

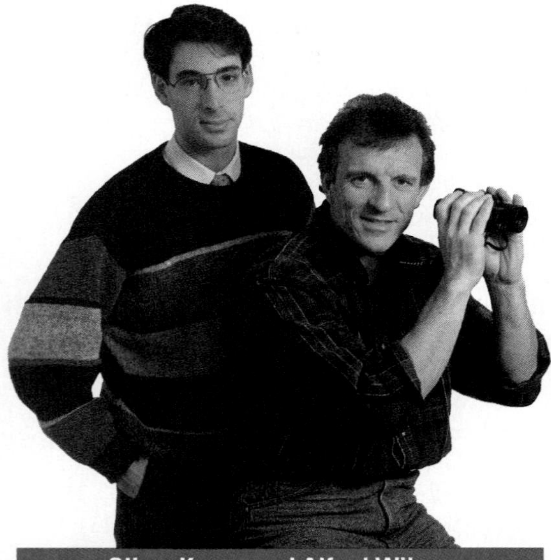

**Oliver Komar and Alfred Wilson**

**Entrepreneurs**
Business Plan, *Explaining the "Nature" of Their Business*
Page 202

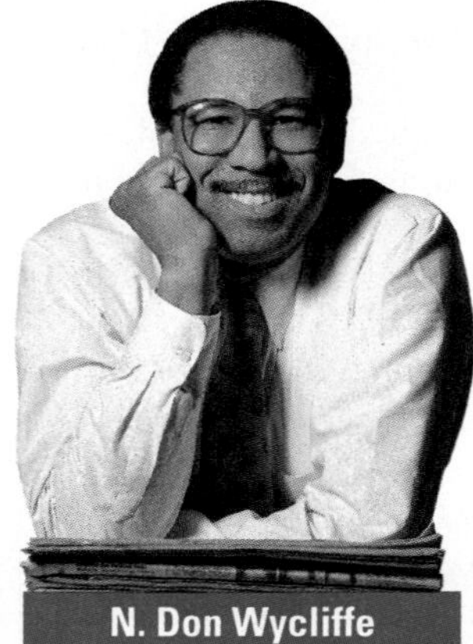

**N. Don Wycliffe**

**Editorial Page Editor**
Editorials, *Building the Editorial Page*
Page 54

**Ramona Austin**

**Curator**
Museum Exhibit, *Shedding Light on Rich Cultures*
Page 114

**Dave Barry**

**Humorist**
Satire, *Humorist Needles Readers to Give Blood*
Page 264

**Steve Fayer**

**Screenwriter**
Screenwriting, *A Prize-Winning Story*
Page 154

# Part 1

# Composition

# Part 1 Composition

UNIT 1

# Personal Writing

Composition

## Lessons

### Personal Writing in the Real World



### Skills and Applications



### *Writing About Literature*



### Writing Process in Action



### *Literature Model*



### Unit 1 Review

UNIT 1 PREVIEW

Case Study

# Personal Writing In the Real World

## A Poet Discovers His Life

**FOCUS: Writing about your life can help you discover aspects of yourself you may have forgotten or never realized.**

Li-Young Lee had accumulated a lifetime of experiences by the age of six, when he immigrated to the United States. His father, a former official in the Chinese government, was a political prisoner in Indonesia when Lee was born. After Lee's father escaped, the family fled, traveling through Singapore, Hong Kong, Macao, and Japan before settling in a Pennsylvania mill town.

Today Li-Young Lee is a poet and author whose works abound with memories from his early life—memories such as the fact that he didn't speak until he was three years old. "We never stayed in any place long enough for me to learn the language," Lee explains.

In 1990, the poet decided to write his life story and publish it in the form of prose memoirs. Lee's memoirs include his family's adventures but focus more on "plain, human things." For example: "On the boat ride from Singapore to Hong Kong we were being chased by the police. . . .Yet what I really want to concentrate on in my writing is this elaborate paper temple my father was making for my sister's eleventh birthday. My father wasn't important because he was a political prisoner but because he made this little temple for his children." Through writing these memoirs, Lee hopes "to come to terms both with my past and with my life here as an American."

*Poet and author Li-Young Lee*

# Prewriting

## REMEMBERING

To write memoirs, a writer must be able to re-create images and feelings. The simplest event may spark long-forgotten memories. The other day, for example, Lee was switching back and forth between English and Chinese as he spoke to his two-week-old niece. Suddenly Lee remembered "the feeling of being inside a language I didn't know."

"Boy, was that a terrible feeling as a child, to hear English being spoken and not understand it at all," Lee says. "But when I had that feeling visited on me again, it felt wonderful, rich, as if it must still be there lodged in me because suddenly it resurfaced."

To capture memories like this one for later exploration, Lee keeps a writer's journal. He says, "My journal helps me remember amazing things that I forgot."

> ***"Being an immigrant is complicated. . . . People tell you these stories about who you are. . . . I kept asking, 'What has this got to do with me?' Part of these memoirs is trying to come to terms with what these stories could really mean to me."***
>
> —Li-Young Lee, poet

*Lee (second child from left) and his family: the impressions upon a young boy become powerful remembrances.*

# Drafting

## COMPOSING

*For Lee, drafting in longhand, below, gives concrete expression to his ideas.*

Lee composed his memoirs by writing in longhand in English.

"I've tried a tape recorder, but it doesn't work for me," he says. "When I'm writing longhand, I may write six sentences. As I'm writing the sixth sentence, my peripheral vision will catch something in the first sentence. There's an echoing, a redoubling that doesn't happen when I speak."

Many writers like to organize their work in advance, but not Lee. When he began to write his memoirs, he had "a very firm sense of what the stories were, what the chronology was going to be. And writing it was just a tedium, just drudgery. I kept thinking, 'This is not why I became a writer.'"

The book became much more interesting to Lee when he abandoned his initial organization. Lee says his memoirs begin with "a very concrete, specific rendering of what happened and then midway through the book, the narrative begins to break down, to become self-reflective and self-questioning. That's the most fun for me."

# Editing

## REFINING

In refining his work, Lee often reads it aloud. "You have to be in touch with the spoken aspect of the language. When children talk, they pause in all the right places. When they write, they don't. I read my work to my wife, too, because I trust her judgment a lot. When she's bored, it's very clear."

Lee sometimes spends "endless hours" laboring over a sentence or passage. "It really is a matter of intense concentration and constant, steady, continuous work." It is work he loves. "I could spend my whole life trying to hear something new inside myself, to think something new, to write something new."

*Lee reads aloud part of his manuscript to his wife, Donna.*

# Reflecting

## LOOKING BACK

"Writing drags up images, memories, and stories that you hardly knew existed inside yourself," says Li-Young Lee. "When I look back at pages I've written a year ago, I'm shocked at what they show."

For example, says Lee, "As I looked back on my writing I realized that every time I described a scene of physical punishment, the voice in the memoir would switch and begin talking from the point of view of the parent and not the child. Now I could have read that in a book and it would not have rung true for me. But here my own writing is throwing it back at me."

Lee uses the image of a mirror to describe the kind of self-discovery he seeks when he looks back at what he has written: "I keep imagining that there must be inside of me one room where there's a mirror, and if I looked in it, it would reflect nothing I'd recognize, but it would be reflecting me after all. The difficulty in writing memoirs is trying to work through stories I've heard all my life to get to some place inside myself that I haven't heard about all my life, and to speak about these stories from that room."

# Responding to the Case Study

### 1. Discussion

**Discuss these questions about Li-Young Lee's writing.**

- How does Lee retrieve and save memories from his early childhood?
- Why does Lee prefer writing the first draft of his memoirs in longhand rather than using a computer or tape recorder?
- What is the challenge that Lee faces when he reads pages he wrote a year ago?
- Describe Lee's view of good writing and the process he uses to maintain the quality of his work.

### 2. Personal Writing

**Write a brief passage that can become part of your own memoirs.**

You might have a vivid memory of some holiday, such as the Chinese New Year celebration shown here. Other possible subjects include the following: a family tradition, a time something went wrong, or a frightening experience. Consider these methods of jogging your memory: jotting down notes in a quiet place; interviewing family members or friends who shared the experience with you; consulting your diary or journal; looking at pictures.

### Grammar Link

**Use commas in compound sentences to avoid run-on sentences.**

Use commas where necessary in the following sentences.

1. Lee is primarily known as a poet but he is a prose writer as well.
2. You may have read that in a book but no one has ever heard about it.
3. Lee began to write his life story and he wrote it in longhand.
4. It was not an easy task and it took longer than expected.
5. Lee lived in five countries before he was six but he knew only one language.

**See Lesson 21.6, page 682.**

LESSON

# 1.1 Personal Writing

# Writing as Self-Discovery

*Songwriter and singer Sting credits much of his success to personal writing. Most of his songs are based on his own memories, dreams or nightmares, and political opinions.*

A vivid nightmare inspired Sting to write the song "The Lazarus Heart." Advice given to him by a seafaring uncle ("Never board a ship unless you know where it's going") became the song "Rock Steady." Sting based the lyrics below on meetings he had with families of South American political prisoners during an Amnesty International tour.

*Literature Model*

Why are these women here dancing on their own?
Why is there sadness in their eyes?
Why are the soldiers here,
Their faces fixed like stone?
I can't see what it is they despise
They're dancing with the missing
They're dancing with the dead
They dance with the invisible ones
Their anguish is unsaid
They're dancing with their fathers
They're dancing with their sons
They're dancing with their husbands
They dance alone They dance alone

Sting, "They Dance Alone"

*What images help to give the lyrics their strength?*

## Write About Yourself

Although it isn't always easy to write about yourself, you may find that learning more about what makes you *you* can be one of the most satisfying aspects of personal writing. To find a topic to write about, choose a start-up technique. You may want to tap into thoughts and memories by freewriting—that is, writing anything that comes to mind. Or you may make a cluster like the one at the right to explore your thoughts. Choose a topic by asking: Which topic is meaningful to me? Which one reveals the most about who I am?

Personal Experiences
Standing up for a cause
Learning right from wrong
Daring to be different
Becoming more independent

As you explore topics, add more branches filled with additional thoughts and ideas. If the branch you have chosen doesn't seem to lead you anywhere, choose another branch. If a new idea comes to you, use it to start another cluster. Don't feel that you have to finish each cluster you start. These clusters are meant to free your mind, not to restrict it.

## Get Focused

Once you've chosen your topic, remember that good writers focus their subjects. Clear, specific language results from: naming particular actions, describing a setting, creating a mood. In the examples below, note how the general words simply frame the scene, while the specific language provides details that bring the scene to life.

Every morning as I walk to school, I see the same group of men sitting on a park bench and overhear their conversation. They make me think about how I will feel when I start to grow old.

There's "The Breakfast Club." I listen to them every morning as I walk to school. What's today's topic? Last night's game? Or the "good old days"? They make me think: "Are these my good old days?"

### Journal Writing

In your journal create a cluster to explore a major decision you've made within the past two years. Place the decision at the center of the cluster. Think about the decision. Add branches filled with any results of the decision, such as changes in your behavior or attitudes.

## Write for Yourself

Personal writing offers you a unique opportunity to make sense of your experiences and to think more deeply about your life. The model below shows how student writer Brenda Marshall shaped a simple memory (derived from the cluster on page 11) into an effective piece of personal writing. Marshall focused on the branch "Learning right from wrong." She visualized a classroom and then an idea came to her—an experience that had happened in French class.

*Note how the conversational tone of the writing pulls the reader into the story.*

*Note the writer's clear, specific language. She writes "began frantically looking for" instead of "couldn't find."*

*How might the writer revise this description of her actions to make the writing more focused?*

### *Student Model*

I was sitting in French class on a Monday morning, trying desperately to wake up. I was especially worried about my sleepiness because I'd have to take a test for which I was only moderately prepared. Fifteen minutes into the class, the teacher began frantically looking for the tests but couldn't find them. She asked if someone would go down to the copy room to try to find them. I, the dutiful student (and the only one who could find the copy room), volunteered.

I went down to the room and found the tests immediately. I took them and headed back upstairs. As I approached the third floor landing, though, I began to wonder. Why should I take the tests back? My class wouldn't want me to, and I didn't want to take this test either. If I told the teacher I couldn't find them, no one would know the difference, and the class would have an extra day to study.

As I turned to walk back to the copy room, though, a moral chain snapped at my neck and pulled me back toward the classroom. I knew that my guilt would be harsher than any failed test. I plodded into the classroom, a moral prisoner, but an unburdened soul.

Brenda Marshall, Newton North High School, Newton, Massachusetts

In addition to the clear, specific language that Marshall uses, note the natural flow of the language and the "real" voice of the writer. The essay sounds as if she is talking directly to the reader. Personal writing allows you to write for yourself, not necessarily with other people in mind. This intimate, informal quality makes personal writing special to both writer and reader.

# 1.1 Writing Activities

## Write a News Feature

You have been asked to write a one-page feature for a special edition of a news magazine that will focus on American high school students. The magazine editors want you to write about a particularly difficult decision you have had to make during your teenage years. Choose a topic you are comfortable with and that is meaningful to you.

- Use clear, specific language.
- Let your own voice come through.

**PURPOSE** To write about a decision you have had to make
**AUDIENCE** Readers of a news magazine
**LENGTH** 1 page

### Grammar Link

**Avoid the use of double negatives—two negative words in the same clause.**

*My class wouldn't want me to, and I did**n't** want to take this test **either** [not neither].*

Rewrite the sentences below, eliminating the double negatives.

1. Haven't you never thought about turning your dreams into music?
2. One British kindergarten teacher wasn't no one who merely thought about it.
3. The teacher, Gordon Sumner, wasn't well known to nobody at the time.
4. But when he transformed himself into Sting the superstar, there wasn't nobody who hadn't heard his music.

**See Lesson 18.6, page 622.**

## Cooperative Learning

In a small group brainstorm another title for the photograph on this page. Discuss the way the photograph makes you feel. Then individually write one paragraph about a personal experience that elicited the same feelings the photograph evokes. Take turns reading your paragraphs. Discuss within the group the effectiveness of each written memory. Does the language clearly describe the experience? Does it sound natural and believable?

George Fiske, *Half Dome and Glacier Point, Yosemite Valley*, 1880

LESSON

# 1.2 Personal Writing
# Using a Journal

*Keeping a journal of any kind helps you stay in touch with your feelings and makes your writing more natural and honest.*

A journal can be a place to talk to yourself about troubling or important issues. Best of all, you don't have to let anyone read what you've written. Forget about what you sound like. Don't let self-consciousness get in the way of recording your thoughts and ideas, although you may want to share your journal writing sometimes.

In the journal entry below Arthur Ashe shares his experiences as one of the first African American professional tennis players.

### *Literature Model*

August 13, 1973

People always ask me how I manage to shift back and forth between black and white societies, but in many ways they miss the point. It is just as much of a change for me to move between my Manhattan apartment and my parents' house out in the Virginia woods as it is for me to move between the black and white worlds. . . . Now my most comfortable world is the tennis tour, where there are so many races and nationalities thrown together that the natural shape and color of things is blurred. It will be a real emotional letdown for me when I finally must leave that society. The largest part of me is part of it.

Arthur Ashe, *Portrait in Motion*

## Choose Any Subject for a Journal

Sports writer Walter "Red" Smith once commented, "There's nothing to writing. All you do is sit down at a typewriter and open a vein." That is, you often have to reach deep within yourself to put your feelings into words, especially when you write in a journal.

Keep in mind, however, that you can use a journal to store a variety of information, from personal thoughts to more academic pursuits. You may want to use a reader-response journal to record your thoughts, impressions, and ideas as you read books for class or for pleasure. You can also keep a learning log to monitor your progress in school or in extracurricular activities that involve learning a skill. Or you might combine all this information into one very full notebook.

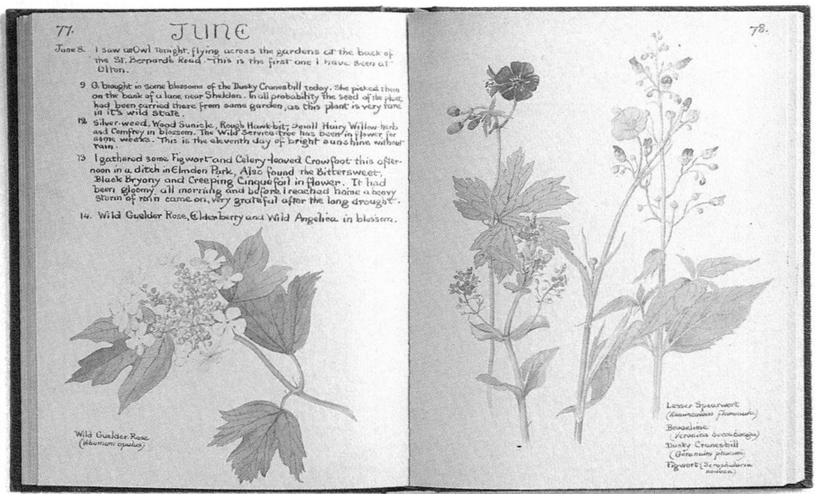


Edith Holden, *The Country Diary of an Edwardian Lady*, 1906

Use your journal as a tool for sharpening your awareness of yourself and the world around you. Record your writing and your thoughts freely in your journal without worrying about handwriting or punctuation. Doodle in your journal; draft a love letter; collect quotations; jot down story ideas; think of beginnings, middles, and ends to stories. Write down unusual pieces of conversation you overhear in a quiet study hall. Write everything that gets you thinking about people and their stories.

Think of your journal as a spacious room in which you store ideas, feelings, and thoughts you can't use immediately but don't want to throw away. When you have a writing assignment but no ideas, a character half-sketched but lacking specific detail, or fragments of ideas for a setting, you may have to go no further than your journal to find what you need to make your writing come to life.

### Journal Writing

Suppose your personal journal is found by historians 200 years from now. What will the contents reveal about you personally other than that you were a teenager living in the 1990s? Write down a short list of details about yourself that would be informative to future readers.

## Make Time to Write

People differ when it comes to when and where to write in their journals. Some prefer writing in the morning when their minds are clear and the day is fresh. Other people write best at night, when they can review the day's events. Whenever possible, carry your journal with you so that you can jot down your immediate impressions if something unexpected happens. Be careful where you leave your journal; you may not want others to see it.

You don't need much time to record your on-the-spot impressions. You don't even have to write in complete sentences. Quickly describe your surroundings: What do you see and hear and touch? How do you feel? If tastes or smells are important to the incident, include them too. Later you can use this material for other writing projects. Read these professional writers' views on journal writing.

> My memory is certainly in my hands. I can remember things only if I have a pencil and I can write with it and play with it. I think your hand concentrates for you. I don't know why it should be so.
>
> Rebecca West
> American novelist

> In this diary I want to talk to myself and let things come as they will. What is it I wish to talk about? Everything that strikes me or that gives me cause for thought.
>
> Fyodor Dostoyevsky
> Russian novelist

> I never travel without my diary. One should always have something sensational to read in the train.
>
> Oscar Wilde
> British playwright

> I keep notes and journals only because I write a great deal, and the habit of writing helps me to manage, annotate, stow away conveniently the references I may need later.
>
> Katherine Anne Porter
> American novelist

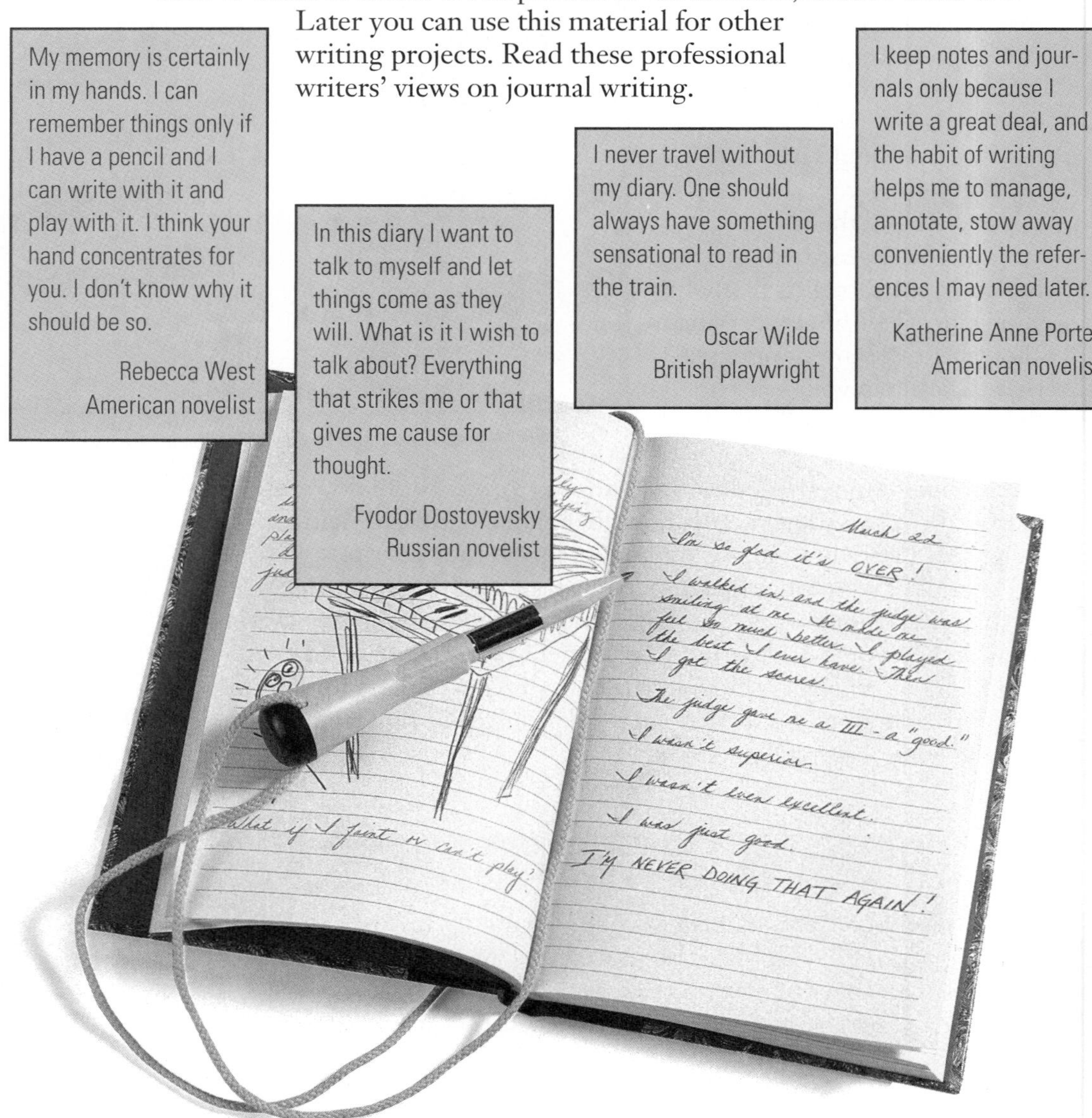

# 1.2 Writing Activities

## Write a Contract

One of the most difficult aspects of journal writing is staying with it. Try writing a contract that will seal your commitment to writing regularly in your journal.

Create a journal, or review the one that you've been keeping. Then write a contract spelling out your goals: the kinds of information you hope to record and the minimum number of entries or amount of time you will spend per week. Be realistic in your goals. Sign and date your contract.

- Use your journal to store information for future writing.
- Record your impressions when you can remember them best.

Gustav Klimt, *Portrait of Maria Beer-Monti, c.* 1915

**PURPOSE** To make a contract with yourself
**AUDIENCE** Yourself
**LENGTH** 1 page

## Cross-Curricular: Art

Imagine that you are looking at artist Gustav Klimt's painting at an exhibit. Write about it as a journal entry. Describe it in enough detail to remember what it looked like. Then write your overall impression of it.

### Grammar Link

**Use the personal pronouns *I* and *me* correctly.**

*People always ask* ***me*** *how* ***I*** *manage to shift back and forth. . . .*

Write each sentence, using the correct pronoun.

1. After he read a few pages of the journal, he decided to show them to Rebecca, Oscar, and (I/me).
2. After he saw some of my journal, he helped Anne and (I/me) with our grammar.
3. He told my friend Fred and (I/me) that journal writing had made him famous.
4. Between you and (I/me), I thought my journal was pretty good.
5. Everyone at the writing conference questioned Katherine and (I/me).

**See Lesson 10.2, page 403.**

LESSON

# 1.3

## Personal Writing
# Learning with a Learning Log

*Keeping a log of the skills you learn both in and out of school can help you remember individual details. Days, months, even years later, you can track your progress and review important names, dates, and places.*

Heather Mike, a Michigan high school student, like the students in the photograph shown here, had a learning experience she wanted to record: working as part of a research team studying the diamondback terrapin, a type of North American turtle. In the excerpt below, notice how writing about her learning experience helped Heather to focus her plans for the future.

### Student Model

For as long as I can remember I have dreamt of becoming a marine zoologist and studying dolphins or whales, preferably in the wild. My experience with the diamondback terrapins only strengthened my determination to follow this dream. I loved working in the field—the satisfaction of catching five turtles after netting a difficult, deep hole, the sense of accomplishment when you see the graphs and charts that resulted from hours of measuring, and the peaceful feeling you get when you release the terrapins and they swim off into the marsh.

Heather Mike, Waverly High School, Lansing, Michigan

*In what way does this learning log entry make Heather's dreams more concrete?*

## Write to Think

On the previous page, Heather described how her learning experience affected her long-range goals, but writing about what you learn can also help you right now. A learning log, a notebook for writing about what you learn in or out of school, can improve your understanding of new information. When you write about what you have learned, you process the information more deeply by moving it into your long-term memory. You may have noticed how much easier it is to understand and remember something after you've put it into your own words.

A learning log is more than just a warehouse for facts, however. You may want to use your learning log to summarize the questions you have about complex chemistry notes or the problems you encounter in a lifesaving class. A learning log enables you to set goals and record the results.

Organize your learning log in the way you find most helpful. You don't have to use full sentences. Just be sure you cover key points. You can abbreviate as much as you like, as long as you can later read and make sense of what you have written. In the model below, the student has chosen to create a double-entry format for his learning log. He has put his notes on one side of the page and his thoughts about his notes on the other side.

*Dates and titles organize the information within the log.*

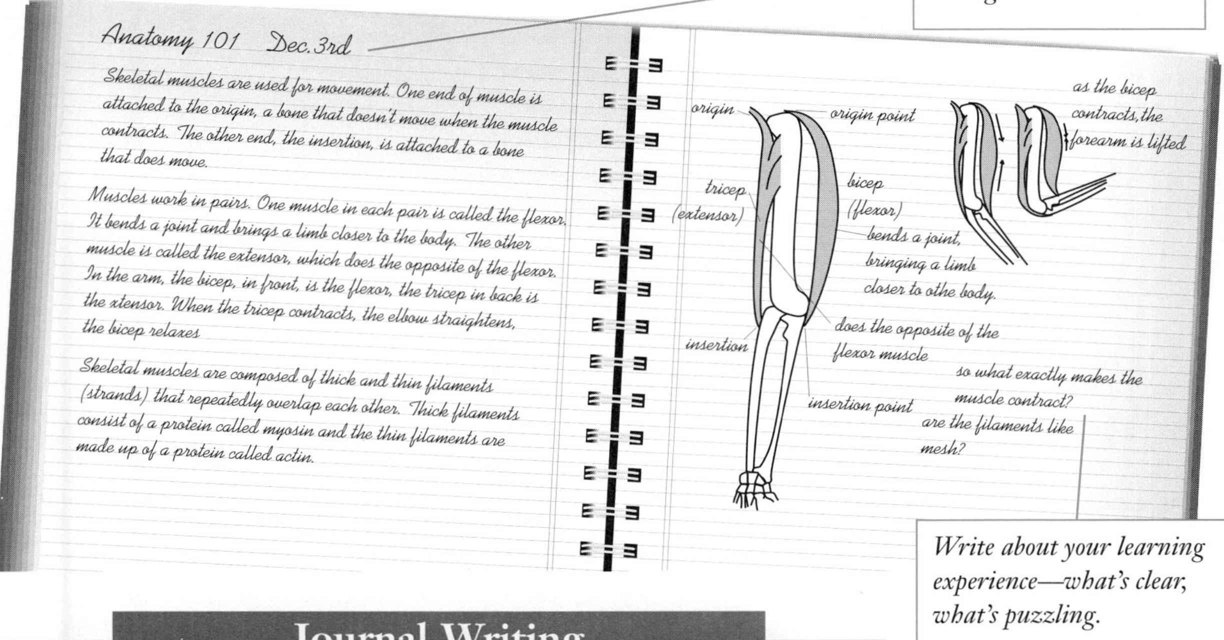


*Write about your learning experience—what's clear, what's puzzling.*

### Journal Writing

Start a learning log by listing subjects or activities you might want to track. Jot down a few notes about why you chose these subjects or activities for inclusion in your learning log.

## Keep It Going

When the assignments begin to pile up, when time starts to grow short, and when the pressure begins to mount, you may be tempted to abandon your learning log. However, in the long run an up-to-date learning log will save you time. For example, when you want to review material in preparation for a test, your learning log will quickly remind you of concepts you found difficult.

Just as you may write in your journal at a specific time every day, try to set aside a specific time to write in your learning log. A study hall may be a good time to review your class notes, or you may want to write in your learning log immediately before you go to sleep at night, as this may help you to recall the material more easily in the morning. Writing at the same time each day will help you establish a routine. After a while, adding to your log will become a natural part of your week.

The longer you maintain your log, the more important your log will become to you. Your experience with a learning log will help you get used to keeping track of important tasks, such as completing college applications, studying for tests and quizzes, and preparing reports or research papers. Use the tricks listed in the following chart to keep your learning log going.

**Learning Log Tricks**

- Date and label each learning log entry.
- Highlight important information.
- Use lists and charts to organize facts.
- Leave space for adding to or revising your log.
- Use abbreviations when possible.
- Review your log to make sure you haven't made mistakes or forgotten to include important information. (This review will also help you remember what you've written.)

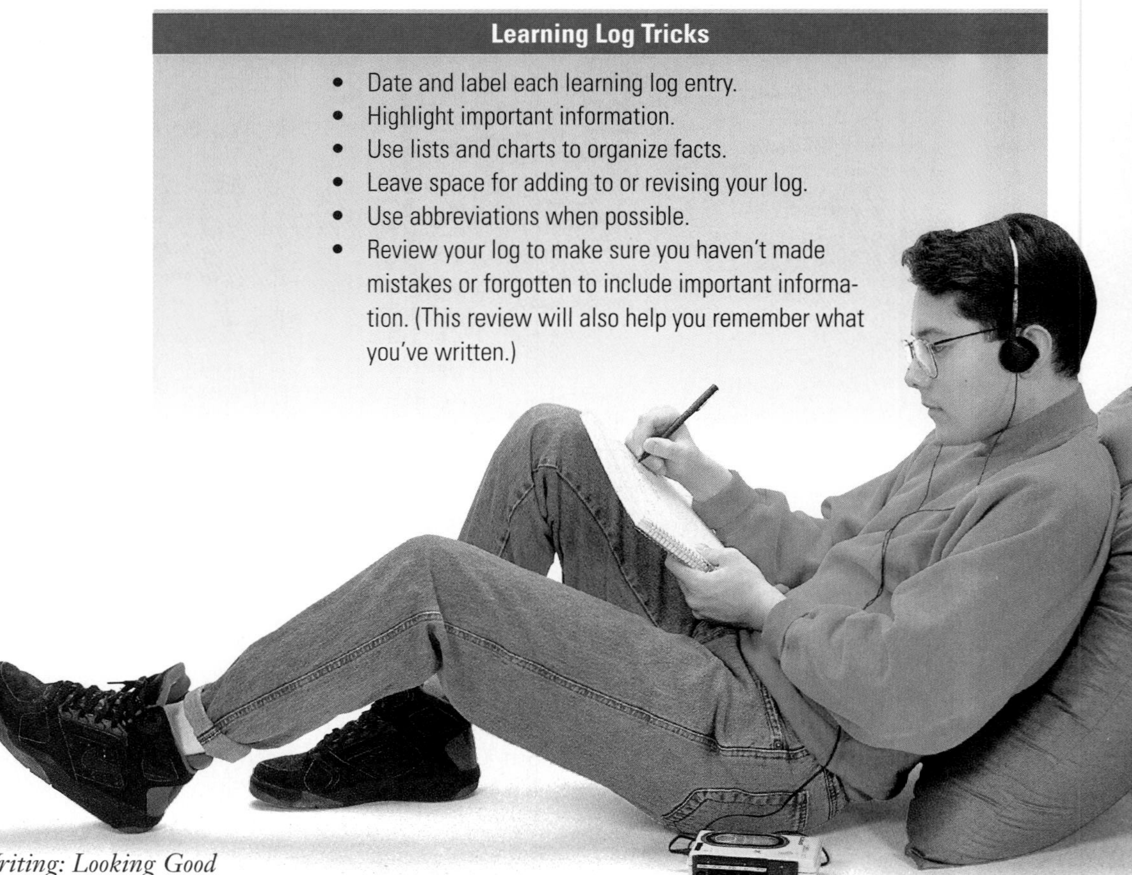

# 1.3 Writing Activities

## Write a Summary

Keep a learning log that monitors your progress in English class over one week. Record any goals or personal challenges you would like to set for yourself. Include what you learn on your own when reading and completing assignments, as well as what you learn in class. Keep track of questions and problems.

At the end of the week, write a summary of your progress. What were the high points of the week? The low points? Did you meet your goals? You may want to share your summary with a guidance counselor, your teacher, a parent, or another adult to get feedback on your progress.

- Organize your learning log in the way you find most helpful.
- Be sure to cover key points.
- Use any method that works for you to keep your learning log going.

**PURPOSE** To monitor your learning by writing in a learning log; to summarize progress
**AUDIENCE** Yourself
**LENGTH** 5–6 pages

**COMPUTER OPTION**

You can use your personal computer as an electronic learning log. Create files for each of your classes. You can use these files to paraphrase and review notes before tests, keep track of assignments, record questions and special problems, and monitor your progress. When you want to write about a particular entry or share your progress with a teacher, print a hard copy of that entry for reference.

## Cooperative Learning

Use your learning logs in cooperative study groups. Review material by sharing your learning log with a group of three or four students. You may want to share your notes, the ways you've summarized the material, study methods you've developed, and the questions you've had about your learning.

As you review your notes and your learning log entries, designate a recorder for the group who can summarize the questions the group members have about the material. Review these questions and try to answer them. Keep these questions and use them when you study for exams. You may want to request input from your teacher.

**Grammar Link**

**Use appositives to present definitions.**

*One end of the muscle is attached to the origin, **a bone that doesn't move when the muscle contracts.***

Expand the following sentences by adding an appositive to define a noun.

1. The hospital's chief surgeon wanted to remove Tim's appendix.
2. The consulting anesthetist agreed with his decision.
3. Tim has a long-standing phobia of hospitals.
4. Recently a well-known philanthropist died on the operating table.
5. Tim hopes that the surgeon will make a small incision.

**See Lesson 12.2, pages 479–480.**

LESSON 1.4

# Personal Writing
# Writing a College Application Essay

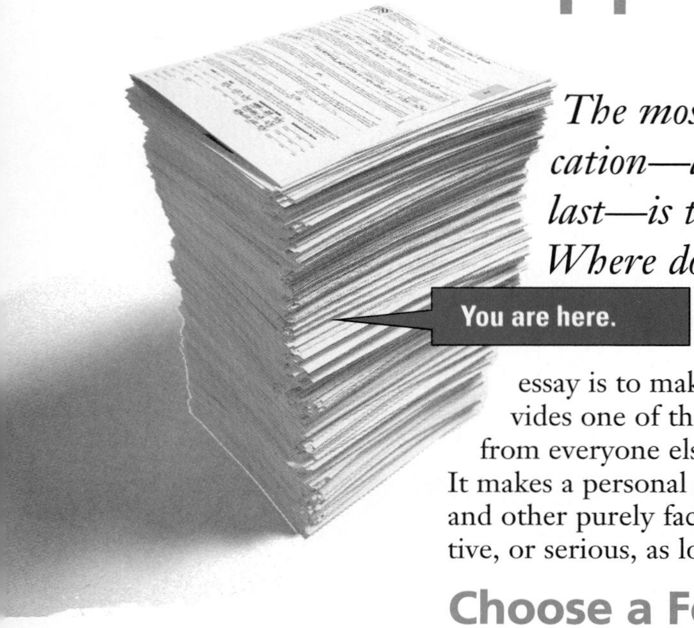

*The most challenging section of a college application—and the section most students leave till last—is that section called "Personal Essay." Where do you begin?*

You are here.

Your challenge in writing a college application essay is to make yours stand out from the others. The essay provides one of the best opportunities to show that you're different from everyone else (and perhaps more worthy of college admission). It makes a personal statement in ways that test scores, school grades, and other purely factual data cannot. Your essay can be funny, imaginative, or serious, as long as it shows who you are—a unique individual.

## Choose a Focus

A college application includes fill-in-the-blanks, short-answer questions, and recommendations from others. However, it also includes a biographical essay which takes time to compose. You may be asked to analyze your talents, your goals, or your personal strengths and weaknesses. In addition, you have to do so concisely and in such a way that a stranger will not only get an idea of who you are but also feel confident that you will excel at the college or university to which you're applying. Where do you begin?

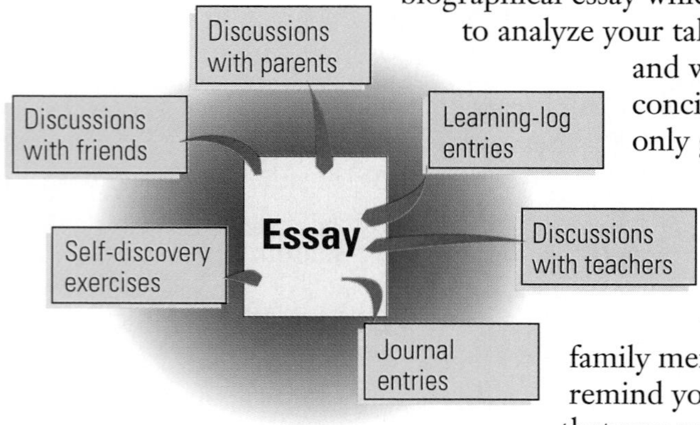

Discussions with parents
Discussions with friends
Learning-log entries
Essay
Self-discovery exercises
Discussions with teachers
Journal entries

One starting point is talking with the people who know you the best—teachers, neighbors, family members—and ask them for ideas. They may remind you of unique experiences or character traits that you may be overlooking. Your journal or your learning log may also give you inspiration. If these possibilities don't excite you, why not try brainstorming or freewriting to generate ideas?

## Put It All Together

When choosing a topic, focus on an aspect of your life that you think will be interesting and memorable. Avoid topics that many others will choose, such as a summer job or vacation, unless you feel that your experience has special interest. Also avoid topics that show you in a negative light. Finally, while your essay can elaborate on a topic mentioned in another part of the application, do not simply repeat information.

Once you have chosen a focus, it's important to relax and write a good story about yourself. Instead of trying to persuade the college that you're great, show them who you are—what you care about, what makes you angry, what the important points in your life have been.

Begin drafting your essay by deciding which details and examples you'll include. Specific details will make your essay more interesting. Use brainstorming, freewriting, or clustering to generate these details.

Like any good story, your essay should be organized. A good way to begin organizing is to brainstorm. The brainstorming sample below is a creative response to the request: "Tell us more about yourself."

*Some people describe me as*
*— always in a hurry*
*— gentle, loving*
*— committed to schoolwork, committed to music*
*— a music lover*

*Activities to include*
*— schoolwork: especially creative writing*
*— karate*
*— piano playing*

Once you develop an informal outline, you can begin drafting. Work on an introductory paragraph that not only states your topic but also captures the attention of the people likely to be reading your essay. Organize your essay into paragraphs that focus on a main idea, providing concrete details to support statements. Finally, create a closing that sums up your ideas and makes the reader remember you.

As you draft, think about the tone of your essay and the image you're presenting. Does the essay sound too negative? Too self-critical? Too boastful? Too pretentious? Remember the story analogy as you write. Your story should interest readers and also sound natural, honest, and positive.

### Journal Writing

List five personal strengths. Circle two strengths that might provide an appropriate focus for a college application. What details and examples can you think of to support your strengths?

## Look Your Best

After drafting your essay, revise it carefully. Consider these questions:

- Does this essay answer the question *and* tell a good story?
- Is it original and interesting?
- Does it sound like me?
- Is the opening engaging and the ending effective?

Put the finished essay aside for a day or two. Then read it aloud so that you hear what the essay will sound like to a stranger.

Carefully edit and proofread your essay before transferring it to the application. Be careful not to let others edit and correct your essay until it no longer sounds like you. If the essay is supposed to be a certain length, count the words. A neat and error-free application will make you look good. The student model below is an original, memorable essay.

*How does the element of mystery help to make this a memorable opening?*

*What makes this line more effective than writing, "I participate in a karate class after school"?*

### *Student Model*

Here she comes again. Just like always—running in, breathless, a stack of books in her arms. She throws the books on top of me and glides on to my bench, screeching to a stop in its center. Then she gently lays her hands in position on my keys, and sighs. "I really shouldn't be here," she tells me. "I have chem to study, and a creative writing paper, and eighty lines of Latin, and a watercolor, and . . ."

She begins to play. It's my favorite, the "Moonlight Sonata." It always reminds me of her—gentle and loving yet deeply passionate. Her fingers press tenderly at first as if my keys were ivory eggshells and ebony velvet. Then she is swept up in the tide of her own emotions and begins to play louder, stronger, faster, her fingers working furiously, faster and faster and then over. She caresses my keyboard, eyes closed, then gasps. "Oh no! It's 3:15! I'm going to be late to karate!"

She jumps and runs out the door without so much as a glance over her shoulder—but that's all right. She'll be here tomorrow. Maybe not at the same time, maybe with different books. But she'll be here. She told me that no matter how hard the courses get, no matter how smothering the work, no matter how little time, she could never give me up. It's wonderful to be loved.

Kimberly I. McCarthy, application to Brown University

# 1.4 Writing Activities

## Write an Essay

You are filling out a college application, and you have to answer one of the following questions or one of your own creation:

1. What is a memorable book you have read in the last year? Why is it memorable?
2. What do you wish to be doing with your life 10 years from now, and how can a college education help you to achieve that goal?
3. What teams, clubs, or organizations are you currently a member of and why are they important to you?
4. If you could have lived during any other period, which era would you choose? Why?

- Begin with a statement that your main idea is an answer to the question.
- Provide several examples, reasons, or details that support your idea.

Draft your essay and share it with a teacher, a parent, an employer, or another adult who knows you well. Revise your essay based on the comments.

**PURPOSE** To write an essay for a college application
**AUDIENCE** College admissions personnel
**LENGTH** 1 page

### COMPUTER OPTION

You can expect your college application essays to go through many, many drafts. Use the Copy function of your word-processing program to save your first draft. Then make a copy of it (either as a new file or on a new page of the existing file), and continue to work on it. Do the same with subsequent drafts, so that you'll always have a record of your initial ideas and the changes you've made.

### Grammar Link

**Use commas to separate three or more words, phrases, or clauses in a series.**

*Writers, teachers, and students get ideas for essays from discussions with friends, discussions with parents, and details in journal entries.*

Add commas to the following sentences where they are needed.

1. The campers looked forward to plenty of fresh air brisk walking and outdoor dining.
2. Neither Juan nor Bob nor Frieda expected to see any fleas ticks or mites.
3. The trip was to be one of pure enjoyment looking at scenery using the maps and taking photographs.
4. To leave the city behind say farewell to modern conveniences and hit the trail were what they wanted.
5. The weather forecast for the mountain area included dewey mornings hot days and cool nights.

**See Lesson 21.6, page 683.**

LESSON

# 1.5 Personal Writing

# Writing a Résumé

*A résumé is a condensed statement of your career objectives and the skills and experiences that you can bring to a job. The tone and organization of your résumé reveal as much about you as your words do.*

**Telephone for the Environment**
State's largest environmental group seeks bright, articulate callers to help p legislation for statewide RECYCLING. Good pay and raise opportunities. Evenings only. Call 555-1532.

**child care**
After-school program at the Mary Finn Elementary School seeks high school student to assist with arts and crafts projects and outdoor activities. Monday through Friday from 3 to 6 P.M. Call 555-8631.

**Internship Positions**
Local law firm offering two summer internship positions to high school students interested in the legal profession. Please send résumé and letter of interest to Frame and Associates, Attorneys at Law, 4 North Street, Southborough, MA 01771 by April 30.

Leaf through the help-wanted ads and you will find job openings in a range of fields. Hundreds of people may apply for one position. Each job applicant will usually submit a similar sheet of paper: a résumé.

## "Know Thyself"

Although a résumé is a professional document, you'll find that writing a résumé involves many of the tasks you use for other types of personal writing. Prewriting techniques such as clustering help you to explore writing topics, and these same techniques will help you to list your various jobs, skills, and interests.

Begin drafting your résumé by writing the easy information: your full name, your address, your telephone number. Then list your educational background, including the highest grade you've completed, the schools you've attended, and any academic awards you have received. Finally, freewrite, cluster, or brainstorm to generate all job-related experiences that come to mind, such as baby-sitting, delivering newspapers, summer jobs, volunteer work. Write down everything you can think of; later you can delete unnecessary information. If you've been a member of a club or held a leadership position, write this information down as well. Include organizations you've been involved with, such as the yearbook staff, student government, drama club, or chess team.

One way to collect ideas for your résumé is to list different ways you can complete the statement "I am . . . ." Each conclusion to this statement should display a positive attribute or accomplishment. The qualities that support your objective most strongly will become the core of your résumé. They will present an employer with a clear portrait of who you are and what you can do.

## Put the Pieces Together

Once you've listed your work experience, skills, and interests, decide which information should be included in your résumé. First, think about the kind of job you're seeking. Read over your list and circle anything that directly relates to that job. Don't worry if nothing seems to match at first. Being co-captain of the tennis team may not seem related to an office job, but it does show that you have had experience both as a team member and leader.

Remember that your résumé will always reveal a lot about your personality as well as your communications skills. It is crucial that you describe everything accurately and concisely. Clear wording and correct grammar will put you in a positive light. Keep these points in mind as you compare the following two résumé entries about working on a school newspaper.

```
I planned and wrote many articles for the paper. I once
talked with the mayor about an article on curfews. I
also spent a lot of time checking dates and names and
looking up information. I always got my articles in on
time.
```

```
Planned and wrote articles. Interviewed community
leaders and conducted research and fact checking. Set
schedules and met deadlines.
```

The first entry doesn't convey a tone that is appropriate to a résumé. First of all, it's not necessary to write in complete sentences. Moreover, the reader knows that *you* did these things, so beginning each statement with "I" is redundant. The second entry summarizes information, replaces "talked with" with "interviewed," eliminates unnecessary details, and sounds more professional.

### Journal Writing

Look through the employment ads in a newspaper. Select three or four ads that interest you, and describe the positions. Jot down experiences that make you a good candidate.

## Attract Attention

Although a résumé presents an individual picture, you can use a standard form to organize your information. The sample below shows one common format. You may want to make slight stylistic revisions according to personal taste, but your résumé should contain all of the sections shown in this sample below. Remember always to include a cover letter with your résumé. When you write your cover letter, be certain that you mention the position you are seeking and add any pertinent information not included in your résumé.

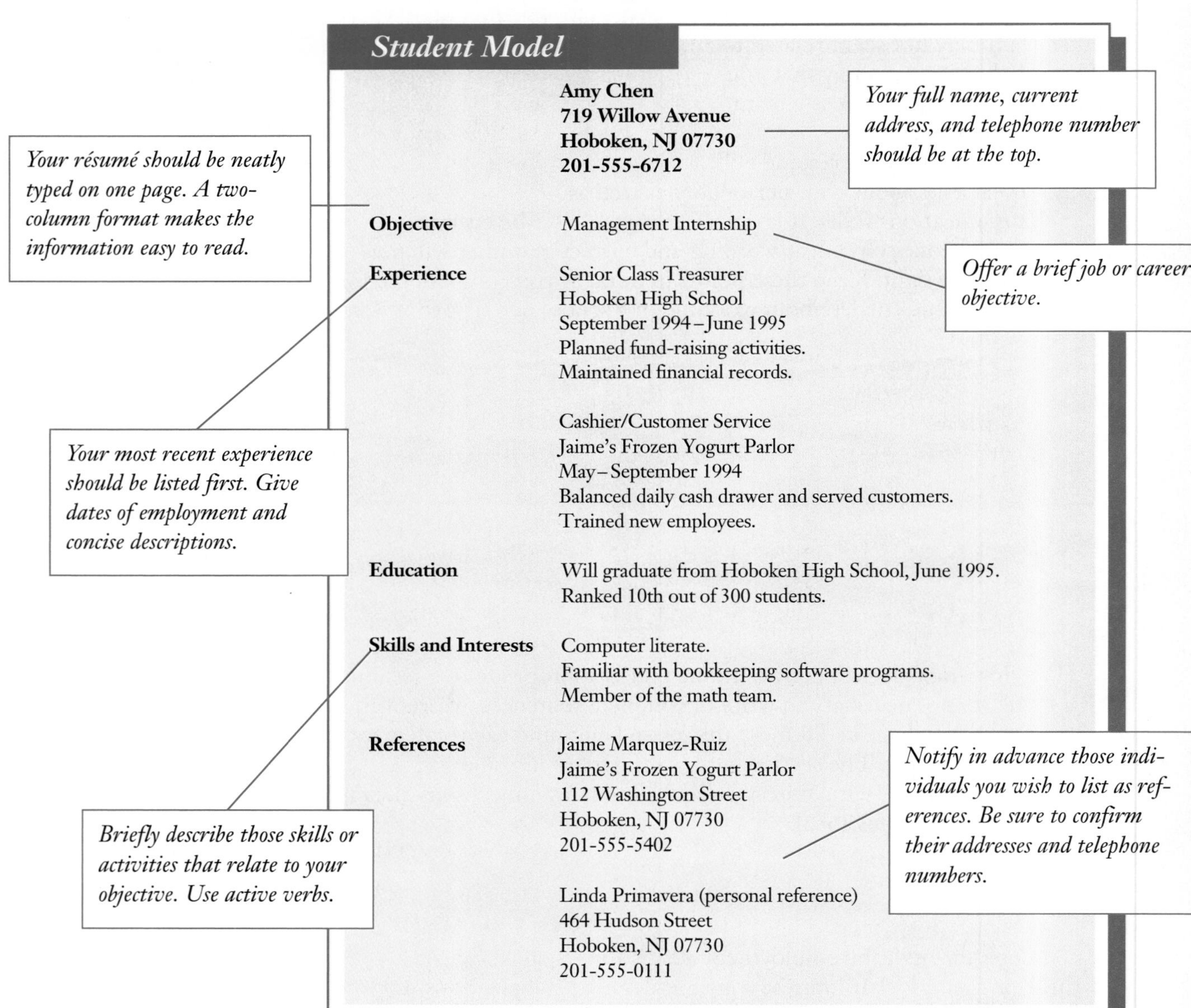

**Student Model**

**Amy Chen**
**719 Willow Avenue**
**Hoboken, NJ 07730**
**201-555-6712**

| | |
|---|---|
| **Objective** | Management Internship |
| **Experience** | Senior Class Treasurer<br>Hoboken High School<br>September 1994–June 1995<br>Planned fund-raising activities.<br>Maintained financial records.<br><br>Cashier/Customer Service<br>Jaime's Frozen Yogurt Parlor<br>May–September 1994<br>Balanced daily cash drawer and served customers.<br>Trained new employees. |
| **Education** | Will graduate from Hoboken High School, June 1995.<br>Ranked 10th out of 300 students. |
| **Skills and Interests** | Computer literate.<br>Familiar with bookkeeping software programs.<br>Member of the math team. |
| **References** | Jaime Marquez-Ruiz<br>Jaime's Frozen Yogurt Parlor<br>112 Washington Street<br>Hoboken, NJ 07730<br>201-555-5402<br><br>Linda Primavera (personal reference)<br>464 Hudson Street<br>Hoboken, NJ 07730<br>201-555-0111 |

*Your full name, current address, and telephone number should be at the top.*

*Your résumé should be neatly typed on one page. A two-column format makes the information easy to read.*

*Offer a brief job or career objective.*

*Your most recent experience should be listed first. Give dates of employment and concise descriptions.*

*Briefly describe those skills or activities that relate to your objective. Use active verbs.*

*Notify in advance those individuals you wish to list as references. Be sure to confirm their addresses and telephone numbers.*

# 1.5 Writing Activities

## Write a Résumé

Leafing through the help-wanted ads in a newspaper, you notice the following advertisement.

Write a résumé to send in response to the advertisement. Be sure to include an objective, your work experience, appropriate skills and activities, and at least two references. Trade résumés with your classmates and offer suggestions for improvement.

**TELEMARKETING POSITION AVAILABLE**

Local firm seeks a bright, articulate individual to conduct telephone research for a major film studio. Four-hour shifts available, nights or weekends. Please send résumé. Good salary. No experience necessary.

- Include important personal information.
- Emphasize personal qualitites that relate to the job you want.

**PURPOSE** To write a job résumé
**AUDIENCE** Potential employer
**LENGTH** 1 page

## Cooperative Learning

Form a résumé-writing group with two or three other students. Exchange résumés with group members and check them against the sample résumé on page 28. Each group member should make a review sheet for each résumé he or she reads. Which elements of the résumé are effective? Which elements need improvement? Exchange your review sheets and discuss your findings with the group. Then each group member can revise his or her résumé based on the comments he or she received.

### Grammar Link

**Capitalize specific names, places, course names, other proper names.**

*I watched* ***Bill Moyers*** *interviewing* ***Dame Rebecca West.***

Capitalize the appropriate words in the paragraph below.

James b. simpson lives at 878 forrest avenue in greenville, north Carolina. He submitted his résumé on may 11, 1995. In addition to the required physics courses, he has taken french and economics. He has worked at borroughs-welcome company for two summers. He expects to graduate in june of this year. He plans to take physics 101 at the local college this summer while he works part time.

**See Lesson 20.2, pages 661–665.**

LESSON 1.6

# Writing About Literature
# Expressing Opinions About Literature

*How you feel about a book is personal; there's no right or wrong opinion. When you share an opinion, however, you need to be ready to defend the position you take.*

## Respond to Reading

You can develop personal responses to literature by paying attention to your impressions while you are reading, not just after you've finished. Keeping a reader-response journal as you read will help. As its name implies, a reader-response journal is a notebook for storing your responses to your reading. In your reader-response journal, ask yourself what you like most about characters and events, and what you like least. Note any striking words, phrases, or descriptions. By writing page numbers, you'll have an easier time finding material later. The following model shows one response to the opening of Charles Dickens's novel *A Tale of Two Cities.*

Once you discover your general attitude toward a piece of literature, find examples from the text to support your opinions. "I liked this book" and "this is a good book" are starting points for your response. However, you will need to offer specific examples—or evidence—in support of the opinions you express.

**Student Model**

"It was the best of times, it was the worst of times." What a great line to start a novel. I don't know much about the French Revolution, so maybe this book will help me learn about what happened.

Student writer Brenda Marshall used the following chart to create the opening paragraphs of an opinion piece about *A Tale of Two Cities.*

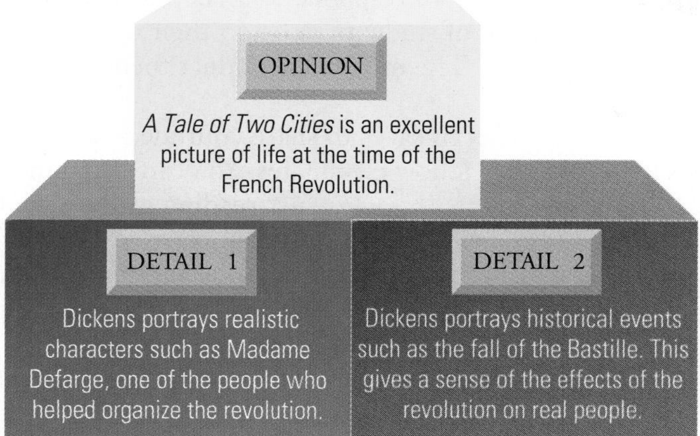

OPINION
A Tale of Two Cities is an excellent picture of life at the time of the French Revolution.
DETAIL 1
Dickens portrays realistic characters such as Madame Defarge, one of the people who helped organize the revolution.
DETAIL 2
Dickens portrays historical events such as the fall of the Bastille. This gives a sense of the effects of the revolution on real people.


## *Student Model*

"It was the best of times, it was the worst of times." So begins *A Tale of Two Cities* by Charles Dickens. In this complex, beautifully written story, Dickens takes us into the lives of the people who will live the triumphs and tragedies of the French Revolution.

One of the novel's most memorable characters is Madame Defarge. Madame Defarge lives in Saint Antoine, a small village near Paris. Unhappy with the inequalities in the French political system, she and her husband conspire with others to overthrow their tyrannical government and to free the prisoners held in the Bastille. As these plans become reality, Madame Defarge quietly records the events into a code in her knitting. As the revolution grows and eventually engulfs the whole of Paris, a triumphant Madame Defarge sits as a spectator to the bloody events, knitting her history.

Brenda Marshall, Newton North High School, Newton, Massachusetts

*What is the writer's opinion of the book?*

*What examples from the book does the writer use to support her opinion?*

## Journal Writing

Keep a reader-response journal as you read your next literature assignment. Ask yourself: What do I find most enjoyable? What do I like least? Which characters are most memorable?

## Share Your Opinions

In the movie *Dead Poets Society*, Robin Williams portrays a dynamic high school English teacher who sparks his students' love of literature. He inspires a small group of students to begin their own reading group, the "Dead Poets Society." The members conduct their meetings in a secret cave.

You don't have to meet in caves to share your ideas about books. You can discuss literature with fellow classmates. You can also join community reading groups, which are often advertised in newspapers and on library bulletin boards. Such discussion groups give participants an opportunity to test their opinions as well as to enrich their understanding by listening to the viewpoints of others. Joining a reading group often proves an invaluable prewriting activity that leads to a richer writing experience. Even in the most casual reading group, however, there are certain discussion rules that you should follow.

**Learn to listen.** This advice doesn't only mean that you are quiet while someone else speaks. It means that you pay close attention to what a speaker is saying. It means interjecting your own ideas at an appropriate time. It means being receptive to comments that others make.

**Allow everyone a chance to speak.** Sometimes you may have to remind someone to let another member express a point, or you may have to encourage the ideas of those who are less aggressive or confident.

**Don't be afraid to disagree.** Conflicting ideas often have interesting outcomes. Both sides gain new insights. A conflicting opinion may cause you to dig more deeply into a book, looking for evidence to support your ideas.

**Be sensitive to others' views.** Most literature can be interpreted and appreciated in various ways and on many levels.

**Find a good leader when you need one.** When a group is small, a leader may not be necessary. Larger groups benefit from a leader whose responsibility is to keep the discussion focused, to encourage all members to contribute, to resolve conflicts, and to sum up.

# 1.6 Writing Activities

## Write a Book Review

You are writing a book review for your high school newspaper. Your review should summarize the book's plot and describe your reaction to the book. Support your views with examples from the book.

Think about the following questions: Did you enjoy the book? Why or why not? Would you recommend it to others? Did the writing remind you of something else you've read?

- State what you like and don't like about the book.
- Write some details—reasons, examples—to explain your opinion.
- If appropriate, compare it to another book.

**PURPOSE** To write a book review
**AUDIENCE** High school students and teachers
**LENGTH** 4–5 paragraphs

## Cross-Curricular: Art

Kenzo Okada painted *Flower Study* shown on this page. A *Time* magazine writer once described Okada's work as follows:

> Okada's palette [choice of colors] has grown increasingly muted and his colors have a weathered look as if time had washed over them again and again, giving them that frail grace that comes only with great age. Nothing is consciously organized; it is Okada's achievement that, in the end, everything still seems in place. This is the chaotic logic of a remotely remembered dream.

State *your* views about the painting as though you were writing for a magazine. Think about whether you agree or disagree with the *Time* writer's opinion. Support your views with specific examples from the painting.

### Grammar Link

**Use correct verbs with compound subjects joined by *and.***

*Unhappy with the inequalities in the French political system, she and her husband* ***conspire*** *with others. . . .*

Supply a correct verb for each of the following sentences.

1. Both the home team and the visiting team ____ to win.
2. Blue and white ____ a good combination for our team's colors.
3. Neither the home team nor the visitors ____ this season.
4. Many a ballplayer, cheerleader, and fan ____ the feeling of defeat.

**See Lesson 16.5, page 572.**

*Kenzo Okada, (Flower Study) - 1958*

LESSON 1.7

# Writing About Literature
# Creative Responses to Literature

*Writing a parody or spoof on a piece of literature allows you to show off your sense of humor. It also requires you to be exceptionally familiar with the object of your spoof.*

In the model below, a writer spoofs Shakespeare's famous soliloquy from *Hamlet.* Read the parody carefully, noting where the writer shows a familiarity with both the content and the form of the original.

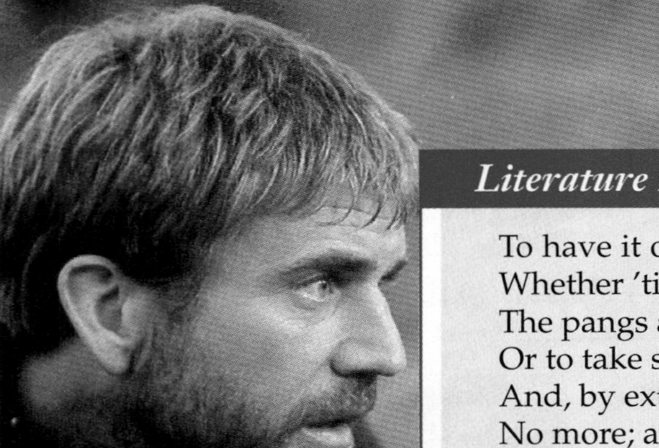

Mel Gibson as Hamlet

*Literature Model*

To have it out or not? that is the question—
Whether 'tis better for the jaws to suffer
The pangs and torments of an aching tooth,
Or to take steel against a host of troubles;
And, by extracting end them? To pull—to tug!
No more; and by a tug to say we end
The tooth-ache, and a thousand natural ills
The jaw is heir to; 'tis a consummation
Devoutly to be wished? To pull—to tug!
To tug—perchance to break! Ay, there's the rub.

C.A.W., *The Brand X Anthology of Poetry*

To test the effectiveness of this parody, compare it with Shakespeare's original "To be or not to be" soliloquy. The best parodies are those that reflect the original work while adding a unique and humorous twist to the language and the storyline.

Let your mind and your imagination wander after you've read a piece of literature. Don't discard any ideas yet, no matter how farfetched. In this way you will often find ideas for your own humorous or even serious parodies and for many other pieces of creative writing as well.

## Find a Rich Springboard

In the previous example, the writer based a piece of humorous writing on a play. You can also use a novel or short story as a springboard for your creative writing. You may choose to adapt a section of a book into a scene for a film or a play. The musical *Les Misérables,* based on Victor Hugo's novel of the same name, is a successful example of how a novel was re-created as a play.

You might also consider writing a story from a different point of view. Virginia Woolf's book *Flush* is an unusual case in point. *Flush* tells the story of poet Elizabeth Barrett Browning's life from the point of view of her dog. Another possibility is altering a well-known fable or story. In the Broadway musical *Into the Woods,* James Lapine and Stephen Sondheim incorporated traditional fairy tales—such as "Cinderella," "Little Red Riding Hood," and "Jack and the Beanstalk"—into a play that explores what "living happily ever after" really means.

The model below shows still another way of responding to fiction. In it, student writer Andrea Dagel imagines herself as a character in F. Scott Fitzgerald's novel *The Great Gatsby.*

### *Student Model*

Although I was accustomed to elegance, I was in awe of the house, the guests, and most of all, the great Gatsby himself. If only I could catch his eye, a spark, perhaps a flame, would grow between us. But I simply could not stand out in such an elegant crowd. That night, however, fate was on my side. As I was about to leave, giving up my fantasy, a clumsy waiter spilled champagne down my dress. The resulting shriek took everyone by surprise. Most important, I was noticed by Gatsby. My humiliation turned to ecstasy when the gracious host gallantly came to my aid—though I must admit I looked less than stunning in his bathrobe.

Andrea Dagel, Centennial High School, Pueblo, Colorado

### Journal Writing

Using the student model above as inspiration, imagine yourself as a character in a book that you've read. Write some phrases that would describe your character's physical appearance and personality traits.

## Find a Creative Response Form

The chart below offers some ideas for creative responses to fiction, but the possibilities are as endless as your imagination. Regardless of the response you explore, the success of your endeavor rests on how well acquainted you are with the original piece of fiction. Become familiar with the setting. Where does the action take place? How does the author describe the location? Analyze the characters in the piece. Do they have personality traits you might highlight? Do they have remarkable physical traits or habits? In the model on page 35, you saw how writer Andrea Dagel highlighted Jay Gatsby's attention to women. Finally, think about the themes and the conflicts. What message is the writer trying to communicate through his or her writing? What message do you want to communicate in your writing? Once you have gathered this prewriting information, you're ready to begin creating your first draft.

**CREATIVE WRITING**
**RESPONSES TO FICTION**

Write a spoof or parody.

Extend the story line—what happens next?

Create an imaginary journal for one of the characters.

Adapt an existing story for a new medium: a film script, a play, a narrative poem.

Rewrite the story from a different point of view.

If you plan to write a parody, be sure to familiarize yourself with the author's word choices, sentence lengths, punctuation, and any trademark idiosyncrasies—such as Mark Twain's use of Missouri dialect. In the model below, student writer Dom Leonardelli uses his knowledge of legal language in a parody of "Goldilocks and the Three Bears." Dom imagines that he is a lawyer prosecuting Goldilocks for the mental anguish she caused his clients, the Bears. Dom wants the jury to award his clients $10 million for their "pain and suffering."

### *Student Model*

One day, a warm summer day, while the Bears were enjoying a family excursion, Goldilocks entered their home at 772 Hot Porridge Way and enjoyed a meal with no intent to pay for it. Under Article 765D, Section 7 of the Fairy Tale Penal Code, that violation is coined, "Defrauding an Innkeeper." She then found comfort via the personal property not allowed either by written or oral permission of the owners. Finally, Goldilocks made her way to the most private place in a home—the bedroom. All of these violation of privacy acts undoubtedly point in favor of my clients. Won't you rule in our favor?

Dom Leonardelli, Centennial High School, Pueblo, Colorado

# 1.7 Writing Activities

## Writing a Parody

You are a storyteller for a kindergartner's birthday party. Select a traditional fable or a fairy tale (such as one by Aesop, the Brothers Grimm, or Hans Christian Andersen), and rewrite it. Your version should change the original story in some way. You might modernize it, alter the moral, change the point of view, or combine the original tale with another fable or fairy tale.

- Show that you know the tale well.
- Be clear about your characters' reactions to things.
- Use the same kind of language and structures the author uses.

**PURPOSE** To write a parody that entertains children in kindergarten
**AUDIENCE** A group of 5-year-olds
**LENGTH** 2–4 pages

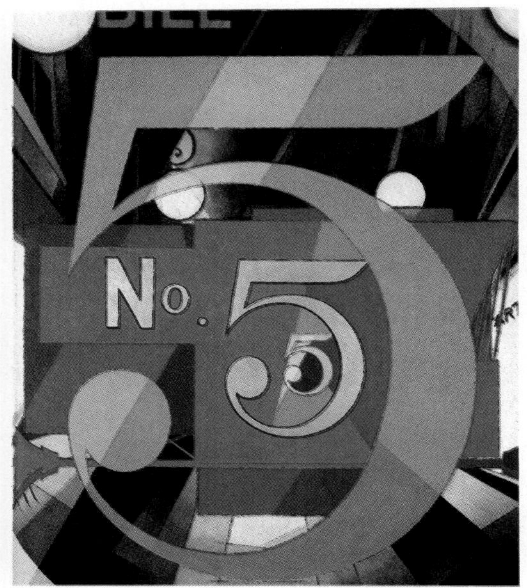


Charles Demuth, *I Saw the Figure 5 in Gold*, 1928

### Grammar Link

**Use commas with introductory clauses.**

***Although I was accustomed to elegance,*** *I was in awe of the house, the guests, and most of all, the great Gatsby himself.*

Add commas to the following sentences where needed.

1. During the time he was on spring break Andrew always tried to get in some sailing.
2. In the winter months that he lived in Chicago it was too windy for sailing.
3. If he went down to the dock he could usually tell what the sailing conditions would be.
4. When he saw the deck of the boat he noticed an old weather-beaten cat sitting there.
5. Although Andrew had no idea whom it belonged to he usually took it along.

**See Lesson 21.6, page 686.**

## Cross-Curricular: Art

American artist Charles Demuth painted *I Saw the Figure 5 in Gold* (1928) as a response to a poem. Write a short story or poem that describes your response to the painting. What is the significance, if any, of the number 5?

UNIT 1

# WRITING PROCESS IN ACTION

## PERSONAL WRITING

In preceding lessons you've learned about the different ways to write about yourself for others and for yourself. Now you can use what you have learned to write a self-portrait.

**• Assignment •**

| | |
|---|---|
| *Context* | *Your school has decided to publish a supplement to the yearbook consisting of personal writing by seniors. It will feature essays inspired by photographs of the writers. To be included, you don't need to write about your official yearbook portrait; you may choose any recent photograph of yourself. What's more, your essay should not merely describe this image of yourself. Instead, the photograph should be a jumping-off point for a new insight about yourself that you wish to share with your classmates.* |
| *Purpose* | *To write a personal essay in which a photograph of yourself is the basis for exploring and sharing an aspect of your personality* |
| *Audience* | *Your classmates, parents, and teachers* |
| *Length* | *2 pages* |

The following pages can help you plan and write your essay. Read through them and then refer to them as you need to. But don't be tied down by them. You're in charge of your own writing process.

# Prewriting

Your first task is to find just the right photograph. If you already have a favorite, fine. If not, conduct your search in one of two ways: without preconceptions, waiting to see which image will "hit you" just right, or with that special favorite look in mind. Once you've found the "face" you want to write about, explore why you've chosen it. The questions on the notepad may help you get started.

Jot down a list of adjectives in answer to the first question or a list of nouns for the second. Try phrases or sentences or whole paragraphs for the third and fourth questions. Do a free and honest exploration.

There are a number of ways to organize your essay. You might want to move from one aspect of your subject to another, always linking each new observation to the last. This approach allows you to delve into past experiences and use them in a chronological organization as you remember them. Or you might choose to organize your essay in order of the importance of your thoughts and impressions. It is likely that your choice of order will be determined by letting your writing flow as you get your ideas down. Whatever order you choose, make sure that you use transition words and phrases to guide your readers from one idea to the next.

You need not restrict yourself to a single image. Look at baby pictures of yourself or photographs of family members to spot similarities and differences. Ask friends and family for their impressions.

Once you've gathered some ideas, reread your notes, looking for patterns of thought and feeling. Now you're ready to ask yourself deeper questions such as: Why does this image of myself appeal to me? Which aspects of my character or personality does it reveal? Which "me" does it present to the audience who looks at it?

Prewriting Questions
- How do I look in the photo?
- What or whom do I look like here?
- What does this photo show about the real me?
- What doesn't it show about the real me?

**Drafting Tip**

The student model in Lesson 1.1 on page 12 provides a good example of the informal approach to drafting that many writers find works best for them.

# Drafting

As you turn your notes into sentences and paragraphs, think about the way you will come across to your readers. A conversational tone and friendly approach is a style that many writers find effective. Use contractions that sound conversational, and have one thought interrupt another as often happens in real life.

In the following excerpt from "My Face," Gail Godwin watches her mother apply makeup to the face that "she was taking out into the world that day."

**Literature Model**

Suddenly I saw her mirror image compose itself into a frightening look. Her eyes widened and gazed into some sorrowful romantic distance; her nostrils dilated; her full lips spread into a weird close-mouthed smile. I knew that, to her, this was her favorite image of herself; I could tell by a kind of relaxed triumph that came over her. "Stop that!" I cried. "Stop looking like that," for as long as she did, my mother was lost to me. . . ."

Gail Godwin, from "My Face"

Although drafting is not the time to agonize over word choice and sentence structure, do consider the voice and tone you will adopt. A comic tone will lead you to make choices that are different from those you would make to convey a serious attitude toward your subject.

Conclude your draft by reinforcing your main idea. You might come full circle, or you could forecast how the future will affect your features. Be sure to include what this close look at yourself has taught you. You might also ponder large questions, as Gail Godwin does in this excerpt from "My Face." Here she focuses on the link between looks and identity and goes on to make us think about the differences between how we see ourselves and how others see us.

**Literature Model**

After all, the mirror shows us the reverse of the self others see. Stand in front of the mirror with someone whose face you know well. His face in the mirror will not look quite the same. It may even look strange to you. Yet this is the face he sees every day. What would be strange for him would be to see his face as you see it at its most familiar.

Gail Godwin, from "My Face"

Revising Checklist

- Have I focused on my topic?
- Have I selected details that best convey my attitude toward my picture?
- Are there any words or images that interfere with a consistent tone?
- Do my introductory and concluding paragraphs successfully perform their functions?
- Are there any places where transitions are needed?

# Revising

To begin revising, read over your draft to make sure that what you've written fits your purpose and your audience. Then have a **writing conference.** Read your draft to a partner or small group. Use your audience's reactions to help you evaluate your work so far. The Revising Checklist can help you and your readers.

# Editing

Once you are happy with the basic content and set-up of your personal essay, **proofread** it carefully for errors in grammar, usage, mechanics, and spelling. Use the Editing Questions below as a guide.

In addition to proofreading, use the self-evaluation list below to make sure your description does all the things you want it to do. When you're satisfied, make a clean copy of your essay and proofread it one more time.

**Revising Tip**

For help on focusing and on selecting details, see Lesson 1.1, page 11 and Lesson 1.4, pages 22–23.

## Self-Evaluation

**Make sure your essay–**

- focuses on one photograph of you that captures the "face" you want to present to the world
- uses the photograph to explore an aspect of your character or personality
- uses details to support the choice of photograph and to convey the personal insight
- uses a method or methods of organization appropriate to the topic and purpose
- follows correct grammar, usage, mechanics, and spelling

*Editing Questions*

- *Have I avoided run-on sentences?*
- *Have I capitalized names, places, course names, and all other proper nouns and adjectives?*
- *Are my compound subjects and verbs in agreement?*
- *Have I used commas with introductory clauses?*
- *Have I checked to make sure words are spelled correctly?*

# Presenting

You can collect the personal essays you and your classmates have written and publish them as a supplement to the yearbook for seniors in your school. Make a bulletin-board display for the cafeteria or library that features the essays along with the photographs of the writers.

## Journal Writing

Reflect on your writing process experience. Answer these questions in your journal: What do you like best about your personal essay? What was the hardest part of writing it? What did you learn in your writing conference? What new things have you learned as a writer?

UNIT 1

# Personal Writing
# Literature Model

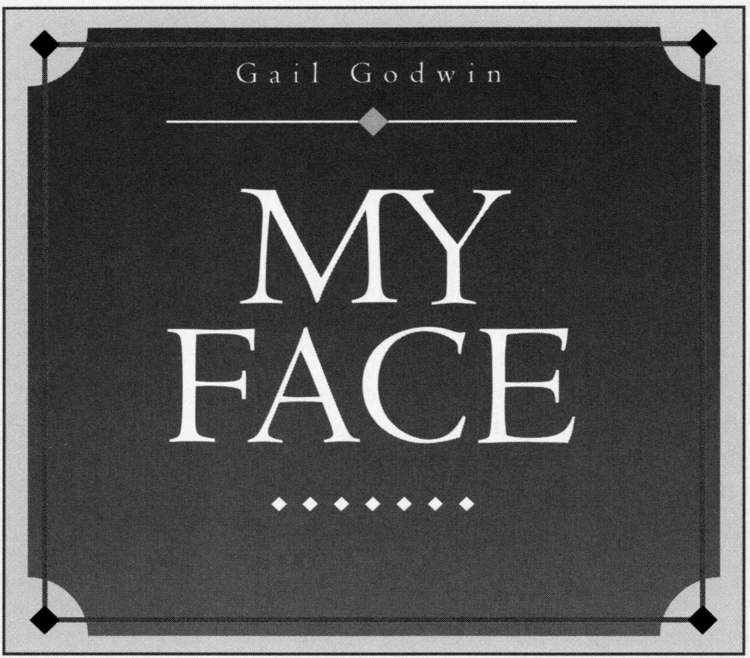


*Prompted by a photographic session for the jacket of her new book, writer Gail Godwin confesses her feelings, thoughts, and fantasies about an important aspect of herself that she presents to the world: her face. As you read, pay attention to how Godwin combines her expressed desire for privacy with her careful self-presentation. Then try the activities in Linking Writing and Literature, on page 51.*

The day has turned out well. More importantly for our purposes, so has my hair. Some years ago I stopped trying to subdue it into the current fashion, and it has since rewarded me by catching the light and air and using them to frame my face for command performances like today.

The photographer arrives on the noon bus and wants to begin

work right away. Out of a cleverly packed kit he brings forth cameras, lights, meters, a tripod, and even a white umbrella. During a session of warm-up shots I pose self-consciously on a chaise longue while he tells me how he went to photograph Auden once and, after only two frames, the great poet rose and said, "All right. That's enough, young man."

"Oh god!" I cry, forgetting "my face" for a few seconds. "What did you do?"

"I was lucky that day. Words saved me. I said, 'But Mr. Auden, in my profession I don't get a chance to revise.' He looked at me for a minute and then said, 'All right,' and sat down again. The only trouble was, he sat down too fast and fell off the chair. But we did get some good pictures, and after the session was over he said, 'If you'll come back again, young man, I'll cook you a chicken dinner.' "

I move to my desk, to recline against the deluxe sprawl of my new IBM and the fading rhododendron blossoms outside the window. The photographer has set up a spotlight and opens the white umbrella. The combination, he explains, makes the face soak up the light. It "fills out the face" with a youthful luminosity. If the need ever arises, he tells me, I can substitute a piece of white poster paper. "Put it on a surface just below your face and it will send up the light in a nice way."

Last week a different photographer walked me into the woods and told me to get comfortable on a rock I had sat down on, in a patch of dappled shade. She retreated on tiptoe and lurked some distance away where she crouched and *waited,* like a nature lover stalking a shy animal. The woods grew still. My hair engaged in a little dance with the breeze. A gnat cruised loudly past my face. What is she waiting for, I thought, watching the face of the photographer. She pursed her lips, she hummed to herself, she smiled mysteriously, she squinted her eyes. I grew almost bored. Then I relaxed and began thinking my own thoughts. Click, she went then. Click. Click.

This photographer stands on a chair behind the white umbrella and asks: "When do you look most like you *like* to look?"

And I think of myself, alone sometimes in this house, how I'll take little intermissions at the bathroom mirror, arranging my face until it suits me. There *is* a look I like. But has anybody ever seen it? If someone did, would that person say, "Ah, what an interesting woman," or, if he/she knew me, "Ah, yes, that's Gail." Or: "Why is that woman posing?" Or: "Why on earth is Gail making that strange face?"

One time, when I was little, I was watching my mother put the finishing touches on the face she was taking out into the world that day. Suddenly I saw her mirror image compose itself into a frightening look. Her eyes widened and gazed into some sorrowful romantic distance; her nostrils dilated; her full lips spread into a weird close-mouthed smile. I knew that, to her, this was her favorite image of herself; I could tell by a kind of relaxed triumph that came over her.

"Stop that!" I cried. "Stop looking like that," for, as long as she did, my mother was lost to me.

As I think these thoughts, the photographer who evoked them with his question takes about a dozen pictures. Later, when I am going over his contacts, I search in vain for my secret favorite look that I have been able to create at the bathroom mirror. What did I expect: that he would be able to evoke the look by getting me to *recall* the look? There are other looks—by which I mean acceptable versions of my face—but I don't see that one. Or perhaps it's there, but it looks different turned around. After all, the mirror shows us the reverse of the self others see. Stand in front of the mirror with someone whose face you know well. His face in the mirror will not look quite the same. It may even look strange to you. Yet this is the face he sees every day. What would be strange for him would be to see his face as *you* see it at its most familiar.

It is not because I am beautiful, or notorious, or even because my face is unusual, that two professional photographers have chosen to ride four hours on the bus, at their own expense, to imprint its image on a dozen rolls of film. No, it is merely because I am an American author soon to have another book published.

I don't know exactly when this practice began of making the contemporary writer a visual object, but it has occurred during my lifetime. During my youthful reading, I rarely knew what the writers looked like—except for the highly visible Hemingway, with his white beard and bare, stocky chest. There was still, I recall, a certain impish elusiveness about writers. They effaced themselves from your imagination, leaving the field free for their characters and *their* stories. As late as 1970, when my first novel was being published and the editor called to ask did I want my picture on the jacket, I replied at once, "Oh, I don't think *my picture* will help the book." I distinctly remember feeling that I would forfeit some of the mystery of a new fictional voice if my face appeared on the book.

My face did not appear on my second novel, either. This novel was about a beautiful woman, so beautiful that stronger, unbeautiful people need her for their various purposes and thus make her their prisoner. The cover artist wisely chose not to depict the particular face of any beautiful woman. If my face had appeared on the back of the book, some skeptical reader might surely have inquired: "What does *she* know about the problems of being extraordinarily beautiful?"

At the editor's suggestion, my third novel did carry my photograph. I was a little disappointed at the one he chose from the contact sheets, but he seemed to feel it would "go well with the book." The heroine of that novel was a woman of 32, intelligent, romantic, and insecure. When she catches a glimpse of her face in a tilted mirror above her beautiful grandmother's coffin, it shocks her. ("It always did when she faced a mirror unexpectedly. It was too alert, too tense, too transparent in what its owner felt.") The photo the editor chose was that of an intelligent-looking woman in her thirties with a closed mouth that stops just short of a smile; she has large, rather dreamy eyes, but their effect is diminished by the pronounced worry line that slashes her brow. My mother hated that picture; she couldn't understand why I would allow anyone to publish a picture that "makes you look old, and not even pretty." The picture startled her: in it, her daughter was lost to her.

Though I have learned not to agonize every time I come across some face of mine that fails to do justice to my wit, charm, and profundity, I still harbor a deep desire for invisibility. In my second novel, Francesca, the beautiful woman, goes to work briefly as the amanuensis (really the cleaning girl) for the ugly "M," a writer who has shaved her head. "M" tells Francesca that she shaved her head so that she would stop looking in the mirror and notice more things about the world.

What "M" meant, of course, was that for an artist there is great value in being invisible. Only when you can stop looking at yourself do you become capable of filling other bodies. Keats, praising this trait in Shakespeare, called it Negative Capability. . . .

One wonders what Jane Austen's comments might have been, had she looked down from Writers' Heaven several months ago and observed the confusion attendant on a paperback release of her early writings. In the first place, she might not have been all that pleased to have her juvenilia published; in the second place, there is her *name*—she who always signed her works "by A Lady"; in the third place, there is a *picture of the author*, in a little oval vignette, above the title, *Love and Freindship* (sic) . . . but wait a moment, who *is* this beautiful, full-bosomed woman in her low-cut gown? One thing for certain: It's not our Jane. But it took the president of the Jane Austen Society to point this out to the embarrassed publisher, who then tracked the error down to the New York Public Library, which had been housing an incorrectly labeled impostress in Jane's file: a portrait of Sarah Austin, a nineteenth-century translator. (Now plain Jane, thin lips pursed, wearing her house cap and high-necked frock, has been instated in her rightful place; but one wonders about that filing error: wishful thinking on somebody's part? After all, Jane has turned out to be a star, and oughtn't a star to look like that pretty lady in the low dress?)

It is time to go through my contact sheets and select one image of myself to appear on the back of my new novel and another image to serve as my "publicity" photo. As I crouch, with magnifying glass over these myriad me's, ruminations and emotions as varied as the poses play through my mind.

1. Would even Lord Byron have been able to face his contact sheets without spasms of self-loathing?
2. A quote from a painter in my fourth novel: "They say people

make their faces after a certain age, but it is also true that before a certain age people's faces help to make them." If, as a teen-ager, I had had my decade's version of, say, Brooke Shields' face, what would I be doing today? Beautiful faces effortlessly open the secrets of other hearts and minds. An alternative route to these secrets—which I always knew I wanted—is via the effort of imagination. If you are beautiful, the world comes to you; but if you have imagination, you can summon the world.

3. Only once in my life has my face opened doors. This was when my favorite uncle William lay dying in the hospital. An extremely popular figure in the community, his room was being besieged by friends, acquaintances, old girlfriends, highway patrolmen, preachers, other judges and lawyers, and a few curiosity seekers. The doctor gave orders that no one but family (and the Reigning Girlfriend) be admitted, and then only for brief sessions. All who were admitted had to be screened by the nurse on duty at the time. But never I. "You can go on in," all the nurses who had never seen me before would say, "anyone can see *you're* one of them."

I have the Godwin face. I have many of my mother's expressions (her sad-romantic gaze; her "polite" look, which is an incongruous combination of silly, pursed mouth and wide, furious eyes; her weird, close-mouthed smile and flaring nostrils when she is being beautiful), but it is the face of my father's family, his lineal features that I see in my photographs—just as, sometimes amused, sometimes alarmed, I see myself in old photographs of his family. There is a sister, in her eighties now, whose girlhood snapshots could pass for some of mine, and, what is even more scary, I have only to sit beside her—queenly, sarcastic old doyen—at a family reunion, and have a preview of myself, at age eighty-three, holding court, as she answers questions about her house ("Yes, it's on the market, but so far nobody's been able to afford it"), accepts compliments on her daughter's food ("Well of course Christine's table is full of good things; she learned *something* at my house"), and on her own skin ("Yes, I've got the pure Powell skin of our mother's family; poor Mose and William got the old sallow Godwin skin"). As I watch her (just now an obsequious cousin has flung himself to his knees beside her and cries, "Hail, Matriarch!") I think: well, I have the nice Powell skin, too, and I also have the large, slashed brow and forehead that will soon make the top part of my face look like a *patriarch,* as hers does now; and I, too, have the long, heavy cheeks that are one day going to shake like an angry bulldog's when I'm on my soapbox, but she *has* lasted (as I intend to), and she still works every day (as I intend to), and she does add to a party (as I hope I shall, at her age).

Odilon Redon, *My Face*, c. 1895–1900

4. A quote from my heroine's friend in my third novel: "You are the type of person who will never be able to see your own face. Your face is a series of impressions, of moods. It will always give more pleasure to others than to yourself."

5. An unvoiced expletive as I X out with a black crayon a certain frame. ("P.S. If there are any frames that you would not like to be seen, please X out on contact sheet," the Photographer-with-the-White-Umbrella has instructed.) Oh, Thomas Pynchon was so shrewd! But it is too late for me to refuse to pose, to steal my image back from old high school files. It is too late for me to be the wise, invisible genie-author, laughing over the reader's shoulder.

I will also never look like a star. (If my work should last, what high-cheekboned, swan-necked, smooth-browed impostress will some visual idealist sneak into my file?) What many a reader will see while reading my books is—let's face it—a younger version of Aunt Thelma posing as my mother. All I can do, at this stage, is to be myself (so the encroaching old face will at least signify the intrinsic me) and to use the black crayon when it is offered: try not to be caught in public with my eyes squeezed shut, with a drink in my hand, or simpering like a fool.

6. A frequent quote from my grandmother. "Fools' names and fools' faces are often seen in public places."

Though the writer in me aspires to the invisibility that will grant me the freedom to imagine myself into anybody, to become Nobody watching and describing the parade of life, the egoist in me hankers for that instant, visible glamour which reveals me a Somebody the moment I enter a room. And, to a degree, the American consumer in me retains a childlike faith in the miracle-working properties of products which, if dotted at the strategic pulse points, thrown across the shoulder or buttoned or belted in the latest fashion, or slathered on my pure Powell skin, will make a roomful of strangers stand up and chant in chorus: "Who *is* that woman who just came in?"

At home alone with my muse, I wear a uniform of old corduroys with the wales rubbed smooth, and any old sweater or shirt. But when I go into the city, I start worrying the day before about how to dress that woman who will always startle me from at least one plate-glass window. One day, I keep vowing, when I have purchased all the right things, I will be able to see Somebody striding along beside me in that window and glimpse at last a glamorous version of myself.

Like the majority of people, my attitude towards my looks wobbles wildly between vanity and despair. But, providentially, my vocation always saves me. In my study, I am invisible. I'm a free-floating consciousness able to go anywhere and see anything without being observed in return. Even when I'm thinking well or lost in the contemplation of other lives, I am temporarily "refined out of existence."

Not long ago, in a moment of anxious vanity ("If I start *today,* I can keep what I have") I sent off to California for an eighteen-dollar book on face-lifting through exercise. ("For women and men over twenty-one," the tactful subhead explained.) Back came a pink volume weighing several pounds and sealed in plastic. I tore off the plastic, read the grudging praise of a prominent plastic surgeon (after all, this book was going to take away some of his business, wasn't it?), and began leafing through the exercises, turning first to my "trouble spots": LOWER CHEEKS, JOWLS, SCOWL.

I began to despair. Knowing my aversion to boredom and routine, could I count on myself to devote fifteen minutes a day for the rest of my life to making faces at myself in a mirror? . . .

Knowing, at this point, that I would probably never open this book again, I transferred my interest to the one really ghoulish aspect of the book and lost myself in its contemplation. On each page where the pretty model was doing her exercise to iron out crows' feet, guard against turkey neck, or restore youthful fullness to the lips, there was an inset of an older woman's face—rather, that part of her face that was in shambles because she had failed to do this particular exercise.

The photos were all of the same poor woman, and I found myself imagining her life. Who was she? (I should point out that she was not grotesque; if you saw her on the street, if you noticed her at all, you would think: just a plain woman, late sixties/early seventies, who hasn't had an interesting life or taken very good care of herself.) But how had she come to lend her face to these pictures? Did anyone tell her beforehand, "You are going to represent the face women don't want to have"? Was she paid well? More money, or less, than the pretty model? Did they just pick her off the street (a California bag lady, glad for the cash), or was she, perhaps, a very well-to-do model whose specialty was admonitory photographs? Was she—it was possible—*the author's mother?* ("Hey, Mom, I have a terrific proposition for you. It will benefit thousands of women, put bucks into our joint account, and you and I will always know I *love* your dear face just the way it is.")

Where was "I" at this moment? Somewhere in California, in a room I was beginning to furnish. Where was the American female, fourth decade, of the incipient bulldog demeanor? Invisible.

I watched Bill Moyers interviewing Dame Rebecca West, age 89, at her home in London. Before and during the interview, the network flashed portraits and photographs of the author in her earlier incarnations: baby sister, young militant, companion of H. G. Wells, banker's wife, woman of accomplishment receiving her honor from the Queen. In all of these stills, you could trace a family resemblance, a continuity-in-retrospect, to the living female Knight on the screen, in her long gown and her pearl choker which tugged at her neck like a self-imposed leash. She was "being good" tonight, but not too good. She made the camera wait while she took her time formulating her answers or remembering the past; she exerted no effort to impress, she even went so far as to demur, or agree politely, if the interviewer switched topics suddenly, or put words into her mouth. She seemed, much of the time, to have become invisible to herself: she was just one big, fluid, rapid mind browsing confidently among whatever ideas were put before her. At one point, because she is hard of hearing, she *lunged* towards Moyers to catch the tail end of his remark, and—for a second—her large head was transformed into a lionlike figure: she became visually, on camera, a sort of mythical beast, heraldic of her accumulated strengths.

Since then, I have been planning *my* heraldic visage; it's much more fun than doing the exercises in the pink book. I've been imagining little scenarios to go with my eighty-year-old mastiff-face. Here is one:

I will have worked very hard at my craft, and because its attendant exercises in Negative Capability have become the priority of my life, I will have rendered myself invisible to me (for large portions of a given day) and visible to others in the various guises they will create for me. To some, I will be a wrinkled old lady (but not as wrinkled as Auden, if I keep using my creams); but to those who see me as a Lady of Letters, my face will have become emblematic of my style ("Don't you just love the thoughts that roam that gashed forehead of hers? And the way her cheeks *quiver* with sensitivity or *rumble* with a wicked wit!").

When the young photographers come, one of them will be after a certain distinctive pouch nobody has quite done justice to on film; another will try to make me shut my eyes or giggle and spill my drink; while another, aspiring to Mythical Photography, will wait for the appearance of my beast in the lens.

I will pose some, wearing a gown of lavender-gray (no jewelry), and reclining among my books and memory artifacts on some dramatic but comfy piece of furniture. One owes an audience a few stage props.

I will get rid of the boring ones quickly by a polite sarcasm or succinct withdrawal of my Presence. ("You look *tired,* young woman." "That will do, young man.")

But if they are swift-witted and charming and very agreeable to me, I will let them tarry while I ruminate aloud, until, through the fissures and gravitational drifts of my old face, they can glimpse the shapes and visions behind it.

I may write something sweet into the flyleaf of one of my books for them. And invite them to stay for supper.

# Linking Writing and Literature

## Readers Respond to the Model

### What makes Gail Godwin's personal essay interesting to you?

**Explore Gail Godwin's personal essay by answering these questions. Then read what other students liked about Godwin's essay.**

1. Gail Godwin raises the issues of self-image and social perceptions that are important for her. Do you think that many people can identify with these issues?
2. What do you think about the way books, films, and other media are published today? Should the emphasis on authors and stars be changed? Why?
3. Choose a paragraph from the selection that you particularly identify with. How has Godwin's writing evoked this response from you?

"My Face" is a collection of thoughts about the author's self-image, and how she wants others to perceive her. "My Face" also reflects the author's views on contemporary literature and how it is publicized. I think many people can identify with the issues she seems to bring up (self-image, society's perceptions). The fact that she makes her insecurities clear in this essay makes her much more real to the reader. I would recommend this selection as an example of contemporary writing. It is written in a very different style from anything I am used to.

***Susannah Levine***

This selection is about a disgruntled author who's upset that pictures of a book's author are kept on the book jacket. She aspires instead "to the invisibility that will grant her the freedom to imagine herself into anybody," but she admits that the egotist in her aspires for the "instant, visible glamour."

***Mathew Isaac***

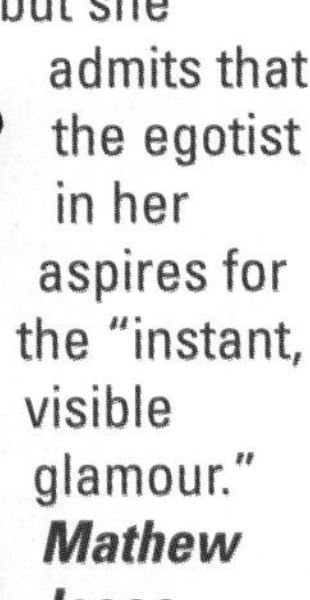

# Unit 1 Review

## Reflecting on the Unit

**Summarize what you learned in this unit by answering the following questions:**

- Which techniques for recalling personal experiences might have been useful to Gail Godwin as she was writing "My Face"? Why do you think so?
- What writing assignment helped you to understand yourself and your experiences better?
- What writing best expresses something unique about you?
- Have you done any personal writing that you would like to reshape later for others to read?

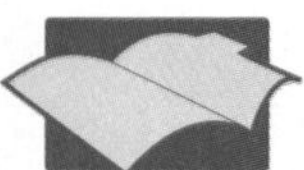

## Adding to Your Portfolio

**Choose one or two selections for your portfolio.**
Look over the personal writing you have done during this unit. Select a completed piece of writing to put into your portfolio. The piece you choose should show some or all of the following:

- Something you did not previously know about yourself
- An understanding of an experience
- Specific rather than general language that makes an experience come to life
- Writing based on ideas generated from freewriting, clustering, or brainstorming

**Reflect on your choice.**
Attach a note to the piece you chose, explaining briefly why you chose it and what you learned from writing it.

**Set goals.**
How can you improve your writing? What will you focus on the next time you write?

## Writing Across the Curriculum

**Make a performance connection.**
Keep a learning log that explores your involvement in a local or school theater group, dance group, or another type of artistic endeavor that involves action and the participation of other people. Describe the people and tasks that come together in a successful performance. What is your role? List what you're learning about the arts, teamwork, and yourself. Describe any insights you're gaining about your own talents and abilities. Write a brief personal essay based on your learning log to share with your fellow performers.

UNIT

# 2 The Writing Process

**Composition**

## Lessons

UNIT
2
PREVIEW

**Case Study**

# The Writing Process in the Real World

## Building the Editorial Page

**FOCUS: Building an editorial page requires a team of writers who research, analyze, debate, then write reasoned opinions.**

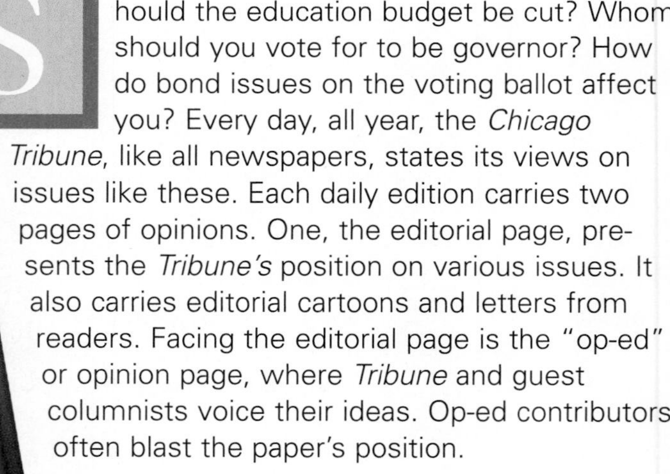

Should the education budget be cut? Whom should you vote for to be governor? How do bond issues on the voting ballot affect you? Every day, all year, the *Chicago Tribune*, like all newspapers, states its views on issues like these. Each daily edition carries two pages of opinions. One, the editorial page, presents the *Tribune's* position on various issues. It also carries editorial cartoons and letters from readers. Facing the editorial page is the "op-ed" or opinion page, where *Tribune* and guest columnists voice their ideas. Op-ed contributors often blast the paper's position.

*N. Don Wycliff*
*Editorial page editor*
Chicago Tribune

*"How do you develop opinions? A good education helps: wide reading; a reasonably thorough acquaintance with philosophy and literature; the varieties of human experience. Then keeping current, reading the newspaper every day. . . . I read everything from Sports Illustrated to New Criterion."*

—N. Don Wycliff

How do all of these ideas get into print every day? Most newspapers have a team called an editorial board; the *Tribune's* board consists of eight writers, a copy editor, two editorial cartoonists, and the page editor, who supervises the team and often writes editorials.

Each writer on the board, including the page editor, specializes in just a few subjects. Former page editor Lois Wille wrote about Illinois and Chicago politics. Don Wycliff, who succeeded her, specializes in social policy and national and international topics.

Every editorial board member reads widely and stays current by interviewing experts in his or her fields. Each day, the page editor and a few writers also meet with various people—representatives of citizen groups, business leaders, public officials, even heads of state—to hear their viewpoints on important issues. One day, the secretary of defense stops by to discuss military spending. Another day, the mayor visits the board to explain the city budget.

*Editorial writers often scan as many as six or seven newspapers a day; they read periodicals and newswire reports and tune in to radio and TV news programs as well.*

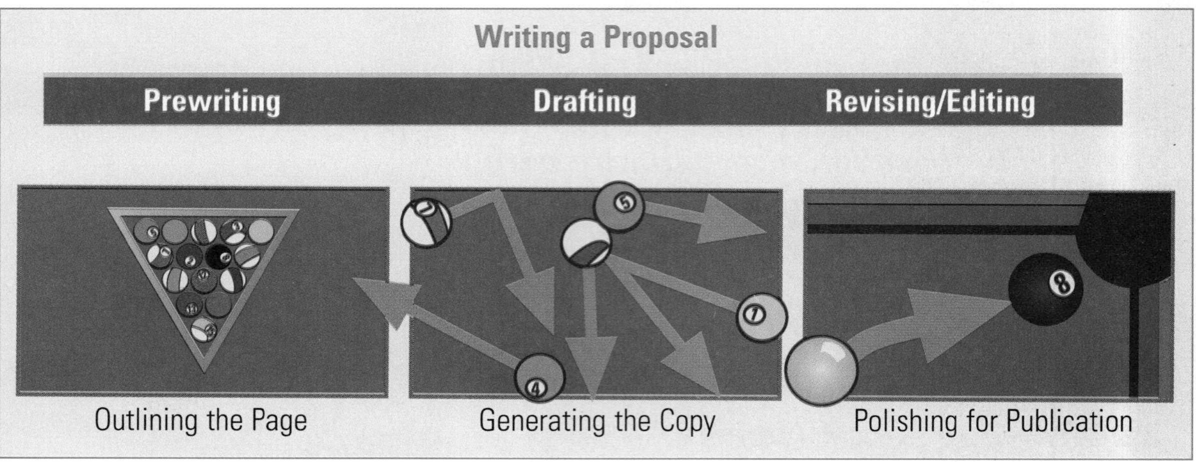


*Wycliff consults with Ellen Soeteber, deputy editorial page editor. Editorial writers must be good at expressing their views—first orally, among themselves, before putting them into print.*

# Prewriting

## OUTLINING THE PAGE

At 10:00 every morning the *Tribune's* editorial board meets in a big conference room four floors above Michigan Avenue. By then, page editor Wycliff and all of the writers have read the Chicago papers, the *New York Times,* the *Wall Street Journal,* and articles in their fields. Discussions are often lively. "People were not selected for the editorial board because they all agreed," says the outgoing editor, Wille. "They were chosen for their good judgment and their curiosity about a range of issues.

The board argues out the topics for the next day's paper, working to keep the page balanced. For instance, the board avoids having coverage of three international topics or three Chicago topics on the page at once.

"I check to see that facts are accurate; that we're not taking off from an unwarranted premise," says Wycliff. "I check that the language be reasonably graceful, if not elegant."

*Soeteber at work: as assistant to Wycliff, she carries out some management duties and writes her own editorials.*

# Drafting

## GENERATING THE COPY

After the meeting, writers head back to their offices to work on their editorials, many of which are due in a few hours. The average editorial runs about five-hundred words (two double-spaced pages).

During prewriting, writers gather an enormous amount of information. In fact, before offering an idea at the morning meeting, they have studied documents, they have read clips of earlier stories, and they have called sources to be sure the facts support their opinions. Now, for the most part, they're ready to sit down at their computers and write. How do they do it?

"First, you frame a good lead," Wycliff says. "When I was a reporter I always figured if I had an hour to do a piece, I'd rather invest forty-five minutes in the lead, and the rest would follow . . . because the lead gives shape to the whole thing. A lead can be long or short, but it's the crucial thing because it tells the reader up front what the piece is about, what your view is, and where you're going to end up.

"After that, you argue the issue through," says Wycliff. "You buttress your opinion, knock down strong points of the other side or concede them—you argue it out."

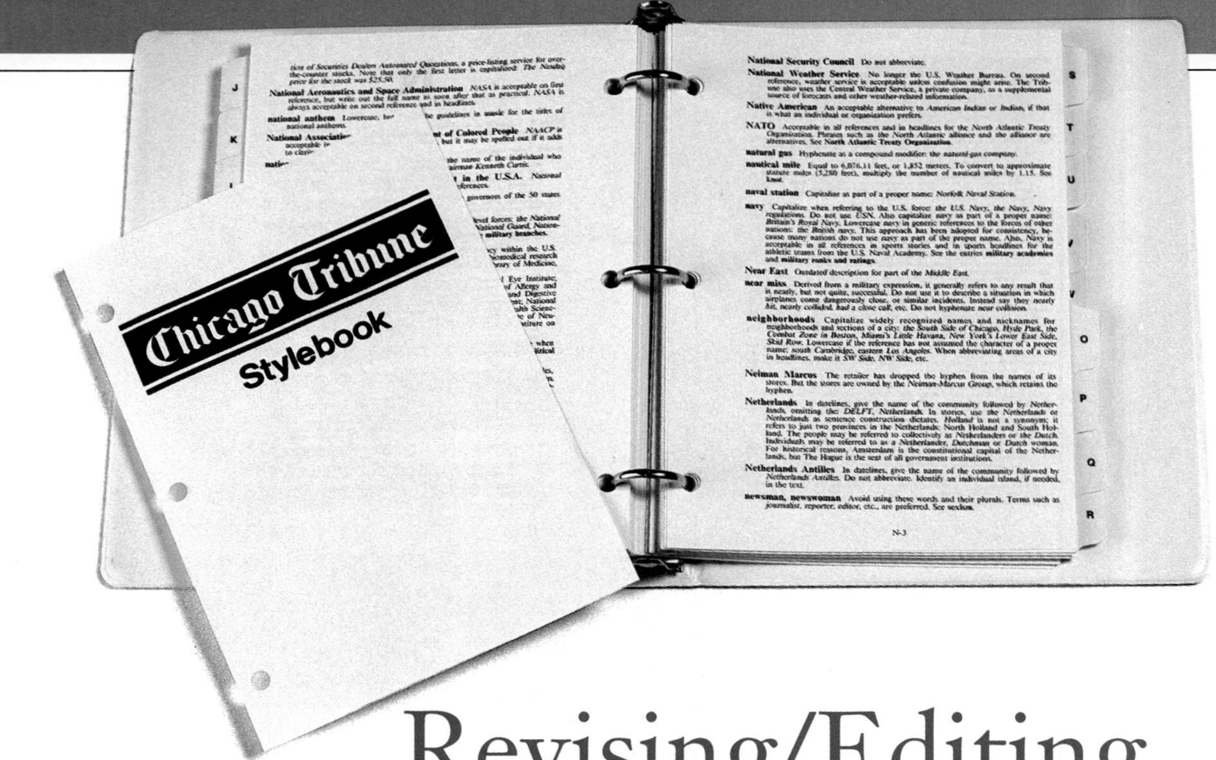


# Revising/Editing

## POLISHING FOR PUBLICATION

*Some major newspapers have their own stylebook (above), which spells out editorial policies on everything from the spelling of foreign city names to whether to hyphenate "teen-ager." Checking for adherence to* Tribune *style is one of the last steps before publication.*

After writers finish their editorials, they push a button, and their copy travels electronically to the editor's computer. There Wycliff reads over the editorials to be sure they support the *Tribune's* policy.

If necessary, he also trims them to fit the space available. When an editorial needs to be cut, Wycliff tries to preserve the flavor of the writer's words and feelings.

Usually, however, the editorials do not require heavy revising. "Most people here are pretty good writers," Wycliff says. "Major changes usually come about because of a difference of opinion about what a piece ought to say."

Once Wycliff gives his okay, the copy travels to the copy editor, who checks it for *Tribune* style: correct punctuation, spelling, abbreviations, and other details. Then the copy zooms electronically to the composing room about a mile away. The editorial board sees the finished pages in the next morning's paper—in time for the 10:00 meeting.

# Responding to the Case Study

**1. Discussion**

**Discuss these questions about editorial writing.**

- Besides reading widely, what else do editorial board members do to stay current?
- How does the editorial board keep each day's page balanced?
- In drafting an editorial, which part is best to focus on because it most affects the whole?
- What situation is likely to lead to heavy revision of an editorial?

**2. Writing an Editorial**

**Write a 250- to 500-word editorial.** Brainstorm topics for editorials, such as banning rock concerts in public parks or sending economic aid to eastern Europe. Choose a topic, research it, and create a list of the pros and cons. Discuss your topic with friends and ask their opinions. Then write the editorial on the topic you choose, using facts from your research to argue your point.

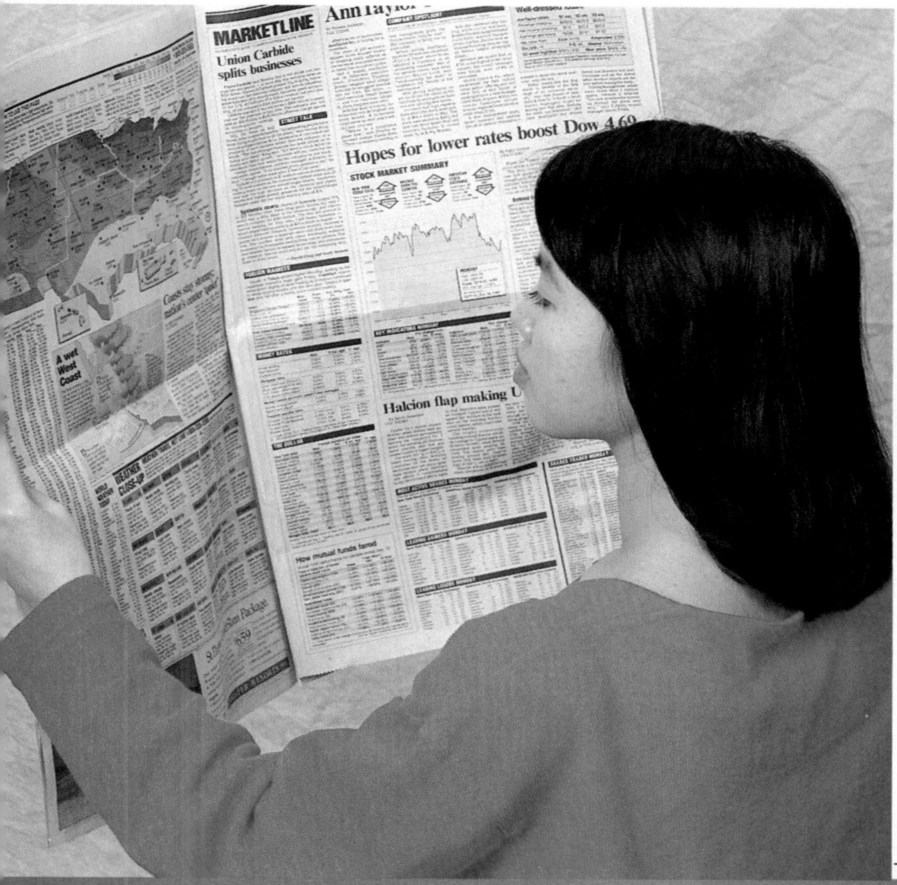

## Grammar Link

**Use specific nouns to convey information clearly.**

*Most writers here have strong **opinions**.*

Use a precise, specific noun to complete the sentences.

1. The editorial page contains some of the best ____ in a newspaper.
2. The editorial page results from a ____ between experts and experienced journalists.
3. Once a lead has been written, the ____ of an editorial is usually established.
4. Some editorials cause strong ____ on the part of readers.
5. Writers gather an enormous amount of ____ before they begin their editorials.

**See Lesson 10.1, pages 397–402.**

LESSON 2.1

# The Writing Process
# An Overview of the Writing Process

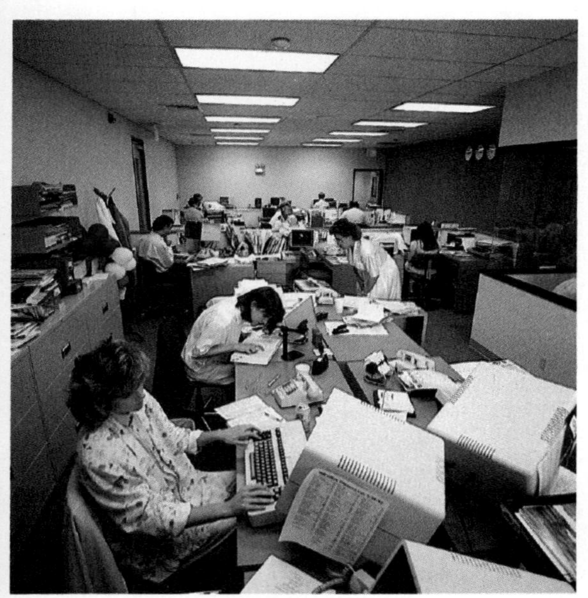

*Writing involves a series of stages in which ideas are formed, words are set down, and the final product is refined and polished. However, stages in the writing process can be repeated or revisited.*

The newsroom is a whirlwind of activity as the final deadline approaches. Computers hum, their screens blinking, as copy editors scan articles for errors. Reporters race to double-check facts in last-minute stories. Within the hour the presses will roll, churning out a newspaper filled with articles.

Professional journalists, and all writers, gather numerous details about a topic through observation, interviews, and research. From this information they build stories. To hold the attention of a diverse audience, journalists revise many times. Finally, their work is presented to you, the reader.

## A Dynamic Process

The writing process is a series of stages that all writers must move through to create their finished product. This process includes prewriting, drafting, revising, editing, and presenting. Although the writing process may sound orderly and predictable, it usually isn't. Writing is a dynamic and sometimes messy process. As you write, you are constantly thinking and discovering new ideas. You are continually evaluating your thoughts and the information you receive, making myriad decisions about what works and what doesn't, and shaping and reshaping your ideas into a unified and coherent whole. In the prewriting stage, you explore ideas, choose a topic, and collect and organize your information. As you draft, you turn your ideas and information into sentences and paragraphs. During revising, you review and refine, grappling with any problems you detect in content and structure. Finally, you edit your work to eliminate errors, and then you present your writing to your audience.

As the illustration on the right shows, writers move in and out of the various stages of the writing process, and this movement is recursive, doubling back on itself, rather than progressing in a straight line from prewriting to presenting.

The model below shows the revision stage in action. Notice how the writer worked with the material to build a coherent and humorous introductory paragraph for the essay.

How did the writer refine the paragraph, and what problems with the content and structure did the writer solve?

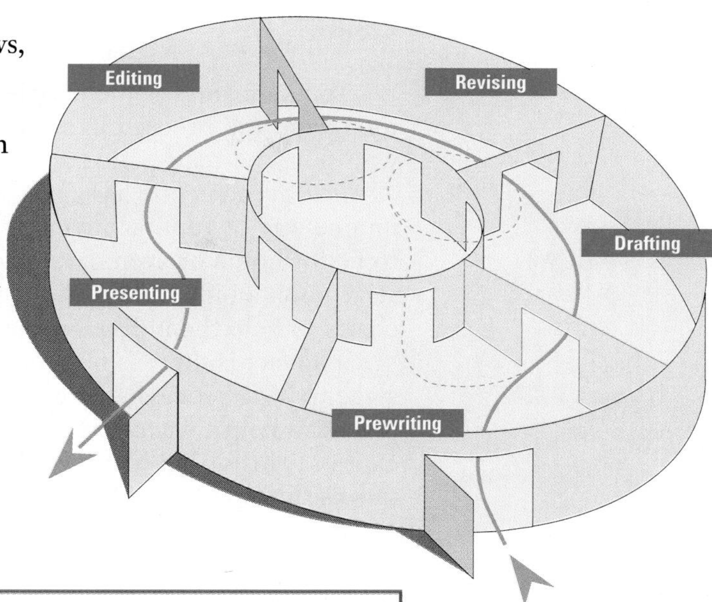


## Model

*Imagine designing and building the ideal school locker.* *Next,* ~~T~~think about the items a high school student needs to store. *Brooms? Arrows? No.* A high school student needs a place for *folders, binders, floppy discs, magazines, paper, tape recorders, coats, jackets, and even an umbrella.* ~~books and many other things.~~ *Now* Picture a designer closet or cabinet--a space filled with cubbyholes and compartments planned to fit the items *actually* stored in that space. ~~That is~~ the ideal ~~school~~ locker. *Apply the same principle, and you are ready to design and build* *First* ~~C~~consider the existing school locker--a space suitable for objects such as arrows, umbrellas, and brooms.

## Journal Writing

What stage of the writing process do you find the easiest? Which stage causes you the most trouble? Why do you think this is so? Do you dislike it? What other thoughts do you have about writing? Jot down your ideas in whatever form seems most suitable.

## Establish Your Personal Writing Process

You may know some people who—when they cook—carefully read the recipe and proceed in an orderly fashion. You probably know others who skim the recipe and substitute ingredients in their own variation.

Just as each cook has an approach to cooking, each writer has a unique way of approaching a writing task. Some writers muse on a topic for hours or even days before they begin to write. Other writers seize upon an idea and begin making lists or creating diagrams and charts to help them develop the idea.

The fact is there is no one "right" approach to writing. The five-stage writing process—prewriting, drafting, revising, editing, presenting—can help a writer create a piece of writing that effectively expresses his or her ideas. Each writer, however, plunges into and moves through the process in a unique way.

In the following excerpt from an interview, professional writer Toni Cade Bambara discusses her writing process.

### *Literature Model*

There's no particular routine to my writing, nor have any two stories come to me in the same way. I'm usually working on five or six things at a time; that is, I scribble a lot in bits and pieces and generally pin them together with a working title. The actual sit-down work is still weird to me. I babble along, heading I think in one direction, only to discover myself tugged in another, or sometimes I'm absolutely snatched into an alley. I write in longhand or what kin and friends call deranged hieroglyphics. I begin on long, yellow paper with a juicy ballpoint if it's one of those 6/8 bop pieces. For slow, steady, watch-the-voice-kid, don't-let-the-mask-slip-type pieces, I prefer short fat-lined paper and an ink pen. I usually work it over and beat it up and sling it around the room a lot before I get to the typing stage. I hate to type—hate, hate—so things get cut mercilessly at that stage. I stick the thing in a drawer or pin it on a board for a while, maybe read it to someone or a group, get some feedback, mull it over, and put it aside. Then, when an editor calls me to say, "Got anything?" or I find the desk cluttered, or some reader sends a letter asking, "You still breathing?" or I need some dough, I'll very studiously sit down, edit, type, and send [it].

Toni Cade Bambara, *Black Women Writers at Work*

# 2.1 Writing Activities

## Write a Paragraph

Write a paragraph that describes how you approach a writing assignment from beginning to end. Examine and write about your own writing process, including the attitudes and emotions you usually experience when you write. Keep in mind the following questions:

- How do you find topics to write about?
- What strategies do you use to gather and organize information?
- How do you revise your work?
- Which stages in your writing process often lead back to others?

**PURPOSE** To explore your own writing process
**AUDIENCE** Yourself
**LENGTH** 1 paragraph

### Grammar Link

**Make sure that the verb of an inverted sentence agrees with the subject.**

*There **is** no particular **routine** to my writing.*

Choose the correct form of the verb in each of these sentences.

1. On the table (lies, lie) the letters you sent me.
2. There (is, are) quite a few solutions to this problem.
3. From the darkness (appear, appears) a shadowy figure.
4. Why (does, do) the very best athletes seek so much publicity?
5. Here (is, are) a study sheet for tomorrow's test.

**See Lesson 16.3, pages 568–569.**

## Cooperative Learning

In a group, discuss the unfinished sculpture by Michelangelo shown on this page. What does the sculpture represent? What does it reveal about the sculpting process? What steps might Michelangelo have followed to get to this point? What might he have done to finish it?

Discuss as a group how the process of creating a work of art, such as the sculpture shown here, is similar to the process of creating a written work. Have one member of the group record the ideas as they emerge from the discussion, and then read them back to the group.

Work independently to write a brief essay comparing and contrasting the writing process and the sculpting process. Use a partner to help you revise and edit your draft. Share your finished essay with the group.

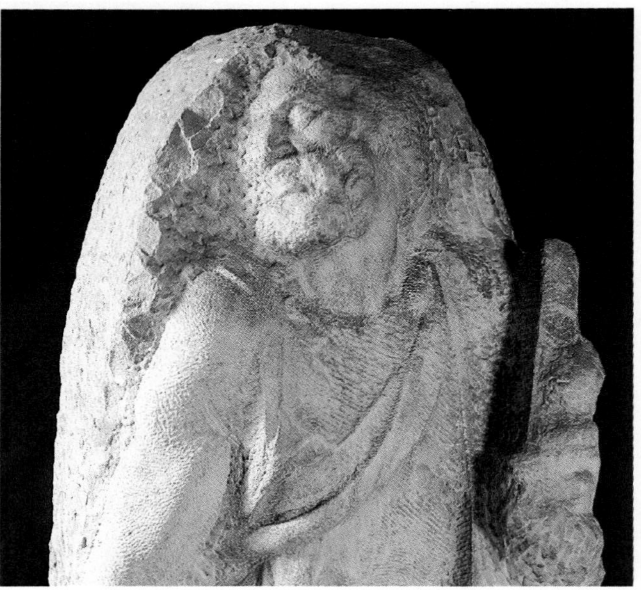

Michelangelo, *St. Matthew*, c. 1520

LESSON

2.2

# The Writing Process
# Prewriting: Finding a Topic

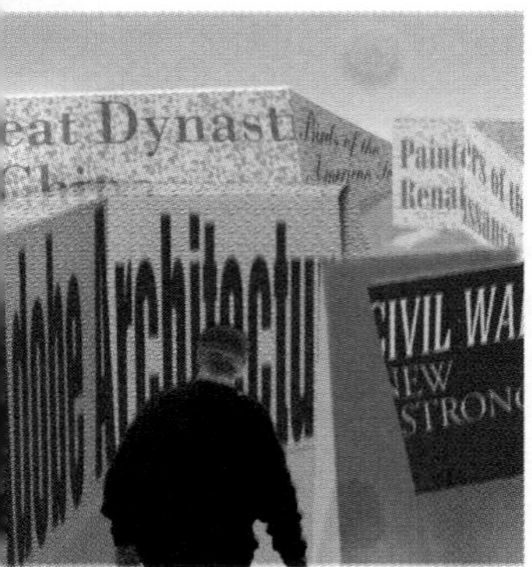


*Most writers have their own ways of exploring topics. Many techniques can help you sort through the maze of ideas. As you experiment with some of these, you'll find the techniques that work best for you.*

## Cluster Related Ideas

Clustering is a very useful technique for finding a writing topic. Begin by writing a word or an idea in the middle of a sheet of paper, as Valerie Stahl did with *building things* in the cluster below. That word or phrase may be a topic assigned to you, something you know you want to write about, or a thought you select at random just to get your ideas flowing. Circle the phrase. Then think of related words and ideas. Write them in bubbles connected to the central bubble.

*From a single phrase, Valerie Stahl has come up with several potential writing topics, from building healthy bodies to building relationships.*

**Student Model**

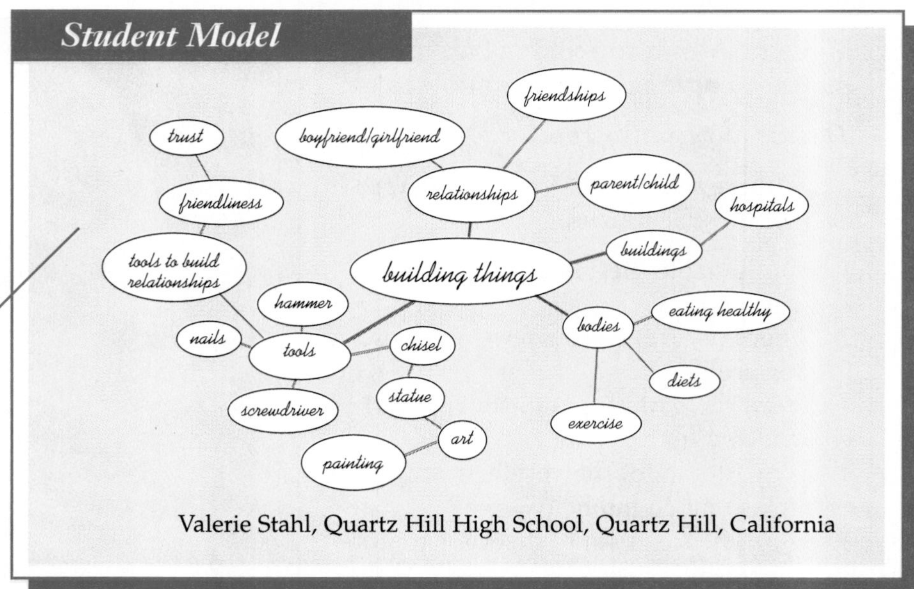


Valerie Stahl, Quartz Hill High School, Quartz Hill, California

As you cluster, your secondary ideas may spawn several related words and phrases, or you may go back and record associations to the original, central idea. Either way, the resulting cluster is not only a group of ideas, but a diagram of how these ideas relate to one another. Of course, you don't need to use all the information in a cluster. What's more, you can use one idea or branch of your original cluster as a new starting place, and cluster again for new topics or for supporting details.

## Brainstorm Topics

In brainstorming, another technique for finding writing topics, you also quickly list ideas as they occur to you. However, when you brainstorm, your ideas often do not follow a particular line of reasoning as they do when you create a cluster. Instead, you can jump from one seemingly unrelated idea to another.

You can brainstorm alone, but brainstorming in a group yields more ideas. Group members toss out ideas as thoughts occur to them, bouncing suggestions off the contributions of others. Because brainstorming is so dynamic, it's important to keep a record of what's said. This list can supply new topics if seemingly promising ideas don't pan out or if they don't provide enough supporting details for the topic the group chooses.

**Brainstorming Together**

The illustration shows the group brainstorming process in action. As you can see, one individual's idea can serve as a spark that ignites the thinking of another group member, and an explosion of ideas can occur. For example, the word *maze* might spark a rhyme, such as *craze* or *daze*, from one group member; a dream about being lost in a maze from another person; and the suggestion of experiments involving mice running through mazes from a third person. The first person, who specializes in word play, might then think of being lost in *a maze* of *maize*, or corn; while the third person might add, "What if it were some kind of mad-scientist experiment?" The topic for a fantasy or science-fiction piece is beginning to take shape.

### Journal Writing

Build your own cluster around a word from the diagram on page 64 or around a term of your choice. Choose a promising topic, and then cluster again for details about that topic.

## Freewrite

Take a sheet of paper and begin writing. About what? Write your thoughts as they occur to you. Write your thoughts about your thoughts. Use sentences or phrases, single words or rhymed pairs, whatever comes to mind. Write for a specified time without stopping.

This technique, called *freewriting*, is another useful way of finding a writing topic. Freewriting gets your ideas flowing. Notice how freewriting helps the following writer to focus on an idea for a writing topic.

***Model***

Start writing. Start thinking. Let's see. I went to see *Camelot* the other night. I love theater—the acting, the sets, the costumes, the music, everything about it. Maybe there's a writing topic here somewhere. I didn't like the actor who portrayed Merlin, though. He just wasn't right. I would have picked someone wiser looking, not stern though. Maybe that would work—casting. How are casting decisions made? How does a casting director build a cast? I could interview casting directors from local theater companies and then write about the process. I'll have to look into this.

Here's another example of freewriting to find a writing topic. How do the approaches of the two writers compare?

***Model***

Write. Think. Ideas. Topics. Wish I were outside instead of here. Could soak up some sun on the football field. Watch the people on the track. Love sports. The Olympics. Training for the Olympics. How? What sport? Maybe ice hockey. Great game. People still talk about U.S. vs. the Soviets 19?? Olympics. U.S. team wins! Was it 1980? Maybe write about that team—who was on it, how they trained, lead up to the final big moment. Wonder what's become of those guys. Have to check it out.

*How did the writer get from wishing to be outside to finding a good topic? Try to find the links between the major ideas in the freewriting samples.*

In freewriting, it's not important whether you use complete sentences as the first writer did, or mostly phrases and single words. Do whatever is most comfortable and natural for you. Your goal is to find a topic that really interests you.

# 2.2 Writing Activities

## Write an Idea Cluster and a Freewrite Paragraph

Create a cluster starting with the central idea "frightening experiences." After you have generated several ideas, review them and choose one as a writing topic. Then freewrite about the topic to discover even more about it.

- Experiment with clustering.
- If necessary, use brainstorming.
- Freewrite for five or ten minutes.

**PURPOSE** To practice prewriting techniques
**AUDIENCE** Yourself
**LENGTH** 1 cluster plus 1 paragraph

### Grammar Link

**Vary the kinds of sentences to make your paragraph more interesting.**

*Start thinking.* ***[imperative sentence]*** *How are casting decisions made?* ***[interrogative sentence]*** *I'll have to look into this.* ***[declarative sentence]***

Rewrite the paragraph below so that it contains at least three different kinds of sentences (declarative, imperative, interrogative, or exclamatory).

It might be hard to approach this subject. I should give myself time for ideas to form. I wonder where my ideas will lead. This is very hard. I don't know how to start.

**See Lesson 13.8, page 512.**

## Cross-Curricular: Art

Look carefully at Fernand Léger's painting *The City* on this page. Freewrite about the images, colors, and shapes. Next, speculate about what Léger thinks of cities; list or cluster the characteristics he seems to focus on. Then do the same for your own reaction to the painting. Finally, select one of the ideas from your prewriting, and write a short paragraph that tells why you think the idea might be a good writing topic.

Fernand Léger, *The City*, 1919

LESSON

# 2.3

The Writing Process

# Prewriting: Establishing Purpose and Audience

*During prewriting you can find a topic, target an audience, and establish a purpose. However, you may vary the order of these activities, depending on the circumstances.*

This song makes me want to dance!
Mommy, please buy me that toy!
Which key does what?



The composer of a song, the developer of a commercial, and the writer of instructions are all aware of an audience and all have a purpose in mind. When you listen, you are part of an audience. What are the different kinds of audiences in these photographs?

## Relate Purpose and Audience

Writers have identified the five purposes shown in the chart below. A rich and complex written work seldom has only one of these aims, but one purpose is usually dominant.

As you define your purpose or purposes, identify a corresponding audience. There are often several audiences for a topic and purpose. For example, a television network's goal is to attract and entertain a wide audience, but entertainment means something quite different to children, teenagers, sports fans, mystery mavens, and current-events connoisseurs. The same topic and purpose can be treated differently, depending on the audience.

**The Five Purposes of Writing**

1. To inform
2. To persuade
3. To amuse or entertain
4. To narrate
5. To describe

## Profile Your Audiences

Identifying several traits of your audience can help you effectively appeal to them in your writing. The illustration on the right shows some characteristics you should consider.

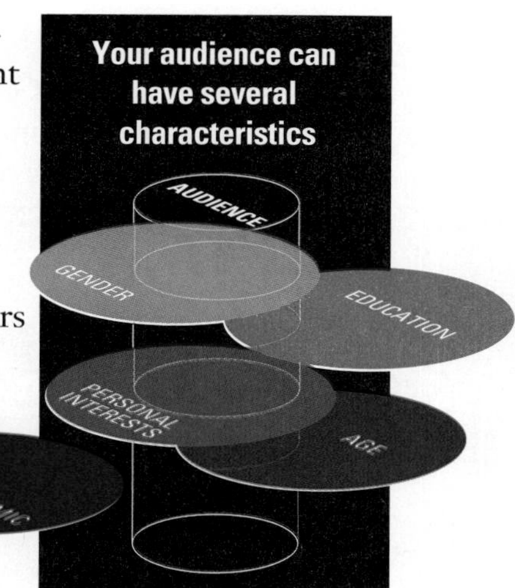


Once you have profiled your readers, you can tailor your writing to the content that will interest them, the style that will hold their attention, and the vocabulary they will best understand. For example, suppose you are writing an informational article about skyscrapers for young children. You might focus on how skyscrapers are built, using an informal style and simple vocabulary. If, on the other hand, your audience is the adult readership of an architectural magazine, you might focus on the development of a single architectural feature, using a formal style and technical language.

Below is an excerpt from a speech by former Congresswoman Barbara Jordan. Notice that she assumes a certain level of knowledge on the part of her audience and uses a formal style, a serious tone, and sophisticated language.

### *Literature Model*

Voting is the supreme privilege of a democracy and more. It is also the obligation of a people who portend to govern themselves . . . a heavy obligation and an exquisite burden. The pundits say that only half of the eligible electorate will vote. I hope they are wrong. A democratic government depends on an informed and enlightened electorate for its legitimacy. That statement is not quite true. The voters may give the government its legitimacy but they may not be informed nor enlightened. It is desirable that they be so. To the extent that people do not vote, to the extent that people are inattentive to the pain, perils, and policies of a democracy, that democracy is at risk.

Barbara Jordan, "Is Our Democracy at Risk?"

*Which words would you change if you were adapting this speech for a junior high school audience? For your classmates? For college students?*

### Journal Writing

Prewrite to identify a potential writing topic related to one of the photographs on page 68. Then write a few questions that you might use to profile your audience for that writing.

## Match Your Main Idea to Purpose and Audience

Once you have a topic, a purpose, and an audience for a piece of writing, you need to narrow your focus—to zero in on what you really want to say and how to say it. In other words, you need to select and refine a main idea that you could express as the topic sentence of a paragraph or the thesis statement of an essay. This main idea must be closely related to your purpose and audience.

*How would you change this ad to make it more appropriate?*

What happens when there is a mismatch among a writer's purpose, target audience, and main idea? The advertisement shown here is an example of such a problem. The purpose of this ad is to convince an audience preoccupied with looking younger to buy and use a skin moisturizer. Think about how you would profile that target audience. Read the main idea conveyed by the content—words and pictures. What changes would you make in the ad to improve the match between your main idea and your purpose and audience?

A good match is important in writing, too. In the model below, the writer's purpose is to inform or explain the tasks of a yearbook photography staff, and the target audience is a group of novice yearbook photographers. As you read, see how well the writer succeeds in matching the main idea to a purpose and audience.

*What is the main idea in this paragraph?*

*The writer provides the novice photographer with plenty of useful examples.*

***Model***

To build a collection of yearbook photographs that truly reflects the life of Washington High School, the photography staff must focus on taking candid shots. What is a "candid" shot? It's the quarterback making a touchdown that wins the game. It's a senior consoling a teary sophomore. It's an art class tramping across campus looking for an interesting perspective. It's a group of students, eating lunch in the cafeteria, arguing about grade requirements for athletes. It's a teacher actually dancing in the talent show. It's any spontaneous happening—silly, sad, serious, maddening—recorded on film that illustrates the 8-to-3 life of Washingtonians. The only way a yearbook photographer can get these shots is to be ever on the lookout, camera in hand (or close by), ready to shoot.

# 2.3 Writing Activities

## Write a Thesis Statement

Use your cluster and freewriting paragraphs about "frightening experiences" to develop your topic into a thesis statement for an essay or story. Develop your thesis statement into the first draft of an opening paragraph with supporting details.

- Determine a purpose: to inform, to persuade, to amuse or entertain, to narrate, or to describe.
- Identify your audience, using the characteristics in the illustration on page 69.
- Develop a main idea that is appropriate for your purpose and audience.
- Express that main idea as a thesis statement, and use it to guide your choice of supporting details.

**PURPOSE** To write a thesis statement about "frightening experiences"
**AUDIENCE** Your choice
**LENGTH** 1 paragraph

## Cooperative Learning

With three classmates create an advertisement with a good match between purpose and audience and the main idea.

First, brainstorm for a list of potential products or services you might advertise. As a group, review the list and choose one product or service for which to create an advertisement. (Review the sample advertisement on page 70.) Then identify your target audience. (Remember that your purpose is to persuade your audience to buy your product or service.) Discuss the audience characteristics that you think are important to consider.

Next, develop a main idea for your advertisement. What key point should you make about the product or service? Work as a group to create the words and pictures for your ad. Divide up the tasks according to the talents of each member. (You may wish to "borrow" the illustration from a magazine.) Finally, ask the class whether they think the purpose, audience, and main idea of your ad are an effective match.

### Grammar Link

**Distinguish between possessive pronouns and contractions that require an apostrophe.**

*A democratic government depends on an informed and enlightened electorate for* ***its*** *legitimacy.*
***It's*** *a senior consoling a teary sophomore.*

Fill in the blanks with *its* or *it's* or *their* or *they're.*

1 ____ not easy facing the first day of school after a lovely summer. 2 Still, returning to school has ____ advantages. 3 You'll find ____ a pleasure to continue friendships you made before summer break. 4–5 Even the discipline of homework will find ____ place in your daily routine, and you'll accommodate your routine to ____ requirements.

6 Not all classes offer the same rewards for all students, depending on ____ interests. 7–9 Even when ____ not keenly interested in a subject, most students do ____ homework assignments so that ____ not in danger of failing the class. 10 In most cases, students see that this is a matter of accepting ____ responsibility.

**See Lesson 21.13 on pages 702–704.**

LESSON

2.4

# The Writing Process
# Drafting: Ordering Your Thoughts

*Just as a landscaper chooses and lays out plants to create a beautiful garden, a writer selects ideas and orders them in an enticing way, leading readers through a satisfying experience.*

In the following passage from *Green Thoughts* by Eleanor Perényi, note the very practical considerations involved in creating the beauty of a perennial garden. Also notice how Perényi links her ideas, arranging them as carefully as her flower beds.

*The transition "much more important" indicates that the previous paragraph was about "choosing plants ahead of time."*

*How does the first sentence preview the order of ideas within this paragraph?*

## Literature Model

Much more important than choosing plants ahead of time is deciding on the location, size and shape of the beds themselves. You can't keep digging up the lawn as you change your mind, or make the belated discovery that the spot you picked is in deep shade all afternoon. A bed can be any length, but no wider than can be reached for weeding by someone on hands and knees. Island beds can be broader than a border beneath a wall, because there is access from both sides. But on no account should any bed be so wide that it must be waded into bodily to get at the plants. As to shape, I prefer the rectangle. For reasons I can no more analyze than defend, I can't abide flower beds with sinuous, irregular outlines.

Eleanor Perényi, *Green Thoughts*

## Create a Sense of Order

As a writer you can choose from many kinds of details—such as examples, facts, statistics, reasons, and concrete or sensory details—to support your main idea. To find supporting details, use the prewriting techniques of clustering, brainstorming, and freewriting.

Your purpose and main idea will determine which kinds of supporting details you decide to include in your draft as well as the order in which you arrange them. Sensory details, for example, can make the description of a garden come to life, while reasons are most useful in arguing a case or explaining why flower beds should be a certain size. Be sure to keep your purpose in mind as you decide how to organize your writing. As you can see from the chart below, some patterns of organization are better suited to particular purposes than others.

| Type of Order | Characteristics | Purpose/Effect |
|---|---|---|
| **Chronological** | Presents events as they happen over time | To explain a process, to narrate a series of events |
| **Spatial** | Presents items in relationships within a place or setting | To describe items in relation to one another or in relation to the viewer |
| **Order of Importance** | Presents information in a hierarchy, or ranking | To persuade, explain, or describe by arranging reasons from least to most, or from most to least, important |
| **Cause and Effect** | Presents events as reason and result, motive and reaction, stimulus and response | To explain an event or series of events in terms of reasons or results, to persuade by stating effects |
| **Compare and Contrast** | Measures items against one another to show how they are alike and how they are different | To show the relationship between items, to persuade by showing the pros and cons of different actions |

Finding the best order for ideas may not be straightforward. During the drafting stage, you may need to return to the prewriting stage to refocus. Don't be concerned about making a U-turn. Ultimately, clarifying your purpose will help you to find a clear, logical way to present your ideas.

### Journal Writing

In your journal, list three potential essay topics and a purpose for each. Then list the type of order you would choose if you were to write about each topic.

# Organize Your Essay

In the conventional organization of an essay, the introductory paragraph "grabs" the reader's attention and makes the main idea clear. The body paragraphs present information that supports the main idea, and the concluding paragraph finalizes the discussion.

While this structure is typical, it is not rigid. Actually, you have many options within this basic structure, and you can even "break the rules" if you do so for a good reason. For example, you might begin with a provocative question, or you might choose to end with such a question. The conventional structure, however, is clear and logical, making your essay easier for you to draft and for your reader to follow.

## The Introduction

Consider your introduction a doorway through which you will lead your reader into your essay. The doorway itself should be appealing, and it should also afford a tantalizing glimpse of what lies beyond. Frequently, the main idea, or thesis, appears in the introduction. You may either imply your thesis or state it explicitly in a thesis statement. Following is a two-paragraph introduction from an essay.

*Notice how Harris draws the reader from the first to the second paragraph, where he states his main idea.*

*Literature Model*

There is no way of deciding the running argument between the people who believe in a liberal arts education and those who believe in a technical education until we ask and answer one prior question.

This question is: What kind of persons do we want our colleges to turn out? Is it enough to "train" students, or do they somehow have to be changed in outlook and attitude? If we decide it is not enough just to "train" students, then we must look to the humanities and social sciences for means of changing them.

Sydney J. Harris, "Science Can't Give Us Everything"

## The Body

In the body of an essay, you support the thesis both in content and in tone. Details should be presented in a definite order that is apparent to the reader, and there should be smooth transitions both within paragraphs and from one paragraph to the next. Read the body of the Harris essay on the following page. Even if you disagree with Harris, take note of how he makes his case.

## *Literature Model*

Literature, history, sociology, philosophy, anthropology—these differ in much more than subject matter from physics, chemistry, engineering, and mathematics. They differ in that the knowledge we have of them affects both the future of the subject and of ourselves.

Our knowledge of the table of atomic weights does not change the atomic system. Our knowledge of algebra or calculus does not affect these mathematical concepts. Our knowledge of metal fatigue and structural stress does not alter those physical laws.

But our knowledge of the humanities and the social sciences is an essential part of those systems. In sociology, for instance, once we truly understand the nature of group pressure and the influence of prejudice, both we and the subject have been modified.

If we know what Shakespeare was getting at in *King Lear,* if we can grasp what was wrong with the Treaty of Versailles, if we see what the existentialists are trying to express—then we are able to utilize this knowledge to reshape our own views of life and to exert influence on those we live with. . . .

The humanities are not "superior" to technical studies because they are more ancient or more "cultural" or more intellectual; these would be poor, and snobbish, reasons for granting them any sort of priority.

They are superior because they expand the imagination, enlarge the personality, enable us to become something different and better than what we were before. Learning a chemical formula does not make a man different; reading Donne's sermons can change his whole life drastically.

Sidney J. Harris, "Science Can't Give Us Everything"

*What is repeated here? Why is it effective?*

*Here Harris summarizes the contrast introduced in earlier paragraphs.*

## Journal Writing

Find an introductory paragraph that you think is especially effective. Paste a copy of it in your journal, and then write a few sentences telling why you think it works well.

## Conclude Your Essay

Imagine for a moment that you have taped a television movie in order to watch it later. Now you've settled down to watch the movie, popcorn in hand. You're caught up in the story, when suddenly the tape ends. You didn't set the timer correctly on your video recorder, so you didn't get the last part of the movie on tape. You're left frustrated, wondering what happened to the character and how the situation was finally resolved.

Readers experience that same kind of frustration when they read a piece of writing that lacks a conclusion. Some writers run down when they get to the end of their essays, forgetting that a good concluding paragraph is as important as the rest of the essay. It may even be more important: not only does the concluding paragraph bring the discussion of the topic to a close, but it's also the writer's last chance to make an impression.

Your conclusion may point out important ideas or emphasize the thesis. Alternatively, you may save the best example, quotation, ironic fact, or humorous anecdote for last. If you choose not to restate your position in your conclusion, make sure that you've stated your case well enough in the body of your essay. Notice how Harris closes his essay first by recalling the question he asked in his opening paragraphs and then by intensifying the contrast he introduced there.

*Literature Model*

Our great need today is not so much for better-trained technicians as it is for well-rounded persons who know how their subject fits into other subjects, and who can relate their experience to some general framework of human experience. Without this, we will breed only a generation of technical barbarians, who do brilliantly what they have been taught to do, but who are blind to the consequences of their actions. This may be an admirable quality in a soldier; it is a disastrous one in a free citizen.

Sidney J. Harris, "Science Can't Give Us Everything"

*The emotional intensity rises in the conclusion. How does Harris create a sense of urgency here?*

Each part of an essay—the introduction, the body, the conclusion—performs an important function in helping a writer present ideas. As you draft, remember that the organization of an essay is not intended to be a rigid prescription. Instead, it offers both writer and reader a clear and logical guide to the main and supporting ideas. While each part has its own special form, function, and characteristics, the final construction should be a well-integrated and harmonious whole.

# 2.4 Writing Activities

## Write a First Draft of Your Introduction

Plan the order of your essay or story about a frightening experience and then write a first draft of your introduction.

Look back at the opening paragraph you wrote. Think about its appeal. Would it make a reader want to go on? Does it express your main idea—either directly or implicitly?

Draft 1–2 paragraphs for an introduction.

- State or imply your main idea clearly.
- Use words that will interest readers.
- Use words and phrases to carry the reader along.

**PURPOSE** To introduce an essay on a frightening experience
**AUDIENCE** Your choice
**LENGTH** 1–2 paragraphs

## Cooperative Learning

Reread the essay "Science Can't Give Us Everything" found on pages 74 to 76. Discuss its content and strategy with a partner paying careful attention to its organization.

Work together with your partner to develop a newspaper opinion column in response to the Harris essay. Your column should be about what particular field or type of education should be stressed in high school. It might recommend stressing anything from art to biology, cooking, geography, or physical fitness. Work together to decide on content and overall organization, then divide the writing responsibilities. One might write the opening and conclusion and the other might write the body. Work together to make the parts fit together smoothly.

### Grammar Link

**Make your subjects agree with their verbs.**

Don't confuse the number of a subject because of an intervening phrase.

*Our **knowledge** of the table of atomic weights **does** not change the atomic system.*

Choose the verb that agrees in number with the subject.

1. Only one project from all of those companies (appears, appear) in this catalog.
2. Sheila, as well as I, (detests, detest) hot summer days.
3. Every exercise and review question completed (brings, bring) me closer to my vacation.
4. Fear, in addition to learned prejudice, (makes, make) some people distrustful of other ethnic groups.
5. Style, perhaps the most important element in holding readers' attention, (contributes, contribute) to the overall impression of the book.

**See Lesson 16.1, pages 565–566, and Lesson 16.6, page 574.**

LESSON

# 2.5 The Writing Process

# Drafting: Writing with Unity and Coherence

*If you have to read a paragraph several times to figure out the connections between ideas, it's likely that the writing lacks two important elements: unity and coherence.*

In the following paragraph from *Unbuilding*, notice how clear the main point is and how carefully David Macaulay guides his readers.

**Literature Model**

By the end of the 1920s the island of Manhattan was the undisputed skyscraper capital of the world. Since the turn of the century its buildings had been forced to grow upward because of both the high cost of land and the desire to build as much rentable floor space as possible on it. The construction of almost two hundred skyscrapers between 1902 and 1929 was made possible by improvements in the quality of steel, in the design of a structural-steel frame which could support both the floors and walls of these buildings, and in the capabilities of the all-important elevator. The erection of higher and higher buildings was encouraged both by increasing confidence in these technological advances and by a growing sense of competition among the buildings' owners.

David Macaulay, *Unbuilding*

## Write with Unity and Coherence

Unity and coherence are related, but they are not the same. A paragraph has unity when each sentence clearly contributes to the main idea expressed in the topic sentence. In the model

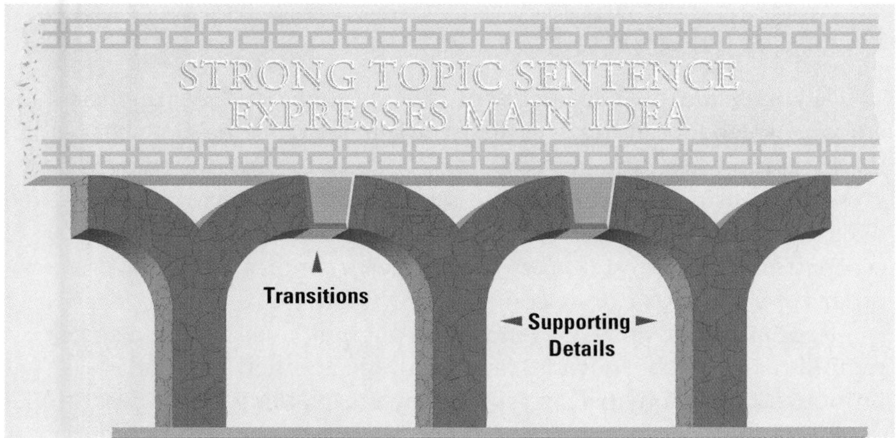


each detail contributes to the explanation of how and why so many skyscrapers were built in Manhattan. A paragraph is coherent when its sentences proceed logically and smoothly with no gaps in reasoning. Transitional words and phrases often indicate the links and relationships between ideas. In the preceding model, Macaulay moves from the need for taller buildings to the technology that made them possible to the attitudes inspired by that technology. Transitions such as *since* and *between* guide the reader through time, while such words as *higher and higher*, *increasing*, and *growing* emphasize the "rise" of the Manhattan skyscraper.

## Build Unity

Writers achieve unity in a paragraph by constructing a strong topic sentence that can serve as the basis for all subsequent sentences. You may express the main idea of a paragraph directly or indirectly. The stated or implied topic sentence allows you to determine which details to use as support; it can also help you to decide how to order these details.

Your purpose helps determine the placement of the topic sentence. When you place it first, you immediately establish the shape of the paragraph. In some cases, however, you may find it more effective to lead up to your topic sentence. Stating a topic sentence directly can sound forced and artificial. In narrative and descriptive writing, for example, the natural flow of the material may convey your meaning without the need for a stated topic sentence. Wherever you place your topic sentence, and whether you state it or not, be sure that all sentences in the paragraph relate to it.

### Journal Writing

In your journal write a strong topic sentence about a favorite building. Make sure to use vivid verbs. Then write two or three supporting sentences that use concrete, relevant details.

## Build Coherence

*Coherence* means "the quality of sticking together." Writing is coherent when readers can move easily from one sentence to the next, reading the paragraph as an integrated whole. You can ensure this smooth progression by using transitional words and phrases. Transitions can introduce illustrations (*for example*), add details (*also*, *in addition*), show comparison or contrast (*although*, *nevertheless*), indicate time or space order (*later*, *above*), or draw conclusions (*therefore*).

Repeating key words or phrases throughout a paragraph also can remind readers how your ideas relate to one another. In some cases, pronouns and synonyms can reinforce while avoiding actual repetition. Such repetition and reinforcement emphasize the sequence of ideas and keep the discussion tied together. In the following passage from Lucy, notice how Jamaica Kincaid uses these devices to achieve coherence.

*What do the words "morning" and "first" have in common? How does their repetition emphasize the narrator's new experience?*

*How does "seeing the sun" function as a transition?*

*Notice how the last sentence brings the ideas and the repeated words together, rounding out the paragraph.*

**Literature Model**

That morning, the morning of my first day, the morning that followed my first night, was a sunny morning. It was not the sort of bright sun-yellow making everything curl at the edges, almost in fright, that I was used to, but a pale-yellow sun, as if the sun had grown weak from trying too hard to shine; but still it was sunny, and that was nice and made me miss my home less. And so, seeing the sun, I got up and put on a dress, a gay dress made out of madras cloth—the same sort of dress that I would wear if I were at home and setting out for a day in the country. It was all wrong. The sun was shining but the air was cold. It was the middle of January, after all. But I did not know that the sun could shine and air remain cold; no one had ever told me. What a feeling that was! How can I explain? Something I had always known—the way I knew my skin was the color brown of a nut rubbed repeatedly with a soft cloth, or the way I knew my own name—something I took completely for granted, "the sun is shining, the air is warm," was not so.

Jamaica Kincaid, *Lucy*

Without being monotonous, the repetition of important nouns and of the pronoun *it* in the passage from *Lucy* stresses the important aspects of the narrator's experience.

# 2.5 Writing Activities

## Write a Draft of Your Essay

Reread your introduction about frightening experiences. What kind of order does it suggest would be necessary? Next, outline your ideas. Consider your conclusion and how it relates to the thesis statement and the body of your essay. Now draft your essay, using your outline as a guide.

- Make each paragraph unified—with each sentence contributing to the main idea
- Choose the most effective order.
- Use transitions to blend sentences.

**PURPOSE** To draft an essay
**AUDIENCE** Your choice
**LENGTH** May vary

## Cross-Curricular: Art

Like writing, works of visual art are expected to conform to standards of unity and coherence. Sometimes, however, artists purposely manipulate the viewer's expectations. Look carefully at the cubist painting and answer these questions:

- How does Picasso challenge expectations?
- Does the painting have unity?
- How does it help you see the human face and human emotions in a new way?

Write a paragraph covering all or some of these issues. Be sure to draft a strong topic sentence. Once you have completed your draft, revise for unity and coherence.

### Grammar Link

**Use the comparative form of adjectives correctly.**

*The erection of **higher** and **higher** buildings . . .*

Complete each sentence with a comparative form of the word in parentheses.

1. After I took the medicine, I felt even ____. (bad)
2. He is ____ than his sister. (blond)
3. She is ____ than most of the other runners. (slow)
4. Ever since you moved to this city, I've felt ____. (happy)
5. The box was ____ than I expected. (heavy)

**See Lessons 18.1–18.2, pages 613–618.**

Pablo Picasso, *Weeping Woman*, 1937

LESSON

# 2.6 The Writing Process
# Revising: Checking Content and Structure

*The first attempt of even the most talented artists, musicians, and writers is seldom a masterpiece. If you consider your drafts as dry runs, dress rehearsals, or tryouts, revising will seem a natural part of the writing process.*

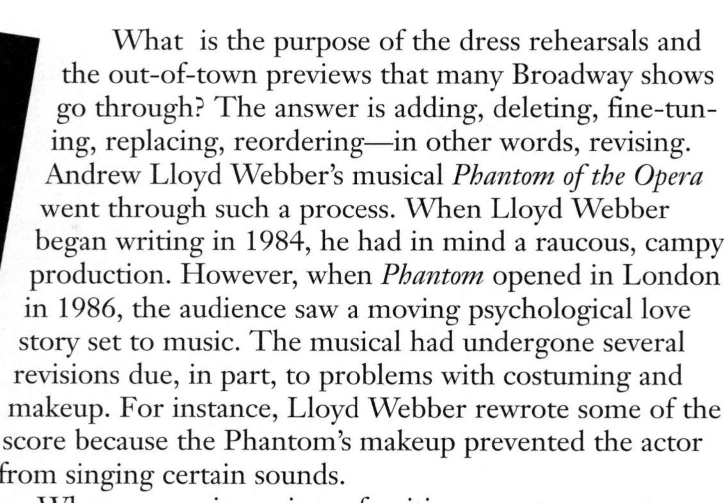

What is the purpose of the dress rehearsals and the out-of-town previews that many Broadway shows go through? The answer is adding, deleting, fine-tuning, replacing, reordering—in other words, revising. Andrew Lloyd Webber's musical *Phantom of the Opera* went through such a process. When Lloyd Webber began writing in 1984, he had in mind a raucous, campy production. However, when *Phantom* opened in London in 1986, the audience saw a moving psychological love story set to music. The musical had undergone several revisions due, in part, to problems with costuming and makeup. For instance, Lloyd Webber rewrote some of the score because the Phantom's makeup prevented the actor from singing certain sounds.

When you revise a piece of writing, you, too, must change aspects of your work in response to your evolving purpose, to fresh ideas, or to newly discovered information.

## Revise Content

Revision is not just an afterthought that gets only as much time as you have at the end of an assignment. Rather, it is a major stage of the writing process, and writers revise every step of the way. Even your decision to switch topics while prewriting is a type of revising. However, don't make the mistake of skipping the revision stage that follows drafting. Always make time to become your own audience and view your dress rehearsal, so to speak. Re*view*ing your work in this way can give you an invaluable perspective.

Revising involves evaluating the effectiveness and appropriateness of all aspects of your writing, clarifying your purpose, and refocusing or elaborating on the facts and ideas you present. When you revise ask yourself the following questions, keeping in mind the audience for whom you are writing: Is my main idea or purpose clear throughout my draft? Do I ever lose sight of my purpose? Have I given my readers all of the information—that is, facts, opinions, inferences—that they need in order to understand my main idea, or do I need to elaborate? Finally, have I included too many details or been redundant?

Below is a page from a manuscript by the novelist and short-story writer Eudora Welty. Notice how she has added and deleted details to bring the passage into sharper focus.

**Revision Checklist for Content**

- Inviting opening; readers enticed.
- Main idea clear—stated or implied.
- Ideas well supported by details.
- No unnecessary information to confuse readers.

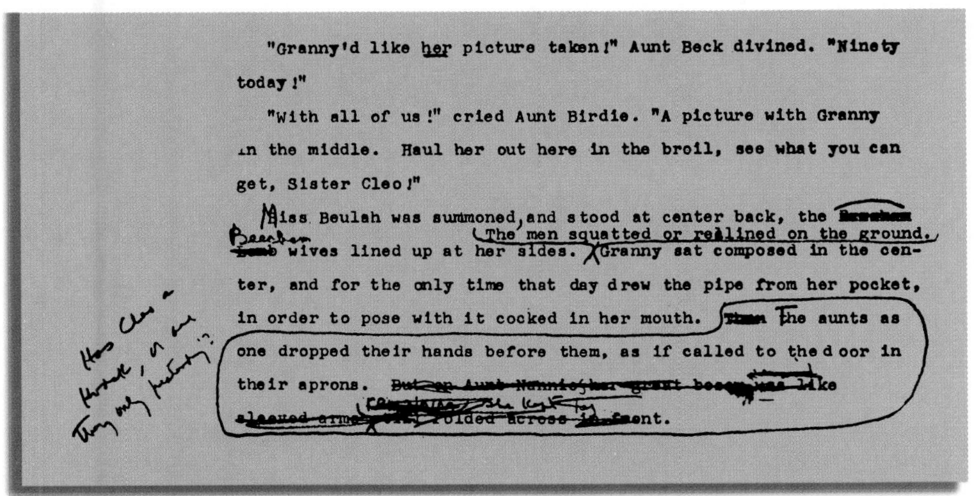
"Granny'd like her picture taken!" Aunt Beck divined. "Ninety today!"

"With all of us!" cried Aunt Birdie. "A picture with Granny in the middle. Haul her out here in the broil, see what you can get, Sister Cleo!"

Miss Beulah was summoned, and stood at center back, the Beecham wives lined up at her sides. The men squatted or reclined on the ground. Granny sat composed in the center, and for the only time that day drew the pipe from her pocket, in order to pose with it cocked in her mouth. The aunts as one dropped their hands before them, as if called to the door in their aprons.

## Journal Writing

Revising is like . . . well, what is revising like? In your journal create several metaphors or similes that express your insights into the revision process. You might start with the comparison to revamping a play that opened this lesson.

## Revise Structure

Although it may appear spontaneous, good writing is carefully structured. If you are not satisfied with the structure of your work, you might do one or more of the following: reorder sentences or paragraphs to improve organization and to clarify relationships among ideas; provide transitions between sentences or paragraphs to enhance coherence; combine paragraphs or sentences to link ideas more closely; or break paragraphs or sentences into several smaller ones to separate and distinguish ideas; In the passage below, notice how the revisions improve the structure of the paragraph.

### *Model*

The actor Carlos Abeyta is many people in one. He <u>is</u> the lonesome cowboy, the greedy entrepreneur, the stoical patient, all roles that have won him numerous awards. ~~In his leisure moments, he likes to garden.~~ In a recent interview, I asked him whether the real Carlos ever gets lost in the shuffle. He smiled ~~weirdly~~ *condescendingly* and said, "All these people you name <u>are</u> the real Carlos. Each time I play a new character, I am rebuilding myself--in a different style, in a different neighborhood--but always from the same basic material." His expression told me that my question was naive. ~~Carlos moved alot as a child and a teen-ager.~~ Perhaps the reason Carlos is at home with so many selves is that he moved nine times before the age of fifteen. "I learned early that I was more than Carlito, my <u>abuela</u>'s good little boy. Moving so much forced me to revise myself over and over. I began to like it--discovering and revising new me's."

**Revision Checklist for Structure**

- **Unity:** All ideas are related to main idea.
- **Coherence:** The flow of ideas is smooth and logical.
- **Transitions:** Sentences and paragraphs are linked.
- **Structure:** Relationship of ideas is clear from the order of presentation.

# 2.6 Writing Activities

## Write a Revision of Your Essay

Have a writing conference with a classmate to help you revise your essay on frightening experiences. Use the checklists on pages 83 and 84 plus the list below to evaluate your content and structure. Make notations about how you will revise your essay.

- Re-evaluate your opening for purpose and audience.
- Check for clarity and economy of ideas.
- Check for unity and coherence.
- Provide additional transitions between ideas, if necessary.
- Check your ending. Is it strong and clear?

**PURPOSE** To improve a piece of writing by revising
**AUDIENCE** A classmate
**LENGTH** Same as the original

Artist unknown, *Mrs. Freake and Baby Mary*, 1670

## Cross-Curricular: Art

Study the portrait below. Write two paragraphs describing the painting for a friend who hasn't seen it. Form an overall impression of it, which you will not explicitly state. Give enough details about the painting to show its content and style. Be sure your description conveys information as well as your overall impression.

### Grammar Link

**Use precise adverbs.**

*He smiled* ***condescendingly****. . . .*

An effective adverb makes the meaning and intent of a sentence more precise.

Create richer images by replacing each boldfaced word with a more precise adverb.

1. The witch laughed **strangely** at the woodcutter.
2. He stared **bravely** at the advancing tiger.
3. She **sadly** kissed him good-bye.
4. The exhausted homeless woman walked **slowly** toward the park.
5. The tired boy waited **quietly** for sleep to come.

**See Lesson 10.5, pages 424–429.**

LESSON **2.7**

# The Writing Process
# Revising: Replacing Clichés, Jargon, and Sexist Language

*When you revise, it's your job to cut out clichés, jargon, and sexist language and to find original, straightforward, and unbiased replacements. The result will be clearer writing that appeals to a wide audience.*

*"She's all work and no play."*

Does the caption of the cartoon at the left *ring a bell* or *hit the nail on the head*? Like the preceding expressions in italic type, the caption is a cliché. In the cartoon, *all work and no play* is used to describe the woman on the left, herself a visual cliché complete with dress-for-success business suit and serious look. The caption of the cartoon also tells you something about the woman speaking.

Clichés, jargon, and sexist language say a great deal about the speaker or writer—none of it good. Stale, pompous, or offensive language can find its way into the drafts of the most careful and well-meaning writers.

## Cut Clichés

A cliché is a stale expression that your reader has heard many times before and doesn't want to hear again. As a writer you need to revise or replace clichés with fresh, original phrases that express your unique point of view. The chart at the right lists some trite, worn-out expressions. Many of them were once vivid, new metaphors, but they have become empty through excessive use. Think of some richer replacements.

**A List of Clichés**

after all is said and done
beyond a shadow of a doubt
depths of despair
few and far between
green with envy
through thick and thin
a word to the wise
sad but true
rude awakening
raging inferno

## Replace Jargon

Jargon is the language of any special group, such as computer buffs or football fans. Those who use jargon for a general audience are often trying to show off their knowledge of a subject. The first of the following letters comes out of a workshop in which writing coach William Zinsser helps professionals to improve their writing. The second letter is a revision of the first.

***Literature Model***

Dear Parent:
We have established a special phone communication system to provide additional opportunities for parent input. During this year we will give added emphasis to the goal of communication and utilize a variety of means to accomplish this goal. Your inputs, from the unique position as a parent, will help us to plan and implement an educational plan that meets the needs of your child. An open dialogue, feedback and sharing of information between parents and teachers will enable us to work with your child in the most effective manner.

William Zinsser, *On Writing Well*

*If you were a parent, how would you react to this letter from your child's principal? Why?*

Dear Parent:
The teachers and administrators of Aztec High know that your involvement in your child's education is critical to our success. As this school year opens, we want to invite you to contact us on a new telephone line we've installed for your use. Call us when you have a question, a suggestion, a complaint, or a compliment. We will use your comments to meet your child's needs more effectively. We believe that opening a dialogue between parents and educators will open a new future for students at Aztec.

*Find the examples of jargon that have been replaced in the revised letter. Then read the two letters aloud to see if you notice any other differences between them.*

### Journal Writing

With a partner brainstorm to compile a list of clichés. When you have five to ten examples, work together to find original ways of expressing the same ideas. List the clichés and their replacements in your journal.

## Eliminate Sexist Language

Sexist words and phrases exist in many published resources because gender related expressions were long considered standard English usage. For example, *businessmen* is often used to denote all persons involved in business. Where does that leave the female executive? Since the 1960s, the feminist movement has made both men and women more aware of sexist stereotypes and language. Most people now replace sexist words such as *poetess* and *actress* with such gender-neutral words as *poet* and *actor* or *performer*.

"Some women to see you, Anne."

Today, the most stubborn case of sexist language remains the use of the pronouns *he*, *him*, and *his* to refer to antecedents of unknown gender, such as *a person*, *a student*, or *a resident*. A rather cumbersome way to avoid this construction is to use the compounds *he or she* and *him or her*. A better way is to reconstruct your sentence so that the plural pronouns *they*, *them*, and *their* can be used. For example, you might write "students love their books" instead of "each student loves his or her books." This solution will not work in all cases; you will have to experiment to find the solution that works.

Beware of solutions that worsen the problems you're trying to fix. Avoid cumbersome constructions, awkward phrasing, and supersensitive reactions. For example, many women are justifiably offended by being called *girls*. However, in the cartoon at the left, Dad may have taken his sensitivity a bit too far!

In the passage below, writer Diana Chang discusses "people who happen to write novels." What linguistic difficulty might she have encountered if she had begun, "A person who happens to write novels"?

*The gender-blind pronoun "one" helps the writer avoid sexist language. In some cases, you might also use "we" to refer to people in general.*

*What difficulty is the singular pronoun "everyone" likely to create in the rest of this sentence?*

### *Literature Model*

People who happen to write novels are nervous. I think one can make this statement without risking storms of controversy. And their nervousness is fully justified, it seems to me. I say "who happen to write novels," meaning to put it just that way, for I really think no one can *will* a novel into existence, and that deep down everyone who attempts to write one recognizes this. . . .

Diana Chang, "Woolgathering, Ventriloquism, and the Double Life"

# 2.7 Writing Activities

## Rewrite to Eliminate Chichés, Jargon, and Sexist Language

Reread your piece on frightening experiences three times. The first time, look for stale expressions. Evaluate words and phrases. Have you heard them before? In your second reading, keep your audience and purpose in mind. Are some expressions too technical or specialized? Finally, scan the essay for sexist language. Read your essay aloud to a conference of several students. Ask them to note any clichés, jargon, or sexist language you may have missed.

- Use fresher expressions for clichés.
- Avoid specialized jargon.
- Restructure sentences to avoid sexist words and expressions.

**PURPOSE** To improve a piece of writing by eliminating clichés, jargon, and sexist language
**AUDIENCE** Students in a writing workshop
**LENGTH** Same as original draft

## Cooperative Learning

Look through newspapers and magazines for examples of political jargon and the clichés of "bureaucratese." Pay particular attention to speeches, direct quotations, and statements from official documents. Cut out two or three of the "best" examples. Then meet with three other students to pool your resources. Discuss and list your examples.

As a group, decide on four examples to revise. Choose pieces that are at least 20 lines long in a newspaper column. Revise one on your own, and then discuss the revisions in your group. Distribute copies of the examples and revisions to your classmates.

### Grammar Link

**Avoid pronouns that lead to the use of sexist language.**

*I think* ***one*** *can make this statement. . . .*

Rewrite the sentences to avoid sexist language.

1. A ballerina needs to devote all her spare time to dancing.
2. The congressmen from several states were opposed to any legislation affecting their constituents.
3. The policeman responding to the 911 call had CPR experience.
4. A writer may find it difficult to be his own audience.
5. A reader may lose interest if he doesn't understand the writer's main point.

**See Lesson 17.6, page 596.**

### COMPUTER OPTION

You may wish to use desk-top publishing for the list that you compiled in the Cooperative Learning activity. Use a personal computer and an appropriate page-layout program to turn your list into a poster or a handout. If you need a laser printer to make your work look just right, neighborhood print and copy shops often have printers that you can use for a small fee.

LESSON **2.8**

# The Writing Process
# Editing: Preparing for Presentation

*Writing, like building a house, is a process. The work isn't complete until it has been inspected for code violations. In the case of a written work, the writer's purpose and audience—plus the practices of standard English—apply.*

**And now the Superstore!**
*unequaled in size*
*unmatched in variety*
*unrivaled inconvenience*

**For Rent:** 6-room hated apartment.

*Offer expires December 31 or while supplies last.*

AUTO REPAIR SERVICE
FREE PICK-UP AND DELIVERY.
TRY US ONCE, YOU'LL NEVER GO ANYWHERE AGAIN

Read the classified ads carefully. It's sometimes surprising how much difference a single letter can make. Even the spaces between words can become significant. As you can see, you're not finished writing until you have edited. Editing applies the finishing touches. It's your last chance to make sure your writing says what you mean and creates a favorable impression.

## Editing—The Last Step

You have several tasks to perform when you edit. In addition to checking spelling, punctuation, capitalization, and grammar, you need to make sure that your sentence structure is solid and varied throughout the piece, and that your word usage suits your purpose and audience. Try to edit your own work *as if you were seeing it for the first time.* Read it over objectively at least twice. Some writers find that reading aloud helps them detect awkward phrasing and faulty sentence structure. Other writers proofread their sentences backward to focus on individual words and to zero in on errors in spelling and capitalization. Try different strategies until you find the method that gets you the best results. No matter what your method, be sure to have a good dictionary and a grammar handbook within reach every time you edit.

## The Editor's Checklist

Since it's easy to forget a detail while applying the finishing touches, people often use some device to jog their memory when a project is near completion. Look over these checklists, and then read the edited passage. Keep in mind that you also have the chance to do some last-minute revising as you edit—the stages of the writing process continually overlap.

**GRAMMAR AND USAGE**

**Verbs**
- Subject-Verb Agreement
- Consistent Tense

**Pronouns**
- Clear Antecedents
- Pronoun-Antecedent Agreement

**Modifiers**
- Correct Placement of Modifiers
- Correct Use of Modifiers in Comparisons

Visitors to Barcelona in the Summer of 1992 saw not only the Olympics but also some of the most unusal structures on Earth. Here, on residentail streets and in wide public squares, stands the controversial work of Antoni Gaudí, the Salvador Dali of architeckure. Gaudí's most famous work, the sagrada familia, is an enormous cathedral started in 1884. It has never been completed. But this circumstance does nothing but add to the mystery and disturbing beauty of the building. Like many of of Gaudí's other creations. It has undulating walls, twisting towers, and buttresses that seem to dissolve into thin air. The whole is asymmetrical, phantasmagorical. One observer said that the sagrada familia looks like a science-fiction sand castle, another said it looks like a giant wedding cake slowly melting in the Catalonian sun.

**SENTENCE STRUCTURE**

**Fragments**

**Run-on Sentences**

**Incorrect Punctuation**

**Nonparallel Structure**

**MECHANICS**

**Punctuation**

**Capitalization**

**SPELLING**

**Check Dictionary**

### Journal Writing

Look over several papers you have written, and use the editing checklists on this page to help you identify your most common errors. List the three errors that you make most often, and then jot down ways to avoid or correct them.

## Proofreading Symbols

You are probably familiar with many proofreading symbols. As you saw on the previous page, these marks serve as a kind of editorial shorthand to remind you of errors you must correct before you present your writing. While you can develop your own proofreading marks, it's best to learn and use the standard symbols shown in the chart below. With these, you can communicate easily with other writers, editors, and printers, thus avoiding troublesome misunderstandings. Use the chart to "translate" the editorial comments and corrections used in the essay below, and notice how the symbols save time and space.

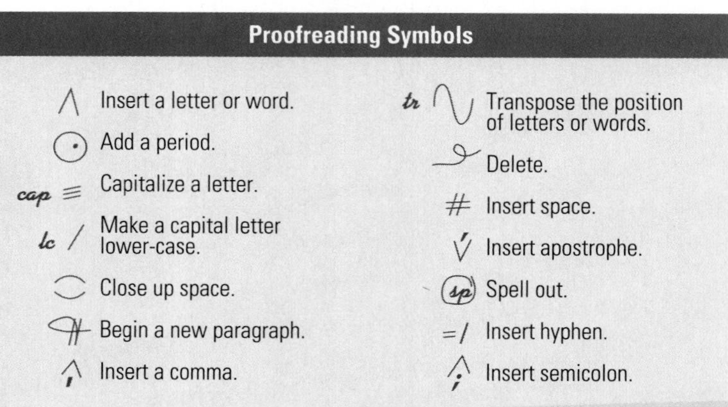

Proofreading Symbols
Insert a letter or word.
Add a period.
cap ≡ Capitalize a letter.
lc / Make a capital letter lower-case.
Close up space.
Begin a new paragraph.
Insert a comma.
tr Transpose the position of letters or words.
Delete.
# Insert space.
Insert apostrophe.
sp Spell out.
=/ Insert hyphen.
Insert semicolon.


*Transposed letters are often the result of a typing error. Proofreading at the word level will help you spot typos.*

*During the editing process, you can catch problems that you missed during revising, such as this awkward phrasing.*

When my eighth grade Art and architecture class lc was assigned to design a building I took the train to boston so that I could sketch the Jonh Hancock building. The Hancock appealed to me mostly because of the controversy surrounding thebuildings windows. ~~Because the building is so tall,~~ this very tall building at first when a crosswind blew against ~~it,~~ their huge panes of glass would be blown out of ~~there~~ frames. This situation caused an immediate threat to anyone walkin on the side walk and was quickly remedied by the builder. Pleased with my ply wood replica of the building, I brought it to class and spoke about the intricate design, and the dangers surrounding the windows. Much to my dismay, my grade on the project was a B. My teacher's comment was, "Your speech was well articulated, btu your Hancock looks like a shoe box."

# 2.8 Writing Activities

## Do a Final Edit

Edit the draft of your essay on frightening experiences. Go over it at least twice, looking for errors first at the sentence level and then at the word level. With the help of a classmate, use the checklist on page 91 for guidance in detecting and marking errors.

- Do subjects and verbs agree?
- Do pronouns and their antecedents agree?
- Have I correctly placed each modifier?
- Have I used correct punctuation?
- Have I capitalized words properly?
- Are all sentences complete?
- Are all words spelled correctly?
- Have I used parallel structure to balance items in a series?

PURPOSE To edit an existing piece of writing
AUDIENCE Your classmate
LENGTH Same as original

From manuscript depicting emperor's life/Tang Dynasty

### Grammar Link

**Avoid dangling or misplaced modifiers.**

*Pleased with my plywood replica . . .,* ***I*** *brought. . . .*

Rewrite the following sentences to avoid dangling or misplaced modifiers.

1. The ruins of Pompeii were of enormous interest to scientists as well as archaeology buffs when they were uncovered.
2. People and animals were found by archaeologists frozen in their tracks.
3. Living at that time and not having any warning about an impending disaster, scientists now understand a great deal more about the people.
4. Many people would visit that area curious about the past.
5. Archaeologists unearthed artifacts and remains using fine tools.

**See Lesson 18.7, pages 623–629.**

## Cross-Curricular: History

Architecture reflects the history, geography, and culture of an area. For example, the building in the painting on this page is clearly Chinese. Working with a small group, explore the connection between buildings and their context. Focus on a style that is well represented in your area, such as the timber-and-stucco Tudor style, or styles featuring adobe, brick, stone, or wood shingles. Then write a report describing the style and analyzing why, when, and where it developed.

LESSON

# 2.9 The Writing Process
# Presenting: Sharing Your Writing

I love ZOWY. It's the coolest station around. I never listen to another. And why should I? ZOWY plays the best music from yesterday and today. I always hear the new releases first, way before my friends who listen to KBOB. Also, what's so great about ZOWY is that they don't play a lot of ads and their DJ's don't talk on and on. But when they do speak, they always have something funny and interesting to say. ZOWY 100.5 FM is the BEST!

Rebecca Robbins, Newton South High School, Newton, Massachussetts

*Some writers see the act of presenting their work as the culmination of all their efforts. Affecting your audience—even if it's only yourself or a close friend—is what writing's all about.*

Presentation is an important part of the writing process. After all, a writer has an audience in mind from the beginning, so presenting the finished piece to that audience is a logical and satisfying way of bringing the process to a close. It will help you as a writer to think through the entire process, from the first glimmer of your original idea and your choice of audience to your presentation. Completing the writing process will give you a satisfying sense of closure.

## Types of Presentation

Just as audiences come in many shapes and sizes, so do presentations. Most, however, fall into one of two categories: formal or informal. As a writer you will have many opportunities to practice and perfect both kinds of presentation. The charts on the opposite page show examples of both formal and informal presentations. As you study them, think about the interplay of purpose, audience, and presentation. How do they affect one another?

## How to Get Your Work Published

Suppose you want to prepare an original writing specifically for publication. What is the procedure? You might begin close to home, with publications such as your school newspaper or literary magazine. Local newspapers and magazines also provide a good opportunity. They usually publish letters to the editor, and opinion pieces from readers often appear on the editorial page. They probably can also suggest a more formal procedure for submitting articles, fiction, or poetry. Telephone the editorial department to find out how to submit your work and to see whether you will receive a fee if your work is published.

Informal Presentation

Keep a journal and periodically read over what you've written.

Read a poem you've written to a friend.

Write a postcard to a relative.

Read an original story to a child.

Write a personal message in a birthday card.

Call a friend and read a "telegram" you've prepared.

FORMAL PRESENTATION

Contribute to a class or school anthology.

Prepare an audiovisual production of a play or skit you've written.

Submit a manuscript to a writing contest.

Write a letter to your local newspaper.

Write and deliver a speech to a group of people.

Write an essay for a college application.

Your English teacher or a librarian might be able to suggest reference materials that can help you locate other appropriate opportunities for publishing. These include such publications as *Writer's Market* and *Market Guide for Young Writers.* These guides will tell you what types of material various publications accept, how to submit your writing, and what fees they pay. Also look in magazines that interest you; the contents page or credits page will probably tell you how to submit material. Other possibilities include writing workshops that publish participants' work and contests sponsored by community groups, corporations, or educational institutions.

### Journal Writing

List the following works and note which ones require a formal presentation and which an informal: a letter to the editor of your school newspaper, a collection of humorous family anecdotes, a letter to a good friend who has moved away, a flyer for a fund-raising concert at your school.

# Select Appropriate Presentation Format

Whether your writing requires a formal or an informal presentation, you still must decide in what manner you will present it. Like a retailer, you have something to "sell" and need an effective marketing strategy. To sell clothing, for instance, department stores present the latest fashions in eye-catching window displays. Writers, too, try to entice their audience with inventive formatting, illustrations, graphics, and other visual or audiovisual flourishes. Of course, a creative format can never substitute for good writing. Any audiovisual effects you use should serve your writing by helping the reader to understand or appreciate it more.

The two facsimiles on this page—a humorous poem and a science text—demonstrate how visual effects (in this case, illustrations and diagrams) can enhance a reader's enjoyment and understanding of a piece of writing. Each image interprets and enhances the accompanying text. However, because the purpose and audience are different in each case, the visuals are also quite different.

MR. MISTOFFELEES

You ought to know Mr. Mistoffelees!
The Original Conjuring Cat—
(There can be no doubt about that).
Please listen to me and don't scoff. All his
Inventions are off his own bat.
There's no such Cat in the metropolis;
He holds all the patent monopolies
For performing surprising illusions
And creating eccentric confusions.
At prestidigitation
And at legerdemain
He'll defy examination
And deceive you again.
The greatest magicians have something to learn
From Mr. Mistoffelees' Conjuring Turn.
Presto!
Away we go!
And we all say: OH!
Well I never!
Was there ever
A Cat so clever
As Magical Mr. Mistoffelees!

Above: T.S. Eliot's *The Naming of Cats* with illustrations by Edward Gorey

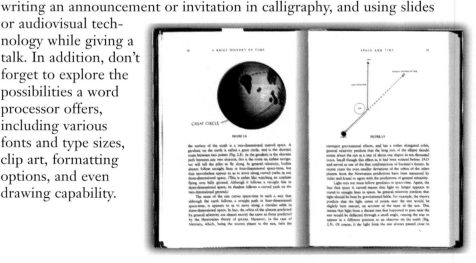

When making decisions about your presentation, be sure that all aspects harmonize. Appropriate presentations might include giving a research report an attractive cover, writing a personal note in longhand so that your personality is revealed, writing an announcement or invitation in calligraphy, and using slides or audiovisual technology while giving a talk. In addition, don't forget to explore the possibilities a word processor offers, including various fonts and type sizes, clip art, formatting options, and even drawing capability.

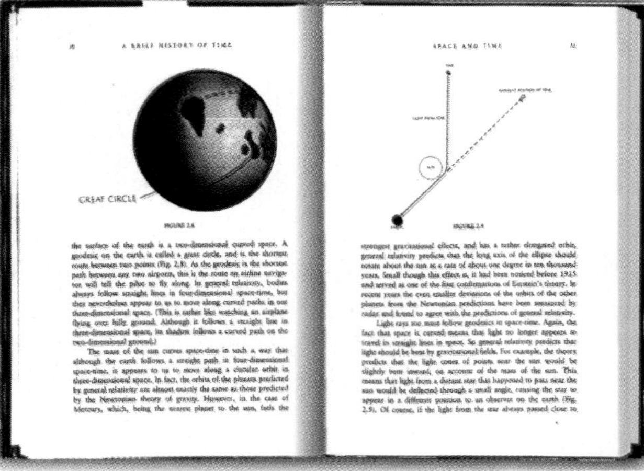

A BRIEF HISTORY OF TIME

GREAT CIRCLE

FIGURE 2.8

the surface of the earth is a two-dimensional curved space. A geodesic on the earth is called a great circle, and is the shortest route between two points (Fig. 2.8). As the geodesic is the shortest path between any two airports, this is the route an airline navigator will tell the pilot to fly along. In general relativity, bodies always follow straight lines in four-dimensional space-time, but they nevertheless appear to us to move along curved paths in our three-dimensional space. (This is rather like watching an airplane flying over hilly ground. Although it follows a straight line in three-dimensional space, its shadow follows a curved path on the two-dimensional ground.)

The mass of the sun curves space-time in such a way that although the earth follows a straight path in four-dimensional space-time, it appears to us to move along a circular orbit in three-dimensional space. In fact, the orbits of the planets predicted by general relativity are almost exactly the same as those predicted by the Newtonian theory of gravity. However, in the case of Mercury, which, being the nearest planet to the sun, feels the

SPACE AND TIME

FIGURE 2.9

strongest gravitational effects, and has a rather elongated orbit, general relativity predicts that the long axis of the ellipse should rotate about the sun at a rate of about one degree in ten thousand years. Small though this effect is, it had been noticed before 1915 and served as one of the first confirmations of Einstein's theory. In recent years the even smaller deviations of the orbits of the other planets from the Newtonian predictions have been measured by radar and found to agree with the predictions of general relativity.

Light rays too must follow geodesics in space-time. Again, the fact that space is curved means that light no longer appears to travel in straight lines in space. So general relativity predicts that light should be bent by gravitational fields. For example, the theory predicts that the light cones of points near the sun would be slightly bent inward, on account of the mass of the sun. This means that light from a distant star that happened to pass near the sun would be deflected through a small angle, causing the star to appear in a different position to an observer on the earth (Fig. 2.9). Of course, if the light from the star always passed close to

Right: Stephen Hawking's *A Brief History of Time*

# 2.9 Writing Activities

## Present Your Work

Imagine that you've been asked to publish your piece on frightening experiences in a newsletter for a national young writers' group. Using the steps below, revise your work to best present both your writing and your designing skills.

- Identify the purpose and audience of your piece, and brainstorm ways to highlight this purpose and attract your audience through visuals.
- Experiment with various layouts, graphs, illustrations, fonts, and type sizes until you find a presentation that clearly enhances your writing. If your piece is long enough, consider inserting headlines with catchy phrasing.
- Using a word processor or a cut-and-paste-by-hand method, incorporate these enhancements into the original piece of writing. If necessary, photocopy the finished product to mask any incision lines.
- Present your enhanced work to classmates acting as the editor and designer of the newsletter. Ask for a response to the additions or changes you've made.
- Your piece may also be appropriate for a fiction or science fiction magazine for young people, or for a community paper or newsletter. Call or write to the publication of your choice for details, then mail it off with a self-addressed, stamped envelope included.

**PURPOSE** To present a piece of writing appropriately
**AUDIENCE** The editor and designer of a newsletter
**LENGTH** Same as original

**COMPUTER OPTION**

You might consider using a computer to enhance the presentation of your essay on frightening experiences. Using this technology, you can add visual appeal with clip art, show scenes from a narration with illustrations, or add italics or boldface to certain words.

Once the presentation of your piece is completed, research some publication possibilities.

### Grammar Link

**Use proper punctuation and capitalization in business letters.**

If you submit your work by mail, you'll want to be sure that you've presented it properly.

Rewrite these addresses for business letters to show correct capitalization.

Dr Evelyn White
PO Box 451
Washington D.C. 20017

mr Sam Davis
Glenley inc
241 west St
Syracuse, New york 13226

Gina Jordan, md
Putney medical group
119 Market st
San francisco California 94118

**See Lesson 20.2, pages 661–665, and Lesson 21.15, pages 708–709.**

LESSON

2.10

# Writing About Literature
# Analyzing Tone

*In speech, tone of voice can reveal feelings and attitude about a topic or a person. Unlike speakers, writers can only rely on words and their arrangement to convey this important message to their audience.*

Albert Pinkham Ryder, *Moonlit Cove*, 1880–90

As you read the following poems, consider how each poet feels about the moon and how that attitude is conveyed.

*Literature Models*

Greatly shining,
The Autumn moon floats
in the thin sky;
And the fish-ponds shake
their backs and flash their
dragon scales
As she passes over them.

Amy Lowell, "Wind and Silver"

*The moon "floats" and "passes" effortlessly. What kinds of feelings or attitudes do these words imply?*

But the moon of the poet
is soiled and scratched, its seas
are flowing with dust.

And other moons are rising,
swollen like boils—

In their bloodshot depth
the warfare of planets
silently drips and festers.

John Haines, from "Moons"

*"Swollen like boils" is a startling and effective image. What other words or phrases evoke disease?*

## Convey Meaning Through Connotation and Denotation

In the poems above, Lowell's moon is majestic; Haines's moon is ugly and diseased. Lowell's tone is serene and admiring; Haines's is disgusted and angry. How do the poets convey these contrasting views?

Connotation is an important conveyor of tone. While the denotation of a word is its literal meaning, connotation is the word's associations. The word *shining* generally has good connotations. Think how different the tone of Lowell's poem would be if she had written *glaring* instead. In addition, the term *dragon scales* adds a fairy-tale quality to the scene. Haines plays off this "poetic" version of the moon. His moon has been *soiled*, a word that has moral connotations beyond the denotation of "not clean." Try reading Haines's lines aloud to get the full effect of the words that suggest infection.

## Identify Techniques

As you have seen, a writer's feelings and attitudes shape tone. Often, writers want their readers to share their feelings and attitudes toward a particular subject. As you read the following passage describing the construction of the railroad in a London suburb, note which words create its tone and how Charles Dickens strives to influence the reader's perception of the event.

**Literature Model**

The first shock of a great earthquake had, just at that period, rent the whole neighborhood to its center. Traces of its course were visible on every side. Houses were knocked down; streets broken through and stopped; deep pits and trenches dug in the ground; enormous heaps of earth and clay thrown up; buildings that were undermined and shaking, propped by great beams of wood. Here, a chaos of carts, overthrown and jumbled together, lay topsy-turvy at the bottom of a steep unnatural hill; there, confused treasures of iron soaked and rusted in something that had accidently become a pond. Everywhere were bridges that led nowhere; thoroughfares that were wholly impassable; Babel towers of chimneys, wanting half their height; temporary wooden houses and enclosures, in the most unlikely situations; carcasses of ragged tenements, and fragments of unfinished walls and arches, and piles of scaffolding, and wildernesses of bricks, and giant forms of cranes, and tripods straddling above nothing.

Charles Dickens, *Dombey and Son*

*Words such as "earthquake," "rent," "undermined," and "carcasses" make it clear that Dickens thinks the railroad is destructive.*

*In addition to "chaos" and "Babel towers," which words and phrases show the confusion and disruption of the human environment?*

In addition to specific word choice, writers can use an extended comparison to express their attitude toward a subject. In the passage above, Dickens compares railroad construction to an earthquake. Look back at the passage, and then read the analysis. Notice how the analysis links Dickens's attitude to his imagery, word choice, and sentence structure. The content of Dickens's description reveals what happened at the construction site; the tone reveals how Dickens feels about it.

## Model

In his description of the construction of the railroad, Dickens turns the idea of progress on its head. Instead of *con*struction, we see *de*struction; instead of an organized wonder of modern engineering, we see disorder and upheaval. The tone of the piece is angry and outraged. Like the scene itself, the rhythm of the paragraph is broken into fragments of descriptive clauses and phrases. However, it is the vivid words and images that best convey Dickens's outrage. The central image of an earthquake—a mindless, destructive force—colors the piece, while phrases such as "undermined and shaking" and "straddling above nothing" reinforce the comparison. Dickens also suggests the *death* of the neighborhood with the word "carcasses," but perhaps the most moving image is the "confused treasures . . . rusted." Something once valuable has been destroyed.

*Citing specific words makes the analysis easier to understand as well as more convincing.*

## Judge Appropriateness

When you analyze literature, look for clues to underlying meaning by identifying the tone that the writer uses. Then judge whether that tone is suitable to the writer's topic, purpose, and audience. For example, what would you think of a real-estate ad for a "shack" with six "cramped" rooms and an "out-of-date" kitchen? You would expect an advertiser to use words with more positive connotations, describing the "shack" as a "quaint cottage" with six "cozy" rooms and a "rustic" kitchen. While the word choice of the first ad is clearly inappropriate for selling real estate, it might be perfect for the "rags" side of a rags-to-riches tale.

When you write about literature, support your analysis with direct reference to the elements, consistency, and appropriateness of tone. Remember that tone indicates the writer's attitude toward his or her audience as well as toward the subject matter.

### Journal Writing

Read a Literature Model in another lesson in this book. Freewrite or jot down notes about what you think the author's attitudes and feelings are. Include the specific words and phrases that led to your conclusion about tone.

# 2.10 Writing Activities

## Analyze the Tone of Your Essay or Story

Analyze the tone of the piece you wrote about frightening experiences. Try to look at it with a fresh eye, as if it had been written by someone else.

Read the lines silently, and jot down your impressions of the tone. Look closely at the words. Do they match your purpose and audience? What connotations do your words and phrases have? Do the connotations relate to your feelings about the topic?

- Decide if your tone expresses your feelings and attitudes.
- Decide if your tone is appropriate for your audience and purpose.
- Revise as necessary.

**PURPOSE** To analyze the tone of the piece you wrote
**AUDIENCE** Yourself
**LENGTH** 1 paragraph

Claude Monet, *The Seine at Giverny, Morning Mists*, 1897

### Grammar Link

**Use a semicolon to separate items in a series if these items contain commas.**

*. . . Babel towers of chimneys, wanting half their height; temporary wooden houses. . . .*

Add semicolons and commas to punctuate the following passage.

She ordered a garden salad which had fresh crisp vegetables a plate of spinach lasagna with tomato sauce grated cheese and mushrooms and a melon sherbet for dessert.

**See Lesson 21.5, pages 680–681.**

## Cross-Curricular: Art

The impressionist painter Claude Monet was particularly interested in the visual and emotional atmosphere created by light. Look carefully at *Morning Mists*, opposite, and write a paragraph describing and analyzing its tone—that is, the feelings Monet has about the scene, how he conveys those feelings, and how he encourages you to share in them.

First look at the colors in the painting, and brainstorm for a list of adjectives that describe the quality of these colors and the feelings they arouse. Do the same for the forms in the painting. Then read over your lists of adjectives and find one or two that seem to capture the tone of the painting. Finally, write a paragraph that describes and analyzes the tone of *Morning Mists.*

UNIT 2

# WRITING PROCESS IN ACTION

## THE WRITING PROCESS

In this unit, you've learned about all of the stages that lead to effective writing, as well as important elements of an essay. Now you can make use of what you've learned. In this lesson you're invited to give your opinion about what constitutes artistic greatness. Don't be afraid to take a personal approach to the subject, but back up your judgments with facts.

### • Assignment •

| | |
|---|---|
| *Context* | *Your class is creating an art review magazine, and you will be a contributing writer. Your topic is "Artistic Greatness." What artist or writer do you most admire? Who, for you, epitomizes artistic greatness? Support your choice in an essay that includes specific references to the artist's or writer's life and work.* |
| *Purpose* | *To write an essay that defines artistic greatness and that uses a particular artist's life and work as an extended example* |
| *Audience* | *Classmates and teachers* |
| *Length* | *No more than 1 page* |

"It is what I have done with where I have been." That is the criterion the artist Georgia O'Keeffe used to evaluate her own life and art.

Think about your own definition of artistic greatness. Whom would you choose to illustrate it? For this assignment, you'll write an essay supporting your choices.

The following pages can help you plan and write your essay. Read through them and then refer to them as you need to. But don't be tied down by them. You're in charge of your own writing process.

# Prewriting

In this essay, you'll support the answers to two questions: (1) Who, in your opinion, is a great artist? (2) What constitutes artistic greatness? Because you have a double-barreled topic, creating two sets of cluster diagrams may prove a good way to begin. Lesson 2.2 can show you how to use clustering to its best advantage. Finally, discuss the topic of artists and greatness with other writers and friends.

Once your research and thinking begin to feel complete, jot down some organizational notes—as formal as a traditional outline or as rough as a list of paragraph topics—before you begin to draft. Keep in mind that the purpose of your essay is to illustrate your idea of what makes this artist, and any artist, great. Experiment with thesis statements and keep your audience in mind throughout your writing process. The college admissions committee wants to know about you even more than about artistic greatness. Therefore, choose your artist, your concept of artistic greatness, and your supporting details carefully. Continue prewriting until you feel you have most of the raw material you need.

*Prewriting Questions*

- *With which artist's work have I had direct, personal experience?*
- *Whose life and work will I be able to research effectively?*
- *What universal quality of greatness does this artist represent?*

# Drafting

Look at the writer Joan Didion's introduction from her essay on Georgia O'Keeffe in the Literature Model on p. 104. She links a startling quotation from O'Keeffe with a personal anecdote showing the impact of the artist's work on a young child. Both the artist's view of herself and the world's response to her art are intriguing; both will drive the essay forward. Note that Didion's introduction suggests her thesis statement, but doesn't state it explicitly. She draws her reader in with quotations by a ninety-year-old woman and a seven-year-old girl, tells them "style is character," but doesn't yet tell them why she thinks O'Keeffe is a great artist. To stir readers, to tantalize, to lead—these are the functions of a strong introduction.

Draft a similar, preliminary thesis statement now, and then build an introductory paragraph around it. Review the principles of unity and coherence in Lesson 2.5. Find a way to lay out the main idea of your argument in a vital and intriguing way.

## Drafting Tip

For more information about different ways to order your ideas, see the chart in Lesson 2.4, page 73.

## Revising Tip

To study actual manuscript marked for revision, see Lesson 2.6, pages 82–85.

### *Literature Model*

"Where I was born and where and how I have lived is unimportant," Georgia O'Keeffe told us in the book of paintings and words published in her ninetieth year on earth. She seemed to be advising us to forget the beautiful face in the Stieglitz photographs. She appeared to be dismissing the rather condescending romance that had attached to her by then, the romance of extreme good looks and advanced age and deliberate isolation. "It is what I have done with where I have been that should be of interest." I recall an August afternoon in Chicago in 1973 when I took my daughter, then seven, to see what Georgia O'Keeffe had done with where she had been. One of the vast O'Keeffe "Sky Above Clouds" canvases floated over the back stairs in the Chicago Art Institute that day, dominating what seemed to be several stories of empty light, and my daughter looked at it once, ran to the landing, and kept on looking. "Who drew it?" she whispered after a while. I told her. "I need to talk to her," she said finally.

Joan Didion, *Georgia O'Keeffe*

The body of your text will contain the details that support your argument. As you draft:

- **Don't forget your audience.** What language is appropriate for them?
- **Think of a way to make your essay personal,** but meaningful to others. Find ways to put yourself in the essay.
- **Stay open.** This is still the time to let your thoughts flow. Follow your plan, but also give your imagination free rein. You can tighten up your work later.

*Revising Checklist*

- *Does my opening paragraph capture the reader's attention?*
- *Are my main idea and purpose easy to understand?*
- *Are my ideas coherent and unified?*
- *Is there any unnecessary information in my essay?*
- *Does my writing use a tone appropriate to my purpose and audience?*
- *Are my ideas presented in the right order?*

# Revising

To begin revising, read over your draft to make sure that what you've written fits your purpose and audience. Then have a **writing conference**. Read your draft to a partner or small group. Use your audience's reactions to help you evaluate your work.

# Editing

Once you are happy with the basic content and set-up of your essay, **proofread** it carefully for errors in grammar, usage, mechanics, and spelling. Use the questions at the right as a guide.

In addition to proofreading, use the self-evaluation list below to make sure your description does all the things you want it to do. When you're satisfied, make a clean copy of your essay and proofread it one more time.

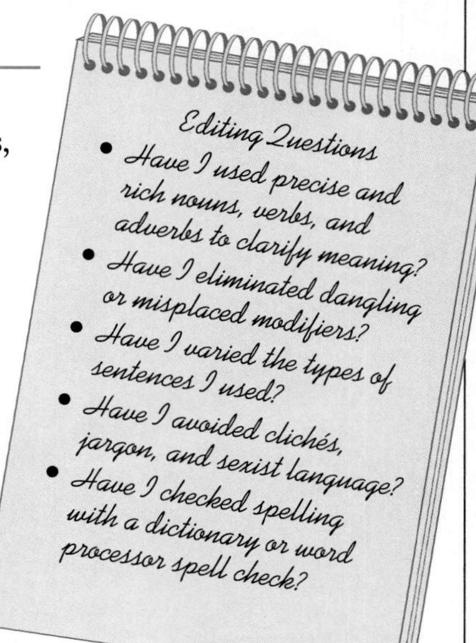

Editing Questions
• Have I used precise and rich nouns, verbs, and adverbs to clarify meaning?
• Have I eliminated dangling or misplaced modifiers?
• Have I varied the types of sentences I used?
• Have I avoided clichés, jargon, and sexist language?
• Have I checked spelling with a dictionary or word processor spell check?


## Self-Evaluation

**Make sure your essay–**

- expresses a clear main idea or opinion and supports it with reasons or evidence
- uses a variety of supporting details
- uses a logical organization
- has a tone that suits purpose and audience
- uses transitions to link ideas
- follows the rules of grammar, usage, mechanics, and spelling

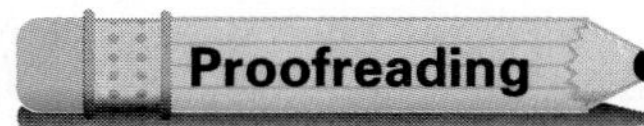


For proofreading symbols, see page 92.

# Presenting

The presentation of a real college essay consists of simply mailing it in. Who knows? Maybe this assignment can be tailored to meet the needs of one of your actual college applications. Whether you use it this way or not, however, share it with a panel of classmates acting as a college admissions committee, and solicit their responses. What you learn may prove valuable.

## Journal Writing

Reflect on your writing-process experience. Answer these questions in your journal: What do you like best about your essay? What was the hardest part of writing it? What did you learn in your writing conference? What new things have you learned as a writer.

UNIT 2

# The Writing Process Literature Model

*"Some women fight and others do not," writes the author of this essay, and then she demonstrates that the artist Georgia O'Keeffe was indeed a fighter. O'Keeffe fought against* them: *the establishment, tradition, stereotypes. She was a nonconformist and a loner in a time (and in a career) when women seldom had the courage, the talent, or the opportunity to take that road. In this essay, Joan Didion celebrates O'Keeffe as a guerrilla "in the war between the sexes."*

"Where I was born and where and how I have lived is unimportant," Georgia O'Keeffe told us in the book of paintings and words published in her ninetieth year on earth. She seemed to be advising us to forget the beautiful face in the Stieglitz photographs. She appeared to be dismissing the rather condescending romance that had attached to her by then, the romance of extreme good looks and advanced age and deliberate isolation. "It is what I have done with where I have been that should be of interest." I recall an August afternoon in Chicago in 1973 when I took my daughter, then seven, to see what Georgia O'Keeffe had done with where she had been. One of the vast O'Keeffe "Sky Above Clouds" canvases floated over the back stairs in the Chicago Art Institute that day, dominating what seemed to be several stories of empty light, and my daughter looked at it once, ran to the landing, and kept on looking. "Who drew it," she whispered after a while. I told her. "I need to talk to her," she said finally.

My daughter was making, that day in Chicago, an entirely unconscious but quite basic assumption about people and the work they do. She was assuming that the glory she saw in the work reflected a glory in its maker, that the painting was the painter as the poem is the poet, that every choice one made alone—every word chosen or rejected, every brush stroke laid or not laid down—betrayed one's character. *Style is character*. It seemed to me that afternoon that I had rarely seen so instinctive an application of this familiar principle, and I recall being pleased not only that my daughter responded to style as character but that it was Georgia O'Keeffe's particular style to which she responded: this was a hard woman who had imposed her 192 square feet of clouds on Chicago.

"Hardness" has not been in our century a quality much admired in women, nor in the past twenty years has it even been in official favor for men. When hardness surfaces in the very old we tend to transform it into "crustiness" or eccentricity, some tonic pepperiness to be indulged at a distance. On the evidence of her work and what she has said about it, Georgia O'Keeffe is neither "crusty" nor eccentric. She is simply hard, a straight shooter, a woman clean of received wisdom and open to what she sees. This is a woman who could early on dismiss most of her contemporaries as "dreamy," and would later single out one she liked as "a very poor painter." (And then add, apparently by way of softening the judgment: "I guess he wasn't a painter at all. He had no courage and I believe that to create one's own world in any of the arts takes courage.") This is a woman who in 1939 could advise her admirers that they were missing her point, that their appreciation of her famous flowers was merely sentimental. "When I paint a red hill," she observed coolly in the catalogue for an exhibition that year, "you say it is too bad that I don't always paint flowers. A flower touches almost everyone's heart. A red hill doesn't touch everyone's heart." This is a woman who could describe the genesis of one of her most well-known paintings—the *Cow's Skull: Red, White and Blue* owned by the Metropolitan—as an act of quite deliberate and derisive orneriness. "I thought of the city men I had been seeing in the East," she wrote. "They talked so often of writing the Great

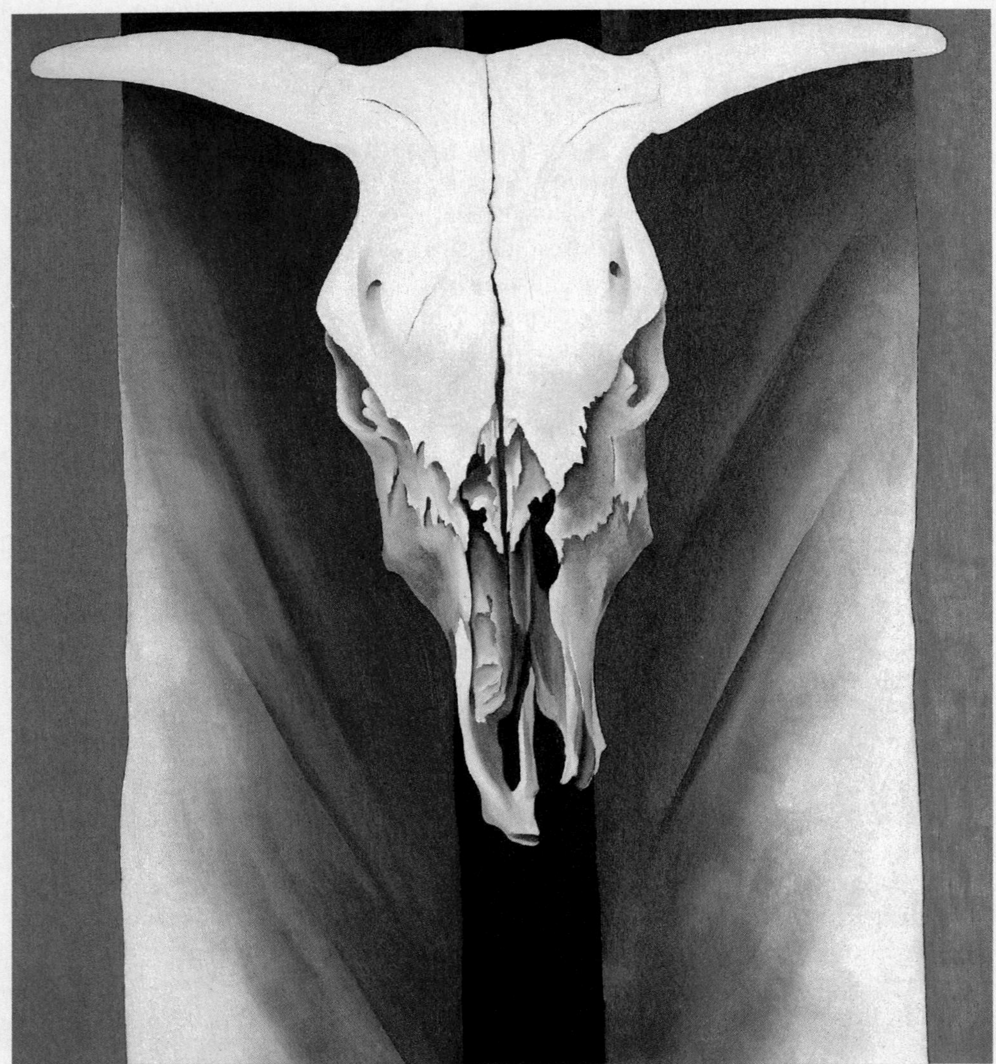

Georgia O'Keeffe, *Cow's Skull: Red, White and Blue*, 1931

American Novel—the Great American Play—the Great American Poetry. . . . So as I was painting my cow's head on blue I thought to myself, 'I'll make it an American painting. They will not think it great with red stripes down the sides—Red, White and Blue—but they will notice it.'"

*The city men. The men. They.* The words crop up again and again as this astonishingly aggressive woman tells us what was on her mind when she was making her astonishingly aggressive paintings. It was those city men who stood accused of sentimentalizing her flowers: "I made you take time to look at what I saw and when you took time to really notice my flower you hung all your associations with flowers on my flower and you write about my flower as if I think and see what you think and see—and I don't." *And I don't.* Imagine those words spoken, and the sound you hear is *don't tread on me.* "The men" believed it impossible to paint New York, so Georgia O'Keeffe painted New York. "The men" didn't think much of her bright color, so she made it brighter. The men yearned toward Europe so she went to Texas, and then New Mexico. The men talked about Cézanne, "long involved remarks about the 'plastic quality' of his form and color," and took one another's long involved remarks, in the view of this angelic rattlesnake in their midst, altogether too seriously. "I can paint one of those dismal-colored paintings like the men," the woman who regarded herself always as an outsider remembers thinking one day in 1922, and she did: a painting of a shed "all low-toned and dreary with a tree beside the door." She called this act of rancor "The Shanty" and hung it in her next show. "The men seemed to approve of it," she reported fifty-four years later, her contempt undimmed. "They seemed to think that maybe I was beginning to paint. That was my only low-toned dismal-colored painting."

Some women fight and others do not. Like so many successful guerrillas in the war between the sexes, Georgia O'Keeffe seems to have been equipped early with an immutable sense of who she was and a fairly clear understanding that she would be required to prove it. On the surface her upbringing was conventional. She was a child on the Wisconsin prairie who played with china dolls and painted watercolors with cloudy skies because sunlight was too hard to paint and, with her brother and sisters, listened every night to her mother read stories of the Wild West, of Texas, of Kit Carson and Billy the Kid. She told adults that she wanted to be an artist and was embarrassed when they asked what kind of artist she wanted to be: she had no idea "what kind." She had no idea what artists did. She had never seen a picture that interested her, other than a pen-and-ink Maid of Athens in one of her mother's books, some Mother Goose illustrations printed on cloth, a tablet cover that showed a little girl with pink roses, and the painting of Arabs on horseback that hung in her grandmother's parlor. At thirteen, in a Dominican convent, she was mortified when the sister corrected her drawing. At Chatham Episcopal Institute in Virginia she painted lilacs and sneaked time alone to walk out to where she could see the line of the Blue Ridge Mountains on the horizon. At the Art Institute in Chicago she was shocked by the presence of live models and wanted to abandon anatomy lessons. At the Art Students League in New York one of her fellow students advised her that, since he would be a great painter and she would end up teaching painting in a girls' school, any work of hers was less important than modeling for him. Another painted over her work to show her how the Impressionists did trees. She had not before heard how the Impressionists did trees and she did not much care.

At twenty-four she left all those opinions behind and went for the first time to live in Texas, where there were no trees to paint and no one to tell her how not to paint them. In Texas there was only the horizon she craved. In Texas she had her sister Claudia with her for a while, and in the late afternoons they would walk away from town and toward the horizon and watch the evening star come out. "That evening star fascinated me," she wrote. "It was in some way very exciting to me. My sister had a gun, and as we walked she would throw bottles into the air and shoot as many as she could before they hit the ground. I had nothing but to walk into nowhere and the wide sunset space with the star. Ten watercolors were made from that star." In a way one's interest is compelled as much by the sister Claudia with the gun as by the painter Georgia with the star, but only the painter left us this shining record. Ten watercolors were made from that star.

# Linking Writing and Literature

## Readers Respond to the Model

### How did Joan Didion create an effective portrait of Georgia O'Keeffe as both a woman and an artist?

**Explore Joan Didion's technique for creating a character portrait by answering these questions. Then read what other students liked about Didion's descriptions.**

1. From what you've read about Georgia O'Keeffe in this essay, in what ways would you say her aggressive character shaped her career as an artist?
2. What details about O'Keeffe's life were most striking—even surprising—to you? How do these details support Didion's main thesis about O'Keeffe?
3. Why do you think Didion shaped the essay around her daughter's reaction to a painting? How does it draw the reader in? Do you think you would have needed to "talk" to O'Keeffe after seeing her painting?

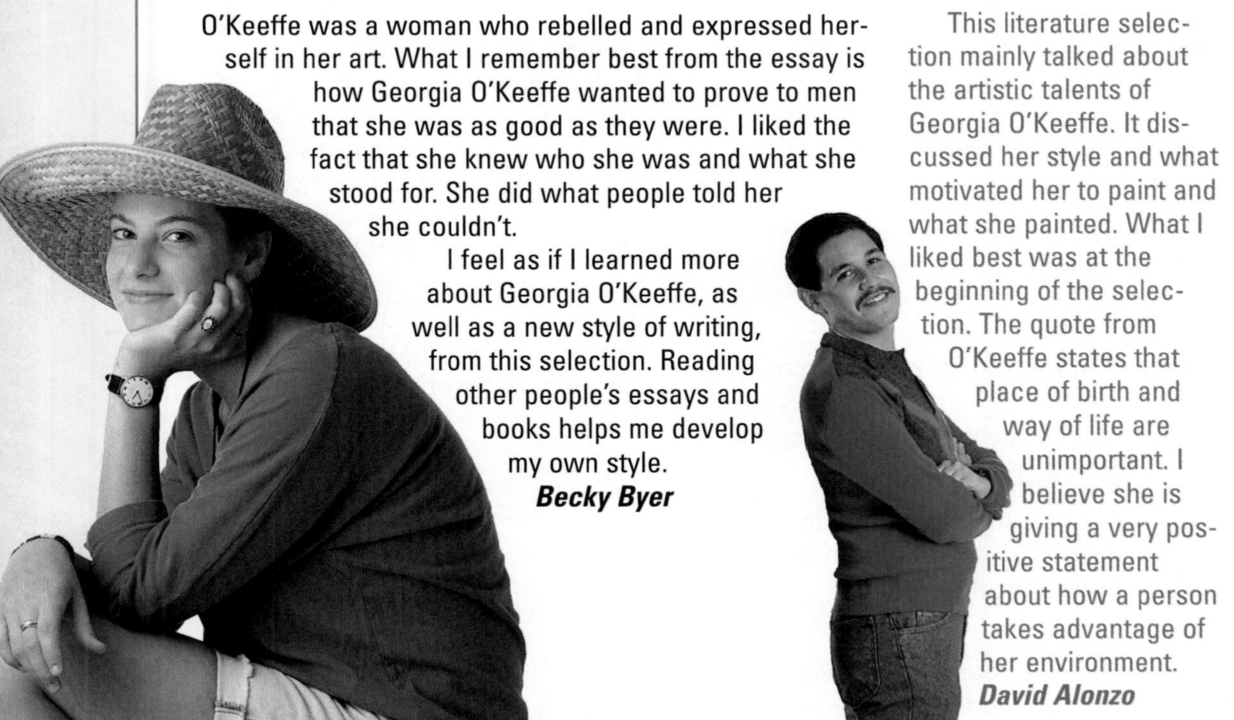

O'Keeffe was a woman who rebelled and expressed herself in her art. What I remember best from the essay is how Georgia O'Keeffe wanted to prove to men that she was as good as they were. I liked the fact that she knew who she was and what she stood for. She did what people told her she couldn't.

I feel as if I learned more about Georgia O'Keeffe, as well as a new style of writing, from this selection. Reading other people's essays and books helps me develop my own style.

***Becky Byer***

This literature selection mainly talked about the artistic talents of Georgia O'Keeffe. It discussed her style and what motivated her to paint and what she painted. What I liked best was at the beginning of the selection. The quote from O'Keeffe states that place of birth and way of life are unimportant. I believe she is giving a very positive statement about how a person takes advantage of her environment.

***David Alonzo***

# Unit 2 Review

## Reflecting on the Unit

**Summarize what you learned in this unit by answering the following questions.**

- How does clustering help develop your ideas during the prewriting process? What if clustering doesn't work? What other prewriting techniques can you try?
- In explaining a process, what kinds of order could you use in an essay?
- What are some techniques for creating a smooth flow of ideas within and between paragraphs?
- How is the way you present your work related to your particular purpose and audience?

## Adding to Your Portfolio

**Choose a selection for your portfolio.**
Look over the writing you did for this unit. Select a completed piece of writing to put in your portfolio. It should show some or all of the following:

- A strong thesis statement and introduction.
- Unified paragraphs.
- Smooth transitions between sentences and paragraphs.
- Correct spelling, punctuation, and attention to other details.
- An attractive and appropriate presentation.

**Reflect on your choice.**
Attach a note to the piece you choose to write, explaining why you took the approach you did and what you learned from writing it.

**Set goals.**
How can you improve your writing? What skill will you focus on the next time you write?

## Writing Across the Curriculum

**Make an art connection.**
Think of how the essay or story you wrote about frightening experiences would work as a film. If your composition was a story, outline the action. Illustrate key scenes by drawing them in order on a storyboard. If your piece was not narrative, but took a persuasive or other approach, plan some key illustrations to enhance it; then draw them. Then write one paragraph explaining how you feel your composition would work as a film.

UNIT 3

# Descriptive Writing

Composition

## Lessons

UNIT 3 PREVIEW

Case Study

# Descriptive Writing in the Real World

## Austin Sheds Light on Rich Cultures

Museum curator Ramona Austin

**FOCUS: Descriptive writing—well researched, detailed, and vivid—can bring to life faraway places, cultures, and eras.**

Straight ahead, past the seven-foot image of an Akan chief, the museum case displayed a king's ransom in gold: earrings as big as oranges; headbands covered with golden moons and stars; carved birds layered with gold leaf. The 150 mysterious, glittering objects told stories of Ghana, Mali, Senegal, and the Ivory Coast—nations of West Africa that once mined most of the world's gold.

Even today, when millions of Americans travel, few have visited these African lands. Fewer still can picture the landscapes or people. But a trip to West Africa, even via a museum, can turn preconceptions upside down. In "Gold of Africa," an exhibit at the Art Institute of Chicago, curator Ramona Austin invited the public to glimpse a part of the real Africa.

"Gold of Africa" was organized in Switzerland and traveled to Chicago in 1991 as part of a three-year tour of American museums. Much of the exhibit remained the same as it traveled from city to city. But as curator, Austin tailored the presentation of the artifacts to suit the size and layout of the Art Institute and the interests of Chicago-area museum goers.

**Putting on the Show**

| Prewriting | Drafting | Revising/Editing |
|---|---|---|
| Planning the Show | Writing the Text | Preparing for the Opening |

> ***"When I was in the forests of Africa, I was in a cathedral of light. . . . not darkness. I realized how much notions of darkness have colored our perceptions of Africa."***
>
> —Ramona Austin

The exhibit traces the history of West African gold cultures from the fourth century, when traders from the north risked crossing the Sahara to buy West African gold. By the ninth century, West African rulers had built huge fortunes, great cities of commerce and learning, and the first of three empires that would survive for centuries. Trade routes fanned out from these empires to the lands of Islam and medieval Europe.

"During the high Middle Ages, West Africa produced from three-quarters to three-fifths of the world's gold," said Austin. "It was a time when Africans had an equal relationship with Europeans. The Africans held back the dispersal of gold or allowed gold to go out in order to control markets. They were skilled economic thinkers."

Austin saw the gold objects as a way to entice people to learn about the history of West Africa. "In our culture gold has tremendous allure. It gave us a very good way to interest people and bring them in."

*Gold sculpture from the border region of Ghana and the Ivory Coast, possibly a trophy from the nineteenth century.*

# Prewriting

## PLANNING THE SHOW

The traveling "Gold of Africa" exhibit included about 150 gold artifacts, mostly from the nineteenth and twentieth centuries, as well as some of the rare ancient gold that has survived the centuries. Large color photographs also accompanied the exhibit; they showed West Africans wearing and using contemporary gold items. Austin's job was to design an environment for these materials that would help visitors understand and experience faraway cultures. To do so, she used visual and verbal techniques.

The curator wanted rooms that visually evoked the mystery and power of gold—that created an atmosphere of suspense as visitors proceeded through the exhibit. Austin wanted the verbal elements of the display to stimulate thinking as well. She felt that the text describing the artifacts should make people feel like explorers in a foreign land. "People have to learn to trust looking, trust their own eyes."

The main planning challenge was displaying so many small, mysterious objects while providing insight into foreign cultures. With the help of an architect and a graphic designer, Austin designed simple, dramatic rooms. The gold pieces would be displayed against rich green panels in each room. Spacious displays would let people get close to the objects to study fine details such as the threads of gold filigree covering tiny golden sculptures and pendants.

Because looking at object after object can become tiring, Austin also devised a dramatic technique to put the items in context: she would hang the large photographs directly above the display cases containing the gold objects. Text in the cases and on the walls would describe the objects and tell fascinating stories about them.

*The exhibit included artifacts, pictures, and text. Detailed descriptions of artifacts, like this unusual ram's head, above, identified the objects' origins and possible uses.*

# Drafting

## WRITING THE TEXT

How do you write for a moving audience? While readers of books are usually seated, museum goers wander from place to place, looking for something to catch their interest. Austin considered the limited attention span of her audience as she created a visual-verbal wall display about West Africa's ancient gold trade.

The display both showed and described in words the accomplishments of Mansa Musa, ruler of Mali during its golden age from 1312 to 1337 and a symbol of Africa's gold culture. Under Mansa Musa's control, the kingdom of Mali covered an area as big as France and Spain. It was famous for its centers of Islamic learning; its influence touched the whole Islamic world and was felt as far away as Europe.

To illustrate this high point in West African history, Austin developed a wall map based on two early European sources. One source was a 1375 map that showed Mansa Musa holding a huge gold nugget. The other was a map of Africa from 1570, when Europeans were still exploring the southern half of Africa. Austin's huge map combined information from these two sources, showing the impact West Africa had on Europeans thousands of miles away.

As Austin drafted the text, she considered her audience of strolling museum visitors. "You see the way this copy is broken up?" she asked, referring to seven short paragraphs of text appearing on the map. "Each section is an idea—a whole idea that I wanted the public to walk away with. People could jump into any part of this text and come away with a whole idea."

*This wall map describes Mansa Musa and his kingdom.*

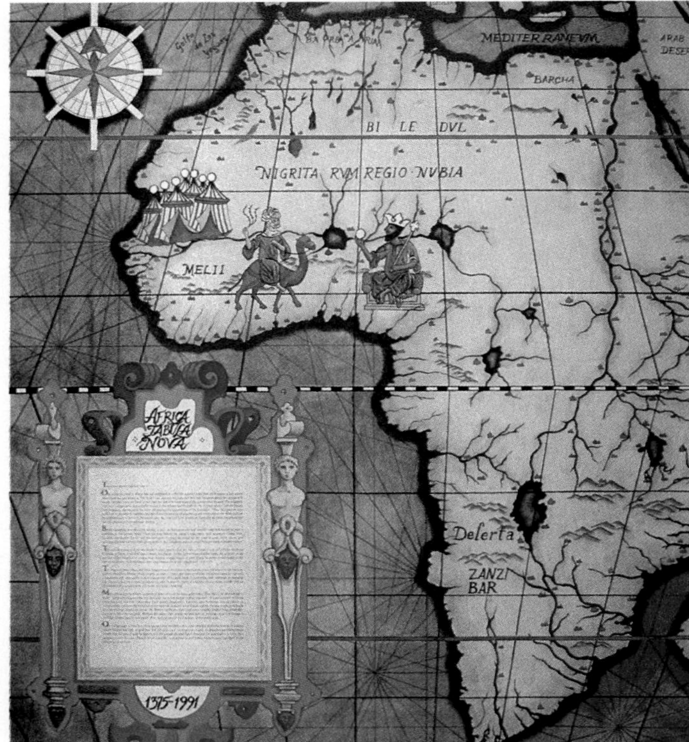

*A dramatic entrance drew visitors to the exhibit.*

# Revising/Editing

## PREPARING FOR THE OPENING

After drafting the text, Austin revised it to polish and tighten the writing. "You can't go on too long," she said. "You can't extend your writing beyond what the situation calls for."

Once Austin was satisfied with the text, she sent it to the education and publications departments at the Art Institute and to scholars for review. Austin used their suggestions to revise her text, simplifying language and correcting facts. Then she sent all the text for the show to be typeset in an attractive and readable style.

As text for the cases and walls came back for proofreading, Austin looked for help. "You need several eyes—three or four people looking at the text all the time. Three people can look at type and not see an error," she said. Catching errors in spelling and grammar was important, too.

Austin's efforts—the planning, designing, research, and descriptive writing—had far-reaching effects: more than 100,000 people saw this exhibit.

*Wall text described items in the display cases.*

# Responding to the Case Study

### 1. Discussion

**Discuss these questions about Ramona Austin's writing.**

- What limitations of her audience did Austin consider when writing her text for the cases and walls? How did her text deal with these limitations?
- Why was it important for each section of the text on the map to contain a main idea?
- What suggestions did the education and publications departments at the Art Institute have for the revisions of Austin's text?
- Why did Austin think it was important for several people to proofread the text?

### 2. Descriptive Writing

**Write a paragraph describing an artifact.**

You are going to write a paragraph about an artifact that is representative of the culture of your community or region. Some items you might consider: products made in your area; items of historical interest; items from nature that symbolize your surroundings; or objects relating to art and entertainment, religion, family life, or education. Bring in the item with a brief but vivid description that tells what the item is made of, its origins, its age, and so on.

### Grammar Link

**Use specific adjectives to describe.**

An *adjective* is a word that modifies a noun or pronoun by limiting its use.

*The 150* ***mysterious, glittering*** *objects told stories of Ghana, Mali, Senegal, and the Ivory Coast—nations of Africa that once mined most of the* ***world's*** *gold.*

Use each adjective in a sentence about "Austin Sheds Light on Rich Cultures."

1. rare
2. ancient
3. contemporary
4. golden
5. visual

**See Lesson 10.4, pages 418–423.**

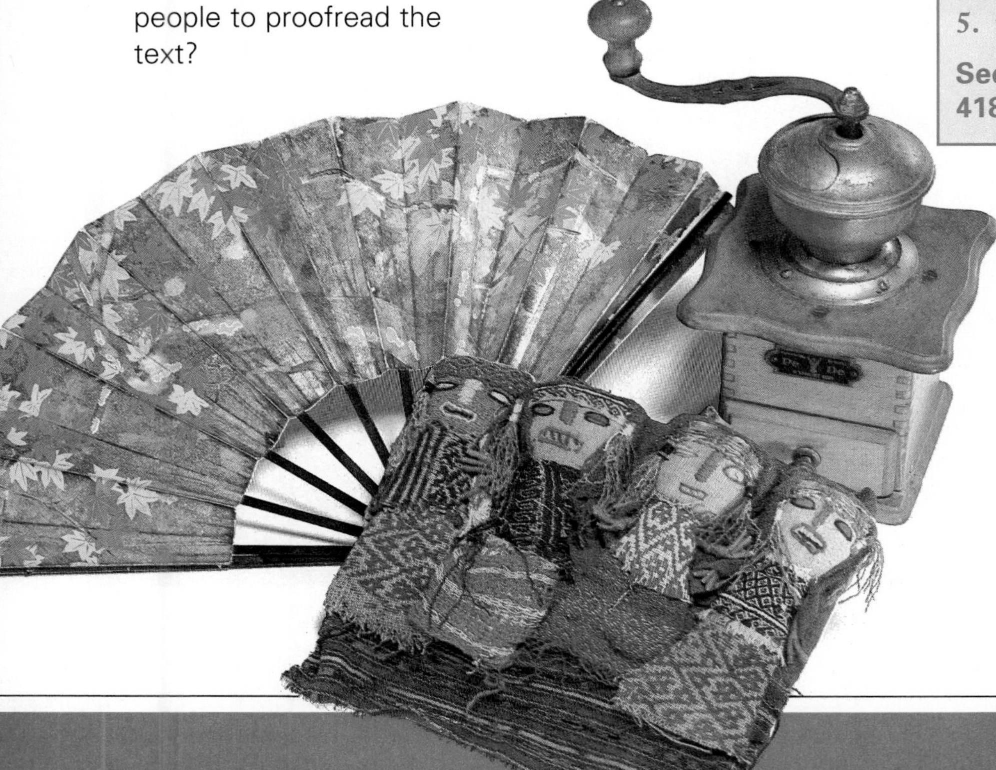

LESSON

# 3.1 Descriptive Writing
# Organizing Descriptions

*To write clear, vivid descriptions, use details that concentrate on the five senses—sight, hearing, smell, taste, and touch. Order your details according to your topic, audience, and purpose.*

## Describe Your Experiences

Can you re-create your experience of looking at this exotic mask from New Guinea, or do you find yourself relying on the standard, "It's hard to describe . . ."? Effective description evokes the sights, sounds, smells, tastes, and textures that inform experience. Carefully chosen sensory details are the tools writers use to re-create experiences for their readers.

As you read the passage below, notice the details Chinua Achebe chooses to re-create the experience of waiting for rain in a Nigerian village.

### *Literature Model*

At last the rain came. It was sudden and tremendous. For two or three moons the sun had been gathering strength till it seemed to breathe a breath of fire on the earth. All the grass had long been scorched brown, and the sands felt like live coals to the feet.

Evergreen trees wore a dusty coat of brown. The birds were silenced in the forests, and the world lay panting under the live, vibrating heat. And then came the clap of thunder. It was an angry, metallic and thirsty clap, unlike the deep and liquid rumbling of the rainy season. A mighty wind arose and filled the air with dust. Palm trees swayed as the wind combed their leaves into flying crests like a strange and fantastic coiffure.

Chinua Achebe, *Things Fall Apart*

*How does the writer convey the idea that the rain is welcome?*

*What impression is created by listing images such as "live coals," a "dusty coat of brown," and "the world lay panting"?*

## Put Things in Order

Re-creating an experience in writing involves more than just listing sensory details. To be effective, a writer must carefully select and order these details. Different methods of organization create different effects. If you want readers to visualize details as they truly exist in relation to one another, you might use spatial order. In this paragraph, follow the writer to the center of a tree-lined pond.

**Spatial Order**

Thick, lush trees frame the scene. In the center a red bridge provides a pathway over the still pond. Standing on the bridge, a young woman pauses to admire the delicate flowers beneath her before crossing to the other side.

When you want to show that some details are more significant than others, use order of importance. In this paragraph, the writer focuses on the young woman.

**Order of Importance**

The focal point of this tranquil scene is a young woman, pausing to admire a spray of bright flowers. The crimson bridge beneath her arches itself across the still pond, while light dances on thick, green treetops.

When you want to organize your details according to the order in which they are experienced, use order of impression. As you read the next example, notice how the writer describes what one sees first, second, and third.

**Order of Impression**

A brilliant red parasol leads the eye directly to the young woman, sheathed in a silk kimono. Next, one notices the small, bright flowers edging the still pond and, finally, the hushed greens that curtain the scene.

### Journal Writing

Select a topic for a descriptive paragraph and brainstorm for the kinds of details you would include. Jot down a possible method of organization and arrange your details accordingly.

## Decide Which Type of Order to Use

You may find using spatial order helpful for describing rooms, objects, and scenes. Order of importance works well when you want to highlight the most important details in a description. Order of impression will help you to describe the order in which you notice details.

Sometimes organization seems to emerge automatically from a topic, and details almost arrange themselves. At other times, you may need to try several methods of organization and choose the one that works best. Don't look for rules to impose on what you write; instead, allow your selection of topic, audience, and purpose to guide your choices. Try to construct a "grand design" by knowing where you're starting and why, where you're going, and what you hope to accomplish along the way.

In the following examples, notice how topic, purpose, and organizational pattern interact to make experiences come to life on the page. In the first passage, the writer uses spatial order to describe the English countryside.

**Prewriting Tip**

When planning a description, consider the point of view you will take. Will the description be from your point of view or from someone else's?

### *Literature Model*

What I saw was principally field upon field rolling off into the far distance. The land rose and fell gently, and the fields were bordered by hedges and trees. There were dots in some of the distant fields which I assumed to be sheep. To my right, almost on the horizon, I thought I could see the square tower of a church.

Kazuo Ishiguro, *The Remains of the Day*

*Words and phrases like "far distance," "bordered," "to my right," and "almost on the horizon" help to indicate the spatial relationships between details.*

As you read the next example, note how the writer uses order of importance to convey the vivid images in the narrator's childhood memories.

### *Literature Model*

Grandfather's little backyard, where hardly anyone ever went except to store odds and ends, was a gloomy jungle of untended plants and trees. But birds, butterflies, and insects frolicked there, and it was the paradise of my childhood. I liked to pluck the delicate cicada skins from the damp mossy tree trunks, to dig earthworms fat as chopsticks from the ground, and to drive clouds of flying baby grasshoppers into the spider webs. ➡

*Comparisons such as "fat as chopsticks" and "like a giant upside-down lotus seedpod" provide concrete visual images.*

And the crab apples that weighed down the tree there were always bigger than store-bought ones.

The grandest sight of all was the hornets' nest in the eaves over Grandfather's window. Like a giant upside-down lotus seedpod, it hung there swarming with more than a hundred busy golden hornets.

Feng Jicai, "The Hornet's Nest"

In the example below, the writer uses order of impression to convey a sense of atmosphere. The details build to create a mysterious scene.

### *Literature Model*

Despite the frantic preparations that had been made to receive them, the mansion still seemed to be under a spell. The Roman-style structure, conceived as the center of a geometric park and grand avenues, was sunk in the riot of a gluttonous jungle growth. The torrid climate had changed the color of the building materials, covering them with a pre-mature patina; nothing was visible of the swimming pool and gardens. The greyhounds had long ago broken their leashes and were running loose, a ferocious, starving pack that greeted the newcomers with a chorus of barking. Birds had nested in the capitals of the columns and covered the reliefs with droppings. On every side were signs of disorder. The Summer Palace had been transformed into a living creature defenseless against the green invasion that had surrounded and overrun it.

Isabel Allende, "Phantom Palace"

*What details create the impression that the disorder is a living thing?*

## Journal Writing

Plan a new descriptive paragraph on the topic you chose in the journal activity on page 121. This time, arrange your descriptive details using a different method of organization.

## Create Topic Sentences

**Revising Tip**

To test how well you have ordered details in a description, read your paragraphs to a classmate. Your listener should "see" a mental picture of what you're describing.

A topic sentence in a descriptive paragraph limits and defines the topic. Topic sentences can serve a variety of additional functions. They can entice or tantalize readers, set the stage for the description that follows, focus the reader's attention in a particular direction, create a mood or impression, add emphasis, or indicate how details are related.

Topic sentences are often placed at the beginning of paragraphs. A topic sentence can also appear in the middle or even at the end of a paragraph. The placement you choose for your topic sentence depends on the function you want that sentence to serve. If you want to establish a mood or prepare readers for what to expect from the paragraph, you might want to place your topic sentence first, as in the model below. On the other hand, if you want to add emphasis or keep your readers in suspense, you might place your topic sentence last.

*Student Model*

The men, women, and children wait for relief, for food, for comfort. There in the crowd stands the impatient child, the hopeful man, and the angry boy with dark eyes and pursed lips. They want their families and their homes and their lives back. They beg for their catastrophe to be our catastrophe.

Allison Batron, Air Academy High School, Colorado Springs, Colorado

When the topic and purpose of your description are clear from the content, you might also use an implied, or suggested, topic sentence. Implied topic sentences are common in descriptive writing. In this model, the writer implies the topic sentence: "The people of Little Italy are full of life."

*Student Model*

At the corner cafes, men are found together speaking of business or playing card games. Bread and wine are always at arm's length. Mothers cook dinner for what looks like an army. Animated expressions complement the busy movement of arms as an Italian woman describes her latest story to anyone who will listen.

Graziella Cirilli, Edison High School, Edison, New Jersey

# 3.1 Writing Activities

## Write a Descriptive Paragraph

Write a descriptive paragraph to enter in a contest sponsored by a national magazine for teens. Use the details in the painting by Jean Béraud below as the basis for your description.

- Choose the details that best serve your purpose.
- Choose an appropriate organization: spatial order, order of importance, order of impression.
- Choose the best place for your topic sentence.

**PURPOSE** To write a descriptive paragraph
**AUDIENCE** Teenage readers of a national magazine
**LENGTH** 1 paragraph

## Cooperative Learning

Working with three other classmates, choose a scene from a familiar short story, book, or movie to dramatize. Discuss the overall mood you want to create and develop a list of details to describe the scene.

Jean Béraud, *Outside the Théâtre du Vaudeville, Paris,* c. 1890

Each group member can then draft a paragraph describing one of the following: setting, props, appearance of the characters, or lighting. Share your paragraph with the other members of your group.

### Grammar Link

**Use commas to set off a nonessential (nonrestrictive) adjective clause.**

*The Roman-style structure,* ***conceived as the center of a geometric park and grand avenues,*** *was sunk in the riot of a gluttonous jungle growth.*

**Do not set off an essential (restrictive) adjective clause.**

*The Summer Palace had been transformed into a living creature defenseless against the green invasion* ***that had surrounded and overrun it.***

Rewrite the following sentences correctly, adding commas where they are needed.

1. The Musée du Louvre which is the world's most famous museum is in Paris.
2. The Vatican Museums which Pope Julius II (1503–1513) founded house many beautiful ancient sculptures.
3. My father who visited the State Hermitage Museum in St. Petersburg was amazed at the exhibition halls.
4. New York City which is host to many museums boasts the Museum of Modern Art.
5. Maria whose parents still live in Madrid visits The Prado whenever possible.

**See Lesson 21.6, pages 684–685.**

LESSON

# 3.2

## Descriptive Writing

# Writing a Unified and Coherent Description

*To write an effective description, use details that reinforce the main idea of the topic sentence of the paragraph. Also, use connecting words or phrases to clarify the relationship among the ideas in the paragraph.*

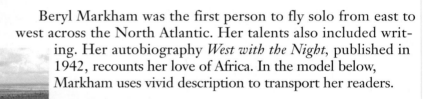

Beryl Markham was the first person to fly solo from east to west across the North Atlantic. Her talents also included writing. Her autobiography *West with the Night*, published in 1942, recounts her love of Africa. In the model below, Markham uses vivid description to transport her readers.

### Literature Model

The Equator runs close to the Rongai Valley, and, even at so high an altitude as this we hunted in, the belly of the earth was hot as live ash under our feet. Except for an occasional gust of fretful wind that flattened the high, cornlike grass, nothing uttered—nothing in the valley stirred. The chirrup-like drone of grasshoppers was dead, birds left the sky unmarked. The sun reigned and there were no aspirants to his place.

We stopped by the red salt-lick that cropped out of the ground in the path of our trail. I did not remember a time when the salt-lick was as deserted as this. Always before it had been crowded with grantii, impala, kongoni, eland, waterbuck, and a dozen kinds of smaller animals. But it was empty today. It was like a marketplace whose flow and bustle of life you had witnessed ninety-nine times, but, on your hundredth visit, was vacant and still without even an urchin to tell you why.

Beryl Markham, *West with the Night*

*What impression is created by the comparison used in the first sentence?*

*What is the main idea of this passage?*

*Markham repeats the central idea and clarifies it by comparing the emptiness of the salt-lick to a deserted marketplace.*

## Create Unity

The effectiveness of Markham's description of the Rongai Valley results from the richness of the word picture she creates. Like a tapestry weaver, Markham intertwines separate pieces—details describing the heat, dust, sun, wind, and animals—with a connecting thread. Each part interacts to form a meaningful whole.

A unified piece of writing uses only those supporting details that reinforce the main idea in the topic sentence. If you cannot see a connection between a detail and the main idea of the paragraph, discard the detail. Eliminating irrelevant details will help unify your writing. When the connection between a detail and the main idea is present but not readily apparent, you may want to explain how this detail relates to the word picture you are creating.

In the illustration below, notice how each detail reinforces the main idea of the topic sentence: an unusually still and deserted landscape. Think of this schematic as a map showing how streets and roads (supporting details) are connected to the major highways (topic sentence).

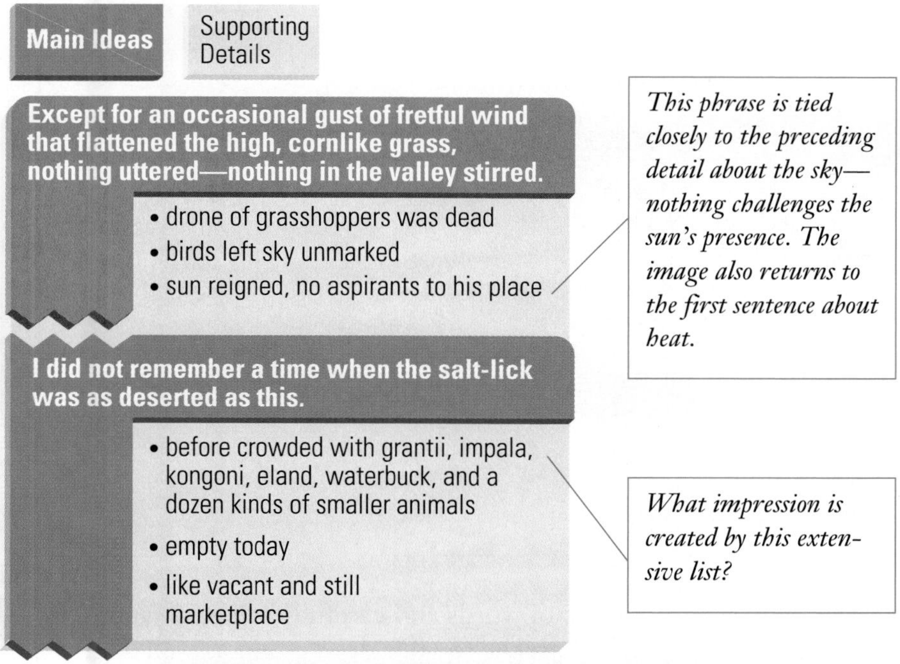

**Main Ideas** | Supporting Details

**Except for an occasional gust of fretful wind that flattened the high, cornlike grass, nothing uttered—nothing in the valley stirred.**

- drone of grasshoppers was dead
- birds left sky unmarked
- sun reigned, no aspirants to his place

*This phrase is tied closely to the preceding detail about the sky—nothing challenges the sun's presence. The image also returns to the first sentence about heat.*

**I did not remember a time when the salt-lick was as deserted as this.**

- before crowded with grantii, impala, kongoni, eland, waterbuck, and a dozen kinds of smaller animals
- empty today
- like vacant and still marketplace

*What impression is created by this extensive list?*

### Journal Writing

Jot down ideas for an impression you would like to create with descriptive writing. Then list some details you might include to support this single impression.

## Achieve Coherence

**Grammar Editing Tip**

When you edit, check to see that the pronouns you use refer clearly to their antecedents. See pages 596–601 for more information on this topic.

A piece of writing is coherent when it has connecting links that clarify the relationships among ideas. A number of strategies can help you achieve coherence, such as using transitional words and phrases, synonyms, repeated words, and pronoun references.

Transitional words and phrases show movement in time, direction. or importance. They also show how one idea or sentence relates to the next. Markham uses words like *when*, *always*, *before*, and *still* to contrast the typically crowded salt-lick with its present emptiness. The chart below lists some of the transitional words and phrases that will help you to achieve coherence in writing.

| Transitional Words and Phrases | | | |
|---|---|---|---|
| **Movement in Time** | | | |
| after a while | currently | immediately | recently |
| afterward | during | in the future | soon |
| at last | finally | later | suddenly |
| at present | first (second, etc.) | meanwhile | then |
| briefly | gradually | now | |
| **Movement in Space** | | | |
| above | beside | inside | over |
| across | beyond | in the middle | to the east |
| among | farther | nearby | toward |
| behind | here | next to | within |
| below | in front of | outside | |
| **Movement in Importance** | | | |
| above all, | finally | in particular | most important |
| equally important | furthermore | indeed | of major concern |
| especially | in fact | moreover | surely |

Well-chosen repetitions of words and carefully selected synonyms can bring emphasis and coherence to your description as well as create parallelism and give the description a cumulative effect. In the model on page 126, note that the repetition of "nothing uttered—nothing in the valley stirred" and the use of the synonyms "deserted," "empty," and "vacant" reinforce the sense of desolation. Beryl Markham eliminates the need for repeating the noun *salt-lick* by using the pronoun *it*. In your writing, use pronouns to replace key words and remind readers of ideas mentioned earlier.

# 3.2 Writing Activities

## Write an Essay Describing a Photograph

From a magazine, select a photograph of a dramatic current event. This photograph will be featured on the cover of the next issue of a national news magazine. You have been asked to write a descriptive essay based on the photograph.

- Use only details that support the topic sentence.
- Use transitional words to make your writing coherent.

**PURPOSE** To write a unified, coherent, descriptive essay based on a photograph
**AUDIENCE** Teenage and adult readers of a national news magazine
**LENGTH** 3–5 paragraphs

### COMPUTER OPTION

If your word processor includes a thesaurus, use it to help you find precise and vivid verbs to replace weak verbs in your descriptive essay. Vivid verbs help keep the attention of your audience. As part of revising your description, circle all weak verbs. Then check for stronger synonyms using the thesaurus option.

### Grammar Link

**A pronoun must agree with its antecedent in number (singular or plural) and gender (masculine, feminine, or neuter).**

Use pronouns to replace key words and remind readers of ideas mentioned earlier.

*I did not remember a time when the **salt-lick** was as deserted as this. Always before **it** had been crowded with grantii, impala, kongoni, eland, waterbuck, and a dozen kinds of smaller animals.*

Write the following sentences, adding an appropriate pronoun. Then underline the antecedent of that pronoun.

1. Many students decided to send ____ college applications to state colleges.
2. Teachers and guidance counselors offered ____ assistance.
3. One student, John, had ____ application returned because it was considered incomplete.
4. Another student, Maria, wants to explore all ____ options before sending in any applications.
5. The deadline for submitting applications to the college office is March 15, and ____ will not be extended.

**See Lesson 17.6, pages 596–601.**

LESSON 3.3

# Descriptive Writing
# Using Figurative Language

*Figurative language is language that is used imaginatively rather than literally. Figurative language can help you present an ordinary subject in a new light.*

Camels are the ships of the desert. Think about that statement. They're awkward and lumbering, but from a distance they may appear to be floating. While shifting desert sands easily trap trucks, camels—like sea vessels—traverse these parched waters effortlessly.

An encyclopedia will give you factual information concerning the camel. Imaginative connections, however, provide a different and exciting kind of understanding.

When you compare camels and ships, you create images. These images, often called figures of speech or figurative language, help others to understand the essence of an idea or to grasp the basic quality of a person, place, or thing.

In the example below, Budd Schulberg uses figurative language to dramatize the boxer's size.

### *Literature Model*

When I stared at Toro that first time the word *giant* . . . didn't occur to me at all. It was *monster* that was in my mind. His hands were monstrous, the size of his feet was monstrous and his oversized head instantly became my conception of the Neanderthal Man who roamed this world some forty thousand years ago. To see him move, slowly, with an awkward loping gait, into the sun-room, bending almost double to come through the doorway, was as disconcerting as seeing one of the restored fossils of primitive man in the Museum of Natural History suddenly move toward you and offer a bony hand in greeting.

Budd Schulberg, *The Harder They Fall*

*What does the comparison to a "monster" or "Neanderthal Man" convey that the word* giant *does not?*

## Create Images with Figurative Language

Figurative language communicates ideas beyond the literal meaning of the words. Use figures of speech such as *simile*, *metaphor*, and *personification* when you want to enrich your writing, create images, add emphasis, evoke emotions, or express fresh and vivid meanings.

Figurative language can be playful, enlightening, witty, or shocking. Figurative language can often communicate in a single phrase a concept or idea that might otherwise take several paragraphs to explain. When used effectively, it is original and full of surprises. The chart at the right defines three kinds of figurative language.

A **simile** associates the qualities of one thing with the qualities of another. The comparison is made by using the word *like* or *as*.
*The rain came from all directions, like music from radios on a crowded beach.*

A **metaphor** equates or identifies one thing with another. The comparison is made directly, without the use of the word *like* or *as*.
*A deafening concert of crashing thunder caused the dog to whimper and the toddler to scream.*

**Personification** assigns human qualities or abilities to animals, objects, or ideas.
*Fat raindrops played drum solos on the overturned buckets.*

As dramatic as figurative language can be, it can also be vague, ineffective, or just plain dull. When the connection you're trying to make between two things doesn't come through clearly to your readers, you obscure the ideas you're trying to communicate or the effects you're trying to create. Mixed metaphors, which ineffectively combine two or more images in a single feature, only confuse readers. Overused similes and metaphors, such as those in the chart at the left, deaden writing, producing stale perceptions.

**DANGER!**
**Bad Figurative Language at Work**

as sly as a fox
as cool as a cucumber
as pretty as a picture
as busy as a bee
as good as gold
as white as snow
as right as rain
as cute as a button

the Last Straw

When using figurative language, decide what impression you want to create for your readers. Relate the details of one thing to specific aspects of the other, helping your readers see something in a new, unexpected light.

**Vocabulary**
**Prewriting Tip**

When you're generating figurative language, try to visualize what your words mean. Sometimes it helps to draw pictures.

### Journal Writing

Revise the examples of bad similes on this page. Create fresh, new images and comparisons that reflect your individual view of the world.

## Write with Imagination

Whether you collect imaginative comparisons along with descriptive details during prewriting or add them during drafting or revising, let metaphors, similes, and personification grow naturally out of your impressions and your material. Don't try to crowd every detail into a comparison. A few well-chosen figures of speech, along with evocative sensory details, will create a far better piece of description than one overloaded with obscure comparisons. Notice the balance between figurative language and sensory detail in the student model below.

### *Student Model*

It was the first day of the new Chinese year, the year of the dragon, and the people of Chinatown were heralding this occasion with an explosive celebration of life. As I walked down the packed street, sound, color, and laughter danced around me.

From across the street, a flash of green caught my eye. A joyous dragon, spanning more than forty feet, pranced its way through the crowd. Although his twenty legs seemed to travel in twenty different directions, the dragon's movements coalesced in a serpentine motion, hypnotizing all who watched his dance.

The dragon's spell was soon broken by the sharp drumming of fireworks exploding on the street underfoot. Light and sound burst forth in chains of sounds that matched the mood of the crowd.

I could not help but be drawn into the whirlpool of emotions that surrounded me. Wave upon wave of joy poured into my soul. I became one with the people and the dragon that danced around and through me. Before this night of joy was over, I knew that the coming year would be a happy one.

Neelesh Chopdekar, Edison High School, Edison, New Jersey

*What impression is created by the writer's use of water images?*

# 3.3 Writing Activities

## Write a Descriptive Essay

A well-known museum has Joan Miró's painting, *Landscape (The Hare)*, in its collection. As an art critic, you must write a descriptive essay to accompany the painting's reproduction in a magazine. Use the reproduction as the basis for your details.

- Use figurative language to create visual images for your readers.
- Balance figurative language with sensory detail.

**PURPOSE** To write a descriptive essay of a painting
**AUDIENCE** Readers of a national art magazine
**LENGTH** 4–5 paragraphs

## Cross-Curricular: American Government

Brainstorm to develop a list of trite similes and metaphors frequently used in political speeches, such as "ship of state," "testing the political waters," "throw the hat into the ring," and "skeletons in the closet." Then brainstorm to develop a list of fresh comparisons. Finally, write a short campaign speech, using the fresh similes, metaphors, and personifications.

Joan Miró, *Landscape (The Hare)*, 1927

### Grammar Link

**Avoid sentence fragments in your writing.**

A **sentence fragment** is an error that occurs when an incomplete sentence is punctuated as though it were a complete sentence.

Fragment: *Although his twenty legs seemed to travel in twenty different directions.*

Fragment: *Hypnotizing all who watched his dance.*

Complete Sentence: *Although his twenty legs seemed to travel in twenty different directions, the dragon's movements coalesced in a serpentine motion, hypnotizing all who watched his dance.*

Rewrite each item below, correcting the sentence fragments. You may need to add words.

1. Some students work and go to school. Need the extra income.
2. Working at part-time jobs after school. Students gain valuable work experience.
3. A student can find a good after-school job at a retail store. Often provides flexible working hours.
4. To juggle both schoolwork and a part-time job. Some students may find it too difficult.
5. Although working and studying can be difficult. They can also learn new skills.

**See Lesson 13.9, page 513.**

LESSON

3.4

# Descriptive Writing
# Using Analogies

*An analogy is an extended comparison between two things that are usually considered dissimilar but that share some common features. When you create an analogy, compare two ideas that have at least three similarities.*

Onto the field they march. Their sweaty faces show the strain of the struggle, their fierce desire to win. They devise a strategy: a blitz, a bomb, or maybe a trap.

Are they soldiers or football players? Who can tell?

Now, stretch your imagination. Think about the ways in which a family is like a corporation or how love is like the sea. You may be surprised at the striking similarities you can find between things that seem very different on the surface.

## Understand Analogies

Analogies are like metaphors because both use vivid images to help make ideas more concrete. While a metaphor consists of a quick comparison, often with intense emotional overtones, an analogy makes an extended comparison, supported point by point with examples and details. Often, an analogy extends through several paragraphs—sometimes through an entire essay.

In addition to being vivid, an analogy clarifies a complex idea or an abstract concept by comparing it to something more familiar. In his short story "The Open Boat," Stephen Crane draws a comparison between riding in a small boat on the open sea and riding a horse.

### Literature Model

A seat in this boat was not unlike a seat upon a bucking bronco, and, by the same token, a bronco is not much smaller. The craft pranced and reared, and plunged like an animal. As each wave came, and she rose for it, she seemed like a horse making at a fence outrageously high. The manner of her scramble over these walls of water is a mystic thing . . . the foam racing down from the summit of each wave, requiring a new leap, and a leap from the air. Then, after scornfully bumping a crest, she would slide, and race and splash down a long incline, and arrive bobbing and nodding in front of the next menace.

Stephen Crane, "The Open Boat"

*Notice how the author's selection of precise verbs clarifies the analogy.*

*One point of similarity is the movement, which is brought to life with similes.*

In the chart below, notice how Crane extends the comparison point by point. Notice also that each element in the analogy supports the main idea of the paragraph: the precariousness of riding in the boat.

### Similarity Chart

**Riding in a Boat**

- unsteady movement
- passengers easily thrown
- passengers climb enormously high waves
- passengers slide and race down long incline
- passengers appear to sail through the air

**Riding a Horse**

- unexpected movement
- rider easily thrown
- rider and horse jump high fences
- rider and horse slide and race down long incline
- rider and horse appear to sail through the air

## Journal Writing

What similarities can you discover between two dissimilar things, such as a school and a factory or time and a river? In your journal make a chart listing similarities and differences.

## Create Analogies

Keep in mind that the success of your analogy depends on your discovering enough similarities to make the analogy convincing. For example, drawing an analogy between bees and people might work, since both are social creatures. An analogy enlightens by pointing out a perceived truth about two subjects and making an extended case for that truth. The checklist below can help you create meaningful analogies.

**Grammar Editing Tip**

As you edit your analogy, check for subject-verb agreement. See Unit 16, pages 564–579.

**Creating Successful Analogies**

- Find a minimum of three similarities between the ideas you are comparing.
- Use specific details and examples, as well as similes and metaphors, to support your comparisons.
- Write a topic sentence that establishes the basis of the comparison.
- Decide on a logical order for the points of the analogy, and use transitions to link them smoothly and clearly.

In the student model below, notice how the writer presents her points in order of importance and uses transitions to link her ideas.

***Student Model***

*The first sentence identifies the two situations being compared.*

*What points of similarity does the writer establish as the basis of this comparison?*

*Notice how transitional words highlight order of importance as the method of organization.*

Reading a novel by William Faulkner is like watching television when my father has the remote control, because both precipitate confusion and agitation and both require a great deal of patience and concentration. A Faulkner novel develops many complex characters. Similarly, the television under my father's roving control reveals numerous characters from every possible program. Faulkner, with his lack of clear transitions, and my father, with his fusion of mismatched programs, tend to blur plot situations after a short time. The most striking similarity, however, is the jumbled presentation of each situation. Faulkner often has no logical chronological order. My father also ensures that each television show is viewed at nonsequential five-minute intervals. Both circumstances guarantee that just as I think I have discovered the meaning of the program or story, I am propelled back into ignorance by one swift and cruel motion.

Kate Jones, Henry Clay High School, Lexington, Kentucky

# 3.4 Writing Activities

## Write an Analogy

Write an article for a local newspaper describing a typical activity of a teenager, such as baby-sitting or getting up in the morning.

- Use an analogy to compare the activity to something else.
- Use specific details.
- Write a topic sentence that establishes the basis of the comparison.
- Use a logical order for the points of the analogy and use transitions to link them.

**PURPOSE** To describe an activity by using an analogy
**AUDIENCE** Newspaper readers
**LENGTH** 2–4 paragraphs

### COMPUTER OPTION

Some computers include word-processing programs that easily create columns. If your computer has this capability, use it to make the similarity chart assigned in the journal activity. Make a note of how to set up the columns so that you can use your computer for other assignments requiring columns.

### Grammar Link

**A verb must agree in number with an indefinite pronoun subject.**

*Reading a novel by William Faulkner is like watching television when my father has the remote control, because* ***both precipitate*** *confusion and agitation and* ***both require*** *a great deal of patience and concentration.*

Write five sentences about reading and five about writing, each using one of the following indefinite pronouns as the subject. Be sure each subject agrees with a present-tense verb.

1. most
2. both
3. several
4. nobody
5. something
6. many
7. either
8. few
9. everybody
10. nothing

**See Lesson 16.7, pages 575–576.**

LESSON

# 3.5 Writing About Literature

# Analyzing Imagery in Descriptive Writing

*Imagery refers to language that appeals to the senses. To analyze descriptive writing, examine the separate images; then determine how they relate to the work as a whole.*

Everald Brown, *Spiritualism*, 1979

## *Literature Model*

The end of the world, as it turned out, was nothing more than a collection of magnificent winter houses on Isle des Chevaliers. When laborers imported from Haiti came to clear the land, clouds and fish were convinced that the world was over, that the sea-green green of the sea and the sky-blue blue of the sky were no longer permanent. Wild parrots that had escaped the stones of hungry children in Queen of France agreed and raised havoc as they flew away to look for yet another refuge. Only the champion daisy trees were serene. After all, they were part of a rain forest already two thousand years old and scheduled for eternity, so they ignored the men and continued to rock the diamond-backs that slept in their arms. It took the river to persuade them that indeed the world was altered. That never again would the rain be equal, and by the time they realized it and had run their roots deeper, clutching the earth like lost boys found, it was too late. The men had already folded the earth where there had been no fold and hollowed her where there had been no hollow, which explains what happened to the river. It crested, then lost its course, and finally its head. Evicted from the place where it had lived, and forced into unknown turf, it could not form its pools or waterfalls, and ran every which way. The clouds gathered together, stood still and watched the river scuttle around the forest floor, crash headlong into the haunches of hills with no notion of where it was going, until exhausted, ill and grieving, it slowed to a stop just twenty leagues short of the sea.

Toni Morrison, *Tar Baby*

## Analyze Descriptive Writing

You can analyze descriptive writing by examining its parts and the way they interact to form the whole. But how do you get started? The first step is to be an active reader. Rather than simply allowing words to pass before your eyes, read with an inquiring mind. Stop, reread, ask questions, and look for connections between ideas in the work and your own experiences. Let the word pictures wash over you, as you note the thoughts that the imagery suggests. Write down everything you think of, keeping in mind that you are looking for possible interpretations rather than a correct answer.

Imagery is a broad term referring to language that appeals to the senses. Examples include metaphor, simile, personification, and analogy. The *Tar Baby* passage, for example, begins with a surprising and puzzling metaphor that compares the end of the world to a collection of beautiful houses. Until you examine the other images in the passage, however, the effect and meaning of the opening metaphor remain unclear. As you analyze the personification of clouds, fish, parrots, daisy trees, and the river, you discover that the opening metaphor refers not to the end of the planet Earth but to the demise of a particular and specific part of the planet. One way to approach this kind of analysis is to create a chart like the one below.

**Vocabulary**

**Prewriting Tip**

As you analyze images, note the precise adjectives the writer chose.

| Image | Type | What Does It Suggest? |
|---|---|---|
| World ending equals magnificent houses. | metaphor | Not end of world literally, but end of wildlife. |
| Clouds and fish convinced. | personification | Understand their habitat is threatened. |
| Parrots agreed. | personification | Had previous experience. Knew about people. |
| Daisy trees unconcerned, rocked snakes in arms. | personification | Thought they were indestructible. Naïve. |

### Journal Writing

Select a descriptive passage from a novel you are now reading or studying in class. Begin an analysis of the images and what they suggest to you by creating a chart like the one above.

**Grammar Editing Tip**

As you edit your literary analysis, check that you have used correct punctuation for quotations. See Lesson 21.11, pages 696–699.

# Write a Literary Analysis

At the center of a literary analysis lies the writer's interpretation of how the descriptive passage achieves particular effects and conveys meaning. Once you've analyzed the separate images and their associations, it's time to look for patterns and relationships. Use the questions in this chart to help you determine how the imagery relates to the work as a whole. These questions will also help you to decide on the main point you want to make in your analysis.

The model below shows the opening paragraphs of an analysis of the *Tar Baby* passage. In the analysis, the writer shows how the imagery in the passage relates to the novel's overall theme.

**Questions to Consider**

- What is the overall effect of the images?
- What do you think the author's purpose was in choosing these images? How do the images relate to the work as a whole?
- What do you want to convey to your readers? Do you want to stress your personal response, or do you want to present a more objective interpretation?
- Which images are most striking or important? Which ones will help you to prove your point?

## *Model*

*The introduction establishes the backdrop of the novel, and the thesis statement shows how the landscape ties in with the theme of conflict.*

In the novel *Tar Baby,* Toni Morrison creates a striking portrait of a Caribbean island and the conflicts that define life there. She portrays the separate worlds of privilege and poverty, residents and winter visitors, African Americans and whites. Even the landscape comes to life in this environment of opposing forces.

*The topic sentence focuses on the imagery, and the second sentence shows how the controlling image influences the passage.*

Morrison gives a voice to the landscape, humanizing it through personification. By making nature feel and think, she vividly illustrates what happens to the natural environment when humans destroy it for their own use. The very first metaphor, in which the end of the world is equated with "a collection of magnificent winter houses," seems like a contradiction until it becomes clear exactly what world is being destroyed.

*How does the use of quotations, paraphrases, and examples from the text add to the effectiveness of this essay?*

The clouds, fish, parrots, and river understand how their existence will be altered by the people clearing the land. Yet, there is conflict even among the natural personalities. The daisy trees remain blindly "serene," believing that as part of "a rain forest already two thousand years old and scheduled for eternity," they are untouchable.

# 3.5 Writing Activities

## Write an Essay Analyzing Imagery

Select a piece of literature that contains imagery: similes, metaphors, personifications, or analogies. Write an essay analyzing the images in the piece.

- Analyze descriptive language
- Interpret patterns and relationships
- Make a main point about the literature

**PURPOSE** To write an essay analyzing the use of imagery in a piece of literature
**AUDIENCE** Your literature teacher
**LENGTH** 1–2 pages

## Cooperative Learning

With a group of three classmates, discuss the painting *Le Rendez-Vous* by René Magritte. Focus first on personal reactions, and then discuss the separate images and their possible meanings. Consider shape, color, size, medium, and style. After the discussion, review notes and resolve questions. Each member can then write an analysis of the painting. Share your essay with your group.

René Magritte, *Le Rendez-Vous*, c. 1938

### Grammar Link

**Use strong verbs to make your writing more precise.**

*The clouds **gathered** together . . . and **watched** the river **scuttle** around the forest floor **crash** headlong into the haunches of hills . . . .*

Replace the weak verb set in boldface in each sentence. You may need to delete or add words to the sentence as you make it stronger.

1. Sometimes, one thunderstorm immediately **sets off** another thunderstorm.
2. Cyclones are storms in which the winds **go** toward the center of an area of low air pressure.
3. After touching down, a tornado's funnel **takes up** debris.
4. An edge of a funnel **can run** into a building.
5. Today, meteorologists **can give** storm warnings to prevent loss of life and damage to property.

**See Lesson 10.3, pages 410–417.**

UNIT 3

# WRITING PROCESS IN ACTION

## DESCRIPTIVE WRITING

In preceding lessons you learned about effective descriptive writing. Now it's time to apply what you've learned. In this lesson, you're invited to write a vivid description of a scenic photograph of your area.

**• Assignment •**

| | |
|---|---|
| *Context* | *A talented photographer is exhibiting scenic photographs of your area. As a writer of the catalog of the exhibition, you've been asked to highlight one photograph in an essay, conveying not only the photograph's physical elements but also its emotional impact.* |
| *Purpose* | *To write a vivid scenic description that suggests a personal reaction* |
| *Audience* | *The readers of a photography exhibition catalog* |
| *Length* | *1–2 pages* |

The following pages can help you plan and write your description. Read through them and then refer to them as you need to. But don't feel tied down by them. You're in charge of your own writing process.

## Prewriting

To begin, think of a place to set up your imaginary camera. If possible, visit the scene and experiment with different perspectives. Even if you can't use direct observation, revisit the scene mentally, and take note of what would be visible from specific vantage points. Remember, you will be writing a description of a photograph of the scene, so you need to find a definite spot from which to visualize it.

To recall and record details of the scene, cluster, brainstorm, or freewrite again. Include similes, metaphors, and personifications to record your impressions and associations. Determine whether your prewriting already contains a pattern of images or if any are suggested to you now. Then select a vantage point for your "camera" and look through its lens. Focus on the details you can see from that point and circle or underline them. Keeping your purpose and audience in mind, ask yourself questions such as those at the right.

If you can answer these questions, you're ready to decide on your controlling idea and fashion the thesis statement that will guide your draft. Don't forget to search through the figures of speech in your prewriting; you may find a thesis statement lurking there. If you can't answer these questions, return to any of the prewriting techniques to generate the answers, or choose another location that will be more inspiring.

*Prewriting Questions*

- *Which details will best re-create this place for my audience?*
- *What is my emotional reaction to this place?*
- *What impression do I want my audience to get from my description?*

## Drafting

Begin by choosing a method of organization for presenting your visual details. Decide, for example, whether you wish to move spatially, or whether you wish to support an overall impression with order of importance. Note how in the following selection Jill Ker Conway uses order of importance to support her overall impression.

**Prewriting Tip**

Lesson 3.3, pages 130–132, has more information about similes, metaphors, and personifications.

***Literature Model***

Very occasionally, where a submerged watercourse rises a little nearer the surface of the earth, a group of eucalyptus trees will cluster. Worn and gnarled by wind and lack of moisture, they rise up on the horizon so dramatically they appear like an assemblage of local deities. Because heat and mirages make them float in the air, they seem from the distance like surfers endlessly riding the plains above a silvery wave. The ocean they ride is blue-grey, silver, green, yellow, scarlet, and bleached gold, highlighting the red clay tones of the earth to provide a rich palette illuminated by brilliant sunshine, or on grey days a subdued blending of tones like those observed on a calm sea.

*The Road from Coorain,* Jill Ker Conway

**Drafting Tip**

Lesson 3.1, pages 120–124, has more information on organizing descriptions.

Because you are writing for a catalog, you need to do more than say what's in the photograph. Your introduction should encourage people not only to look carefully at this landscape but also to appreciate it the way you do. You may wish to save details about the exhibit and the photograph until later, beginning instead with your emotional reaction or a striking image. Make your audience feel that they are at the site or viewing the photograph directly.

As you draft the body of your essay, follow the pattern of organization you chose, but don't be afraid to stop and choose another organizing principle if the first one doesn't work. Also, even though drafting is not the time to belabor each word, do consider the connotations of the words you choose and how they contribute to your tone and the impression you want to create.

Finally, think about what you want your conclusion to accomplish. You may want to fix an image in the minds of your audience, evaluate either the scene itself or the photograph of it, or provide insight into your feelings about the place. You might also close with information about the exhibit.

**Revising Tip**

For help with transitions, see Lesson 3.2, pages 126–127.

## Revising

To begin revising, read over your draft to make sure that what you've written fits your purpose and audience. Then have a **writing conference**. Read your draft to a partner or small group. Use your audience's reactions to help you evaluate your work so far. The Revising Checklist can help you and your partner or group.

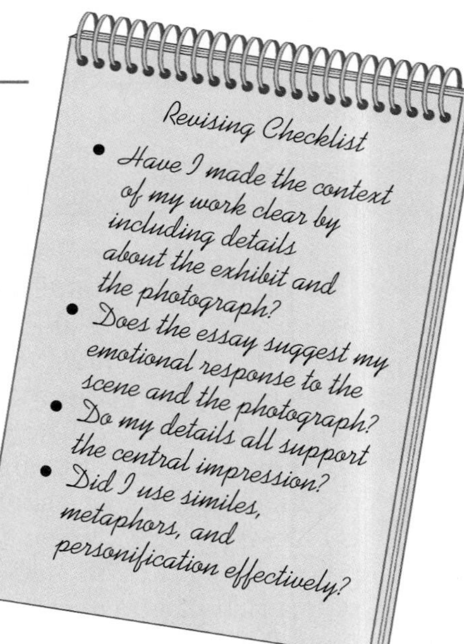

Revising Checklist
• Have I made the context of my work clear by including details about the exhibit and the photograph?
• Does the essay suggest my emotional response to the scene and the photograph?
• Do my details all support the central impression?
• Did I use similes, metaphors, and personification effectively?

# Editing

Once you are pleased with the basic content and set-up of your description, proofread it carefully for errors in grammar, usage, mechanics, and spelling. Use the questions at the right as a guide.

Editing Checklist
• Did I punctuate restrictive and nonrestricive adjective clauses correctly?
• Did I use clear antecedents for pronouns?
• Did I avoid using sentence fragments?
• Did I check subject-verb agreement for indefinite pronouns used as subjects?
• Did I check the spelling of all words I'm unsure of?



## Self-Evaluation

**Make sure your description—**

- views the scene from one particular vantage point and is limited to what would be revealed or suggested in a photograph
- uses vivid language and evocative figures of speech to bring the scene to life and to reveal its emotional impact
- orders details in a way that complements the purpose and audience of the description
- is unified and coherent
- follows the rules of grammar, usage, mechanics, and spelling

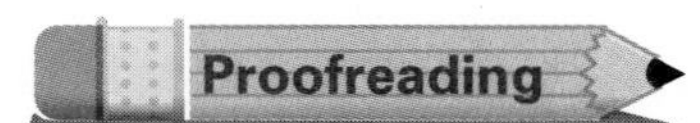


For proofreading symbols, see page 92.

# Presenting

You might want to take a photograph of the scene that served as the basis of your description and post it in your classroom along with a clean copy of your essay. You also might want to organize an exhibit of your class's pictures and texts in the school cafeteria or library or even somewhere in your community. Eventually you could include the photographs and essays in a special class catalog.

**Editing Tip**

Lesson 13.9, page 513, has more information on avoiding sentence fragments.

**Presenting Tip**

Work closely with your classmates to ensure the neatness of the texts, photographs, and displays.

## Journal Writing

Reflect on your writing process experience. Answer these questions in your journal: What do you like best about your descriptive writing? What was the hardest part of writing your description? What did you learn in your writing conference? What new things have you learned as a writer?

UNIT 3

# Descriptive Writing
# Literature Model

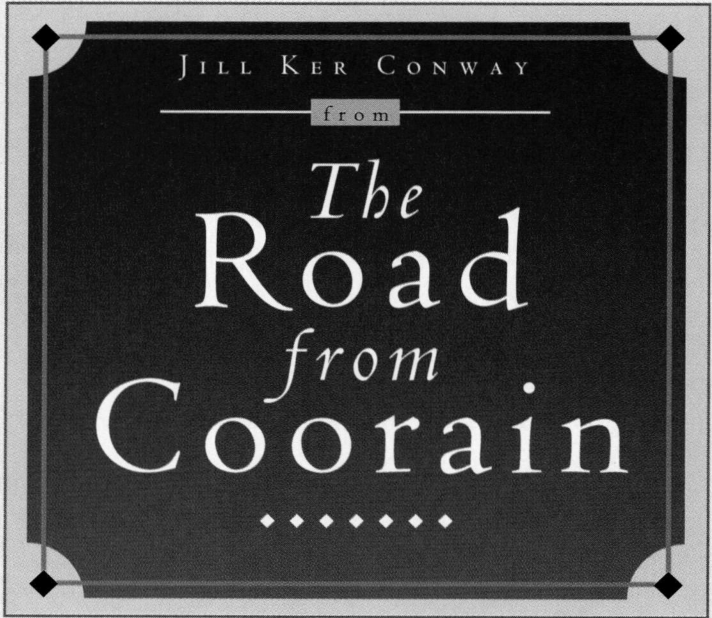

JILL KER CONWAY
from
The Road from Coorain


*Like a photographer, Jill Ker Conway focuses different-sized lenses on the Australian landscape to achieve different effects. Whether examining plant growth at ground level or the ever-present horizon from a distance, she creates a vivid portrait of the colors and textures of a complex, though spare, environment. After you read the selection, try the activities in Linking Writing and Literature on page 151.*

The western plains of New South Wales are grasslands. Their vast expanse flows for many hundreds of miles beyond the Lachlan and Murrumbidgee rivers until the desert takes over and sweeps inland to the dead heart of the continent. In a good season, if the eyes are turned to the earth on those plains, they see a tapestry of delicate life—not the luxuriant design of a book of hours* by any means, but a tapestry nonetheless, designed by a spare modern artist. What grows there hugs the earth firmly with its extended system of roots above which the plant life is delicate but determined. After rain there is an explosion of growth. Nut-flavored green grass puts up the thinnest of green spears. Wild grains appear, grains which develop bleached gold ears as they ripen. Purple desert peas weave through the green and gold, and bright yellow bachelor's buttons cover acres at a time, like fields planted with mustard. Closest to the earth is trefoil clover, whose tiny, vivid green leaves and bright flowers creep along the ground in spring, to be replaced by a harvest of seed-filled burrs in autumn—burrs which store within them the energy of the sun as concentrated protein. At the edges of pans of clay, where the topsoil has eroded, live waxy succulents bearing bright pink and purple blooms, spreading like splashes of paint dropped in widening circles on the earth.

Above the plants that creep across the ground are the bushes, which grow wherever an indentation in the earth, scarcely visible to the eye, allows for the concentration of more moisture from the dew and the reluctant rain. There is the ever-present round mound of prickly weed, which begins its life a strong acid green with hints of yellow, and then is burnt by the sun or the frost to a pale whitish yellow. As it ages, its root system weakens so that on windy days the wind will pick it out of the earth and roll it slowly and majestically about like whirling suns in a Van Gogh painting. Where the soil contains limestone, stronger bushes grow, sometimes two to three feet high, with the delicate narrow-leaved foliage of arid climates, bluish green and dusty grey in color, perfectly adapted to resist the drying sun. Where the soil is less porous and water will lie for a while after rain, comes the annual saltbush, a miraculous silvery-grey plant which stores its own water in small balloonlike round leaves and thrives long after the rains have vanished. Its sterner perennial cousin, which resembles sagebrush, rises on woody branches and rides out the strongest wind.

Very occasionally, where a submerged watercourse rises a little nearer the surface of the earth, a group of eucalyptus trees will cluster. Worn and gnarled by wind and lack of moisture, they rise up on the horizon so dramatically they appear like an assemblage of local deities. Because heat and mirages make them float in the air, they seem from the distance like surfers endlessly riding the plains above a silvery wave. The ocean they ride is blue-grey, silver, green, yellow, scarlet, and bleached gold, highlighting the red clay tones of the earth to provide a rich palette illuminated by brilliant sunshine, or

* **book of hours:** a prayer book hand-painted by medieval monks with illustrations in brilliant colors

Edward Officer, *On the Plains of the Darling*, 1907

on grey days a subdued blending of tones like those observed on a calm sea.

The creatures that inhabit this earth carry its colors in their feathers, fur, or scales. Among its largest denizens are emus, six-foot-high flightless birds with dun-grey feathers and tiny wings, and kangaroos. Kangaroos, like emus, are silent creatures, two to eight feet tall, and ranging in color from the gentlest dove-grey to a rich red-brown. Both species blend with their native earth so well that one can be almost upon them before recognizing the familiar shape. The fur of the wild dogs has the familiar yellow of the sun-baked clay, and the reptiles, snakes and goannas, look like the earth in shadow. All tread on the fragile habitat with padded paws and claws which leave the roots of grass intact.

On the plains, the earth meets the sky in a sharp black line so regular that it seems as though drawn by a creator interested more in geometry than the hills and valleys of the Old Testament. Human purposes are dwarfed by such a blank horizon. When we see it from an island in a vast ocean we know we are resting in shelter. On the plains, the horizon is always with us and there is no retreating from it. Its blankness travels with our every step and waits for us at every point of the compass. Because we have very few reference points on the spare earth, we seem to creep over it, one tiny point of consciousness between the empty earth and the overarching sky. Because of the flatness, contrasts are in a strange scale. A scarlet sunset will highlight grey-yellow tussocks of grass as though they were trees. Thunderclouds will mount thousands of feet above one stunted tree in the foreground. A horseback rider on the horizon will seem to rise up and emerge from the clouds. While the patterns of the earth are in small scale, akin to complex needlepoint on a vast tapestry, the sky is all drama. Cumulus clouds pile up over the center of vast continental spaces, and the wind moves them at dramatic pace along the horizon or over our heads. The ever-present red dust of a dry earth hangs in the air and turns all the colors from yellow through orange and red to purple on and off as the clouds bend and refract the light. Sunrise and sunset make up in drama for the fact that there are so few songbirds in that part of the bush. At sunrise, great shafts of gold precede the baroque sunburst. At sunset, the cumulus ranges through the shades of a Turner seascape before the sun dives below the earth leaving no afterglow, but at the horizon, tongues of fire.

Except for the bush canary and the magpie, the birds of this firmament court without the songs of the northern forest. Most are parrots, with the vivid colors and rasping sounds of the species. At sunset, rosella parrots, a glorious rosy pink, will settle on trees and appear to turn them scarlet. Magpies, large black and white birds with a call close to song, mark the sunrise, but the rest of the day is the preserve of the crows, and the whistle of the hawk and the golden eagle. The most startling sound is the ribald laughter of the kookaburra, a species of kingfisher, whose call resembles demonic laughter. It is hard to imagine a kookaburra feeding St. Jerome or accompanying St. Francis. They belong to a physical and spiritual landscape which is outside the imagination of the Christian West.

The primal force of the sun shapes the environment. With the wind and the sand it bakes and cleanses all signs of decay. There is no cleansing by water. The rivers flow beneath the earth, and rain falls too rarely. In the recurring cycles of drought the sand and dust flow like water, and like the floods of other climates they engulf all that lies in their path. Painters find it hard to capture the shimmer of that warm red earth dancing in the brilliant light, and to record at the same time the subtle greens and greys of the plants and trees. Europeans were puzzled by the climate and vegetation, because the native eucalyptus trees were not deciduous. The physical blast of the sun in hot dry summers brought plants to dormancy. Slow growth followed in autumn, and a burst of vigorous growth after the brief winter rainy season. Summer was a time of endurance for all forms of life as moisture ebbed away and the earth was scorched. Winter days were like summer in a northern climate, and spring meant the onset of unbroken sunshine. On the plains, several winters might go by without a rainy season, and every twenty years or so the rain might vanish for a decade at a time. When that happened, the sun was needed to cleanse the bones of dead creatures, for the death toll was immense.

The oldest known humans on the continent left their bones on the western plains. Nomadic peoples hunted over the land as long as forty thousand years ago. They and their progeny left behind the blackened stones of ovens, and the hollowed flat pieces of granite they carried from great distances to grind the native nardoo grain. Their way of life persisted until white settlers came by bullock wagon, one hundred and thirty years ago, to take possession of the land. They came to graze their flocks of sharphooved sheep and cattle, hoping to make the land yield wealth. Other great inland grasslands in Argentina, South Africa, or North America were settled by pastoralists and ranchers who used forced labor: Indian peons, Bantus, or West African slaves. On Australia's great plains there were no settled native people to enslave. The settlers moved onto the plains long after the abandonment of transportation from Great Britain, the last form of forced labor available in the Antipodes. As a result, the way of life that grew up for white settlers was unique.

# Linking Writing and Literature

## Readers Respond to the Model

### What makes Jill Ker Conway's description effective?

**Explore Jill Ker Conway's description by answering these questions. Then read what other students remembered about Conway's description.**

1. Jill Ker Conway never explicitly states her emotional response to her environment, but she suggests it throughout this excerpt. How does she feel about the western plains of New South Wales? Which details indicate her personal reactions?
2. What do you think it would be like to live in such a landscape? Do you think you would find it overwhelming, depressing, exhilarating, or inspiring? Explain.
3. Choose a descriptive section that you find particularly effective. What imagery—metaphors, similes, personifications, analogies—makes this section so effective?

The author's description of the kangaroos and emus is the most interesting part of this literature selection. The mood seems sad, though, because Conway says that the plains of New South Wales will eventually be taken over.
***Aimee Hart***

The descriptions made this selection unique. The author made excellent use of detail in her description of the grasslands. The effect was almost poetic! The author's use of metaphors and similes really conveys a picture of how the grasslands look. It is obvious that she finds her subject matter beautiful.
***Michelle Kalski***

# Unit 3 Review

## Reflecting on the Unit

**Summarize what you learned in this unit by answering the following questions.**

- How would you define effective descriptive writing?
- What are the different methods of organization for descriptive writing?
- How can you achieve a unified and coherent description?
- What is figurative language and when should you use it?
- What is an analogy? When should you use it?
- What appeals to you about Jill Ker Conway's description in her book *The Road from Coorain?*

## Adding to Your Portfolio

**Choose a selection for your portfolio.** Look over the descriptive writing you have done during this unit. Select a piece of writing to put into your portfolio. The piece you choose should show one or more of the following:

- vivid, sensory details and rich, evocative, figurative language
- an effective organization for your topic, audience, and purpose
- an effective topic sentence or thesis statement
- connecting words or phrases that clarify the relationships among the ideas

**Reflect on your choice.** Attach a note to the piece you chose, explaining briefly why you chose it and what you learned from writing it.

**Set goals.** How can you improve your writing? What skill will you focus on the next time you write?

## Writing Across the Curriculum

**Make a geography connection.** Research additional information on the western plains of New South Wales. Then write a descriptive paragraph about one section or feature of the plains for your classmates. Gather your details about this section or feature and formulate your main point. Choose an appropriate method of organization. Be sure to revise your paragraph for your topic, purpose, and audience. Check for unity and coherence.

UNIT

# 4 Narrative Writing

Composition

## Lessons

### Narrative Writing in the Real World



### Skills and Applications



### *Writing About Literature*



### Writing Process in Action



### *Literature Model*



### Unit 4 Review

UNIT
4
PREVIEW

Case Study

# Narrative Writing in the Real World

## Fayer Develops a Prize-winning Story

**FOCUS: Whether for film or print, writing a dramatic narrative requires a careful choice of storytelling details.**

In the mid-1970s, Steve Fayer worked as a writer for Blackside, Inc., a black-owned production firm that sought to develop a two-hour television program on the civil rights struggles of the 1950s and 1960s. Although support for the initial project was withdrawn, Blackside's president, Henry Hampton, remained determined to tell the story of African Americans' battle for equality. In 1983, Hampton asked Fayer to return to Blackside to help develop what would become a six-hour, award-winning series, *Eyes on the Prize.*

Fayer wrote two episodes of *Eyes on the Prize*—its name taken from a stirring civil rights song. The series aired in 1987 and drew wide acclaim, including two Emmy awards. This success opened the way for a second Eyes series in 1990. Fayer was even more deeply involved in helping to structure the sequel.

*Screenwriter Steve Fayer*

***"We tried to tell stories that would allow an audience to enter the history of the civil rights movement and to relive it.'***

—Steve Fayer, screenwriter for *Eyes on the Prize*

"Working on *Eyes* changed the way I felt about myself," he says. "I'm not as courageous as the people in the civil rights movement, but I'm no longer comfortable with myself unless I speak out when speaking out is called for."

At Blackside, the lengthy process of producing *Eyes on the Prize* began with a seminar. Historians and other participants met with the film's staff for group discussions and lectures—what Fayer terms "a process of immersing ourselves in the history." Meanwhile, researchers compiled a collection of background readings for the seminar participants.

Writers, writer-producers, film archivists, researchers, and editors worked together to develop *Eyes on the Prize.* Fayer says the team approach "can be kind of frustrating to somebody who likes working alone. But there is no way that one person can have the entire vision. A series like this can take thirty or forty people hunting for music, for archival footage, for interviews, for still shots. We needed people to talk to scholars and to uncover special collections of film or university archives. Making a documentary is an extraordinarily complex undertaking."

*Steve Fayer (facing page) stands at a sculpture dedicated to Martin Luther King Jr. The work of King and other activists helped African Americans gain political power. One example of that rise to power was Harold Washington (below), mayor of Chicago, 1983–1987.*

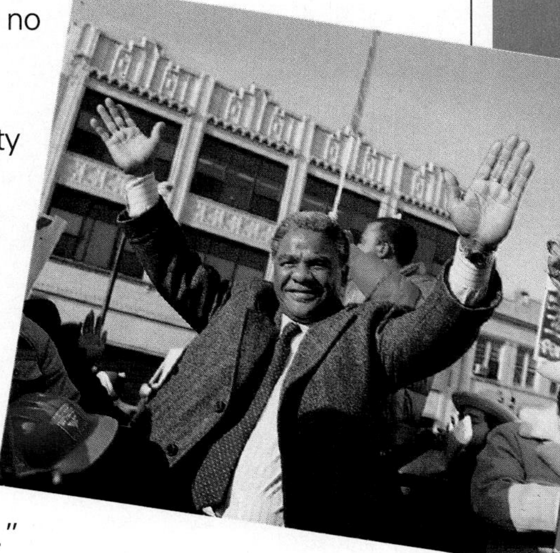

# Prewriting

## DEVISING A STRATEGY

Writers often find that the best way to tell a story is to let people tell it in their own words. For *Eyes on the Prize,* production teams interviewed scores of civil rights activists. The result was often riveting. But getting subjects to tell their stories can be tough.

Interviewing, says Fayer, is a fine art. "Sometimes you know the story's locked up inside the person, but you can't get it. For one of the greatest interviews in the first series, the guy was so nervous he could hardly speak. We had to stay there and 'burn the film'—let it roll—until we could see him relax."

The writers had to decide not only who should tell the story but also how to tell it. One episode depicts the 1963 civil rights march on Washington, D.C., where Martin Luther King Jr. gave his famous "I have a dream" speech. Fayer and his colleagues—producers Callie Crossley and Jim DeVinney, who wrote the episode—wanted to do more than just relate facts.

Fayer recalls, "There was great opposition to this march. People feared it would lead to violence; there was controversy about what speeches should be given; there was also fear that no one would come. Now we could have just told you that on August 28, 1963, there was a march on Washington and 250,000 people came. But we wanted the audience to enter the drama of the march and to understand that its success wasn't foreordained."

So through the voice of the narrator, writers told of the worry that the crowd would not be large enough to attract the nation's attention. Then they wove in participants' memories of behind-the-scenes controversy. Out of this dramatic tension came the climactic moment of King's historic address.

*Production teams accumulated hundreds of hours of videotaped interviews of participants in the civil rights movement; the interviews helped form the basis of the series.*

# Drafting

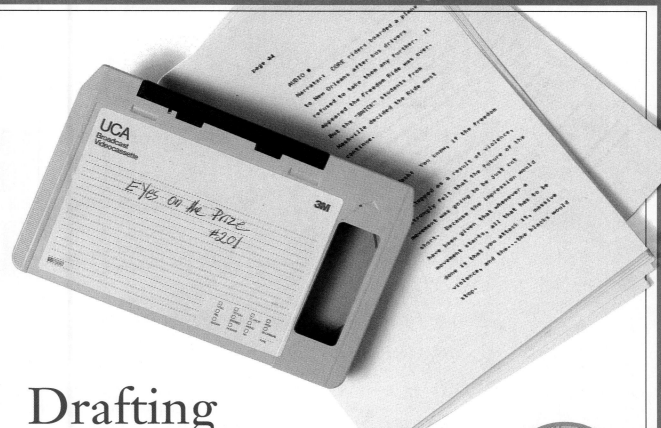

## WRITING THE SCRIPT

While "talking heads" can provide dramatic, primary-source narrative, some information is best told quickly and succinctly by a narrator. The screenwriter writes the narration that knits segments of the film together and gives the audience "context for what they're watching," Fayer says.

To keep the audience from becoming bored, he explains, the screenwriter must avoid telling viewers what they can already see on the screen. Instead, the writer should provide information that the audience cannot know or provide for itself—explaining, for example, why the march on Washington was successful and what happened as a result of it.

Documentary script writing resembles other forms of narrative writing. Fayer made his own list of more than a dozen *do*'s and *don't*s of writing; many of his rules apply well to either medium. For example, "Avoid the passive voice and abstract words ending in *-ing* or *-ion.* Write simple declarative sentences with action verbs to tell what's happening. Follow basic dramatic structure by including conflict, character, and resolution."

*The script is written in a way that cues the narrator and makes unfamiliar words easy to read. For example, the acronym SNCC (Student Nonviolent Coordinating Committee) appears in the script as SNICK—as the acronym is pronounced—so the narrator is less likely to stumble over it during recording.*

# Revising/Editing

## CUTTING AND COLLABORATING

In filmmaking as in publishing, tough decisions must be made about what to include in the story and what to cut. "Some documentarians have a tendency to try to tell everything," says Fayer. "But film is not a good medium for cataloging things."

Revising can be a frustrating process for a screenwriter. Says Fayer, "Sometimes a film is edited so that the particular lead-ins and lead-outs and audio cues you wrote are now in different positions or don't exist anymore. If you're serious about what you're doing, you're really bending your brain to come up with the right words. And then when those words are no longer needed, it can break your heart." In the first *Eyes* series, Fayer revised his narration to fit the producer's and editor's film cuts. In the second series, however, he was more involved in preplanning.

Collaboration among writers, producers, and editors was crucial. "In *Eyes,* we all stepped on each other's territory," Fayer explains. "For example, a writer might say, 'What would happen if you shortened that cut by three or four frames? Wouldn't it speed up the action; wouldn't it bring us closer to where we want to be?' It was wonderful to be part of that process. What we ended up with was something that had an impact on the way people looked at the world and at their own history."

*Fayer with colleagues Judy Richardson and Henry Hampton in the video-editing room at Blackside, Inc. In a team effort, members must consider what is best for the film overall.*

# Responding to the Case Study

**1. Discussion**

**Discuss these questions about Steve Fayer's writing.**

- According to Fayer, why is a team approach essential in developing and producing a documentary series?
- Why does Fayer think that interviewing is a fine art?
- Why did Fayer and his colleagues want to do more than just relate the facts surrounding the historic civil rights march on Washington, D.C.?
- What does Fayer say about the role of the screenwriter and the purpose of the narration?
- What does Fayer think is the benefit of collaborating during the editing stage?

**2. Narrative Writing**

**Write a narrative script for a brief videotape that tells your life history.** Select visual elements that will appear in the film. Visual images can include still photographs, special objects such as keepsakes, interviews with parents and friends, and excerpts from movies or tapes. Link the visuals together with a well-constructed script. Remember, since you can't tell everything, choose your stories carefully. In your script, put your visual clues in parentheses at appropriate points: (My first baby photo with Mom and Dad), or (Still shot from the movie *The Red Shoes,* which inspired my love of ballet).

## Grammar Link

**Use the active voice instead of the passive voice in most cases.**

A *verb* is in the active voice when the subject of the sentence performs the action.

Active: The producers approved the script.
Passive: The script was approved by the producers.

Steve Fayer cautions writers to *avoid the passive voice:* active voice creates a stronger impression.

Rewrite each sentence so that the verb is in the active voice.

1. Historical archives were examined by a team of researchers.
2. Memories of the march were relived by participants.
3. Background information was given by the narrator.
4. The documentary was broadcast by public television stations.
5. The script was praised by critics and viewers.

**See Lesson 15.7, pages 553–554.**

LESSON

# 4.1 Narrative Writing

# Setting the Narrative Landscape

*Everyone loves a story. Some narratives are true, others are clearly fiction, yet most have the same basic elements: characters, plot, point of view, theme, and setting.*

At first glance, setting may not seem important to narrative, but think about how the climate, neighborhood, number of rooms, and condition of a house affect the moods, actions, and personalities of the people who live there. Then see how West Indian writer Jamaica Kincaid uses setting in the opening of her novel *Lucy*.

## *Literature Model*

It was my first day. I had come the night before, a gray-black and cold night before—as it was expected to be in the middle of January, though I didn't know that at the time—and I could not see anything clearly on the way in from the airport, even though there were lights everywhere. As we drove along, someone would single out to me a famous building, an important street, a park, a bridge that when built was thought to be a spectacle. In a daydream I used to have, all these places were points of happiness to me; all these places were lifeboats to my small drowning soul, for I would imagine myself entering and leaving them, and just that—entering and leaving over and over again—would see me through a bad feeling I did not have a name for. I only knew it felt a little like sadness but heavier than that. Now that I saw those places, they looked ordinary, dirty, worn down by so many people entering and leaving them in real life, and it occurred to me that I could not be the only person in the world for whom they were a fixture of fantasy. It was not my first bout with the disappointment of reality and it would not be my last.

Jamaica Kincaid, *Lucy*

*The setting is ominous: dark, cold, and difficult to see.*

*Notice the stark contrast between Lucy's expectations and what she now sees. How do you think this contrast will affect her life? How might it affect the novel?*

## Set the Scene

In narrative writing, use the details of setting to create mood and develop reader expectation about character and action. As the diagram below shows, the elements of setting—time, place, weather, historical period, and cultural milieu—should all work together in your narrative.

As you write, consider how each element of setting can contribute to your purpose. Take *place*, for example. Many particular sites have associations for readers, and you can give these feelings and opinions to your characters. Jamaica Kincaid's Lucy imagined New York as a glamorous place where she might find salvation. Now she is dismayed at how ordinary it appears. She is also surprised by the *weather*. Coming from the tropical Caribbean, she is unprepared for the cold of a New York winter. This contrast in climate subtly points to a more important adjustment Lucy will have to make: to a new *cultural milieu*. Her experiences and values growing up on a small West Indian island are very different from those she will find in a large, fast-paced northern city.

Through all stages of your writing process, consider how comfortably your characters fit into their surrounding culture. If you want them to reflect their cultural milieu, pay particular attention to attitudes, accent, dress, and typical activities. If you portray characters ill at ease in their surroundings, as in *Lucy*, you can use the characters' reactions to comment on the society they find themselves in or the one they left behind. In addition, don't forget how closely tied culture is to *historical period*. New York in the 1790s or the 1890s would have presented different sets of conditions for a West Indian to adjust to. You might even make a historical period and its culture—such as California in the sixties or your high school today—the focus of your narrative.

### Revising Tip

When you're revising your description of the setting, eliminate details that don't help to create mood, establish conflict, propel plot, or hint at theme.

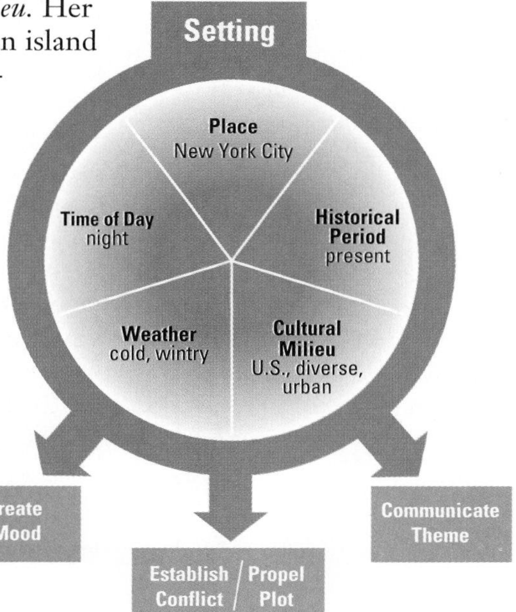

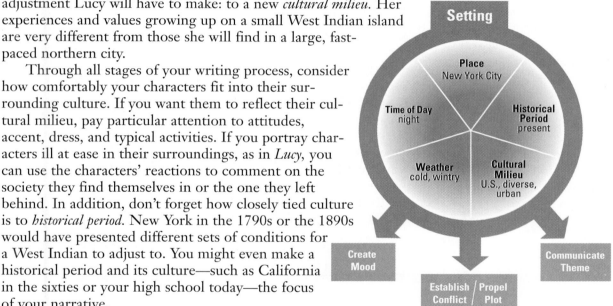

### Journal Writing

Think about a narrative you have enjoyed recently. What was the setting and what role did it play in the story? List some descriptive words and phrases that might capture this setting. If possible, go back to the original book or story and compare your language with that used by the writer.

## Create a Mood

Jamaica Kincaid's description of New York creates a mood or atmosphere of unease and disappointment. Writers often use the device of a character seeing a place for the first time to create atmosphere. When you're creating mood in a narrative, remember that word choice can be as important as the locale itself. Look at the way Elizabeth A. Stager creates mood in her story "Liquid Black."

### *Student Model*

*What effect do the words "cradle," "harbor," and "warm" have on the mood of the piece?*

The electricity was out. Not just in our house but all around the lake. Spots of light flickered behind the dark patches we knew to be trees; we made our way down to the lake by flashlight. On the dock we found a sort of cradle, a harbor from the darkness, and yet a place at one with it. The warm soft boards of the pier were comforting in their solidity. An old worn hand sheltering us and holding us up. We crowded in a circle underneath LauraLe's big Indian blanket. Robby was there, and Tommy. Me, Danny, Laura, LauraLe, Adam. All of us in a circle on the dock.

*The word "kissed" suggests that the boat, the water, and the dock are in harmony.*

At night there are no waves on the lake, but somehow we could hear its presence in the heavy quiet, and in the way our voices sounded. A motor boat purred along the opposite shoreline, its green warning light twinkling faintly. Long moments later, its tiny wake kissed the beams beneath our dock.

Elizabeth A. Stager, Kettering Fairmont School, Kettering, Ohio

Notice how Elizabeth uses words that evoke safety and comfort to set the scene. The chart below shows how two different moods can be created for the same desert setting.

| Two Moods of the Desert | |
|---|---|
| UPBEAT<br>Location Is Inviting | NEGATIVE<br>Location Is Hostile |
| Rich golds of the sunset, aroma of mesquite on the fire, clear music of the mission bells | Sharp needles of cacti, parched streambed, threatening hiss of a snake |

## Establish Conflict

When you hear the word *conflict*, do you think of a war, an argument, or other negative situations? In actuality, conflict is not always bad. When you race another swimmer, you're engaged in a form of conflict.

Conflict is at the heart of narrative. It is what sets the plot in motion and causes changes in the characters. Setting can take on an important role in establishing conflict. As in many adventure novels, setting can play a direct role in the conflict: a mountain to be climbed or a wilderness to be tamed. Setting can contribute to conflict in more subtle ways, too. It can represent the characters' internal struggles: a thunderstorm, for example, might symbolize the clash of emotions within a character. Conflict can even take the form of an individual struggling to overcome her dissatisfaction with her new neighborhood, as in the passage below.

**Vocabulary**

**Editing Tip**

Overused modifiers detract from the words they modify. When editing, replace words such as *particularly, really*, and *very* with more specific words. For example, instead of *very hot*, you might say *blistering*.

***Literature Model***

The moving men jumped out of the front of the van and began to unload the back. Mattie paid the driver and got out of the cab. The moist gray air was as heavy as the sigh that lay on her full bosom. The ashen buildings were beginning to fade against the gentle blanketing of the furry gray snow coming from the darkening sky. The sun's dying rays could be felt rather than seen behind the leaden evening sky, and snow began to cling to the cracks in the wall that stood only six feet from her building.

Mattie saw that the wall reached just above the second-floor apartments, which meant the northern light would be blocked from her plants. All the beautiful plants that once had an entire sun porch for themselves in the home she had exchanged thirty years of her life to pay for would now have to fight for light on a crowded windowsill.

Gloria Naylor, *The Women of Brewster Place*

*What do the words "ashen" and "dying rays" suggest?*

*The contrast between her old home and her new one is accomplished in only a few words.*

## Journal Writing

Choose a locale, such as a forest, a crowded city street, or your classroom. Brainstorm, freewrite, or cluster for vivid words that set two contrasting moods for the locale you selected. For your setting, create a diagram like the one on page 161.

## Communicate a Theme

The theme of a novel or story is the insight into human life that the writer conveys through the narrative. It is often called the controlling idea. The way a writer describes a setting can tell you a great deal about the theme of a novel. Look, for example, at the opening of O. E. Rölvaag's novel *Giants in the Earth*. Like his characters, Rölvaag was a Norwegian immigrant to the Great Plains of the United States.

*What kind of impression does the covered wagon leave on the prairie grass? What does that impression suggest about the future success of settlers on the prairie?*

*Which words suggest how people and animals are dwarfed by the seemingly endless prairie?*

*Without any landmarks, people have no way to judge their progress.*

### *Literature Model*

It was late afternoon. A small caravan was pushing its way through the tall grass. The track that it left behind was like the wake of a boat—except that instead of widening out astern it closed in again.

"Tish-ah!" said the grass. . . "Tish-ah, tish-ah". . . Never had it said anything else—never would it say anything else. It bent resiliently under the trampling feet; it did not break, but it complained aloud every time—for nothing like this had ever happened to it before. . . "Tish-ah, tishah" it cried, and rose up in surprise to look at this rough, hard thing that had crushed it to the ground so rudely, and then moved on. . . .

The caravan seemed a miserably frail and Lilliputian thing as it crept over the boundless prairie toward the sky line. Of road or trail there lay not a trace ahead; as soon as the grass had straightened up again behind, no one could have told the direction from which it had come or whither it was bound. The whole train—Per Hansa with his wife and children, the oxen, the cow, and all—might just as well have dropped out of the sky.

O. E. Rölvaag, *Giants in the Earth*

From the opening paragraphs, it's clear that Rölvaag's novel will deal with the insignificance of human beings when confronted with a vast, unchanging, and uncaring natural world. When you're writing a narrative, think carefully about how your characters relate to their environment. Is the specific place—including its inhabitants and cultural values—friendly or hostile? Even if the setting itself is neutral, think about how you can use it to show your feelings about life in general. One way to zero in on the telling details is to imagine you're designing a stage set or cinematic setting for your story. Ask yourself how you could create mood and hint at theme through scenery, props, color, and sound. Then use concrete, evocative words to describe these details.

# 4.1 Writing Activities

## Describe a Story Setting

Use the painting *Diner with Red Door* as the setting for a story. First, describe it as it might appear at the beginning of a story about a character who anticipates failure or disappointment. Then describe the same setting as it might appear at the end of the story, after the character has had some unexpected success or reward.

- Choose some details from the setting that create a mood.
- Use concrete words that evoke the mood or feeling.
- Express a theme or controlling idea through the words and details you choose to describe the setting.

**PURPOSE** To use description to create mood
**AUDIENCE** Your teacher and classmates
**LENGTH** 2–4 paragraphs

Ralph Goings, *Diner with Red Door*, 1979

### Grammar Link

**Make tenses compatible, especially past and past perfect.**

*. . . no one* ***could have told*** *the direction from which it* ***had come*** *or whither it* ***was bound****.*

Rewrite the sentences to show that one event preceded another event.

1. The immigrants traveled a great distance, and they wanted to rest and settle down.
2. They planted crops where only wild grass grew.
3. They survived hardships and now looked forward to a better life.

**See Lesson 15.4, pages 545–548, and 15.6, pages 551–552.**

## Cross-Curricular: Journalism

With a partner, choose a brief but dramatic newspaper story, and discuss how you might rewrite the story if it were the opening for a fictional narrative. Concentrate on setting—the mood you want to create and the details of time and place you need to add. On your own, write the opening of your fictional narrative. Then exchange papers and discuss the differences between newspaper reporting and writing fiction.

LESSON

# 4.2 Narrative Writing

# Ordering Time in a Narrative

Helen Lundeberg, *Double Portrait of the Artist in Time*, 1935

*Writers manipulate our expectations about time. Often they use flashbacks to show the complicated relationship between past and present. They also use fantasies, dreams, and flash-forwards to offer glimpses of events to come.*

*Literature Model*

My father said he saw him years later playing in a tenth-rate commercial league in a textile town in Carolina, wearing shoes and an assumed name.

"He'd put on fifty pounds and the spring was gone from his step in the outfield, but he could still hit. Oh, how that man could hit. No one has ever been able to hit like Shoeless Joe."

Three years ago at dusk on a spring evening, when the sky was a robin's-egg blue and the wind was soft as a day-old chick, I was sitting on the verandah of my farm home in eastern Iowa when a voice very clearly said to me, "If you build it, he will come."

The voice was that of a ballpark announcer. As he spoke, I instantly envisioned the finished product I knew I was being asked to conceive. I could see the dark, squarish speakers, like ancient sailors' hats, attached to aluminum-painted light standards that glowed down into a baseball field, my present position being directly behind home plate.

W. P. Kinsella, *Shoeless Joe*

*"Years later" alerts us to some unnamed event that occurred before the sighting that begins the book.*

*"Three years ago" begins the basic narrative that will lead to the present.*

*How does the narrator project himself into the future?*

## Create a Plot

A narrative is comprised of a series of events. Plot is the writer's arrangement of those chronological events to dramatize a particular conflict or theme. Writers don't always begin a narrative with the event that happened first, since this event is not always the one that best sets the mood, introduces the conflict, or has high interest for the reader. Many highly successful narratives, such as *The Adventures of Huckleberry Finn*, proceed more or less chronologically; others, such as *The Scarlet Letter*, begin with a dramatic event and then only gradually reveal the preceding events.

Few if any novels, stories, or even movies take place in "real time." In other words, depictions of events do not take as long as the actual events. For example, a seven-hour drive from Chicago to Cleveland in *Shoeless Joe* is covered in a single sentence. A few pages later, however, a brief argument in a restaurant is allotted several paragraphs. Extending a single moment of confrontation so that it takes longer to read about than it would have taken to occur creates suspense or emotional tension.

Once you take one event out of chronological time, you have to decide how to order the remaining events. Look at the chart below. It shows the chronological events and the plot of classic "whodunit" mysteries, such as those of Agatha Christie. Does the plot look familiar? Many mystery novels, movies, and TV shows use this arrangement of events to keep readers or viewers on the edge of their seats.

### Presenting Tip

When reading your narrative aloud, pause before shifts in time. Use your voice or other dramatic devices the way filmmakers use fade-outs—to alert your audience to flashbacks or flash-forwards in time.

### Grammar Editing Tip

When editing your narrative, you can refer to the material about verb tenses in Lessons 15.3 through 15.6, pages 541–552.

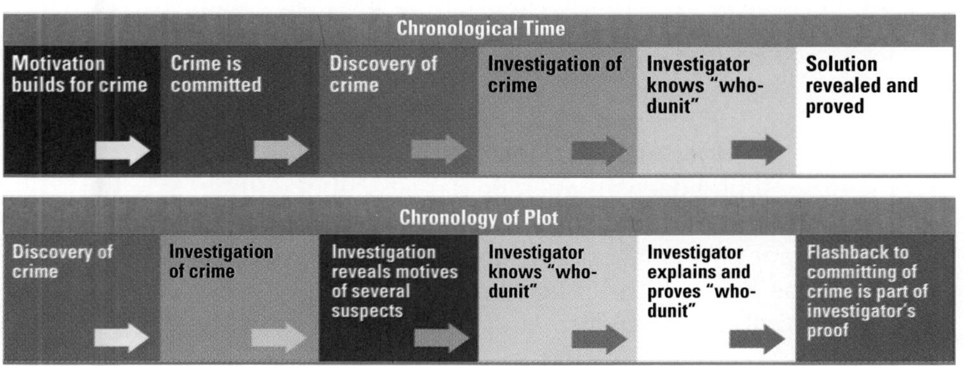


### Journal Writing

List the events of a recent day in the order in which they occurred. Then choose a purpose, such as showing the typical day of a twelfth grader or revealing a particular characteristic of yourself, your school, or your peers. Rearrange and list the events of the day to suit your purpose.

## Order a Narrative Chronologically

Chronological narratives are the easiest to understand; they allow readers to experience the story the same way they live their lives. They are also best for building certain kinds of suspense: Will the characters or won't they . . . be successful at escaping the evil genius, winning the election, overcoming a handicap, or resolving a problem? These stories also allow for surprise endings, such as those in tales by Saki or O. Henry. Because they are well suited to showing character development and other kinds of cause and effect, chronological narratives are often used for history and biography. Think about stories you might wish to tell, and decide which ones would be most effectively told in chronological order.

In the movie *Spellbound*, Gregory Peck plays a man with amnesia who has been accused of murder. Dream sequences and flashbacks help him and psychoanalyst Ingrid Bergman to reveal his true history.

## Order a Narrative with Flashbacks

You know all the signs: the music, the dreamy look on the character's face, the fade-out. These are the filmmaker's way of introducing a flashback. While the most familiar examples of flashbacks are cinematic, the technique has long been popular with novelists. Edith Wharton's 1911 novel *Ethan Frome* is told entirely in flashback. The reader discovers the story behind Frome's disability just the way the narrator learns the story. In addition to having a character relate past events to the narrator, you can use a character's musings and memories to introduce flashbacks. Whichever device you use, be sure that your reader will not get "lost in time." Notice how student writer Cheryl S. Fletterick uses verb tenses to alert readers to the flashback in her story about her grandfather's death.

*How does the first sentence whet the reader's interest?*

*The immediate switch to flashback provides information about the narrator, who is also the main character.*

### *Student Model*

We have some bad news," the voice said as the front door opened. "Real bad," echoed another voice.

It had been an average day at school with an average amount of homework. After school, I stopped at my grandparents' house to say hello and tell them where I was going. I just poked my head down the staircase, mumbled my plans, and a few seconds later I was gone and ready for an afternoon at the mall.

I returned home later in the evening to an unusually quiet home. Wondering where everyone was, I called my grandparents, but there was no answer. Seeing how late it was getting, I began my homework. When I heard the key in the door, I went to greet my mother.

"Cheryl," she said again, "we have some bad news."

Cheryl S. Fletterick, South Windsor High, South Windsor, Connecticut

# 4.2 Writing Activities

## Write a Personal Narrative

Suppose that a question on your college application asks you to write a narrative that reveals something about yourself, something that is not shown by your grades or your test scores. For example, you could write about an important occasion in your life, such as receiving an award for a special achievement, a hobby or an activity you are involved in, or any important event in which you have participated. Develop a plot outline to assist you in ordering events. Then write the narrative.

- Identify events that should be told in chronological order.
- Use flashback to relate earlier events or talk about a character.
- Write a first sentence to engage the reader's interest.

**PURPOSE** To order time in a personal narrative
**AUDIENCE** Your teacher and classmates
**LENGTH** 1–2 pages

### Grammar Link

**Punctuate possessive nouns correctly.**

Cheryl**'s** mother
her grandparent**s'** house

Rewrite the sentences correctly, adding apostrophes where they are needed.

1. My mothers news stunned me.
2. The only death I had ever experienced was a great-uncles, and I had hardly known him.
3. Some of my friends have mourned over their pets deaths.
4. Deaths inevitability is hard to accept.
5. Death gives us an opportunity to celebrate a persons life.

**See Lesson 21.13, pages 702–704.**

### COMPUTER OPTION

You can use your computer to facilitate the ordering and reordering of the events of a narrative without having to recopy them or to edit and re-edit on the same page. As you're planning and prewriting for any of the activities on this page, you might list the events chronologically, as they occur in real time. Save that list for reference, and then copy it as the basis for manipulating the order of events. Each time you work out a possible plot, you can save and print out that list of events; you'll then be able to compare your plot to the original chronology. If you change your mind in the drafting stage, you can still use the cut-and-paste option to move events around in your manuscript.

LESSON

# 4.3 Narrative Writing

# Building Narrative Suspense

Ralph Gibson, *Hand at Door*, 1970

*Suspense is the uncertainty about the outcome of events in a story—what makes a reader's pulse quicken. Writers create suspense in many ways—but the result is always the pressing desire to read on to the end.*

In the painting by Ralph Gibson, suspense beckons the viewer to discover what lurks behind the door. The following excerpt from a D. H. Lawrence story illustrates how a writer can build suspense.

*The "strange anxiety at her heart" suggests the horrible event to come.*

*The action slows down to a crawl with sensory description of the mother's thoughts, feelings, impressions.*

*What is the effect of the repetition of "know" and "knew"?*

### *Literature Model*

It was about one o'clock when Paul's mother and father drove up to their house. All was still. Paul's mother went to her room and slipped off her white fur cloak. She had told her maid not to wait for her. . . .

And then, because of the strange anxiety at her heart, she stole upstairs to her son's room. Noiselessly she went along the upper corridor. Was there a faint noise? What was it?

She stood, with arrested muscles, outside his door, listening. There was a strange, heavy, and yet not loud noise. Her heart stood still. It was a soundless noise, yet rushing and powerful. Something huge, in violent, hushed motion. What was it? What in God's name was it? She ought to know. She felt that she knew the noise. She knew what it was.

Yet she could not place it. She couldn't say what it was. And on and on it went, like a madness.

Softly, frozen with anxiety and fear, she turned the door-handle.

D. H. Lawrence, "The Rocking-Horse Winner"

## Create Suspense in Narrative

Perhaps you've heard people call suspense stories or movies *cliff-hangers*. The origin of the word *suspense* is related to the physical condition of being suspended, or left hanging, and the anxiety associated with this uncertain state. At its most extreme, suspense creates physical tension, but it also raises many questions in readers' minds. *Will they escape? Will she find out what he's done? Will he realize the truth? Who did it? Are they on our side? Why did it happen?* Questions like these lurk behind suspense—whether the suspense is of physical danger, revelation, betrayal, or painful self-knowledge. The desire to find answers to these questions keeps us reading.

How can you, as a writer, create the suspense that will keep the attention of your readers? You can use an eerie setting to add suspense, or you can slow down time at a crucial moment with precise description, flashbacks, or changes of scene. An unnerving surprise will make your readers wonder whether another surprise may be on the way. You can also create suspense through foreshadowing, a hint of what's to come. Early in "The Rocking-Horse Winner," for example, Lawrence tells us that "the house came to be haunted by the unspoken phrase: *There must be more money!*" The word *haunted* foreshadows death and horror. Bear in mind that you walk a fine line when you use foreshadowing or withhold information: too many hints spoil the surprise; too few may leave your reader lost and annoyed or fail to create suspense at all.

**Drafting Tip**

When you're drafting, use foreshadowing to create reader anticipation for any kind of outcome. For example, the sun breaking through the clouds can foreshadow success.

### Journal Writing

Find a suspenseful passage in a book or a story. Note the techniques the writer used for creating suspense. Think about and jot down notes on how such techniques would translate to a visual medium such as film, television, or theater.

## Use Delaying Tactics

As you know from television, anything that slows down or cuts off the action at a crucial moment creates suspense. It's the case of the well-placed commercial or "Tune in next week. . . ." Writers use various literary devices to delay "the next installment." D. H. Lawrence used detailed description to slow down the scene you read on page 170. A flashback can also tease out a scene. Another delaying tactic is used by Tony Hillerman in his novel *Talking God.* At a critical moment, Hillerman ends a chapter; the next chapter takes us to a new location and a new set of characters. It's almost as though he'd taken a break for a commercial! Notice how the following model also delays important information.

> ***Model***
>
> The envelope was the first thing Laura saw when she opened the mailbox. It was white and rich among the garish catalogs and dull bills. Even before she saw Richmond's Hotel & Beach Resort in sea-green italics, she knew that this was what she'd been waiting for.
>
> She hesitated. Why had Cynthia heard so much sooner?
>
> In the house she poured a glass of water. Sitting at the table, she touched the heavy, pebbly paper and felt like crying. Life would go on if she didn't get this job. But it wouldn't be the same life, not the same life at all.
>
> On New Year's Eve she and Cynthia and Mark and Steve had made a circle under the mistletoe at midnight. They hugged each other and decided to apply for jobs to the same beach resort that summer. It would be their last summer together as high school students, their last summer before they scattered in different directions.
>
> "Don't be such a baby," Laura muttered. But as she started to slide a pencil under the flap, the phone rang.
>
> "Did it come?" breathed Cynthia's eager voice. "Oh, Laura. It won't be the same if all four of us aren't together!"

*Why is "this was what she'd been waiting for" such a good device for the beginning of a suspenseful story?*

*Flashback slows down the action and makes us wait to find out what's in the envelope.*

*Think of at least two ways in which the phone call increases suspense.*

When you set out to write a suspenseful narrative, try making a plot outline showing the events in the order in which you will present them. Then decide what you want your readers to wonder about: an upcoming event, a psychological change, or the revelation of a past event. Consider the best way to delay this information while increasing the readers' desire to find out. Be careful that you don't delay so much that your audience will lose interest. Finally, revise your draft to make sure that it is not choppy or confusing.

# 4.3 Writing Activities

## Write a Suspenseful Story

As a feature writer for your school newspaper, you contribute to the column "Senior Year: A Time of Suspense." For this week's edition, write a suspenseful story, either fiction or nonfiction, about a competitive sports event, a character facing a personal challenge, or a topic of your own choosing.

- Use foreshadowing to hint at what is to come.
- Avoid telling too much too soon.
- Use some delaying tactics to build suspense.
- Don't delay so much that you lose your readers' interest.

**PURPOSE** To write a suspenseful narrative
**AUDIENCE** Readers of your school newspaper
**LENGTH** 1–2 pages

Andrew Wyeth, *Winter*, 1946

### Grammar Link

**Avoid run-on sentences.**

Run-on sentences can distract or confuse your readers' train of thought.

*My brother reads horror stories, he likes the scary feelings he gets.*

*My brother reads horror stories; he likes the scary feeling he gets.*

Correct the following run-on sentences.

1. The movie bored us it lacked suspense.
2. It was a frightful crime and the culprit was never caught.
3. That TV show is sensational children should not watch it.
4. The score was tied, three minutes of overtime remained.

**See Lesson 13.10, pages 514–517.**

## Cross-Curricular: Art

Look carefully at *Winter* by Andrew Wyeth. Think about who the person in the painting might be, where he's going and why, and what he's thinking. Freewrite notes about how he got there and what might happen next. Include any visual hints in the painting that suggest these ideas. Finally, write a short story opening that builds suspense. Base it on this scene.

LESSON

# 4.4 Narrative Writing
# Using Point of View

*As an experienced reader, you know that the choice of narrator determines what you learn, when you learn it, and how you feel about the characters and their situations. When you read, always consider from whose point of view you are watching events unfold. Read the passage below, and think about whose perspective you are getting.*

### Literature Model

There. She had it at last. The weeks it had devoted to eluding her, the tricks, the clever hide-and-go-seeks, the routes it had in all sobriety devised, together with the delicious moments it had, undoubtedly, laughed up its sleeve—all to no ultimate avail. She had that little mouse.

It shook its little self, as best it could, in the trap. Its bright black eyes contained no appeal—the little creature seemed to understand that there was no hope of mercy from the eternal enemy, no hope of reprieve or postponement—but a fine small dignity. It waited. It looked at Maud Martha.

She wondered what else it was thinking. Perhaps that there was not enough food in its larder. Perhaps that little Betty, a puny child from the start, would not, now, be getting fed. Perhaps that, now, the family's seasonal housecleaning, for lack of expert direction, would be left undone. . . .

Maud Martha could not bear the little look.

Gwendolyn Brooks, "Maud Martha Spares the Mouse"

*Whose personality is revealed by "delicious moments," "laughed up its sleeve," and similar phrases that describe the mouse?*

*Maud Martha's imagination is turning the real mouse into a kind of fairy-tale mouse. The more she sees it in human terms, the more she sympathizes with it.*

Although the writer refers to Maud Martha in the third person—as "she"—you experience her change in attitude for yourself because you, the reader, are clearly inside her mind.

## Choose a Storyteller

Once you have a story in mind, you may find that you automatically slip into one point of view or another without giving the decision much thought. It may just feel right to have a character narrate the story or, on the other hand, to use a more distant narrator who can jump from New York City to the Sahara, keeping the reader up to date on the action in both locations. Nevertheless, it's a good idea to be aware of the characteristics of each point of view.

**Point of View**

| Point of View | Narrator | Characteristics |
|---|---|---|
| **First Person** uses *I* | Character in the story | Involved in action; knows only what this character could logically know; may be unreliable or misleading |
| **Third Person** uses *he, she, they* | Not a character in the story | More distance from story than first person |
| **Omniscient** | All-knowing narrator | Can see into the minds of all characters |
| **Limited** | Not all-knowing; takes perspective of one character | Views world through the eyes of this character |

## Use First-Person Narration

First-person point of view lends immediacy and allows the reader to experience the story as the character is experiencing it. If the narrator is also the main character, the reader has the advantage of knowing an important character's thoughts and motivations. On the other hand, some first-person narrators are not reliable reporters or interpreters of events. For example, Huck himself is the narrator of *The Adventures of Huckleberry Finn*, and part of the novel's effect comes from his naive misunderstanding of the society around him. A minor character may also be an effective narrator. In Arthur Conan Doyle's stories, Dr. Watson tells the story. This device allows Holmes to solve the case while Doyle withholds information until just the right moment.

**Grammar Editing Tip**

At the editing stage, check subject-verb agreement in your narrative. For assistance, you can refer to unit 16, pages 564–579.

### Journal Writing

To explore how point of view affects setting, characters, action, and theme, think of a familiar story, such as a fairy tale or a fable, told in a limited third-person point of view. List ways in which this story would be different if told in the first person.

## Use Third-Person Narration

**Vocabulary**

**Revising Tip**

During the revision stage, make sure that you tailor tone and vocabulary to suit your narrator's personality. Also check that your point of view is consistent, and eliminate information that the narrator could not know.

With third-person point of view, the narrator is outside the story yet may still choose his or her distance. "Maud Martha Spares the Mouse" is an example of third-person limited narration in which the distance between narrator and character is almost nonexistent. The story is told as it is experienced by a character, and the author does not intrude with commentary.

When you use third-person omniscient narration, you can give the narrator—and the reader—access to the thoughts of several or all of the characters, to the past and the future, and to all locales. Your all-knowing narrator, however, may or may not tell all. Omniscient narrators sometimes withhold information or express opinions that are different from those of the characters.

As you read the paragraphs below, notice the changes Zev Alexander made when he retold the anecdote from a different point of view.

*Student Model*

Max boarded the bus and paid the fare. He took a seat next to an elderly man, took off his mittens, and let his feet swing in the air. Staring down at him, the man could sense Max's nervousness. Max took out a bag of cookies his mom had baked for him and offered one to the stranger. The gray-haired fellow pleasantly said, "No. Thank you, but my teeth can't chew them." Max was a little upset by the man's condition, and he watched the senior citizen slowly and painfully depart the bus at the next stop. The aged man knew that he had left an impression on the future.

My first step onto the bus was filled with fear. I had never taken the bus alone before, but I was reassured by an old guy who smiled at me, so I sat next to him. I couldn't help noticing the many wrinkles on his face and the obviously out-of-style clothes he wore. I took out my cookies and thought that Mom would have wanted me to offer him one. He said no, mentioning not being able to chew well. I couldn't imagine not being able to chew sweets. I was feeling a little uncomfortable, but he got off soon. He walked away slowly as if it hurt him to move. It was really sad, and I realized I was lucky to be young and healthy.

Zev Alexander, Classical High School, Providence, Rhode Island

# 4.4 Writing Activities

## Rewrite a Fairy Tale or Fable

Tell a fairy tale or fable from a different point of view. Refer to the list you made in your journal (as suggested on page 175), and choose one character in the story to be your narrator. Refine your prewriting planning by deciding what the character would be most interested in. Then draft your story. After you have revised and edited it, present it to your class as a dramatic reading.

- Tell the events your character would know.
- Keep to your point of view.
- Color the dialogue and events to reflect the storyteller's personality.

**PURPOSE** To retell a fairy tale or fable from a different point of view
**AUDIENCE** Readers of *Fractured Fables*
**LENGTH** 4 paragraphs

## Cooperative Learning

Meet with three classmates to discuss a painting that shows at least two people interacting, such as Jean Béraud's painting on page 125. Consider what the characters are like and how you know. Discuss what you think the relationships among the characters seem to be. You may not agree on all points.

Next, each member of the group should select a character from the painting. Each student should write a first-person narrative about the activity in the painting from the point of view of his or her character. Be sure to include your character's opinions of the other characters.

Meet again and listen to all the narratives. Discuss the advantages and disadvantages of each point of view.

### Grammar Link

**Choose the correct case form of the personal pronoun.**

Note the use of the correct case forms of personal pronouns in the following sentences from Zev Alexamder's anecdotes.

*Max boarded the bus and paid the fare.* ***He*** *took a seat next to an elderly man, took off* ***his*** *mittens, and let* ***his*** *feet swing in the air.*

For each of the following sentences, choose the correct personal pronoun from each pair in parentheses.

1. Between you and (I, me), I enjoy reading Gary Soto's poems and recollections.
2. When he started writing children's books, his happiest fans were (we, us).
3. It is (he, him) whom other writers also enjoy reading.
4. My friend told my brother and (I, me) that Gary also produces films for children.
5. Gary has many fans, and he often asks (they, them) to comment on his books.
6. One reader had read *Baseball in April* and said that (he, him) had really liked it.
7. Did he give (we, us) a copy of his poetry book *A Fire in My Hands*?
8. He gave (they, them) a talk on how to write books for children.
9. Bob and (she, her) learned a lot from the talk.
10. A few friends came up to speak with Bob and (she, her) afterward.

**See Lesson 17.1, pages 587–589.**

LESSON

4.5

# Narrative Writing

# Writing a Short-Short Story

*Short stories are usually crafted to be read in one sitting. Short-short stories require only a few moments of reading time—a fact you will notice as you read the brief but complete modern fable below. As short as it is, it is long enough to get the job done, the characters revealed, and the point made.*

## Literature Model

"Do not ride your bicycle around the corner," the mother had told the daughter when she was seven.

"Why not!" protested the girl.

*Note that she is called "the mother," not given a particular name.*

"Because then I cannot see you and you will fall down and cry and I will not hear you."

"How do you know I'll fall?" whined the girl.

"It is in a book. The Twenty-Six Malignant Gates, all the bad things that can happen to you outside the protection of this house."

*Is this a real book? What is the mother really telling the daughter?*

"I don't believe you. Let me see the book."

"It is written in Chinese. You cannot understand it. That is why you must listen to me."

"What are they, then?" the girl demanded. "Tell me the twenty-six bad things."

But the mother sat knitting in silence.

"What twenty-six!" shouted the girl.

The mother still did not answer her.

"You can't tell me because you don't know! You don't know anything!" And the girl ran outside, jumped on her bicycle, and in her hurry to get away, she fell before she even reached the corner.

*Why does the girl fall so soon?*

Amy Tan, *The Joy Luck Club*

## Examine the Characteristics of the Short-Short Story

Like miniature paintings, short-short stories hold an entire world in a tiny package. Naturally, they do not have the complexity of a novel or a longer story. Because of limited space, the details included must be very carefully chosen. In this regard, short-short stories are similar to poems.

Short-short stories can have a tremendous impact because of their brevity. Many rely on surprise endings for their "punch." In a fable the ending leads to a moral. In a joke the surprise ending is the punch line, and it leads to a laugh. Many others, such as ghost stories, strive for that pleasurable *frisson*, or shiver of fear. Several kinds of traditional short-short stories were originally told rather than written. Therefore, they grab the listener's attention right away and don't let go.

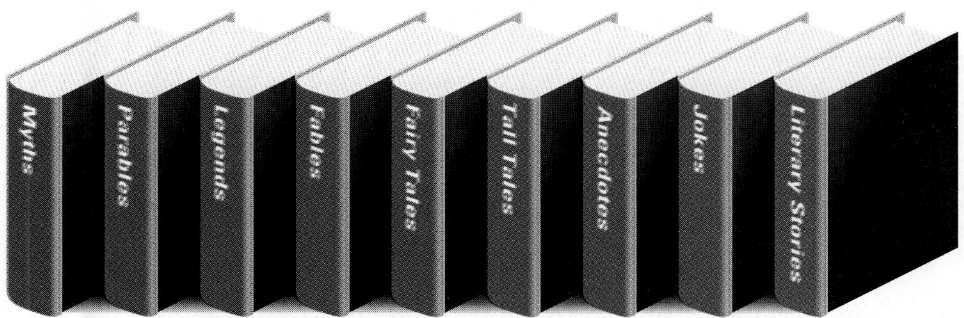


Whether you're creating a short-short story or your own version of one of the classics illustrated above, focus carefully on your purpose and be prepared to pare down the conflict and action and to use symbols to "sum up" a complex idea. The key is to establish the conflict immediately, give universality to the characters and situation, and then resolve the conflict in a powerful and unexpected way. Short-short stories need only the essentials of setting. The plot should be simple and concentrated, containing only essential events. The few characters can be "types" or symbols. The fabled ant and grasshopper, for example, represent particular personality traits. Characters can also represent the average person, as Amy Tan's mother and daughter represent all mothers and daughters. Even the briefest tale can provide important insights.

### Drafting Tip

As you draft a story, don't worry about whether it's "good" or "bad," too long or too short. Try to write without censoring yourself. There will be time to cut and change when you revise.

### Journal Writing

List past experiences that you might be able to turn into stories. Jot down notes for setting, character, plot, point of view, and theme for each of them. Then evaluate each story idea for its suitability as a short-short story. Choose one, and save your prewriting.

## Draft a Short-Short Story

Many modern short-short stories deal with internal or psychological issues without such symbols as the tortoise and the hare or the dangerous wolf hiding in the forest. You may find it easier to write in this more modern mode, or you may appreciate the immediate impact provided by familiar symbols.

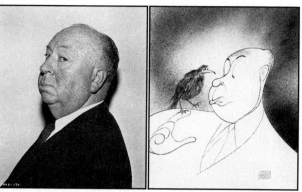

It takes Hirschfeld only a few lines to "capture" Alfred Hitchcock.

Writer William Peden compares short-short stories to "the click of the camera, the opening or closing of a window, a moment of insight." You may thus want to begin your prewriting at the end, with the startling discovery, the insight, the moral, the chilling conclusion, or the punch line. Then ask yourself: How can I achieve this effect? In other cases, a real event, person, or issue may be your inspiration. Then ask yourself: How can I reveal the essence of this experience or character in the most economical way? What is really essential to my meaning?

Once you begin drafting, however, don't be afraid to include too much; let your creativity flow freely.Your hardest work will be in revising, as you pare down the setting to eliminate all but a few props, use only the most telling details, and see how much of the plot you can delete and still have a clear and compelling story.

If you're stuck for an idea for a short-short story, you might take off from a traditional fairy tale or fable, as Brenda Marshall did.

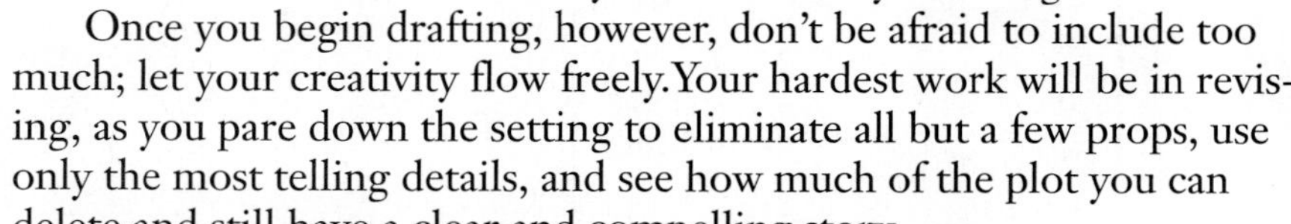

### *Student Model*

I never thought I'd find a frog by the side of the road, just because I was thinking about such things. Yet as I pushed my red ten-speed up the hill, there he was, just sitting there, looking as though he'd been waiting for me all my life. His green coat shimmered in the August heat, and I thought of my water bottle, forgotten in the sink at home. As I watched him, I remembered that dumb old fairy tale, with the prince and all that, but pretended to myself not to care. He stared at me and I stared back. The hill became steeper, but I was strong, and didn't slow down. I was nearly alongside him before I noticed. When I did, I screamed out loud. His beady eyes were stuck, staring blankly at the world. An accidental twist of my bike tire sent the stiff corpse tumbling down the embankment.

Brenda Marshall, Newton North High School, Newton, Massachusetts

# 4.5 Writing Activities

## Write a Short-Short Story

Write a short-short story based on the Vermeer painting. First, decide whether the moment depicted by Vermeer will be the result of the action of your story or the incident that sets it in motion. Next, freewrite about the moment and the character of the woman and the letter writer. Then write one or more drafts. Be sure to pare your story down to its essentials during the revision stage.

- Establish the conflict immediately.
- Give universality to the characters and situation.
- Make sure your plot is simple and concentrated.
- Resolve the conflict in a powerful and unexpected way.

**PURPOSE** To write a short-short story
**AUDIENCE** Your classmates
**LENGTH** 1–2 pages

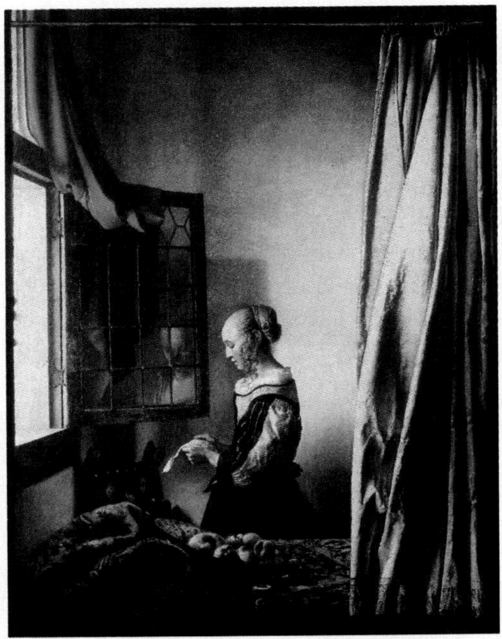

Jan Vermeer, *Girl Reading Letter at an Open Window*, c. 1660

### Grammar Link

**Punctuate direct quotations correctly.**

*"How do you know I'll fall?" whined the girl.*

Rewrite the direct quotations, using correct punctuation.

1. That computer game is dynamite Sandy exclaimed.
2. My sister downloaded it from an online service said Matt.
3. Do you ever surf the Internet asked Luke.
4. With a chuckle Rita replied You could say I'm in the fast lane on the Information Superhighway.

**See Lesson 21.11, pages 696-699.**

## Cooperative Learning

Work with a partner to find a photograph with great impact. Discuss which details give it impact and how these visual details may be translated into words. Then work on your own to write a short-short story based on the photograph. Exchange papers, and discuss the similarities and the differences between your two stories.

LESSON 4.6

# Writing About Literature
# Analyzing a Narrative for Film Adaptation

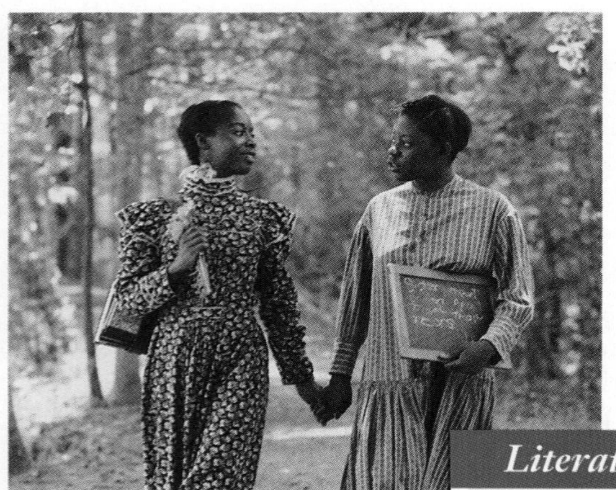

*The relationship between an orginal book and its film adaptation can be very complex. A moviegoer never really "sees" the novel on which a film is based.*

The photograph is a still from the film *The Color Purple*, based on Alice Walker's acclaimed novel. In the interview below, film director Steven Spielberg recalls Walker's response to the filming of one scene.

### Literature Model

**Spielberg:** [Alice Walker] came down as sort of a spiritual counselor. She never said, "That's not accurate. That's not what my grandmother was like"—although she did sometimes have those feelings. It would get back to me through three or four people that she felt Whoopi had lost her accent and would I listen more carefully.

She was on the set when I shot the scene where Mister is separating Nettie and Celie. I did the master in one shot because I wanted everyone to experience what the separation was like. I didn't want to have to say, "OK, go down the steps of the porch. Cut. Have lunch." I wanted the actors to feel the horror. And you can't do that when you piecemeal a scene. So I did it in one shot, and I turned to Alice and she was a wreck. Really crying. And that was good for me because I wanted to impress her. This was her book; she'd won the Pulitzer Prize.

I knew I had a responsibility to *The Color Purple*, and yet I didn't want to make the kind of movie from the novel that some people wanted me to. Because that's not who I am.

"Dialogue on Film: Steven Spielberg," *American Film*

*Spielberg's technique helps actors live the story they are shooting.*

*Adapting a novel to film often raises the question, Whose story is it—the novelist's or the filmmaker's?*

# Explore How Narrative Translates into Film

Both the book and movie versions of *The Color Purple* were popular and successful. However, many filmmakers have learned the expensive lesson that a great book does not necessarily make a great movie.

Films are not made directly from books. They are made from screenplays, which have no narrative exposition. Films must substitute action and dialogue for what the narrator of a novel might tell you directly. Director John Huston turned B. Traven's novel *The Treasure of the Sierra Madre* into the screenplay for the classic 1948 movie. The illustration below shows three versions of the scene in which Curtin (Humphrey Bogart) rescues Dobbs (Bruce Bennet) from a caved-in mine.

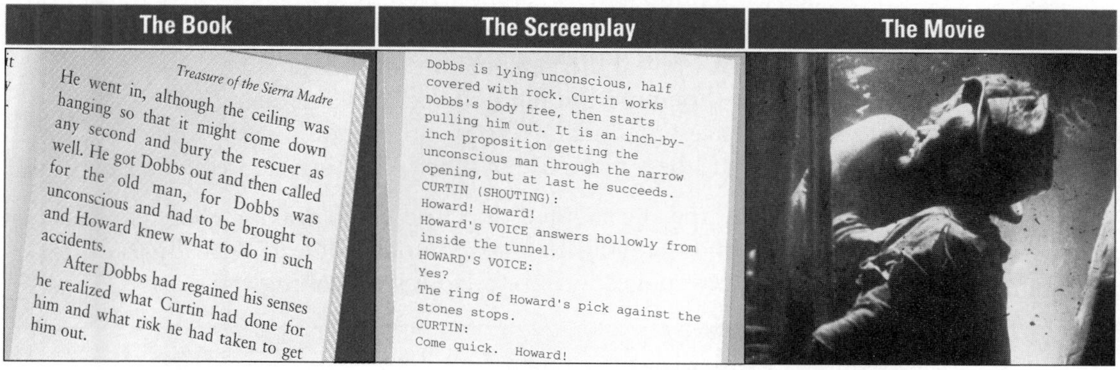

**The Book**

*Treasure of the Sierra Madre*

He went in, although the ceiling was hanging so that it might come down any second and bury the rescuer as well. He got Dobbs out and then called for the old man, for Dobbs was unconscious and had to be brought to and Howard knew what to do in such accidents.

After Dobbs had regained his senses he realized what Curtin had done for him and what risk he had taken to get him out.

**The Screenplay**

```
Dobbs is lying unconscious, half
covered with rock. Curtin works
Dobbs's body free, then starts
pulling him out. It is an inch-by-
inch proposition getting the
unconscious man through the narrow
opening, but at last he succeeds.
CURTIN (SHOUTING):
Howard! Howard!
Howard's VOICE answers hollowly from
inside the tunnel.
HOWARD'S VOICE:
Yes?
The ring of Howard's pick against the
stones stops.
CURTIN:
Come quick.  Howard!
```

**The Movie**

Screenplay writers must use a different approach than novelists do because their words will either be spoken by actors or be translated into sound effects, scenery, actions, props, music, lighting, and so forth. What's more, a novel can sprawl over 600 pages, while a film is considered long if it exceeds two hours. Filmmakers may have to condense long periods of time and the adventures of many characters.

On the other hand, working in film has its advantages. As Steven Spielberg says, the filmmaker is "a painter and a writer and a musician." The audience of a movie can respond to a setting directly, without the intervention of words. Music can help to create atmosphere without slowing the action. Actors can show emotion so effectively that they practically enter into a relationship with the audience. For all of these things to happen, however, many adaptations must be made.

## Journal Writing

Recall some novels and short stories you have enjoyed. Think about what made them "a good read." Note which ones you think would make good movies and why. Save your notes.

## Plan a Film Adaptation

**Prewriting Tip**

In the prewriting stage of an adaptation for film, break your story into three to five scenes. Draw an appropriate number of large circles, and jot ideas for setting, dialogue, and action in each circle.

**Grammar Editing Tip**

At the editing stage, check your adaptation for misplaced and dangling modifiers. You can refer to Lesson 18.7, pages 623-629.

Now that you've decided to adapt your favorite novel into a hit movie, think about what you like most about the book. Focus on this element throughout the adaptation process. Identify how less important elements of the novel may need to be altered or cut to highlight your desired effect. Ask yourself questions such as these:

- How should I show setting? Merely as background or with long, panning shots that make it practically a character in the movie?
- Does the novel have too many characters to keep track of in a movie? Too few to be interesting? Can several minor characters be combined into one? Should some be eliminated? Some added?
- Are there too many subplots for a movie? Can they be condensed, eliminated, or summarized in dialogue? Does the action jump around? How can I indicate these jumps?
- How can I reveal the personalities of the characters without access to their thoughts? Should I add actions and dialogue, use voice-overs, have other characters give their opinions?
- How can I best make use of music, lighting, and cinematography?

Choose the appropriate question, and begin making changes. You will probably find that your first adaptations will lead logically to others, as in Jamie Luce's suggestions for adapting a Hemingway story.

***Student Model***

**Memo:** Filming Ernest Hemingway's "Soldier's Home"—The setting should be late fall. Emphasize bare trees and overcast skies to give the feeling of loneliness and alienation.

Showing Harold walking home from the train station alone will help to emphasize the fact that the celebration of the soldiers' heroic return from WWI is over.

Highlight the change in Harold's personality since his tour in Europe. This could be accomplished by adding a character—a good friend who was not drafted for medical reasons. He could tell how upbeat and friendly Harold used to be.

Flashbacks to Harold's tour of duty could emphasize the war's effect on him. Lead into flashbacks with small, ordinary instances, such as baby screaming, car going by, sight of train.

Jamie Luce, Shaker Heights High School, Shaker Heights, Ohio

*Notice how Jamie focuses on the most important aspects of the story, such as loneliness and alienation, and then looks for cinematic ways to reveal or emphasize them.*

# 4.6 Writing Activities

## Write a Scene

Read a short story by Jamaica Kincaid or D. H. Lawrence (see excerpts on pages 160 and 170) or by an author of your own choosing. Select a scene from the story, and turn it into a screenplay by changing all the narration into dialogue, descriptions of action, sound effects, props, and other cinematic elements. Use the questions on page 184 as a guide.

- Include brief descriptions of the setting.
- Provide information, from a narrator, about any important events that preceded this scene.
- Write dialogue that reveals the characters' personalities and moves the story along.

**PURPOSE** To write a screenplay based on a scene from a short story
**AUDIENCE** Your teacher and classmates
**LENGTH** 1–2 pages

### COMPUTER OPTION

When you're part of a script-writing team, you will be involved with many sections, versions, and revisions of material. You can use your PC to help file, copy, and combine these elements.

Your computer can help you save and catalog the drafts done by each member of the group so that they can be easily found, read, revised, and printed. It can combine a number of documents by different writers to produce a single script and then print enough copies for the group's consideration. Finally, you can use your search-and-replace function to make changes throughout the script, such as fixing the spelling of a name.

### Grammar Link

**Use correct principal parts of verbs. Do not confuse the past and past participle.**

*I **did** it in one shot.*

Complete the sentences, using the correct form of the verb in parentheses.

1. Filming on a sequel to the train film ________ in Arizona last week. (begin)
2. An unknown screenwriter has ________ the screenplay for the sequel. (write)
3. The casting director ________ the ideal actors for more than 200 parts. (find)
4. The producer has ________ a director who is well-known for her outdoor epics. (choose)
5. The original novel was adapted heavily before it ________ the requirements for a good film. (fit)

**See Lessons 15.1–15.2, pages 537–540.**

UNIT 4

# WRITING PROCESS IN ACTION

## NARRATIVE WRITING

In preceding lessons, you have learned about the art of narrative writing—how to establish setting, order time, build suspense, and employ different points of view. You've also had the chance to write a short-short story and plan how you would adapt a literary work for film. In this lesson you're invited to apply the skills you've learned and write about an important "chapter" in your life, an event that represents a turning point.

### • Assignment •

| | |
|---|---|
| *Context* | *Imagine that years from now you are composing your memoirs from journals you kept faithfully from childhood on. Scanning these journals, you notice that there are several important events that have changed the course of your life or dramatically altered your thinking. You've decided to write a short narrative about one of these turning points to share with a general audience. Your ultimate goal is to write a longer narrative of which this piece will become a chapter.* |
| *Purpose* | *To write a narrative about a pivotal event in your life* |
| *Audience* | *People who want to know about the events that have shaped your life* |
| *Length* | *2 pages* |

The following pages can help you plan and write your narrative. Read through them, and then refer to them as you need to. But don't be tied down by them. You're in charge of your own writing process.

# Prewriting

What has happened in your life? A look at the general shape of your experiences will help you to see points of departure, moments of truth. Begin by drawing a time line or chronological chart of the events of your life. Once you have listed the major events, lace your history with details. The prewriting questions will help you get started.

Study your time line, searching for moments or periods that represent turning points. Choose two of these, and apply a prewriting technique, such as clustering, to help you explore the events. Then select the one that shows the most promise. Think about who your audience will be and how you can help them understand not only the turning point itself but also the emotional implications. Notice how Christy Brown uses setting to represent metaphorically the mixture of anguish and excitement he felt after his first unsuccessful attempt to write. Then consider the setting of your own turning point. Can you use it to convey mood the way Brown does?

*Prewriting Questions*

- *What details of my early childhood are interesting?*
- *What major events—moves, educational attainments, discovered talents, travels—helped shape my life?*
- *What memorable occasions stand out in my mind?*
- *Which individuals have influenced me most?*
- *Whom can I consult for information or insight?*

*Literature Model*

The stillness was profound. The room was full of flame and shadow that danced before my eyes and lulled my taut nerves into a sort of waking sleep. I could hear the sound of the water-tap dripping in the pantry, the loud ticking of the clock on the mantelshelf, and the soft hiss and crackle of the logs on the open hearth.

Christy Brown, *My Left Foot*

Remember, you can also use character and point of view to suggest the significance of your pivotal event. Since your former self is actually a character in your narrative, experiment with narrative voice until the tone rings true.

# Drafting

### Drafting Tip

You can refer to Lesson 4.2, pages 166–168, for organizational strategies and to Lesson 4.3, pages 170–172, for tips on creating suspense.

To get started, ask yourself what point you want to make about the pivotal event in your life. Think carefully about the idea you most want to get across, and write it down as a complete sentence. Then, with this idea in focus, begin to organize your material. Consider how you can engage your readers' interest through the technique of building suspense.

Once you have decided on a pattern and perhaps jotted down a rough plotline, begin drafting. Don't worry now about finding just the right word or about whether your point of view is consistent. Just let your writing flow to get your ideas down. If you run into a snag, go back to prewriting: seek fresh details, or reimmerse yourself in the mood.

### Revising Tip

For help with maintaining a consistent narrative voice, see Lesson 4.4, pages 174–176.

# Revising

To begin revising, read over your draft to make sure that what you have written fits your purpose and your audience. Then have a **writing conference**. Read your draft to a partner or small group. Use your audience's reactions to help you evaluate your work so far. In addition, you can use the following questions to help you.

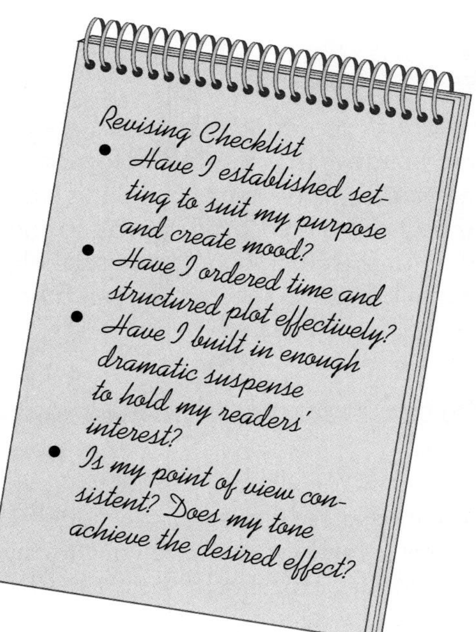

Revising Checklist
• Have I established setting to suit my purpose and create mood?
• Have I ordered time and structured plot effectively?
• Have I built in enough dramatic suspense to hold my readers' interest?
• Is my point of view consistent? Does my tone achieve the desired effect?

# Editing

Once you are happy with the basic content and set-up of your narrative, **proofread** it carefully for errors in grammar, usage, mechanics, and spelling. Use the editing checklist at the right as a guide.

In addition to proofreading, use the self-evaluation list below to make sure your narrative does all the things you want it to do. When you're satisfied, make a clean copy of your narrative and proofread it once again.

Editing Checklist
• Are most of my verbs in the active voice?
• Did I avoid shifting tenses needlessly?
• Did I write possessive pronouns and direct quotations correctly?
• Have I checked spelling and looked up any words I was unsure of?


## Self-Evaluation

**Make sure your narrative—**

- focuses on a pivotal event in your life
- effectively uses setting and point of view to show the emotional impact of that event
- clearly shows why this is a turning point in your life
- uses plot and other suspense-creating devices to create and hold reader interest
- follows correct grammar, usage, mechanics, and spelling

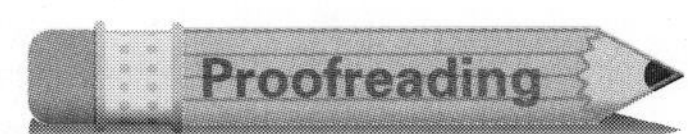


For proofreading symbols, see page 92.

# Presenting

You might want to share your writing with someone you interviewed during prewriting or with someone who played a role in the turning point you chose to narrate. You might also ask someone who knows very little about you to read and comment on your work. An objective opinion is particularly valuable if you plan to submit your narrative for publication.

### Journal Writing

Reflect on your writing process experience. Answer these questions in your journal: What do you like best about your narrative? What was the hardest part of writing it? What did you learn during the writing conference? What new things have you learned as a writer?

UNIT 4

# Narrative Writing
# Literature Model

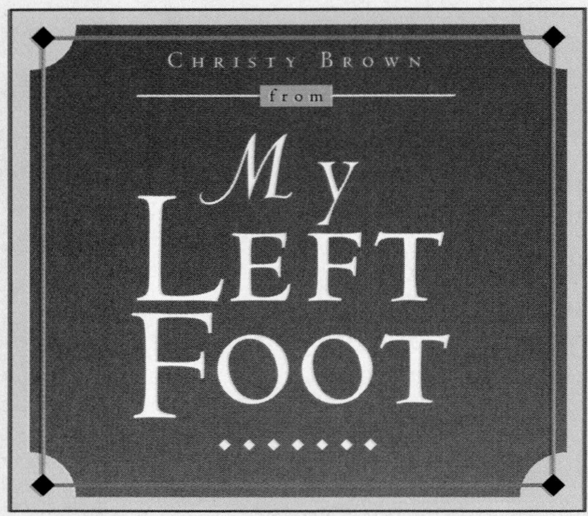


*Christy Brown's story would have had a very unhappy ending if his family had listened to the experts and abandoned their belief in him. In the following selection from his autobiography,* My Left Foot, *Brown tells about the physical limitations he was born with and how he overcame them in a most ingenious way one cold December afternoon. As you read, pay close attention to how Brown uses narrative techniques. Then try the activities in Linking Writing and Literature on page 199.*

I was born in the Rotunda Hospital, on June 5th, 1932. There were nine children before me and twelve after me, so I myself belong to the middle group. Out of this total of twenty-two, seventeen lived, four died in infancy, leaving thirteen still to hold the family fort.

Mine was a difficult birth, I am told. Both mother and son almost died. A whole army of relations queued up outside the hospital until the small hours of the morning, waiting for news and praying furiously that it would be good.

After my birth mother was sent to recuperate for some weeks and I was kept in the hospital while she was away. I remained there for some time, without name, for I wasn't baptized until my mother was well enough to bring me to church.

It was mother who first saw that there was something wrong with me. I was about four months old at the time. She noticed that my head had a habit of falling backwards whenever she tried to feed me. She attempted to correct this by placing her hand on the back of my neck to keep it steady. But when she took it away back it would drop again. That was the first warning sign. Then she became aware of other defects as I got older. She saw that my hands were clenched nearly all of the time and were inclined to twine behind my back; my mouth couldn't grasp the teat of the bottle because even at that early age my jaws would either lock together tightly, so that it was impossible for her to open them, or they would suddenly become limp and fall loose, dragging my whole mouth to one side. At six months I could not sit up without having a mountain of pillows around me; at twelve months it was the same.

Very worried by this, mother told my father her fears, and they decided to seek medical advice without any further delay. I was a little over a year old when they began to take me to hospitals and clinics, convinced that there was something definitely wrong with me, something which they could not understand or name, but which was very real and disturbing.

Almost every doctor who saw and examined me, labelled me a very interesting but also a hopeless case. Many told mother very gently that I was mentally defective and would remain so. That was a hard blow to a young mother who had already reared five healthy children. The doctors were so very sure of themselves that mother's faith in me seemed almost an impertinence. They assured her that nothing could be done for me.

She refused to accept this truth, the inevitable truth—as it then seemed—that I was beyond cure, beyond saving, even beyond hope. She could not and would not believe that I was an imbecile, as the doctors told her. She had nothing in the world to go by, not a scrap of evidence to support her conviction that, though my body was crippled, my mind was not. In spite of all the doctors and specialists told her, she would not agree. I don't believe she knew why—she just knew without feeling the smallest shade of doubt.

Finding that the doctors could not help in any way beyond telling her not to place her trust in me, or, in other words, to forget I was a human creature, rather to regard me as just something to be fed and washed and then put away again, mother decided there and then to take matters into her own hands. I was her child, and therefore part of the family. No matter how dull and incapable I might grow up to be, she was determined to treat me on the same plane as the others, and not as the "queer one" in the back room who was never spoken of when there were visitors present.

That was a momentous decision as far as my future life was concerned. It meant that I would always have my mother on my side to help me fight all the battles that were to come, and to inspire me with new strength when I was almost beaten. But it wasn't easy for her because now the relatives and friends had decided otherwise. They contended that I should be taken kindly, sympathetically, but not seriously. That would be a mistake. "For your own sake," they told her, "don't look to this boy as you would to the others; it would only break your heart in the end." Luckily for me, mother and father held out against the lot of them. But mother wasn't content just to say that I was not an idiot, she set out to prove it, not because of any rigid sense of duty, but out of love. That is why she was so successful.

At this time she had the five other children to look after besides the "difficult one," though as yet it was not by any means a full house. There were my brothers, Jim, Tony and Paddy, and my two sisters, Lily and Mona, all of them very young, just a year or so between each of them, so that they were almost exactly like steps of stairs.

Four years rolled by and I was now five, and still as helpless as a newly-born baby. While my father was out at bricklaying earning our bread and butter for us, mother was slowly, patiently pulling down the wall, brick by brick, that seemed to thrust itself between me and the other children, slowly, patiently penetrating beyond the thick curtain that hung over my mind, separating it from theirs. It was hard, heart-breaking work, for often all she got from me in return was a vague smile and perhaps a faint gurgle. I could not speak or even mumble, nor could I sit up without support on my own, let alone take steps. But I wasn't inert or motionless. I seemed indeed to be convulsed with movement, wild, stiff, snake-like movement that never left me, except in sleep. My fingers twisted and twitched continually, my arms twined backwards and would often shoot out suddenly this way and that, and my head lolled and sagged sideways. I was a queer, crooked little fellow.

Mother tells me how one day she had been sitting with me for hours in an upstairs room, showing me pictures out of a great big storybook that I had got from Santa Claus last Christmas and telling me the names of the different animals and flowers that were in them, trying without success to get me to repeat them. This had gone on for hours while she talked and laughed with me. Then at the end of it she leaned over me and said gently into my ear:

"Did you like it, Chris? Did you like the bears and the monkeys and all the lovely flowers? Nod your head for yes, like a good boy."

But I could make no sign that I understood her. Her face was bent over mine, hopefully. Suddenly, involuntarily, my queer hand reached up and grasped one of the dark curls that fell in a thick cluster about her neck. Gently she loosened the clenched fingers, though some dark strands were still clutched between them.

Then she turned away from my curious stare and left the room, crying. The door closed behind her. It all seemed hopeless. It looked as though there was some justification for my relatives' contention that I was an idiot and beyond help.

They now spoke of an institution.

"Never!" said my mother almost fiercely, when this was suggested to her. "I know my boy is not an idiot. It is his body that is shattered, not his mind. I'm sure of that."

Sure? Yet inwardly, she prayed God would give her some proof of her faith. She knew it was one thing to believe but quite another to prove.

I was now five, and still showed no real sign of intelligence. I showed no apparent interest in things except with my toes—more especially those of my left foot. Although my natural habits were clean I could not aid myself, but in this respect my father took care of me. I used to lie on my back all the time in the kitchen or, on bright warm days, out in the garden, a little bundle of crooked muscles and twisted nerves, surrounded by a family that loved me and hoped for me and that made me part of their own warmth and humanity. I was lonely, imprisoned in a world of my own, unable to communicate with others, cut off, separated from them as though a glass wall stood between my existence and theirs, thrusting me beyond the sphere of their lives and activities. I longed to run about and play with the rest, but I was unable to break loose from my bondage.

Then, suddenly, it happened! In a moment everything was changed, my future life molded into a definite shape, my mother's faith in me rewarded and her secret fear changed into open triumph.

It happened so quickly, so simply after all the years of waiting and uncertainty that I can see and feel the whole scene as if it had happened last week. It was the afternoon of a cold, grey December day. The streets outside glistened with snow; the white sparkling flakes stuck and melted on the window-panes and hung on the boughs of the trees like molten silver. The wind howled dismally, whipping up little whirling columns of snow that rose and fell at every fresh gust. And over all, the dull, murky sky stretched like a dark canopy, a vast infinity of greyness.

Inside, all the family were gathered round the big kitchen fire that lit up the little room with a warm glow and made giant shadows dance on the walls and the ceiling.

In a corner Mona and Paddy were sitting huddled together, a

few torn school primers before them. They were writing down little sums on to an old chipped slate, using a bright piece of yellow chalk. I was close to them, propped up by a few pillows against the wall, watching. It was the chalk that attracted me so much. It was a long, slender stick of vivid yellow. I had never seen anything like it before, and it showed up so well against the black surface of the slate that I was fascinated by it as much as if it had been a stick of gold.

Suddenly I wanted desperately to do what my sister was doing. Then—without thinking or knowing exactly what I was doing, I reached out and took the stick of chalk out of my sister's hand—*with my left foot.*

I do not know why I used my left foot to do this. It is a puzzle to many people as well as to myself, for, although I had displayed a curious interest in my toes at an early age, I had never attempted before this to use either of my feet in any way. They could have been as useless to me as were my hands. That day, however, my left foot, apparently on its own volition, reached out and very impolitely took the chalk out of my sister's hand.

I held it tightly between my toes, and, acting on an impulse, made a wild sort of scribble with it on the slate. Next moment I stopped, a bit dazed, surprised, looking down at the stick of yellow chalk stuck between my toes, not knowing what to do with it next, hardly knowing how it got there. Then I looked up and became aware that everyone had stopped talking and were staring at me silently. Nobody stirred. Mona, her black curls framing her chubby little face, stared at me with great big eyes and open mouth. Across the open hearth, his face lit by flames, sat my father, leaning forward, hands outspread on his knees, his shoulders tense. I felt the sweat break out on my forehead.

My mother came in from the pantry with a steaming pot in her hand. She stopped midway between the table and the fire, feeling the tension flowing through the room. She followed their stare and saw me, in the corner. Her eyes looked from my face down to my foot, with the chalk gripped between my toes. She put down the pot.

Then she crossed over to me and knelt down beside me, as she had done so many times before.

"I'll show you what to do with it, Chris," she said, very slowly and in a queer, jerky way, her face flushed as if with some inner excitement.

Taking another piece of chalk from Mona, she hesitated, then very deliberately drew, on the floor in front of me, *the single letter "A."* "Copy that," she said, looking steadily at me. "Copy it, Christy."

I couldn't.

Alexander Calder, *Letter A*, 1943

I looked about me, looked around at the faces that were turned towards me, tense, excited faces that were at that moment frozen, immobile, eager, waiting for a miracle in their midst.

The stillness was profound. The room was full of flame and shadow that danced before my eyes and lulled my taut nerves into a sort of waking sleep. I could hear the sound of the water-tap dripping in the pantry, the loud ticking of the clock on the mantelshelf, and the soft hiss and crackle of the logs on the open hearth.

I tried again. I put out my foot and made a wild jerking stab with the chalk which produced a very crooked line and nothing more. Mother held the slate steady for me.

"Try again, Chris," she whispered in my ear. "Again."

I did. I stiffened my body and put my left foot out again, for the third time. I drew one side of the letter. I drew half the other side. Then the stick of chalk broke and I was left with a stump. I wanted to fling it away and give up. Then I felt my mother's hand on my shoulder. I tried once more. Out went my foot. I shook, I sweated and strained every muscle. My hands were so tightly clenched that my fingernails bit into the flesh. I set my teeth so hard that I nearly pierced my lower lip. Everything in the room swam till the faces around me were mere patches of white. But—I drew it—*the letter "A."* There it was on the floor before me. Shaky, with awkward, wobbly sides and a very uneven centre line. But it *was* the letter "A." I looked up. I saw my mother's face for a moment, tears on her cheeks. Then my father stooped down and hoisted me on to his shoulder.

I had done it! It had started—the thing that was to give my mind its chance of expressing itself. True, I couldn't speak with my lips, but now I would speak through something more lasting than spoken words—written words.

That one letter, scrawled on the floor with a broken bit of yellow chalk gripped between my toes, was my road to a new world, my key to mental freedom. It was to provide a source of relaxation to the tense, taut thing that was me which panted for expression behind a twisted mouth.

Having taught me to draw the letter "A" with my foot, mother next set out to teach me the whole alphabet in much the same way. She was determined to make use of the opportunity so miraculously presented to her and to help me communicate with the rest through the written word, if not through the spoken one.

My memory of the way she set about this is quite clear. She would bring me up into the front bedroom any day she wasn't too busy with the household, and spend hours teaching me one letter after the other. She would write down each letter on the floor with a piece of chalk. Then she would rub them out with a duster and make me write them down again from memory with the chalk held between my toes. It was hard work for both of us. Often she would be in the pantry cooking the dinner when I'd give a howl to make her come up to see if I had spelt a word correctly. If I was wrong, I'd make her kneel down, her hands covered with flour, and show me the right way to do it. I remember the first thing I learned to write was my initials: "C. B." though I'd often become confused and put the "B" before the "C." Whenever anyone asked me what my name was I'd grab a piece of chalk and write "C. B." with a great flourish.

Soon afterwards I learnt to write my full name instead of just two initials. I was tremendously proud of myself when I could do this. I felt quite important.

I was now going on six, and soon I got tired of just writing my own name. I wanted to do something else—something bigger. But I couldn't, because I couldn't read. I didn't exactly know what being able to read meant. I just knew that Jim could do it, Tony could do it, that Mona and Peter could do it, and that made me want to do it too. I think I was jealous.

Slowly, very painfully, I ploughed through the whole twenty-six letters with my mother and gradually mastered each of them in turn. One thing that gave mother great encouragement at this time was my ability to listen and watch attentively when she was sitting by my side giving me lessons. My attention seldom wavered.

I remember us sitting in the big horse-haired armchair before a big fire one winter's evening. The baby was asleep in the pram on the other side of the hearthstone. The two of us were alone in the dim-lit kitchen, while my father was at a bricklayers' meeting and my sisters and brothers out playing on the streets. My mother had Peter's schoolbook in her hand and she was reading little stories about the poor children of Lir who were turned into swans by their wicked stepmother, about Diarmud and Graine and the King who turned everything he touched into gold. She read on to me till the shadows had made the room dark and little Eamonn stirred and cried in his sleep. Then she got up and switched on the lights. The spell broke and the enchantment was gone.

Knowing the alphabet was half the battle won, for I was soon able to put letters together and to form little words. After a while I began to know how to put words together and form sentences. I was getting on. But it wasn't as easy or as simple as it sounds. Mother had by now seven other children to care for besides myself. Fortunately she had a real ally in my sister Lily, or "Titch," as the others nicknamed her. She was the eldest and the little mother of the circle, a small, wiry kid with flowing black curls and flashing eyes. She could be very sweet when she liked—quite a proper little angel. But she wasn't very angelic when she was roused. She realized my mother's tough situation quicker than any grown woman would, and responded. She busied herself looking after the others so that mother could spend more time with me. She cooked, and washed and dressed the smaller ones and made sure the bigger ones washed behind their ears every morning before setting out for school. Perhaps she was just a shade too zealous, for often Jim or Tony would slink, shame-faced, into the kitchen, bearing testimony to little Lily's earnest housewifery in the form of swollen ears or black eyes.

I still could not speak intelligibly, but by now I had a sort of grunting language which the family understood more or less.

Whenever I got into difficulties and they couldn't make out what I was saying, I'd point to the floor and print the words out on it with my left foot. If I couldn't spell the words I wanted to write I flew into a rage, which only made me grunt still more incoherently.

Although I couldn't talk very much at seven years old, I was now able to sit up alone and crawl about from place to place on my bottom without breaking any bones or smashing any of mother's china. I wore no shoes or any other kind of footwear. My mother had tried to make me used to having my feet covered from an early age, saying I looked very much neglected barefooted. But whenever she put anything on my feet I always kicked them off again quickly. I hated having my feet covered. When mother put shoes or stockings on my feet I felt as any normal person might feel if his hands were tied behind his back.

As time went on I began to depend more and more on my left foot for everything. It was my main means of communication, of making myself understood to the family. Very slowly it became indispensable to me. With it I learned to break down some of the barriers that stood between me and the others at home. It was the only key to the door of the prison I was in.

# Linking Writing and Literature

## Readers Respond to the Model

## How would you describe the impact that Christy Brown's narrative had on you?

**Evaluate Christy Brown's narrative by answering these questions. Then read what other students liked about Brown's narrative.**

1. Reread the scene beginning on page 193 that describes the afternoon Christy discovered his "road to a new world." Why does he remember it in such detail? Which details about that afternoon stick in your mind? How do these details contribute to the way you feel about Christy and the members of his family?
2. Christy's mother is an important part of his life. What motivated her? Why did she reject the advice of doctors and friends and continue to believe in Christy's intelligence? What do you think her feelings were that December afternoon? How do you think she treated Christy as he matured?
3. From the selection, choose a paragraph that had a great impact on you. Describe your personal response, and comment on the devices that the author uses to achieve this effect.

This literature selection was about a boy who is physically handicapped. While the rest of his family was ready to send him to an institution, his mother always believed in him. What I remember most clearly is when Christy wrote the letter *A* and proved to the family that he was not mentally defective.

Christy Brown created the mood of this selection by showing the great love that his mother had for him. She was incredibly strong. Throughout the selection the author speaks of how his mother believed in him and would never give up on him. I would definitely recommend this selection to a friend. It is an excellent piece of work. It shows the power of love. Everyone should have a great mother like that. A parent's love should be unconditional and everlasting!

***David Alonzo***

The story is memorable because it is unlike anyone else's. Christy Brown starts off by explaining his situation and builds up to the point where he proves to everyone that he is not an "idiot." The story is sad, but it is also exciting. You want to know what happens next. This story has so much feeling and inspiration that I can't imagine people reading it and feeling as if they will not amount to anything. The story makes you want to have goals and fulfill those goals.

***Becky Byer***

# Unit 4 Review

## Reflecting on the Unit

**Summarize what you learned in this unit by answering the following questions.**

- What are the basic elements of narrative writing?
- What are the purposes of setting?
- What plot devices can you use in narrative writing?
- What suspense-creating devices are effective in narrative writing?
- What are the different points of view you can use in narrative writing?
- What makes a short-short story unique?

## Adding to Your Portfolio

**Choose a selection for your portfolio.**
Look over the writing you did for this unit. Choose a piece of writing for your portfolio. The writing you choose should show one or more of the following.

- successfully integrated narrative elements: setting, character, plot, theme, and point of view
- flashbacks, flash forwards, or foreshadowing or other devices to insert past or future events into the plot
- suspense achieved by withholding information, foreshadowing, or using delaying tactics
- a consistent narrative voice

**Reflect on your choice.**
Attach a note to the piece you chose, explaining briefly why you chose it and what you learned from writing it.

**Set goals.**
How can you improve your writing? What skill will you focus on the next time you write?

## Writing Across the Curriculum

**Make a technology connection.**
Project yourself into a futuristic world in which technology reigns. Write a high-impact short story about life in a high-tech world. Use your knowledge about recent advances to create a setting that you might expect to find in the twenty-first century.

UNIT

5

# Expository Writing

Composition

## Lessons

UNIT
5
PREVIEW

Case Study

# Expository Writing in the Real World

## Explaining the "Nature" of Their Business

**FOCUS: An effective business plan uses well-chosen facts and statistics to generate interest in a product.**

If Alfred Wilson and Oliver Komar don't answer their office phone, they've probably gone birding. Avid bird enthusiasts since childhood, Komar and Wilson developed an educational VCR game, "Gone Birding!" which allows novices and experts to test their knowledge of North American birds.

"Gone Birding!" challenges players to identify birds seen on a videocassette and progress around a game board using glassy "eggs" as game pieces. The board, a map of the United States and Canada, marks key birding sites. Players draw cards that give information about each site and the wildlife found there. "Surprise Cards" bestow good or bad fortune on the players: you might have an unexpectedly good sighting in Florida; you might miss seeing several species in Wyoming due to forest fires. The player to accumulate the most bird sightings wins.

To produce their game, Wilson and Komar established themselves as president and vice president, respectively, of a new company, Rupicola Productions, named after an exotic South American bird. Then the partners set out to raise the start-up

*Game designers Oliver Komar (left) and Alfred Wilson (right)*

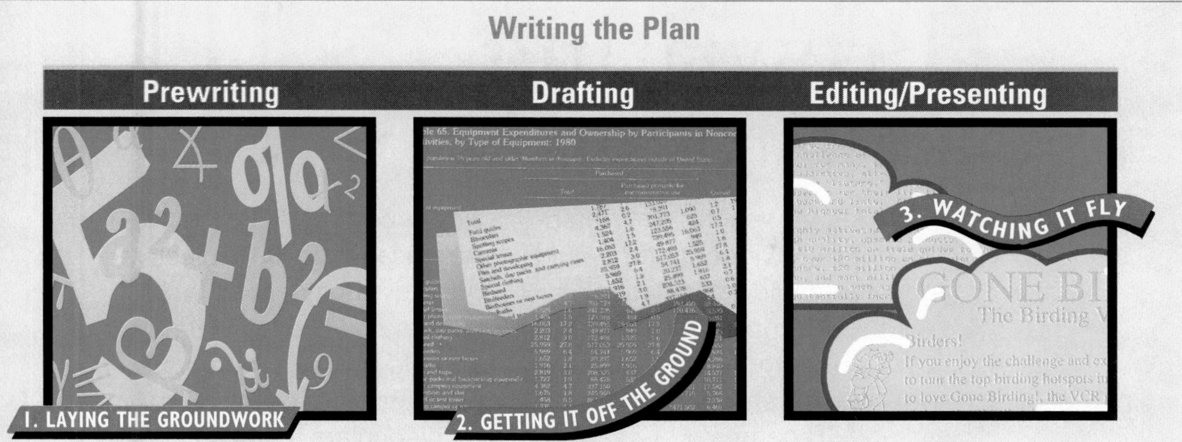


> ***"We really took very seriously every word we wrote in the business plan because we knew that this was our ticket to the future. We'd invested a couple of years of our time at virtually no pay to try to make a business. And we knew that the only way we were going to finance this business was through a well-written business plan."***
>
> —Oliver Komar, vice president and co-founder of Rupicola Productions

funds needed to design and produce the game. The money would cover filming, hiring well-known hosts, producing advertising, and manufacturing the game.

Rupicola's first step in fundraising was to write a business plan stating the company's objectives and identifying the potential market for the game.

Wilson and Komar designed their business plan to explain their game to two types of investors: wealthy people who shared their love of birdwatching but knew little about VCRs, and companies that had money to invest but knew almost nothing about birdwatching.

# Prewriting

## LAYING THE GROUNDWORK

To show wealthy birdwatchers that their video game would appeal to a wide population, Wilson and Komar included statistics on the growing videocassette market and the success of earlier VCR games. For example, their 1987 document cited a research firm's prediction that 85 percent of all homes would have VCRs by 1995. Wilson chuckles, "Today we wouldn't have the same problem explaining what a VCR is. Probably just one sentence would do it."

Their other audience, venture-capital companies, needed to be told of the existing market for birdwatching products. "Whenever possible we used quotes from the United States governments or from magazines like *Time* or *Life* about the size of the birding market," Wilson says. Their business plan cites these figures: "*Birding* magazine reports that 11 million Americans of all ages actively go birdwatching. . . . In 1980, birders spent over $18 million on field guides to birds and other wildlife, over $80 million on binoculars, over $55 million on bird feeders, $20 million on birdhouses, $26 million on birdbaths. . . ."

Wilson and Komar studied how to write a business plan by reading other successful plans. "We were careful to follow a format that's standard for business plans," says Komar. "Of course, every business plan has to be customized for the situation." Most business plans include product descriptions, projected profits, and other data, such as information on competition—"although in our case," says Wilson, "there wasn't any."

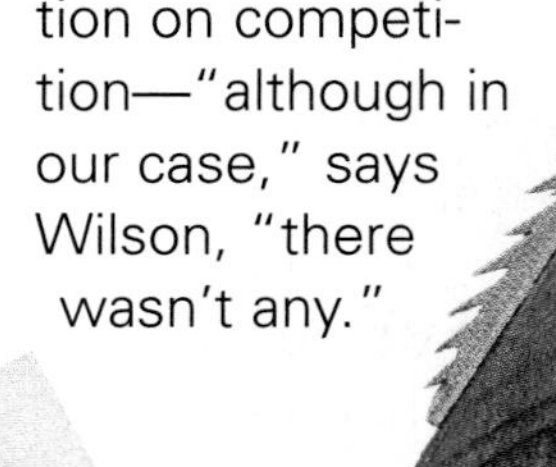

# Drafting

## GETTING IT OFF THE GROUND

Wilson and Komar wrote independent first drafts of each section of their business plan. Then they brought their drafts together, took the best parts from each, and combined them.

Oliver Komar says the partners have never viewed the writing as "a competitive thing" in which each seeks to prove that he can write better than the other. "On many occasions we've taken something I've written and expanded it based on what Alf has written," he explains, "and I've always felt in the end it was much better. We worked endlessly on the plan to improve it."

The two businessmen contribute to the writing in different ways. "My strength is directness," Komar explains. "I get to the point as quickly as possible, and I don't take too many words to say what needs to be said."

Alfred Wilson agrees. "Ollie's writing style is somewhat more organized. Mine is more conversational and perhaps more colorful than is usual for a businessman."

# Editing/Presenting

## WATCHING IT FLY

The two partners extended their collaborative effort to include many other people. For example, they talked to others who had started companies. Says Wilson, "We could have written many pages about things that were really enthusiastic about, but venture capitalists advised us to keep the plan brief. So we had to do a lot of editing of each chapter."

When the partners disagreed about how to write a section, they sought outside opinions. "We got our families and friends involved in reviewing and editing everything we did," says Wilson. "What we were after was the most effective piece of writing, not something that was less effective but all ours."

The $500,000 Wilson and Komar needed to produce "Gone Birding!" was raised by their effective business plan. In its first year, advertisements for the game ran in fifteen magazines.

"Most business plans don't get financed," says Komar. Now, he says, "we've sold 'Gone Birding!' to over 350 stores and to customers directly though phone sales." It all started with a well-written business plan.

# Responding to the Case Study

## 1. Discussion

**Discuss these questions about Komar and Wilson's writing.**

- For what two audiences was this business plan written? How were they similar and different?
- How did Komar and Wilson use other sources of information to create their plan?
- What made the collaboration between these two writers successful?
- What difficulties did Komar and Wilson face in 1987 that they might not face today? What challenges might they encounter if they were writing a new plan?

## 2. Expository Writing

**Develop a business plan to get start-up funds for your own product, such as a new game or a service not found in your area.** Incorporate the basic elements of a business plan, including a product explanation, facts about the potential market, and ideas about production and distribution. The young entrepreneurs shown below are creating a business plan for a new T-shirt venture.

## Grammar Link

**Make subjects and verbs agree.**

When the subject of a sentence is a noun of amount, use a singular verb form if the noun refers to a total that is considered to be one unit. Use a plural verb form if the noun refers to a number of individual units.

*The **$500,000** Wilson and Komar needed to produce "Gone Birding!" **was** raised by their effective business plan.* (one unit)

Use the form of the verb in parentheses that correctly completes each sentence.

1. Four dollars _____ (is/are) the cost of the blank video cassette.
2. The first four dollars earned by the store _____ (is/are) displayed behind the counter.
3. Two months _____ (has/have) passed since I submitted the report.
4. Three months _____ (is/are) the average response time.
5. Thirty minutes _____ (feel/feels) like a long time for a commercial.

**See Lesson 16.4, page 571.**

LESSON **5.1**

# Expository Writing

# Writing an Expository Essay

*Expository writing lets writers share information and explanations directly with an audience.*

*Literature Model*

Women and men especially shy away from a new hair style, color, or permanent wave because they are afraid they will be stuck with it until it grows out. Now there is a high-tech way to get a preview. A California company, New Image Industries, has developed a computer system that superimposes hair styles on the video image of a salon client's face. The machines cost up to $22,500 and can be programmed with 400 styles.

The customer is photographed with hair tucked into a stocking cap. The picture is displayed on the video screen and hair in selected styles is added; the hair can be modified with an electronic stylus. What results is an approximation, since the hair is not the client's. Some computers record the consultation on video; others take instant photographs of the client wearing different styles.

Anne-Marie Schiro, "New Hairdo, No Angst," *New York Times*

## Define Expository Writing

The news article above uses precise language and accurate facts to tell readers about New Image Industries, a business started by young entrepreneurs John Hallorand and Kirk Lamar. In order to obtain financing, Hallorand and Lamar used expository writing. They wrote a business plan to explain their idea and convince others it was worth backing.

You use expository writing all the time. When you write a term paper or answer an essay question on a test, you're often using expository writing. When you tell about the process of a physics experiment, define commonly used computer terms, give written directions, explain the causes and effects of the California gold rush, or write about the differences between literary characters such as Heathcliff and Catherine, you're using expository writing.

Suppose that you're looking for a way to earn extra money, and you decide to start your own word-processing business. Like New Image Industries creators Hallorand and Lamar, you will have to find a way to finance your fledgling business. While researching various financing possibilities, you discover that several local businesses may be willing to help you get your business started. You decide to write a letter to the owner of each business, explaining your idea and the kind of assistance you need. When you write these letters, you will use expository writing to communicate your ideas.

**Kinds of Expository Writing**

**Explaining a process:** Explains a sequence of events

**Showing a cause-and-effect relationship:** Explains how one event or action causes other things to happen

**Dividing and classifying:** Divides a topic into categories

**Defining:** Explains the meaning of a term or an idea

**Comparing and contrasting:** Explains by pointing out similarities and differences between items

Expository writing informs an audience by presenting information and explaining concepts and ideas. It involves examining a subject by breaking it down into parts, examining those parts, and showing how they relate to one another. The chart above lists kinds of expository writing. Depending on your subject, your audience, and your purpose for writing, you may want to use one or a combination of these kinds of writing to convey your information. If, for example, you want to explain how you will run your word-processing business, you might write an essay that explains a process. If you want to explain why you're starting the business, a cause-and-effect essay would be more appropriate. To describe and define the kinds of services your business will provide, you might write a defining essay. Or, if you want to distinguish your business from other similar ventures, you might write a comparison-and-contrast essay.

## Journal Writing

Brainstorm to get ideas for a small business. In your journal jot down your best idea. Then make a detailed list of the steps you would follow to make your business a reality. Include ideas about people and businesses that might offer assistance to a dynamic new enterprise.

## Plan and Draft an Expository Essay

During the prewriting stage of an expository essay, establish your topic and your purpose—that is, the goal of your writing. Other prewriting steps include identifying your audience and determining the best method of organizing your essay. In an essay explaining your plan for a new business, your purpose might be to present your idea in a way that is interesting, informative, and persuasive. You could organize your essay by summarizing why you decided to start your own business and explaining what you need in order to get started.

Next you must gather details that will support your purpose. It often helps to ask yourself who, what, when, where, why, and how, about your topic as you prewrite. Knowing your audience will help you determine what details to include.

To begin drafting, compose a one-sentence thesis statement that clearly expresses your main idea. Use this statement to guide you through the drafting stage. Discard any details that do not support your thesis statement. Remember to use transitional words and phrases, such as *first, however, because, on the other hand, after, finally, most important, next*, and *since*, to show how the ideas in your essay are related and organized.

*What facts support the writer's contention that a market exists for a word-processing business?*

*Notice the one-sentence thesis statement, clearly expressing the main idea of the essay.*

*Notice how key words are repeated as a way of linking ideas between paragraphs.*

**Model**

Although many high school students have some computer skills, they often lack the typing skills and the equipment needed to produce clean, professional-looking term papers. Many of my neighbors hand-write business letters because they, too, lack either a computer or the skill to operate one. Finally, local small businesses often don't have enough staff to process all the documents they need on a daily basis. These situations represent an opportunity for a new business that I propose starting: Quick/Right Word Processing.

In order to begin Quick/Right Word Processing, I'll need about $1,450 to purchase equipment and supplies. A used computer will cost about $900; a second-hand, letter-quality printer an additional $450; and business cards, stationery, and other supplies about $100. I have some money; however, I'll need an additional $1,200 to get the business started. Once I have made the initial investment in equipment, I will meet my ongoing expenses from sales and use whatever profit is left to pay back the loan with interest.

# 5.1 Writing Activities

## Write an Expository Essay

Write an essay explaining your plans for starting a small business that will be run in a vacant local building. Choose one of the following services or select an idea of your own: coaching sports, automobile repair, grooming pets.

Address your essay to the owner of the building whose space you will rent in order to begin this new enterprise.

- Decide which kind of expository writing is most appropriate for your purpose.
- Compose a thesis statement that clearly expresses your main idea.
- Use details that support your thesis statement.

**PURPOSE** To write an expository essay proposing a business to be operated in a local building
**AUDIENCE** The owner of the building
**LENGTH** 4 paragraphs

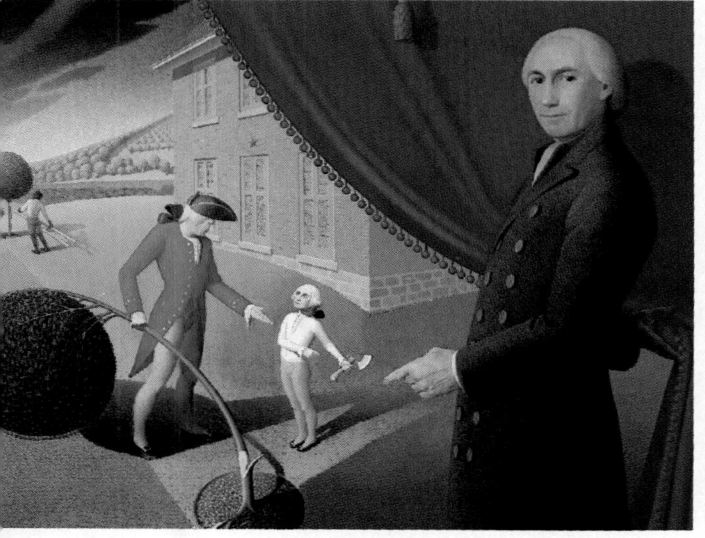

Grant Wood, *Parson Weems's Fable*, 1939

## Cross-Curricular: Art

Look closely at Grant Wood's painting, *Parson Weems's Fable.* Notice how the artist depicts the famous story of Washington and the cherry tree, which was first told by Parson Weems in his popular *Life and Memorable Actions of Washington.* What is happening in the painting? Brainstorm to get a list of ideas. Then choose one idea and use it to write an expository essay explaining the painting.

### Grammar Link

**Make sure that an indefinite pronoun subject agrees with the noun to which it refers.**

***Many*** *of my neighbors* ***hand-write*** *business letters. . . .*

Use the form of the verb in parentheses that correctly completes each sentence.

1. Most of the business plan _____ (was/were) devoted to market analysis.
2. Everyone who has read the plan _____ (agree/agrees) that it is succinct and effective.
3. One of the items _____ (emphasize/emphasizes) the importance of advertising.
4. All of the details _____ (support/supports) the main idea of the plan.

**See Lesson 16.7, page 575.**

LESSON 5.2

# Expository Writing
# Writing Instructions

*Effective instructions are straightforward, precise, and clearly organized. Writers who use obscure language or garbled logic end up with confusing instructions. Would this manual help you program a VCR?*

**Advanced Features**

**Setting Your VCR for Timer Recording**

- Press OPERATE and load a cassette. Then set INPUT/SELECT to TV and set REC to either SP or EP. NOTE: If you use timer recording to record external sources, set INPUT/SELECT to AUX and enter the channel number.
- Press PROG. NO. The display will change to the *Timer Set Mode.* Now enter data into the NO. 1 program memory.
- Press CHANNEL. The PROG indicator will flash. Set to the channel you wish to record.

Making assumptions about an audience is a trap many people fall into when writing instructions. The writer of the above guide mistakenly assumes that all readers will easily understand technical language. The resulting jargon makes the writing very difficult to follow. Now imagine yourself using the following model to set up a VCR to record your favorite program. Are these steps easier to follow?

*Model*

Instructions for timer-activated VCR recording:
- Turn on power. Red light signals power is on.
- Insert blank cassette
- Set INPUT SELECT button to TUNER position.
- Set the timer program by completing the following steps:

1. Check to be sure that the clock is already set to show the correct day and time. See pg. 13 for directions for setting the clock. ➡

2. Lift lid located on the left side of recorder. Press TIMER SET button.

3. The letter displayed indicates the title assigned to the program you want your VCR to record. If no other programs have been set, the display shows the letter A, blinking. If other programs have already been set, the display moves ahead in alphabetical order and shows the next unused letter.

4. Press NEXT button.

## Write Your Way Out of the Maze

When explaining a process, you should lead your readers in a clear, step-by-step fashion through each stage of the process. For example, imagine that you have been asked to write instructions explaining how to set up an aquarium. Your audience will be children who have had relatively little experience with fish. Since the first step in writing instructions about any topic is to gather information, start by looking in books, magazines, or other reference sources and taking careful notes. Also, watch someone who is setting up an aquarium or, even better, set up an aquarium yourself. Make your observations, and write down each step as you complete it, omitting no details.

**Questions to Ask Yourself Before Drafting**

?

- Who is my audience?
- What does my audience know about the topic?
- What are the steps in the process?
- Have I arranged the steps in the best order?
- What other information does my audience need?

Next, list the steps of the process and arrange them in chronological order. Always keep your audience in mind, asking yourself what concepts they already understand and what concepts need to be explained. Before you begin to draft instructions, you may want to make a list of questions and answers like those in the list above. This will prevent you from leaving out any important steps or overestimating what your audience knows about your subject.

### Journal Writing

Think about the last time you had to explain a process or give directions, either orally or in writing. In your journal jot down what you were trying to explain, what you may have had to repeat, and any changes you might make if you were to give the same explanation today.

## Draft Instructions

**Grammar**

**Drafting Tip**

Writing in simple sentences can help you break a process into steps. Use simple sentences in your first draft. You can always combine them to form compound or complex sentences later in the writing process. Review simple sentences in Lesson 13.3, page 501.

When drafting a set of instructions, pay special attention to the thesis statement. It prepares your readers by telling them what process you will describe and where the step-by-step information will lead.

Keeping your audience in mind will help you stay on target while you draft. Think about what your readers already know and what information you will need to explain to them. Be sure to break the stages of your process into easy-to-follow steps. Use short, clear sentences. Trying to pack too much information into any one step will make your instructions difficult to follow.

Define any terms your audience may not know. Never use complicated terms or difficult words when easy-to-understand, "user-friendly" language will do the job. Help the reader see the step-by-step progression of the instructions by using transitional words such as *first*, *next*, *after*, and *finally* to signal movement to a new stage.

As part of the revising stage, review your notes to be sure you have not omitted any steps or explanations. Try following your instructions exactly as you have written them. Look for steps you have left out, unclear or fuzzy directions, and unnecessary information.

Notice how Ashley Brady uses short sentences, transitions, and user-friendly language in her instructions for setting up an aquarium.

*The thesis statement identifies the process being explained.*

*Has the writer explained why certain steps are necessary?*

*User-friendly language keeps instructions easy to understand. "Poisoning" is easier to understand than "toxic reaction," for example.*

### *Student Model*

In order to create a beautiful aquatic environment, follow these simple steps. First, rinse gravel for the bottom of the tank in water to remove any excess dust. You'll need about five pounds of gravel for a ten-gallon aquarium. Then fill the tank three-quarters full with tap water. At this time, you can arrange the gravel and add decorations such as plants.

After this step is completed, continue filling the aquarium with tap water to within two inches of the rim. Next, add one drop of chlorine neutralizer per half gallon of tap water to prevent the chlorine in the tap water from poisoning the fish. Finally, allow the aquarium to sit for forty-eight hours (two days) before introducing the fish into the aquarium. This will allow the chlorine in the tap water to be neutralized and the temperature to stabilize.

Ashley Brady, Henry Clay High School, Lexington, Kentucky

# 5.2 Writing Activities

## Write a Feature Article

Your article, aimed at incoming high school students, should discuss how new students can make the most out of their high school years. In order to bring a fresh twist to a traditional topic, write your article in the form of a "recipe for success." Instead of giving instructions for cooking food, you will list the ingredients and explain the steps needed to create a happy and successful high school experience.

- Use clear, straightforward language.
- Write simple sentences to describe each step.
- Select transitional words that show the relationship between steps.

**PURPOSE** To write a feature newspaper article
**AUDIENCE** Incoming high school students, as well as other readers of your school paper
**LENGTH** 3 paragraphs

## Cooperative Learning

How can a grassroots political organization achieve its goals? Work with a small group of students to create an instruction booklet that describes several strategies for achieving political goals. First, discuss a goal your group might like to achieve, such as increasing the penalties for driving while intoxicated. Then brainstorm a list of strategies your group could use to achieve success, such as poster or letter writing campaigns or door-to-door canvassing. Each group member should choose one idea and write instructions for carrying out that strategy. Put your instructions together to form a booklet. Then work together to create an introduction for your ideas.

### Grammar Link

**Use simple sentences in the imperative to communicate instructions clearly.**

*Lift lid located on the left side of recorder. Press TIMER SET button.*

Rewrite each complex sentence as several simple sentences. Write imperative sentences when effective.

1. You should always read the manual before you try to operate any new equipment because every device is different and reading the instructions tells you about unique features.
2. Although many people have difficulty setting their VCRs, you will find that it's really not that hard if you just follow these instructions.
3. After recording, you should press STOP and then you can press EJECT to load another cassette, or press REWIND to play back what you have recorded.
4. When I showed you how to operate the CD player, I forgot to point out a few important steps, including turning the machine on by pressing POWER.

**See Lesson 13.3, page 501, and Lesson 13.8, page 512.**

LESSON 5.3

# Expository Writing

# Explaining Causal Relationships

*When you look for reasons and explanations for events or conditions, you are exploring causal relationships. Think about the subjects that pique your curiosity and make you ask "Why?"*

Writer Frederick Lewis Allen wondered why farmers in 1932 went to such extremes to stop farm foreclosures. In some parts of the country, farmers would march together to the scene of a foreclosure sale and drive off prospective bidders. They would then bid for items at ridiculously low prices and later return all purchases to the former owner. Notice how Allen's paragraph provides information that explains these unusual actions.

*Literature Model*

The farmers were rebellious—and no wonder. For the gross income of American agriculture had declined from nearly 12 billion dollars in 1929—when it had already for years been suffering from a decline in export sales—to only 5 1/4 billions in 1932. While most manufacturing businesses dropped their prices only a little and met slackened demand with slackened production, the farmer could not do this, and the prices he got went right to the cellar. Men who found themselves utterly unable to meet their costs of production could not all be expected to be philosophical about it.

Frederick Lewis Allen, *Since Yesterday*

*What reasons does the writer give for the farmers' rebellious mood?*

## Explain Cause-and-Effect Relationships

Cause-and-effect writing gives reasons and explanations for events, conditions, or behavior. It answers the need most of us have to understand the world around us. The preceding model explains the mood of

American farmers during the Great Depression by listing some of the events that caused it. Most often you will use cause-and-effect writing to inform and explain, although you may also use it for persuasive or speculative purposes.

Almost any time you want to explain "why" in writing, you will use some form of cause-and-effect exposition.

Sometimes cause-and-effect relationships are stated simply, as in the model on page 216, with one or several causes leading directly to an effect. Often, however, they are more complex. Sometimes the relationship takes the form of a causal chain, in which an effect turns into a cause that produces other effects, and so on. In other cases a single cause may have multiple effects, as in the following model by Frank Trippet.

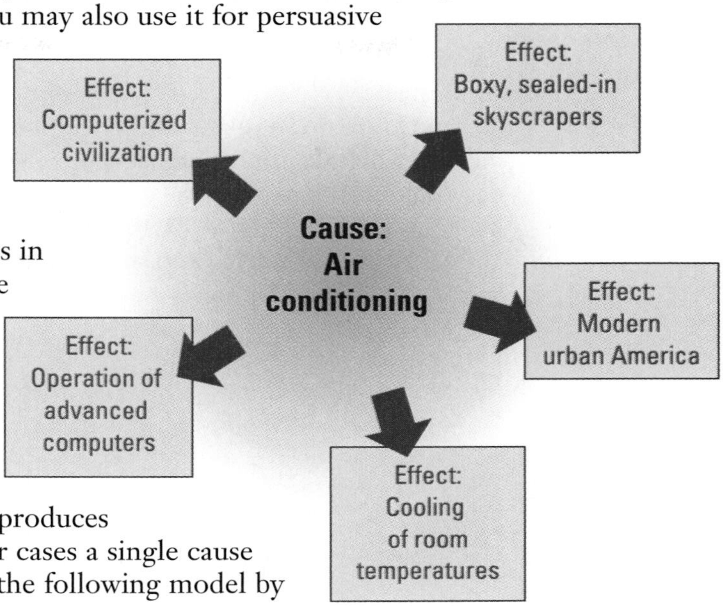

## Literature Model

Many of its byproducts are so conspicuous that they are scarcely noticed. To begin with, air conditioning transformed the face of urban America by making possible those glassy, boxy, sealed-in skyscrapers on which the once humane geometrics of places like San Francisco, Boston, and Manhattan have been impaled. It has been indispensable, no less, to the functioning of sensitive advanced computers, whose high operating temperatures require that they be constantly cooled. Thus, in a very real way, air conditioning has made possible the ascendancy of computerized civilization.

Frank Trippet, "The Great American Cooling Machine"

## Journal Writing

Think about the subjects you are studying that require cause-and-effect analysis. Jot down assignments you have completed in other subjects that required cause-and-effect writing.

## Troubleshoot Essays

When planning a cause-and-effect essay, begin by listing the event or condition you want to explain. Then brainstorm to generate ideas about either its causes or its effects. Think carefully about the causes and effects you have listed. You may find it helpful to diagram or demonstrate these relationships graphically. Check to be sure you have not drawn any faulty conclusions. It may help to ask yourself the following questions.

| Faulty Cause-and-Effect Relationships | |
|---|---|
| **• Have you assumed a cause-effect relationship when there is none?** | *I can get into any college in the country; my mother knows everyone.* |
| **• Have you assumed only one cause when many causes may be appropriate?** | *The team lost the pennant because of the umpire's bad call.* |
| **• Have you incorrectly assumed a causal relationship between two events that immediately follow each other?** | *Unemployment skyrocketed once he began his term as governor. He should do the state a favor and resign.* |

Make sure you have not oversimplified cause-and-effect relationships. Seldom does an important effect have one, single cause. The statement "The North won the Civil War because it had superior manpower and resources" oversimplifies a complex event. One way to avoid oversimplification might be to write: "One of the major reasons the North won the Civil War was that the Union could survive staggering losses of men and equipment while the South could not."

Distinguish between long-term and short-term causes and effects. A short-term cause or effect is a single, immediately identifiable event; a long-term cause or effect may be less easy to pinpoint but in the long run is more important. For example, a short-term effect of a recession is an increase in unemployment; a long-term effect is a weakened economy.

Also distinguish between primary (most important) and secondary (ancillary) effects. In the following model, the author discusses some of the secondary effects of the 1941 German blitz campaign in Britain.

*A primary effect of the blitz was the death of British citizens.*

### *Literature Model*

By the end of January 1941, approximately sixty thousand British citizens had died in the war, nearly half of them civilians. The blitz was producing some curious side effects. ➡

The divorce rate in Britain reportedly was down some fifty percent, but the cities witnessed a distressing jump in the rate of juvenile crime, attributable primarily to the destruction of the schools and social centers, and the relaxation of parental authority as fathers went off to military service or worked overtime in defense factories. Londoners became much more willing to speak to strangers in the street. Telephone wires in the city repeatedly got crossed, allowing callers to listen in on one another's conversations. . . . Accidents abounded during the nightly blackouts; pedestrians kept getting poked in the eye by passersby with raised umbrellas; bicycles careened into one another or against unexpected obstacles, leading the government to post placards and take out newspaper ads warning people to wear white at night.

William K. Klingaman, *1941: Our Lives in a World on the Edge*

*Notice that the writer cites evidence supporting a cause-and-effect relationship.*

## Plan a Cause-and-Effect Essay

Use your cause-and-effect diagram as the basis for an outline. Review your notes and identify the most significant causes or effects. It may help to ask yourself the following questions: Who was responsible? Who was affected? Did the event have economic or social ramifications?

Compose a thesis statement that clearly states your topic. Because cause-and-effect essays need a logical structure, you will almost always write the essay in chronological order. You can also use reverse chronological order. For example, you might begin with an effect and trace it back to its original cause.

As you write, use paragraphs with strong, clear topic sentences and relevant supporting details. Be careful not to overstate your case. Many causal relationships cannot be proven conclusively. Consider, for example, the following: "The unresolved Iranian hostage situation caused President Carter to lose his bid for reelection." Qualifying an overstatement, in this case by changing *caused* to *may well have caused*, will add credibility to your essay.

### Drafting Tip

As you draft your essay, think about your audience. What do your readers know about the topic? What background information do they need?

### Journal Writing

Think about an occurrence in your life that set off a series of multiple effects. In your journal create a diagram that shows the relationship between the event and its effects on your life.

## Grammar Revising Tip

Many transitional expressions, such as *consequently, primarily,* and *finally,* are conjunctive adverbs and should be set off with commas. Refer to Lesson 10.7, page 438, for more information.

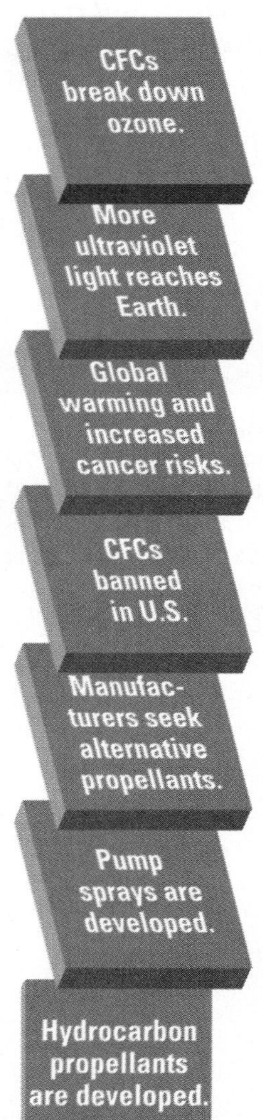
CFCs break down ozone.
More ultraviolet light reaches Earth.
Global warming and increased cancer risks.
CFCs banned in U.S.
Manufac-turers seek alternative propellants.
Pump sprays are developed.
Hydrocarbon propellants are developed.

# Write About Causal Relationships

Use transitional words and phrases, such as those listed in the chart below, to signal cause-and-effect relationships and to indicate degrees of certainty and levels of importance. You can also use repetition.

**Transitions in Cause-and-Effect Writing**

| Cause and Effect | Degrees of Certainty | Levels of Importance |
|---|---|---|
| as a result | certainly | above all |
| because | may | equally important |
| consequently | necessarily | finally |
| due to | perhaps | first |
| if . . . then | possibly | initially |
| leads to | probably | last |
| therefore | undoubtedly | primarily |
| thus | unquestionably | second |

Notice how transitional words and repetition are used in the following model to make the cause-and-effect relationships clear.

### *Model*

Many products such as hair sprays, shaving creams, and antiperspirants use chlorofluorocarbons (CFCs) as aerosol propellants. In the 1970s, however, scientists learned that CFCs have a devastating effect on the environment. CFCs break down ozone in the upper atmosphere, thus allowing increased levels of ultraviolet light to reach Earth. The intensified ultraviolet light rays, in turn, cause global warming and increased risks of skin cancer.

Consequently, in 1978, the United States government banned the use of CFCs as propellants, and in Europe and other parts of the world CFC usage began to decline. As a result, manufacturers of products requiring aerosol propellants have been forced to seek alternatives to CFCs.

The common pump spray is one solution. It offers environmental safety but is not as convenient as an aerosol and does not give the fine mist spray needed for certain products. Another alternative is the use of simple hydrocarbons, but although hydrocarbons don't harm the atmosphere, they're flammable and produce too wet a spray for certain products such as antiperspirants.

# 5.3 Writing Activities

## Write a Cause-and-Effect Essay

As part of a college application form, you are asked to write a brief autobiographical essay. You decide to focus on a single event and the many effects it had on your life. Before you begin drafting your essay, check your ideas for faulty conclusions. Then write a cause-and-effect essay explaining the effects of this event.

- Use chronological order as you describe the chain of events clearly.
- Use transitional words to signal causal relationships.
- Check your writing for overstatement and oversimplification.

**PURPOSE** To write an autobiographical essay showing cause and effect
**AUDIENCE** College admissions board
**LENGTH** 4 paragraphs

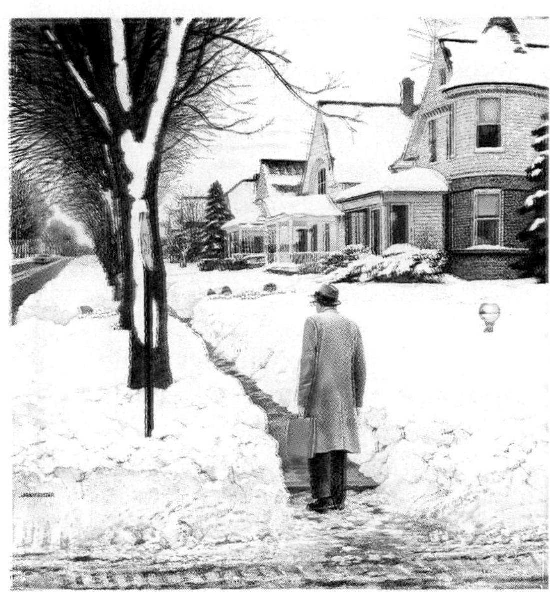

John Falter, *Snowball*, 1959

## Cross-Curricular: Art

Look carefully at John Falter's painting *Snowball*. How does the painter suggest a series of causes and effects? What is happening? What do you think will happen next? Write a cause-and-effect essay in which you speculate, or try to predict, how the situation pictured in the painting will unfold.

### Grammar Link

**Use a comma or semicolon with conjuctive adverbs.**

Use a semicolon to separate main clauses joined by a conjunctive adverb. Use a comma to set off conjunctive adverbs that begin a sentence or clause.

***Thus,*** *in a very real way, air conditioning has made possible the ascendancy of computerized civilization.*

Punctuate each sentence.

1. Early railroad lines shaped the American population moreover they were the main channels for commerce.
2. Undoubtedly the rail system expansions of the nineteenth century led to population redistribution.
3. As a result many cities in the West grew larger.
4. Consequently the U.S. legislature changed however these changes were not immediate.
5. Certainly the airplane has also had a major effect on population nevertheless the railroad's impact is still visible throughout America.

**See Lesson 21.5, pages 680–681, and Lesson 21.6, pages 682–690.**

LESSON 5.4

# Expository Writing
# Explaining by Using an Analogy

*An analogy is a comparison that makes an explanation easier to follow. Writers often use analogies to relate an unfamiliar topic to another more familiar one.*

*What comparison is the author making?*

**Model**

An electronic database works on the same principle as a telephone book. Like telephone books, electronic data bases list information, but with some significant differences. Perhaps you have had the experience of trying to find a telephone number when you have only the last name (Brown) and a street address. Using a telephone book, you have no alternative other than to look through all the listings for Brown until you find the correct address. Databases eliminate this drudgery. Using an electronic database, you could search by street, or, even better, combine the information you have (Brown plus street address) and ask for only those listings that include the name "Brown" and "14 Appletree Lane." Chances are, you would have your telephone number in seconds flat.

## Use an Analogy to Clarify Your Topic

An analogy is an extended comparison. You might use an analogy to compare two objects, people, places, or ideas. Rather than pointing out a single common trait between two topics, an analogy identifies multiple similarities. An effective analogy can be carried through one or several paragraphs, or even through an entire essay.

Analogies add color and variety to expository writing. They can help clarify complex, abstract, or unusual ideas. An analogy clarifies by comparing a difficult idea to a simpler one. In the following model, the writer uses an analogy to dramatize and explain the British colonization of Australia in 1787.

## *Literature Model*

One may liken this moment to the breaking open of a capsule. Upon the harbor the ships were now entering, European history had left no mark at all. Until the swollen sails and curvetting bows of the British fleet came round South Head, there were no dates. The Aborigines and the fauna around them had possessed the landscape since time immemorial, and no other human eye had seen them. Now the protective glass of distance broke, in an instant, never to be restored.

Robert Hughes, *The Fatal Shore*

*What two things does the writer compare?*

*Notice how the analogy is extended throughout the paragraph.*

*How does the last sentence tie the analogy together?*

Suppose you want to explain the process of writing and decide to use an analogy to clarify your explanation. Begin your search for an analogy by brainstorming. Ask yourself: What is the process of writing like? Is it like electricity? A journey? Mining? A bridge? In this beginning stage, write down all the ideas that occur to you.

One way to evaluate a possible analogy is to construct an analogy frame. List specific details from the topic you want to explain in one column. In the second column, list corresponding details from your analogous topic. The analogy frame lets you quickly assess whether you have enough material and whether your specific comparisons are substantial. The following analogy frame charts some of the similarities between the processes of mining and writing.

**Revising Tip**

Before revising, have a friend read your analogy draft and check that the comparison is clear. Revise to clarify.

**Analogy Frame**

| **Comparison:** Mining | **Comparison:** Writing |
|---|---|
| It requires you to dig deeply. | It requires you to dig deeply within yourself. |
| It is exhausting work. | It is exhausting work. |
| The more you mine, the more proficient you will become at it. | The more you write, the more proficient you will become at it. |

## Journal Writing

In your journal test an analogy by developing an analogy frame. List as many similarities as you can for each of your subjects.

**Grammar**

**Drafting Tip**

Many analogies will use the words *like* or *as* to join the two things being compared. Consult page 644 of the Usage Glossary to review the correct use of these words.

## Write an Analogy

Before you begin to draft an analogy, think about how you will arrange your details. Consider chronological order, spatial order, order of importance, or another organizational pattern that will suit your subject.

Begin your analogy with a topic sentence that clearly states what you're comparing. Use transitional words such as *so it is*, *like*, *similar to*, *just as*, and *likewise* to give your essay coherence. Notice the strong topic sentence and chronological arrangement used in the model below.

*What two things are being compared?*

*Notice how the phrases "enjoy my part" and "walk by the center of the stage" extend the analogy.*

***Literature Model***

The stretch of Hudson Street where I live is each day the scene of an intricate sidewalk ballet. I make my own first entrance into it a little after eight when I put out the garbage can, surely a prosaic occupation, but I enjoy my part, my little clang, as the droves of junior high school students walk by the center of the stage dropping candy wrappers.

Jane Jacobs, "The Uses of Sidewalks"

As you write, keep in mind what you want to explain. Don't allow the analogy to take charge. Suppose, for example, that Jane Jacobs had compared the physical stamina of her neighbors to that of ballerinas. Not only does the comparison not hold up, but it detracts from the purpose of the essay: to show the rhythm of life on Hudson Street.

*What two things does Conrad compare?*

*Notice the images that extend the analogy.*

***Literature Model***

Going up that river was like traveling back to the earliest beginnings of the world, when vegetation rioted the earth and the big trees were kings. An empty stream, a great silence, an impenetrable forest. The air was warm, thick, heavy, sluggish. . . . The broadening waters flowed through a mob of wooded islands; you lost your way on that river as you would in a desert, and butted all day long against shoals, trying to find the channel, till you thought yourself bewitched and cut off forever from everything you had known once—somewhere—far away—in another existence perhaps.

Joseph Conrad, *Heart of Darkness*

# 5.4 Writing Activities

## Write an Analogy

Write an editorial for your school newspaper in which you compare gossip to a virus. Construct an analogy frame to help you find similarities between a gossip and a virus. You might ask yourself, for example, how both gossip and a virus could effect the smooth functioning of a group or committee. Check your analogy frame for accuracy and continue writing your essay.

- Extend the analogy throughout your writing.
- Relate details in a logical order.
- Keep your analogy in mind, but don't let it overwhelm your writing.

**PURPOSE** To compare two things, using an analogy
**AUDIENCE** Readers of the school newspaper
**LENGTH** 2 paragraphs

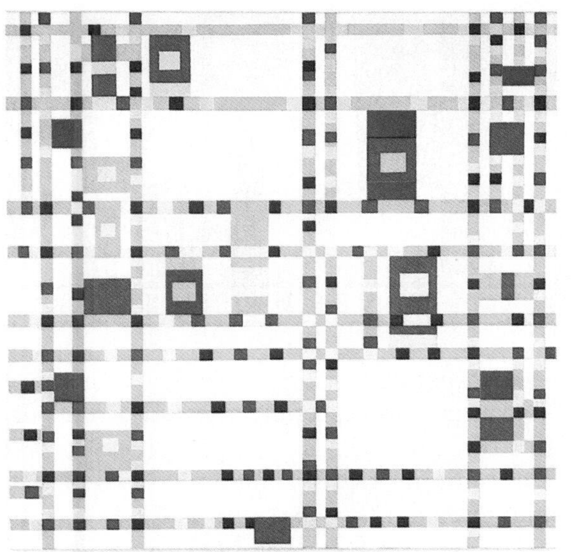

Piet Mondrian, *Broadway Boogie-Woogie*, 1942–43

## Cooperative Learning

Work with a small group of students to discuss the painting *Broadway Boogie-Woogie* by Piet Mondrian. What comparisons do you think the artist is making? Talk about different analogies that could be discussed. Each group member should then write a brief essay explaining the painting by using an analogy. Gather the essays and read them together. Discuss how exploring more than one analogy deepens your experience with the painting.

### Grammar Link

**Use pronouns that are consistent with the person of your writing.**

This sample from Jane Jacob's writing uses the first person:

***I** make **my** own first entrance into it a little after eight when **I** put out the garbage can . . .*

Rewrite each sentence below, using pronouns as indicated in the parentheses.

1. He looked at himself in the glass tube as though it were a mirror. (first person)
2. After collecting several mold samples, I placed labels on all of the vials that were mine. (third person, female)
3. She told herself that her experiment was bound to succeed. (second person)
4. You never expect that your results will completely contradict your hypothesis. (first person)
5. When you analyzed your data, you found that your assumptions were incorrect. (third person, male)

**See Lesson 10.2, page 403.**

LESSON 5.5

# Expository Writing
# Using Visuals That Speak

*Visuals can organize, clarify, and expand many different kinds of data. How many words would it take you to describe the drawing below? Do you think your words would have the same impact?*

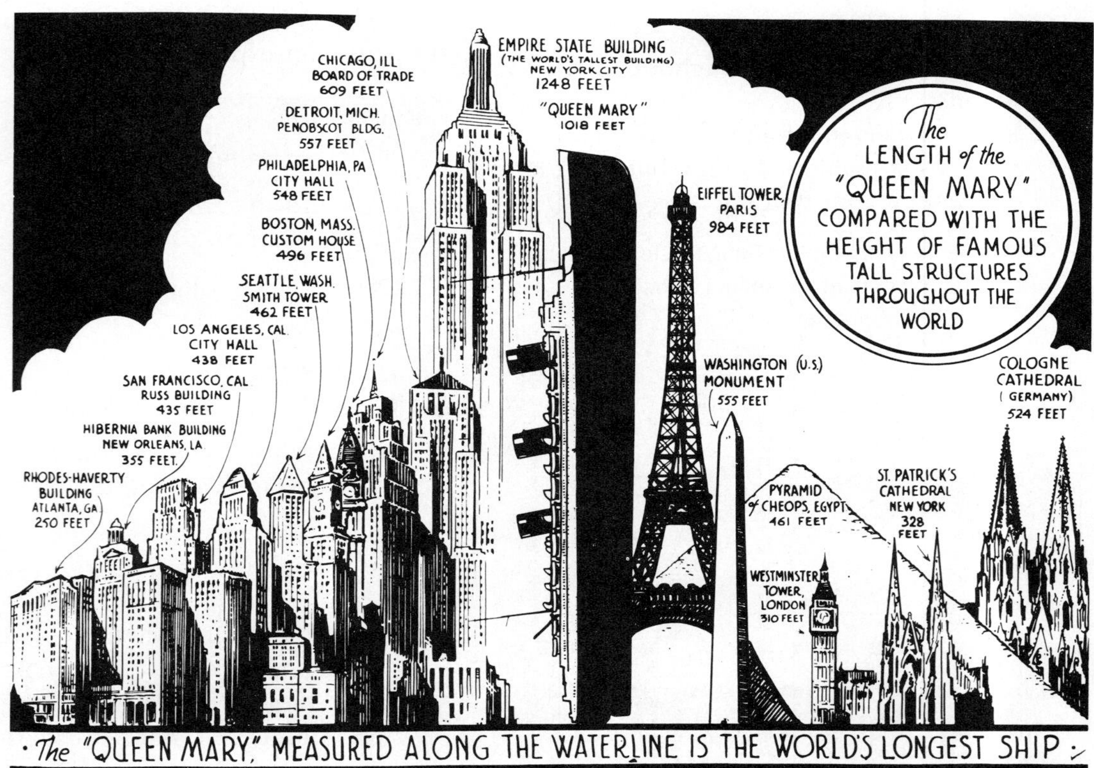


Well-organized and clearly expressed writing is the key to good communication. Still, an appropriate and carefully selected picture or visual can indeed be "worth a thousand words." Graphs, charts, maps, time lines, diagrams, or slides can transform a simple rehearsal of facts into a powerful and dramatic statement. For example, an essay could easily state that the *Queen Mary* is 1,018 feet long, but readers gain a far more vivid impression of that statistic when they see the scale drawing above.

## Use Visuals to Enhance a Message

A visual representation of data can often help you illustrate an important point. Readers appreciate visuals that condense complicated information and make patterns quickly recognizable. A history report on the American economy after World War II, for example, can have greater impact if you include a chart depicting the Gross National Product before and after the war. Similarly, a map showing how high-pressure systems affect the jet stream will clarify a report on weather patterns.

Visuals can be used to illustrate a variety of concepts and abstract ideas. For example, during the fourteenth century, the bubonic plague struck Europe, leaving millions of people dead in its wake. This idea can easily be expressed in words, but if you want to dramatize the extent of the devastation over a period of time, you might use a graph like the one shown below.

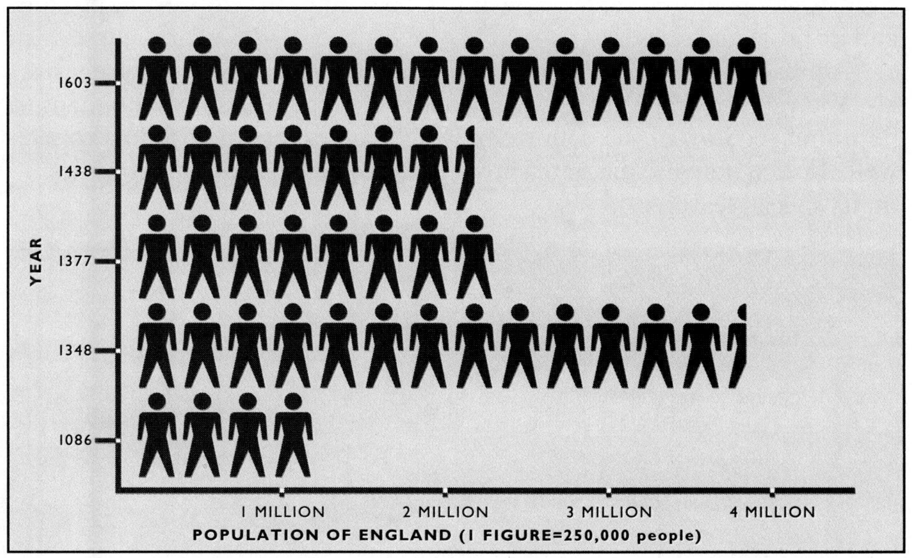


Strong visuals can convey in a glance the essence of an idea that might take several paragraphs to express in words. Visuals work particularly well with statistical data, comparative information, changes or patterns recorded over an extended period of time, complex processes, and geographical relationships.

### Journal Writing

Brainstorm a list of different types of visuals. For example, you might include graph styles, such as bar graphs, circle graphs, pictographs, and so on. Next to each type of visual, jot down some ideas about the kinds of data the visual can effectively express.

# Create a Presentation

**Grammar**

**Drafting Tip**

A clear, concise title can help focus your readers on the information you want them to get out of a visual. See Lesson 20.2, page 664, to review capitalization rules for titles.

In business writing, visuals play a crucial role in communicating information. Learning to use effective visuals will help you meet writing goals at school and in the workplace.

Imagine, for example, that you represent a small computer company that has developed a pocket computer called "Grades at a Glance" which allows users to record their grades by subject. At the press of a button, students can learn their current cumulative grade in any subject. Your company wants to interest a larger manufacturer in financing the production and marketing of your product. Your task is to create a vivid, powerful presentation that both explains and sells your product.

Think about the kind of information you must communicate. You need to talk about how the computer works, what it looks like, what special features it includes, and who will buy it. You also need to tell prospective backers your estimate of how much the computer will cost to produce and its projected sales.

A presentation of this type provides many opportunities to use visuals. You can use graphs to project production costs and sales, and maps to point out sections of the country in which you expect the product to sell well. Notice how the diagram shows the product and focuses attention on its special features.

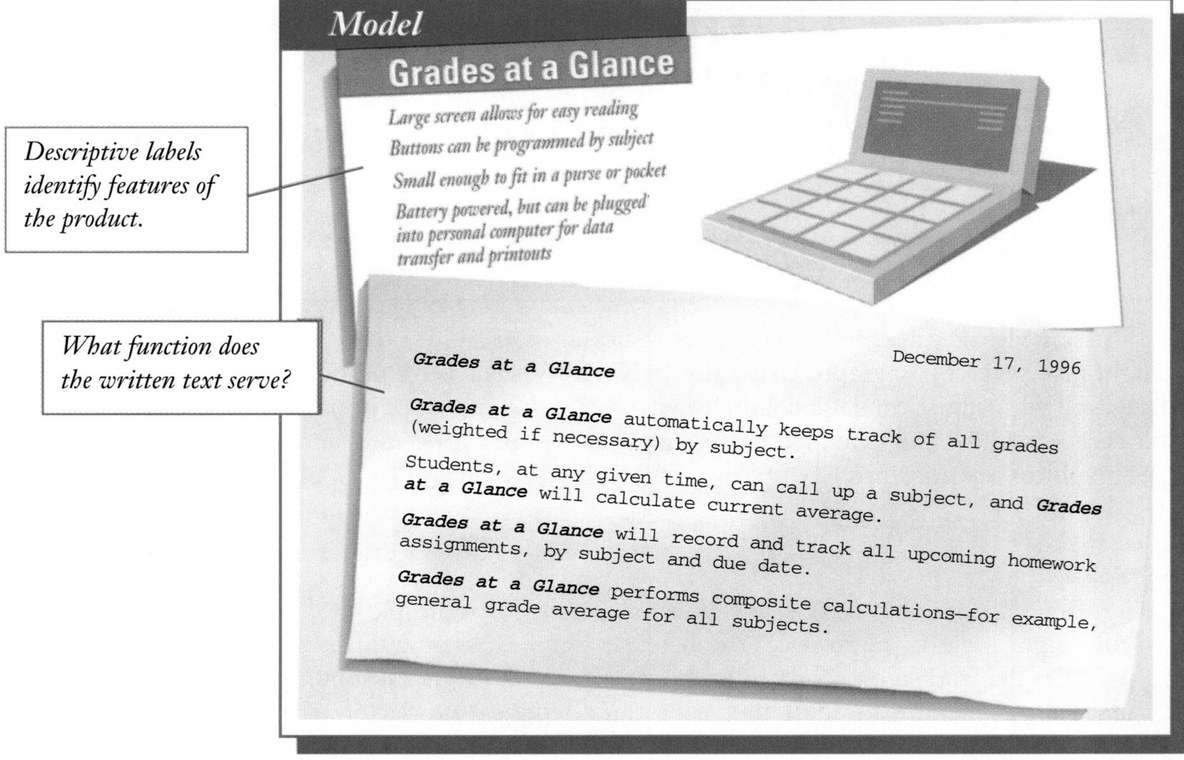

*Model*

Descriptive labels identify features of the product.
What function does the written text serve?
Grades at a Glance
Large screen allows for easy reading
Buttons can be programmed by subject
Small enough to fit in a purse or pocket
Battery powered, but can be plugged into personal computer for data transfer and printouts



**Grades at a Glance** December 17, 1996

**Grades at a Glance** automatically keeps track of all grades (weighted if necessary) by subject.

Students, at any given time, can call up a subject, and **Grades at a Glance** will calculate current average.

**Grades at a Glance** will record and track all upcoming homework assignments, by subject and due date.

**Grades at a Glance** performs composite calculations—for example, general grade average for all subjects.

# 5.5 Writing Activities

## Present Survey Results in a Visual

Create a survey that will interest readers of your school newspaper. Base your survey on one of these topics, or use your own ideas: Whom do you admire most? How many former U.S. presidents can you name? Rank school activities in order of preference.

As you analyze the results of your survey, think about how you can use a visual to convey information to your readers.

- Choose a visual form that matches the data you are presenting.
- Use a title and clear labels to focus readers' attention.
- Use your text to support and explain your visual.

**PURPOSE** To present survey results using a visual and writing
**AUDIENCE** Newspaper readers
**LENGTH** 2–3 paragraphs

### COMPUTER OPTION

You may use your computer to help you create a visual to show the results of your survey. Check to see what graphic capabilities are available on your personal computer. Most database and many word-processing programs include graph-making functions. You can also use drawing software to create your own images, "clip art" software to cut and paste images into your work, or a scanner to add images from other sources, such as newspapers, photographs, and encyclopedias.

### Grammar Link

**Capitalize important words in the title of a visual.**

Do not capitalize prepositions, articles, or conjunctions shorter than five letters in a title, unless they are the first or last word of the title. Capitalize the first word of a subtitle following a colon.

*Grades at a Glance*

Capitalize each of the following visual titles.

1. building the great wall of china
2. distribution of income across the population: the united states from 1900 to 1990
3. pennant winners in the American league, 1960 to 1990
4. a bird's eye view of Yosemite national park
5. how a hydroelectric dam works
6. the ages of the signers of the declaration of independence
7. America's most popular television programs, by region
8. an artist's view of a volcano exploding
9. playgrounds: number and acreage by state, 1985 and 1995
10. important milestones in the history of flight

**See Lesson 20.2, pages 660–665.**

LESSON

5.6

# Expository Writing
# Explaining Problems, Proposing Solutions

*Expository writing can present clear and creative solutions to all kinds of problems.*

A good problem solver is inventive, persistent, and flexible. Engineer, poet, and architect R. Buckminster Fuller explored an incredible variety of modern problems. His 1933 car design, the Dymaxion, offered such innovative features as a conic front to reduce wind resistance and a three-wheel design to facilitate parking in awkward spaces. Lloyd Steven Sieden gives us a glimpse of the thought process that led Fuller to add front-wheel drive to the Dymaxion.

### *Literature Model*

Fuller discovered that front-wheel-drive pulling propulsion provided an enormous advantage over the commonplace rear-wheel-drive pushing, and he illustrated that advantage using an ordinary wheelbarrow. When passing over obstacles, a wheelbarrow pushed from behind can be dangerous, as its front wheel strikes an obstacle and it lurches backward into the stomach of the person pushing. However, if that same wheelbarrow is turned around and pulled, a person actually lifts it over bumps as it is pulled, and the problem disappears.

Once the simple beauty of that shift became apparent to Bucky, he immediately reconsidered his ideas and designed his vehicle to include a single, rear steering tire pulled by two front tires so that it would embody a more natural steering pattern as well as the propulsion strategy of the pulled wheelbarrow.

Lloyd Steven Sieden, *Buckminster Fuller's Universe: An Appreciation*

## Identify Problems and Solutions

The first step to finding a creative and effective solution is to identify and limit the problem. Consider the following dilemma. Two people share a bedroom. One wants to sleep; the other wants to read. If the reader turns on the light, the other person will find it impossible to sleep.

Begin by identifying the problem. State the general problem first. Then narrow your scope, and identify a specific problem to solve.

| General Problem | Specific Problem |
|---|---|
| People need a way to read in bed without disturbing other people sleeping in the same room. | Find a way to illuminate only the page being read without excess or undirected light falling on someone who's sleeping. |

After identifying the problem, brainstorm a list of possible solutions. Try not to limit yourself; keep an open mind and let your ideas flow. Compare the advantages, disadvantages, and practicality of each. A chart may provide a useful focus for your evaluation.

| Possible Solutions | Evaluations of Possible Solutions |
|---|---|
| Print books with luminous ink that will glow in the dark. | Present books don't have luminous ink. Books would have to be reprinted. |
| Put a smaller, lower wattage bulb in the bedside lamp. | Reducing light from bulb would make reading uncomfortable and cause eyestrain. |
| Put a narrow, cone-shaped shade on bedside lamp to focus light more directly on page. | Reader would have to sit too close to bedside table in order to get sufficient light for reading. |
| Design a light-weight lamp that can be clipped onto a book. Attach to this lamp an opaque shade that directs light only onto the page. | Solution: 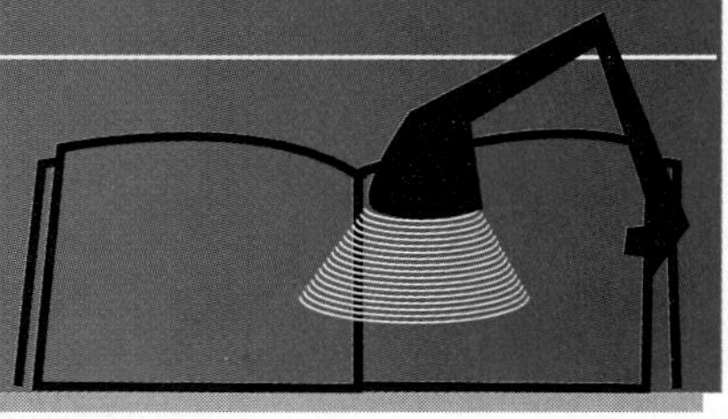 |

### Journal Writing

Think about something that you recently complained about at home or at school. What problem had you identified? In your journal describe the problem in general terms. Then state a specific problem that you could solve.

# Write a Problem-Solution Essay

**Revising Tip**

When revising, be sure to develop your proposal logically. Have you demonstrated that the problem is significant? Have you shown that your solution is practical?

After you have defined and limited the problem, brainstormed to develop possible solutions, and filled in a problem-and-solution chart to evaluate your ideas, you are ready to draft your essay. As a first step, identify the most intriguing ideas in your notes. You may decide to emphasize an interesting problem, highlight an ingenious solution, or treat both aspects equally. Your choice will be determined, in part, by your readers and your assessment of their needs and interests. They may need to be convinced that a problem exists. Sometimes the problem will be obvious, but the solution will require extensive explanation.

Think about how you will engage your readers. An example, anecdote, or even a statistic or fact can help grab your readers' attention. A strong thesis statement should zero in on the problem. Review your chart to find supporting details. Keep your purpose in mind, choose language that will speak directly to your audience, and use transitions to link your ideas. The model below was developed from the chart on page 231.

***Model***

*Does the writer succeed in engaging the reader in the opening paragraph?*

Most people have nights when they just can't sleep. Often, that's a good time to read, but people who share a room with others can't even turn to a book for relief during a long, sleepless night. Switching on a light that's bright enough to read by will awaken anyone nearby. Then there are two people who can't sleep, and one of them will be really grouchy because he or she was awakened from a good night's sleep by an inconsiderate insomniac. Now there's a solution to this vexing problem: the battery-powered clip-on reading light.

*Which is given more emphasis in this proposal, the problem or the solution?*

The battery-powered clip-on reading light has many advantages over the bedside lamp and other lighting fixtures. First, the lamp is lightweight, so it can be clipped right to the book instead of sitting two or three feet away on a table. The clip-on reading light uses batteries, thus eliminating potential problems with tangled electrical cords. Because it is located just a few inches from the page, only a small amount of light is required for comfortable reading. In addition, a well-designed, opaque shade focuses the light on the book where it's needed, rather than scattering it all over the room. The combination of these characteristics gives the insomniac one hope in a long, dismal night: a chance to read a good book, or even a dull one that's sure to induce sleep.

*What facts or evidence has the writer included to illustrate the advantages of the clip-on light?*

# 5.6 Writing Activities

## Write a Problem-Solution Essay

Write a letter to a local newspaper proposing a solution to one of the following problems or another of your choosing: graffiti in your school or community; the unfair advantage of height in the sport of basketball; school buildings sitting unused for three months each year; an underused public transportation system.

Make sure your letter explains the problem and tells how you think it can be solved.

- Identify and limit the problem.
- List and evaluate possible solutions.
- Choose an emphasis that makes sense for your topic.

**PURPOSE** To write a letter presenting an effective solution to a community problem
**AUDIENCE** Newspaper readers
**LENGTH** 3–4 paragraphs

## Cooperative Learning

Do you have a pet peeve? Work with a small group to brainstorm solutions to an everyday problem, such as people talking during a movie. Discuss each solution, using a chart like the one on page 231. Bounce ideas off your group members and evaluate all of their ideas carefully. Then work together to write an essay in which you propose a solution for this annoyance.

### Grammar Link

**Make subjects and verbs agree.**

Make sure that the subject and verb agree, even when intervening expressions, such as *in addition to*, *as well as*, or *plus*, appear between the subject and verb. These intervening expressions do not affect the number of the subject.

*You may find that a **chart**, together with your ideas, **provides** a useful focus for your evaluation.*

Use the form of the verb in parentheses that correctly completes each sentence.

1. His ideas, together with his stamina, _____ (make, makes) him a brilliant problem solver.
2. After many experiments, the scientist, as well as her colleagues, _____(realize/realizes) that they need to redefine the problem.
3. You will find that those articles, plus the book I lent you, _____ (give/gives) a full overview of the subject.
4. A single troublesome problem, accompanied by a list of possible solutions, _____ (provide/provides) a good starting place for an essay.
5. Your insights, in addition to your curiosity, _____ (prepare/prepares) you to find solutions.

**See Lesson 16.6, page 574.**

LESSON 5.7

# Expository Writing
# Writing an Analysis

"Hey! 'Made in the U.S.A.'!"

*A thoughtful, logical analysis begins with a clear perspective and then digs into a subject to find relevant ideas and details.*

Analysis reflects the writer's perspective. Consider these statistics: Between 1965 and 1980, American motor vehicle production dropped by about 28%. During the same period, production in Western Europe and Japan increased by about 26% and 488% respectively. A politician, an economist, and a historian might each interpret these figures differently. In the model below, columnist Brock Yates offers his analysis.

### Literature Model

Not one of us enjoys witnessing the current agonies of the Big Three. The broad economic ramifications of their flagging business aside, it is painful to listen to the incessant gloating of our associates from Europe and Japan as they revel in U.S. automotive misfortunes.

Still, there is no disputing their reasons for smugness. Detroit fell woefully behind the Japanese in the 1970s and 1980s, and no amount of chauvinism can refute that reality.

Fortunately, the system is beginning to correct itself. . . . Moreover, a depressing record of shoddy quality is being diligently corrected. The Big Three have long enjoyed world-class climate-control systems and automatic transmissions, and this year 56 percent of domestic-brand cars will offer driver-side air bags, as opposed to but 8 percent of the Japanese transplants. Our products rank high by most measurements of safety, and our fuel-economy standards are surprisingly good when compared with all but the smallest imports. These are all reasons for optimism, but hard times still lie ahead.

Brock Yates, "I'm innocent, pal," *Car and Driver*

*What is the main idea of this essay?*

*What is the writer's perspective?*

## Learn to Analyze

Analysis occurs anytime you look at a subject closely from a particular perspective and interpret what you see. When you examine a short story by sorting images into meaningful categories, you're analyzing. When you interpret statistical information, you're analyzing. In the previous model, Brock Yates analyzed the decline of the American automobile industry by viewing it from the perspective of American workmanship. In the model that follows, the writer examines the United States automobile industry from the perspective of how it is managed.

### Drafting Tip

As you draft, make sure your readers understand your perspective. Give background information that will help your readers understand your reasoning.

### *Literature Model*

The inability of Detroit's carmakers to stem the Japanese advance has raised unsettling questions about America's ability to compete in manufacturing and fueled an often emotive debate about America's economic decline. In fact, the failure of Detroit's carmakers at home may have more to do with their sclerotic bureaucracies, acrimonious labor relations, and myopic bosses than any general American inability to keep up. GM's and Ford's foreign operations, managed more nimbly because of their distance from Detroit, have been skillful enough to ride a booming European market, though both companies have also benefitted from restrictions on the Japanese in Europe. Other American manufacturers, such as Xerox and many computer companies, have competed successfully against Japanese rivals by learning from them.

Cocooned in Detroit, the Big Three's top managers have been less responsive. Too often GM, Ford, or Chrysler have opted for a quick fix diversification or management fad. And, most ominously, they seem to have lost touch with the American consumer.

*The Economist*, April 1990

*How does the perspective offered here differ from that of Brock Yates?*

### Journal Writing

Imagine that you are looking at the latest model of a high-priced sports car. First consider the point of view of an artist, then that of a parent with four young children, and finally that of a professional car racer. Jot down what you might notice looking at the sports car from these perspectives.

## Analyze a Text

When you are asked to analyze a subject or a text you will often be given a perspective from which to base your analysis. In an American history class, for example, you might be asked to analyze the April 14, 1912, *Titanic* tragedy from the perspective of its emotional impact on the American public. In literature class you might be asked to analyze the tone in Langston Hughes's poem "Theme for English B." Suppose you were asked to analyze the following text from your own perspective. How would you begin?

### *Literature Model*

Whenever she looked at Joy this way, she could not help but feel it would have been better if the child had not taken the Ph.D. . . . Mrs. Hopewell thought it was nice for girls to go to school and have a good time but Joy had "gone through." . . . The doctors had told Mrs. Hopewell that with the best care, Joy might not see forty-five. She had a weak heart. Joy had made it plain that if it had not been for this condition, she would be far away from these red hills and good country people. She would be in a university, lecturing to people who knew very well what she was talking about. And Mrs. Hopewell could very well picture her there, looking like a scarecrow and lecturing to more of the same. Here she went all day in a six-year-old skirt and a yellow sweatshirt with a cowboy on a horse embossed on it. She thought this was funny; Mrs. Hopewell thought it was idiotic and showed simply that she was still a child. She was brilliant but she didn't have a grain of sense. It seemed to Mrs. Hopewell that every year she grew less like other people and more like herself—bloated, rude, and squint-eyed. She said such strange things! To her own mother she had said—without warning, without excuse, standing up in the middle of a meal with her face purple and her mouth half full—"Woman! do you ever look inside? Do you ever look inside and see what you are not? . . ." She had cried sinking down again and staring at her plate, "Malebranche was right: we are not our own light!" Mrs. Hopewell had no idea to this day what brought that on. She had only made the remark, hoping Joy would take it in, that a smile never hurt anyone.

Flannery O'Connor, "Good Country People"

## Choose a Perspective

First, reread the story so that you know where the excerpted section occurs and how it fits in with the overall content of the story. In this case, the paragraph appears midway in the story. It focuses on the character of Joy, a thirty-year-old woman who wears an artificial leg, the result of injuries incurred in a childhood hunting accident. Joy thinks of herself as an intellectual, devoid of romantic and childish illusions. Joy takes great pride in her ability to see and face the truth. In the excerpt on page 236, Joy is speaking to her mother, Mrs. Hopewell, a cheerful woman with a generally optimistic, somewhat naive, philosophy of life. The interchange between Joy and her mother takes place just prior to the arrival of Manley Pointer, the young man who deceives Joy.

As you consider various perspectives, keep your mind open to new ideas. What intrigues you about the story? Characterization? Tone? Prose style? Setting? Reread the story several times. Ask questions, take notes, and make as many connections as possible. You might want to use a chart like the one below to develop a list and test possible approaches to your analysis.

**Grammar**
**Drafting Tip**

Active verbs can strengthen your analysis. Instead of saying that a character was influenced by jealousy, you might say that jealousy drove the character to action. See Lesson 15.7 on page 553 to review the voice of verbs.

**Possible Perspectives**

| Type | Focus | Elements |
|---|---|---|
| Character Analysis | Joy | Major traits, appearance, action, what she says about herself, what others say about her, change and development |
| Imagery | Blindness | Meaning and effect, frequency and type, connection with other images |
| Dramatic Irony | Joy | Her perception of herself, how others perceive her, what her behavior reveals |

### Journal Writing

Think of a historical topic that interests you. Jot down perspectives you might use to analyze that topic. Indicate the perspective you think would provide the most interesting approach.

## Put Your Perspective in Writing

To begin drafting your analysis, consider how your reading relates to ideas you have studied in class. Your teacher will probably expect to see classroom discussion topics reflected in your analysis. Suppose that for the last several weeks your teacher has stressed the use of irony—the contrast between appearance and reality—in short stories. As you review your class notes, you see that you had already noticed irony in the excerpt. You may then decide to use irony, specifically dramatic irony, as the perspective from which you will analyze the excerpted text.

Compose a thesis statement that clearly states the main idea of your essay. Often, limiting your topic in this way can be one of the most difficult parts of this type of assignment. Use your thesis statement to guide your choice of supporting details. When appropriate, quote from the text.

Notice how the writer in the model below uses the perspective of dramatic irony in the opening paragraphs of an analysis of Flannery O'Connor's short story, "Good Country People."

### *Student Model*

*Find the thesis statement in this opening paragraph.*

*Notice how choosing a perspective helps to organize this type of essay.*

Joy Hopewell, a thirty-year-old woman disabled since childhood, takes great comfort in her advanced degrees and regards with unconcealed disdain the uneducated "good country people" around her. Joy considers her mother naive and superficial, Mrs. Freeman a dim-witted busybody, and the Bible salesman, Manley Pointer, a fool and buffoon. Ironically, while Joy sees herself as so much more perceptive than the residents of the small southern town where she lives, of all the characters in Flannery O'Connor's short story, she is the most blind, the most superficial in her assessment of people. Mrs. Hopewell correctly saw that as Joy grew older, she grew more bitter and less able to see ("squint-eyed") what was going on around her.

The test of Joy's perception and ability to "look and see" what she is not comes in the person of the duplicitous Manley Pointer. Joy sizes him up, assumes he is well-meaning but stupid, and agrees to talk with him only to prove to herself her own moral and intellectual superiority. Manley Pointer, by contrast, observes Joy carefully, "like a child watching a new fantastic animal at the zoo." Joy's need to feel herself superior to compensate for her physical handicap blinds her to the world around her and, in particular, to the wiles of Manley Pointer.

# 5.7 Writing Activities

## Write an Analysis

For a school art writing contest, write an analysis of the painting *La Méridienne* (Midday Nap) from the perspective of mood. Consider color and shape, positioning of figures, placement of tools, the activity of the animals, the artist's use of texture and light, and other factors that influence the mood of the painting.

- Make your perspective clear in your thesis statement.
- Support your analysis with specific examples.
- Revise to exclude details that do not relate to your thesis statement.

**PURPOSE** To analyze van Gogh's painting from the perspective of mood
**AUDIENCE** Writing contest judges
**LENGTH** 2–4 paragraphs

## Cooperative Learning

Working with three other students, choose a current political topic and discuss various perspectives from which you might analyze the topic. Each group member will write a brief analysis of the subject from a different perspective. Then share your work with the group and discuss how perspective affects the impact of each essay.

Vincent van Gogh, *La Méridienne*, 1889–1890

### Grammar Link

**Use *good* and *bad* as adjectives.**

*Badly* is always an adverb; *well* can be used as an adverb or an adjective.

*. . . our fuel-economy standards are surprisingly* ***good*** *when compared with all but the smallest imports.*

Complete each sentence with the correct word in parentheses.

1. Because she was coming down with a cold, Maggie did not look _____ (good/well).
2. Her doctor gave her some _____ (good/well) advice when he recommended rest.
3. She knew that she had a _____ (bad/badly) flu.
4. Maggie felt _____ (bad/badly) that she missed dance practice due to fatigue.
5. Her cough sounded _____ (bad/badly).
6. She knew that if she had gone, she would have danced _____ (bad/badly).
7. If she recovers in time, she knows that she will perform _____ (good/well) at the upcoming recital.
8. Her medication mixes _____ (bad/badly) with rigorous exercise.

**See Lesson 18.5, page 621.**

LESSON

# 5.8 Expository Writing
# Writing a Business Letter

*A business letter is a formal communication tool that you can adapt to meet many specific purposes. As you follow a career path after high school, you will have many opportunities to use business letters effectively.*

You will often write business letters to people you do not know. Your writing makes a first impression for you. A well-organized, succinct letter will encourage a prompt and positive response. Consider how this letter's tone and content reflect the writer's enthusiasm and competence.

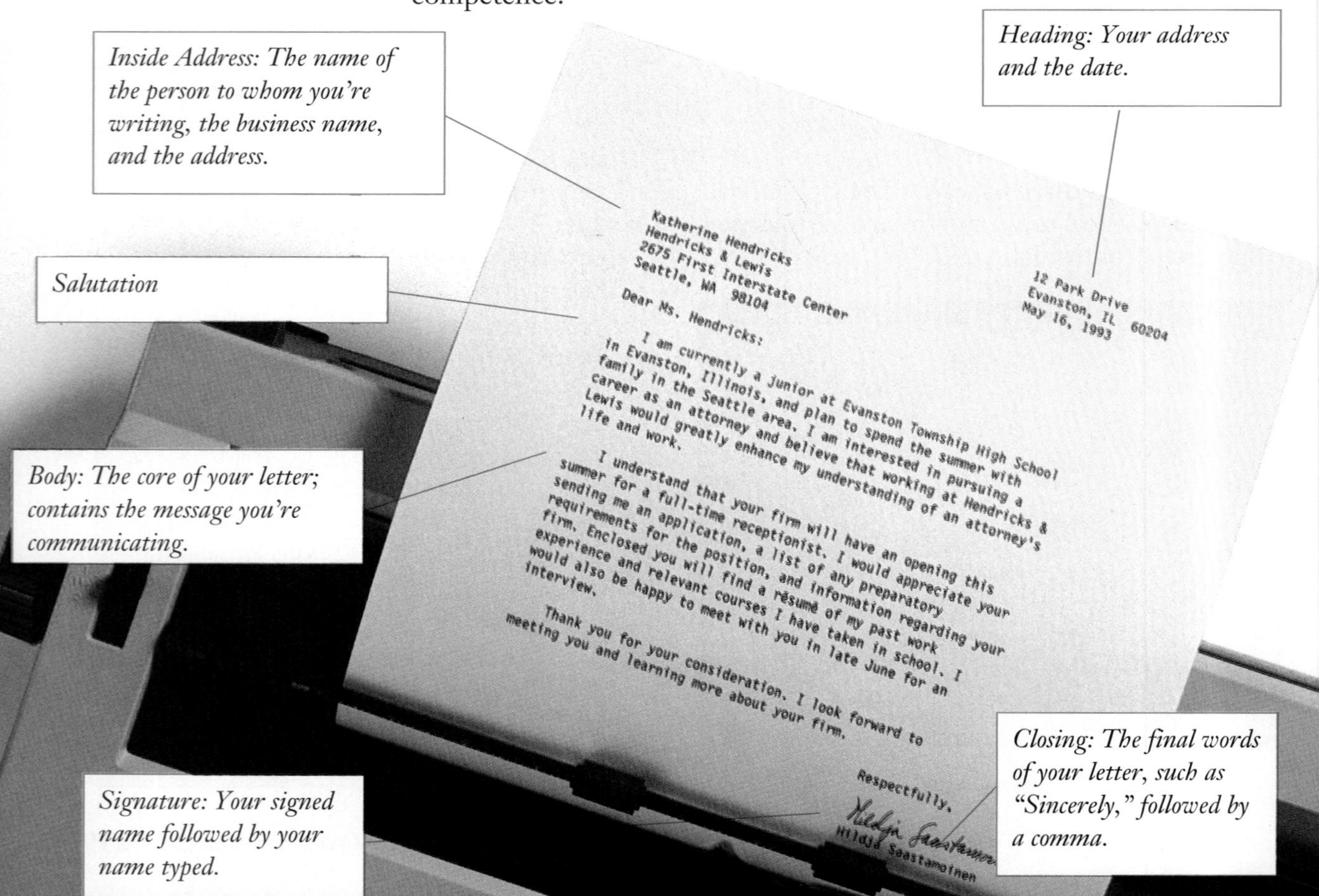
Inside Address: The name of the person to whom you're writing, the business name, and the address.
Heading: Your address and the date.
Salutation
Body: The core of your letter; contains the message you're communicating.
Closing: The final words of your letter, such as "Sincerely," followed by a comma.
Signature: Your signed name followed by your name typed.

12 Park Drive
Evanston, IL 60204
May 16, 1993

Katherine Hendricks
Hendricks & Lewis
2675 First Interstate Center
Seattle, WA 98104

Dear Ms. Hendricks:

I am currently a junior at Evanston Township High School in Evanston, Illinois, and plan to spend the summer with family in the Seattle area. I am interested in pursuing a career as an attorney and believe that working at Hendricks & Lewis would greatly enhance my understanding of an attorney's life and work.

I understand that your firm will have an opening this summer for a full-time receptionist. I would appreciate your sending me an application, a list of any preparatory requirements for the position, and information regarding your firm. Enclosed you will find a résumé of my past work experience and relevant courses I have taken in school. I would also be happy to meet with you in late June for an interview.

Thank you for your consideration. I look forward to meeting you and learning more about your firm.

Respectfully,

Hildja Saastamoinen

## Know Why to Write a Business Letter

A business letter is a formal letter written either to communicate information or to request action. Business letters provide a direct and effective means of communicating on a wide range of topics. Knowing how to write a business letter is a skill you'll find useful throughout your life.

Use the business letter format whenever you want to inquire, make a request, complain, order a product or make an order adjustment, apply for employment, or explain your views on a subject. Whatever your specific purpose, whether to ask about a job opening as Hildja did on page 240 or to protest your state representative's recent vote on an important issue, business letters have one universal purpose: to get results.

| Types of Business Letters | | |
|---|---|---|
| **Inquiry or Order Letter** | **Complaint Letter** | **Opinion Letter** |
| • Be brief.<br>• State request clearly.<br>• Give reasons for your request.<br>• Make your request specific and reasonable.<br>• Include your phone number or a self-addressed, stamped, return envelope. | • Identify exact product or service.<br>• Accurately describe the problem.<br>• Request a specific solution.<br>• Be polite.<br>• Keep a copy of your letter until your complaint has been addressed. | • Identify and summarize the issue.<br>• State your opinion and support it with reasons and facts.<br>• Summarize your main points and, if possible, offer a solution. |

When you write a business letter, always keep your specific goal or purpose clearly in mind. Business letters are not necessarily about business, but they do mean business, so don't let them wander off the subject. Because the tone of the business letter is formal, avoid slang, contractions, and clichés. Do not use excessively wordy expressions. "Thank you," for example, is preferable to "I wish to express my gratitude." Remember to be courteous and polite, regardless of your purpose.

### Editing Tip

Always edit business letters very carefully. Errors in spelling, punctuation, or typing may undermine the effectiveness of your message.

### Journal Writing

Think about a business letter you might want to write. List the person or organization to whom you will address your letter and the reason you want to write it.

## Presenting Tip

If you are using a word processor to create a neat final copy, stick with one font. Using too many fonts will give your letter a more casual, informal look. Choose a font that looks serious and traditional instead of one that's "fun."

# Format a Business Letter

Business letters are usually written in one of two forms: the modified block form or the full block form. The letter on page 240 follows the modified block form. In this format, the heading, closing, and signature are aligned along the right margin. All other elements are aligned along the left margin. Paragraphs are indented.

In letters using the full block form, all elements are aligned along the left margin. Paragraphs are not indented. Both full block and modified block form allow extra space between paragraphs and each element of the letter. In both formats, letters should be single spaced. Leave extra space for your signature between the closing and your typed name. The letter below uses the full block form.

144 Franklin Street
Jamaica Plain, MA 02130
September 30, 1993

Sports Editor
Boston Globe
135 Wm. T. Morrissey Blvd.
Boston, MA 02106

Dear Editor:

*Notice the clear topic sentence stating the subject of the letter.*

I think there should be playoffs in high school football. First, there should be playoff games between the top four teams in each of the six divisions. The winners would be division champions and eligible for the State playoffs.

*How does the writer anticipate and solve potential problems?*

The playoffs between the six division champions should be held at Foxboro Stadium and begin two weeks from the day the teams last played. The three playoff games would take place in the following order: Division 1 vs. Division 4, Division 2 vs. Division 5, and Division 3 vs. Division 6. The three winning teams would all be given one week's rest. For the State Championship, the first two teams to play against each other will be determined by lottery. Each of the three winning teams would pick one of three tickets. The tickets would be marked REST, PLAY, and PLAY. The two teams with the PLAY tickets would compete against each other first. The winner of this game would play the one remaining team for the State championship.

Sincerely,

Kyvah Johnston

# 5.8 Writing Activities

## Write a Business Letter

What would you like to see on television that is not currently available? Think about a concrete suggestion you would like to make for new programming, and write a serious business letter to a network that you think will be responsive to your idea. Explain your suggestion clearly, and tell why you think it would benefit the network. Send it, and keep a copy of your letter until you have received a response.

- Choose direct, concise language to communicate your idea.
- Use a formal tone.
- Set up your letter in the modified or full block form.

**PURPOSE** To write a business letter suggesting a programming idea
**AUDIENCE** Television network programmers
**LENGTH** 2–3 paragraphs

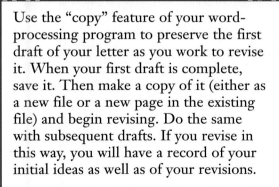

### COMPUTER OPTION

Use the "copy" feature of your word-processing program to preserve the first draft of your letter as you work to revise it. When your first draft is complete, save it. Then make a copy of it (either as a new file or a new page in the existing file) and begin revising. Do the same with subsequent drafts. If you revise in this way, you will have a record of your initial ideas as well as of your revisions.

### Grammar Link

**Punctuate a business letter properly.**

Use commas correctly in addresses. Use a colon after the salutation of a business letter, and follow the closing with a comma.

*Evanston, IL 60204*
*Dear Ms. Hendricks:*
*Respectfully,*

Punctuate each address, salutation, or closing.

1. Dear Dr. Brownell
2. Yours
3. Ada OK 74820
4. Dear Consumer Affairs Department
5. Bellevue WA 98004
6. Dear Ms. Wallis
7. Arlington VA 22209
8. Dear Division of Motor Vehicles
9. To Whom It May Concern
10. Sincerely

**See Lesson 21.4, page 679, and Lesson 21.6, page 689.**

LESSON

5.9

# Expository Writing
# Comparing and Contrasting Opinions

*Carefully weighing evidence will help you evaluate contrasting opinions.*

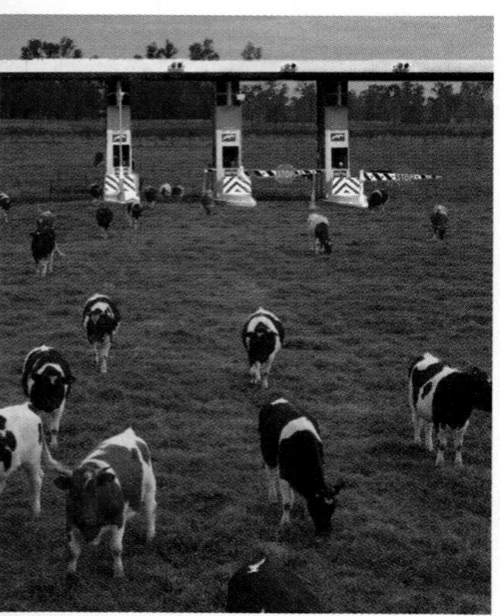

To evaluate contrasting viewpoints, you need to assess each opinion thoroughly. Consider the grazing-rights debate. For more than a century, some ranchers have grazed their cattle on public land, paying a fee for the privilege. Critics claim that ranchers do not pay fair market value for the use of this land.

*What facts and reasons does the writer use to support his point of view?*

### *Literature Model*

Last year, the Government's grazing management program registered a net loss of $50 million. This subsidy helped support the 23,000 ranchers who lease permits to graze on 268 million acres of public land in the 16 Western states—ranchers who produce less than 5 percent of the country's beef.

In the valley where I live in southwestern New Mexico, a neighbor bought a ranch 10 years ago. He bought 80 acres of private land. Attached to this was a Forest Service permit to graze 280 cows on 38,400 acres in the Gila National Forest. The permit cost him about $1,000 per cow—$280,000, which he paid to the previous owner (not to the Forest Service). He spent $100,000 more to buy cattle to stock his ranch. From his point of view, he has spent too much money—and he works too hard—to be considered a welfare recipient.

My friend also claims, as do most ranchers, that the difficulty of grazing on rugged Federal land—plus the costs he must share with the Government to build fences and to provide water tanks—brings him well up to the price of a private lease.

Sharman Apt Russell, "The Myth of the Welfare Rancher," *New York Times*

## Recognize Opinions

When you read editorial articles, watch how the writer uses facts to support an opinion. Russell argues that ranchers pay fair fees for grazing rights. George Wuerthner, a biologist and former park ranger, presents an opposing point of view in the model that follows. As you read, notice that although both writers address many of the same points and use much of the same factual data, they reach very different conclusions.

### *Literature Model*

Western ranchers paid $35 million for the public lands they used that year [1989], which works out to about one sixth to one eighth as much as they might have paid to lease equivalent private land. Grazing fees for the same year covered less than 45 percent of the federal costs of range management and improvement.

Near Oregon's Whitehorse Butte, for example, one rancher pays an annual fee of $18,000 for the use of 126,000 acres of public land. To mitigate the environmental impacts of this ranch, the BLM [Bureau of Land Management] plans to build a water pipeline, drill a well, and construct 16 miles of fence. Dollars weren't mentioned when the agency announced its decision to go ahead with the project in July, but $174,000 was the price tag the agency had put on an earlier, similar version of the plan. Annual maintenance costs for the pipeline had been set at $14,000.

For tolerating and paying for most of such developments, the public doesn't even receive all of the $18,000 annual fee in return. By law, half of all grazing fees must be used to finance more "improvements" like the pipeline. Another 12 percent goes to the county grazing board. After these deductions, the public treasury receives only $6,800—about five cents an acre.

George Wuerthner, "The Price Is Wrong," *Sierra*

*What is the writer's major argument?*

**Grammar Editing Tip**

Statistics are often expressed numerically. Unless a sentence begins with them, use numerals to express numbers that would be written in more than two words. Refer to Lesson 21.16 on pages 710–711 to review the rules for using numbers and numerals.

### Journal Writing

Think about an issue you understand well. In your journal list facts related to the issue. Pick one of these facts and jot down notes about how a student with a different viewpoint might use these same facts to support his or her opinion.

## Evaluate Opinions

Many issues have two or more strong sides. It's not always clear what's right, whose logic is strongest, and which facts are accurately interpreted. A careful analysis that compares each argument point-by-point can help you to understand different points of view and form a judgment concerning the validity of various opinions. A Venn diagram can help you to see what any two arguments have in common and where they diverge.

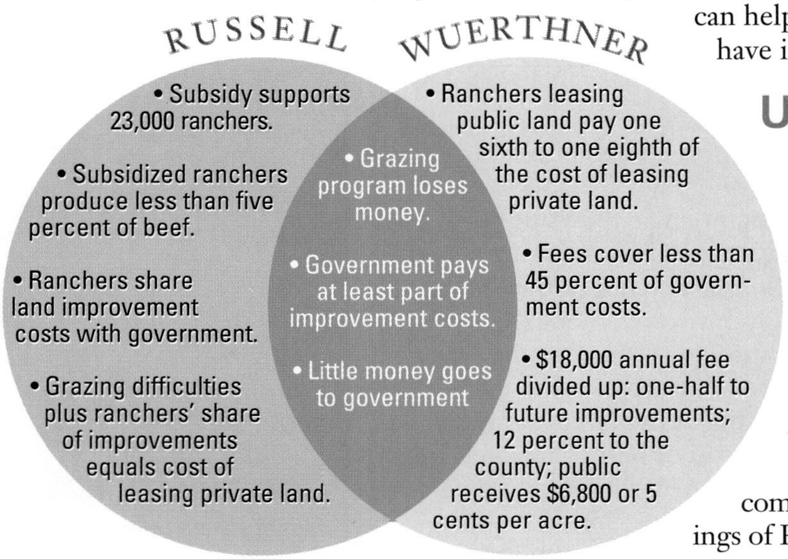

RUSSELL

- Subsidy supports 23,000 ranchers.
- Subsidized ranchers produce less than five percent of beef.
- Ranchers share land improvement costs with government.
- Grazing difficulties plus ranchers' share of improvements equals cost of leasing private land.

RUSSELL and WUERTHNER

- Grazing program loses money.
- Government pays at least part of improvement costs.
- Little money goes to government

WUERTHNER

- Ranchers leasing public land pay one sixth to one eighth of the cost of leasing private land.
- Fees cover less than 45 percent of government costs.
- $18,000 annual fee divided up: one-half to future improvements; 12 percent to the county; public receives $6,800 or 5 cents per acre.

## Understand Bias

When you evaluate opinions, be alert for bias. Ask the following kinds of questions to test the validity of the writing: Is the source reliable? Does the writer cite facts to support a particular point of view? Are the facts current and accurate? Does the evidence support or contradict what you know? Is the evidence complete? In the following model, the writer compares and contrasts the merits and failings of Russell's and Wuerthner's arguments.

### *Model*

George Wuerthner cites numerous statistics to back up his claim that ranchers leasing federal land fail to pull their weight financially. Perhaps the most compelling figure Wuerthner quotes is the total price paid by Western ranchers for public land in 1989 compared with what it would have cost to lease that land privately.

What Wuerthner's figures fail to consider is that ranchers' fees for leasing federal land are determined not by acreage but by the number of cattle they graze on that land. Sharman Russell lists the actual expenses of a rancher with 280 cows grazing on 34,000 acres of land. From the point of view of this rancher, federal grazing permits are anything but a free ride. Furthermore, Wuerthner makes no mention of the quality of federal grazing lands, specifically, that the terrain is rugged and far from ideal for grazing.

Wuerthner's statistics are impressive but misleading since they tell only half the story and leave out important details.

*According to the writer, how does Wuerthner's essay show bias?*

# 5.9 Writing Activities

## Write a Comparison-and-Contrast Essay

Write an essay for your school newspaper comparing and contrasting the two points of view about Christopher Columbus reflected in the excerpts below. Indicate the author of each opinion as you discuss it by using a tag phrase, such as *Berliner's notes*, or *According to Erdich and Dorris.*

- Recognize and analyze opinions in each excerpt.
- Evaluate how well the writers support their opinions.
- Look for indications of bias.

**PURPOSE** To write an essay comparing and contrasting two points of view
**AUDIENCE** School newspaper readers
**LENGTH** 2–4 paragraphs

Did Columbus "discover" America? Yes, in every important respect. This does not mean that no human eye had been cast on America before Columbus arrived. It does mean that Columbus brought America to the attention of the civilized world, that is, to the growing, scientific civilizations of Western Europe.

The result, ultimately, was the United States of America. It was Columbus' discovery for Western Europe that led to the influx of ideas on which this nation was founded—and on which it still rests.

Michael S. Berliner,
"Columbus as Well as Western Civilization Should Be Honored," *Boston Herald*

Columbus only discovered that he was in some new place. He didn't discover America. . . . The best way to celebrate Columbus . . . would be to begin keeping over four hundred treaties [with Native Americans] that were made and never kept. . . . If some of the treaties were kept, perhaps through returning some of the land from the public domain to Native American communities, that land itself would mean that standards of living would rise. It really comes down to the land.

Louise Erdrich and Michael Dorris interview,
Bill Moyers, *A World of Ideas*

### Grammar Link

**Make sure that your comparisons are complete.**

Unclear

*These ranchers pay lower rates than any tax-payers.*

Clear

*These ranchers pay lower rates than any* ***other*** *taxpayers.*

Rewrite each sentence to correct the incomplete comparisons.

1. The government land is usually less expensive than any land.
2. The ranchers' concerns are no more vital than anyone's.
3. I feel that Wuerthner's figures are more impressive than Russell.
4. Russell's argument is more supportive of the ranchers than Wuerthner.
5. My opinion is less extreme than everyone.

**See Lesson 18.4, page 619.**

LESSON 5.10

# Expository Writing
# Comparing and Contrasting Biographies

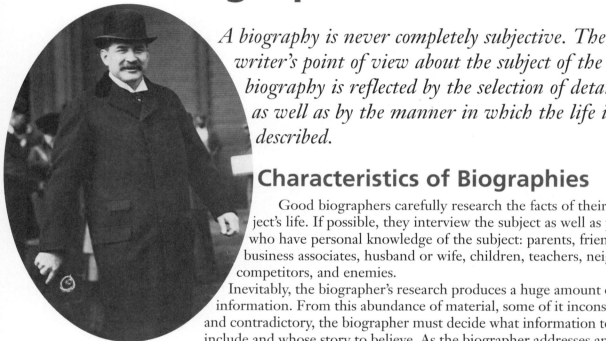

*Financier*
*John Pierpont Morgan*

*A biography is never completely subjective. The writer's point of view about the subject of the biography is reflected by the selection of details as well as by the manner in which the life is described.*

## Characteristics of Biographies

Good biographers carefully research the facts of their subject's life. If possible, they interview the subject as well as people who have personal knowledge of the subject: parents, friends, business associates, husband or wife, children, teachers, neighbors, competitors, and enemies.

Inevitably, the biographer's research produces a huge amount of information. From this abundance of material, some of it inconsistent and contradictory, the biographer must decide what information to include and whose story to believe. As the biographer addresses and resolves these dilemmas, an outline of the person's life emerges. Although the biographer strives for accuracy and a truthful rendering, biographies are necessarily colored by the writer's perceptions and interpretations.

Separate biographies about the same person often draw very different conclusions based on similar factual material. When two biographies about the same person exist, they can be compared and contrasted. John Pierpont (J.P.) Morgan (1837–1913) was a financial wizard who cut a colorful figure with his legendary appetite for money, power, and beautiful art. Few men of his time, including the President himself, were more respected. Notice the similarities and differences between the following two excerpts.

### Literature Model

Morgan had vision and surpassing imagination. Add to these incredible audacity, sublime self-confidence, unqualified courage, amazing virility of mind and body, and a personality that can only be described as overwhelming. Small wonder, then, that this man, part poet, part pirate, grew (in the estimation of himself and others) almost into a God; and, as a God, ruled for a generation the pitiless, predatory world of cash.

Morgan was a colossal adventurer in the realm of reality. He took what he wanted. His code was his own. He did things that today could not be defended in law or morals. But, for his time and generation, he played the game and played it fairly.

John K. Winkler, *Morgan the Magnificent*

### Literature Model

He [Morgan] did not have feet of clay, but a glittering carapace. He wore a helmet of mirrors that blinded all true sight of him and his own insight. This was not self-deception: before the age of psychiatry, the inner eye was blinkered. He was a plutocrat who protested, in the English fashion, that he was an aristocrat. He was believed because most men at that time believed that the fittest ruled, if not the best.

He demonstrated the odd moral fragmentation that enables the voracious to consider money one thing and its effect on other human lives another. He believed that he had the right to take as much income from other people as he judged fair.

Andrew Sinclair, *Corsair: The Life of J. Pierpont Morgan*

### Drafting Tip

When drafting an essay, keep your organization clear. Outline your material first and stick to your outline.

## Journal Writing

Imagine two friends each writing a biography about you. In your journal jot down how you think the biographies would differ.

## Compare and Contrast Biographies

If you were preparing a comparison-and-contrast essay, you would want to take careful notes as you read the biographies on page 249, asking yourself questions to help you observe in greater detail. You might organize your notes with a graphic organizer like the one below.

| Comparison Frame | |
|---|---|
| **Winkler:** Emphasizes the larger-than-life character of Morgan; views him in positive terms | **Sinclair:** Emphasizes Morgan's character flaws |
| Vision, imagination, and self-confidence | Blind to his own faults |
| Colossal adventurer | Moral fragmentation |
| Lived by his own code; took what he wanted | Ignored the suffering of others |
| Played the game fairly | Believed in taking as much as he judged fair |

The model that follows compares and contrasts the two biographers' assessments, using information from the complete biographies.

*Notice the strong thesis statement identifying the key idea of the essay.*

*What details from the two biographies does the writer use to support the thesis statement?*

### *Model*

Although neither Winkler nor Sinclair would argue the historical importance and contribution of John Pierpont Morgan, they do differ in their assessment of Morgan's ethics and character. Winkler casts Morgan's larger-than-life appetite for money and power in positive terms and cites as evidence examples of Morgan using his tremendous influence to benefit the public good, as he did when he unofficially led the country through the Panic of 1907. Winkler portrays Morgan as a Herculean figure and forgives him his faults because "he played the game and played it fairly."

Sinclair, on the other hand, focuses on Morgan's habit of separating business from all other aspects of his life. As Sinclair sees it, this "odd moral fragmentation" allowed Morgan to satisfy his voracious appetite for money and power without having to consider the effect his actions might have on the lives of other people. Sinclair sees Morgan as historically important, but not necessarily admirable.

# 5.10 Writing Activities

## Write a Comparison-and-Contrast Essay

Write an essay for an art students' club comparing and contrasting the two self-portraits done by the artist Rembrandt. The portraits, completed about twenty-five years apart, represent not only how the artist saw himself, but how he wished others to see him. Notice color, light, facial expression, clothing, and the position and stance of the subject.

- Identify the important similarities and differences between the two portraits.
- Describe the overall impression of each portrait.
- Give your opinion about which portrait offers the "truer" picture. Support your opinion.

**PURPOSE** To compare and contrast two portraits of the same subject
**AUDIENCE** Art students' club
**LENGTH** 2–4 paragraphs

Rembrandt, *Self-portrait after Titian's "Ariosto,"* 1640

Rembrandt, *Self-portrait at Kenwood, London,* c. 1665

### Grammar Link

**Make compound subjects and verbs agree.**

When a sentence has a compound subject joined by *or* or *nor*, use a verb that agrees with the subject closer to the verb.

*Neither the biography nor the **articles were** completely subjective.*

Write the verb in parentheses that correctly completes each sentence.

1. Either Morgan or his fellow businessmen _____ (control/controls) New York City politics.
2. Neither the writers nor their editor _____ (seem/seems) to believe that Morgan was admirable.
3. Nevertheless, either the author or the readers _____ (interpret/interprets) what is written.
4. Usually the critics or the public _____ (praise/praises) the author's efforts.

**See Lesson 16.5, pages 572–573.**

## Cooperative Learning

Work with a small group of students to discuss a famous person. You might choose a well-known performer, athlete, or politician. Two members of the group should present a brief oral biography of the person, telling all of the facts that they know about the subject. After the presentations, discuss how the two biographies were similar and different. Each group member should then write an essay comparing and contrasting the two presentations.

UNIT 5

# WRITING PROCESS IN ACTION

## EXPOSITORY WRITING

In preceding lessons you've learned how expository writing can help you explore causal relationships, analyze and solve problems, include an important visual, and compare and contrast different points of view. You've also learned about some special uses for expository writing, such as writing instructions, analogies, and business letters. In this assignment, you will apply what you have learned by writing an essay that explores the connections between an invention and its effects.

### • Assignment •

| | |
|---|---|
| Context | Entrants in this year's Inventor's Day contest should answer this question: What technological innovation has had the strongest influence on your personal life or on society as a whole? Winning entries will be read at the awards ceremony. |
| Purpose | To write an expository essay that explores the logical connection between an invention and its consequences |
| Audience | A panel of judges who are teen-age and adult inventors |
| Length | 1–2 pages |

The next pages can help you plan and write your entry. Read through them and then refer back to interesting ideas as you write. But remember that they are only a guide. Your personal writing process might lead you in other directions and toward different discoveries.

# Prewriting

What inventions couldn't you live without? Use clustering, brainstorming, or freewriting to help you decide on a technological innovation you can write about. Focus on the tools you use every day, considering both major and minor inventions, from the automobile to the paper clip. The prewriting questions at the right may help you get started.

After selecting your invention, think about its effects. Collect your ideas and information from research in chart or note form. Answering *who*, *what*, *where*, *why*, and *how* questions will also help you zero in on specific, important details.

Before you start to draft, reread your notes, keeping in mind your purpose, audience, and the main idea you want to communicate. This overview of your notes should help you develop a thesis statement; if it does not, return to your favorite prewriting techniques to get more concrete information.

Prewriting Questions

- How might the world be different if this invention did not exist?
- What are the positive and negative effects of the invention?
- What analogy could I use to describe the invention?
- From what perspective will I write?
- Would a visual enhance my essay?

# Drafting

To begin drafting, review the method of organization you will use in your essay. Remember that each section has a specific function:

- Introduction: You need to grab your reader's attention, as well as provide a clear, accurate thesis statement that prepares a reader. You should also leave a few clues about the approach you will take in your essay.
- Body: Present the details that support your thesis statement. Keep your audience in mind. Define unfamiliar terms and include any necessary background information.
- Conclusion: You want to leave your readers with a sense of completeness without belaboring the obvious. In addition to summarizing the main points of your essay, you might also want to express a judgment or a realization. Notice on the next page how Henry Kisor uses a personal perspective to close an article about electronic discussion groups.

**Drafting Tip**

For help with explaining casual relationships and writing an analysis, see Lesson 5.3, page 216, and Lesson 5.7, page 234.

*Literature Model*

For me, computer-chatting was a staggering revolution in communications. For the first time I could participate in group talks without worrying about whether people could understand my speech, whether they would listen to what I had to say rather than how I said it, and whether I could follow the bouncing ball of conversation among a large number of people.

Henry Kisor, from *What's That Pig Outdoors?*

Remember the goal of drafting: getting your ideas down on paper. Don't be too hard on yourself while you're writing. You'll be able to fix awkward sentences or fuzzy ideas when you revise.

# Revising

**Revising Tip**

For help with transitions and identifying faulty cause-and-effect relationships, see Lesson 5.3, page 216.

Start revising by reading over your first draft while considering your audience and purpose. During a **writing conference**, read your draft to a partner or small group. Use your audience's reaction to help you evaluate the effect of your writing. Use the Revising Checklist questions to focus your thinking.

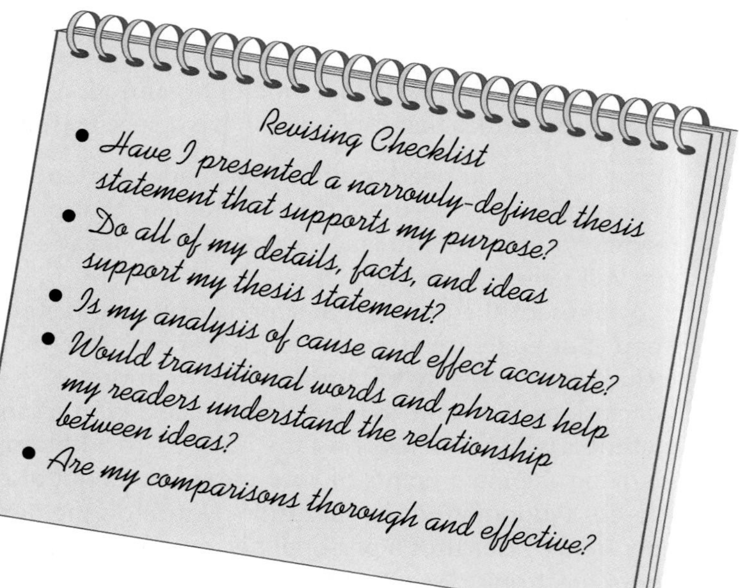

Revising Checklist
• Have I presented a narrowly-defined thesis statement that supports my purpose?
• Do all of my details, facts, and ideas support my thesis statement?
• Is my analysis of cause and effect accurate?
• Would transitional words and phrases help my readers understand the relationship between ideas?
• Are my comparisons thorough and effective?

# Editing

When you are happy with the basic content and set-up of your essay, **proofread** it carefully for errors in grammar, usage, mechanics, and spelling. Use the questions at the right as a guide.

In addition to proofreading, use the Self-Evaluation list below to make sure your essay does all the things you want it to do. When you're satisfied, make a clean copy of your essay and proofread it one more time.

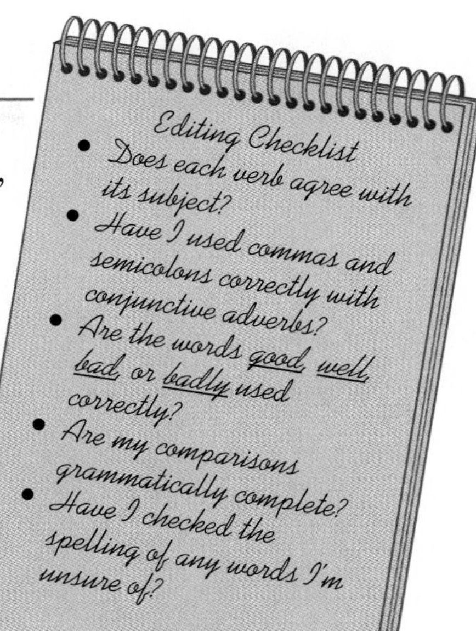

Editing Checklist
• Does each verb agree with its subject?
• Have I used commas and semicolons correctly with conjunctive adverbs?
• Are the words good, well, bad, or badly used correctly?
• Are my comparisons grammatically complete?
• Have I checked the spelling of any words I'm unsure of?


## Self-Evaluation

**Make sure your essay—**

- explains how a technological innovation has affected society or your life
- uses effective examples, incidents, facts, and reasons
- states the purpose clearly in the introduction, supports the thesis statement in smooth, well-organized body paragraphs, and concludes effectively
- uses vocabulary and reasoning suitable to the audience
- follows correct grammar, usage, mechanics, and spelling

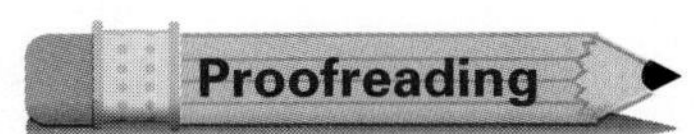


For proofreading symbols, see page 92.

# Presenting

You and your classmates might consider sponsoring an Inventor's Day by holding a school assembly in which selected essays are presented as speeches. As you plan the event, discuss how visuals such as slides, transparencies, and posters could turn the speeches into powerful and dramatic demonstrations.

## Journal Writing

Reflect on your writing process experience. Answer these questions in your journal: What do you like best about your essay? What was the most difficult stage of writing it? What did you learn in your writing conference? What new strategies have you learned for writing?

UNIT 5

# Expository Writing
# Literature Model

*Henry Kisor once rushed to the window in alarm because he confused his son's question, "What's that big loud noise?" with "What's that pig outdoors?" In this essay, Henry Kisor uses expository writing to describe how computer-based communications have enlarged the world for hearing-impaired people. As you read, notice how Kisor uses specific details and analogy to communicate his ideas. Then try the activities in Linking Writing and Literature on page 261.*

It is not only the elevating of public consciousness about the hearing-impaired that has freed us from centuries of isolation. For many of us the microchip is probably the greatest aid to communication the twentieth century has yet provided. It has made possible hearing aids of sophistication, miniaturization, and power unheard of in the days when I toted that heavy Bakelite brick and its batteries in a harness. It has led to medical advances such as cochlear implants, tiny devices that when surgically placed within the inner ear help certain hearing-impaired patients to overcome the greatest frustrations of soundlessness.

The microchip has also made possible inexpensive, small, noiseless, durable, and easily obtainable replacements for the huge, clattering old teletype machines that a generation ago first allowed deaf people to "talk" with one another on the telephone. Today's TDD—short for "Telecommunications Device for the Deaf"—looks like a lightweight portable typewriter with a keyboard and two rubber cups into which a telephone handset is inserted. It's simply a computerized version of the teletype, its eight-inch-wide roll-paper printer replaced by an electronic digital readout that displays a single glowing line of text. (Some TDDs can also print out text on narrow cash-register paper.)

All deaf residents of Illinois are now entitled to a free TDD, thanks to a five-cent-a-month charge applied to all phone bills in the state. Most government offices, libraries, and other public institutions also have TDDs. Partly as an exercise in corporate noblesse oblige and partly to win the business of deaf people, a growing number of private firms are installing the machines and publicizing their phone numbers.

Why not? A TDD does not tie up a phone line. The device sits unobtrusively next to the phone until it's needed. It's easy to tell when a call from a TDD is coming in; the caller presses its space bar repeatedly, sending distinctive beeps. And, though technophobes may fret, little training is required to operate the machine; one simply turns it on, places the telephone handset into the rubber cups, and taps away on the keyboard.

In the early 1980s, when the telephone companies first began renting TDDs to the deaf for a low monthly charge and to businesses and institutions for a bit more, I persuaded the *Sun-Times* to try an inexpensive three-month experiment: renting a TDD for me at the office while I obtained another for home. At the very least I'd be able to call home and talk with my family, just as my co-workers did. Perhaps, if the TDD became widely used, it would be a boon to me in other ways as well.

And it was. Before long I bought a lightweight, booksized, battery-operated portable TDD that I could take on the road, calling from phone booths and hotel rooms to my home or even to the paper, where I'd arrange for another editor to keep the office TDD by her desk in case I should call. The *Sun-Times* pronounced the experiment successful and kept the TDD.

I've used TDDs to make airline and hotel reservations and to call public libraries to obtain information about authors. Every other week I use one to touch base with my parents in Pennsylvania; they bought a $200 TDD just to communicate with their deaf son eight hundred miles away. Being able to speak with each other without resorting to the aid of a third party is a mutual comfort. And now my son Colin has my old portable TDD with him at college, and calls home occasionally for a father-son shmooze.

As for reaching people who might not deal with enough deaf customers to warrant owning or renting a TDD—dentists and doctors as well as pizza parlors come to mind—deaf communities in many cities have organized "relay stations" of hearing volunteers, many of them physically handicapped and housebound. These volunteers take TDD calls from the deaf and relay them by voice to their destinations, then call TDD users back with the responses. In 1990 Illinois put into operation a professional relay system with two 800 numbers, one for TDDs and one for voice, so that no callbacks are needed. Rather, the relay operators "translate" simultaneously between the two parties, and the better operators are so skilled that their services as go-betweens are virtually unobtrusive.

In Illinois at this writing, the relay service will handle only intrastate calls, not long-distance ones. I've begun to use the state relay service to call local writers and ask them to review books for the *Sun-Times*, but must rely on my assistant for out-of-state calls. Within a few years, however, thanks to federal legislation recently enacted, a network of relay systems will crisscross the United States. And I will be able to speak directly not only with authors and reviewers all over the United States but also editors and publicity directors in New York City, the capital of the publishing profession. In some ways, I'll be able to "work the phones" just like any hearing journalist.

TDDs indeed have opened a wide door on the closed world of the deaf, helping end a great deal of its isolation. But for the time being, TDDs are still specialized devices for handicapped users. They're not the kind of appliance one finds in every home or business; their use is still limited to a tiny portion of the American population. And for technical reasons, due to their teletypewriter heritage, they are slow. It's easy for a fast typist to outrun a TDD's transmission rate; when that happens, the message becomes garbled and unreadable.

The personal computer has revolutionized not only my professional but my personal life as well. When I bought that Osborne 1 in 1982, it was intended strictly as a writing machine. But before long I added to my system a modem, a device that allows two computers to exchange information over the phone. It allowed me to transmit articles and columns written at home on the Osborne to the big mainframe computer at the *Sun-Times* so that I would not have to retype them at the office.

Bridget Riley, *Aurulum*, 1977

But there are other uses for a modem. Soon I discovered that I could use it to communicate with other people—*hearing* people. The vehicle is the electronic bulletin board system—"BBS," for short. These are personal computers, owned by hobbyists, that employ modems and special software to turn themselves into glorified answering machines for other computers. One can call a BBS with one's own computer and modem, and then type in a password in order to read messages, public and private, other people have left on the system. The best analogue for a BBS is a kind of electronic rural general store. People drop in from all over to set a spell, picking up gossip with their video screens and passing on their own chitchat with their keyboards. They can even "talk" with the proprietor of the system, taking turns typing away at their keyboards, their sentences following one another on-screen.

It wasn't long before I figured out that all one needed to "keyboard-talk" with another computer user was ordinary modem software on the computers at both ends of the phone line. At prearranged times I could call a fellow computer user and "chat" with him. This is very much like using a TDD, but without technical problems. Computers are much faster than TDDs; even the fastest typist can't outrun a computer's transmission rate. And the large screen of the computer is much more efficient than the TDD's single-line display.

Most important, the personal computer and modem are universal appliances, not special devices associated with a particular handicap, as TDDs are for the deaf. For the first time, they enabled me to "talk" on the phone with the *hearing* world at large—with fellow members of my own culture. To me they were truly an instrument of liberation.

Before long I discovered that these computer conversations need not be expensive long-distance calls, either. They can be conducted through organizations called videotex services that maintain phone connection in cities everywhere. These services are by day large computer database services for business and industry, and by night information exchanges for computer hobbyists. For an hourly charge (twelve to fifteen dollars is typical) plus the cost of a local call, personal computer users can call up a videotex service, send "electronic mail" to other subscribers around the country, and pick up their own. They can also make use of a feature called "Chat," in which hundreds of computer users around the country and in foreign lands can "talk" simultaneously with their keyboards. The conversation can be a giant free-for-all like a citizens band radio colloquy, or a private one-to-one conversation, or a "conference call" limited to two, three, or more persons.

For me, computer-chatting was a staggering revolution in communications. For the first time I could participate in group talks without worrying about whether people could understand my speech, whether they would listen to what I had to say rather than how I said it, and whether I could follow the bouncing ball of conversation among a large number of people.

# Linking Writing and Literature

## Readers Respond to the Model

## How does Henry Kisor use expository writing to communicate his ideas?

**Explore Henry Kisor's essay by answering these questions. Then read what other students liked about Kisor's writing.**

1. What audience do you think Kisor has in mind for his essay? How does he present appropriate background information, facts, and statistics?
2. Find an analogy in the essay. How does this comparison help you understand the main idea of this section?
3. One focus of this essay is the effects of the microchip. How does Kisor illustrate this causal relationship? Is his logic clear and persuasive?

This selection was enlightening and informative. The selection was factual and for the most part, objective. Generally I prefer more subjective material, but in this instance, the article was interesting. Use of first-person point of view allowed the author to interject his own views into the piece.
***Mathew Isaac***

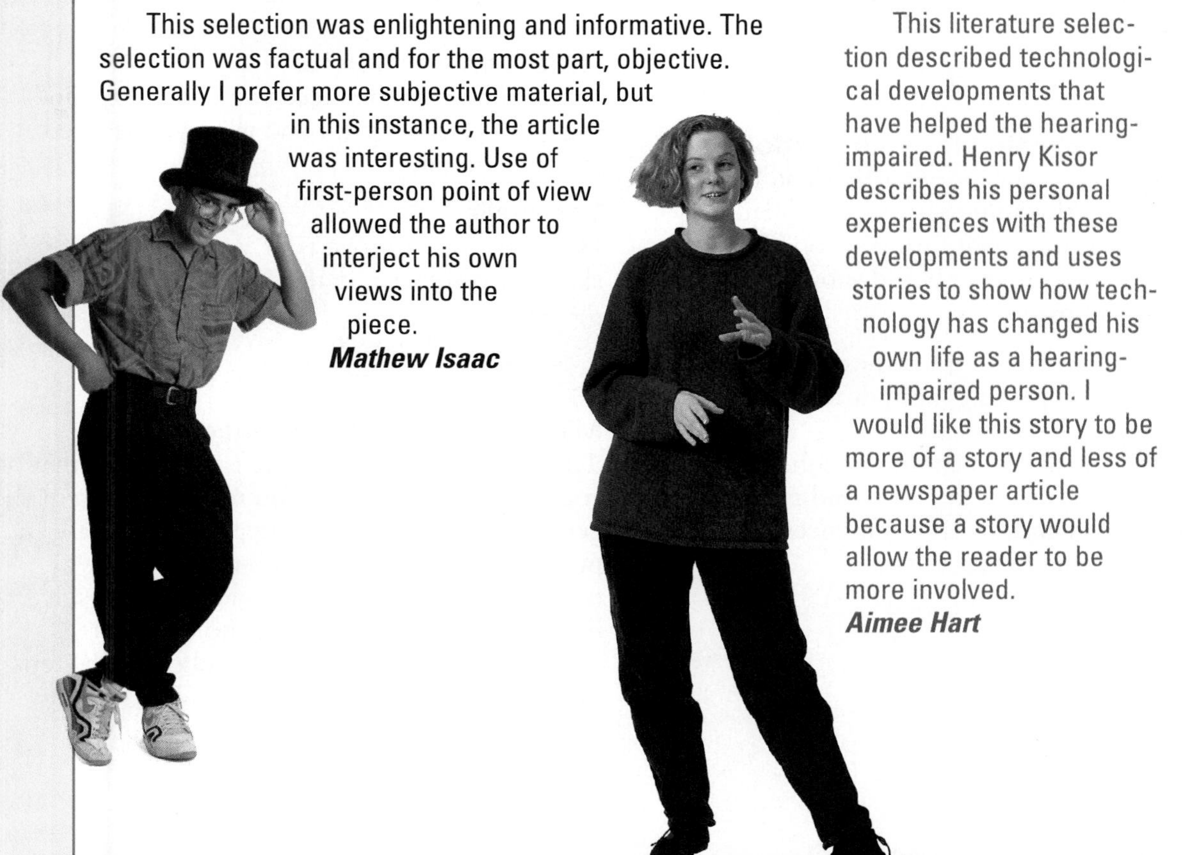

This literature selection described technological developments that have helped the hearing-impaired. Henry Kisor describes his personal experiences with these developments and uses stories to show how technology has changed his own life as a hearing-impaired person. I would like this story to be more of a story and less of a newspaper article because a story would allow the reader to be more involved.
***Aimee Hart***

# Unit 5 Review

## Reflecting on the Unit

**Review what you have learned in this unit by answering the following questions.**

- How can expository writing present facts and details in an engaging way? Cite examples from the unit models.
- When writing instructions, how can you make your steps easy to follow?
- What traps should you watch for when writing about causal relationships or problems and solutions?
- What steps can you take if you are asked to analyze a passage?

## Adding to Your Portfolio

**Choose a selection for your portfolio.**
Look over the expository writing you have done during this unit. Select a completed piece of writing to put into your portfolio. The piece you choose should show some or all of the following:

- a strong, clearly-defined thesis statement
- effective supporting facts, details, statistics, and ideas
- transitions that contribute to coherence
- carefully analyzed thoughts and reasons
- logical conclusions and inferences
- an order that makes sense

**Reflect on your choice**
Attach a note to the piece you chose, explaining why you selected it and what you learned from writing it.

**Set goals**
How can you improve your writing? What skill will you focus on the next time you write?

## Writing Across the Curriculum

**Make a mathematics connection.**
Think of a difficult mathematics problem that you know how to solve. You might select a geometric proof, a graphing problem, or a puzzle like creating a magic square. Write an essay explaining the problem and how to solve it. Make sure that someone who does not already know the solution can follow each step in your writing.

UNIT

6

# Persuasive Writing

Composition

## Lessons

UNIT 6 PREVIEW

Case Study

# Persuasive Writing in the Real World

## Humorist Needles Readers to Give Blood

**FOCUS: Like all persuasive writing, effective satire must be well structured in order to sway readers.**

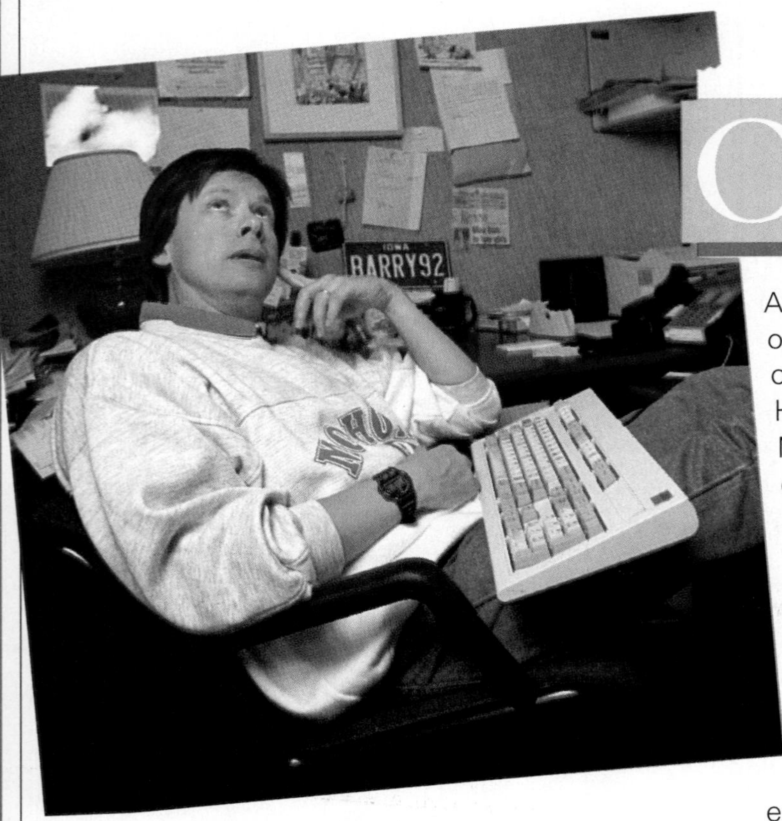


*Humor columnist Dave Barry*

Out in the office behind his house, Dave Barry is sweating over his newspaper column. His feet are propped up on his desk, and his computer keyboard sits on his lap. As Barry taps out a phrase, it materializes on his nineteen-inch computer screen in oversized letters. Nah, that doesn't work. He tries something else, thinks about it. Nope. Not funny. He looks over at his two dogs, Ernest and Zippy, and they stare back. No ideas there.

Why all this toil and doubt? Where are all the laughs? Is this the life of a humor columnist?

"The making of an idea into something that's funny and readable is slow and agonizing and mechanical work," Barry says. "I go back to my office every day—I mean *every* day. And I write. I try a sentence and don't like it and try it again. I change this character or that

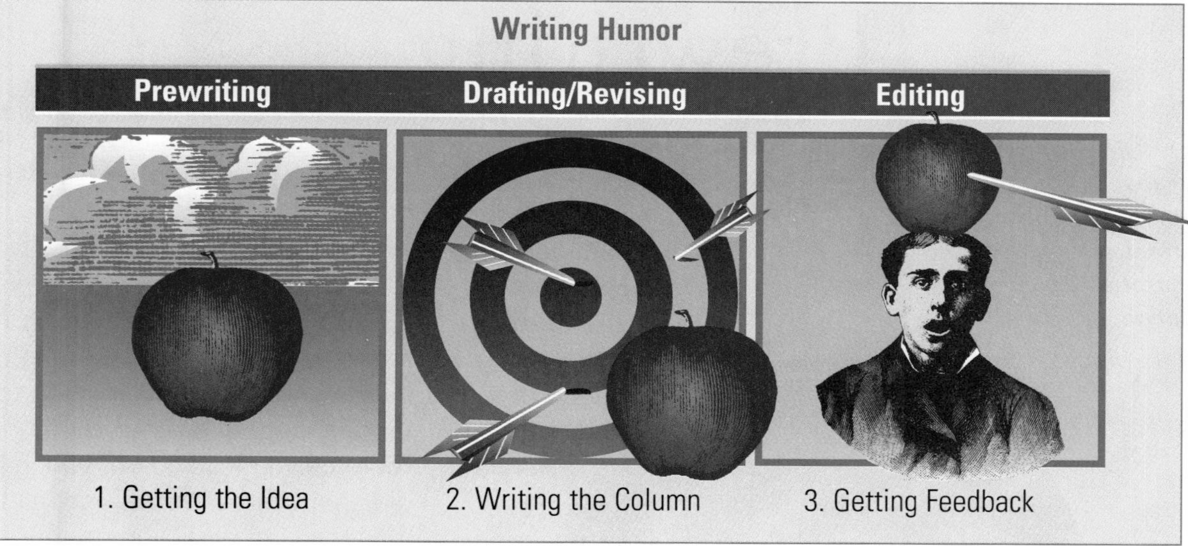


wording and then try it again, and hours and hours later there's something there."

The result of Barry's hard work is a dozen books and many articles, but mainly a hilarious weekly column that is syndicated in more than four hundred newspapers. Barry's popularity springs from his knack for taking everyday subjects—men's cologne, household disasters, flying—and turning them into what he calls his "fish in the face" style of humor. "My humor is the opposite of dry humor," Barry says. "It's wet humor. I don't go for subtle, and I don't go for ironic, and I don't go for witty wordplay. I like to really hit readers in the face."

Day after day, Barry ponders the silliness of life and works to make his readers laugh. But one of Barry's columns also carried a gentle message. In this particular article the humorist tried to persuade nervous people, like him, to donate blood.

> ***"If you're writing humor to persuade, don't preach. Bear in mind that the audience you're trying to reach is as smart and sensitive and decent as you are."***
>
> —Dave Barry, humor columnist

# Prewriting

## GETTING THE IDEA

*Barry sits atop the letters that pour in to him constantly. Many readers share stories that provide inspiration for his columns.*

The idea for the column on blood donation took shape slowly, as many of Barry's ideas do. "When I went down to give blood at the *Miami Herald* blood drive, I was probably aware that it was a potential topic for a column," says Barry. "But most of the time I won't realize until later that a certain event is something I'm going to write about. Like if my bathroom ceiling falls down, which it did about three weeks ago, all I was thinking was, 'Oh no, my bathroom ceiling fell down. What am I going to do?' Not until later did I think, 'Well, maybe I can write a column about this.' "

Sometimes Barry gets his ideas for topics from newspapers, magazines, videos, movies, or other popular-culture media. In fact, says Barry, topics are everywhere. "You can write about time, changing classes at school, grocery shopping, whatever. It's just a question of finding what's funny in the situation. In the case of donating blood, I wouldn't have written this column if I didn't think I could make it funny," Barry explains. "It happens to be a topic that involves a terror of medical things, which is a good topic for humor because most people have it."

# Drafting/Revising

BLOOD DRIVE

## WRITING THE COLUMN

"In this case I was telling a story: I'm going and giving blood," Barry says. But at first, confronting the blank computer screen, "All I was really thinking about was how to get a funny opening."

To snag his readers, Barry went to the heart of his dilemma: Would he give blood this time, or would he chicken out again? Barry captured this sweaty moment of decision by using the present tense: "OK, this is it," he wrote. "The last day of the Red Cross blood drive . . ."

Barry did not use an outline; he began with some rough ideas and let the writing flow. He flashed back to the day his terror of needles began—when Mrs. Hart, his first-grade teacher, cheerfully announced that Dr. Jonas Salk had invented the polio vaccine. Then she marched everybody off to the cafeteria to get their shots. "I decided to go back to when I was a kid," Barry explains, "because everybody was a kid once, and everybody remembers getting shots."

Barry also mined the built-in humor of childhood. "Humor comes from the idea that as a kid you don't know what polio is. All you know is that they're sticking needles in your arm and therefore whoever is doing that is bad. You have it completely backward."

The columnist did not fire off a quick, complete draft and revise it later. As usual, Barry revised as he went along. "I'll write the first sentence and I'll rewrite and rewrite and rewrite; then I'll write the first two sentences and rewrite them both. I'm a real rewriter. I never leave anything alone."

From his childhood agonies, Barry moved his tale to the Red Cross blood drive room at the *Miami Herald.* His tone intensified from nervous to terrified to ranting. He imagined horrors, such as his blood overflowing the collection bag and streaming downstairs into the Classified Advertising Department. Just as important, Barry based the climax of his story on the truth: as the Red Cross nurse held his arm and took aim with the needle, Barry fainted.

*With typical exaggeration, Barry depicts being inoculated with a needle "the size of a harpoon."*

# Editing

## GETTING FEEDBACK

Two editors read Barry's column before it ran—mainly to be sure it was funny, that the jokes worked. First was Barry's wife, Beth, a professional editor. "Beth usually marks up the copy a fair amount," Barry says. "She's really into the logic of things, and even absurdity has a sort of internal logic.

"After I dealt with her objections I turned in the column to the magazine at the *Miami Herald,* and my editor did the same thing. He's almost exclusively interested in whether the column is funny." Both editors also checked to be sure Barry didn't use jokes or approaches from previous columns.

Once Barry revised this column, he and his editors agreed it was funny. But was it persuasive? "I don't have any figures, but the Red Cross sure liked the column," says Barry. "I think it works because it's honest, even though it's full of exaggerations," he adds. "It confronts the fact that most people don't give blood because most people are afraid to.

"I also think the lack of preachiness makes this column effective," he says. "You have to be a very, very skilled writer with an extremely good cause to just sit there and tell people what to think and have them not resent it. You need to tell stories, you need to use humor, you need something to persuade people, other than just you telling them. Because after all, who are *you*?"

### EXCERPT FROM BARRY'S COLUMN

. . . There I was, enjoying life and drawing unrecognizable pictures for my mom to put on the refrigerator, when suddenly——you never know when tragedy is going to strike——Mrs. Hart announced in a cheerful voice that somebody named "Dr. Salk" had discovered a "vaccine" for "polio." I had no idea what any of this meant. All I knew was that one minute I was having a happy childhood, and the next minute they were lining us all up in alphabetical order, with You Know Who in front, and marching us to the cafeteria, where we encountered a man——I assumed this was Dr. Salk——holding a needle that appeared to be the size of a harpoon.

"You'll hardly feel it!" said Mrs. Hart, this being the last time I ever trusted a grown-up. . . .

Of course I am no longer a little boy: I'm a grown-up now, and I'm aware of the medical benefits of inoculations, blood tests, etc. I'm also aware that the actual physical discomfort caused by these procedures is minor. So I no longer shriek and cry and run away and have to be captured and held down by two or more burly nurses. What I do now is faint. Yes. Even if it's just one of those procedures where they prick your finger just a teensy bit and take barely enough blood for a mosquito hors d'œuvre.

"I'm going to faint," I always tell them.

"Ha ha!" they always say. "You humor columnists are certainly . . . "

"Thud," I always say. . . .

# Responding to the Case Study

**1. Discussion**

**Discuss these questions about Dave Barry's writing.**

- What kinds of subjects does Barry prefer to write about in his column?
- Where does Barry get the ideas for his column?
- Barry describes his humor as "wet humor." What does he mean by this?
- In the column on giving blood, how did Barry get his readers' attention?
- Describe Barry's technique for revising his writing.
- When Barry edits his column, what kind of help does he seek?

**2. Persuasive Writing**

**Write an analysis of a humorist's style and effectiveness.** Watch or listen to humorous commentators on TV or radio news programs. What subject or issue did the humorist discuss? What kind of humor did the commentator use? Wordplay? Exaggeration? Did the humorist persuade you to accept his or her point of view? How? Write a two-to-four-paragraph analysis of the humorist's style and effectiveness.

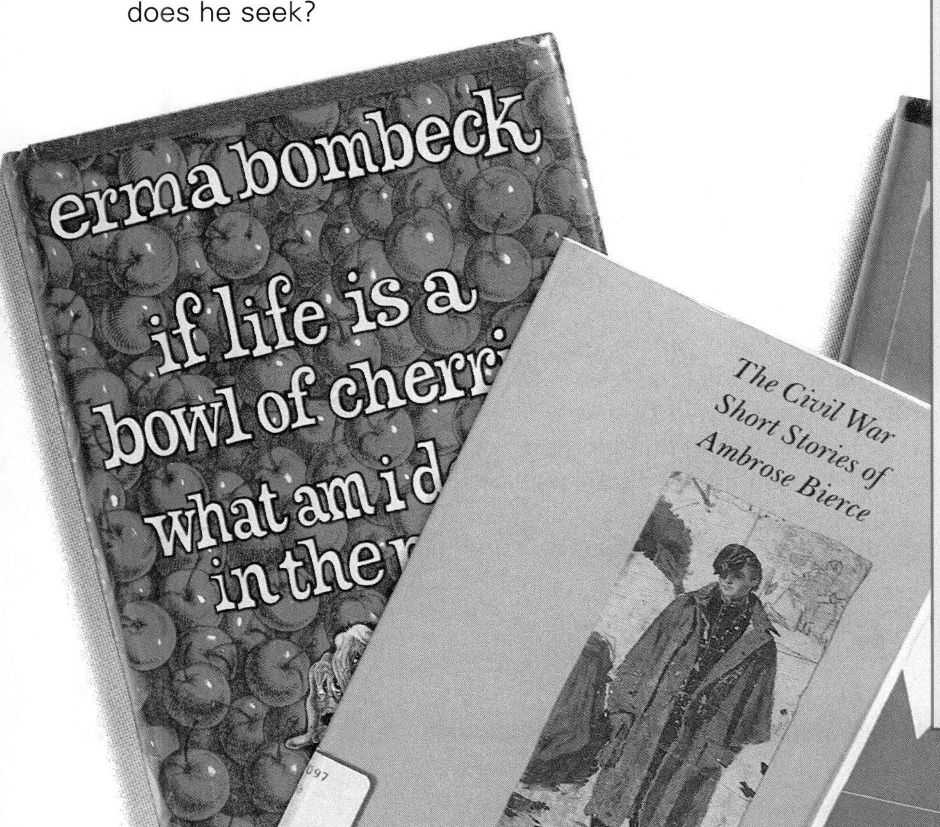

erma bombeck
if life is a
bowl of cherr
what am i d
in the
The Civil War
Short Stories of
Ambrose Bierce


## Grammar Link

**Use commas correctly with restrictive and nonrestrictive participles.**

Participles and participial phrases that are essential to the meaning of a sentence are not set off by commas. Notice how Dave Barry uses essential participial phrases:

*He imagined horrors, such as his blood overflowing the collection bag and streaming downstairs into the Classified Advertising Department.*

Use commas where appropriate to set off participles or participial phrases in the following sentences.

1. The trooper having walked to the car window wrote a speeding ticket.
2. The man driving the car seemed to cooperate.
3. The crying baby in the backseat didn't help matters.
4. Exhausted the driver drove off.

**See Lesson 21.6, pages 682–690.**

LESSON 6.1

# Persuasive Writing
# Writing a Persuasive Essay

*One way to persuade people to see your point of view is to use humor. In the model below, Mike Royko uses humor to persuade readers that contemporary art is absurd.*

Laughter often gets people's attention and makes them more receptive. For example, in the 1970s some people felt that pop art was taken too seriously. *Esquire* magazine expressed disdain for the style by drowning pop artist Andy Warhol in a soup can, the subject of some of his paintings.

### *Literature Model*

I hesitate to comment on contemporary art because when I've done it in the past, art experts have called me a boor and a Philistine, which hurt my feelings. . . .

Now I've come across another contemporary art story, which I've been trying to understand.

An art lecturer at Harvard has assigned her students to make sculptures from chicken bones. . . . She gave each of the students in her Fundamentals of Sculpture Class a live chicken and told them to take it home and keep it around as a pet for one day.

Then they were to take it to a slaughterhouse, watch it being killed and processed, and have it for dinner.

And after picking the bones clean, they were to use them to create a work of art.

The teacher explained that her goal is to bring the artist and the object closer together. . . .

[A] student said that having the live chicken stay overnight in her dormitory was an enlightening experience. As she put it: "It's better to eat something that you had a relationship with because you respect the fact that it was alive."

Mike Royko, *Dr. Kookie, You're Right*

*When Royko pokes fun at himself as well as at experts, what kind of writing does he lead you to expect?*

## Topic, Issue, and Audience

Your purpose in writing a persuasive essay is to influence your audience to think or act in a certain way. You may wish merely to give your readers a new perspective on a general topic, such as modern art or high school education, or you may wish to take a strong stand on a controversial issue arising from a general topic that interests you. If you do the latter, be sure the issue is worth discussing and one on which there are differing opinions. When you diagram the two sides of an issue, as shown in the chart, you should be able to support each side with at least two or three reasons. If the balance of support leans heavily in one direction, that issue may be a poor choice because most people will already agree. If the issue is insignificant, it won't hold your interest as a writer or the interest of your audience. Finally, take a *yes* or *no* position on the issue.

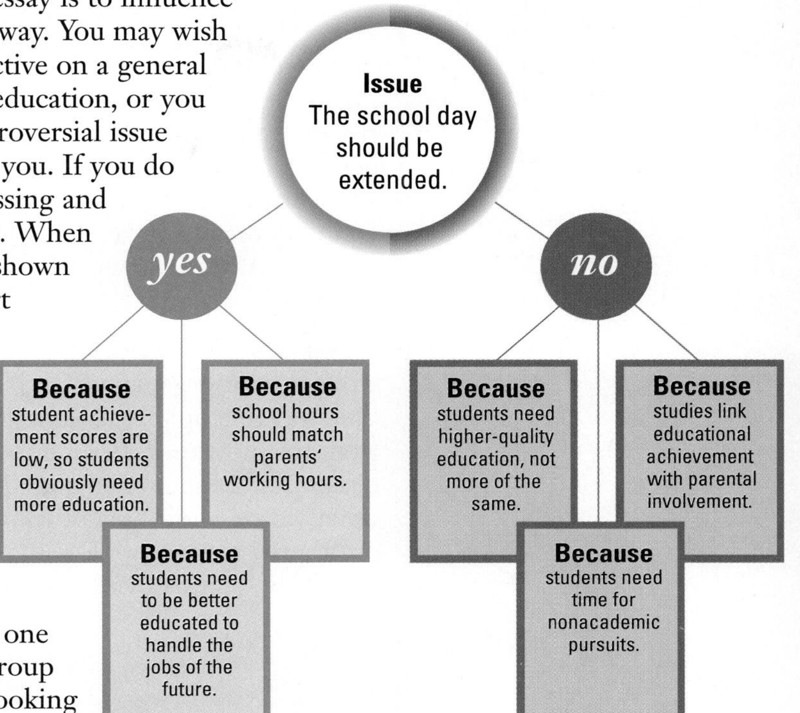

Issue
The school day should be extended.
yes
no
Because student achievement scores are low, so students obviously need more education.
Because school hours should match parents' working hours.
Because students need to be better educated to handle the jobs of the future.
Because students need higher-quality education, not more of the same.
Because studies link educational achievement with parental involvement.
Because students need time for nonacademic pursuits.

A particular topic or issue, such as the one in the chart, may be insignificant to one group of people, such as new college graduates looking for jobs, and yet be of great interest to another audience, such as parents of school-age children. Audience also affects how you treat your topic. The identity of your readers will influence the attitude you show toward your subject and the evidence you choose.

When you're prewriting, consider questions such as these:

- Who makes up my probable audience?
- What are their general interests?
- What do they already know about the topic?
- What is likely to be their opinion on this topic and why?

Imagine you're writing about extending the school day. Think about how your attitude and evidence might change if your audience were fellow students, parents, or the Taxpayers' Alliance of your town.

### Presenting Tip

Depending on your topic, you might submit a persuasive essay to your school or local newspaper or send it to the appropriate government agency.

### Journal Writing

Brainstorm for three issues for a persuasive essay, and diagram the opposing sides for each issue. If your first issues don't look promising, experiment with others. Finally, circle the issue that you might want to use for a persuasive essay.

## Organize Your Essay

**Revising Tip**

When revising a persuasive essay, be sure transitional words and phrases make your argument clear and easy to follow.

You are probably already an expert on a number of persuasive strategies. You use them in disagreements with friends, in pleas for permission, and in other persuasive opportunities of everyday life. Several organizational strategies are also available to you when you write a persuasive essay. Before you choose a strategy, you need to be sure of your goal or stance. Therefore, you may want to use a thesis statement to summarize the opinion you wish your audience to have or the action you wish them to take. Then jot down the most basic support for your position. A thesis statement can provide a focus for your prewriting, drafting, and revising.

**Using Order of Importance** One of the most common and effective strategies for organizing a persuasive essay is using order of importance. One way to employ this strategy is to rank and discuss your evidence from the most to the least important. Then, to undercut the opposition, discuss and refute arguments that may be made against your position. In other words, show how or why these arguments are illogical, impractical, or otherwise unsound. Finally, end with a strong conclusion that your readers will remember or that will spur them to action.

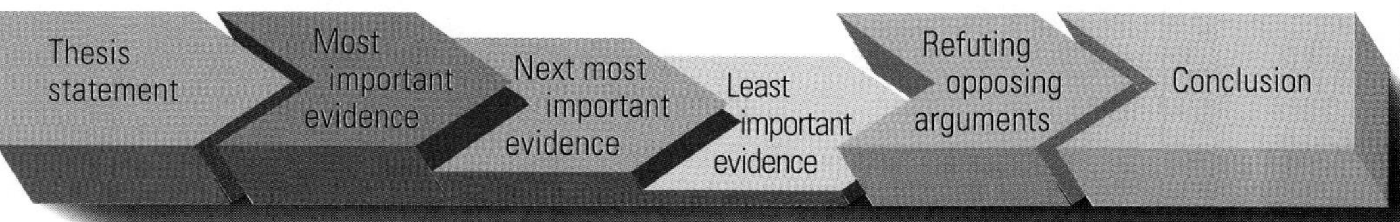


**Refuting Opposing Arguments First** As an alternative to stating your own position first, as in order of importance, you might begin your persuasive essay by analyzing and refuting the arguments of the opposing side. This organizational pattern is especially effective with highly controversial issues. By debunking the opposition first—perhaps with humor as Mike Royko did on page 270—you make your audience more receptive to your ideas. After you refute opposing arguments, clearly state your own position and support it with evidence. Even if you refute opposing arguments first, you can still use a clever opening device, such as the anecdote Ellen Goodman employs in the essay on page 273.

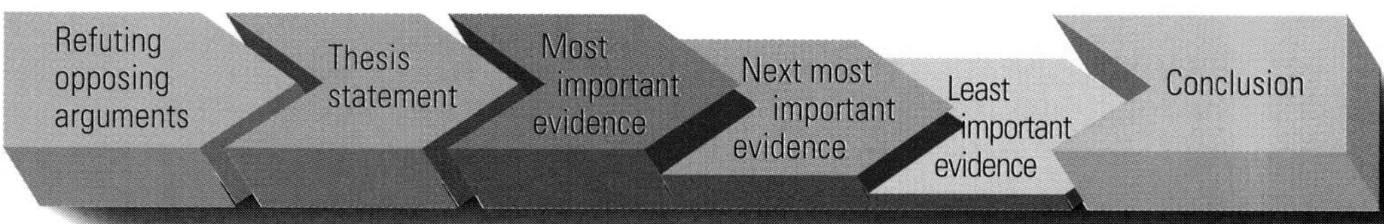

## *Literature Model*

The bill had been paid long ago and yet the notices kept arriving, threatening to repossess Christmas and cut off my plastic life-sustaining equipment.

Finally the specialist had gone to the root of the problem. All fixed up, he said proudly, and then proceeded to explain what had gone wrong. You guessed it: "It was a blip in the computer."

Now I don't know about the rest of the hi-tech consumer world out there, but I have heard this one too many times. When this explanation comes over the telephone or over the television, when I hear it from the space-lab *Columbia* or the District of Columbia, I harbor a small nagging suspicion about the role that the computer is playing in society. I think the role is called scapegoat.

Remember back when that Iowa woman was declared dead by Medicare, although otherwise in fine fettle? What killed her? Computer error. . . . Virtually everything that goes awry in our earthly lives—aside from lost love and a fallen soufflé—is now blamed on some computer or other. In the whodunit of modern life, the computer is the butler. The silent butler.

Frankly I am not so quick with a judgment of guilty against the computer anymore. At least on this planet, some of the mistakes are just too whimsical or charming for the mind of a machine.

Ellen Goodman, "The Scapegoat Computer"

Refuting opposing arguments

*What is the first hint that Goodman doesn't believe the specialist's explanation?*

Refuting opposing arguments

*"The butler did it" is a cliché of mystery stories.*

Refuting opposing arguments

*What might be the reason that the specialist in the first paragraph, as well as others, blames the computer for so many errors?*

After mocking the position that computer error is the source of virtually all that goes wrong, Goodman states her own position: "I'm not suggesting that the computers never make a botch of things. . . . But it's too handy a victim. The computer can't yell. It has a cursor but it can't tattle." In a final jibe at contemporary society, she suggests a legal defense fund to protect the rights of this mechanical scapegoat.

## Journal Writing

Choose one of the persuasive-essay topics for which you diagramed opposing arguments. In your journal, jot down ideas for organizing a persuasive essay on this topic.

## Examine a Complete Essay

To see one of the organizational strategies for persuasive writing in action, look at the following essay.

### *Model*

It seems that everyone concerned about the educational crisis is looking for quick fixes. A prime example of the quick-fix mentality is the proposal to extend the school day.

Refuting opposing arguments

Proponents of the extended school day argue that because student achievement scores are so low, students need to spend more time in school. But if students aren't acquiring basic knowledge and skills under the present system, it's unlikely that more of the same will help. Those in favor of the extended school day also point out that longer days will benefit working parents who worry about their children coming home to an empty house, but the emphasis here is misplaced. The focus should be on what benefits students, not their parents. Finally, proponents of the lengthened day argue that today's students need to be even better educated to handle the jobs of tomorrow. This point is moot, however, if students aren't measuring up to standards of the past anyway.

Thesis statement

The extended school day is not the answer to today's educational crisis. What's needed is higher-quality education, greater parental involvement, and a continued balance between academic and nonacademic activities.

Most important evidence

Students at many good private schools still get high test scores and go on to do well in college. These schools have the same hours as other schools. The standards and quality of instruction at public schools should be raised to the level of the better private schools.

Next most important evidence

Parental involvement must go hand in hand with higher-quality education. Studies have shown that a major factor in students' achievement is how much concern parents show for their children's education.

Refuting opposing arguments

These two factors will do most to improve education, and they do not preclude preserving a balance between students' schoolwork and their involvement in sports and other interests. Like adults, students need balanced lives.

Conclusion

The educational crisis is real, but it won't be cured by easy solutions. We can't jump on every bandwagon that rolls by. And the extended school day is just another bandwagon.

# 6.1 Writing Activities

## Write an Editorial

Your town is considering a law that would make jaywalking a crime. That means pedestrians who cross the street against the light or in the middle of the block could get ticketed just as motorists get ticketed for disobeying traffic signals.

Write a persuasive editorial for the local newspaper that argues for or against passage of that law.

- Gather information in the form of a chart.
- Identify evidence in favor of and against your position.
- Use one of the organizational strategies described on page 272.
- Present a strong conclusion.

**PURPOSE** To persuade for or against making jaywalking a crime
**AUDIENCE** Readers of the local newspaper
**LENGTH** 1–2 pages

### Grammar Link

**Use correct principal parts of verbs.**

*Finally the specialist* ***had gone*** *to the root of the problem.*

In each sentence below, use the correct principal part of the verb in parentheses.

1. We didn't (know) when he would (give) the test papers back.
2. Last semester we always (know) when he had (give) papers back to the other class.
3. He (go) right past our classroom yesterday.
4. The class (know) that he (go) home without a word.
5. He (give) us a disturbing smile before he (go) home.

**See Lesson 15.1, page 537.**

## Cross-Curricular: Art

Look carefully at the scene in the painting by Paul Cézanne. Then write a short essay persuading someone to visit this site.

Before writing your essay, determine what the audience for your argument will be. You might target a friend, retirees or college students looking for a vacation site, or business people searching for a meeting location.

Paul Cézanne, *The Gulf of Marseilles,* 1883–85

LESSON

# 6.2 Persuasive Writing

# Analyzing and Using Evidence

*A writer needs to present strong evidence to persuade readers to change their minds or to take action. Both of the following paragraphs suggest the same solution to the growing problem of trash disposal. As you read, decide which paragraph is more convincing and why.*

*Does this paragraph answer the question: What's wrong with throwing everything away?*

*What is the effect of all these numbers on the reader?*

### *Model*

Americans have developed a throwaway mindset. We're too accustomed to throwing away everything. You name it; we throw it away. Many people think recycling is the answer, but it's not enough. We need to reduce the amount of waste we produce as well. We need to change our disposable lifestyle. And one way to do that is to discourage the throwaway habit by charging households and businesses for the amount of trash they create.

We live in a throwaway society. Each day, all day long, we dispose of things—napkins, paper bags, diapers, juice boxes, razors—more than three pounds of trash per person per day. Of the approximately 160 million tons of garbage Americans produce each year, only about 10 percent is recycled. The rest goes into about 6,000 landfills, one-third of which are nearly full. What's more, people don't want pollution-causing landfills started in their communities. More recycling can help, but it won't be enough. We also need to produce less trash, and one way to encourage people to reduce the amount of trash they produce is to charge them for it.

The second paragraph is more specific and uses concrete examples and statistics as evidence. The first paragraph lacks supporting evidence.

## Identify Forms of Evidence

You know what kind of evidence the criminal investigator looks for: the tell-tale scratch on the windowsill, the too-tight alibi, the almost perfect signature. Like a detective's case, the persuasive essay can succeed or fail based on the strength of its evidence. That evidence may take different forms, including any of the following:

- **Firsthand observations**—accounts from original sources. They may be your observations or someone else's. *Senior George Jackson states, "I tried to run track and work last year, but I didn't have time to do my homework."*
- **Informed opinions**—the judgments of experts or authorities. *Pediatrician Susan Holmes warns parents of the relationship between stress and poor health in teenagers.*
- **Examples**—individual instances that demonstrate a general point. *Many students work after school. Junior Anna Flores bags groceries from 4 to 9 P.M. each school day.*
- **Reasons**—underlying facts or causes that provide logical sense for a premise or occurrence. *Students who work full time clearly do not have the opportunity for extracurricular activities that nonworking students have.*
- **Facts**—statements that can be proven true. *In the past century, a person's average life expectancy has increased dramatically.*
- **Statistics**—numerical facts. *In 1955, 60 percent of American households consisted of a nuclear family with two or more school-age children, a working father, and a housewife mother.*

To construct an effective essay, support your position with the best evidence you can find. Just as the orb is supported by the pillar in the illustration above, so is an effective argument supported by evidence.

Building a case—gathering reliable evidence—requires research. Use library sources such as reference books, other nonfiction books, magazines, newspapers, and videotapes. You might also interview experts or people involved in the issue or call government or private organizations for information.

**Prewriting Tip**

When you do research, gather as much information as you can. It's easier to select from an abundance than to stretch out too little information.

### Journal Writing

Use the headlines in your local newspaper to find an issue for a persuasive essay. Then list the kinds of evidence and the sources you might use to write an effective essay on this topic.

## Grammar Editing Tip

When preparing an essay with numerous abbreviations used as words, make sure they are punctuated properly (see in the Student Model: S.A.T., PC). For assistance, refer to pages 708–709 of Lesson 21.15 in Grammar, Usage, and Mechanics.

# Evaluate Evidence

Hearsay, personal opinion, speculation, or name-calling are unacceptable in a persuasive essay, and can only undermine your case. Reliable evidence should be *relevant*, *unbiased*, *up-to-date*, *complete*, and *verifiable* in several independent sources.

Look at the student essay below. As you read, note whether it contains reliable evidence and how humor contributes to its effectiveness.

### *Student Model*

*Verifiable statistic*

*Humorous alliteration*

*Thesis statement*

*Sarcasm and exaggeration for humorous effect*

*Up-to-date statistic*

*Logical reasoning*

*Forceful conclusion*

As schools continue relying on computers to be instant cure-alls for the problems in education, is it any wonder that newspapers report test scores of American students are falling? There are as many as 27 million of these microchip monsters in the schools, and when they're poorly used, they are not the benefit they could be. Schools need to integrate computers into a multifaceted curriculum rather than just plugging them in and expecting them to come alive and teach well.

There is now one computer for every sixteen students. It is easy for a teacher merely to allow one of these oversized video games to be the sole educator and let the students' brains turn to mush. We cannot afford to produce a generation that can score millions on video games but cannot print their names on the S.A.T. It is critical that we do not forget the archaic teaching method of the past: reading. Books are not only better for stimulating youngsters' brains, they never go "down" or run out of disc space. Schools now devote over four billion dollars every year to computers. They need to divert some of their budgets to an even more archaic educator: teachers. There is no substitute for the human interaction gained from instruction by a living, breathing organism instead of a microchip. A teacher's salary may look immense next to the $500 price tag of a PC, but the ability teachers have to work with and around problems makes up for the cost of employing real people.

Computers are here to stay and can offer advantages to the modern classroom; however, if schools want to maintain high standards, they should not let artificial intelligence replace human brains as the thinkers of choice.

Padraic Romfh, Rangeview High School, Aurora, Colorado

# 6.2 Writing Activities

## Write an Editorial

You're a writer for your school newspaper. Right before deadline, you are asked to write the editorial for or against laws requiring people to use seat belts in cars. Since time is short, decide on your position as early in your preparation as possible.

- Support your position with evidence that is relevant, unbiased, up-to-date, complete, and verifiable.
- Present an adequate amount of evidence.
- Use different forms of evidence from the list on page 277.

**PURPOSE** To persuade for or against mandatory seatbelt laws
**AUDIENCE** Readers of the school newspaper
**LENGTH** 2–4 paragraphs

Adolph Gottlieb, *Blues*, 1962

## Cooperative Learning

Do modern works of art, such as Adolph Gottlieb's painting *Blues*, have artistic merit? Discuss this issue with three of your classmates. Appoint one member of the group to act as moderator and another member to take notes on the discussion. Have each group member write out a plan—including a thesis statement, the main points of evidence, and the order of the evidence—for a short persuasive essay. As a group, select one plan, and then appoint one person to draft the essay and another to revise it.

### Grammar Link

**Make sure that verbs agree with subjects that are nouns of amount.**

*Of the approximately 160 million tons of garbage Americans produce each year, only about **10 percent is** recycled.*

Rewrite the following sentences, using the verb form that agrees with the subject.

1. A hundred dollars (is) a lot if you spend it carefully.
2. When I counted the bills, a hundred dollars (is) in my wallet.
3. Three days (has) passed since we saw the sun.
4. Ten clowns (is) the most that can fit in that little car.
5. Seventy points (is) too much to give for that essay.

**See Lesson 16.4, pages 570–571.**

LESSON 6.3

# Persuasive Writing

# Detecting Errors in Logic

*Logic is the process of clear and organized thinking that leads to a reasonable conclusion.*

An editorial making fun of a political candidate's appearance probably wouldn't persuade you to vote against him. You'd realize that such an essay, like the cartoon on this page, illustrates faulty logic. A candidate's looks have nothing to do with qualifications for the job.

As you read the following essay, consider how effective the argument is and whether there is any faulty logic.

**Model**

The scientific evils of *1984* are being acted out today in animal research laboratories across the country. Brainy, cold-hearted scientists in their clean white coats inject helpless baby animals with drugs that wreak havoc on them. These poor young animals live their entire, though often short, lives confined in tiny cages. And for what reason? So that scientists can find a better diet pill for humans who eat too much? Animal research simply feeds human vanity and is inexcusable. This inhumane research must be stopped.

When people demonstrated against animal research at the local university, the head of the research unit left town. Obviously, university officials are afraid to face the opposition. But a security guard at the university joined the demonstrators, showing that opposition may be having an effect.

The comparison between George Orwell's novel *1984* and current animal research is inaccurate. In *1984*, science was used to control human behavior, not for animal research.

## Identify Logical Fallacies

A commercial featuring a teenager wearing Brand X jeans and surrounded by a group of admirers is supposed to convince you that wearing this garment will make you popular, but you can easily spot this fallacy, or error in logic. In persuasive essays similar logical fallacies weaken or destroy the credibility of an argument.

| Common Logical Fallacies | | |
|---|---|---|
| | **Fallacy** | **Example** |
| **Stereotyping** | Ascribing characteristics to an entire group | Brainy, cold-hearted scientists |
| **False Analogy** | Making an inaccurate comparison between two situations, ideas, people, or things | The scientific evils of *1984* are being acted out today in animal research laboratories across the country. |
| **Loaded Words** | Using emotion-filled words to appeal to people's feelings | *Helpless baby* animals, *poor young* animals |
| **Overgeneralization** | | |
| Limited Sample | Drawing a conclusion about an entire group from a very small sample of the group | So that scientists can find a better diet pill for humans who eat too much? Animal research simply feeds human vanity. |
| Unrepresentative Sample | Drawing a conclusion about an entire group from a sample that is not part of the group or is not typical of the group | But a security guard from the university joined the demonstrators, showing that opposition may be having an effect. |
| **Oversimplification** | | |
| False Cause | Attributing a cause-and-effect relationship simply because one event follows another | When people demonstrated against animal research at the local university, the head of the research unit left town. Obviously, university officials are afraid to face the opposition. |
| Only Cause | Attributing only one cause when there are many causes | And for what reason? So that scientists can find a better diet pill for humans who eat too much? |

### Journal Writing

Find two or three magazine advertisements that contain logical fallacies that you can paste in your journal. Over each ad, write a label identifying each fallacy, such as "loaded words," and briefly write an explanation of how it is used.

## Revise for Errors in Logic

**Drafting Tip**

During the drafting stage, look for faulty logic in opposing arguments. A good way to refute an opposing argument is to point out a logical fallacy.

Logical fallacies may creep into the drafts of even the best writers. You may be particularly prone to overstate your case when you feel strongly about an issue. Of course, you should try to be fair and logical whenever you write and speak. However, when you're drafting an essay that will be carefully revised, you can afford to let your momentum carry you along. Then it will be especially important to scrutinize your draft and to revise any errors in reasoning.

The following draft contains a number of errors in logic. Note how the writer has revised the draft to eliminate these errors.

*How else might you have eliminated* stereotyping *here?*

*Note the* oversimplification: only cause. *What other words are often used in this kind of logical error?*

*Note the* oversimplification: false cause. *What might be one real cause for decreased funding?*

The animal rights movement is ~~filled with~~ misguided ~~extremists~~. Many Dramatic advances in modern medicine, including the elimination of deadly childhood diseases and the increase in life expectancy, are ~~all~~ in large part due to animal research. Consider this partial list of medical benefits from animal research: vaccines against diphtheria, measles, mumps, polio, rubella, whooping cough; the elimination of smallpox; treatment for diabetes; the control of infection; and organ transplants. Some of these medical advances have extended to veterinary medicine as well, as vaccines and surgical techniques that were developed through animal research are used on farm animals and pets.

Today, the struggle to find treatments for cancer and Alzheimer's disease depends heavily on animal research. ~~But as the animal rights movement has gained momentum, funding for medical research has decreased. It's clear that these activists are standing in the way of human health~~. *With funding for medical research declining, we must carefully consider where our dollars will make the most difference.*

Notice how easily the writer corrected some logical fallacies and gained credibility in this draft simply by adding or deleting a few words.

# 6.3 Writing Activities

## Write a Humorous Essay

Are pet owners too permissive or too strict, overprotective or too busy to spend time with their pets? As a guest columnist for the magazine *Parents of Pets*, write a humorous persuasive essay identifying the weakness and proposing how pet owners might correct it. If you feel comfortable doing so, you might take the "voice" of a dog, a cat, or another animal.

To guard against overgeneralizations in your essay, identify the sample you're basing your argument on. For example, perhaps the sample is your family and several families in your neighborhood.

- Do not oversimplify.
- Do not use humor in place of or at the expense of logic.
- Revise your essay to elminate the logical fallacies found in the chart on page 281.

**PURPOSE** To persuade with humor
**AUDIENCE** Pet owners
**LENGTH** 6–8 paragraphs

### COMPUTER OPTION

You can use your PC to design a simple pie chart, graph, or other visual representation to accompany the humorous essay you wrote for *Parents of Pets*. If you have the appropriate software, you can also illustrate the article with simple drawings. A page-layout option will allow you to design and create a facsimile of the magazine page that carries your article.

## Cooperative Learning

Meet with three classmates and discuss the "logic" of advertising. Then have each group member bring in two magazine ads that depend primarily on visual images rather than words. Select two ads that best illustrate faulty evidence or errors in reasoning. Have two members of the group work on each ad: one should write a brief analysis of the methods of persuasion used in the ad, and the other should "translate" the ad into a written form for use as a radio advertisement.

### Grammar Link

**Use commas and semicolons in series.**

*Consider this partial list of medical benefits from animal research: vaccines against diphtheria, measles, mumps, polio, rubella, whooping cough; the elimination of smallpox; . . .*

Punctuate the following paragraph, making sure to use commas and semicolons in series.

The kitchen lacked the most basic equipment: pots and pans a colander to drain spaghetti measuring spoons potholders a table that we could use as a work surface sharp knives and bowls. We decided that for the time being we would have to rely on frozen dinners whatever we could buy in cans, such as beans corned beef tuna fish and soup and whatever prepared food we could get at the market like sandwiches and salads.

**See Lesson 21.5, pages 680–681.**

LESSON

6.4

# Persuasive Writing
# Using Inductive and Deductive Reasoning

*There are two major types of logical thinking, inductive reasoning and deductive reasoning. Writers use both to build persuasive arguments.*

The famous fictional detective Sherlock Holmes loved to display his incredible reasoning powers. He would often astound his friend Watson by correctly "guessing" the hometown, occupation, previous adventures, day's activities, marital status, and emotional state of a new client. Holmes could turn a scuffed boot, a muddy trouser cuff, a rare silk tie, and a tiny scar into an accurate biography of the stranger.

## *Models*

Did you know that the heart medicine digitalis is produced from the purple foxglove plant? The Mexican yam is the source of cortisone, a drug used in treating arthritis and other diseases. Antibiotics, insulin, and pain relievers are also derived from plants and animals. What other medicines might be obtained from as yet unstudied endangered species? Clearly, preserving the diversity of plants and animals on the earth is important to human life.

Many plants and animals that have not yet been studied by scientists are now facing possible extinction. In the past, antibiotics, heart drugs, and other medicines that come from plants and animals have extended the average person's life expectancy. Therefore, preserving the diversity of plant and animal life on the earth is important to human life.

The first example demonstrates inductive reasoning, using specific facts to draw a general conclusion. The second illustrates deductive reasoning, using a universal statement and a related fact to draw a conclusion.

## Use Inductive Reasoning

You are probably familiar with inductive reasoning from having read about scientific studies and political polls. When you use inductive reasoning, you move from specific facts or observations to a general conclusion. To construct an inductive argument, follow these three steps: (1) Begin with a series of facts. (2) Study the facts, looking for a connection among them. (3) Draw a conclusion or a generalization.

Many inductive conclusions generalize about a population based on a sample. A population is the whole class of events, objects, or people at issue. A sample is the segment of this population that is actually examined. To be valid, a conclusion must be based on a sample that is both large enough and representative of the population. Although the gathered facts may not *prove* a conclusion, they can support the conclusion to a greater or lesser degree.

You may have seen headlines such as this one: One Hundred ABCville Citizens Taken Ill; Health Department Searches for Cause.

The diagram shows how the Health Department might test 15 people to determine what caused the illness for all 100. If the sample is selected randomly from the entire 100, it will be fairly representative of the population. Many studies rely on samples even smaller than 15 percent of the population and still get sufficiently accurate results.

**Drafting Tip**

When you are drafting an inductive argument, clearly identify the population at issue and the makeup of the sample.

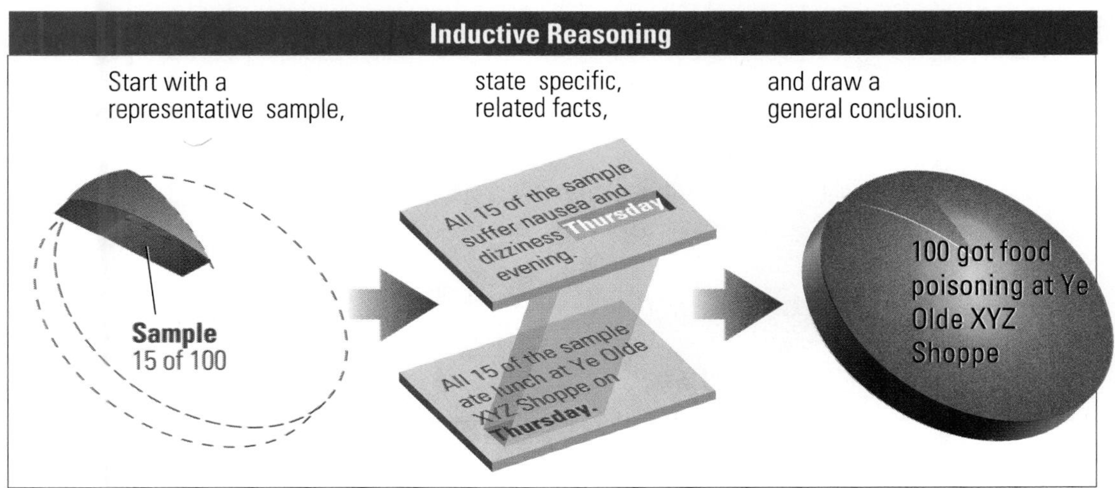
Inductive Reasoning
Start with a representative sample,
state specific, related facts,
and draw a general conclusion.
Sample
15 of 100
All 15 of the sample suffer nausea and dizziness Thursday evening.
All 15 of the sample ate lunch at Ye Olde XYZ Shoppe on Thursday.
100 got food poisoning at Ye Olde XYZ Shoppe

### Journal Writing

What generalization could you make about the clothing styles of the students in your school by observing twenty of them at random? Draw a pie chart in your journal to show the sample that you think would be large enough and representative.

## Use Deductive Reasoning

How did Sherlock Holmes "guess" the biographical details of strangers? By deduction, my dear Watson. He used a wide range of generalizations about people, such as *farmers have calloused hands and sunburns* but *factory workers have calloused hands and no sunburns*. When Mr. X appeared, Holmes used his powers of observation to note such details as the style of clothes worn, the condition of fingernails, the color of the mud on shoes. Then he combined the details with a generalization, and reached a conclusion about Mr. X.

When you use deductive reasoning, begin with a generalization, state a related fact, and draw a conclusion based on the generalization and the fact. As the illustration below shows, deductive reasoning moves from a general statement to a more specific conclusion.

Many deductive arguments can take the form of a syllogism, a three-part formal statement, somewhat like the math equation "If A equals B, and B equals C, then A equals C." As you may know, the three parts of a syllogism are called the major premise, the minor premise, and the conclusion. Notice how the likelihood of a particular case of food poisoning can be predicted by deduction.

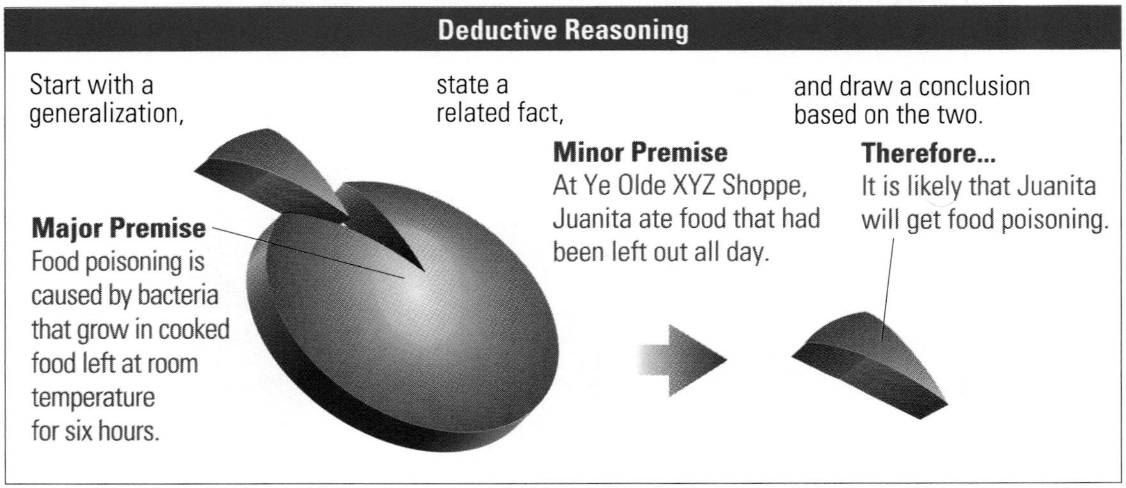

Deductive Reasoning
Start with a generalization,
state a related fact,
and draw a conclusion based on the two.
Major Premise
Food poisoning is caused by bacteria that grow in cooked food left at room temperature for six hours.
Minor Premise
At Ye Olde XYZ Shoppe, Juanita ate food that had been left out all day.
Therefore...
It is likely that Juanita will get food poisoning.


You are probably familiar with the kind of deductive reasoning shown above. It is the reasoning behind many health warnings phrased, "If you don't get enough ________, you will get ________."

A syllogism is said to be valid when it follows the rules of deductive reasoning. In addition, the major premise must be a universal statement that covers all or none of the population, never a part. No valid conclusion can be drawn from this major premise: Many dogs chase cats.

A syllogism may be valid without being true. In the next example, the major premise is untrue; therefore, although the syllogism is valid, it is not true.

**Valid but Untrue Syllogism**

*Major Premise:* All dogs chase cats.
*Minor Premise:* Holly is a dog.
*Conclusion:* Holly chases cats.

The following syllogism is both valid and true. The major premise is a universal statement that is true. The minor premise is also true, and the conclusion follows from the major and minor premises.

**Valid and True Syllogism**

*Major Premise:* A diet high in fat is unhealthful.
*Minor Premise:* A typical teenager's diet is high in fat.
*Conclusion:* A typical teenager's diet is unhealthful.

The following model written by Martin Luther King Jr. demonstrates the use of deductive reasoning in a persuasive argument.

### *Literature Model*

How does one determine whether a law is just or unjust? A just law is a man-made code that squares with the moral law or the law of God. An unjust law is a code that is out of harmony with the moral law. To put it in the terms of St. Thomas Aquinas: An unjust law is a human law that is not rooted in eternal law and natural law. Any law that uplifts human personality is just. Any law that degrades human personality is unjust. All segregation statutes are unjust because segregation distorts the soul and damages the personality. It gives the segregator a false sense of superiority and the segregated a false sense of inferiority.

Martin Luther King Jr., "Letter from Birmingham Jail"

King's argument can be stated in the following syllogism.

*Major Premise:* Any law that degrades human personality is unjust.
*Minor Premise:* Segregation damages human personality.
*Conclusion:* Segregation statutes are unjust.

## Journal Writing

Create two syllogisms in your journal: one that is valid but not true and one that is both valid and true. Jot down why each syllogism is valid and why one is true and the other is not.

**Grammar Drafting Tip**

When constructing syllogisms, you can refer to the material about order of subject and predicate on pages 457–459 of Lesson 11.4 in Grammar, Usage, and Mechanics.

## Evaluate Inductive and Deductive Arguments

**Vocabulary**
**Editing Tip**

When you edit a persuasive essay, be sure to use qualifiers, such as ***many, some,*** and ***most,*** to limit your generalizations where appropriate.

As a writer and as a reader, consumer, and voter, you'll need to evaluate the soundness of the logic in persuasive writing. The chart summarizes questions to ask when evaluating inductive and deductive arguments. For inductive arguments, evaluate the specific evidence to see whether it leads logically to the conclusion. For deductive arguments, evaluate both premises to determine the truth and validity of the conclusion. Any argument should also be checked for logical fallacies, or errors in reasoning, which are discussed on pages 280–282.

**Questions to Ask in Evaluating Arguments**

**Inductive Argument**

1. What are the specific facts or evidence from which the conclusion is drawn?
2. Is each fact or piece of evidence accurate?
3. Do the facts form a representative and sufficiently large sample?
4. Do all of the facts or the evidence lead to the conclusion?
5. Does the argument contain any logical fallacies?

**Deductive Argument**

1. What are the major premise, the minor premise, and the conclusion?
2. Is the major premise a universal statement?
3. Are both premises true?
4. Does the conclusion follow logically from the major and the minor premises?
5. Does the argument contain any logical fallacies?

You may use inductive and deductive arguments in both serious and humorous persuasive writing. Note the model below.

### *Student Model*

A wise Jefferson Elementary School graduate once said, "Success may be measured by the logo on your tennis shoes." This statement is not only profound, but true. Recent surveys show that 90 percent of all people between the ages of nine and thirteen believe that the proper athletic footwear now will have a critical effect on their future. It would seem, therefore, that parents should listen to their kid's plea for the $128 sneakers, if they really want what is best for their child.

Chadwick Jennings Fleck, Howland High School, Warren, Ohio

# 6.4 Writing Activities

## Write a Persuasive Paragraph

Using deductive reasoning, complete the following syllogism by supplying a logical conclusion. Then write a persuasive paragraph expanding on the argument presented in the syllogism. Bring your paragraph to life with examples, quotes, or anecdotes.

| | |
|---|---|
| *Major premise:* | Anyone who professes concern about the environment should recycle. |
| *Minor premise:* | Students at Central High School say that they care about the environment. |
| *Conclusion:* | |

- Present a valid conclusion that logically follows the major and minor premises.
- Eliminate logical fallacies in the argument.
- Use qualifiers, such as *many*, *some*, and *most*, to limit generalizations.

**PURPOSE** To derive and present a logical conclusion
**AUDIENCE** Your classmates and teacher
**LENGTH** 1 paragraph

## Cross-Curricular: History

Your history teacher has assigned your class to write a paper on gender roles. Choose one of the following topics, or a topic of your own, and outline an inductive argument. You may need to do some research to find specific facts for your argument. Then write a brief persuasive essay, using inductive reasoning to support your position.

- Historically, have behavioral differences between the sexes been considered a result of biological differences or social conditioning?
- Should women be allowed to perform combat duty in the armed services?

### Grammar Link

**Punctuate restrictive and nonrestrictive clauses correctly.**

Adjective clauses introduced by the word *that* are restrictive and should not be set off by commas. Nonrestrictive clauses often begin with *which* and should be set off with commas.

*Many plants and animals* ***that*** *have not yet been studied by scientists are now facing possible extinction.*

Rewrite each sentence below, completing the adjective clause. If it is nonrestrictive, use the word *which* and set off the clause with commas. If it is restrictive, use the word *that.* Then underline the complete adjective clause.

1. All attention was focused on the stage ____ became a symbol of the earth itself.
2. The Native American dance group ____ performed that night was world famous.
3. We began to notice differences in the dances ____ were performed without pause.
4. Audience members applauded the dances ____ they wanted to see repeated.
5. After the performance, everyone wanted to examine the costumes ____ included multicolored fringe and feathers.

**See Lesson 21.6, pages 682–690.**

LESSON

# 6.5 Persuasive Writing
# Writing a Satirical Essay

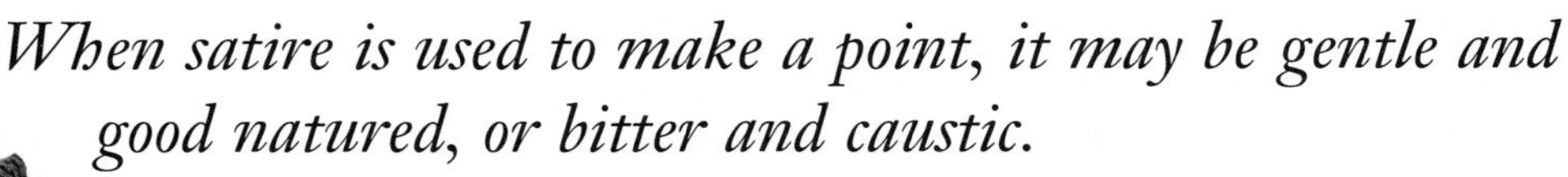

*When satire is used to make a point, it may be gentle and good natured, or bitter and caustic.*

In her essay "Packing," Erma Bombeck describes her husband's packing: "If there is a bar mitzvah, ten-kilometer run, costume party, fire in the hotel, bowling tournament, western cookout, or rain for forty days and forty nights, he's ready." Although she doesn't state her point directly, her opinion of her husband's strategy is clear. As you read the following essay, ask yourself what it has in common with the Bombeck piece.

### *Student Model*

We, the sports fans of America, sure are lucky to live in the 1990s!!! . . . I'm a baseball fan, and I'm glad I wasn't around twenty, thirty, even fifty years ago. Today's athletes are so much better (I know because they always say so) and they play the game for the best motivation of all, themselves. None of this "love of the game" stuff. Imagine a major-leaguer being able to buy only three or four cars. That's just not how it should be. Today, ball players are paid thousands of dollars to stand in the outfield artificial turf and watch three balls hit to infielders. Then they get to go to the plate and hit meaningless fly balls and blame their .250 batting averages on a "bad back." Hey, it beats the olden days when players would simply play and strive to excel because they loved the game. Who wants to see Babe Ruth hit sixty home runs, Lou Gehrig play 2,100 games in a row, and players like Musial, Koufax, Williams, Mantle, and Yastrzemski play their hearts out for their love of the game and their intense desire to make the game enjoyable for the fans? Give me a break. I want to see players stand in front of a microphone and exclaim, "I am the greatest of all times; why did I only get a Porsche?"

Reuben Ehrlich, Air Academy High School, USAFA, Colorado

*What is the "real" answer to this question?*

## How Writers Use Satire

Satire is a form of persuasion that uses humor to criticize and change society. Both the Bombeck piece and Reuben's essay are satires. By *not* saying what they mean, they make their meaning perfectly clear, and their dry humor easily skewers their targets. A satirist may take aim at anything: a human foible, a social practice, or a political plan. For example, you might target people or institutions that inspire unquestioning fear or loyalty. If you make them look ridiculous, you encourage a real examination of whether they deserve that devotion and respect. Humor can be a surprisingly powerful weapon.

**The Weapons of Satire** When you write satire, your weapons include irony, exaggeration, and understatement. Writers create irony by saying the opposite of what they mean, as Reuben Ehrlich does when he praises the motivation of today's athletes. Exaggeration involves overstatement for effect; it's unlikely, for example, that Erma Bombeck's husband is *really* ready for all the events she lists. Deliberate understatement, representing something as less important than it really is, can also hit home, as Reuben shows when he downplays the achievements of outfielders.

**Finding Subjects for Satire** Satire has long been a popular form of entertainment as well as a weapon of social criticism. In ancient Greece, for example, crowds flocked to the plays of Aristophanes, who poked fun at the customs and political figures of his day. When you're looking for a subject for satire, think of the targets of the satirists you enjoy on TV and in newspapers. Also, become a sharp observer of the world around you. You can find countless potential subjects for satire, ranging from how people celebrate holidays to who sits where in the cafeteria.

### Journal Writing

What current social issues do you think are particularly suited to satirical treatment? Think about issues close to home as well as issues in the news, and list them in your journal along with the satirical weapon that would be best for each.

## Plan a Satirical Essay

**Drafting Tip**

As you draft, don't try to be funny in every line—that's a strain for you and for the reader. Also, consider whether your humor suits your intended audience.

When you write satire, it's easy to get carried away by exaggeration or humor and stray from your point. The result will be off target and not very funny. That's why a thesis statement is important. You don't have to include it in your essay, but use it to provide a focus as you write. Explore your topic by asking yourself questions such as: Is anything absurd about this situation? Would it become absurd if exaggerated slightly? Would understatement be more effective? How might I create irony by using comparisons or by stating the opposite of what I think? Generate some examples of irony, exaggeration, and understatement that might be useful in making your point. Then think about how to shape your examples into a convincing and amusing essay.

As you can see from the following passage, a well-aimed satire can hit a very particular target while it also comments on society at large.

### *Literature Model*

*What is the target of these overblown or exaggerated claims for a new product?*

A new aid to rapid—almost magical—learning has made its appearance. Indications are that if it catches on, all the electronic gadgets will be so much junk. The new device is known as Built-in Orderly Organized Knowledge. The makers generally call it by its initials, BOOK.

*How does the irony here help you take a new look at something very familiar?*

Many advantages are claimed over the old-style learning and teaching aids on which most people are brought up nowadays. It has no wires, no electric circuits to break down. No connection is needed to an electricity power point. It is made entirely without mechanical parts to go wrong or need replacement.

*These understatements call to mind an image of a comfortable and relaxed era.*

Anyone can use BOOK, even children, and it fits comfortably into the hands. It can be conveniently used sitting in an armchair by the fire.

How does the revolutionary, unbelievably easy invention work? Basically BOOK consists only of a large number of paper sheets. These may run to hundreds where BOOK covers a lengthy program of information. Each sheet bears a number in sequence, so that the sheets cannot be used in the wrong order. To make it even easier for the user to keep the sheets in the proper order, they are held firmly in place by a special locking device called a "binding."

R. J. Heathorn, "Learn with BOOK"

Through satire, Heathorn makes fun of our society's worship of technology and our insatiable appetite for the "new" and "improved."

# 6.5 Writing Activities

## Write a Scene for a TV Show

Choose a television program that you think is spoofable. Write a brief statement describing the elements of the show that you want to satirize. Using the elements from your statement as "targets," write a scene for a satire of the show.

- Use exaggeration, understatement, or irony—whichever best hits your target.
- Write a thesis statement.
- Maintain your focus by not overusing any of the "weapons" of satire.

**PURPOSE** To spoof a TV show
**AUDIENCE** Your classmates and teacher
**LENGTH** At least 1 scene

Duane Hanson, *Tourists*, 1970

## Cross-Curricular: Art

Look at Duane Hanson's satirical sculpture. What did you think it was satirizing before you read the name *Tourists?* Consider these questions: How successful is this sculpture as satire? Which methods of satire does Hanson employ? How is the visual satire different from a satirical essay? Using the sculpture as well as your own experience, write a satirical essay about tourists.

### Grammar Link

**Be sure that verbs agree with subjects when the subject is qualified by the word *each*.**

*Each sheet bears a number in sequence. . . .*

Use the correct form of the verb in parentheses in each of the following sentences.

1. Each tourist (is) required to carry his or her own bags.
2. Each tour guide and his or her group (have) an identity card.
3. Am I mistaken, or (do) each bus and its passengers (require) one tour guide?
4. Each bag and its owner (have) one identification number.
5. Each bus driver and his or her passengers (stay) in the same hotel.

**See Lesson 16.5, pages 572–573.**

LESSON

# 6.6 Persuasive Writing
# Creating a Satirical Cartoon

"You majored in English, Brinwell. Write us up a nice little request for higher appropriations."

*If a picture can be worth a thousand words, a satirical cartoon—combining a few deftly drawn lines with equally few and aptly chosen words—can speak volumes.*

What are the targets of the cartoons on this page? What do the pictures "say" about their subjects? How do the words amplify the drawing, or vice versa? Consider how many words you would need to describe the progression of emotions revealed by Cathy's facial expressions below.

Like satirical writing, satirical cartoons comment on political and social issues, often zeroing in on particular events, people, or groups. Satirical cartoonists, like writers, may employ irony, exaggeration, or understatement to create humor and to criticize their subject. The added dimension of visual satire may give them more immediate impact and may make them more memorable than an essay on the same subject.

Study your favorite cartoons, and note how they convey attitudes and emotions as well as action. Focus on one feature, such as eyebrows, and see how anger, puzzlement, surprise, or dismay can be expressed. Then cut out realistic photographs from magazines, and experiment with conveying similar emotions by altering only the eyebrows on each photo.

## Identify the Elements of a Satirical Cartoon

Satirical cartoons take two main forms: the single-panel cartoon and the multipanel comic strip. In both forms, cartoonists may use any of a number of elements to convey their viewpoints. The most important of these elements are caricatures, symbols, analogies, labels, captions, and dialogue.

In a caricature, the artist exaggerates some physical features of a subject, creating a comic effect. For instance, in the caricature of rock star Mick Jagger, the artist has played up Jagger's most distinctive facial features. Caricature is often an important part of a political cartoon.

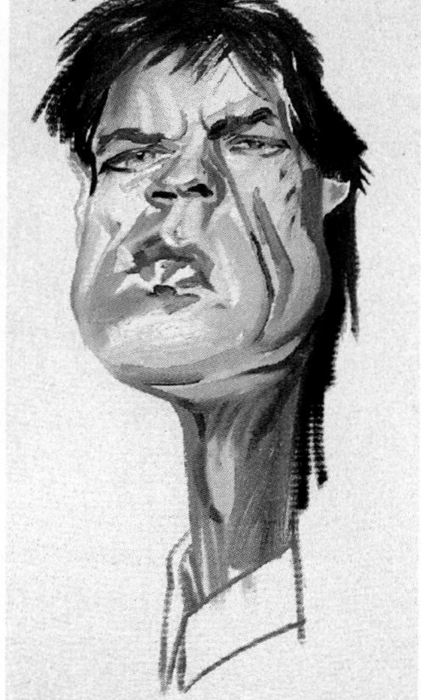

Illustration by Philip Burke

A symbol is an object that represents something else, such as a group, an event, or an idea. Political cartoonists often use an elephant to stand for the Republican party, a donkey for the Democratic party, and Uncle Sam for the United States. By using symbols, a cartoonist can quickly convey complex ideas in a single picture.

Another economical way to convey a complex idea is by making an analogy. An analogy is an extended comparison that shows or implies multiple similarities. For example, a political cartoonist has compared the downfall of communism to the extinction of the dinosaurs. An apt analogy is a shortcut that helps dramatize the cartoonist's point of view. For more about analogies, see Unit 5, Lesson 4.

Labels are words *on* pictures, while captions are phrases or sentences *below* pictures. Cartoonists use labels to identify particular symbols, caricatures, characters, or ideas that may not be readily apparent. They use captions to help convey the main idea of a cartoon or to show the words of a character. In comic strips, the point of a cartoon is often conveyed through dialogue, which is conversation that appears in speech balloons.

### Drafting Tip

When writing a caption, you can refer to the material about using interjections on page 441 of Lesson 10.8 in Grammar, Usage, and Mechanics.

### Journal Writing

In a newspaper or magazine, find a satirical cartoon that contains a caricature. In your journal, describe the caricature and explain what the cartoonist is trying to convey about the person.

## Make a Satirical Cartoon

What is being satirized in the cartoon below? How does it "work"? This cartoon is based on a comparison or analogy; it manages to satirize both the sneaker ads aimed at teen-agers and the dress-for-success ads aimed at executives. It takes a gentle poke at business practices. The cartoon works because the analogy is immediately clear, and it's both apt and incongruous, thus creating humor. You can translate what makes this cartoon work into guidelines for creating your own cartoon.

*The characters are easily recognizable; the briefcase (visual) and the wing tip shoes (words) make it clear that they are all business people.*

*The words can be quickly read and easily understood.*

**Choose a limited subject.** Consider subjects that are familiar to your audience and that can be encapsulated in a few words and images. Try characters, actions, or ideas that become laughable with only a little exaggeration or an unlikely comparison.

**Create simple, easy-to-recognize characters.** Aim your satire at targets that can be "summarized" in a few easily recognized images. You might choose a single person, such as a rock star, or a group or institution—such as businesspeople, a nation, Congress, or basketball players. Labels or dialogue can help identify characters, but remember that the less "work" your audience has to do, the more effective your cartoon will be.

**Use only simple actions.** Consider straightforward, uncomplicated actions for your characters. While the actions may be symbolic, such as pumping up for a business deal, it should be clear what the character in the drawing is doing.

**Use words sparingly.** While brief, simple dialogue may be necessary to get your point across, make sure it's easy to understand and doesn't take up much room. If you rely too heavily on dialogue, you're really creating an illustrated story or play instead of a cartoon. Labels and captions, too, should be minimal and easy to understand.

**Revise and simplify.** Eliminate all that is extraneous and rework your cartoon until its impact is as immediate as possible.

### Revising Tip

Cartoons are primarily visual. Whenever possible, use a visual clue, such as a briefcase, rather than the label "businesswoman."

# 6.6 Writing Activities

## Create a Satirical Cartoon

Imagine that you are a cartoonist with an opposing viewpoint on the same subject satirized in one of the cartoons in this lesson. First, use the five-step process described on page 296 to evaluate the cartoon. Be sure you know what the cartoon symbolizes. Observe carefully how the cartoonist uses specific elements of art and writing.

Now create a cartoon expressing your own viewpoint. You may be able to borrow many of the words and images from the original cartoon.

- Use the elements of satirical writing—irony, exaggeration, or understatement.
- Choose a limited subject.
- Create simple, easy-to-recognize characters.
- Use only simple actions.
- Use words sparingly.
- Revise and simplify.

**PURPOSE** To create a satirical cartoon
**AUDIENCE** Your classmates and teacher
**LENGTH** 1–8 panels

### COMPUTER OPTION

Are you having trouble doing the drawing for the assignment? You may be able to create the images for your cartoon on your computer. Many software companies publish floppy disks of "clip art," various illustrations in many different categories, that you can copy and paste electronically. You can also use drawing software programs to create your own images. These are fun to use and relatively easy to learn. The finished product may look professionally produced.

### Grammar Link

**Use commas, when needed, with introductory words, nouns of direct address, and tag phrases.**

*Well, could you cut a new roast. . . ?*

*You majored in English, Bromwell.*

*You've completed your cartoon, haven't you?*

Add an introductory word, a noun of direct address, or a tag phrase to each of the following sentences, and use a comma if it's necessary.

1. Charles Addams was a famous cartoonist?
2. He did most of his work for *The New Yorker* magazine.
3. When one of his cartoons was rejected, his editor said to him, "It's a bit too grim."
4. I saw it later and thought it was very funny.
5. The magazine continues to publish his cartoons.
6. Those Addams family movies are based on his cartoons?
7. Some say the movies are funnier than the cartoons.
8. I'm telling you, nothing is funnier than his cartoons.

**See Lesson 21.6, pages 682–690.**

LESSON

# 6.7 Writing About Literature Analyzing a Critical Review

*The whole point of a critical review is to persuade. The goal is to persuade others to do or not do something or to go or not go someplace.*

How do you decide what movies to see? Are you influenced by critical reviews in newspapers or magazines? As you read the following review, decide whether it would persuade you to see *Breaking Away.*

***Literature Model***

Here's a sunny, goofy, intelligent, little film about coming of age in Bloomington, Indiana. It's about four local kids, just out of high school, who mess around for one final summer before facing the inexorable choices of jobs or college or the Army. One of the kids, Dave (Dennis Christopher), has it in his head that he wants to be a champion Italian bicycle racer, and he drives his father crazy with opera records and ersatz Italian.

His friends have more reasonable ambitions: One (Dennis Quaid) was a high school football star who pretends he doesn't want to play college ball, but he does; another (Jackie Earle Haley) is a short kid who pretends he doesn't want to be taller, but he does; and another (Daniel Stern) is one of those kids like we all knew, who learned how to talk by crossing Eric Sevareid with Woody Allen. . . .

*Breaking Away* is a movie to embrace. It's about people who are complicated but decent, who are optimists but see things realistically, who are fundamentally comic characters but have three full dimensions. It's about a Middle America we rarely see in the movies, yes, but it's not corny and it doesn't condescend. Movies like this are hardly ever made at all; when they're made this well, they're precious cinematic miracles.

Roger Ebert, Review of *Breaking Away*

*Is this information tantalizing, or do you think it gives too much away?*

*Film Critic Roger Ebert*

## The Purposes and Conventions of Reviews

Critical reviews are basically persuasive. They often convince people to read a particular book or not to see a particular movie. In so doing, they make use of other types of writing. For example, reviews may use narration to give readers an idea of the plot, or they may use description in their discussion of setting, cinematography, or character. In both cases, however, the narration and description should be in service of the basic purpose of a critical review: to evaluate and recommend.

While critical reviews give readers the information they need in order to choose among all the new books and movies that come out each year, they should also be interesting and entertaining in their own right. Critics, however, have a responsibility to be accurate and fair and not merely to show off their own wit or cleverness.

Like other forms of writing, critical reviews follow certain conventions. The chart on the right highlights some of these conventions as they apply to movie reviews. Use the checklist to evaluate an individual review as well as to decide whether the reviewer is worth reading again. In some cases, you will be able to answer these questions better after having seen the movie. Then you'll know whether to read and follow the advice of that reviewer again.

**Checklist for a Movie Review**

1. Does the review focus on the movie (rather than on a side issue that happens to be important to the reviewer)?
2. Does it give enough information about the movie so I know whether I want to see it, or does it spoil my enjoyment by telling too much?
3. Does it evaluate the movie according to the criteria usually used for that genre, such as strength of storyline, acting, direction, cinematography, and emotional impact?
4. Does the review zero in on specifics that interest me, such as an individual actor, a particular locale, the emotional impact, and the cinematography?
5. If it gives details of the reviewer's personal reaction to the movie, does that reaction help me decide whether or not I want to see the movie?
6. Is the review interesting and worth reading in its own right?

### Journal Writing

Think about some of the informal movie or book "reviews" that you've heard in conversations with friends, teachers, or relatives. Jot down notes about those that were particularly convincing, and explain why these reviews influenced you. Which of the conventions above did these "reviewers" follow?

## Evaluate a Critical Review

*"What movie should we see tonight?"*

*"I read a great review of Spielberg's new movie in the paper."*

*"Oh, that reviewer just likes everything Spielberg does. But then again, so do I. Let's go see it."*

What's the point of being able to judge the merit of a critical review? Because critics often differ, you need to decide for yourself which critic's advice to follow. You also want to have a sense of how knowledgeable and fair each reviewer is—and how entertaining to read. You may even find that you enjoy the style of someone who hates the books or movies that you love. Reading well-thought-out and well-written reviews can also sharpen your own critical abilities and give you ideas for your own writing.

The model below shows how the checklist on page 299 might be used to evaluate the entire Roger Ebert review of *Breaking Away*, which was excerpted on page 298. The typed remarks were made before the writer saw the movie. The handwritten notes were added afterward. Note that the model concludes with a general comment about the reviewer.

**Drafting Tip**

You might turn an evaluation of a critical review into a letter to the editor agreeing or disagreeing with a review you've read in a newspaper.

Roger Ebert on Breaking Away

What I thought of the review:

— Gives enough information to interest me, but it seems as though I know practically the whole story already. *Oops—there were a few surprises left!*

— Described personalities, not plot.

— I like movies about teenagers if they're realistic, so the review helped here.

— His enthusiasm was contagious. *I loved it too—guess he couldn't help gushing.*

— Interesting, well-written review--entertaining to read.

Overall, I like Ebert's style and would read him again. *And we agreed on this movie, so I'll check his opinions before I decide where to spend my time and money.*

# 6.7 Writing Activities

## Write a Comparative Essay

Look through current magazines and newspapers and find two reviews, by different reviewers, of a movie. Use the checklist on page 299 to evaluate them. Then write a short essay discussing which reviewer's advice you would be more likely to follow and which reviewer you would prefer to read for entertainment. (They may not be the same.)

- Look for accurate and fair judgments.
- There should be a balance between information and opinion.
- Look for ideas for your own writing.

**PURPOSE** To analyze two critical reviews
**AUDIENCE** Your classmates and teacher
**LENGTH** 1–2 pages

## Cooperative Learning

Meet with three classmates to consider the fate of Richard Serra's steel sculpture, below, which ran 120 feet long and 12 feet high and inspired fierce controversy when placed in front of an office building. Employees petitioned its removal. The sculpture was eventually removed in 1989.

Select some local or well-known national artwork and, jointly, write a critical review of it. Make a case for why the taxpayer should or should not have paid for it.

### Grammar Link

**Use consistent tenses in your writing. Notice that Roger Ebert's review of *Breaking Away* is almost all written in the present tense.**

Rewrite the following paragraph to make the verb tenses consistent.

In an early scene of the film, which opened today, Frederick leads his sheep down the mountain to sell so that he can buy medicine for his sick mother. By the time he returned home, she has already died. Flashbacks in black and white reveal that Frederick never likes caring for sheep anyway, but the economic loss will be substantial. He uses the money from the sale of the sheep to buy a camcorder. He wanted to make videos for years. So far, there is nothing believable about this movie. It appears that the filmmaker was giving us an unwanted glimpse of his own youth.

**See Lesson 15.6, pages 551–552.**

Richard Serra, *Tilted Arc*, 1981

UNIT 6

# WRITING PROCESS IN ACTION

## PERSUASIVE WRITING

In preceding lessons you've learned about the kinds of techniques and strategies that can make persuasive writing effective. You've also had the chance to convince your readers of your point of view with your writing. Now it's time to make use of what you learned. In this lesson, you're invited to write a persuasive essay about the importance of cultural characteristics to a person's character.

### • Assignment •

| | |
|---|---|
| *Context* | *Your school offers an elective called International Relations: the Microcosmic View. The current course theme is fundamentals: what makes people, communities, or nations what they are. You've been given a great deal of freedom in selecting your topic for a persuasive essay that incorporates anecdote and, if possible, humor. You're asked to consider not only your own experience but also that of others so that your conclusion will appeal to a diverse audience.* |
| *Purpose* | *To write a persuasive essay supporting the position that a particular cultural ingredient is of paramount importance in making people who they are* |
| *Audience* | *A group of high school students from around the world who are studying cultural similarities and differences* |
| *Length* | *3–5 pages* |

The following pages can help you plan and write your persuasive essay. Read through them and then refer to them as you need to. But don't be tied down by them. You're in charge of your own writing process.

WRITING PROCESS IN ACTION

# Prewriting

You are asking, "What personal and cultural ingredients most influence a person's development?" Use this question or one you've phrased for yourself to help you begin prewriting. As you prewrite keep in mind that the ingredient you write about should have general applicability and potential for debate. Subjects you might consider include language, family structure, education, government, entertainment, and physical environment.

After using the question above or one of your own to get images and ideas percolating, begin to focus your prewriting to look for a pattern or a spark to ignite the single idea that can become your thesis.

Now use your thesis statement as a touchstone in selecting supporting details. If all of the details you have generated during prewriting come solely out of your own experience, do some research related to your thesis to find out what experts think, or interview friends, family members, teachers, and others to gather not only facts and opinions but also anecdotes.

Remember that you're rounding up details that will serve a specific persuasive purpose and speak to a designated audience.

Prewriting Options

- To help find your thesis, select what seems to be a central idea and create a cluster of words and ideas around it.
- Ask someone to brainstorm your subject with you, tossing out the subjects mentioned above.
- Take a sheet of paper and begin freewriting, putting down your thoughts as they occur to you.
- Consider both your own interests and those of your audience.

**Prewriting Tip**

For help with deciding on a topic, see Lesson 6.1, page 271.

# Drafting

Every essay needs a structure, an organizational plan, but this is particularly important in building a persuasive argument. Start your plan with your thesis. Write it down, and experiment with the order of these supporting ideas. Given your thesis, which pattern proves most forceful or most compelling: chronological, order of importance, cause and effect, or comparison and contrast?

Once you've decided on an organizational pattern, pack the structure with plenty of supporting details for each persuasive point. Remember that you are required to use anecdotes and encouraged to use humor.

After creating an outline or an informal plan for your essay, the next step is to decide on your opening. Consider your stance and your tone; they are particularly important in persuasive writing. Notice how Amy Tan in "Mother Tongue" disarms her readers by first confessing a shortcoming and then asserting her credentials.

**Drafting Tip**

For help in organizing your essay, see Lesson 6.1, page 272.

*Literature Model*

I am not a scholar of English or literature. I cannot give you much more than personal opinions on the English language and its variations in this country or others.

I am a writer. And by that definition, I am someone who has always loved language. I am fascinated by language in daily life. I spend a great deal of my time thinking about the power of language—the way it can evoke an emotion, a visual image, a complex idea, or a simple truth. Language is the tool of my trade. And I use them all—all the Englishes I grew up with.

Amy Tan, "Mother Tongue"

**Drafting Tip**

For help in drafting your essay, see the examples in Lesson 6.1 on pages 273 and 274.

**Revising Tip**

For help with errors in logic, see Lesson 6.3, page 281, and Lesson 6.4, page 288.

Having equipped yourself with a general map of the area you want to cover, you're ready to draft. Don't trouble yourself over grammar or word choice now; doing so can interrupt the spontaneous flow of ideas. Writing freely, however, doesn't mean writing wildly, so keep your purpose and audience in clear focus. Imagine a "personal reader" (face and all) whom you wish to convince, and marshal your persuasive skills to that purpose.

Revising Checklist

- Have I supported my position with the best evidence I can find?
- Have I identified any logical fallacies that could compromise the credibility of my essay?
- Would using inductive or deductive reasoning strengthen my argument?
- Are irony, exaggeration, and understatement used where appropriate?

## Revising

To begin revising, read over your draft to make sure that what you have written fits your purpose and your audience. Then have a **writing conference**. Read your draft to a partner or small group. Use your audience's reactions to help you evaluate your work so far. The checklist questions at the left can help you and your audience.

# Editing

Once you are happy with the basic content and set-up of your persuasive essay, **proofread** it carefully for errors in grammar, usage, mechanics, and spelling. Use the questions at the right as a guide.

In addition to proofreading, use the self-evaluation list below to make sure your essay does all the things you want it to do. When you're satisfied, make a clean copy of your description and proofread it one more time.

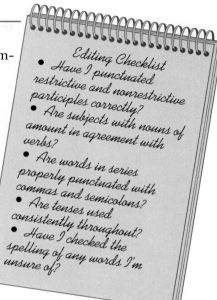

Editing Checklist
- Have I punctuated restrictive and nonrestrictive participles correctly?
- Are subjects with nouns of amount in agreement with verbs?
- Are words in series properly punctuated with commas and semicolons?
- Are tenses used consistently throughout?
- Have I checked the spelling of any words I'm unsure of?

## Self-Evaluation

**Make sure your persuasive essay—**

- makes a case for the importance of a particular influence on personal or cultural identity
- supports a clear thesis with appropriate evidence
- contains no errors in logic
- uses an anecdote or illustration
- uses humor effectively
- follows correct grammar, usage, mechanics, and spelling

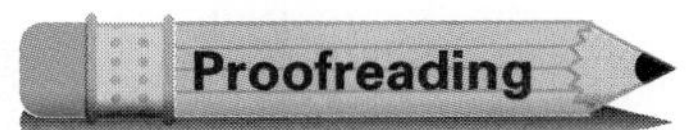


For proofreading symbols, see page 92.

# Presenting

You can contribute the persuasive essay you have written to a school or local publication. If the subject and tone are appropriate, you might submit it as a sample of your writing when you apply to colleges. Begin by asking a friend or family member to read your essay and criticize it frankly.

**Presenting Tip**

For help in deciding on how to present your essay, see Lesson 2.9, pp. 94–96.

## Journal Writing

Reflect on your writing experience. Answer these questions in your journal: What do you like best about your essay? What was the hardest part of writing it? What did you learn in your persuasive writing conference? What new things have you learned as a writer?

UNIT 6

# Persuasive Writing
# Literature Model

*In* "Mother Tongue" *Chinese-American writer Amy Tan writes about the difference between the standard English she learned in school and the "broken" English her mother spoke at home. In the following essay, Tan explores the effects of growing up with many "Englishes" and persuades us with wit and insight that language, for better or worse, shapes us and the world we live in.*

I am not a scholar of English or literature. I cannot give you much more than personal opinions on the English language and its variations in this country or others.

I am a writer. And by that definition, I am someone who has always loved language. I am fascinated by language in daily life. I spend a great deal of my time thinking about the power of language

—the way it can evoke an emotion, a visual image, a complex idea, or a simple truth. Language is the tool of my trade. And I use them all—all the Englishes I grew up with.

Recently, I was made keenly aware of the different Englishes I do use. I was giving a talk to a large group of people, the same talk I had already given to half a dozen other groups. The nature of the talk was about my writing, my life, and my book, *The Joy Luck Club.* The talk was going along well enough, until I remembered one major difference that made the whole talk sound wrong. My mother was in the room. And it was perhaps the first time she had heard me give a lengthy speech, using the kind of English I have never used with her. I was saying things like, "The intersection of memory upon imagination" and "There is an aspect of my fiction that relates to thus-and-thus"—a speech filled with carefully wrought grammatical phrases, burdened, it suddenly seemed to me, with nominalized forms, past perfect tenses, conditional phrases, all the forms of standard English that I had learned in school and through books, the forms of English I did not use at home with my mother.

Just last week, I was walking down the street with my mother, and I again found myself conscious of the English I was using, the English I do use with her. We were talking about the price of new and used furniture and I heard myself saying this: "Not waste money that way." My husband was with us as well, and he didn't notice any switch in my English. And then I realized why. It's because over the twenty years we've been together I've often used that same kind of English with him, and sometimes he even uses it with me. It has become our language of intimacy, a different sort of English that relates to family talk, the language I grew up with.

So you'll have some idea of what this family talk I heard sounds like, I'll quote what my mother said during a recent conversation which I videotaped and then transcribed. During this conversation, my mother was talking about a political gangster in Shanghai who had the same last name as her family's, Du, and how the gangster in his early years wanted to be adopted by her family, which was rich by comparison. Later, the gangster became more powerful, far richer than my mother's family, and one day showed up at my mother's wedding to pay his respects. Here's what she said in part:

"Du Yusong having business like fruit stand. Like off the street kind. He is Du like Du Zong—but not Tsung-ming Island people. The local people call putong, the river east side, he belong to that side local people. That man want to ask Du Zong father take him in like become own family. Du Zong father wasn't look down on him, but didn't take seriously, until that man big like become a mafia. Now important person, very hard to inviting him. Chinese way, came only to show respect, don't stay for dinner. Respect for making big celebration, he shows up. Mean gives lots of respect. Chinese custom. Chinese social life that way. If too important won't have to stay too long. He come to my wedding. I didn't see, I heard it. I gone to boy's side, they have YWCA dinner. Chinese age I was nineteen."

You should know that my mother's expressive command of English belies how much she actually understands. She reads the *Forbes* report, listens to *Wall Street Week,* converses daily with her stockbroker, reads all of Shirley MacLaine's books with ease—all kinds of things I can't begin to understand. Yet some of my friends tell me they understand 50 percent of what my mother says. Some say they understand 80 to 90 percent. Some say they understand none of it, as if she were speaking pure Chinese. But to me, my mother's English is perfectly clear, perfectly natural. It's my mother tongue. Her language, as I hear it, is vivid, direct, full of observation and imagery. That was the language that helped shape the way I saw things, expressed things, made sense of the world.

Lately, I've been giving more thought to the kind of English my mother speaks. Like others, I have described it to people as "broken" or "fractured" English. But I wince when I say that. It has always bothered me that I can think of no way to describe it other than"broken," as if it were damaged and needed to be fixed, as if it lacked a certain wholeness and soundness. I've heard other terms used, "limited English," for example. But they seem just as bad, as if everything is limited, including people's perceptions of the limited English speaker.

I know this for a fact, because when I was growing up, my mother's "limited" English limited *my* perception of her. I was ashamed of her English. I believed that her English reflected the quality of what she had to say. That is, because she expressed them imperfectly her thoughts were imperfect. And I had plenty of empirical evidence to support me: the fact that people in department stores, at banks, and at restaurants did not take her seriously, did not give her good service, pretended not to understand her, or even acted as if they did not hear her.

My mother has long realized the limitations of her English as well. When I was fifteen, she used to have me call people on the phone to pretend I was she. In this guise, I was forced to ask for information or even to complain and yell at people who had been rude to her. One time it was a call to her stockbroker in New York. She had cashed out her small portfolio and it just so happened we were going to go to New York the next week, our very first trip outside California. I had to get on the phone and say in an adolescent voice that was not very convincing, "This is Mrs. Tan."

And my mother was standing in the back whispering loudly, "Why he don't send me check, already two weeks late. So mad he lie to me, losing me money."

And then I said in perfect English, "Yes, I'm getting rather concerned. You had agreed to send the check two weeks ago, but it hasn't arrived."

Then she began to talk more loudly. "What he want, I come to New York tell him front of his boss, you cheating me?" And I was trying to calm her down, make her be quiet, while telling the stockbroker, " I can't tolerate any more excuses. If I don't receive the check immediately, I am going to have to speak to your manager when I'm in New York next week." And sure enough, the following week there we were in front of this astonished stockbroker, and I was sitting there red-faced and quiet, and my mother, the real Mrs. Tan, was shouting at his boss in her impeccable broken English.

We used a similar routine just five days ago, for a situation that was far less humorous. My mother had gone to the hospital for an appointment, to find out about a benign brain tumor a CAT scan had revealed a month ago. She said she had spoken very good English, her best English, no mistakes. Still, she said, the hospital did not apologize when they said they had lost the CAT scan and she had come for nothing. She said they did not seem to have any sympathy when she told them she was anxious to know the exact diagnosis, since her husband and son had both died of brain tumors. She said they would not give her any more information until the next time and she would have to make another appointment for that. So she said she would not leave until the doctor called her daughter. She wouldn't budge. And when the doctor finally called her daughter, me, who spoke in perfect English—lo and behold—we had assurances the CAT scan would be found, promises that a conference call on Monday would be held, and apologies for any suffering my mother had gone through for a most regrettable mistake.

I think my mother's English almost had an effect on limiting my possibilities in life as well. Sociologists and linguists probably will tell you that a person's developing language skills are more influenced by peers. But I do think that the language spoken in the family, especially in immigrant families which are more insular, plays a large role in shaping the language of the child. And I believe that it affected my results on achievement tests, IQ tests, and the SAT. While my English skills were never judged as poor, compared to math, English could not be considered my strong suit. In grade school I did moderately well, getting perhaps B's, sometimes B-pluses, in English and scoring perhaps in the sixtieth or seventieth percentile on achievement tests. But those scores were not good enough to override the opinion that my true abilities lay in math and science, because in those areas I achieved A's and scored in the ninetieth percentile or higher.

This was understandable. Math is precise; there is only one correct answer. Whereas, for me at least, the answers on English tests were always a judgment call, a matter of opinion and personal

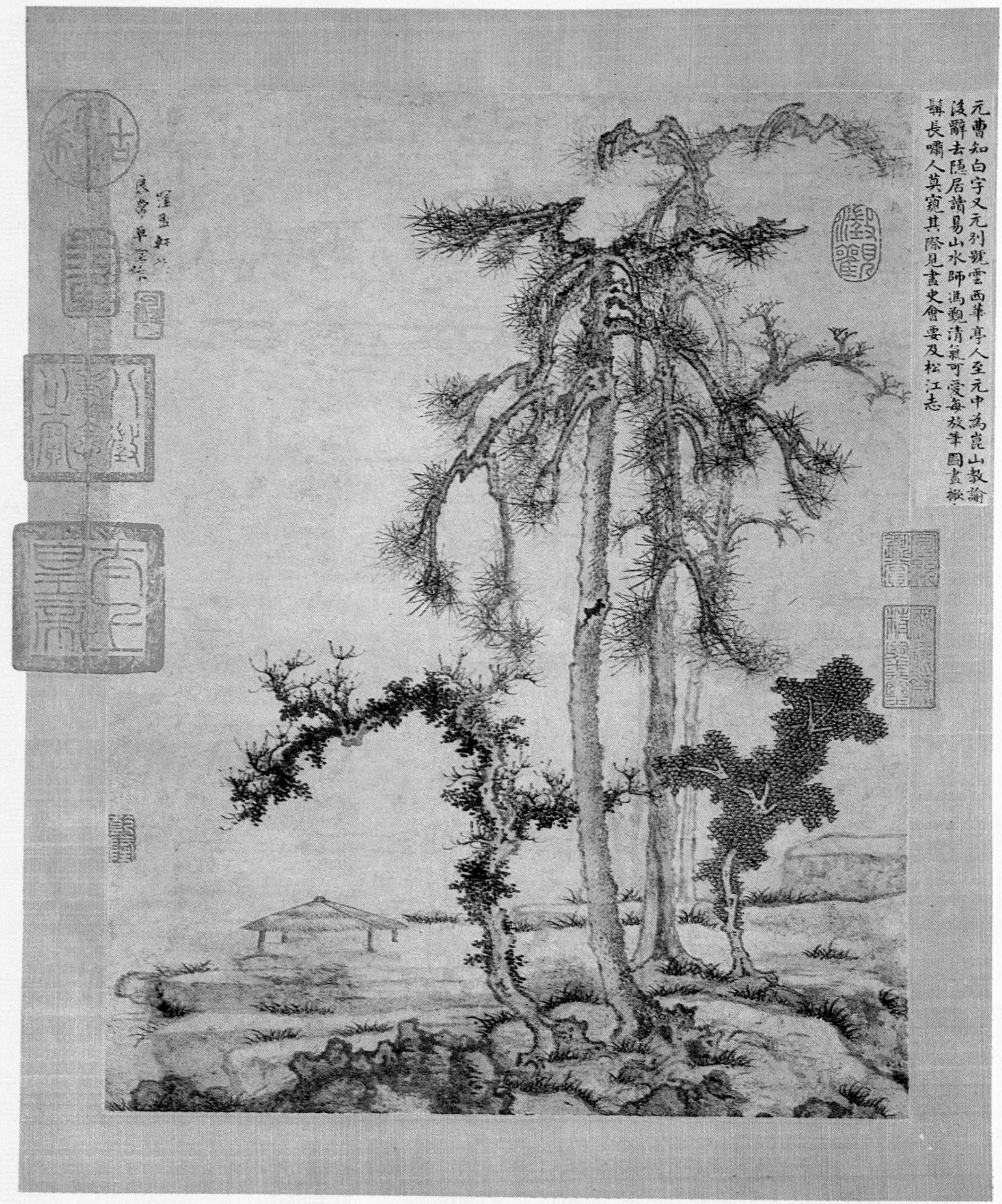


Ts'ao Tche-Po, *Pavilion near Pine Trees*, 1272–1355

experience. Those tests were constructed around items like fill-in-the-blank sentence completion, such as, "Even though Tom was ____, Mary thought he was ____." And the correct answer always seemed to be the most bland combinations of thoughts, for example, "Even though Tom was shy, Mary thought he was charming," with the grammatical structure "even though" limiting the correct answer to some sort of semantic opposites, so you wouldn't get answers like, "Even though Tom was foolish, Mary thought he was ridiculous." Well, according to my mother, there were very few limitations as to what Tom could have been and what Mary might have thought of him. So I never did well on tests like that.

The same was true with word analogies, pairs of words in which you were supposed to find some sort of logical, semantic relationship—for example, "*Sunset* is to *nightfall* as ________ is to ________." And here you would be presented with a list of four possible pairs, one of which showed the same kind of relationship: *red* is to *stoplight, bus* is to *arrival, chills* is to *fever, yawn* is to *boring.* Well, I could never think that way. I knew what the tests were asking, but I could not block out of my mind the images already created by the first pair, "*sunset* is to *nightfall*"—and I would see a burst of colors against a darkening sky, the moon rising, the lowering of a curtain of stars. And all the other pairs of words—red, bus, stoplight, boring—just threw up a mass of confusing images, making it impossible for me to sort out something as logical as saying: "A sunset precedes nightfall" is the same as "a chill precedes a fever." The only way I would have gotten that answer right would have been to imagine an associative situation, for example, my being disobedient and staying out past sunset, catching a chill at night, which turns into feverish pneumonia as punishment, which indeed did happen to me.

I have been thinking about all this lately, about my mother's English, about achievement tests. Because lately I've been asked, as a writer, why there are not more Asian Americans represented in American literature. Why are there few Asian Americans enrolled in creative writing programs? Why do so many Chinese students go into engineering? Well, these are broad sociological questions I can't begin to answer. But I have noticed in surveys—in fact, just last week—that Asian students, as a whole, always do significantly better on math achievement tests than in English. And this makes me think that there are other Asian-American students whose English spoken in the home might also be described as "broken" or "limited." And perhaps they also have teachers who are steering them away from writing and into math and science, which is what happened to me.

Fortunately, I happen to be rebellious in nature and enjoy the challenge of disproving assumptions made about me. I became an English major my first year in college, after being enrolled as premed. I started writing nonfiction as a freelancer the week after I was told by my former boss that writing was my worst skill and I should hone my talents toward account management.

But it wasn't until 1985 that I finally began to write fiction. And at first I wrote using what I thought to be wittily crafted sentences, sentences that would finally prove I had mastery over the English language. Here's an example from the first draft of a story that later made its way into *The Joy Luck Club,* but without this line: "That was my mental quandary in its nascent state." A terrible line, which I can barely pronounce.

Fortunately, for reasons I won't get into today, I later decided I should envision a reader for the stories I would write. And the reader I decided upon was my mother, because these were stories about mothers. So with this reader in mind—and in fact she did read my early drafts—I began to write stories using all the Englishes I grew up with: the English I spoke to my mother, which for lack of a better term might be described as "simple"; the English she used with me, which for lack of a better term might be described as "broken"; my translation of her Chinese, which could certainly be described as "watered down"; and what I imagined to be her translation of her Chinese if she could speak in perfect English, her internal language, and for that I sought to preserve the essence, but neither an English nor a Chinese structure. I wanted to capture what language ability tests can never reveal: her intent, her passion, her imagery, the rhythms of her speech and the nature of her thoughts.

Apart from what any critic had to say about my writing, I knew I had succeeded where it counted when my mother finished reading my book and gave me her verdict: "So easy to read."

# Linking Writing and Literature

## Readers Respond to the Model

### What makes Amy Tan's persuasive essay effective?

**Explore Amy Tan's essay about language by answering these questions. Then read what other students liked about Tan's essay.**

1. How did Amy Tan feel about calling the stockbroker for her mother? What does this anecdote tell you about Tan and her mother, about immigrant families, about our society in particular, or about human nature in general?
2. Tan describes at length her performance on, and reactions to, tests such as the SAT. What is her point here about language?
3. How is the phrase "mother tongue" a play on words in this essay? What is your "mother tongue"? What makes up the private jokes, nicknames, expressions, and family stories known only within your household? How do you think this family language has shaped the way you view the world?

Tan never got hostile. She said she rebelled, but she never sounded angry. "Mother Tongue" was always friendly and evoked sympathy from me.

***Arthur Housinger***

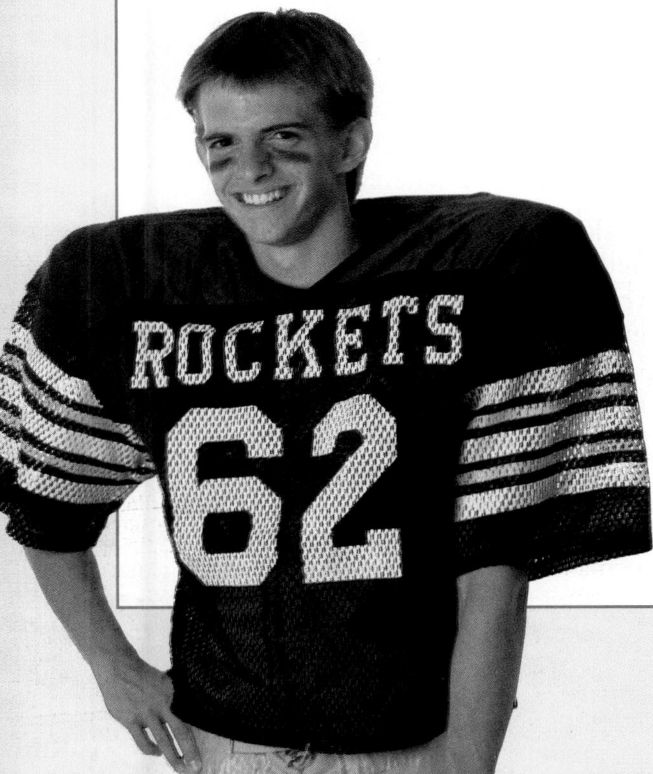


In this selection, Amy Tan talks about what it was like to grow up in a home where "broken" English was spoken. I liked Tan's thoughts about why so many Asian Americans are steered toward careers in math and science. I also enjoyed Tan's discussion about why her scores on exams like the SATs were only average or poor. I could relate to the difficulty of the SATs as I have taken them recently.

***Susannah Levine***

# Unit 6 Review

## Reflecting on the Unit

**Summarize what you learned in this unit by answering the following questions.**

- Compare the persuasive techniques of Dave Barry in his humorous column with those of Amy Tan in "Mother Tongue." Which could you use more effectively in your own writing?
- How can identifying and evaluating evidence early in the writing process make your writing easier and better?
- Do you understand the difference between inductive and deductive reasoning? Can you use both in your writing?

## Adding to Your Portfolio

**Choose selections for your portfolio.**
Look over the persuasive writing you have done during this unit. Select a completed piece of writing to put into your portfolio. The piece you choose should show some or all of the following:

- organization by order of importance first or by refutation of opposing arguments first
- reliable evidence
- sound logic
- use of inductive or deductive logic
- satire created by exaggeration, understatement, or irony
- a successful match of purpose, audience, and type and order of evidence

**Reflect on your choice.**
Attach a note to the piece you chose, explaining briefly why you chose it and what you learned from writing it.

**Set goals.**
How can you improve your writing? What skill will you focus on the next time you write?

## Writing Across the Curriculum

**Make a geography connection.**
Select a country that you've visited or one that you'd like to visit and write two or three paragraphs to persuade others to visit it as well. Do some research to find out the more attractive features of the country: the hospitable people, the pleasant climate, the fine cuisine, the scenery, or the favorable exchange rate of the dollar. Explain why your audience should choose your country rather than another. Try to make your case with accurate facts, clear logic, and humor.

UNIT 7

# Research Paper Writing

Composition

## Lessons

### RESEARCH PAPER WRITING

### Skills and Applications



### Unit 7 Review

LESSON 7.1

# Research Paper Writing

# Prewriting: Planning and Researching

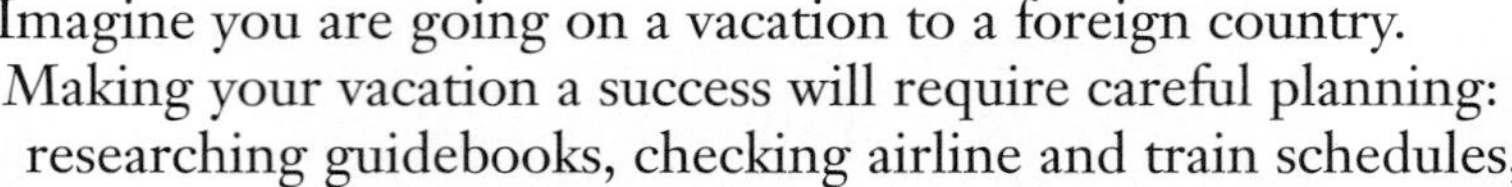

Imagine you are going on a vacation to a foreign country. Making your vacation a success will require careful planning: researching guidebooks, checking airline and train schedules, arranging an itinerary, and contacting hotels. In spite of all the work involved in planning, the result will be an entertaining, rewarding vacation.

Similarly, a research paper is a demanding project that can be made more manageable and enjoyable through careful planning. This unit is meant to serve as a guide to exploring a research topic of your choice.

As you probably know, creating a research paper is different from writing other kinds of papers. Rather than writing exclusively about your own experiences and opinions, when you prepare a research paper, you examine and evaluate the ideas of others. You will present your findings in your paper, giving credit to ideas that you borrow. A research paper is, nevertheless, similar to other kinds of writing in that you use the stages of the writing process. You should plan ahead and give yourself enough time for each stage.

The chart below suggests a six-week writing process. The actual time that you spend on your research paper may vary, depending on your paper's required length and the availability of library resources. Your teacher can help you to plan your time.

**Five Steps in Planning a Research Paper**

1. Set a schedule
2. Determine a purpose
3. Select a topic
4. Choose a central idea
5. Identify research questions

| Week 1 | Week 2 | Week 3 | Week 4 | Week 5 | Week 6 |
|---|---|---|---|---|---|
| Prewriting: Planning, Researching, and Outlining | | | Drafting | Revising | Editing and Presenting |

Paper Due

## Choose and Limit a Topic

Your first step in writing a research paper is to choose a specific topic. Your teacher may assign you a general subject area from which to choose a specific topic, or you may choose your own. Because you will spend many hours working on your paper, it is important to choose a topic covering a significant issue that will sustain your interest.

To find a topic, think about what you have read lately. Perhaps some issue or event piqued your curiosity. What would you like to learn more about? Try brainstorming or freewriting to get ideas. You might also browse through encyclopedias and books to generate ideas.

Next, limit your topic so that you can explore it adequately in a paper of the assigned length. Scanning tables of contents and indexes of books will indicate how broad your topic is, how it can be broken down into subtopics, and how much information is available on the topic. Your topic should not be so broad that you can't cover it in a short paper, nor so narrow that you can't find enough research materials.

Marie-Corinne Gilbert, a student at Santa Catalina School in Monterey, California, is interested in Russian history. Throughout this unit you will see examples of notes, outlines, and drafts leading to a finished research paper on a topic in Russian history—Mikhail Gorbachev, Peter the Great, and the modernization of Russia—that she prepared during the Gorbachev era. You can read her finished paper on pages 342–347.

**Prewriting Tip**

Jot down unfamiliar terms. You will need to define them in the body of your paper.

**Limiting a Topic**

| Too General | Limited | Too Limited |
|---|---|---|
| Europe's Industrial Revolution | Child labor in English coal mines | English Child Labor Law of 1802 |
| World War I | Gas warfare in World War I | Belgian cannon styles in World War I |
| The modernization of Russia | Reformers: Peter the Great and Gorbachev | Modern tractor production in Russia |

## Get the Big Picture

Once you have selected a topic, reading about it in general reference books will help you to think of different ways to approach it. You may see an aspect of your topic that relates to your own interests; for example, if your topic is music and the arts, and you're interested in foreign affairs, you might want to write about the ways cultural exchange programs among nations can affect diplomatic relations. Note possible research sources as you read.

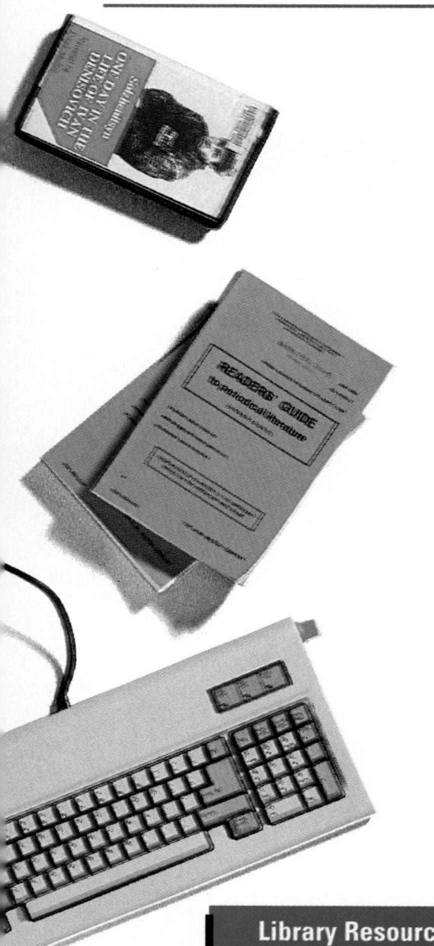


As you learn more about your topic, you should begin to develop your paper's central idea, which is the purpose of your research. Even though this central idea will probably change as you do more research, a central idea will guide your efforts. If you are open to changing your central idea, you will be more likely to find interesting and useful information as you do library research.

To devise a central idea, begin by asking yourself general questions about your topic, such as the following: What effect did this event or person have on society? Why did this event occur as it did? Why is it important now? What is interesting or unique about the topic? Don't rush to answer these questions too early, or you will limit your ability to explore all the aspects of your central idea. As you begin finding answers, refine your questions so that they are more precise and explore something unique about your topic.

## Identify Sources

While you are exploring your topic, you should gather perspectives on it from various sources. Most large libraries will have not only printed resources, such as books, magazines, journals, newspapers, and pamphlets, but also nonprint resources, such as tapes of radio programs, television programs, and films.

You can find most library resources by using the card catalog, the computer catalog, or the microfiche listings. Additionally, special references, such as the *Guide to Historical Literature*, will direct you to books in certain fields of study. Magazine articles can be located by using the *Readers' Guide to Periodical Literature*. Many newspapers, such as *The New York Times* and the *Washington Post*, publish indexes of their articles.

**Library Resources**

- Newspaper indexes
- Almanacs
- On-line computer services
- Films and videotapes
- Card catalog
- *Readers' Guide to Periodical Literature*
- Biographical encyclopedias, *Who's Who*
- Recordings, interviews

Some of your sources will be primary, or original, sources such as letters, interviews, and historical documents. Others will be secondary sources, which are writings about a primary source, such as a critic's review, a historical essay, or a biography. Primary sources have immediacy and authority; secondary sources have perspective and, often, a more impartial analysis.

## Prepare a Working Bibliography

As you write down the names of promising sources to consult, you will be creating a working bibliography. When you locate a source, first skim it for an idea of the topic it covers and the scope and depth of detail it provides. If a source seems to have useful information, create a complete bibliography card for it by recording the source's cataloging information, as shown below. Use one index card for each source. Write down the author, title, city of publication, publisher, and date, and all other information that will identify that source.

Number your bibliography cards consecutively. Later, you will use these numbers in your notes to identify your sources. Here are some examples of bibliography cards for a paper on Peter the Great and Mikhail Gorbachev. Later, using the information on your bibliography cards, you will also prepare a list of your sources, called a *works cited page*, at the end of your paper. If you are thorough now in recording source information, you can avoid returning to the library to fill in missing information.

**Drafting Tip**

Check the formats for the works cited on page 333 to see what items of information you should record for each type of source.

### What to Write on Bibliography Cards

Note the following information for books: author's name, title of a part of a book (for example, you might use information from a preface or from a work in an anthology), title of the book, name of the editor or translator (if there is one), the edition (if there is one), the number of the volume and the name of the series (for books that are one of a series), the city of publication, the publisher's name, the publication date, and page numbers of a work that is part of a collection of works within a book.

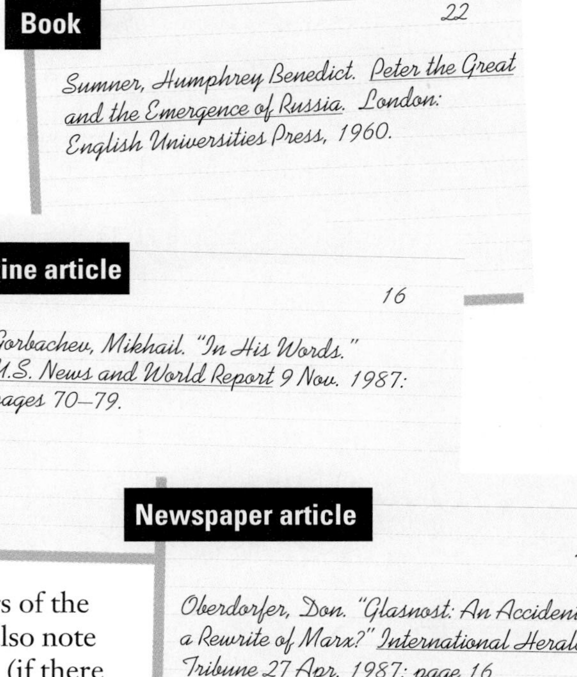

Book
22
Sumner, Humphrey Benedict. Peter the Great and the Emergence of Russia. London: English Universities Press, 1960.
Magazine article
16
Gorbachev, Mikhail. "In His Words." U.S. News and World Report 9 Nov. 1987: pages 70–79.
Newspaper article
41
Oberdorfer, Don. "Glasnost: An Accident or a Rewrite of Marx?" International Herald Tribune 27 Apr. 1987: page 16.


For periodical sources, note the author's name, title of the article, the name of the periodical, the date of publication and the page numbers of the article. If the periodical is a newspaper, also note the edition and section of the newspaper (if there is either) in which the article appears (such as section D).

**Evaluating Sources** Before you take notes, evaluate them for blatant bias. If a source's bias detracts from the objectivity of your paper, you may not want to use it unless you present one or more opposing views. To detect bias, ask yourself whether you think the source is treating the topic fairly. Does the author make unqualified assertions? Are the views of the author often disputed? Answering these questions will help you to choose the best sources.

## Take Notes

As you reread sources for your research paper, look for concepts, statements, and quotations that illustrate aspects of your central idea. After you read a source, evaluate it before taking notes.

**Three Ways of Taking Notes** When you find useful information, write it on a four-by-six-inch index card. Be sure that each note card identifies the source (use the number of the bibliography card that corresponds to each source) and the page number on which you found the information. In the examples that follow, notice that there are three different ways to take notes: paraphrasing, summarizing, and quoting directly.

*When you **summarize,** focus only on key points and concepts. Be sure to include enough detail so that your note card will be meaningful when you refer to it later. Label your note card "summary."*

*"Page 771" indicates the information appears on that page of the source. Full bibliographic information is on card # 3 (indicated by the number in the upper-right corner).*

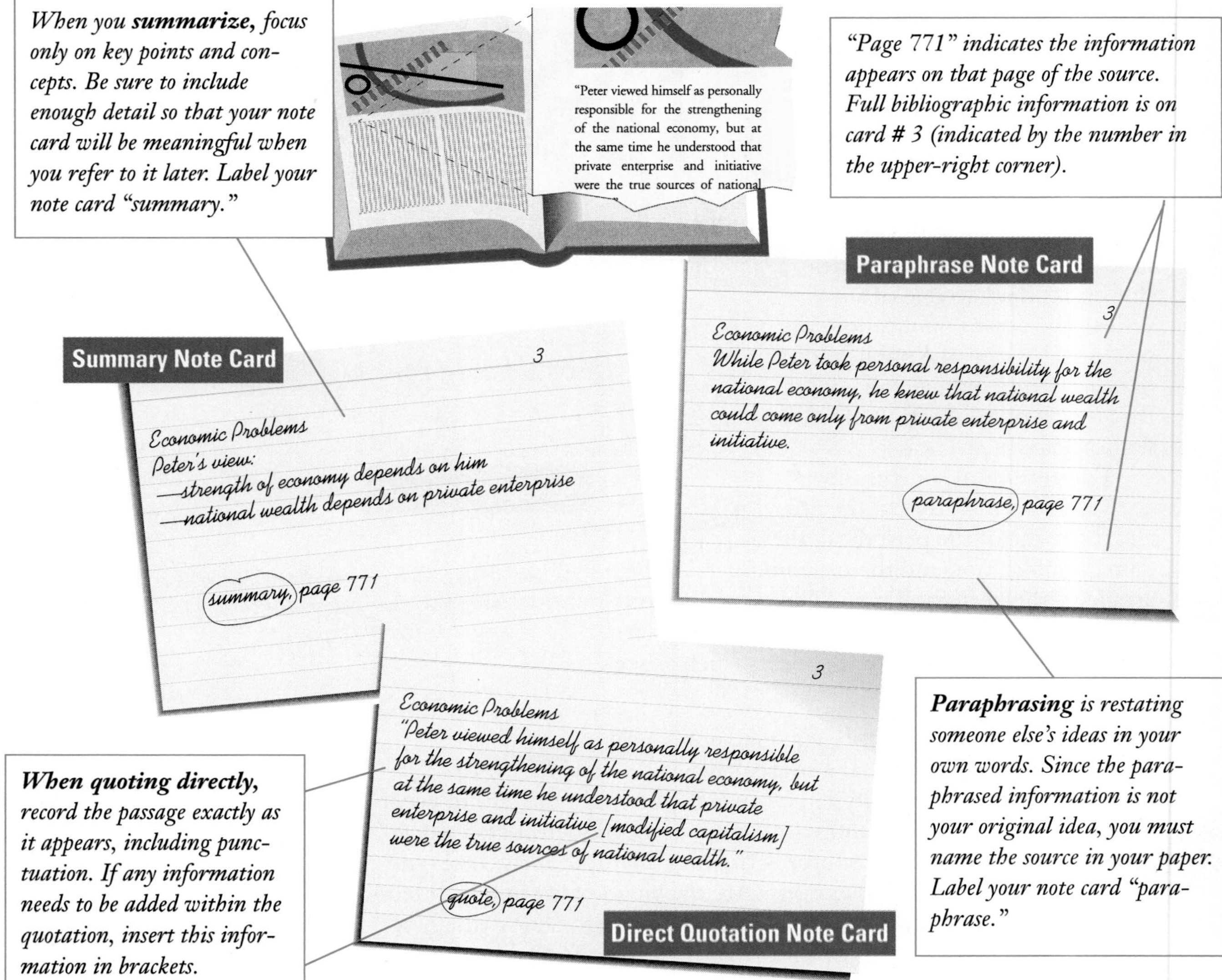

"Peter viewed himself as personally responsible for the strengthening of the national economy, but at the same time he understood that private enterprise and initiative were the true sources of national
Paraphrase Note Card
3
Economic Problems
While Peter took personal responsibility for the national economy, he knew that national wealth could come only from private enterprise and initiative.
paraphrase, page 771
Summary Note Card
3
Economic Problems
Peter's view:
—strength of economy depends on him
—national wealth depends on private enterprise
summary, page 771
3
Economic Problems
"Peter viewed himself as personally responsible for the strengthening of the national economy, but at the same time he understood that private enterprise and initiative [modified capitalism] were the true sources of national wealth."
quote, page 771
Direct Quotation Note Card


*When quoting directly, record the passage exactly as it appears, including punctuation. If any information needs to be added within the quotation, insert this information in brackets.*

***Paraphrasing** is restating someone else's ideas in your own words. Since the paraphrased information is not your original idea, you must name the source in your paper. Label your note card "paraphrase."*

**Avoiding Plagiarism** Plagiarism is presenting the ideas or statements of another writer without crediting the original source. In fact, the word *plagiarism* comes from the Latin word *plagiarius*, which means "kidnapper." Plagiarism is theft, even when it is unintentional. Professional journalists and writers have lost their jobs, and certainly their credibility, because they plagiarized.

Plagiarism can occur in several ways. Obviously a writer commits plagiarism if he or she quotes a source without using quotation marks or paraphrases a source without giving credit. Plagiarism also occurs when a writer summarizes a source's ideas or observations without giving credit to the source. Can you always avoid plagiarism just by naming your source? No. If you substitute a few of your own words in a direct quotation and call it a paraphrase, you have commited plagiarism because most of the words are still the source's words, not yours. To avoid paraphrasing a source too closely, look away from the source as you take notes on it. After you have written your paraphrase, reread the source to make sure that you have used your own words.

Taking notes carefully and documenting them clearly can help you to avoid plagiarism. On each note card be sure to indicate whether your notes are a direct quotation, a paraphrase, or a summary. If you combine two kinds of notes on one note card, for example, a paraphrase of a source followed by your own conclusion, be sure that you label both clearly on the card.

# 7.1 Writing Activities

## Skills Practice

1. In this list of topics, identify whether each is too general, sufficiently limited, or too limited for a seven-page paper.

- The Battle for Palestine, 1947 to Present
- The Role of Spain in History
- Central American Archaeological Finds
- Economic Reform in Mexico, 1975–1990

2. Suppose you want to write a report on the causes of fluctuating exchange rates between the United States and Canada. Which of the following sources do you think might have the most useful information about this topic? Why or why not?

- *Reader's Digest*
- the *Toronto Globe and Mail*
- *Newsweek*
- video series, *Vacationing in Canada*
- textbook, *Fundamentals of Economics*
- the *Wall Street Journal*

## Your Research Paper

Now select a topic for your own research paper, and write three to seven research questions about it. After your teacher approves your choice of topic, begin your research. Prepare your bibliography cards, and hand them in to your teacher.

LESSON

# 7.2 Research Paper Writing
# Prewriting: Developing an Outline

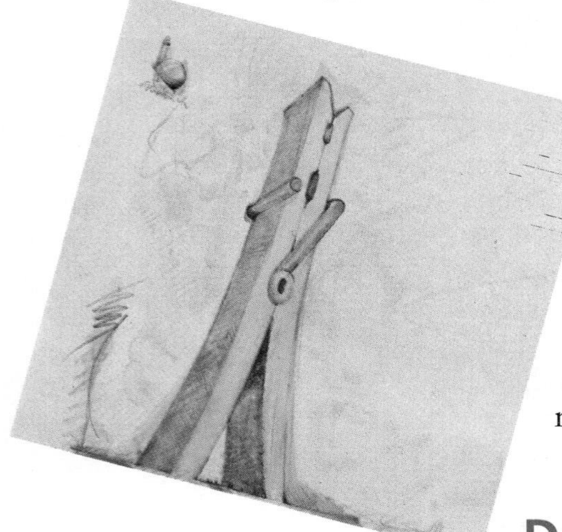

Claes Oldenburg, Sketch for *Clothespin*

Good planning makes any challenging project more manageable. For example, when preparing to create a large sculpture or painting, an artist first visualizes it in a series of sketches. Once satisfied that the sketches capture the overall vision of his or her ideas, the artist begins the work using the sketches as guides.

In the same way, writing a research paper can be made easier if you organize your notes and your thoughts into an outline. Refine your outline until it reflects your ideas accurately, and then use it to guide your writing.

## Develop an Outline

You can organize your ideas in many ways. Your topic and the information that you have collected may suggest a method of organization. For example, if your topic centers on a historical event, you may choose chronological order, which is the order in which things happen in time. Alternatively, you might want to use cause and effect, which is an arrangement that shows how one idea or event (the cause) directly determines another (the effect). Another popular method of organization is order of importance, the arrangement of items by degrees, such as less important to more important. Also, you may use one method of organization, such as chronological order, for main ideas, and use another method of organization, such as cause and effect, for details.

A working outline will help you to organize the information you have already collected and will guide your future research. Since this is a working outline, you can easily adapt it as you do more research and as some ideas become more, or less, important.

Look at the following outline for Marie-Corinne Gilbert's research paper, which appears on pages 342–347.

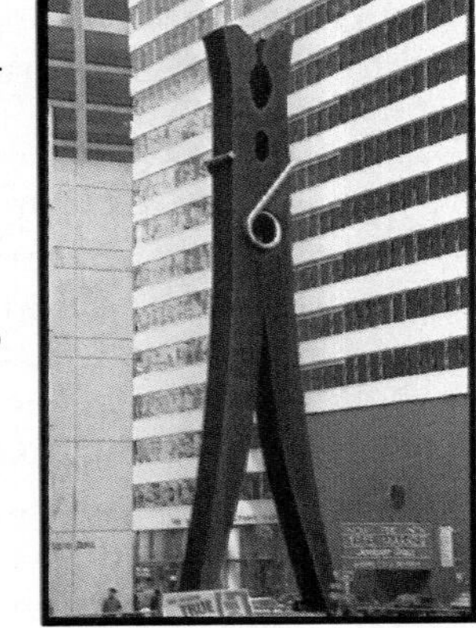

Claes Oldenburg, *Clothespin*, 1945

```
   I.   Personality traits
        A. Peter the Great
           1. Energy and enthusiasm
           2. Indomitable will
           3. "Common touch"
        B. Mikhail Gorbachev
           1. Eager for change
           2. Stubborn nature
           3. "Common touch"
  II.   Attitudes toward the West
        A. Western-style dress
        B. Russian beliefs maintained
           1. Peter and torture of prisoners
           2. Gorbachev and opposition
 III.   Attitudes toward women
        A. Peter's time
           1. Women in seclusion
           2. Peter eases restrictions
           3. Wife maintains high profile
        B. Gorbachev's time
           1. Advocate of women's rights
           2. Wife in the public eye
  IV.   Obstacles to reform
        A. Problems from predecessors
           1. Peter's Russia 200 years behind
              a. Mongol occupation
              b. Medieval philosophies
           2. Gorbachev's bureaucratic mess
              a. Military might
              b. Central planning
              c. Needs planning and management
        B. Torpor and fear of foreigners
```

*Use roman numerals for main headings. Use capital letters for subheadings, and indent. Use numbers and lower-case letters for items beneath subheadings.*

*Leaders' traits and attitudes are in parallel organization; why is this treatment effective?*

*In what order are obstacles placed?*

Each roman numeral heading of the above outline first examines Peter the Great and then Mikhail Gorbachev. This organization allows point-by-point comparisons and contrasts of the two men. What if the outline considered all aspects of Peter the Great and then presented all those of Mikhail Gorbachev? Readers would have to remember details from one half of the paper to the next.

To organize the notes you have taken so far, sort them into major categories. Then ask yourself which ideas support other ideas. Also consider the order in which events occur. Group your notes in the most effective way, and base your working outline on the groupings.

## Consider Alternative Forms of Organization

The traditional outline is not the only method for organizing a research paper. You may find that other methods are more suited to your topic or to your way of thinking. A graphic such as the one shown below can also be used to organize information.

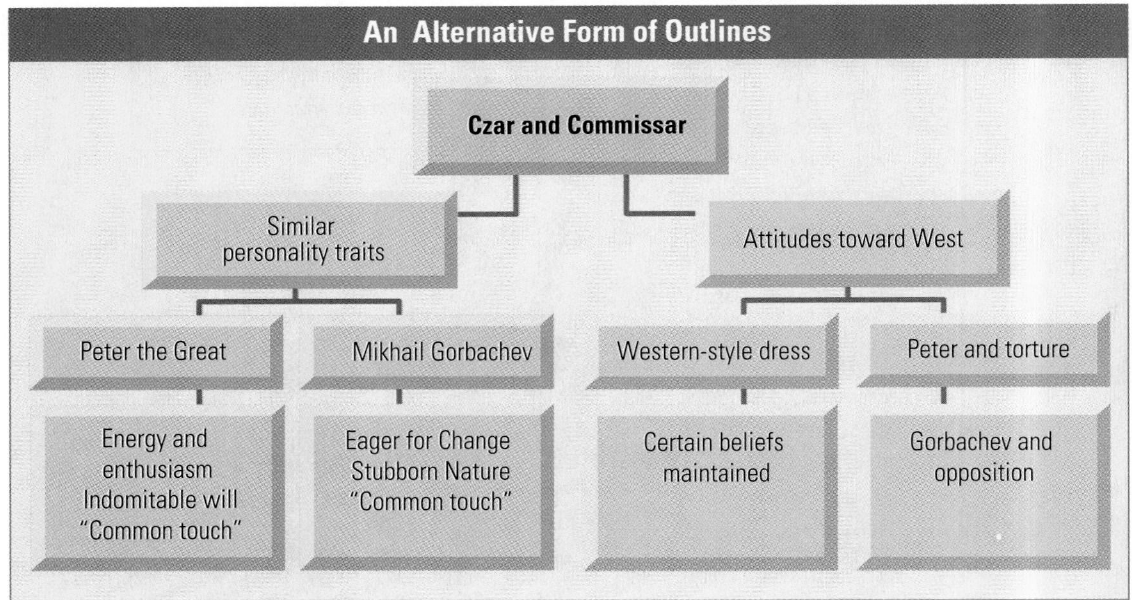


## Develop a Thesis Statement

**Drafting Tip**

Try using more than one method of organization. For example, put main ideas in chronological order; use cause and effect for details.

Until now, your efforts have been guided by questions and a central idea about your topic. Now you should focus specifically on your central idea and turn it into a thesis statement. As you may know, a thesis statement is a concise, clearly focused single sentence stating an idea that you prove or illustrate through your writing (see pages 68–70). The thesis statement also reveals your perspective on your topic and may even preview your arrangement of information for readers.

To prepare a thesis statement, follow these three steps. First, examine your central idea and refine it to reflect the information that you gathered in your research. The information that you found may be very different from what you expected to find. Next, consider your approach to the topic. What is the purpose of your research? Are you proving or disproving something? Illustrating a cause-and-effect relationship? Offering a solution to a problem? Examining one aspect of the topic thoroughly? Predicting an outcome? Finally, revise your central idea to reflect your approach and polish your wording.

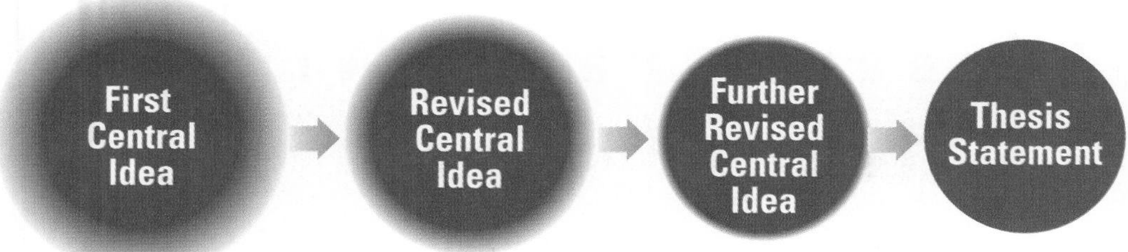


The central idea of the student research paper on pages 342–347 might have been "Peter the Great and Mikhail Gorbachev were two great Russian reformers." A revised central idea could have been "They conducted their reforms in different ways because of the eras in which they lived and the state of their nation." The final thesis statement is "Although Peter and Gorbachev often reacted to their problems differently, their reforms and goals for Russia have much in common."

Of course, you should adapt your thesis statement as you write so that it reflects the direction that your paper is taking. Don't be boxed in by your thesis statement.

# 7.2 Writing Activities

## Skills Practice

1. Organize this information into three categories; then supply a heading for each, and arrange them into a working outline.

- The European Union (EU) presently consists of fifteen member countries.
- The effectiveness of the EU's operations can be seen in the rapid economic growth that member nations have enjoyed since its beginnings in the 1950s.
- EU members have abolished all trade tariffs among themselves.
- The EU is a major economic unit, with more people and higher industrial output than the United States.
- Future EU goals include forming a political union.
- Since its founding, members of the EU have enjoyed large increases in their per capita income, volume of trade, and total value of goods and services produced.
- The EU's purpose is to improve members' standards of living by forming a single market for economic resources.
- In the near future, capital, resources, and workers will be able to move as freely within the EU as they do among the states in the United States.

2. Rewrite the following central idea as a concise, single-sentence thesis statement.

> The United States built the Panama Canal. Because of this, some people in the United States thought it was wrong to return control of the canal to Panama. The ceding of the canal was in America's best interest.

## Your Research Paper

Prepare a working outline for the research paper that you began in Lesson 7.1, and draft a thesis statement for it.

LESSON 7.3

# Research Paper Writing
# Drafting

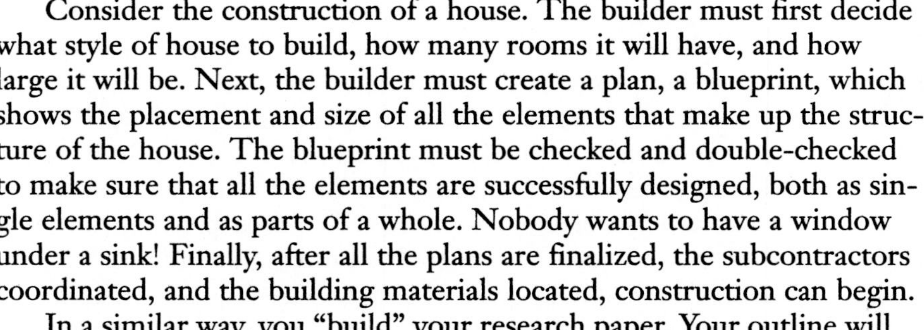

Consider the construction of a house. The builder must first decide what style of house to build, how many rooms it will have, and how large it will be. Next, the builder must create a plan, a blueprint, which shows the placement and size of all the elements that make up the structure of the house. The blueprint must be checked and double-checked to make sure that all the elements are successfully designed, both as single elements and as parts of a whole. Nobody wants to have a window under a sink! Finally, after all the plans are finalized, the subcontractors coordinated, and the building materials located, construction can begin.

In a similar way, you "build" your research paper. Your outline will serve as your blueprint and your note cards as your building materials. Your tools will be your writing skills.

## Write from an Outline

You may want to begin by arranging your note cards so that they parallel the order of the headings in your outline. In addition to the body paragraphs that your note cards suggest, your paper should have an introduction and a conclusion. You may find it easier to write these portions after you have drafted the body of the paper. Next, decide whether you want to write the body of your paper from beginning to end, or whether you want to tackle certain sections first. You will probably not draft your entire paper at one sitting. Most writers draft their papers over a period of several days.

Before you write the text for each section of your outline, reread the note cards for that section, making sure each idea belongs in that section. When you use information from a note card in your draft, include the number of the note card immediately after the information. You will use the numbers later to document your sources.

Although you will credit your research sources where appropriate, try to use your own words and ideas as often as possible. Not every note card will result in a separate statement or outline entry. As shown on the next page, Marie-Corinne Gilbert used more than one note card to support a single outline entry.

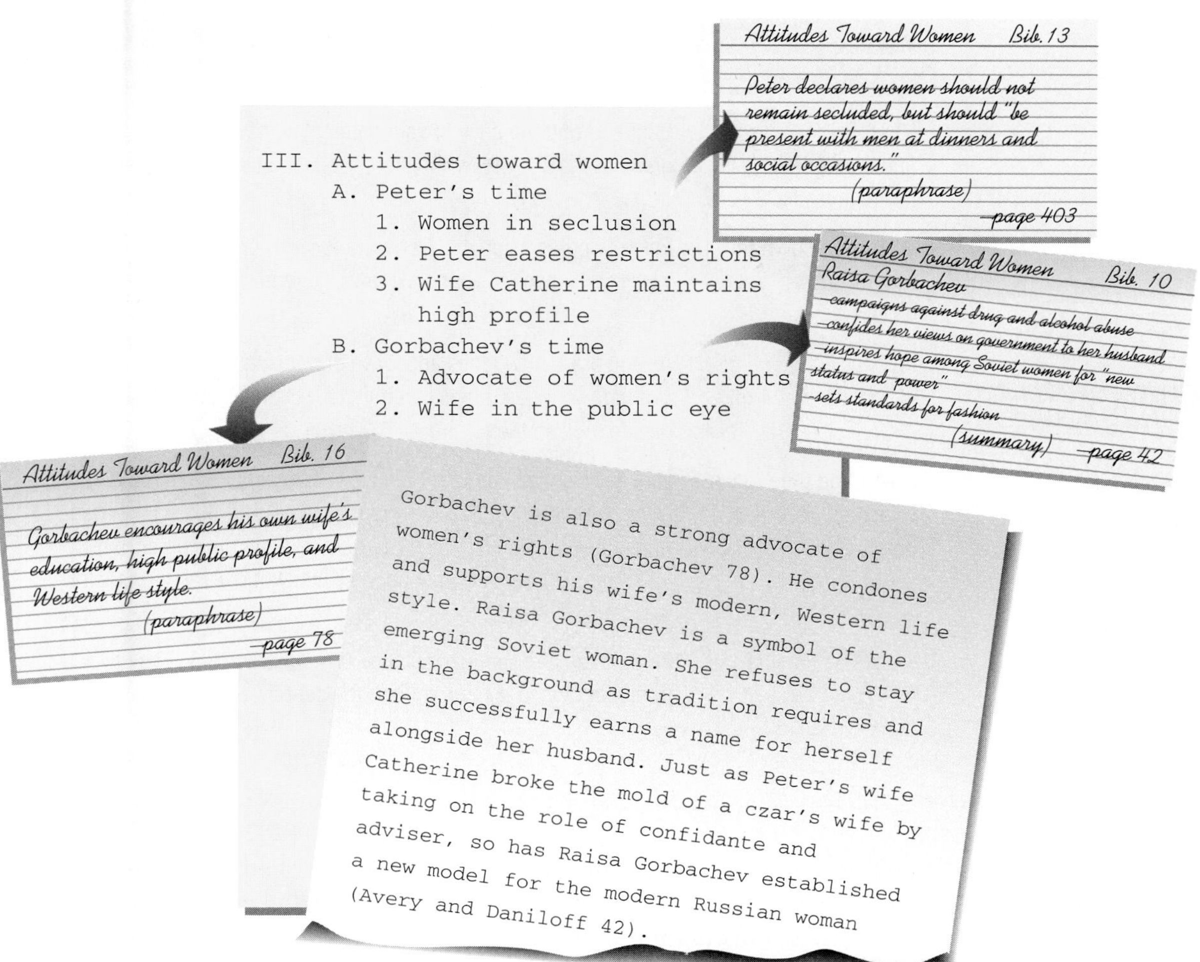

Attitudes Toward Women Bib. 13
Peter declares women should not remain secluded, but should "be present with men at dinners and social occasions."
(paraphrase)
page 403
III. Attitudes toward women
A. Peter's time
1. Women in seclusion
2. Peter eases restrictions
3. Wife Catherine maintains high profile
B. Gorbachev's time
1. Advocate of women's rights
2. Wife in the public eye
Attitudes Toward Women Bib. 10
Raisa Gorbachev
-campaigns against drug and alcohol abuse
-confides her views on government to her husband
-inspires hope among Soviet women for "new status and power"
-sets standards for fashion
(summary)
page 42
Attitudes Toward Women Bib. 16
Gorbachev encourages his own wife's education, high public profile, and Western life style.
(paraphrase)
page 78
Gorbachev is also a strong advocate of women's rights (Gorbachev 78). He condones and supports his wife's modern, Western life style. Raisa Gorbachev is a symbol of the emerging Soviet woman. She refuses to stay in the background as tradition requires and she successfully earns a name for herself alongside her husband. Just as Peter's wife Catherine broke the mold of a czar's wife by taking on the role of confidante and adviser, so has Raisa Gorbachev established a new model for the modern Russian woman (Avery and Daniloff 42).


In the example above, information on the note cards is not simply dropped into the draft. Information from three of the note cards is reworded to effectively develop the main idea of this section of the draft. Notice that, in the paper, source identification immediately follows information taken from the note cards.

## Manage Information

As you write your first draft, concentrate on getting your ideas down in a complete and logical order. Don't try to find the "perfect" word or phrase, and don't worry about mistakes in spelling, usage, or mechanics. You will fix those errors when you revise and edit your draft.

You may need to do some problem solving as you draft. Some problems have obvious solutions. For example, if you discover that you need more facts to support a main idea, the obvious solution is to go back to your sources and get more facts. Other solutions are not so obvious. The following chart lists common writing problems and possible solutions.

| Solving Drafting Problems | |
|---|---|
| **Problem** | **Solution** |
| I just can't seem to find the right words for the introduction. | Begin writing the body of your paper first. After you have a fuller grasp of the subject, writing an introduction should be easier. |
| When I sit down to write, I get writer's block. | Put your notes aside and freewrite for ten minutes to warm up. You'll come back to your draft ready to write. |
| I feel as if my outline is limiting my writing. | As you draft, new ideas and ways of thinking will often arise. Evaluate your new ideas carefully, and change your outline if you decide to keep them. |
| I can't find the proper transitions between paragraphs. | Look for a single important idea that connects both paragraphs. (How are things similar? Different? Linked in time or in the reactions they produced?) Use that idea to connect the paragraphs: "Similarly, Gorbachev must address many of the same problems that Peter the Great faced." |
| I feel as if I'm just listing the ideas of other writers. | Paraphrase and summarize more. Use other writers' work to support your own ideas, not to limit the content of your paper. |

**Editing Tip**

Use transitional expressions (see the Grammar section) to connect paragraphs and sentences.

## Draft Introductions and Conclusions

Your paper's introduction and conclusion work together to frame your research paper. The introduction can be a good place to use a special bit of information that you have found in your research, perhaps a little-known fact, a vivid description, or a funny anecdote that you want to highlight. In your conclusion, you may wish not only to summarize your main points, but also to tell how your research points to important new questions to explore. The following introduction poses a question to create immediate interest in the topic and to pull readers into the paper. To find an answer to the question, readers must continue through the paragraph. Read the introduction to Marie-Corinne Gilbert's research paper on page 342.

*The thesis statement concisely states the topic and the writer's approach to it.*

> What will our generation do when fossil fuels, such as gasoline, oil, and coal, are depleted? Advocates of nuclear energy claim that without nuclear power plants, the future will see us shivering in the dark. Survivors of the Chernobyl disaster can testify, however, to the risks of nuclear power. The solution to the energy crisis lies in safe, alternative fuel sources: the sun, the wind, and the oceans.

Use the chart on the following page as a guide when you draft your introduction and conclusion.

| Traits of Effective Introductions and Conclusions | |
|---|---|
| **Introduction** | **Conclusion** |
| Contains a clear, concise thesis statement | Restates the thesis statement |
| Grabs and keeps the reader's interest | Reviews the main points of the paper |
| Identifies your approach to the topic | Notes the significance of the research |
| Presents a bit of enticing background information on unfamiliar subjects | Identifies possible implications for the future |

# 7.3 Writing Activities

## Skills Practice

Based on the following outline and notes, write a paragraph on the founding of the United Nations. Determine which notes are relevant to each outline section.

I. Founding of the United Nations
   A. Inter-Allied Declaration
      1. Meeting of representatives
      2. Purpose of meeting
   B. Atlantic Charter
      1. Declarations of Charter
      2. Aims of Charter
   C. Dumbarton Oaks Conference
   D. San Francisco Conference
      1. UN Conference on International Organization
      2. Disagreements among Big Three

- During World War II, ten European countries who opposed Nazi Germany signed the Inter-Allied Declaration on June 12, 1941.
- The Inter-Allied Declaration pledged to work for a free and peaceful world.
- The Inter-Allied Declaration was followed by the Atlantic Charter, which was signed by Franklin Roosevelt and Winston Churchill, August 14, 1941.
- Declarations of the Atlantic Charter included disarmament and economic cooperation among nations.
- Aims of the Atlantic Charter were approved by the signatories of 26 nations in the Declaration by the UN on Jan. 1, 1942.
- August–October 1944: Dumbarton Oaks Conference was held at the Dumbarton Oaks estate outside Washington, D.C.
- Representatives of China, Great Britain, the Soviet Union, and the U.S. met to plan a global peacekeeping organization.
- Certain basics of the future United Nations, such as the establishment of a permanent security council, were agreed to at Dumbarton Oaks.
- United Nations Conference on International Organization is held in San Francisco, April 25, 1945. Fifty nations attend. Major disagreements occur between the Big Three (United States, Britain, Russia) and the smaller nations.

## Your Research Paper

Using your working outline and note cards, prepare a first draft of the research paper you have been working on throughout this unit. Save your note cards.

LESSON

# 7.4 Research Paper Writing
## Citing Sources

When people fail to give credit to the sources from which they have taken ideas, the consequences can be disastrous. In 1988, a candidate for the presidency of the United States was forced to withdraw from the race when it was discovered that parts of some of his speeches were plagiarized from a British politician. In a similar instance, the director of a university's journalism program was forced to resign after not giving proper credit in a speech.

Besides avoiding plagiarism, giving credit to (also called *documenting* or *citing*) your sources makes your own writing more authoritative. If you make an assertion and cite sources who are experts in the field, your own point will be more believable. Similarly, if you cite respected publications in your research, your own viewpoints will command more respect.

How can you thank a man for giving you what's already yours? How then can you thank him for giving you only part of what's already yours?

*Malcolm X*
*Oxford Union Society debate*
*December, 1964*

## Document Information

Generally, you will need to name the sources of words, ideas, and facts that you borrow. Readers should be able to discern your ideas and those of your sources. In addition to citing books and periodicals from which you take information, cite song lyrics, letters, and dialogue from plays. Also credit original ideas that are expressed graphically in tables, charts, and diagrams. For some topics, you may want to include visual aids, such as photocopies of photographs, graphics, or artwork, to enhance your readers' understanding. You can cite the sources of visual aids when you refer to them in the text of your research paper.

Although you need to document your sources whenever you use someone else's exact words or paraphrase an idea, you need not cite every bit of information that you use. For example, you don't need to cite the source of well-known sayings ("There will always be an England") or common knowledge (The United Nations is headquartered in New York City). All other information should be cited. The chart on the next page illustrates the kinds of information that require citation.

| Is Citation Needed? | |
|---|---|
| **Type of Information** | **Explanation** |
| "Gorbachev seemed eager to stop talking about change and to begin making it happen." | Yes. Always cite direct quotation, regardless of how well known the content. |
| . . . but the Stalinist system of central planning has caused the U.S.S.R. to fall far behind in technological and industrial advances. | Yes. Always cite your paraphrase of another writer's conclusion, based on that writer's research and analysis. |
| Peter and Gorbachev may still be considered advanced thinkers in relation to the majority of Russian society at their respective times. | No. Don't cite paraphrase of general information since you are providing details that can be found in many common sources. |
| Every year nearly one million Soviets leave their villages and move to overcrowded cities; currently, fifty-two cities have populations in excess of 500,000. | Yes. Always cite statistics and analyses that are not common knowledge. |
| During the Mongol Occupation (1240–1480) . . . | No. Dates of the Mongol Occupation can be found in most reference books on the subject. |
| The rapid advance of modern science, however, can render technology obsolete virtually overnight . . . . | No. The rapid pace of technological advancement is common knowledge. |

**Prewriting Tip**

For periodicals, bibliography cards should identify the page numbers of the article; note cards should identify the page(s) from which you took information.

You should also consider your readers when you cite sources. Even if you find that some of your information is common knowledge, you should cite one of the sources for your readers' sake; they may want to read more about the idea and can refer to that source.

## Format Your Citations

You can cite your sources in one of three ways: parenthetical documentation, endnotes, or footnotes. While your teacher may assign one particular style of documentation, all styles serve the same purpose: to give credit to your sources and to make them accessible to your readers.

Citations should follow as closely as possible after the borrowed information. It should be easy for the reader to identify the ideas that are being cited. With any type of documentation, simply replace the number of the note card that you wrote on your draft with the proper documentation format. To avoid omitting a citation, place a check mark on each note card as you use it. Save your note cards so you can double-check citations in your finished paper.

# Insert Parenthetical Documentation

**Editing Tip**

Underline book and periodical titles if you are using a typewriter; put them in italic type if you are using a word processor.

Parenthetical documentation consists of two main elements: the author's name and the page number or numbers on which the information is found. This information is put in parentheses within the body of the paper. Full identification of the source is given in the list of works cited at the end of a paper.

To avoid awkward breaks in sentences, put the documentation at the end of a clause or a sentence. The reference is put in parentheses and comes before commas and periods, but after quotation marks. For example, "The population decreased 40% in 20 years" (Davis 67).

The chart below shows forms of parenthetical documentation.

| Source | Parenthetical Documentation |
|---|---|
| **One author**<br>(Massie 110) | Documentation shows that the author is Massie and the information is on page 110 of the source. (See the corresponding works cited entry on page 333.) |
| **Two authors**<br>(Avery and Daniloff 42) | Use this form for a source with two or three authors. For more than three authors, use the last name of the first author, followed by *et al.* and the page number(s): (Davis et al. 44–47) |
| **No author**<br>("Driving" 166) | If no author is listed, use the name of the editor if there is one. If not, use an abbreviated version of the source's title. |
| **Authors listed more than once in the works cited**<br>(Bialer, "Gorbachev" 40) | Use this form if you cite more than one source by the same author. The source's title is abbreviated after the author's name and a comma. (See Works Cited on page 334.) |
| **Author's name in text**<br>(178–180) | When you use the author's name in your writing and it is clear where the material originated (for example, "Thompson's studies on this question indicate . . ."), insert only the page number in parentheses to document the source. |

*Page numbers in parenthetical documentation indicate just the pages from which information is taken. Page numbers in works cited entries are for the page span of the entire periodical article or anthologized work.*

# List Works-Cited Entries

The works you cite are included in alphabetical order at the end of your paper. The entries more fully identify your parenthetical sources. These entries contain the publishing information that you recorded on your bibliography cards. For sources that do not specify an author or an editor, begin the entry with the title of the book, article, pamphlet, or tape, disregarding such words as *A*, *An*, and *The* when alphabetizing.

The chart that follows illustrates the formats for various sources for Marie-Corinne Gilbert's research paper.

| Type of Source | Works-Cited Entry |
|---|---|
| **Book with one author** | Massie, Robert K. *Peter the Great: His Life and World.* New York: Ballantine, 1985. |
| **Book with two authors** | Doder, Dusko, and Louise Branson. *Gorbachev: Heretic in the Kremlin.* New York: Viking, 1990. |
| **Anthology with an editor but no author** | Reddaway, Peter, ed. *Uncensored Russia.* London: Jonathan Cape, 1972. |
| **Work (with author) in anthology (with editor)** | Besançon, Alain. "Emperor and Heir, Father and Son." *Peter the Great Changes Russia.* 2nd ed. Ed. Marc Raeff. Lexington: Heath, 1972. 160–170. |
| **Encyclopedia article, no author** | "Gorbachev, Mikhail Sergeyevich." *Encyclopedia Americana.* 1990 ed. |
| **Magazine article** | Franklin, Daniel. "The Soviet Economy." *The Economist* 9 Apr. 1988: 48–49. |
| **Newspaper article** | Wicker, Tom. "In the West's Interest." *The New York Times* 18 Feb. 1987, late ed.: A15. |
| **Government publication with no specified author** | United States. Office of the Chief of Naval Operations. *Understanding Soviet Naval Developments.* Washington, GPO, 1985. |
| **Films and videotapes** | *The Soviet People Speak Their Minds.* Dir. Dimitri Devyatkin. MPI Productions, 1984. |
| **Personal interviews** | Strauss, Hector. Personal interview. 5 Nov. 1990. |

*Use this order, as it applies, for books: authors' names, title of anthologized work, title of book, number of edition, name of editor, volume, city of publication, publisher's name, publication date, page numbers*

*Use this order, as it applies, for periodicals: authors' names, title of article, name of periodical, series number, date of publication, newspaper edition, page numbers of the complete article.*

In the preceding chart, shortened forms of publishers' names are used. Some abbreviated names are easy to arrive at, for example, *Ballantine* for *Ballantine Books, Inc.*, *Viking* for *Viking Press*, and *GPO* for *Government Printing Office*. For the correct shortened forms of other publishers' names, you may need to ask your teacher. You may also have noticed that dates of weekly periodicals and newspapers are written without punctuation in the order of *day*, *month* (abbreviated), and *year.*

Update your works-cited entries as you revise your paper. You will probably drop some entries and add others. Your final list of works cited should contain only those sources used in your final revision.

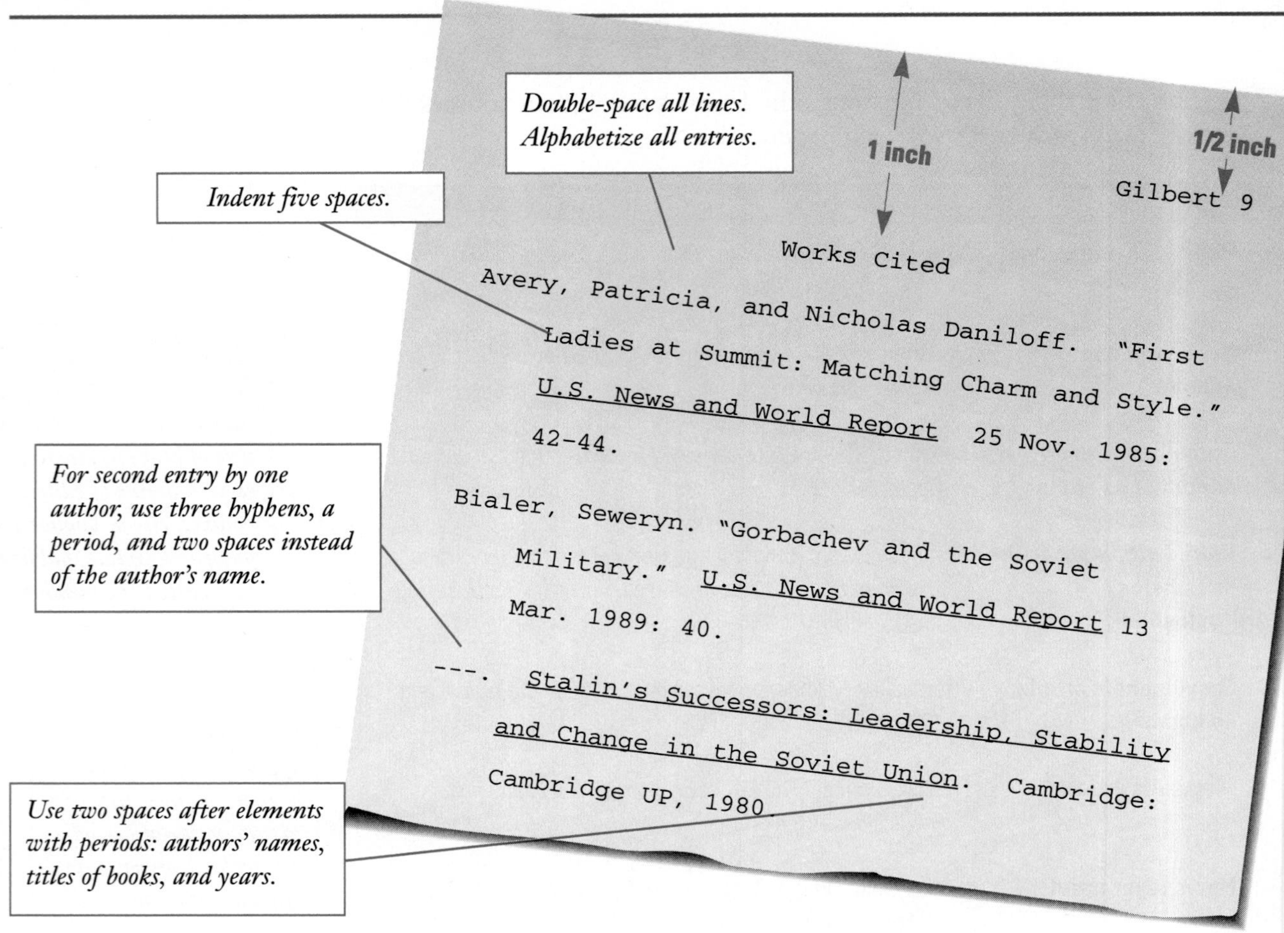

Double-space all lines.
Alphabetize all entries.
Indent five spaces.
1 inch
1/2 inch
Gilbert 9
Works Cited
Avery, Patricia, and Nicholas Daniloff. "First
Ladies at Summit: Matching Charm and Style."
U.S. News and World Report 25 Nov. 1985:
42-44.
For second entry by one author, use three hyphens, a period, and two spaces instead of the author's name.
Bialer, Seweryn. "Gorbachev and the Soviet
Military." U.S. News and World Report 13
Mar. 1989: 40.
---. Stalin's Successors: Leadership, Stability
and Change in the Soviet Union. Cambridge:
Cambridge UP, 1980.
Use two spaces after elements with periods: authors' names, titles of books, and years.


## Explore Other Styles of Documentation

Your teacher may want you to use a method of documentation other than parenthetical documentation and a list of works cited. Whatever method you use, make sure you give credit to your sources.

**Endnotes** Throughout the body of a paper, number each source cited consecutively, with a superscript number (typed one-half line above the rest of the line). Each number should correspond to a reference in the endnotes on a separate page titled "Notes" at the end of the research paper. The notes are numbered consecutively and contain the complete publishing information for each source.

**Footnotes** Like endnotes, these are marked by consecutive superscript numbers, but the information is placed at the bottom (or "foot") of the page that contains the reference.

After you document a work the first time, use a short form—just the author's last name and page numbers—in subsequent notes. See an example of footnote styles on the following page.

## Endnote and Footnote Styles

### In Text

. . . as *Time* magazine once noted, "Gorbachev seemed eager to stop talking about change and to begin making it happen."[4] Gorbachev, often called stubborn and opinionated,[5] reflects Peter's frequent unwillingness to accept contrary ideas or criticisms from others.

### Corresponding Endnotes and Footnotes

[4] John Moody, "Back to Work, Comrades," *Time* May 17, 1987: 41.

[5] Mortimer B. Zuckerman, "Gorbachev: The Rest of the Story," *U.S. News and World Report* Dec. 21, 1987: 84–85.

*How do these formats differ from those used for works-cited entries?*

# 7.4 Writing Activities

## Skills Practice

The following list contains the sources for the information in the paragraphs that follow. Insert the proper parenthetical documentation in the paragraphs at the corresponding number. Then correctly format the sources into a list of works cited.

**(1)** An article, "Grenada," with no author that appears in the 1990 edition of *World Book Encyclopedia.*

**(2)** Magazine, *U.S. News and World Report.* Article "From Bad to Worse for U.S. in Grenada," by writer James N. Wallace. Date of issue—October 31, 1983. The article appears on page 35 only.

**(3)** Dennis Mullin, writer, in *U.S. News and World Report.* Article "Why the Surprise Move in Grenada—and What Next?" Date of issue—November 7, 1983. The information is from page 34; the article is on pages 33–35.

Grenada, a Caribbean island nation, gained its independence from Great Britain in 1974. Its government operated under a constitutional monarchy until a coup led by Maurice Bishop overthrew this system in 1979. (1)

Bishop, who had been called "charismatic but frequently inept," (2) was viewed unfavorably by many people. President Reagan said that Bishop's regime "bears the Soviet and Cuban trademark, which means it will attempt to spread the virus among its neighbors." (2) When Bishop was overthrown by his aides in October 1983, the island's military buildup continued. Other Caribbean nations grew concerned that "the upheaval and leftist sentiment would engulf the rest of the region" if the U.S. did not act. (3)

After an official request from the Organization of Eastern Caribbean States (OECS), U.S. forces invaded the island. Despite the quick military success, many observers in the U.S. and elsewhere expressed doubt as to the legality of the operation. (3)

## Your Research Paper

Prepare the documentation for the sources in your research paper. Insert documentation in your draft and create a works-cited page, a notes page, or footnotes.

LESSON

# 7.5 Research Paper Writing
# Revising

Like all great writers, the American poet Ezra Pound understood how essential the revision process is to effective writing. In his letters he tells of an inspiration he had for a poem after watching people on a Paris subway platform. He worked hard to find words that were lovely enough to describe the sudden emotion he had felt. He wrote a thirty-line poem and then destroyed it. A year later, still searching for the perfect expression, he wrote a fifteen-line poem, which he later revised into a single sentence:

> The apparition of these faces in
> the crowd;
> Petals on a wet, black bough.

Although brief, this poem, "In a Station of the Metro," conveys more wonder and passion than Pound's longer versions of the poem.

While a poem is very different from a research paper, the goals of revision are the same. First, think about the organization of your paper as a whole. You may want to rearrange sections or paragraphs in a more effective or more logical order. Next, look at the development of details. Some ideas may need more support, while redundancies need to be eliminated. Finally, consider your individual word choices. Your revision should clarify your ideas and improve the flow and cohesiveness of your writing.

Notice how the passage above, from the model paper on page 342, might have been revised and improved in the stages shown.

### Revising a Passage

**1** Peter was able to retain ~~full~~ *autocratic* control over *Russian* policy. ~~in Russia. This included policies at home and abroad~~ *both foreign and domestic policy*. Gorbachev is *greatly* influenced ~~to a great extent~~ by Western public opinion. Gorbachev does not ~~have the~~ *possess Peter's* absolute power. ~~of Peter and the other Czars.~~

**2** *Although* Peter was able to retain autocratic control over Russian policy, ~~This included~~ both foreign and domestic, ~~policy.~~ Gorbachev is greatly influenced by Western public opinion. He does not possess Peter's absolute power.

**3** Although Peter was able to retain autocratic control over Russian policy, both foreign and domestic, Gorbachev ~~is~~ greatly influenced by Western public opinion. ~~He~~ does not possess ~~Peter's~~ *this* absolute power *and is*

# Revise the Research Paper

The first step in revising your draft is to set it aside for a day or two. Distancing yourself from your paper will give you perspective and will make you more objective about your writing.

When you come back to your paper, reread it several times. In the first reading, check to see whether you have accidentally omitted any sections of your outline. In each subsequent reading, focus on a different aspect of revision. Start with the "big picture" of organization, and then consider the details, such as word choices.

Before revising, you may wish to share your draft with other students. They will see your draft with "new eyes" and can point out areas where your meaning is unclear or where ideas need more support.

Try using the questions in the following chart as a starting point for revision. After you answer these questions, begin revising your paper. If you are writing a long paper, you may want to tackle your revision in sections rather than all in one sitting.

**Revising Tip**

Your arguments will sound stronger if you use the active voice. For a review of the active voice, see Lesson 15.7, page 553.

## √ Revision Checklist

1 **Do the main ideas in the body of the paper support the thesis statement?** Look for at least one place where the connection between a main idea and the thesis statement is not strong, and circle it.

2 **How could the order of main ideas be improved?** Experiment. Make a copy of your paper, cut it apart, and put main ideas in another order to see whether they work better.

3 **Which main ideas need more support?** Think of what your readers *don't* know. Look for at least one idea that needs more support, and circle it.

4 **Which details need to be expanded, eliminated, or clarified?** Think of what your readers will want to know or will find convincing. Look for at least three details that need improvement, and underline them.

5 **What features of the introduction will make readers want to read the rest of the research paper?** Keep revising your introduction until the answer is clear.

6 **Where can transitions from paragraph to paragraph and from idea to idea be made stronger?** Look for at least three places that need stronger transitions, and underline them.

7 **Which clauses can be tightened to eliminate wordiness? Which individual words are not as strong or as precise as they should be?** Find at least ten clauses and ten words that need improvement, and place a check mark beside each.

8 **Does the conclusion sum up main ideas and reiterate the purpose of the paper?** Keep revising the conclusion until it does.

## Analyze a Revision

Here's how a page of the draft of the research paper on page 342 might be revised. Notice that vague words have been replaced with more precise words. Also, notice that some information, while interesting, is deleted because it is not directly relevant and impedes the flow of ideas.

***Model***

The Soviet Union presents a paradox of modern technology. In some areas, [such as aerospace] the Soviet Union equals, if not surpasses, many Western nations. ~~Aerospace is one example. The Soviets were the first to launch a communications satellite–the infamous Sputnik–into space, and stayed on a par with the United States in the race to put a man on the moon.~~ Yet, at the same time, ~~the nation~~ [it] lacks a ~~good~~ reliable telephone system. The very structure of the Soviet system precludes the possibility of keeping up with rapid technological changes because it does not ~~generally~~ supply the incentive for workers to develop these new ideas. [Therefore] The Soviet Union is very dependent on the [West and] ~~United States,~~ Japan, ~~Great Britain, Germany, and other Western nations~~ to supply this [technology], and this [dependence] is not new in Russian history. Peter the Great faced this problem in the area of advanced shipbuilding techniques for his [expanding] Navy and weaponry for his reformed Army. Peter's ability to update his technology and keep it for twenty years served as ~~an~~ [a great] advantage to him in ~~bringing~~ [modernizing] Russia ~~up to date~~. Once he acquired this technology, [however] he did not face the possibility of its becoming obsolete in only a few year's time, as does Gorbachev. The [rapid] advance of modern science can render technology obsolete virtually overnight.

*This is an interesting fact, but it's not relevant to this paper.*

*Keep vague words such as "generally," "usually," and "somewhat" to a minimum.*

*Why is it more concise to say "the West"?*

## Revise a History Paper

When your topic is the history of a foreign country or its culture, you should take extra precautions to ensure that your writing is fair, accurate, and free from nationalistic bias. Using Lesson 7.1 as a guide, examine your sources for cultural or political bias; some experts are outspoken in their opinions on forms of government or historic figures.

You should also be aware that certain words, ideas, and even statistics may be used differently in other cultures. For example, what the British refer to as a "public" school is actually a private school in the United States. Unemployment statistics and gross national product statistics are calculated differently in other countries.

Finally, you should recognize that a sign of progress in one country may be a sign of problems in another. For example, rising crop exports in the United States signal a healthy economy, while in a poor country, this may mean that people can't buy inexpensive basic staples, such as rice and wheat, because such staples are exported.

# 7.5 Writing Activities

## Skills Practice

On a separate sheet of paper, revise the following passage for clarity, coherence, and readability.

The two most powerful economic forces in Asia are Japan and South Korea. They share certain similarities in the way they do business. International trade is the main focus of both countries. Government involvement in the operation of certain industries is very high, and they face increasing pressure from the United States and other Western nations to open their markets to goods produced by these nations. Japan and South Korea are also active trading partners. They invest in each other's economy.

However, tensions between the two countries often arise. These are a result of historic confrontations. The effect of these confrontations continues to the present day. Japan annexed Korea in 1910. Trying to increase its influence in the Asian basin, Japan asserted that Korea was a province of Japan historically. To enforce this, efforts were made to eradicate Korean culture and prohibit any use of the language there. Land and businesses were also seized. (In actuality, Japan and China have both struggled for control of Korea throughout history, each claiming it as their province.) After Japan was defeated in World War II, South Korea and North Korea were separated. People in Japan of Korean heritage are not treated as full citizens to this day.

## Your Research Paper

Now begin revising your research paper. First consider major elements, such as the overall method of organization, and then examine supporting details and individual word choices. If you write using a computer, you can print out a clean copy at each stage and eliminate the confusion of a single, heavily marked draft.

You may wish to work in groups to gain other perspectives on your paper. Remember, however, that your paper is your own.

LESSON

# 7.6 Research Paper Writing
# Editing and Presenting: A Model Paper

When a book publisher accepts an author's manuscript, the process of turning it into a bound book begins. First, an editor works with the author to revise the manuscript's content and structure. Then the pages are typeset. Next, the pages are given to a proofreader who marks omitted information, misspellings, usage errors, and incorrect documentation. Only after the book has been thoroughly checked by many people, including the author, is it printed and sold.

You have already done what a writer and an editor do. Now, you need to make the final proofreader's check before you present your paper to readers.

## Use the Final Editing Checklist

After you have revised your paper, proofread it several times, looking for a different kind of flaw each time. Read your paper once for sense, looking for mistakes in usage, omitted words, and transposed elements. Read again for typing and punctuation errors. It's a good idea to devote one reading just to detecting spelling errors. Finally, proofread your citations, cross-checking your bibliography cards, note cards, and first draft as necessary. The checklist on this page can help you to catch any remaining problems.

**Presenting Tip**

Use a plastic cover to give your research paper a professional look. It will also protect the paper against accidents.

**Final Editing Checklist**

- ☐ *Are words omitted?*
- ☐ *Do typing errors exist?*
- ☐ *Are grammar and usage correct?*
- ☐ *Is punctuation correct?*
- ☐ *Are all words spelled correctly and consistently?*
- ☐ *Are proper names capitalized?*
- ☐ *Are unfamiliar words defined or explained?*
- ☐ *Is each source properly documented?*
- ☐ *Is your name on each page?*

## Present Your Paper

If you use a separate title page, format your paper to resemble the model. On separate lines, center your name and the date under the title.

Before you turn your paper in, check to make sure that you have all the elements of a complete paper, as shown here.

You may wish to make a photocopy of your paper to use if you apply for a job that entails written communication, or to serve as a springboard for a more in-depth paper in a future college course.

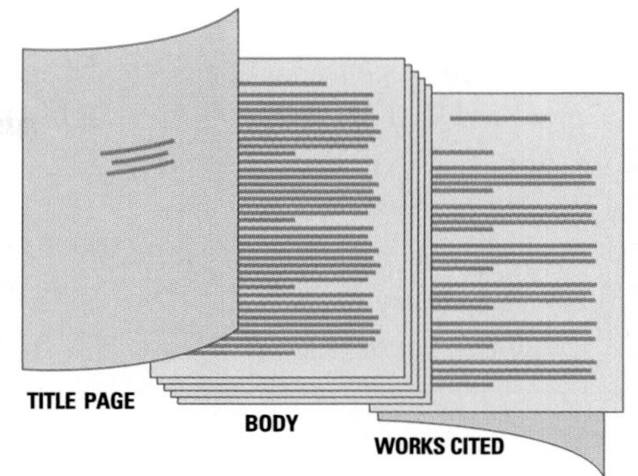


# 7.6 Writing Activities

## Skills Practice

Rewrite each of the following sentences, correcting errors in grammar, usage, spelling, and mechanics.

1. The Philippines have been an independent nation after 1946.
2. The position of the united nation's secretary general has many responsibilities; including meadiating general sessions.
3. The Caribbean Basin Initiative was intended to substantially increase economic interdependence among them.
4. The Sinai peninsula has been the sight of many armed armed confrontations through-out history.
5. Even countries with a mutuel langauge and culturel history, can dissagree over Economics.
6. Despite establishment of political neutrality in the year of 1815, Switzerland was involved in many diplomatic operations since then.
7. The united Kingdom consists of England, Scotland, Wales, and, northern Ireland.
8. Peru is the third-largest country in south America.
9. Rachel Carson's book, "Silent Spring," is her most famous; it documents the impact of pesticides on wild life and domestic animals.
10. A inventor may obtain a patent in one country but the legal rights may not be upheld in another country.
11. Recyling is one of the best known ways to cut down on the consumtion of earth's natural resources.
12. In East Gray, Maine highly dangerous cancer-causing chemicals from landfills seeped into the ground and contaminated local well water. Ralston 132.

## Your Research Paper

Finally, you're ready to edit your research paper and prepare it for readers. After you have carefully proofread your paper several times, turn in the final version to your teacher. You may also be asked to turn in your bibliography cards, note cards, and drafts.

## Student Model



*This research paper was first published by* The Concord Review, *a quarterly review of essays by secondary students of history in the English-speaking world.*

*What assumptions about the content of this paper can you make after reading the thesis statement?*

*Note the parenthetical documentation format.*

*How does this transition connect ideas?*

Marie-Corrine Gilbert
Russian History

Czar and Commissar:
Peter the Great, Mikhail Gorbachev,
and the Modernization of Russia

Peter the Great and Mikhail Gorbachev are two of the greatest reformers in Russian history. Both men inherited backward societies burdened by colossally inefficient bureaucracies, and many similarities can be found in their personalities and reforms. The reforms of both men stemmed from their mutual goal of modernizing the Russia of their respective times. Although Peter was able to retain autocratic control over Russian policy, both foreign and domestic, Gorbachev does not possess this absolute power and is greatly influenced by Western public opinion. Although Peter the Great and Mikhail Gorbachev often reacted to their problems differently, their reforms and goals for Russia have much in common.

The condition of Russia and the reforms enacted during their respective terms of power illustrate the numerous similarities between the two men. Not surprisingly, they share many personality traits. Peter the Great (1682–1725), a man of limitless energy and enthusiasm, implemented sweeping reforms to force Russia out of its backward ways and to transform it into a nation equal to its European counterparts. His indomitable will provided the driving force behind the transformation of Russia during the eighteenth century. Mr. Gorbachev (b. 1931) also evidences a strong desire for reform, and, as *Time* magazine once noted, "Gorbachev seemed eager to stop talking about change and to begin making it happen" (Moody 41). Gorbachev, often called stubborn and opinionated (Zuckerman 84), reflects Peter's frequent unwillingness to accept contrary ideas or criticisms from others. Both these men also possess what is fre-quently referred to as the "common touch." Gorbachev enjoys mingling with crowds, talking and shaking hands, and wanting to know the real people of Russia, not just the statistics that represent them. Peter not only talked with the people, he worked with them and among them in shipyards and workshops. As a result, both Peter and Gorbachev altered public perceptions of their offices and roles (Massie 110).

One of the most important qualities shared by these two men can be found in their attitudes toward the West. One of Peter the Great's notable trademarks consisted of his habit of wearing European clothes in a time when most Russians still favored traditional dress (Troyat 98). Had it not been for his enormous height, ➡

estimated to have been six feet, seven inches, he could have blended into any urban crowd in Western Europe. Similarly, Gorbachev, abandoning the baggy suits of his predecessors, "looked in his Western suit with cutaway flybacks, like one of the crowd of Americans on the pavement" (Zuckerman 84). This, however, can mislead the casual observer to conclude erroneously that both men completely adopted Western values or attitudes (Zuckerman 84). Peter often indulged in the more primitive aspects of the old Russian mentality, such as his willingness not only to allow, but also to inflict torture on prisoners, including his own son (Besançon 160–170). Gorbachev also displays some characteristics of the old Soviet mentality, as seen in his slowness to loosen emigration restrictions or to allow opposition political parties. Peter the Great and Gorbachev both outwardly displayed many Western ideals, while inwardly maintaining many traditional Russian beliefs.

*Why is this background detail important?*

Nonetheless, Peter and Gorbachev may still be considered advanced thinkers in relation to the majority of Russian society at their respective times. Peter modified society's low opinion of women and brought them out of seclusion. Prior to Peter's time, women lived in a haremlike environment, but he eased restrictions on women, allowing them to be educated and also to be socially acknowledged by men (Massie 403). The role of Peter's second wife, Catherine, illustrates this revised outlook toward women, for Catherine not only appeared at state functions with her husband, but she also accompanied Peter on his numerous journeys and military campaigns. Gorbachev is also a strong advocate of women's rights (Gorbachev 78), and reveals his beliefs in this area through condoning and supporting his wife's modern, Western life style. Raisa Gorbachev symbolizes the emerging Soviet woman, refusing to be thrust into the background as tradition dictates and successfully earning a name for herself alongside her husband. Just as Peter's wife Catherine broke the silent, faceless mold of a czar's wife by assuming the role of confidante and adviser, so has Raisa Gorbachev established a new model for the modern Russian woman (Avery and Daniloff 42).

*What is the function of this transitional sentence?*

*How is this paragraph organized? Why is it effective?*

These two men both faced many obstacles to their reforms in the complicated and often backward societies in which they lived. Peter the Great and Gorbachev inherited similar problems from their predecessors, and both came to power during periods of virtual stagnation in Russian society. Peter faced the formidable task of creating a modern European nation out of a country that was, intellectually and culturally, two centuries behind Western Europe. During the Mongol occupation (1240–1480), Russia essentially missed important European developments such as the Renaissance ➡

*What details do you expect to come after this sentence?*

and the beginnings of modern market economies. As a result, the Russia of Peter's day attempted to rival the West while relying primarily on medieval philosophies and practices. Gorbachev also confronts this need to move into the future, noting that what the Soviet Union needs is "genuinely revolutionary and all-embracing transformations in society because there is simply no other path for us. We cannot retreat. There is nowhere to retreat to" (Lih 309). However, while the retardation of Peter's time was caused by the outside forces of the Mongols, Gorbachev confronts problems with internal origins. The Soviet Union equals the rest of the world in military might, but the Stalinist system of central planning has caused the U.S.S.R. to fall far behind in technological and industrial advances (Beissinger 341). The unbending bureaucracy and hard-line Soviet mentality represent main obstacles in Gorbachev's path to reform, for "by far the central problem, the key to the entire emergency, has to do with the need to reform the whole system of central planning and management" (Bialer, *Stalin* 291). Gorbachev, like Peter, must overcome both institutional torpor and historic xenophobia in order to achieve the goal of modernization.

*Why is the book title abbreviated in this citation?*

Many of the same societal problems Gorbachev must address can also be found in Peter's era. Gorbachev has introduced reforms, such as increasing the price while reducing the production of alcohol, in an attempt to lower the alarming rate of alcoholism in the Soviet Union. Alcoholism and chronic drunkenness result in low productivity among a negligent and lethargic work force. Alcohol abuse also influenced Peter and his society because, even then, drunkenness was pervasive. Unlike Gorbachev, however, Peter himself seemed to have encouraged overindulgence in alcohol through his revels with the "Drunken Synod" (Massie 124). Despite their differing views on the "virtues" of alcohol, neither Peter nor Gorbachev surmounted the problem of alcohol abuse. There seems to be the classic, self-perpetuating cycle in the Russian use of alcohol: the people are unhappy; so they drink, which results in poor job performance, which leads to dissatisfaction and disillusionment, and thus more drinking. Besides alcoholism, the major concerns of Gorbachev consist of reforming a failing economy plagued by an apathetic work force, and the need to increase agricultural production. He also faces a severe shortage of consumer goods, decreasing morale within the military, an increasing infant mortality rate, and a declining life expectancy, illustrating the need for more advanced medical care and technology (Daniloff 24). Peter's generation also encountered a high infant-mortality rate, a very low life expectancy, and the need for radical socioeconomic change. Although similar problems were present in ➡

*Note how this transition introduces Gorbachev's problems by repeating an idea from the previous paragraph.*

*What is the function of this sentence?*

their respective societies, Peter and Gorbachev often reacted differently to the situation at hand.

Peter the Great, though he frequently worked among the common people, remained, above all, an autocrat. Life and death hinged on his word, and he could make any law at will. However, due to a lack of consistently reliable communication, these laws were not always enforced. The Russian empire was too large and the communication system too primitive to allow effective oversight of every region. While Gorbachev enjoys the advantage of instant communication, he does not possess Peter's absolute power. Gorbachev must rely upon the support of the Politburo, the bureaucracy, and even the people in order to implement his policies. Therefore, Gorbachev's road to reform is paved with kinder words than Peter's. *Glasnost* (openness) and *perestroika* (restructuring) are the key words in the new Russian reform lexicon. Glasnost retains the support of the intellectuals, but the problem Gorbachev now faces is that as the people possess more rights to free speech, their economic distress results in strikes and protests that ironically jeopardize the success of further economic reform. The problem of free speech resulting in heightened unrest appears in the numerous Soviet republics that are demanding increased autonomy. The primary reasons for the "decline of the Soviet military's authority and prestige are democratization and Glasnost" (Bialer, "Gorbachev" 40).

*What other methods could the writer have used to explain the meaning of relevant foreign words?*

The Soviet Union presents a paradox of modern technology. In some areas, such as aerospace, the Soviet Union equals, if not surpasses, many Western nations, yet at the same time it lacks a reliable telephone system. The very structure of the Soviet system precludes the possibility of keeping up with rapid technological changes because it does not supply the incentive for workers to develop these new ideas. Therefore, the Soviet Union is very dependent upon the West and Japan to supply this technology, and this dependence is not new in Russian history. Peter the Great faced this problem in the area of advanced shipbuilding techniques for his expanding navy and weaponry for his reformed army. Once he acquired this technology, however, he did not face the possibility of its becoming obsolete in only a few years' time, as does Gorbachev. Peter's ability to update his technology and keep it for twenty years served as a great advantage to him in modernizing Russia. The rapid advance of modern science, however, can render technology obsolete virtually overnight, thus making Gorbachev's modernizing efforts more difficult because he must foster an ongoing relationship with the West, which can sometimes tie his hands both at home and abroad. ➡

Peter and and Gorbachev also faced similar economic problems on their road to reform. In the years preceding Peter's reign, Russian commerce and industry were not highly developed. "Scattered through towns were small factories and workshops for household implements, handicrafts and tools which met the needs of tsar, boyars, and merchants" (Massie 791). Inspired by his journey west, Peter decided to expand Russian industry. His desire for more advanced industrial capacity stemmed from his love of the military, as he needed guns and cannons to improve his army, and he wanted these armaments to be manufactured in Russia. Peter established powder mills and cannon foundries, along with a new textile industry, placing high import duties on foreign goods such as cloth to protect his new industries. Peter encouraged foreign craftsmen and businessmen to live in Russia and assist in his efforts. However, the reason for the success of Peter's industries lies in his realization that "private enterprise and initiative were the true sources of national wealth" (Massie 791).

*Why do you think the writer usually begins each point of comparison with Peter the Great?*

*This quotation describes the economic reality of the time.*

As in Peter's day, the modern Russian economy desperately needs reform, but Gorbachev has yet to embrace fully Peter's understanding of the role of private initiative. Gorbachev, confronted with a nation in severe economic decline and stagnating under an immense bureaucracy, introduced *Glasnost* and *perestroika* to attain his top priority, economic reform and revitalization. Gorbachev seeks to shift power from the central planning committees to a more local level. He condensed the Central Committee's twenty-six departments down to six, hoping to make problems more manageable. One of the most crucial phases for economic reform began in the summer of 1987, when the Central Committee approved a reform plan that will gradually decrease the power of Gosplan, the planning agency. Whether or not this effort succeeds depends upon the changing of attitudes as well as methods, which Peter comprehended as well as Gorbachev does (Galuszka 78).

In the meantime, Gorbachev faces the serious possibility of losing support and being deposed by his Politburo opponents if he does not produce fairly rapid results. Current economic conditions in the U.S.S.R. reflect the enormity of the situation: shortages of consumer goods have increased, the living standard has declined, and inflation and the deficit have grown. Lacking Peter's absolute power and ability to resort to the military to en-force his reforms, Gorbachev faces having the old system come apart before he can develop a new system that is ready to replace it.

*How does this transition bridge two ideas?*

The reforms of Peter the Great and Mikhail Gorbachev reflect their goals and aspirations for Russia during their respective eras. On their ascent to power, both the Czar and the President/General ➡

Gilbert 6

Secretary faced a nation in desperate need of socio-economic reform, and both strove mightily to bring the necessary changes. The chief difference thus far has been that Peter's absolute power served as a substantial advantage in imposing his reforms. Gorbachev must overcome opposition in the Politburo and among the Soviet public in ways more subtle, discreet, and diplomatic than those employed by Peter. Only time will tell which of these men served Russia more favorably, but one thing is certain for now: "Peter the Great, tsar for 43 years, transformed Russia. Mikhail the Modern will have to stay in power almost as long to do as much" (Franklin 48).

*What main points are summarized in the conclusion?*

*This colorful quotation from a journalist makes the ending memorable.*

Examples of Works Cited

Avery, Patricia A., and Nicholas Daniloff. "First Ladies at Summit: Matching Charm and Style." *U.S. News and World Report* 25 Nov. 1985: 42–44.

Beissinger, Mark R. "The Age of the Soviet Oligarchs." *Current History* Oct. 1984: 305–342.

Besançon, Alain. "Emperor and Heir, Father and Son." *Peter the Great Changes Russia.* 2nd ed. Ed. Marc Raeff. Lexington, Mass.: Heath, 1972. 160–170.

Bialer, Seweryn. "Gorbachev and the Soviet Military." *U.S. News and World Report* 13 Mar. 1989: 40–42.

---. *Stalin's Successors: Leadership, Stability and Change in the Soviet Union.* Cambridge: Cambridge UP, 1980.

Daniloff, Nicholas. "Ahead for Andropov: Troubles on All Sides." *U.S. News and World Report* 29 Nov. 1982: 24–26.

Franklin, Daniel. "The Soviet Economy." *The Economist* 9 Apr. 1988: 48–49.

Galuszka, Peter. "Reforming the Soviet Economy." *Business Week* 7 Dec. 1987: 76–78.

Gorbachev, Mikhail. "In His Words." *U.S. News and World Report* 9 Nov. 1987: 70–79.

Lih, Lars T. "Gorbachev and the Reform Movement." *Current History* Oct. 1987: 309–338.

Massie, Robert K. *Peter the Great: His Life and World.* New York: Ballantine, 1985.

Moody, John. "Back to Work, Comrades." *Time* 17 May 1987: 41.

Troyat, Henri. *Peter the Great.* Trans. Joan Pinkham. New York: Dutton, 1987.

Zuckerman, Mortimer B. "Gorbachev: The Rest of the Story." *U.S. News and World Report* 21 Dec. 1987: 84–85.

*Double-space all lines on your works cited page.*

# Unit 7 Review

## Reflecting on the Unit

**Summarize what you have learned in this unit by answering the following questions:**

- What are three ways to organize your ideas when developing an outline?
- How does prewriting help a research paper writer to focus?
- What are some important elements that should be contained in a research paper's conclusion?
- Why are citations important in a research paper?
- Can you always avoid the accusation of plagiarism simply by naming your sources?

## Adding to Your Portfolio

**Choose a selection for your portfolio.**
Look over the writing you have done for this unit and add it to your portfolio. You may also want to select either your outline, your research notes, or your revised draft as examples of writing processes to keep in your portfolio. The writing process should demonstrate all or some of the following:

- a thesis statement synthesizing the research and approach to the topic
- main ideas that support the thesis statement
- an organization that helps strengthen and advance the thesis statement and main ideas
- research sources noted within the body of the research paper and detailed at the end
- a conclusion that sums up the main ideas and reiterates the purpose of the paper.

**Reflect on your choice.**
Attach a note to the writing process example you chose, explaining why you chose it and what you learned from writing it.

**Set goals.**
How can you improve your writing?
What skill will you focus on the next time you write?

## Writing Across the Curriculum

**Make a history connection.**
Choose a topic from within the student research paper on pages 342–347. For example, you might choose the status of women in Russian society during the reign of Peter the Great. List your topic, a central idea, research questions, and some possible sources for a research report on the subject.

UNIT
# 8

# Style Through Sentence Combining

Composition

## Lessons

### Skills and Applications

UNIT 8

Sentence Combining

# Style Through Sentence Combining

You know the feeling. Hunched over your rough draft, you stare at sentences that look like snarled spaghetti. Should you start over? How will you ever untangle the mess? Is there no hope?

Take heart. One approach that has worked for millions of students is sentence-combining practice. This approach helps you learn revising skills such as adding, deleting, and rearranging ideas, which can help you transform sentences into more readable structures. Research on sentence combining indicates that such practice transfers to your real writing and improves its overall quality.

Of course, sentence-combining practice won't extend the deadline for your research paper or cure confused thinking. But if you need help in smoothing out your sentences—improving their readability, variety, and style—here's an approach that deserves your attention.

## A Workshop on Style

In this unit, you will find two types of sentence-combining exercises. The first type consists of clusters of short sentences that you will combine into longer ones. The second type, drawn from literature selections in this book, is set up in an unclustered format.

The first type of combining gives you practice in creating descriptive, narrative, expository, and persuasive paragraphs. You can combine each cluster of short sentences into one single sentence, or you can leave a cluster partially combined—or combine two or more clusters together. The idea, always, is to take risks and create the best sentences you can, writing them in your journal or as your teacher directs.

Exercises on facing pages deal with the same topic or situation. Think of these exercises as "bookends" for the writing you will do. After you have combined sentences into paragraphs, your task is to connect the paragraphs into a longer essay or story. Doing so will help you transfer sentence-combining skills to your own writing.

The second type of exercise, drawn from literary passages, invites you to test your skills against those of a professional writer. As you do these unclustered exercises, you will need to figure out the ideas that belong logically together. After you have completed the sentence-combining exercises, you can check your version against the author's original.

By studying similarities and differences in the two passages, you will learn a great deal about your own style. Sometimes you will prefer the professional writer's sentences. Why, specifically, are they "better" than yours? But sometimes you will prefer your own style. Then you can build on this writing skill, trying it out in your own stories and essays. Both types of exercises will help you improve your writing.

## Explore Your Own Style

Sentence-combining practice helps when you revise your real writing. You know that sentences are flexible instruments of thought, not rigid structures cast in concrete. The simple fact that you feel confident in moving sentence parts around increases your control of the writing process.

To acquire this sense of self-confidence—one based on your real competence in combining and revising sentences—you can try strategies like those described below.

1. *Vary the length of your sentences.* Work for a rhythmic, interesting balance of long and short sentences, remembering that brevity often has dramatic force. Use this knowledge.
2. *Vary the structure of your sentences.* By using sentence openers on occasion—and by sometimes tucking information in the middle of a sentence—you can create stylistic interest.
3. *Use parallelism for emphasis.* Experiment with repeated items in a series—words, phrases, and clauses—to understand how structural patterns work and how you can use them to advantage.
4. *Use interruption for emphasis.* Colons, semicolons, dashes, commas, parentheses—all of these are useful tools in your stylistic tool kit; knowing how to use them well matters.
5. *Use unusual patterns for emphasis.* It may never have occurred to you to sometimes reverse normal sentence patterns. Such a strategy can work—if you know how to use it.

Of course, the whole point of sentence-combining practice is to improve your revising and editing skills. Therefore, when it comes time to rework a draft, it's important to apply what you have learned about combining and revising.

The same holds true when you are responding to the writing of your peers. If you spot a passage that can be improved with stylistic tinkering, simply write SC (for sentence combining) in the margin. This will be a cue to apply some of the skills learned in this unit.

# 8.1 Descriptive Writing

## Exercise A: Farmhouse

**Directions** Combine each cluster of numbered items into one or more sentences. Combine clusters, if you wish.

**1.1** Just ahead was the farmhouse.
**1.2** This was where the road ended.
**1.3** The road was gravel.
**1.4** The road was sun baked.

**2.1** Its porch now sagged.
**2.2** The porch was once proud.
**2.3** Its chimney had begun to cave in.
**2.4** The chimney was brick.

**3.1** The windows stood dark.
**3.2** The windows stood empty.
**3.3** The windows were unshuttered.
**3.4** The windows had no one behind them.

**4.1** Its siding was gray.
**4.2** The gray was weathered.
**4.3** Its siding was the color of ash.

**5.1** Roses grew thick on a picket fence.
**5.2** Roses grew wild on a picket fence.
**5.3** The fence was sagging.
**5.4** The fence now enclosed weeds.
**5.5** The weeds were knee-deep.

**6.1** An oak tree lay in the side yard.
**6.2** It was blackened from a lightning strike.
**6.3** It was splintered from a lightning strike.
**6.4** A row of poplars grew to the north.
**6.5** The poplars were untrimmed.
**6.6** They were like shaggy giants.

**7.1** Nothing moved around the house.
**7.2** The only sound was the wind's whisper.
**7.3** The whisper was breathless.
**7.4** The whisper came through the trees.

### Writing Tip

For cluster 3 try several opening words—***unshuttered, standing, dark and empty, with,*** and ***the***—before settling on one sentence.

**Invitation** Describe Anna, the person seeing the farmhouse, as clearly as you can.

## Exercise B: Anna's Memory

**Directions** Combine each cluster of numbered items into one or more sentences. Combine clusters, if you wish.

**1.1** Anna remembered sitting beside her dad.
**1.2** He drove the pickup to town.
**1.3** He drove in the darkness.
**1.4** The darkness was in the early morning.

**2.1** The truck had rattled down the road.
**2.2** The truck had bounced down the road.
**2.3** It had headed toward the Farmer's Market.
**2.4** The Farmer's Market was lit by floodlights.
**2.5** The floodlights were bluish.

**3.1** There they would find men in overalls.
**3.2** The men were thick-shouldered.
**3.3** They wheeled berries over the docks.
**3.4** They wheeled peaches over the docks.
**3.5** They wheeled melons over the docks.
**3.6** The docks were concrete.

**4.1** Then would come breakfast.
**4.2** It was at a café across from the market.
**4.3** The café was grease spattered.
**4.4** The café was friendly.

**5.1** Anna would sometimes have pancakes.
**5.2** The pancakes were perfectly round.
**5.3** She would soak them with maple syrup.
**5.4** The maple syrup was sticky-sweet.

**6.1** Her father had finished his eggs.
**6.2** He would sip his coffee.
**6.3** He would exchange jokes with the cook.
**6.4** He would exchange gossip with the cook.

**7.1** Afterward would come the drive back.
**7.2** This was in the day's gathering heat.
**7.3** Dust had billowed up from behind.

**Invitation** Describe the scene that Anna drives back to with her father. Share your text with a writing partner.

### Writing Tip

In sentence 7.3 try ***with*** as a connector, delete ***had***, and change ***billowed*** to ***billowing***.

## Exercise C: Man in a Café

**Directions** Combine each cluster of numbered items into one or more sentences. Combine clusters, if you wish.

**1.1** Emile was a small man.
**1.2** He was carefully dressed.
**1.3** He sat alone in a café.
**1.4** The café was dockside.
**1.5** It had a view of the sea.

**2.1** Hair was combed across his baldness.
**2.2** His hair was wispy.
**2.3** His hair was thinning.
**2.4** He studied white triangles.
**2.5** They were on a blue horizon.

**3.1** He wore a navy blazer.
**3.2** The blazer was double-breasted.
**3.3** He wore a white shirt.
**3.4** The white shirt was crisp.
**3.5** He wore a burgundy ascot.
**3.6** The ascot had a matching hanky.

**4.1** He was like an actor in a play.
**4.2** The play was strange.
**4.3** He adjusted his sunglasses with care.
**4.4** His care was exquisite.

**5.1** On one hand was a jeweled ring.
**5.2** The hand was pale.
**5.3** The hand was uncalloused.
**5.4** The ring glinted in the light.
**5.5** The light was apricot-colored.

**6.1** He finished his cappuccino.
**6.2** He touched a napkin to his mouth.
**6.3** His gesture was elegant.
**6.4** His gesture was practiced.
**6.5** He squinted at his watch.
**6.6** It had a glittering gold face.

### Writing Tip

To experiment with sentence openers, consider using ***like*** to open cluster 4 and ***finishing*** to open cluster 6.

**Invitation** Describe what you see happening *before* this scene. Then link "Man in a Café" to "Limousine" on the next page.

## Exercise D: Limousine

**Directions** Combine each cluster of numbered items into one or more sentences. Combine clusters, if you wish.

**1.1** The street was almost deserted.
**1.2** The street was next to the café.
**1.3** The only exception was an elderly couple.
**1.4** They were out for an afternoon stroll.

**2.1** A limousine eased up to the curb.
**2.2** The limousine was white.
**2.3** The limousine had blackened windows.
**2.4** The curb was dockside.
**2.5** No parking was allowed there.

**3.1** Sunlight gleamed along its fenders.
**3.2** The fenders were seamless.
**3.3** The fenders were long.
**3.4** Sunlight played across its grill.
**3.5** The grill was chrome.

**4.1** The car had whitewall tires.
**4.2** The car had spoked wheel covers.
**4.3** The car had twin antennas.
**4.4** The antennas were for TV reception.
**4.5** The antennas were for a telephone.

**5.1** Its engine murmured.
**5.2** The murmur was quiet.
**5.3** The old couple shuffled by.
**5.4** They were enjoying the sunset.

**6.1** Then a side window dropped.
**6.2** The side window was darkened.
**6.3** This revealed a silhouette inside.
**6.4** The silhouette was shadowy.

**7.1** In the distance lay the sun.
**7.2** It oozed orange across the water.
**7.3** It oozed red across the water.

### Writing Tip

For sentence variety avoid using three participle phrases in a row (***enjoying, revealing, oozing***) in clusters 5, 6, and 7.

**Invitation** Write an ending for "Man in a Café" and "Limousine" that uses description effectively. Share your text with a writing partner.

## 8.2 Narrative Writing

### Exercise A: Food for Thought

**Directions** Combine each cluster of numbered items into one or more sentences. Combine clusters, if you wish.

**1.1** Alex slipped on a light jacket.
**1.2** He checked his wallet.
**1.3** He headed for the parking lot.
**1.4** His VW van was parked there.

**2.1** Rain had begun to fall.
**2.2** It made rivers on the windshield.
**2.3** The rivers were tiny.
**2.4** The rivers were trickling.

**3.1** The wipers swept left to right.
**3.2** They set up a rhythm.
**3.3** The rhythm was steady.
**3.4** They smeared the road film.
**3.5** They smeared the dead bugs.

**4.1** He drove out to the main highway.
**4.2** He then turned west.
**4.3** He angled through an industrial area.
**4.4** The industrial area was grim.
**4.5** He had once worked there.

**5.1** Clouds hung low on the horizon.
**5.2** Their underbellies rubbed the rooftops.
**5.3** The underbellies were gray.
**5.4** Rain hissed beneath the VW's tires.

**6.1** His destination was a truck stop.
**6.2** The truck stop was familiar.
**6.3** It was lit by red neon.
**6.4** He would have breakfast there.

**7.1** He ordered coffee.
**7.2** He ordered scrambled eggs.
**7.3** He clicked a ballpoint pen into action.
**7.4** He listened to inner thoughts.

**Writing Tip**

Try ***where*** as a connector in cluster 1 and elsewhere in this exercise. To make an absolute in cluster 5, change ***rubbed*** to ***rubbing.***

**Invitation** Become Alex for a moment and try writing a free verse poem. Use your poem to link "Food for Thought" and "Old Friends."

## Exercise B: Old Friends

**Directions** Combine each cluster of numbered items into one or more sentences. Combine clusters, if you wish.

**1.1** Alex chewed on a crust of toast.
**1.2** The crust was rubbery.
**1.3** Alex looked up from his poem.
**1.4** The poem was slender.
**1.5** He had scrawled it on a napkin.
**1.6** The napkin was paper.

**2.1** A semi had just pulled in.
**2.2** It was grimy from its morning run.
**2.3** The trucker climbed down.
**2.4** He cocked his cap to one side.
**2.5** He began thumping tires with a hammer.

**3.1** Diesel exhaust had spread in a banner.
**3.2** The banner was greasy.
**3.3** The banner was black.
**3.4** It was along the top of the trailer.

**4.1** The driver hesitated along the highway.
**4.2** He waited for traffic to clear.
**4.3** He then loped toward the truck stop.
**4.4** His gait was awkward.
**4.5** His gait was stiff-legged.
**4.6** It was as if he might be in pain.

**5.1** Inside the café he grinned at Alex.
**5.2** He shuffled across the linoleum.
**5.3** The linoleum was gritty.
**5.4** He broke into chatter.
**5.5** The chatter was nonstop.

**6.1** Alex sipped coffee from a mug.
**6.2** The coffee was lukewarm.
**6.3** The mug was ceramic.
**6.4** Alex folded up his thoughts.
**6.5** Alex pocketed them.

**Invitation** Create a dialogue between Alex and the truck driver. Share your text with a writing partner.

### Grammar Writing Tip

To make an absolute in cluster 4, delete ***was*** in sentences 4.4 and 4.5 and then join with ***and.*** For more on absolutes, see page 487.

## Exercise C: On the Edge

**Directions** Combine each cluster of numbered items into one or more sentences. Combine clusters, if you wish.

**1.1** Jan stood uncertainly atop a slope.
**1.2** The slope was steep.
**1.3** The slope was untracked.
**1.4** Jan summoned up her courage.

**2.1** Behind her were laughs from her friends.
**2.2** Behind her were taunts from her friends.
**2.3** They said she had lost her nerve.

**3.1** She whirled around.
**3.2** She shouted back at them with defiance.
**3.3** Her defiance was head strong.

**4.1** Then she flexed her knees.
**4.2** She took several deep breaths.
**4.3** She checked her bindings.

**5.1** She had second thoughts.
**5.2** She studied the area below.
**5.3** It was a bowl-shaped run.
**5.4** Only experts were allowed there.

**6.1** The slope was beyond her ability.
**6.2** She was attracted by its challenge.
**6.3** The challenge was dangerous.
**6.4** She was attracted by its powder snow.
**6.5** The snow shimmered with ice crystals.

**7.1** She bit her lip hard.
**7.2** She felt the pull of gravity.
**7.3** The pull was inexorable.
**7.4** She asked herself what she was doing.

**8.1** Off to one side was another trail.
**8.2** It was safer and easier.
**8.3** Her friends had decided to take it.

### Writing Tip

In clusters 1 and 8 consider using paired modifiers after the noun headwords, ***slope*** and ***trail***, rather than before them.

**Invitation** Narrate what Jan notices and thinks about as she faces a difficult challenge. Link this narration to "Downhill Skier."

## Exercise D: Downhill Skier

**Directions** Combine each cluster of numbered items into one or more sentences. Combine clusters, if you wish.

**1.1** She traversed from left to right.
**1.2** Her body was crouched and ready.
**1.3** She chose a downhill angle of attack.

**2.1** She felt herself gather speed.
**2.2** She felt herself gather momentum.
**2.3** Her knees were locked tight.
**2.4** Her body was relaxed.

**3.1** She swooped over a low rise.
**3.2** The rise was near the trees.
**3.3** She was momentarily airborne.
**3.4** She was perfectly in control.
**3.5** This was thanks to adjustments.
**3.6** The adjustments were in mid-air.

**4.1** She loved the jump's weightlessness.
**4.2** It was a floating feeling.
**4.3** It was like being knee-deep in snow.
**4.4** The snow was feathery.
**4.5** The snow was freshly fallen.

**5.1** She first dipped one pole.
**5.2** She then dipped the other.
**5.3** She made a series of arcs.
**5.4** The arcs were birdlike.

**6.1** Snow rose in plumes.
**6.2** The plumes were powdery.
**6.3** She skied beyond herself.
**6.4** She headed for a steep area.
**6.5** She would surely face trouble there.

**7.1** She felt panic rise within her.
**7.2** She tried to slow down.
**7.3** It was now too late.

### Grammar Writing Tip

In sentences 2.3 and 2.4, you can delete ***were*** and ***was*** to create parallel absolutes. For more on absolutes, see page 487.

**Invitation** Narrate a conclusion to this story. Then share your text—"On the Edge" plus "Downhill Skier"—with a writing partner.

## 8.3 Expository Writing

### Exercise A: Understanding Stress

**Directions** Combine each cluster of numbered items into one or more sentences. Combine clusters, if you wish.

**1.1** To be alive is to experience stress.
**1.2** Everyone faces problems at school.
**1.3** Everyone faces arguments with friends.
**1.4** Everyone faces arguments with family.
**1.5** Everyone faces conflicting demands on time.

**2.1** Emotions associated with stress include anger.
**2.2** Emotions associated with stress include anxiety.
**2.3** These are accompanied by increased blood pressure.
**2.4** These are accompanied by increased heart rate.
**2.5** These are accompanied by increased muscle tension.

**3.1** Such effects are our "fight or flight" response.
**3.2** The effects are physiological.
**3.3** The response is genetically encoded.
**3.4** We share this response with other animals.

**4.1** Human beings once faced threats in two ways.
**4.2** The threats were physical.
**4.3** They stood their ground and fought.
**4.4** They ran for safety.

**5.1** Extra energy was needed to survive.
**5.2** Extra alertness was needed to survive.
**5.3** The body responded by releasing two hormones.
**5.4** One hormone was adrenaline.
**5.5** The other hormone was noradrenaline.
**5.6** These pumped more blood to the brain and muscles.
**5.7** These triggered blood-clotting mechanisms.

**6.1** We rarely face the same threats as early humans.
**6.2** We are equipped with the same physiology.
**6.3** The physiology is activated by stress.

**7.1** Exercise is one good way to reduce stress.
**7.2** Relaxation techniques can also prove valuable.

**Writing Tip**

In cluster 4 try a colon for stylistic effect. In cluster 5 try using a pair of dashes to set off the names of hormones.

**Invitation** Describe how you feel after vigorous exercise such as basketball or another sport. What happens to your level of stress?

## Exercise B: Exercise Matters

**Directions** Combine each cluster of numbered items into one or more sentences. Combine clusters, if you wish.

**1.1** Regular exercise has many benefits.
**1.2** The benefits are physiological.
**1.3** These include reduced risk of heart disease.
**1.4** These include lowered blood pressure.
**1.5** These include lowered cholesterol levels.

**2.1** Particularly helpful are aerobic activities.
**2.2** They condition the heart to pump blood.
**2.3** The blood is oxygen-rich.
**2.4** They condition muscles to use oxygen.

**3.1** Many activities create a "training effect."
**3.2** These activities include jogging.
**3.3** These activities include swimming.
**3.4** These activities include cycling.
**3.5** These activities include aerobic dance.
**3.6** The "training effect" strengthens the heart.

**4.1** This training effect is developed over time.
**4.2** Exercise sessions last from fifteen to sixty minutes.
**4.3** Sessions occur from three to five days per week.

**5.1** The heart gradually becomes stronger.
**5.2** It actually pumps more blood per beat.
**5.3** This decreases the heart rate while resting.
**5.4** This decreases the heart rate while exercising.

**6.1** The physiological effects are important.
**6.2** Other benefits include improved self-esteem.
**6.3** Other benefits include lessened anxiety.
**6.4** The benefits are psychological.
**6.5** The benefits are more difficult to measure.

**7.1** Regular exercise clearly reduces stress.
**7.2** It may also relieve symptoms of depression.
**7.3** This is according to some clinical reports.

### Writing Tip

In cluster 6 consider using a connector such as ***while*** or ***although***.

**Invitation** Can relaxation strategies or other techniques help reduce daily stress? Focus on one such technique in a follow-up paragraph.

## Exercise C: Insect Communication

**Directions** Combine each cluster of numbered items into one or more sentences. Combine clusters, if you wish.

**1.1** Insects use an array of tactics.
**1.2** The array is bewildering.
**1.3** The tactics are for communication.

**2.1** Fireflies emit a cold light.
**2.2** Glow worms emit a cold light.
**2.3** They use the light to summon mates.
**2.4** They use the light to discourage predators.

**3.1** Many moths possess a sense of smell.
**3.2** Many butterflies possess a sense of smell.
**3.3** The sense is extraordinary.
**3.4** It enables them to interpret faint odors.
**3.5** The odors are over a mile away.

**4.1** Crickets produce sound by stridulation.
**4.2** Locusts produce sound by stridulation.
**4.3** Cicadas produce sound by stridulation.
**4.4** They rub rough surfaces on their legs.
**4.5** They rub rough surfaces on their wings.
**4.6** They rub rough surfaces on their abdomens.
**4.7** They rub rough surfaces on their thoraxes.

**5.1** Termites secrete substances from their skin.
**5.2** Termites are both blind and deaf.
**5.3** The substances are fatty.
**5.4** The substances communicate their rank.
**5.5** Their rank is in the termite community.

**6.1** Ant species communicate in various ways.
**6.2** These include tactile sensations.
**6.3** The sensations are from their antennae.
**6.4** These include exchanges of food.
**6.5** The exchanges are mouth-to-mouth.
**6.6** These include scent from trails.
**6.7** The trails are chemical.

### Grammar
### Writing Tip

In either cluster 2, 4, 5, or 6, consider using single (or paired) dashes for stylistic emphasis. For more on dashes, see page 691.

**Invitation** Human beings also use many communication tactics. Identify as many as you can in a follow-up paragraph. Then share your paragraph with a partner.

## Exercise D: Honeybee Boogie

**Directions** Combine each cluster of numbered items into one or more sentences. Combine clusters, if you wish.

**1.1** Honeybees communicate through a dance.
**1.2** The dance is highly expressive.
**1.3** The dance is genetically programmed.

**2.1** A bee discovers a food source.
**2.2** It returns to the hive.
**2.3** It is dusted with pollen.
**2.4** It is perfumed with nectar.

**3.1** It dances on the comb's vertical wall.
**3.2** It attracts the attention of fellow workers.

**4.1** The dance specifies two kinds of information.
**4.2** One kind is the distance of the food supply.
**4.3** The other is the direction of the food supply.

**5.1** The food is less than eighty-five feet away.
**5.2** The finder bee executes a series of figures.
**5.3** The series is swift.
**5.4** The figures are circular.

**6.1** The food lies at a greater distance.
**6.2** The finder bee promenades in a straight line.
**6.3** This is broken at intervals by pirouettes.
**6.4** The pirouettes are to right and left.
**6.5** The finder bee wags its abdomen in a tempo.
**6.6** The tempo communicates distance.

**7.1** Equally remarkable is the honeybee's strategy.
**7.2** The strategy is for communicating direction.

**8.1** A bee circles.
**8.2** A bee promenades.
**8.3** It dances at an angle from the vertical axis.
**8.4** This angle specifies the direction of food.
**8.5** The direction is in relation to the sun's location.

**Grammar**
**Writing Tip**

In cluster 4 try using either a dash or colon for emphasis. For more on dashes, see page 691; for more on colons, see pages 678–679.

**Invitation** Do you consider the dance of the honeybee a language? Why or why not? Write a follow-up paragraph to this exercise, and share it with a writing partner.

# 8.4 Persuasive Writing

## Exercise A: Now Hear This

**Directions** Combine each cluster of numbered items into one or more sentences. Combine clusters, if you wish.

**1.1** Hearing loss is a problem.
**1.2** The hearing loss is noise-induced.
**1.3** The problem is growing.
**1.4** The problem is among teenagers.

**2.1** Many adolescents wear sunglasses.
**2.2** The sunglasses are for eye protection.
**2.3** Few protect their ears from loud noises.
**2.4** Few protect their ears from loud music.
**2.5** These can cause damage.
**2.6** The damage is permanent.

**3.1** Most do not know something.
**3.2** Exposure to 85 decibels causes hearing loss.
**3.3** The exposure is prolonged.
**3.4** The hearing loss is gradual.
**3.5** Exposure to 100 decibels can cause damage.
**3.6** The damage is irreversible.

**4.1** Rock concerts often create sounds.
**4.2** They are amplified to 110 decibels.
**4.3** Equally scary are personal stereos.
**4.4** These funnel their blasts into the ear.
**4.5** The funneling is direct.

**5.1** Cassette players easily produce 110 decibels.
**5.2** These headphones are strapped to the skull.
**5.3** The decibels are destructive.
**5.4** The decibels assault the tiny hair cells inside the ear.
**5.5** The assault is unrelenting.
**5.6** The hair cells are delicate.

**6.1** And "boom cars" can produce 130 decibels.
**6.2** The cars are equipped with huge speakers.
**6.3** The cars are equipped with huge amplifiers.
**6.4** This is a self-destructive level of noise.

**Writing Tip**

In cluster 3 delete ***something*** and use ***that*** as a connector. In clusters 4 and 5 change the words ***direct*** and ***unrelenting*** into adverbs.

**Invitation** Describe an experience in which you may have risked injuring your hearing, either temporarily or permanently. Share it with a writing partner.

## Exercise B: Hearing Loss

**Directions** Combine each cluster of numbered items into one or more sentences. Combine clusters, if you wish.

**1.1** The ear is an organ.
**1.2** The organ is amazingly flexible.
**1.3** It was not designed to withstand abuse.
**1.4** It was not designed to withstand assaults.

**2.1** Sudden noise damages the ear.
**2.2** The noise is intense.
**2.3** It is like a gunshot.
**2.4** It is like a dynamite blast.

**3.1** More insidious is sustained noise.
**3.2** The noise comes from chain saws.
**3.3** The noise comes from vacuum cleaners.
**3.4** The noise comes from jackhammers.
**3.5** The noise comes from stereo systems.

**4.1** A barrage flattens hair cells.
**4.2** The barrage is prolonged.
**4.3** The barrage is repeated.
**4.4** The hair cells are tiny.
**4.5** They transmit sound to the auditory nerve.

**5.1** The hairs begin to wilt.
**5.2** A person hears a buzzing sound.
**5.3** A person hears a ringing sound.
**5.4** These sounds are known as tinnitus.

**6.1** Hair cells can recover with rest.
**6.2** The cells are in the inner ear.
**6.3** Continued assaults weaken them.
**6.4** Continued assaults kill them.

**7.1** These cells do not regenerate.
**7.2** The result is permanent hearing loss.

### Writing Tip

In clusters 1 and 6 try several connectors—***but, yet, however, while, although***—before settling on one. Check punctuation.

**Invitation** Laws protect the hearing of workers in noisy work places, but in many communities no laws cover recreational noises. Should such laws be enacted?

## Exercise C: Free Speech

**Directions** Combine each cluster of numbered items into one or more sentences. Combine clusters, if you wish.

**1.1** Americans enjoy freedom of speech.
**1.2** Americans enjoy freedom of religion.
**1.3** Americans enjoy freedom of assembly.
**1.4** This is thanks to the First Amendment.
**1.5** It is part of our Bill of Rights.

**2.1** But our history makes something clear.
**2.2** Free speech is not absolutely protected.
**2.3** This is especially in times of war.
**2.4** This is especially in times of crisis.
**2.5** The crisis is domestic.

**3.1** One example is the Espionage Act of 1917.
**3.2** One example is the Sedition Act of 1918.
**3.3** These acts created penalties for expression.
**3.4** It might promote "contempt" for government.
**3.5** It might promote "scorn" for government.

**4.1** Charles Schenck was arrested for distributing leaflets.
**4.2** Charles Schenck was a socialist.
**4.3** The leaflets protested the World War I draft.
**4.4** The Supreme Court upheld his conviction.

**5.1** Justice Holmes wrote the Court's decision.
**5.2** Speech can be curbed under certain conditions.
**5.3** It shows a "clear and present danger."
**5.4** The danger might cause "substantive evils."

**6.1** A false cry of "Fire!" in a crowded theater is a crime.
**6.2** It is not an exercise of free speech.
**6.3** This is according to Holmes's famous ruling.

**7.1** We take freedom of speech for granted.
**7.2** We hardly give it a second thought.
**7.3** It has often been tested by the courts.
**7.4** The courts must balance one freedom against others.

### Writing Tip

In sentence 2.1 delete ***something*** and use ***that*** as a connector. In cluster 5 use a connector such as ***if*** or ***when***.

**Invitation** We often focus on the right of free speech. Do certain responsibilities accompany that right? Express your views in writing.

## Exercise D: Symbolic Speech

**Directions** Combine each cluster of numbered items into one or more sentences. Combine clusters, if you wish.

**1.1** The courts have considered "symbolic speech."
**1.2** The courts have protected citizens' rights.
**1.3** The courts have expanded citizens' rights.
**1.4** The rights are under the First Amendment.

**2.1** One important case focused on a student.
**2.2** The student was thirteen years old.
**2.3** The student was Mary Beth Tinker.
**2.4** She wore a black armband to class.
**2.5** Her aim was to protest the Vietnam War.

**3.1** Mary Beth's parents supported her action.
**3.2** They opposed U.S. involvement in Vietnam.
**3.3** Their opposition was vigorous.
**3.4** They took active political stands.

**4.1** The girl was suspended from school.
**4.2** Her action violated school rules.
**4.3** Her action was symbolic.
**4.4** Her action was wearing a black armband.
**4.5** Her action created a "disruptive influence."
**4.6** This was according to school officials.

**5.1** The Supreme Court weighed conflicting claims.
**5.2** One was centered on school district rights.
**5.3** The rights are to maintain classroom control.
**5.4** The other was centered on First Amendment rights.

**6.1** The Court finally ruled in the student's favor.
**6.2** It said that students have basic rights.
**6.3** The rights are guaranteed under the Constitution.

**7.1** The ruling stipulated something.
**7.2** The state must respect the rights of students.
**7.3** Students must respect their obligations.
**7.4** Their obligations are to the state.

### Writing Tip

In sentence 2.2 hyphenate ***thirteen-year-old*** when you use it as a noun or modifier. In sentences 5.2 and 5.4 combine by deleting ***was***.

**Invitation** What other forms of symbolic speech do you think are protected by the First Amendment? Write a persuasive paragraph about First Amendment protection.

## 8.5 Literature Exercises

### Exercise A

**Directions** Scan the sentences below. The unnumbered ones come directly from *My Left Foot*, by Christy Brown. The numbered sentences are adapted from Brown's book. Decide which of the numbered sentences belong together, and combine them in your own way. Then compare your sentences with the originals on pages 190–198.

It happened so quickly, so simply after all the years of waiting and uncertainty that I can see and feel the whole scene as if it had happened last week.

1. It was the afternoon of a cold day.
2. The day was grey.
3. The day was in December.
4. The streets outside glistened with snow.
5. The white flakes stuck on the window-panes.
6. The white flakes melted on the window-panes.
7. The white flakes sparkled.
8. The white flakes hung on the boughs of the trees.
9. The white flakes were like molten silver.
10. The wind howled dismally.
11. The wind whipped up little columns of snow.
12. The columns whirled.
13. The columns rose at every fresh gust.
14. The columns fell at every fresh gust.
15. And over all was the sky.
16. The sky was dull and murky.
17. The sky stretched like a dark canopy.
18. The sky was a vast infinity of greyness.

Inside, all the family were gathered round the big kitchen fire that lit up the little room with a warm glow and made giant shadows dance on the walls and ceiling.

19. Mona and Paddy were in the corner.
20. Mona and Paddy were sitting huddled together.
21. A few school primers were before them.
22. The primers were torn.
23. They were writing down little sums.
24. They wrote on a slate.
25. The slate was old and chipped.
26. They used a bright piece of yellow chalk.

## Exercise B

**Directions** Scan the sentences below. The unnumbered ones come directly from *The Road from Coorain*, by Jill Ker Conway. The numbered sentences are adapted from Conway's book. Decide which of the numbered sentences belong together, and combine them in your own way. Then compare your sentences with the originals on pages 146–150.

The creatures that inhabit this earth carry its colors in their feathers, fur, and scales.

1. Among its largest denizens are emus.
2. They are flightless birds.
3. They stand six feet high.
4. They have dun-grey feathers.
5. They have tiny wings.
6. Among its largest denizens are kangaroos.
7. Kangaroos are silent creatures.
8. They are like emus.
9. They stand two to eight feet tall.
10. They range in color from the gentlest dove-grey.
11. They range in color to a rich red-brown.

Both species blend with their native earth so well that one can be almost upon them before recognizing the familiar shape.

12. The wild dogs have fur.
13. It has the familiar yellow of the sunbaked clay.
14. The reptiles look like the earth in shadow.
15. The snakes look like the earth in shadow.
16. The goannas look like the earth in shadow.
17. All tread on the fragile habitat.
18. All have padded paws.
19. All have padded claws.
20. These leave the roots of grass intact.

On the plains, the earth meets the sky in a sharp black line so regular that it seems as though drawn by a creator interested more in geometry than the hills and valleys of the Old Testament.

21. Human purposes are dwarfed by such a horizon.
22. The horizon is blank.
23. We see it from an island in a vast ocean.
24. We know we are resting in shelter.

## Exercise C

**Directions** Scan the sentences below. The unnumbered ones come directly from *Georgia O'Keeffe*, by Joan Didion. The numbered sentences are adapted from Didion's book. Decide which of the numbered sentences belong together, and combine them in your own way. Then compare your sentences with the originals on pages 106–110.

1. Some women fight.
2. Others do not fight.
3. Georgia O'Keeffe was like so many guerrillas.
4. The guerrillas are successful.
5. The guerrillas are in the war between the sexes.
6. Georgia O'Keeffe seems to have been equipped early.
7. Her equipment was an immutable sense of who she was.
8. Her equipment was a fairly clear understanding of something.
9. She would be required to prove who she was.
10. Her upbringing was conventional on the surface.
11. She was a child on the Wisconsin prairie.
12. She played with China dolls.
13. She painted watercolors with cloudy skies.
14. Sunlight was too hard to paint.
15. She listened every night to her mother read stories.
16. She listened with her brothers and sisters.
17. The stories were of the Wild West.
18. The stories were of Texas.
19. The stories were of Kit Carson.
20. The stories were of Billy the Kid.
21. She told adults she wanted to be an artist.
22. She was embarrassed about something.
23. They asked her what kind of artist she wanted to be.
24. She had no idea "what kind."
25. She had no idea what artists did.

She had never seen a picture that interested her, other than a pen-and-ink Maid of Athens in one of her mother's books, some Mother Goose illustrations printed on cloth, a tablet-cover that showed a little girl with pink roses, and the painting of Arabs on horseback that hung in her grandmother's parlor.

26. She was in a Dominican convent at age thirteen.
27. She was mortified.
28. The sister corrected her drawing.

UNIT 9

# Troubleshooter

Composition Lessons

Use Troubleshooter to help you correct common errors that you might make in your writing. You can indicate the errors on your paper using the handwritten codes in the left-hand column. Then the Table of Contents below will help you locate solutions to correct errors.

## 9.1 Sentence Fragment

### PROBLEM 1

### *Fragment that lacks a subject*

*frag* Lauren ruined her new sweater. Put it in the washing machine.

**Solution**

**Lauren ruined her new sweater. She put it in the washing machine.**

Add a subject to the fragment to make it a complete sentence.

### PROBLEM 2

### *Fragment that lacks a complete verb*

*frag* From the darkened room came a flickering light. The television set.

*frag* We expect to make the playoffs this year. The team winning most of its games.

**Solution A**

**From the darkened room came a flickering light. The television set was still on.**

**We expect to make the playoffs this year. The team is winning most of its games.**

Add either a complete verb or a helping verb to make the sentence complete.

**Solution B**

**From the darkened room came a flickering light—the television set was still on.**

**We expect to make the playoffs this year because the team is winning most of its games.**

Combine the fragment with another sentence.

## PROBLEM 3

### *Fragment that is a subordinate clause*

*frag* Kim wants to visit Africa. Because her ancestors came from there.

*frag* Miray wrote a letter to the editor. Which was published.

**Solution A**

**Kim wants to visit Africa because her ancestors came from there.**

**Miray wrote a letter to the editor, which was published.**
Combine the fragment with another sentence.

**Solution B**

**Kim wants to visit Africa. Her ancestors came from there.**

**Miray wrote a letter to the editor. Her letter was published.**
Rewrite the fragment as a complete sentence, eliminating the subordinating conjunction or the relative pronoun and adding a subject or other words necessary to make a complete thought.

## PROBLEM 4

### *Fragment that lacks both a subject and a verb*

*frag* The new department store will open. On Labor Day.

**Solution**

**The new department store will open on Labor Day.**
Combine the fragment with another sentence.

***If you need more help in avoiding sentence fragments, see Lesson 13.9, page 513.***

## 9.2 Run-on Sentence

### PROBLEM 1

*Comma splice—two main clauses separated only by a comma*

*run-on* Most of the guests left the party at nine, we stayed to help clean up.

**Solution A**

**Most of the guests left the party at nine. We stayed to help clean up.**

Replace the comma with an end mark of punctuation, such as a period or a question mark, and begin the new sentence with a capital letter.

**Solution B**

**Most of the guests left the party at nine; we stayed to help clean up.**

Place a semicolon between the two main clauses.

**Solution C**

**Most of the guests left the party at nine, but we stayed to help clean up.**

Add a coordinating conjunction after the comma.

### PROBLEM 2

*Two main clauses with no punctuation between them*

*run-on* An airplane was passing overhead its roar caused the windows to rattle.

**Solution A**

**An airplane was passing overhead. Its roar caused the windows to rattle.**

Separate the main clauses with an end mark of punctuation, such as a period or a question mark, and begin the second sentence with a capital letter.

**Solution B**

**An airplane was passing overhead; its roar caused the windows to rattle.**

Separate the main clauses with a semicolon.

**Solution C**

**An airplane was passing overhead, and its roar caused the windows to rattle.**

Add a comma and a coordinating conjunction between the main clauses.

## PROBLEM 3

### *Two main clauses with no comma before the coordinating conjunction*

*run-on* Local roads were flooded by the storm and airline traffic was delayed.

*run-on* We packed the sandwiches and fruit but we forgot the juice.

**Solution**

**Local roads were flooded by the storm, and airline traffic was delayed.**

**We packed the sandwiches and fruit, but we forgot the juice.**

Add a comma before the coordinating conjunction to separate the two main clauses.

*If you need more help in avoiding run-on sentences, see Lesson 13.10, pages 514–517.*

# 9.3 Lack of Subject-Verb Agreement

## PROBLEM 1

### *A subject that is separated from the verb by an intervening prepositional phrase*

*agr* A blending of strong voices make the chorus unusually good.

*agr* Regulations in that industry protects workers.

Do not mistake the object of a preposition for the subject of a sentence.

**Solution**

**A blending of strong voices makes the chorus unusually good.**

**Regulations in that industry protect workers.**

Make the verb agree with the subject, which is never the object of a preposition.

## PROBLEM 2

### *A predicate nominative that differs in number from the subject*

*agr* Japanese gardens was her great joy.

**Solution**

**Japanese gardens were her great joy.**

Ignore the predicate nominative, and make the verb agree with the subject of the sentence.

## PROBLEM 3

### *A subject that follows the verb*

*agr* On the table was several piles of paper.

*agr* Here comes the two stars of the show.

**Solution**

**On the table were several piles of paper.**

**Here come the two stars of the show.**

In an inverted sentence look for the subject *after* the verb. Then make sure the verb agrees with the subject.

**PROBLEM 4**

## *A collective noun as the subject*

```
agr    The student council (meet) on a regular basis.
agr    The team (is) issued lockers.
```

**Solution A**

**The student council meets on a regular basis.**

If the collective noun refers to a group as a whole, use a singular verb.

**Solution B**

**The team are issued lockers.**

If the collective noun refers to each member of a group individually, use a plural verb.

**PROBLEM 5**

## *A noun of amount as the subject*

```
agr    Two dollars (are) the bus fare.
agr    Ten years (makes) a decade.
```

**Solution**

**Two dollars is the bus fare.**

**Ten years make a decade.**

Determine whether the noun of amount refers to one unit and is therefore singular or whether it refers to a number of individual units and is therefore plural.

## PROBLEM 6

### *A compound subject that is joined by* and

agr Blue and red makes purple.

agr Ham and eggs are a popular breakfast.

**Solution A**

**Blue and red make purple.**

If the parts of the compound subject do not belong to one unit or if they refer to different people or things, use a plural verb.

**Solution B**

**Ham and eggs is a popular breakfast.**

If the parts of the compound subject belong to one unit or if both parts refer to the same person or thing, use a singular verb.

## PROBLEM 7

### *A compound subject that is joined by* or *or* nor

agr Neither the chairs nor the sofa need cleaning.

**Solution**

**Neither the chairs nor the sofa needs cleaning.**

Make the verb agree with the subject that is closer to it.

## PROBLEM 8

### *A compound subject that is preceded by* many a, every, *or* each

agr Many a stuffed animal and toy were in the baby's playpen.

When *many a*, *each*, or *every* precedes a compound subject, the subject is considered singular.

**Solution**

**Many a stuffed animal and toy was in the baby's playpen.**
Use a singular verb when *many a*, *each*, or *every* precedes a compound subject.

## PROBLEM 9

### *A subject that is separated from the verb by an intervening expression*

*agr* Linda's job, in addition to her schoolwork, take all her spare time.

Certain expressions, such as *as well as*, *in addition to*, and *together with*, do not change the number of the subject.

**Solution**

**Linda's job, in addition to her schoolwork, takes all her spare time.**
Ignore an intervening expression between a subject and its verb. Make the verb agree with the subject.

## PROBLEM 10

### *An indefinite pronoun as the subject*

*agr* Each of my nieces have written to thank me.

Some indefinite pronouns are singular, some are plural, and some can be either singular or plural, depending upon the noun they refer to. (See page 575 for a list of indefinite pronouns.)

**Solution**

**Each of my nieces has written to thank me.**
Determine whether the indefinite pronoun is singular or plural, and make the verb agree.

***If you need more help with subject-verb agreement, see Lessons 16.1 through 16.8, pages 565–579.***

# 9.4 Lack of Pronoun-Antecedent Agreement

## PROBLEM 1

### *A singular antecedent that can be either male or female*

ant A responsible government official listens closely to his constituents.

Traditionally a masculine pronoun has been used to refer to an antecedent that may be either male or female. This usage ignores or excludes females.

**Solution A**

**Responsible government officials listen closely to their constituents.**

Reword the sentence so that both the antecedent and the pronoun are plural.

**Solution B**

**Responsible government officials listen closely to constituents.**

Reword the sentence to eliminate the pronoun.

**Solution C**

**A responsible government official listens closely to his or her constituents.**

Reword the sentence to use *he or she*, *him or her*, and so on.

## PROBLEM 2

### *A second-person pronoun that refers to a third-person antecedent*

Seiji and Lou like that restaurant because you get generous portions at a reasonable price.

Do not refer to an antecedent in the third person using the second-person pronoun *you.*

**Solution A**
**Seiji and Lou like that restaurant because they get generous portions at a reasonable price.**
Use the appropriate third-person pronoun.

**Solution B**
**Seiji and Lou like that restaurant because diners get generous portions at a reasonable price.**
Use an appropriate noun instead of a pronoun.

## PROBLEM 3

### *A singular indefinite pronoun as an antecedent*

```
ant    Each of the girls had their own sleeping bag.
ant    Neither of the men took off their coat.
```

*Each, everyone, either, neither,* and *one* are singular and therefore require singular personal pronouns.

**Solution**
**Each of the girls had her own sleeping bag.**

**Neither of the men took off his coat.**
Don't be fooled by a prepositional phrase that contains a plural noun. Determine whether the indefinite pronoun antecedent is singular or plural, and make the noun agree.

***If you need more help with pronoun-antecedent agreement, see Lesson 16.7, pages 575–576, and Lesson 17.6, pages 596–601.***

## 9.5 Lack of Clear Pronoun Reference

### PROBLEM 1

### *A pronoun reference that is weak or vague*

ref Our baseball team won, which was its reward for much hard work.

ref The violent hurricane flooded roads and toppled trees, and that made driving impossible.

ref Many students hope to earn all *A*'s, but it is difficult to achieve.

Be sure that *this*, *that*, *which*, and *it* have a clear antecedent.

**Solution A**

**Our baseball team won the championship trophy, which was its reward for much hard work.**

Rewrite the sentence, adding a clear antecedent for the pronoun.

**Solution B**

**The violent hurricane flooded roads and toppled trees, and those conditions made driving impossible.**

**Many students hope to earn all *A's*, but their goal is difficult to achieve.**

Rewrite the sentence, substituting a noun for the pronoun.

### PROBLEM 2

### *A pronoun that refers to more than one antecedent*

ref Carlos told Jake that he had been elected captain.

ref The actors expect the crew to be on time, but they often come late.

**Solution A**
**Carlos told Jake that Jake had been elected captain.**
Rewrite the sentence, substituting a noun for the pronoun.

**Solution B**
**Although the actors often come late, they expect the crew to be on time.**
Rewrite the sentence, making the antecedent of the pronoun clear.

## PROBLEM 3

### *The indefinite use of* you *or* they

ref To increase fitness, you have to exercise regularly.

ref At the turn of the century, they had few household conveniences.

**Solution A**
**To increase fitness, an individual has to exercise regularly.**
Rewrite the sentence, substituting a noun for the pronoun.

**Solution B**
**At the turn of the century, there were few household conveniences.**
Rewrite the sentence, eliminating the pronoun entirely.

*If you need more help in making clear pronoun references, see Lesson 17.7, pages 602–605.*

# 9.6 Shift in Pronoun

## PROBLEM

### *An incorrect shift in person between two pronouns*

```
pro    Along the hiking trail they unexpectedly found
       a place where you can picnic and swim.

pro    I believe that one should take responsibility
       for their actions.

pro    If one sets priorities carefully, you will
       usually succeed.
```

Incorrect pronoun shifts occur when a writer or speaker uses a pronoun in one person and then illogically shifts to a pronoun in another person.

**Solution A**

**Along the hiking trail they unexpectedly found a place where they can picnic and swim.**

**I believe that one should take responsibility for one's actions.**

**If one sets priorities carefully, one will usually succeed.**
Replace the incorrect pronoun with a pronoun that agrees with its antecedent.

**Solution B**

**Along the hiking trail they unexpectedly found a place where hikers can picnic and swim.**

**I believe that people should take responsibility for their actions.**
Replace the incorrect pronoun with an appropriate noun.

*If you need more help in eliminating incorrect pronoun shifts, see Lesson 17.6, pages 596–601.*

# 9.7 Shift in Verb Tense

## PROBLEM 1

### *An unnecessary shift in tense*

shift t Every day Lily walks the dog and fed the cat.

shift t Ari swung, and he gets a hit.

When two or more events occur at the same time, be sure to use the same verb tense to describe each event.

**Solution**

**Every day Lily walks the dog and feeds the cat.**

**Ari swung, and he got a hit.**

## PROBLEM 2

### *A lack of correct shift in tenses to show that one event precedes or follows another*

shift t By the time the plane finally took off, we sat on the runway for an hour.

When events being described have occurred at different times, shift tenses to show that one event precedes or follows another.

**Solution**

**By the time the plane finally took off, we had sat on the runway for an hour.**

Shift from the past tense to the past perfect tense to indicate that one action began and ended before another past action began. Use the past perfect tense for the earlier of the two actions.

***If you need more help with shifts in verb tenses, see Lesson 15.4, pages 545–548, and Lesson 15.6, pages 551–552.***

## 9.8 Incorrect Verb Tense or Form

### PROBLEM 1

***An incorrect or missing verb ending***

*tense* Last week it rain three days out of four.

*tense* Soo Li has always wonder about prehistoric civilizations.

**Solution**

**Last week it rained three days out of four.**

**Soo Li has always wondered about prehistoric civilizations.**
Add *-ed* to a regular verb to form the past tense and the past participle.

### PROBLEM 2

***An improperly formed irregular verb***

*tense* Eduardo flinged his jacket on the chair.

*tense* Has the play been casted yet?

Irregular verbs form their past and past participle in some way other than by adding *-ed*. Memorize these forms, or look them up.

**Solution**

**Eduardo flung his jacket on the chair.**

**Has the play been cast yet?**
Use the correct past or past participle form of an irregular verb.

### PROBLEM 3

***Confusion between the past form and the past participle***

*tense* The team has beat all its opponents handily.

*tense* Santha has already drank the water.

**Solution**

**The team has beaten all its opponents handily.**

**Santha has already drunk the water.**

Use the past participle form of an irregular verb, not the past form, when you use the auxiliary verb *have*.

## PROBLEM 4

### *Improper use of the past participle*

| | |
|---|---|
| *tense* | Unfortunately, the program (begun) early. |
| *tense* | Callie (swum) across the lake twice today. |
| *tense* | The chorus (sung) this song in many other concerts also. |

The past participle of an irregular verb cannot stand alone as a verb. It must be used with the auxiliary verb *have*.

**Solution A**

**Unfortunately, the program has begun early.**

**Callie has swum across the lake twice today.**

**The chorus has sung this song in many other concerts also.**

Add the auxiliary verb *have* to the past participle to form a complete verb.

**Solution B**

**Unfortunately, the program began early.**

**Callie swam across the lake twice today.**

**The chorus sang this song in many other concerts also.**

Replace the past participle with the past form of the verb.

***If you need more help with correct verb forms, see Lesson 15.1 and Lesson 15.2, pages 537–540.***

## 9.9 Misplaced or Dangling Modifier

### PROBLEM 1

#### *A misplaced modifier*

*mod* Unmowed for several weeks, the neighbors complained about our lawn.

*mod* A woman passed by leading a springer spaniel in a long black dress.

Modifiers that modify the wrong word or seem to modify more than one word in a sentence are called misplaced modifiers.

**Solution**

**The neighbors complained about our lawn, unmowed for several weeks.**

**A woman in a long black dress passed by leading a springer spaniel.**

Move the misplaced phrase as close as possible to the word or words it modifies.

### PROBLEM 2

#### *The adverb* only *misplaced*

*mod* Isabel only sings the refrain in that song.

The meaning of your sentence may be unclear if the word *only* is misplaced.

**Solution**

**Only Isabel sings the refrain in that song.**

**Isabel sings only the refrain in that song.**

**Isabel sings the refrain only in that song.**

Place the adverb *only* immediately before the word or group of words it modifies. Note that each time *only* is moved in the sentence, the meaning of the sentence changes.

## PROBLEM 3

### *A dangling modifier*

*mod* Standing on the observation deck, the view could be seen for miles.

*mod* After trying the combination several times, the lock finally opened.

*mod* Disappointed that vacation would soon end, September came all too quickly.

Dangling modifiers do not seem logically to modify any word in the sentence.

**Solution**

**Standing on the observation deck, Lionel could see the view for miles.**

**After trying the combination several times, Jennifer finally opened the lock.**

**Disappointed that vacation would soon end, we felt that September came all too quickly.**

Rewrite the sentence, adding a noun to which the dangling phrase clearly refers. Often you will have to add other words, too.

***If you need more help with misplaced or dangling modifiers, see Lesson 18.7, pages 623–629.***

## 9.10 Missing or Misplaced Possessive Apostrophe

### PROBLEM 1

### *Singular nouns*

*poss* The Congress votes affect the nations future.

**Solution**

**The Congress's votes affect the nation's future.**

Use an apostrophe and an *-s* to form the possessive of a singular noun, even one that ends in *-s*.

### PROBLEM 2

### *Plural nouns ending in -s*

*poss* The shoppers cars jammed the parking lot.

**Solution**

**The shoppers' cars jammed the parking lot.**

Use an apostrophe alone to form the possessive of a plural noun that ends in *-s*.

### PROBLEM 3

### *Plural nouns not ending in -s*

*poss* Michelle plans to attend a womens college.

**Solution**

**Michelle plans to attend a women's college.**

Use an apostrophe and an *-s* to form the possessive of a plural noun that does not end in *-s*.

## PROBLEM 4

### *Pronouns*

poss Is this anybodys jacket?

poss The blue station wagon is their's.

**Solution A**

**Is this anybody's jacket?**

Use an apostrophe and an *-s* to form the possessive of a singular indefinite pronoun.

**Solution B**

**The blue station wagon is theirs.**

Do not use an apostrophe with any of the possessive personal pronouns.

## PROBLEM 5

### *Confusion between* its *and* it's

poss The cat lay on the rug, washing it's paws.

poss Let us know when its time to leave.

The possessive of *it* is *its*. *It's* is the contraction of *it is*.

**Solution**

**The cat lay on the rug, washing its paws.**

**Let us know when it's time to leave.**

Do not use an apostrophe to form the possessive of *it*. Use an apostrophe to form the contraction of *it is*.

*If you need more help with apostrophes and possessives, see Lesson 17.1, pages 587–589, and Lesson 21.13, pages 702–704.*

## 9.11 Missing Commas with Nonessential Element

### PROBLEM 1

***Missing commas with nonessential participles, infinitives, and their phrases***

com José being naturally optimistic was not troubled by the news.

com Thoroughly prepared Monica stepped confidently up to the balance beam.

com To be well informed Mariko reads the newspaper daily.

**Solution**

**José, being naturally optimistic, was not troubled by the news.**

**Thoroughly prepared, Monica stepped confidently up to the balance beam.**

**To be well informed, Mariko reads the newspaper daily.**
Determine whether the participle, infinitive, or phrase is truly not essential to the meaning of the sentence. If so, set off the phrase with commas.

### PROBLEM 2

***Missing commas with nonessential adjective clauses***

com The documentary which must have been difficult to film examines efforts to save the panda's habitat.

**Solution**

**The documentary, which must have been difficult to film, examines efforts to save the panda's habitat.**
Determine whether the clause is truly not essential to the meaning of the sentence. If so, set off the clause with commas.

## PROBLEM 3

### *Missing commas with nonessential appositives*

com Janine Chiang a third-year medical student spoke about careers in health care.

**Solution**

**Janine Chiang, a third-year medical student, spoke about careers in health care.**

Determine whether the appositive is truly not essential to the meaning of the sentence. If so, set off the appositive with commas.

## PROBLEM 4

### *Missing commas with interjections and parenthetical expressions*

com Gee it's good to see you.

com You have heard certainly that Beth won the election.

**Solution**

**Gee, it's good to see you.**

**You have heard, certainly, that Beth won the election.**

Set off the interjection or parenthetical expression with commas.

***If you need more help with commas and nonessential elements, see Lesson 21.6, pages 684–686.***

## 9.12 Missing Commas in a Series

**PROBLEM**

***Missing commas in a series of words, phrases, or clauses***

s com — The recipe calls for tomatoes garlic basil and chicken breasts.

s com — Lem glanced at his notes took a deep breath and began to speak.

s com — The Colorado River runs through the Grand Canyon along the California-Arizona border and into the Gulf of California.

s com — Seagulls were riding the breeze floating lazily on the water and squabbling noisily over scraps of food.

s com — Maria plays guard Kassandra is a forward and Eula is the goalie.

**Solution**

**The recipe calls for tomatoes, garlic, basil, and chicken breasts.**

**Lem glanced at his notes, took a deep breath, and began to speak.**

**The Colorado River runs through the Grand Canyon, along the California-Arizona border, and into the Gulf of California.**

**Seagulls were riding the breeze, floating lazily on the water, and squabbling noisily over scraps of food.**

**Maria plays guard, Kassandra is a forward, and Eula is the goalie.**

When there are three or more elements in a series, use a comma after each element, including the element that precedes the conjunction.

***If you need more help with commas in a series, see Lesson 21.6, pages 682–683.***

# Part 2

# Grammar, Usage, and Mechanics

UNIT

# 10 Parts of Speech

Grammar

## Lessons

# 10.1 Nouns

**A noun is a word that names a person, a place, a thing, or an idea.**

| | |
|---|---|
| PERSON | wife, chaplain, Harriet Tubman, vice president, Dad |
| PLACE | hospital, porch, seashore, Korea |
| THING | whale, tooth, cactus, compact disc |
| IDEA | solitude, 1761, conscience, Renaissance |

**A concrete noun names an object that occupies space or that can be recognized by any of the senses.**

oxygen taxi planets music mint

**An abstract noun names an idea, a quality, or a characteristic.**

happiness trouble loyalty intelligence equality

A singular noun refers to one person, place, thing, or idea. A plural noun refers to more than one person, place, thing, or idea.

| | |
|---|---|
| SINGULAR | niece, wish, berry, shelf, bacterium |
| PLURAL | nieces, wishes, berries, shelves, bacteria |

The possessive form of a noun indicates possession, ownership, or the relationship between two nouns.

| SINGULAR POSSESSIVE | PLURAL POSSESSIVE |
|---|---|
| a **girl's** locker | the **girls'** lockers |
| a **dish's** pattern | the **dishes'** pattern |
| a **mouse's** tail | the **mice's** tails |

## Exercise 1 Identifying Nouns

On your paper write each of the twenty-five nouns that appear in the following paragraph.

### *Literature: Mother and Daughters*

[1]The child . . . is moving rapidly towards the mouth of the river where the ocean makes big whirlpools near the rocks. . . . [2]Pilar stands at the edge of the water surrounded by two servants and several . . . children, who call, . . . then stand quietly around their mother. [3]She is immobile, only the lace around her neck quivers. . . . [4]She is slender and tall, with an easy grace, like a palm. [5]Her eyes are thoughtful, even in fear. [6]As Santiago approaches the fast-moving figure at the mouth of the river, Pilar reaches for a small hand at her side and holds tightly to it.

From *Cantando bajito (Singing Softly)* by Carmen de Monte Flores

## Exercise 2 Supplying Abstract and Concrete Nouns

For each concrete noun in items 1–5, write an abstract noun that names an idea with which the concrete noun can be associated. For each abstract noun in items 6–10, write a concrete noun that has the quality of the abstract noun.

**SAMPLE ANSWERS** dancer—grace
helplessness—baby

1. cream
2. sunrise
3. siren
4. pillow
5. mildew
6. sorrow
7. fame
8. timidity
9. enthusiasm
10. fashion

## Exercise 3 Completing Sentences with Nouns

Fill in each blank with a noun. Be sure that your completed sentences make sense.

1. Sachi's ________ has a new ________.
2. The blue ________ has white ________.
3. The ________ gave a(n) ________.
4. ________ is my favorite ________.
5. The ________ wrote a(n) ________.

## Exercise 4 Making Nouns Plural and Singular

Change each of the following words to its singular form if it is plural and to plural if it is singular. Consult a dictionary if necessary.

1. proof
2. data
3. crises
4. studio
5. echo
6. basis
7. ally
8. radius
9. canoe
10. cilia
11. dwarf
12. alumnus
13. oasis
14. termini
15. piano
16. alley
17. belief
18. tomato
19. convoy
20. roof

## Exercise 5 Using Plural and Singular Nouns

Complete each sentence with the correct singular or plural form of one of the words listed in Exercise 4. Write your answer on a separate sheet of paper.

1. France and Britain were _____ during World War I.
2. The main train _____ in Rome stands beside an ancient wall.
3. For many years, _____ were considered poisonous.
4. AIDS has become an international health _____.
5. Many artists have _____ in old warehouses.

## Exercise 6 Making Singular Nouns Show Possession

Write the correct form of the ten nouns in the following paragraph that should show possession.

Mount Godwin-Austin other name is much shorter and much simpler to remember. It is K2, one of western Himalaya mountain peaks. K2 was actually T.G. Montgomerie choice of names. Working for the Survey of India in 1856, Montgomerie measured the mountain and labeled it K2 to signify that it was one of Karakorum Range thirty-five summits. The peak position straddles the border between China and Jammu and Kashmir. K2 is currently under the Pakistani government control. K2 fame lies in the fact that it is the second tallest mountain in the world, rising 8611 m. Mount Everest is its only superior at a towering 8848 m. Mt. Everest, like K2, exists in the Himalayan Mountains. A visitors description of K2 includes words such as *icy* and *awesome*. The mountains surface contains limestone, and its base is granite. Between 1892 and 1954, eight expeditions were made to K2. The eighth, made by Achille Compagnoni and Lino Lacedelli, two members of an Italian expeditionary team, was the first successful journey to K2 summit.

## Exercise 7 Using the Apostrophe Correctly

Proofread the following paragraph for twenty incorrectly written plural nouns, singular nouns, plural possessive nouns, and singular possessive nouns. Copy each mistake and its sentence number onto your paper. Then write the correct form beside each word.

[1]Mr. Jones' distributed the dissecting trays and tool's. [2]The tools' included scalpels, tweezers, and scissor's. [3]Mr. Jone's had planned this activity weeks' before. [4]Three student's parents, all members of the medical profession, had come to serve as Mr. Jones's assistant's. [5]The assistants jobs were to supervise the students' during the activity and to offer guidance or a demonstration to any student who asked for it. [6]The biology class' would be locating the heart, the kidney's, the liver, and the brain. [7]Two vascular surgeon's nurses were among the assistants. [8]One of the nurses' discussed the importance of keeping ones composure while dissecting the frog. [9]Mr. Jones hoped the experience would help his student's better understand the interrelationship of the organ's of the body, information that he would eventually relate to mens, women's, and childrens biological features. [10]He also wanted the students to know that dissecting an animal is a learning tool, not an activity meant to repulse the participant's.

## Exercise 8 Choosing Correct Possessive Forms

For each item, write the correct possessive form from the two choices in parentheses.

1. My young nephew Ernie fell out of a tree, and the (boy's/boys') arm was broken.
2. The (children's/childrens') toys were scattered all over Aunt Josephine's front lawn.
3. Cousin (Gina's/Ginas') husband told jokes that helped everyone relax at the gathering.
4. Joan and Alice are twins. According to their mother, the two (sister's/sisters') three hobbies in life are talking on the phone, combing their hair, and reading exercise magazines.
5. Uncle Pete, who is a traveling salesperson for a petroleum company, says a (salesperson's/salespersons') car should be comfortable, expensive, and fully loaded.

# Proper and Common Nouns

A **proper noun** is the name of a particular person, place, thing, or idea.

A **common noun** is the general—not the particular—name of a person, place, thing, or idea.

Proper nouns are usually capitalized; common nouns are usually not capitalized.

| PROPER NOUNS | |
|---|---|
| PERSON | Uncle Max, Dame Agatha Christie, Confucius, Vincent van Gogh |
| PLACE | Jupiter, Pacific Ocean, India, National Gallery of Art, California |
| THING | Mercedes-Benz, Passover, *West Side Story,* U.S. Government Printing Office |
| IDEA | Presbyterianism, Harlem Renaissance, Jazz Age, Medieval Period |

## Exercise 9 Matching Proper Nouns with Common Nouns

On your paper match the numbered proper nouns on the left with the lettered common nouns on the right.

| | |
|---|---|
| **1.** Adirondacks | **a.** writer |
| **2.** Cleopatra | **b.** religion |
| **3.** Muhammad Ali | **c.** queen |
| **4.** Michelangelo | **d.** university |
| **5.** Harvard | **e.** artist |
| **6.** Catholicism | **f.** athlete |
| **7.** Louvre | **g.** mountains |
| **8.** *Wall Street Journal* | **h.** museum |
| **9.** Maya Angelou | **i.** river |
| **10.** Rio Grande | **j.** newspaper |

## Exercise 10 Writing with Proper Nouns

Think about the important people, places, things, and ideas in your life. Make a list of ten proper nouns that name some of these important people, places, things, and ideas. Include at least two examples of each of the four categories of nouns. Use each proper noun in a sentence.

## Collective Nouns

A **collective noun** names a group.

| | | | |
|---|---|---|---|
| crew | (the) club | community | (an) army (of ants) |
| staff | (the) jury | chorus | (the) panel (of judges) |

A collective noun may be considered either singular or plural. When it refers to a group as a whole, it should be regarded as singular. When it refers to the individual members, it should be regarded as plural.

| | |
|---|---|
| SINGULAR | The **council** meets every Monday afternoon. |
| | A **family** of robins is nesting here. |
| PLURAL | The **council** have decided to split into two groups. |
| | The **family** of robins are leaving one by one. |

### Exercise 11 Identifying Collective Nouns

On your paper list the five collective nouns in the following paragraph.

*Tracking a Mountain Lion*

[1]Racing from different directions, a pack of baying hounds close in on the mountain lion and corner it near some rocks. [2]A team of conservationists rushes from their trucks, and a veterinarian shoots a tranquilizing dart into the cat. [3]The group quickly logs the cat's vital statistics and then fastens a radio collar on it to track its home range. [4]They are trying to see what effect, if any, the cat has on the local cows. [5]The conservationists are hoping to prove that mountain lions are not necessarily responsible for the decreases in the local herd of cows and flock of sheep.

### Exercise 12 Review: Identifying Nouns

On your paper list the forty nouns in the following sentences. Write *CN* next to any collective nouns.

*Novice Spelunkers*

1. Several members of the senior class read about the recently discovered human bones.
2. A colony of bats lives in the cave where the explorers discovered the bones.
3. A small school of fish swims in an adjacent stream.
4. A flock of rare birds nests above the entrance to the subterranean passage.
5. A scout troop has visited the site, but the scouts did not disturb any of the relics.
6. The youngsters had looked for the hideout of pirates, but their leader had kept the relics safe.
7. A group from my anthropology class visited the site where we found the bones as well as illustrations on the walls.
8. The group concluded that an ancient culture had made the drawings.
9. One picture of a herd of buffalo included two calves.
10. Our group shared our observations with the archeology club.

## Exercise 13 Review: Creating Sentences with Nouns

Write five sentences about your favorite restaurant. Rely especially on concrete nouns to convey a vivid picture of a place where you enjoy eating.

## Exercise 14 Review: Nouns

On your paper complete each sentence by filling in the twenty blanks with the kinds of nouns specified in italics. Be sure that your completed sentences make sense.

1. *proper* found a *common* in the *concrete*.
2. The reading of *common* is popular in my *collective*.
3. The *collective* meets on *abstract*.
4. I saw three *common* swim across the *concrete* to *proper*.
5. *proper* wrote a famous *common* entitled *proper*.
6. On a rainy *common* I like to stay at home and eat *concrete*.
7. A *collective* of lions is a beautiful and fearsome *common* on the plains of *proper*.
8. *proper* is a good friend known for her *abstract*.
9. The *abstract* is a period of time known for its *abstract.*
10. *concrete* can be dangerous to *common* if treated with *abstract*.

## Exercise 15 Review: Forming the Plural and Possessive Forms of Nouns

Draw four columns labeled *singular, singular possessive, plural,* and *plural possessive.* Write the underlined noun in each sentence under the correct heading. Then write the noun's other forms under the other headings.

1. The Roman emperor Domitian built a vast palace on one of the hills of Rome.
2. The trees' leaves are turning red and gold.
3. Have you ever seen how animals behave before an earthquake?
4. We watched the fish's colorful tail disappearing under the rock.
5. The potatoes rolled off the truck and spilled over the roadway.
6. On winter nights we could sometimes hear the howl of a solitary wolf.
7. The dodo is a bird that has been extinct for centuries.
8. I could see from the packages' condition that they had been left out in the rain.
9. The line was an extension of the radius of a circle.
10. The captain's log revealed no awareness of the impending disaster.
11. Sonia has worked for years as a children's book illustrator.
12. It is his belief that he can conquer the mountain.
13. Some townspeople fled to the country to avoid the plague.
14. Don't forget to turn off the water when you brush your teeth!
15. Will you be buying new water glasses?

## 10.2 Pronouns

A **pronoun** is a word that takes the place of a noun, a group of words acting as a noun, or another pronoun. The word or group of words that a pronoun refers to is called its **antecedent.**

Poet Lance Henson has published twelve books in which **he** celebrates the rich heritage of the Cheyenne. [The pronoun *he* takes the place of the noun *Lance Henson.*]

After Aretha and Ted gathered signatures on the petition, **they** signed **it themselves.** [The pronouns *they* and *themselves* take the place of the nouns *Aretha* and *Ted;* the pronoun *it* takes the place of *petition.*]

How **many** in this class have already written **their** essays? [The pronoun *their* takes the place of the pronoun *many*, which stands for an unspecified number of people in the class.]

The approximately seventy-five pronouns in the English language fit into one or more of the following categories: personal and possessive pronouns, reflexive and intensive pronouns, demonstrative pronouns, interrogative pronouns, relative pronouns, and indefinite pronouns.

## Personal and Possessive Pronouns

A **personal pronoun** refers to a specific person or thing by indicating the person speaking (the first person), the person being addressed (the second person), or any other person or thing being discussed (the third person).

Like nouns, personal pronouns can be singular or plural.

| Personal Pronouns | | |
|---|---|---|
| | Singular | Plural |
| FIRST PERSON | I, me | we, us |
| SECOND PERSON | you | you |
| THIRD PERSON | he, him, she, her, it | they, them |

FIRST PERSON — The coach asked **me** to pitch. [*Me* refers to the person speaking.]

SECOND PERSON — Ask Maria to show **you** where the gym is. [*You* refers to the person being addressed.]

THIRD PERSON — **She** gave **them** a tour of the school. [*She* and *them* refer to the persons being discussed.]

Third-person singular pronouns express **gender.** *He* and *him* are masculine; *she* and *her* are feminine; *it* is neuter (neither masculine nor feminine).

The personal pronouns that indicate possession or ownership are called **possessive pronouns.** They take the place of the possessive forms of nouns.

| Possessive Pronouns | | |
|---|---|---|
| | **Singular** | **Plural** |
| FIRST PERSON | my, mine | our, ours |
| SECOND PERSON | your, yours | your, yours |
| THIRD PERSON | his, her, hers, its | their, theirs |

Some possessive pronouns must be used before nouns; others can stand alone.

| | |
|---|---|
| USED BEFORE A NOUN | This is **your** ticket. |
| USED ALONE | This ticket is **yours.** |

## Exercise 16 Using Personal and Possessive Pronouns

Improve the following paragraph by replacing the underlined word or words with personal or possessive pronouns. Write your answers on your paper.

### *Animated Cartoons*

[1]Animated cartoons can reproduce anything that the reader of this passage can imagine in the reader's mind. [2]An animated cartoon achieves the cartoon's effects through a simple technique. [3]Cartoon artists draw the artists' pictures on a large board. [4]In each picture the figure changes the figure's position slightly. [5]If Bugs Bunny winks Bugs Bunny's eye, Bugs Bunny would be drawn in the first picture with Bugs Bunny's eye open. [6]In the next picture Bugs Bunny's eye would be half closed. [7]In the following picture Bugs Bunny's eye would be completely closed. [8]The camera operator films these individual pictures in the pictures' proper sequence. [9]When the individual frames are run through a projector, the frames' rapid projection creates the illusion of movement. [10]As the readers of this passage view the animated cartoon, the readers' eyes seem to see Bugs Bunny's eye wink.

## Exercise 17 Forming Possessive Pronouns

Write the possessive form(s) of each of the following personal pronouns. Remember that some personal pronouns have more than one possessive form. Also, some personal pronouns share the same possessive forms.

SAMPLE ANSWER us—our, ours

1. I
2. you
3. he
4. she
5. it
6. we
7. they
8. me
9. him
10. her

## Reflexive and Intensive Pronouns

The reflexive and intensive pronouns are formed when *-self* or *-selves* is added to certain personal and possessive pronouns.

| Reflexive and Intensive Pronouns | | |
|---|---|---|
| | **Singular** | **Plural** |
| FIRST PERSON | myself | ourselves |
| SECOND PERSON | yourself | yourselves |
| THIRD PERSON | himself, herself, itself | themselves |

A **reflexive pronoun** refers to a noun or another pronoun and indicates that the same person or thing is involved.

I promised **myself** that I would practice more.

She taught **herself** to play the guitar.

The band members organized the parade by **themselves.**

An **intensive pronoun** adds emphasis to another noun or pronoun.

You **yourself** can't answer that riddle.

Juan **himself** painted his room.

I wrote that poem **myself.**

We **ourselves** are quite well.

### Exercise 18 Identifying Antecedents of Reflexive and Intensive Pronouns

Write the noun or pronoun to which the reflexive or intensive pronoun in each sentence refers.

*Building Homes for the Homeless*

1. Maria herself constructed the two bedrooms in the rear of the Habitat for Humanity house.
2. You can paint the room yourself, or you can work on another project.
3. I gave myself a pat on the back for installing the kitchen plumbing without any help.
4. The oldest worker in the group pulled himself up the ladder and attached the gutters.
5. We ourselves completed the two-bedroom dwelling in less than three days.

## Demonstrative Pronouns

A **demonstrative pronoun** points out specific persons, places, things, or ideas.

| Demonstrative Pronouns | | |
|---|---|---|
| SINGULAR | this | that |
| PLURAL | these | those |

**This** is the record I want.
Play **that** again.
**These** were left here after last night's party.
My records are newer than **those.**

**Exercise 19** Writing with Demonstrative Pronouns

Write five sentences describing a sport you enjoy as a participant or as a spectator. Write your sentences as if you are speaking to someone who can see what you are describing. Use a demonstrative pronoun in each sentence. Use each of the four demonstrative pronouns at least once.

SAMPLE ANSWER That is the pitcher's mound.

**Exercise 20** Using Reflexive, Intensive, and Demonstrative Pronouns

Supply the appropriate reflexive, intensive, or demonstrative pronoun for each blank. On your paper write the pronoun, and identify it as *reflexive*, *intensive*, or *demonstrative*.

***Jackie Robinson, Major Leaguer***

[1]After researching the life of Jack Roosevelt Robinson (1919–1972), I came to feel that ________ who understand the man's historic importance will consider him a hero. [2]I learned, first of all, that Robinson was an all-around athlete; ________ are the sports in which he excelled in college: baseball, football, and basketball. [3]Following three years of service in the U.S. Army, Robinson was signed by Branch Rickey ________, president of the Brooklyn Dodgers, to play baseball for Rickey's team. [4]Thus, Robinson found ________ in a position to break the "color line" in the major leagues.

[5]On April 11, 1947, when Robinson played his first game for the Dodgers, his teammates ________ did not unanimously support his presence. [6] ________ was the first time in the twentieth century that an African American had played major league baseball. [7]By enduring intense scrutiny and abuse, Robinson proved ________ a courageous leader. [8]During a ten-year career that included six World Series, he earned for ________ the respect of his peers and the public. [9]In 1962 we witnessed his election to the Baseball Hall of Fame; ________ alone is a great accomplishment. [10]Yet I believe Robinson's importance transcends sports: American society ________ became fairer and more open because of Robinson's courage.

## Interrogative and Relative Pronouns

An **interrogative pronoun** is used to form questions.

| who? | whom? | whose? | what? | which? |
|---|---|---|---|---|

**Who** are the captains?
**Whom** should I ask to help me?
**Whose** did you use?
**What** did you find?
**Which** of these models did you build?

To add emphasis, you can use the intensive forms of the interrogative pronouns: *whoever, whomever, whosoever, whatever,* and *whichever.*

**Whoever** could have done this?

A **relative pronoun** is used to begin a special subject-verb word group called a subordinate clause (see Unit 13).

| who | whose | whomever | that | what |
|---|---|---|---|---|
| whom | whoever | which | whichever | whatever |

Dolley Payne, the woman **who** married James Madison, was born in North Carolina. [The relative pronoun *who* begins the subordinate clause *who married James Madison.*]

Dolley Madison rescued a portrait of George Washington from the White House, **which** the British burned in 1814. [The relative pronoun *which* begins the subordinate clause *which the British burned in 1814.*]

The first personal message **that** was sent over Morse's telegraph was from Dolley Madison. [The relative pronoun *that* begins the subordinate clause *that was sent over Morse's telegraph.*]

### Exercise 21 Distinguishing Between Interrogative and Relative Pronouns

On your paper list the interrogative and relative pronouns that appear in the following sentences, and label each of them as *interrogative* or *relative.*

***Yo-Yo Ma, Celebrated Cellist***

1. Yo-Yo Ma is the name of a cellist whose performances have won critical acclaim and prestigious awards.
2. What other cellist of this generation has so delighted lovers of chamber music?
3. Born in France in 1955, Yo-Yo Ma is an international celebrity whose father was also a musician.
4. Who among us can claim to have made a musical debut at Carnegie Hall at age nine?
5. Leonard Rose was the teacher who instructed Ma at the Juilliard School in New York City.

# Indefinite Pronouns

An **indefinite pronoun** refers to persons, places, or things in a more general way than a noun does.

Sally seems to like **everyone.** [The indefinite pronoun *everyone* refers to people in general.]

I'm hoping that **someone** can help me. [The indefinite pronoun *someone* does not tell you to whom it refers.]

When we counted the coins, we discovered that **some** were missing. [The indefinite pronoun *some* has the specific antecedent *coins.*]

| Some Indefinite Pronouns | | | |
|---|---|---|---|
| all | either | much | others |
| another | enough | neither | plenty |
| any | everybody | nobody | several |
| anybody | everyone | none | some |
| anyone | everything | no one | somebody |
| anything | few | nothing | someone |
| both | many | one | something |
| each | most | other | |

## Exercise 22 Identifying Indefinite Pronouns

Write the indefinite pronouns in each of the following sentences about the history of Native American reservations.

1. Someone in my class is researching Native American history, especially the establishment of reservations.
2. No one realized in the beginning that the land allocated for reservations would eventually shrink.
3. The government cautioned everyone who traveled westward to beware of attacks.
4. When the two earliest reservations were developed, both were on land that white settlers wanted.
5. However, neither comprised enough land to warrant white aggression.
6. The government asked everybody living on reservations to change their ways and become more like the white settlers.
7. Most mistrusted the white government.
8. Of all the Native American leaders, one did come forth to demand that the old treaties designating certain boundaries be respected.
9. When government officials scrutinized the treaties for loopholes, they found plenty.
10. Each provided the means by which the United States government could force the Native Americans onto smaller sections of land.

## Exercise 23 Review: Using Interrogative, Relative, Indefinite, Reflexive, Demonstrative, and Personal Pronouns

The following questions and statements are missing twenty pronouns. Add them according to the directions in parentheses. Write your answers on your paper.

### *In the News*

1. __________ will it take to end the strike __________ has crippled two major airlines? (Use an interrogative pronoun; use a relative pronoun.)
2. __________ has decided to play basketball for the University of North Carolina Tarheels. (Use a personal pronoun.)
3. Nearly __________ will be glued to their television sets tonight as the movie stars __________ made us laugh, weep, and sit on the edge of our seats last year line up for their Oscars. (Use an indefinite pronoun; use a relative pronoun.)
4. Do __________ think __________ will oversee the merger, or does she plan to allow her business manager to handle it all __________? (Use a personal pronoun; use a personal pronoun; use a reflexive pronoun.)
5. __________, folks, is exactly what police say happened to __________ the minute he stepped off the plane. (Use a demonstrative pronoun; use a personal pronoun.)
6. __________ craves chocolate as much as __________ does. (Use an indefinite pronoun; use a personal pronoun.)
7. __________ do __________ think was elected? (Use an interrogative pronoun; use a personal pronoun.)
8. __________ __________ will make the reservation. (Use a personal pronoun; use a reflexive pronoun.)
9. The club welcomes __________ __________ who have an interest in cycling. (Use an indefinite pronoun; use a demonstrative pronoun.)
10. Make sure to send __________ to __________. (Use an indefinite pronoun; use a personal pronoun.)

## Exercise 24 Review: Using Pronouns

Write ten sentences about a movie you have seen recently. Try to use pronouns from all the categories you studied in this lesson.

## Exercise 25 Review: Pronouns

On your paper list in order the twenty-five pronouns that appear in the following paragraph. Identify each as *personal*, *possessive*, *reflexive*, *intensive*, *demonstrative*, *interrogative*, *relative*, or *indefinite*.

### *A Family of Labradors*

[1]Sandpiper, our Labrador retriever, had nine puppies in November. [2]We set ourselves the task of naming the puppies after different birds. [3]Our neighbors, who love birds, lent us their bird encyclopedia. [4]They themselves own Whippoorwill, the father of Sandpiper's litter. [5]They are proud of Whippoorwill, who has won prizes in hunting-dog field trials. [6]Whippoorwill's owners, who know a good pup when they see one, chose the biggest pup of all as theirs. [7]Several of my friends chose pups, too. [8]Now which of the remaining pups do I myself want? [9]All are beautiful. [10]Making a choice will be one of the hardest tasks that I will ever have.

## 10.3 Verbs

**A verb is a word that expresses action or a state of being and is necessary to make a statement.**

The acrobats **soared.**
The motor **stopped.**
We **dream** in color.
This writer **is** also an athlete.

Unlike other parts of speech, a verb changes form to express time. Various *tense* forms indicate the present, the past, and the future.

| | |
|---|---|
| PRESENT TENSE | I **own** a personal computer. |
| PAST TENSE | I **owned** a personal computer. |
| FUTURE TENSE | I **will own** a personal computer. |
| PRESENT TENSE | I **drink** orange juice. |
| PAST TENSE | I **drank** orange juice. |
| FUTURE TENSE | I **will drink** orange juice. |
| PRESENT TENSE | I **am** a student. |
| PAST TENSE | I **was** a student. |
| FUTURE TENSE | I **will be** a student. |

### Exercise 26 Locating Past Tense Verbs

As you read the following sentences, write all the past tense verbs you find. Some sentences contain more than one past tense verb.

#### *Constantinople's Church*

1. Emperor Justinian commanded his architects to design the most spectacular religious building of all time.
2. The architects were Anthemius of Tralles and Isidore of Miletus.
3. Many parts of the Roman Empire sent rare and costly building materials.
4. Construction of the Church of Hagia Sophia, or Holy Wisdom, began in A.D. 532.
5. Workers completed the church in about five years.
6. Later, an earthquake damaged the dome of the church, and workers built a new and even higher dome.
7. When the Turks conquered Constantinople, they covered over the beautiful and colorful mosaics that decorated the walls.
8. In 1935 Hagia Sophia became a museum.
9. Workers uncovering the mosaics found many beautiful pictures.
10. Constantinople (now Istanbul) was a city on the Bosporus, a strait that connects the Black Sea and the Sea of Marmara.

## Exercise 27 Adding Verbs to Make Sentences

On your paper write ten complete sentences by supplying a verb for each of the blanks in the items below.

### *Summertime in the Park*

1. Let's ________ the famous park around the corner.
2. Visitors ________ around the well-kept grounds.
3. The landscaping is beautiful: willowy trees ________ over walkways, filtering the harsh summer sunlight.
4. Peacocks ________ across the lush lawns.
5. Tropical birds ________ in the trees.
6. Brillantly colored butterflies ________ among the shrubs and flowers.
7. Children ________ in imaginatively designed playgrounds.
8. Groups of friends ________ in high-spirited voices.
9. A strolling band ________ diners in the outdoor restaurant.
10. Diners ________ their meal by the fragrant rose garden.

## Exercise 28 Identifying Verb Tenses

Copy each verb you supplied to complete Exercise 27. Next to each verb, write the verb's tense: *present tense*, *past tense*, or *future tense*.

SAMPLE ANSWER visit—present tense

## Exercise 29 Using Verb Tenses

On your paper write the appropriate tense of the verb given in parentheses.

[1]The Emperor penguin has been an interesting subject of study for many years. [2]Recently, a researcher (to be) in the Arctic, studying the behavior of those penguins. [3]As she watched, something (frighten) the flock and they all (scurry) from an area of the ice. [4]Although she (can) not see the cause of their alarm, she was certain there (to be) a reason. [5]Then she (notice) that one penguin (remain), apparently in distress and unable to move. [6]As she (approach) to give assistance, she (observe) that the ice all around the penguin (to be) quite mushy. [7]With a hearty tug she (pull) the bird free, but (attach) to its underside (to be) several animals she (have) never seen before. [8]All (fall) away back toward the the mushy water, but she (manage) to capture one before it (escape).

[9]Called an ice borer, this animal (measure) approximately six inches and (have) an extremely high rate of metabolism, which allows it to maintain a body temperature of over ninety degrees. [10]On its head is a grooved, raised plate that is even hotter—almost 120°F. [11]Using its head plate, the ice borer (tunnel) through the ice searching for the prey it eats to maintain its body heat. [12]Finding a large animal such as a seal or penguin, the borers quickly melt the ice around their victim. [13]While it remains helpless and trapped in the mush, a group of borers seize the prey from below and make a quick meal of it.

# Action Verbs

An **action verb** tells what someone or something does.

Action verbs can express either physical or mental activities.

| | |
|---|---|
| PHYSICAL ACTION | The workers **cheered** the announcement.<br>The manager **arrived** at the plant early. |
| MENTAL ACTION | Both sides **considered** the new agreement.<br>Each side **believed** in the necessity of new productivity incentives for the employees. |

A **transitive verb** is an action verb that is followed by a word or words that answer the question *what?* or *whom?*

Lapidaries **cut** gems. [The action verb *cut* is followed by the noun *gems*, which answers the question *cut what?*]

An **intransitive verb** is an action verb that is *not* followed by a word that answers the question *what?* or *whom?*

The knife **cut** quickly and with precision. [The action verb is followed by words that tell *how*.]

**Exercise 30** **Recognizing Action Verbs**

Write on your paper the action verb in each of the following sentences. Indicate whether each action verb is used as a *transitive* or an *intransitive* verb.

***Foreign Flora and Fauna in Florida***

1. Many foreign plants and animals thrive in Florida.
2. Most of these foreign plants and animals arrive in freighters or in someone's luggage.
3. Naturalists recognize fifty varieties of foreign animals in Florida.
4. Siamese catfish crawl out of Florida canals.
5. The Brazilian water hyacinth chokes Florida waterways.
6. In southern Florida, Colombian iguanas scamper through Australian pines.
7. Rhesus monkeys from India find a home in Silver Springs.
8. Florida's lakes and canals teem with some thirty different species of foreign tropical fish.
9. The fierce South American piranhas sometimes escape from tropical-fish dealers.
10. Cuban tree frogs consume insects harmful to citrus trees.

**Exercise 31** **Creating Sentences with Transitive and Intransitive Verbs**

For each verb below write two sentences. First, use the verb as a transitive verb. Then use it as an intransitive verb.

1. hide
2. climb
3. gather
4. scream
5. run

## Exercise 32 Using Irregular Verb Forms

Complete the sentences by choosing an appropriate irregular verb from the chart provided. Notice that irregular verbs do not add *-ed* to form the past or past participle forms. Some change spellings; others do not change at all.

| PRESENT | PAST | PAST PARTICIPLE |
|---|---|---|
| begin | began | has/have begun |
| burst | burst | has/have burst |
| come | came | has/have come |
| drink | drank | has/have drunk |
| give | gave | has/have given |
| ring | rang | has/have rung |
| see | saw | has/have seen |
| throw | threw | has/have thrown |
| do | did | has/have done |

### *The Championship Game*

1. The referee will __________ the basketball into the air to start the game.
2. Have you ever __________ a more eager bunch of players?
3. Each team, apprehensive but primed, __________ to the center of the freshly varnished court.
4. Spectators __________ from mammoth cups and ate popcorn, pizza, and nachos in the stands.
5. The bell to start the game has already __________ .
6. The coach _________ the waiting substitute some last-minute guidance before sending him into the game.
7. The enthusiasm in the superdome _________ to swell.
8. The coaches have _________ all they can to prepare the players for this championship match.
9. Have the cheerleaders __________ their stunts yet?
10. The woman sitting next to me has already __________ two soft drinks.
11. A bell __________ as the last three-point shot was attempted.
12. Half-time has _________ , and my team is behind by three points.
13. The referees have __________ that player out of the game for fighting.
14. We _________ a number of celebrities sitting a few rows behind the team.
15. As my team savored its first championship, I _________ with pride.

## Exercise 33 Identifying Correct Irregular Verb Forms

Read the following sentences. If the underlined irregular verb form is correct, write *correct* on your paper. If the irregular verb form is incorrect, write the correct form on your paper.

### *Take Me Out to the Ballpark*

1. The President of the United States threw the ball that <u>begun</u> the game.
2. The most powerful pitcher <u>come</u> to the mound and dug his heels into the earth.
3. The umpire <u>give</u> the batter a moment to adjust his hat.
4. Has the pitcher already <u>showed</u> the fans his most impressive throws, or has he got a new trick up his sleeve today?
5. Anxious players sat in the dugout and <u>drank</u> from squeeze bottles.

## Linking Verbs

A **linking verb** links, or joins, the subject of a sentence (often a noun or pronoun) with a word or expression that identifies or describes the subject.

The most common linking verb is *be* in all its forms, including *am, is, are, was, were, will be, has been,* and *was being.*

A symphony **is** a work for musical instruments.
The plots of operas **are** often tragic.
Samuel Barber **was** an American composer.
Barber's music **has been** popular for years.

Several verbs other than the forms of *be* can function as linking verbs. Notice how the linking verbs in the following sentences link the subject with a word in the predicate.

The pitcher **appeared** tired during the last inning of the baseball game.
(The verb *appeared* links *pitcher* to *tired.*)
She **stayed** calm during the storm.
(The verb *stayed* links *she* to *calm.*)

| Other Linking Verbs | | | |
|---|---|---|---|
| appear<br>become<br>feel | grow<br>look<br>remain | seem<br>smell<br>sound | stay<br>taste |

**Exercise 34** **Recognizing Linking Verbs and the Words They Connect**

Read the following sentences. Write the linking verb in each sentence. Then write the words that the linking verb is connecting.

***Anwar al-Sadat***

1. Anwar Sadat, Egyptian military leader and president from 1970 until 1981, grew popular with many people in the United States when he worked toward peace in the Middle East.
2. During his campaign for peace, he became the first Arab leader to recognize Israel.
3. Sadat's life looked bleak in the 1940s, when he was jailed twice during World War II for making contacts with the Germans.
4. Sadat rose to power for the first time in 1964, when he became vice president of Egypt.
5. Islamic fundamentalists felt bitterly angry about Sadat's recognition of Israel in 1979, and they assassinated Sadat in 1981.

## Exercise 35 Identifying Action Verbs and Linking Verbs

On your paper write the verb that appears in each of the following sentences. Then identify each verb as either an *action verb* or a *linking verb*.

### *Rio de Janeiro, City of Pleasures*

1. Rio de Janeiro, once Brazil's capital, now plays a new role as a center of tourism.
2. Its beautiful forests, mountains, and beaches attract tourists from all over the world.
3. Because of the city's tropical climate, its spectacular beaches stay open year-round.
4. Sugar Loaf, a conical mountain in Guanabara Bay, is Rio's landmark.
5. Atop Mount Corcovado a 124-foot statue of Christ the Redeemer overlooks the city.
6. Rio de Janeiro remains an important center of culture, industry, and commerce in Brazil.
7. With a capacity of two hundred thousand fans, Rio's Maracaña Stadium illustrates the dedication of Brazilians to their national sport, soccer.
8. Brazilians are also passionate about the samba, the dance music of Rio's world-famous carnival.
9. During the four days and four nights of carnival, local samba clubs offer prizes for the most unusual and beautiful costumes.
10. With colorful parades and all-night street dances, Rio seems especially joyous during this carnival season.

## Exercise 36 Replacing Linking Verbs with Lively Action Verbs

Rewrite the following sentences. Omit the linking verb in each sentence and replace it with a lively action verb. You may add, rearrange, or delete words, as you create vivid sentences.

**SAMPLE** I was tired.
**ANSWER** I experienced extreme fatigue after jogging ten miles in the afternoon sun.

### *Ozone*

1. Ozone is pale blue and highly toxic.
2. The boiling point of ozone is -111.9 degrees Celsius, and its melting point is -192.5 degrees Celsius.
3. Ozone is a strongly magnetic form of oxygen and more active chemically than ordinary oxygen.
4. Ozone is beneficial in disinfecting air, purifying water, and bleaching specific foods.
5. Crops and humans are in jeopardy from the shrinking ozone layer.

## Exercise 37 Identifying Verb Tenses

Make a list of the action verbs you used in Exercise 36. Next to each verb, write its tense: present, past, or future.

## Verb Phrases

The verb in a sentence may consist of more than one word. The words that accompany the main verb are called **auxiliary,** or helping, **verbs.**

A **verb phrase** consists of a main verb and all its auxiliary, or helping, verbs.

| Auxiliary Verbs | |
|---|---|
| FORMS OF *BE* | am, is, are, was, were, being, been |
| FORMS OF *HAVE* | has, have, had, having |
| OTHER AUXILIARIES | can, could |
| | do, does, did |
| | may, might |
| | must |
| | shall, should |
| | will, would |

Auxiliary verbs affect the meaning of the main verb in many ways. The most common auxiliary verbs, the forms of *be* and *have*, help the main verb to express various tenses.

I **am walking.**
I **have walked.**
I **had been walking.**

Other auxiliary verbs are used to create questions or to indicate possibility, obligation, or permission.

**Did** Yussuf **drive**?
Denise **could have driven** there.
I **should be driving** home now.
No one **may drive** without a license.

**Exercise 38** **Using Verb Phrases in Interrogative Sentences**

Write five interrogative sentences about flying an airplane. (Interrogative sentences ask questions and very often begin with an auxiliary verb.) Each sentence must include one of the verb phrases listed below.

**1.** is leaving
**2.** had seemed
**3.** should move
**4.** does sing
**5.** have thought

## Exercise 39 Identifying Verb Phrases

On your paper write each verb phrase that appears in the following sentences. (Two of the sentences have more than one verb phrase.) Put parentheses around the auxiliary verbs in each phrase. (A word or words that interrupt a verb phrase are not considered part of the verb phrase.)

### *Computer Games*

1. Computer games can entertain children and adults.
2. In some electronic baseball games the player is always batting against the computer's pitches.
3. In one baseball game the player might stretch a double into a triple.
4. In another game the player could turn a single into a tag at second base.
5. If the salesperson will let you, you probably should try several different games at the store.
6. The player can also participate in some electronic football games.
7. In some of these football games, you can change plays even at the line of scrimmage.
8. People with spelling problems have benefited from electronic spelling games with human voices.
9. People who have used these games have actually improved their spelling.
10. An electronic word game can even challenge two players at once.

## Exercise 40 Creating Sentences with Vivid Verbs

Write five sentences that describe a parade, a circus act, or some other spectacle. Choose very specific action verbs and verb phrases to convey a vivid sense of the event.

## Exercise 41 Verbs

On your paper write the verb or verb phrase in each sentence in the following passage. Then identify each verb or verb phrase as an *action verb* or a *linking verb*. Also identify each action verb as *transitive* or *intransitive*.

### *Bringing the Wilderness to City Dwellers*

[1]Some great parks are becoming natural havens for American city dwellers. [2]For example, visitors to San Francisco's Golden Gate Recreation Area can surf within view of the Golden Gate Bridge. [3]San Franciscans are discovering forest and mountain trails only an hour's ride from the inner city. [4]Urban parks bring the wilderness to city dwellers all over our country. [5]Nearly three thousand miles to the east, residents of New York City are visiting the Gateway National Recreation Area. [6]Swimmers, fishermen, and picnickers alike can benefit from the facilities at this recreational area. [7]For many New Yorkers a visit to the Gateway National Recreation Area can be the first opportunity for a peek at a striped bass. [8]Already millions of New York City residents have visited Gateway. [9]Recently the National Park Service has established urban recreational areas in other large cities. [10]In the years ahead, then, more and more urban Americans will be participating in wilderness experiences relatively close to home.

## 10.4 Adjectives

An **adjective** is a word that modifies a noun or pronoun by limiting its meaning.

**thunderous** applause　　**silent** approval
**scarlet** jacket　　**this** hospital

An adjective often answers one of three questions about a noun or pronoun.

- *What kind?* (Descriptive words such as colors and nationalities)
- *Which one?* (Words that point out, such as *this, that,* and *first*)
- *How many?* (Number words, such as *four, twenty-two,* and *several*)

You can consider possessive pronouns—such as *my*, *your*, and *our*—as adjectives because they modify nouns in addition to serving as pronouns: *my* car, *your* vacation, *our* project. You can also consider possessive nouns as adjectives: *Della's* piano.

**Exercise 42** **Classifying Adjectives**

Divide your paper into three columns. Label your columns *What kind? Which one?* and *How many?* Read the following list of phrases. The first word in each phrase is the adjective. The second word is the noun being modified by the adjective. Decide which question (*What kind? Which one? or How many?*) the adjective answers about the noun. Then write each phrase under the appropriate column heading.

1. snow-white car
2. the first day
3. the other man
4. few people
5. table leg
6. myriad hypotheses
7. last week
8. this rope
9. one minute
10. sumptuous dinner

**Exercise 43** **Identifying Possessive Pronouns and Possessive Nouns**

Write the possessive pronouns and possessive nouns that are functioning as adjectives in the following sentences. Next to each possessive pronoun or possessive noun, write the noun or pronoun it modifies.

1. Dr. Ho's method of surgery is quite unique.
2. His training in the uses of herbs as anesthetics is not widely accepted.
3. Dr. Ho's colleague, Dr. Samuels, says she is willing to try the herb concoctions.
4. Dr. Sanchez, however, prefers to continue using her conventional anesthetics.
5. The medical field's wide array of techniques offers patients many choices.

Adjectives may be used in various positions in relation to the words they modify.

How **comfortable** this chair is!
This **comfortable** chair is my favorite.
This chair is **comfortable.**
Everyone finds this chair **comfortable.**
This chair, **comfortable** despite its age, is my favorite.

### Exercise 44 Noting the Placement of Adjectives

Write the adjectives you find in each sentence. Next to each adjective, write B if the adjective comes *before* the noun or pronoun it modifies. Write A if the adjective comes *after* the noun or pronoun it modifies. Do not list the words *a, an,* or *the.*

***The Dayak***

1. The aboriginal inhabitants of Borneo, the third-largest island in the world, are named the Dayak.
2. A tropical island in southeastern Asia, Borneo is mountainous for the most part and receives abundant rainfall each year.
3. There are six groups of Dayak, the oldest groups being the Penans, Kenyahs, and Klemantans.
4. The Kayans, Ibans, and Muruts are more recent arrivals to the island.
5. The Ibans, fierce and courageous, are famous as pirates and conquerors.

### Exercise 45 Finding Adjectives

On your paper list the twenty adjectives that appear in the following passage. Count possessive pronouns as adjectives in this exercise, but do not count the words *a, an,* and *the.*

***Literature: A Sunday Ritual***

[1]*Now I lay me down to sleep* . . . there will be new shoes in the morning. [2]New shoes and an old dress white as new . . . and hair perfect as heat and grease can press it. [3]There will be hands to shake as she rises from the curb onto the one broad step that took you off Homewood Avenue, which was nowhere, to the red doors of the church that were wide enough to let the whole world in but narrow too, narrower than your narrow hips, child, eye of the needle straight and narrow. . . . [4]Hands to help her across the threshold, through the tall red doors, from hard pavement that burned in summer, froze in winter. . . .

From "The Tambourine Lady" by John Edgar Wideman

### Exercise 46 Creating Sentences with Adjectives

Select five of the adjectives from the sentences in Exercise 45. Write five sentences of your own, using each adjective.

Many adjectives have different forms to indicate their degree of comparison.

| POSITIVE | COMPARATIVE | SUPERLATIVE |
|---|---|---|
| tall | taller | tallest |
| lazy | lazier | laziest |
| difficult | more difficult | most difficult |
| bad | worse | worst |
| good | better | best |
| little | less or lesser | least |
| much | more | most |
| many | more | most |
| far | farther | farthest |

Positive Degree (No comparison)
Jo's routine is **difficult** to execute.

Comparative Degree (Comparison of two nouns or pronouns)
Fernando's routine is **more difficult** to execute than Jo's routine is.

Superlative Degree (Comparison of three or more nouns or pronouns)
Kim executes the **most difficult** routine of all the team members.

## Exercise 47 Improving Incorrect Comparisons

Read the following comparison sentences. If a sentence is correct, write *correct*. If a sentence has an incorrect comparison, rewrite the sentence, correcting the comparison. (Note that adjectives never add both *-er* or *-est* and *more* or *most*.)

### *Coffee, Tea, or Cola?*

1. Coffee, which many people like best, is the common name for a genus of trees that has thirty species.
2. Arabian coffee plants are most common to the Americas—where two thirds of the world's supply of coffee is grown—than to any other area of the world.
3. Coffee is cultivated in more cooler regions than tea or cola, but frost can easily damage coffee trees.
4. Cola is a more common name for certain tropical trees of the same family as the cacao.
5. Cola trees are the taller of the three plants from which these beverages come.
6. Do you know which contains more caffeine—coffee, tea, or cola beverages?
7. Which is the tastier of these three beverages?
8. Many people think coffee is more flavorful than tea.
9. Yet most people like iced tea gooder than iced coffee.
10. How farthest would you travel on a hot day for a cold cola drink?

## Articles

**Articles** are the adjectives *a*, *an*, and *the*. *A* and *an* are called indefinite articles. *The* is called a definite article.

| | |
|---|---|
| **INDEFINITE** | I am **a** landscaper. |
| | I planted **an** evergreen. |
| **DEFINITE** | I am **the** landscaper. |
| | I planted **the** evergreen. |

**Exercise 48** **Indentifying Articles**

Write the articles found in the following sentences. Label each article *definite* or *indefinite*.

***A. J. Foyt***

1. A. J. Foyt is a retired professional automobile racer.
2. He was the first four-time winner of the Indianapolis 500 and a fierce contestant who drove a number of different kinds of racing cars.
3. Foyt drove midgets, stock cars, sports cars, and the mighty Indy race cars.
4. Foyt also won the Daytona 500 in 1972 and the 24 Hours of Le Mans in 1967.
5. A person who could handle crashes and injuries and continue to race, Foyt was famous for racing long past the age most racers retire.

## Proper Adjectives

A **proper adjective** is formed from a proper noun and begins with a capital letter.

Nguyen Trai was a **Vietnamese** writer.

We have used the **Gregorian** calendar since 1752.

You can change many proper nouns into proper adjectives by using the suffixes *-an*, *-ian*, *-n*, *-ese*, *-ish*, and *-i*.

| PROPER NOUN | PROPER ADJECTIVE | PROPER NOUN | PROPER ADJECTIVE |
|---|---|---|---|
| Poland | Polish | Africa | African |
| Thomas Jefferson | Jeffersonian | Pakistan | Pakistani |

**Exercise 49** **Forming Proper Adjectives**

Write a proper adjective formed from each of the following proper nouns. Consult a dictionary if you need help.

1. Sweden
2. Queen Victoria
3. Venice
4. Alexander Hamilton
5. Panama
6. Kenya
7. Japan
8. George Washington
9. Chile
10. Ireland

## Exercise 50 Writing Comparative and Superlative Forms of Adjectives

Write the comparative and superlative forms of the following adjectives. (Reminder: Do not add *-er* or *-est* to adjectives that form the comparative and superlative forms by means of *more* and *most.*) Then choose five of them and write sentences using the comparative and superlative forms of the adjective.

1. loose
2. lovely
3. funny
4. wise
5. harmful
6. lazy
7. desirable
8. gentle
9. intelligent
10. desolate
11. many
12. favorable
13. absorbent
14. bad
15. simple
16. far
17. gracious
18. witty
19. practical
20. much

## Exercise 51 Changing Proper Nouns into Proper Adjectives

In the sentences below, convert the proper nouns that should be proper adjectives. Write the proper adjectives on your paper in the order in which they appear in the sentences.

### *European Vacation*

1. Europe is sometimes considered one of the seven continents of the world; however, it is really the western fifth of the Eurasia landmass that is composed principally of Asia countries.
2. The Europe population comprises the second largest population of any continent in the world.
3. The northernmost point of the Europe mainland is a Norway town called Nordkinn, and the southernmost point is a Spain town called Punta de Tarifa.
4. From west to east, the Europe mainland extends from the Portugal town of Cabo da Roca to the northeastern slopes of the mountains known as the Urals, located in Russia and Kazakhstan.
5. Europe overflows with ancient history, beginning with the Greece and Rome civilizations that offered the world a massive and innovative concoction of fine art, literature, government, and philosophy.

## Exercise 52 Using Adjectives to Enliven Sentences

With the exception of articles, the sentences below contain no adjectives. Rewrite the sentences, adding vivid adjectives to modify the nouns or pronouns.

### *Hurricane!*

1. Hurricanes originate over oceans.
2. They move along a path.
3. Aircraft fly into hurricanes to study the wind.
4. Hurricanes have eyes.
5. During a hurricane, there is damage.

## Exercise 53 Creating Sentences with Adjectives

Write five sentences about a favorite place you recall from your childhood. Describe it as vividly as you can. As you write, consider the variety of adjectives available for use in your sentences:

- adjectives that answer *What kind? Which one?* or *How many?*
- adjectives that compare by adding *-er, -est, more,* or *most*
- possessive pronouns and possessive nouns used as adjectives
- proper adjectives formed from proper nouns

## Exercise 54 Identifying Adjectives

On your paper write the twenty-five adjectives, including articles, that appear in the following paragraph.

### *Walt Disney*

[1]Walt Disney had a long, productive career. [2]Although his artistic training was limited to a few courses at an artists' school, Disney created the famous characters Mickey Mouse and Donald Duck. [3]Disney's films earned him international recognition, for the Disney style was rich in color and humor. [4]Films like the masterful *Cinderella* and innovative *Fantasia* are still enjoyed around the world. [5]Critics have acclaimed Disney as one of the greatest figures in modern American popular culture.

## Exercise 55 Review: Identifying Nouns and Adjectives

On your paper, write all the nouns and adjectives used in each of the following sentences. Do not include articles.

| | | |
|---|---|---|
| **SAMPLE** | Alex opened the squeaky hood of his car. | |
| | Nouns | Adjectives |
| **ANSWER** | Alex, hood, car | squeaky, his |

### *Henry Ross Perot*

1. Henry Ross Perot, an American business executive, ran for the United States presidency in 1992.
2. Perot was born in Texarkana, Texas, in 1930, and his alma maters are Texarkana Junior College and the U. S. Naval Academy.
3. His talent for sales surfaced when he was still a child.
4. Young but ambitious, Perot went door-to-door and sold Christmas cards, magazines, newspapers, and used saddles.
5. While at the U. S. Naval Academy, Perot's academic performance was average, but his classmates elected him best all-around midshipman and class president for life.
6. After his discharge from the navy, Perot sold computers for IBM.
7. During Perot's fifth year with IBM, he sold his year's quota of computers before the end of January.
8. After a while in an administrative position, Perot realized he wanted his own company.
9. Perot took all the money he had and established Electronic Data Systems.
10. Perot's business doubled annually, and eventually he sold the ever-growing industry to General Motors for 2.5 billion dollars.

## 10.5 Adverbs

**An adverb is a word that modifies a verb, an adjective, or another adverb by making its meaning more specific.**

Note how adverbs are used in the following sentence to modify an adjective (*few*), a verb (*have planned*), and an adverb (*successfully*):

**Very** few people have **ever** planned a trip **so** successfully.

Adverbs indicate *when, where, how*, and *to what degree.*

We are driving to Georgia **today.**
Drive **backward** by putting the car into reverse.
We were **profoundly** disturbed by the announcement.

Study these examples of adverbs and the questions they answer:

| How? | When? | Where? | To What Extent? |
|---|---|---|---|
| hurriedly | then | here | so |
| sorrowfully | finally | nearby | often |
| steadily | yesterday | underground | very |

### Exercise 56 Locating Adverbs

The following sentences are divided into three sections. In the first section the adverb in each sentence modifies the verb. In the second section the adverb in each sentence modifies an adjective. In the third section the adverb in each sentence modifies another adverb. Write the adverb in each sentence and the word it modifies.

*In the Path of Destruction*

**Section One: Adverbs That Modify Verbs**

**1.** The tornado approached slowly from the east.
**2.** We evacuated our house quickly.
**3.** Heavy clouds were gathering overhead.
**4.** Then came a rumbling noise like that of a train.

**Section Two: Adverbs That Modify Adjectives**

**5.** We grew extremely nervous as we watched the distant funnel.
**6.** The mass exodus of fellow townspeople imprinted a very terrifying image on my mind.
**7.** People were leaving their houses at an incredibly slow pace.

**Section Three: Adverbs That Modify Other Adverbs**

**8.** Some people gathered dangerously close to the twister and took pictures.
**9.** At first, our car rocked rather gently from side to side as the winds increased.
**10.** The car jerked really violently as the tornado passed near us.

Like adjectives, some adverbs use different forms to signify degrees of comparison.

| POSITIVE | COMPARATIVE | SUPERLATIVE |
|---|---|---|
| leaped **high** | leaped **higher** | leaped **highest** |
| steps **gracefully** | steps **more gracefully** | steps **most gracefully** |
| skis **well** | skis **better** | skis **best** |
| swam **far** | swam **farther** | swam **farthest** |
| sang **badly** | sang **worse** | sang **worst** |

**Positive Degree** (No comparison)
Donna pitched **well** in the softball game.

**Comparative Degree** (Comparison of two actions)
Brook pitched **better** than Donna did.

**Superlative Degree** (Comparison of one action with two or more other actions)
Yvette pitched **the best** of all the pitchers in the bull pen.

## Exercise 57 Improving Incorrect Comparisons

Read the following comparison sentences. If a sentence is correct, write *correct*. If a sentence has an incorrect comparison, rewrite the sentence, correcting the comparison. (**Note:** Never drop the -ly from an adverb. Either add *more* or *most* in front of the adverb, or change the *y* to an *i* and add *-er* or *-est* to the end of the adverb.)

### *Flying the Friendly Skies for Nothing*

1. Business people travel more fast by plane than by car or train.
2. They also more often choose those airlines that offer frequent flier points.
3. Some frequent flier programs are conducted better than others.
4. Of all the programs offered in the United States, the one that runs the more smoothly attracts the most participants.
5. The program that gives business fliers the most points per trip draws trade the best of all.
6. When an airline changes its policies most unexpectedly, travelers become dissatisfied with that company.
7. After business fliers hear that an airline is offering a better frequent flier package than it did in the past, fliers begin to talk most positively about using that airline.
8. The closer an airline gets to reducing or abolishing its frequent flier activities, the most slowly it sells tickets.
9. Since some airlines perform more badly than others in important areas such as on-time arrivals and keeping track of luggage, frequent flier points may be an enticement to travel with those airlines.
10. Airlines that retrieve lost luggage more slowly than others are nightmares for frequent travelers.

## Exercise 58 Writing the Comparative and Superlative Forms of Adverbs

Write the comparative and superlative forms of the following adverbs. Reminders: Do not add *-er* or *-est* to adverbs that form the comparative and superlative forms by means of *more* and *most.* Also, do not drop the *-ly* on adverbs that end in *-ly*. Often, dropping the *-ly* turns an adverb into an adjective. (For example, *slowly* is an adverb; *slow* is an adjective.)

1. well
2. seldom
3. slowly
4. violently
5. unexpectedly
6. loosely
7. early
8. close
9. soon
10. often
11. late
12. loudly
13. noisily
14. suddenly
15. quickly
16. low
17. straight
18. kindly
19. graciously
20. far

## Exercise 59 Identifying Modifiers

Read the following sentences. Look at the underlined words. Decide if each word is an adjective or an adverb. Write your answers on your paper in the order that the words appear in the sentences.

### *The Eyes Have It*

1. The inconvenience of conventional eyeglasses led to the invention of plastic corrective lenses worn directly on the eyeball.
2. Contact lenses have the clear advantage of being more carefully protected by the shape of the skull than eyeglasses are.
3. Contact lenses also provide a desirable alternative for persons unhappy with conventional glasses for cosmetic reasons.
4. Most modern contact lenses are plastic, and they cover only the cornea of the eye.
5. Recent innovations such as these are hailed by some physicians and criticized by others.

## Exercise 60 Identifying Adverbs

On your paper write the twenty adverbs that appear in the following paragraph. Then write the word or words each adverb modifies. (An adverb can modify a verb, an entire verb phrase, an adjective, or another adverb.)

### *First Victory*

[1]Although she had entered competitions before, Marilyn had never taken first place in a race. [2]She waited quite nervously at the starting line, flexing her arms and legs repeatedly. [3]Before Marilyn felt entirely ready, the starter raised his pistol high above his head. [4]The pistol exploded noisily, and its echo resounded even more piercingly off the school building. [5]With expressions grimly set, the runners rapidly circled the track. [6]Marilyn found that she was running tirelessly and effortlessly. [7]Soon she neared the front of the pack. [8]For the first time in her life, no one would leave her behind. [9]She pulled ahead with every powerful stride. [10]To the sound of cheers, she crossed the finish line first and waved triumphantly to the crowd.

You may place an adverb that modifies a verb in different positions in relation to the verb. If an adverb modifies an adjective or another adverb, however, you must place it immediately before the word it modifies.

| | |
|---|---|
| MODIFYING A VERB | **Apparently** he ate last. |
| | He **apparently** ate last. |
| | He ate last, **apparently.** |
| MODIFYING AN ADJECTIVE | Yogurt is **very** good for you. |
| MODIFYING AN ADVERB | **Only** rarely do I eat dessert. |

## Exercise 61 Locating Adverbs That Modify Verbs

Copy the following sentences. Draw an arrow from the adverb to the verb being modified. If the sentence contains a verb phrase, the adverb modifies all the words in the phrase.

1. Trained seals will graciously provide hilarious and unbelievable performances.
2. Trainers frequently drop tiny fish into the seals' mouths.
3. Do you think seals ever tire of those same seafood treats?
4. If a seal performs badly, the show remains enjoyable.
5. Since seals have fins for feet, they can clap rapidly, a most humorous trick.

## Exercise 62 Locating Adverbs That Modify Adjectives

Copy the following sentences. Draw an arrow from the adverb to the adjective being modified. Then circle the noun or pronoun being modified by the adjective.

1. Strangely moody, house cats are often overlooked as trainable.
2. Ordinary cats can be unusually good performers, however.
3. A truly excellent example of a group of trained cats is located in Key West, Florida.
4. These cats' abilities are too good to be believed by the many people who have seen the cats perform on television or during sidewalk shows in Key West.
5. Their trainer has taught them a rather large number of tricks.

## Exercise 63 Locating Adverbs That Modify Other Adverbs

Copy the following sentences. Draw an arrow from the adverb modifying another adverb in each sentence to the adverb being modified. Then circle the verb being modified by that adverb.

1. Dogs are almost always hungry.
2. They may bark too eagerly for food.
3. Dogs, however, will wait somewhat longer than people.
4. Trained dogs have performed really well when they knew that food was to be their reward.
5. One dog howled a tune very loudly to receive his food.

## Exercise 64 Positioning Adverbs

Rewrite each of the following sentences, using the verb-modifying adverb that appears in parentheses. Then rewrite each sentence again, placing the same adverb in a different position.

### *Richard Allen, Religious Leader*

1. Born a slave before the American Revolution, Richard Allen showed his religious leanings. (quickly)
2. Allen's eloquent preaching converted his own master, a Delaware farmer. (soon)
3. The farmer freed Allen and his family. (gratefully)
4. Allen traveled and preached to listeners of all races. (fervently)
5. Beginning in 1784 he worked with Bishop Francis Asbury, a Methodist evangelist. (diligently)
6. Crowds of free African Americans responded to his preaching at Saint George's Church in Philadelphia. (enthusiastically)
7. In reaction to discrimination there, Allen's congregation established its own organization in 1787. (proudly)
8. Allen argued for a majority of his parishioners to remain within the Methodist Church. (persuasively)
9. In 1794 Bishop Asbury blessed the new congregation's building. (formally)
10. Allen presided over the establishment of the African Methodist Episcopal Church, which today has over two million members. (eventually)

## Exercise 65 Identifying Adverbs

On your paper write each of the twenty adverbs that appear in the following paragraph. Then write the word or words that each adverb modifies.

### *Elizabeth Gray Vining, Royal Tutor*

[1]Elizabeth Gray always wanted very much to be a writer. [2]She eagerly took to writing during her years at Germantown Friends School in Philadelphia. [3]The young student was "exceedingly gratified" when a story she really intended for children was published in a church magazine. [4]Graduating from Bryn Mawr College in 1923 when she was only twenty, Gray immediately began looking for a job. [5]Finally, she took a teaching position and began to work hard on what was eventually published as *Meredith's Ann*, her first novel for girls. [6]She later attended Drexel Institute, earning a degree in library science, and in 1926 she moved to North Carolina to work as a librarian. [7]There Gray wrote several acclaimed history books for young people and was married to Morgan Vining. [8]In 1933, after only four years of marriage, her husband was killed in an automobile accident. [9]Elizabeth Gray Vining's highly unusual appointment as tutor to Crown Prince Akihito of Japan took place in 1946. [10]Wanting his son to learn English, the emperor quite surprisingly chose Vining as the boy's teacher. [11]Subsequently she also taught Akihito's brothers, sisters, and classmates. [12]In her book *Windows for the Crown Prince*, Vining vividly describes her years as a royal tutor in Japan.

# Negative Words as Adverbs

The word *not* and the contraction *-n't* are considered adverbs. Other negatives can function as adverbs of time, place, and degree.

I ca**n't** be late. The bus is **nowhere** in sight.

**Some Common Adverbs That Convey a Negative Meaning**

| | | | |
|---|---|---|---|
| no | none | never | scarcely |
| never | nothing | hardly | barely |

In your writing, avoid using the adverbs above with other negative words.

INCORRECT We **can't hardly** wait until our trip to Germany.
CORRECT We **can hardly** wait until our trip to Germany.

INCORRECT I **never** told **no one** where you hide your spare car key.
CORRECT I **never** told **anyone** where you hide your spare car key.
OR
I told **no one** where you hide your spare car key.

## Exercise 66 Avoiding the Use of Double Negatives

For each sentence below, select a word from the pair in parentheses. Your choice should create a sentence that contains only one negative. Write your choices on your paper.

### *Climb Every Mountain*

1. There wasn't (no, any) easy trail to take up the mountain.
2. I (can, can't) barely understand why the hiking club chose this mountain for its hike.
3. When I looked for a safe way to cross the stream, I found that there (wasn't, was) none.
4. My hiking partner doesn't want to carry (nothing, anything) except her water bottle.
5. The hiking club didn't consider attempting (any, no) out-of-state trips this year.

## Exercise 67 Rewriting Incorrect Sentences

The sentences below contain double negatives. Rewrite them to create five correct sentences. There will be more than one way to rewrite each incorrect sentence.

### *Jack Nicholson*

1. Hard work doesn't mean nothing to an accomplished actor such as Jack Nicholson.
2. He probably doesn't have no free time because he is so busy starring in films, directing movies, or writing screenplays.
3. Nicholson doesn't rarely play comical characters; instead he chooses sinister parts.
4. While watching Nicholson in *One Flew Over the Cuckoo's Nest*, I wasn't scarcely able to contain my anger at the way he was treated by the hospital personnel.
5. Nicholson won't accept no acting parts that underplay his outstanding ability.

# 10.6 Prepositions

**A preposition is a word that shows the relationship of a noun or pronoun to some other word in a sentence.**

My grandmother's apartment is **below** ours. [*Below* shows the spatial relationship of one apartment to another.]

The windows shook **during** the earthquake tremors. [*During* indicates the time relationship between the shaking and the tremors.]

The bus driver waited **for** me. [*For* shows the connection between the verb *waited* and the pronoun *me*.]

*meaning "except"

| Commonly Used Prepositions | | | |
|---|---|---|---|
| aboard | beside | into | through |
| about | besides | like | throughout |
| above | between | near | to |
| across | beyond | of | toward |
| after | but* | off | under |
| against | by | on | underneath |
| along | concerning | onto | until |
| amid | despite | opposite | unto |
| among | down | out | up |
| around | during | outside | upon |
| as | except | over | with |
| at | excepting | past | within |
| before | for | pending | without |
| behind | from | regarding | |
| below | in | respecting | |
| beneath | inside | since | |

**A compound preposition is a preposition that is made up of more than one word.**

| Compound Prepositions | | |
|---|---|---|
| according to | because of | next to |
| ahead of | by means of | on account of |
| along with | in addition to | on top of |
| apart from | in front of | out of |
| aside from | in spite of | owing to |
| as to | instead of | |

Prepositions begin phrases that generally end with a noun or pronoun called the **object of the preposition.**

Seami painted a portrait **of my mother.**
Clarice spoke **to the group.**
**In the fall**, Zack returned to school.
The box **of dishes** was too heavy and nearly broken **on one side**.
She looked **in the car** and saw a sleeping puppy **on the seat**.
**Since last week,** Sadie has been complaining **about a sore wrist.**

## Exercise 68 Identifying Prepositions

List prepositions in the following sentences. Some prepositions consist of more than one word. (The numeral at the end of each item indicates the number of prepositions in that sentence.)

### *Home-Grown Weather Forecasting*

1. For short-range forecasts, private citizens can be more accurate at times than the weather bureau. (2)
2. Swallows fly higher in fair weather than before a storm. (2)
3. You can even tell the correct temperature by the number of chirps made by a cricket. (3)
4. If you add thirty-seven to the number of times a cricket chirps in fifteen seconds, you will know the correct temperature in degrees Fahrenheit. (4)
5. Bees return to their hives because of an approaching storm and stay inside them until the end of the storm. (4)
6. According to my uncle, before a storm some of the joints in his left leg begin aching. (4)
7. Farmers north of the equator know that when the wind shifts and clouds appear in the southwest, rain or snow may follow within twenty-four hours. (3)
8. A combination of heat and high humidity often means a summer thunderstorm. (1)
9. For those who look at a barometer, a sudden drop in pressure foretells the coming of a storm. (4)
10. Lacking practical forecasting skills, many of us just listen to the radio. (2)
11. Not until the nineteeth century did weather predicting become a science. (1)
12. Precise measurements of the atmosphere are of the greatest importance in meteorology. (3)
13. During the 1800s, progress was made in the areas of thermodynamics and hydrodynamics. (3)
14. Instruments for observing and measuring the atmosphere were developed. (1)
15. Weather stations at various points around the world constantly gather weather data. (2)
16. According to ancient records, weather observations were made and recorded in the fourteenth century, but they were neither systematic nor extensive. (2)
17. By the seventeeth century, record keeping became more systematic, and documents were kept that covered large areas. (1)
18. Even when people did keep accurate weather records, they had no easy way of communicating their data to other areas. (2)
19. By means of the telegraph, invented during the mid-nineteenth century, weather data could finally be sent to a central area and studied; thus, forecasts were made. (3)
20. Now, owing to more accurate forecasts, people who live near approaching storms can be warned about them well in advance. (4)

## Exercise 69 Identifying Adjective Phrases and Adverb Phrases

Prepositional phrases that modify nouns or pronouns are called adjective phrases. Prepositional phrases that modify verbs are called adverb phrases. The following sentences contain both types of prepositional phrases. Write the prepositional phrases found in each sentence. Then write the noun, pronoun, or verb modified by the phrase. Some sentences contain several phrases. Some sentences may contain no phrases. Write *no phrase* if none is present.

**SAMPLE** I bathed the dog in a big, metal tub.
**ANSWERS** in a big, metal tub; bathed
**SAMPLE** Angeline bought the puppy with the yellow fur.
**ANSWERS** with the yellow fur; puppy

### *Labrador Retrievers*

1. The Labrador retriever originated in Newfoundland, Canada.
2. During the early part of the nineteenth century, the dogs were imported to England.
3. Until 1887, these animals were called Newfoundland dogs.
4. Several other dogs were called Newfoundlands at that time; accordingly, to distinguish the imported retrievers from the rest, the imports became known as Labrador retrievers.
5. In 1903, the Kennel Club of England acknowledged the Labrador retriever as a breed.
6. The male Labrador retriever usually grows to a height of two feet at the shoulders and weighs around seventy pounds.
7. Labs have short hair with black, yellow, or chocolate coloring.
8. The dog's fur is nearly impenetrable by water.
9. Labs were originally trained for retrieving killed or wounded game such as aquatic birds.
10. Today, many people have a difficult time stopping their Labrador retrievers from fetching articles that do not belong to them, such as shoes, rugs, and decorative yard ornaments.

## Exercise 70 Identifying Adjective Phrases and Adverb Phrases

Use the following ten prepositions in ten sentences of your own. Develop a variety of prepositional phrases, some that modify nouns or pronouns and some that modify verbs. Add adjectives and adverbs wherever necessary. Be creative.

1. down
2. against
3. opposite
4. by means of
5. according to
6. for
7. throughout
8. concerning
9. in spite of
10. on account of

# 10.7 Conjunctions

A **conjunction** is a word that joins single words or groups of words.

## Coordinating Conjunctions

A **coordinating conjunction** joins words or groups of words that have equal grammatical weight in a sentence.

| Coordinating Conjunctions | | | | | | |
|---|---|---|---|---|---|---|
| and | but | or | nor | for | yet | so |

The road twisted **and** turned. [joins words]
The cat was not in the closet **or** under the bed. [joins phrases]
Stay on the path, **but** be careful of the ice patches. [joins clauses]
We had to wait a long time in the rain, **for** the bus was late. [joins clauses]
I will not forget to pack my lunch for tomorrow, **nor** will I neglect to set my alarm. [joins clauses]
He woke up late, **yet** he got to the dentist's office on time. [joins clauses]

### Exercise 71 Identifying Coordinating Conjunctions

Write the coordinating conjunction(s) that appear in each of the following sentences.

*Responsibilities of Airline Dispatchers*

1. Airline dispatchers are concerned with the safety of planes and millions of passengers.
2. The pilot and the dispatcher are two of the authorities who can cancel or delay a flight.
3. Dispatchers are trained thoroughly, for they control hundreds of lives at one time.
4. Dispatchers must be at least twenty-three years old, but few are so young.
5. A college education is essential to an airline dispatcher, and courses in meteorology and physics are valuable.
6. Many dispatchers have also been pilots or radio operators.
7. The dispatchers' day is a long one, for they must discuss flight conditions with the next person on duty.
8. Before permitting a plane to take off, the dispatcher checks the plane's fuel capacity and weight.
9. There are no hasty decisions in the work of an airline dispatcher, nor are there irreversible orders.
10. Flight conditions may change, yet the dispatcher must never lose track of all the variables affecting a flight.

# Correlative Conjunctions

**Correlative conjunctions** work in pairs to join words and groups of words of equal weight in a sentence.

| Correlative Conjunctions | |
|---|---|
| both . . . and<br>either . . . or<br>just as . . . so | neither . . . nor<br>not only . . . but (also)<br>whether . . . or |

Correlative conjunctions can make the relationship between words or groups of words clearer and more emphatic than coordinating conjunctions can.

| COORDINATING CONJUNCTIONS | CORRELATIVE CONJUNCTIONS |
|---|---|
| She **and** I have the same birthday. | **Both** she **and** I have the same birthday. |
| I have a sister **and** a brother. | I have **not only** a sister **but also** a brother. |
| I do not want cake **or** punch. | I want **neither** cake **nor** punch. |
| He invited me to the party **and** danced with me. | **Not only** did he invite me to the party, **but** he **also** danced with me. |

**Exercise 72** **Identifying Correlative Conjunctions**

Write both parts of the correlative conjunctions that appear in the following sentences.

**SAMPLE** Either you will have to mow the yard, or you will have to trim the bushes.
**ANSWERS** Either . . . or

### *The American Melting Pot*

1. A good percentage of famous Americans can claim not only European or African heritage but also Native American ancestry.
2. One of these is the former baseball star Dick Allen, who is both African American and Native American.
3. Johnny Bench, who is one-eighth Choctaw, was not only the Rookie of the Year in 1968 but also the Most Valuable Player in 1970.
4. Whether you know James Garner from *The Rockford Files* or remember him from commercials, you may not know that he is descended from Native Americans in Oklahoma.
5. Poverty defeated neither Johnny Cash nor Loretta Lynn, who claim Cherokee blood.

6. Just as Cash and Lynn are part Cherokee, so is the singer Dolly Parton.
7. The well-known humorist Will Rogers, who was one-eighth Cherokee, appeared both on stage and in films.
8. Neither prejudice nor an arduous struggle for success dampened the optimism of comedienne Moms Mabley, an African American who also had Cherokee ancestors.
9. Artist Robert Rauschenberg had both a German and a Cherokee grandparent.
10. Many of Jessamyn West's stories are about either her father's Comanche ancestors or her mother's British forebears.

## Exercise 73 Identifying Words Joined by Correlative Conjunctions

Write the correlative conjunctions in the following sentences. Then write whether *words*, *phrases*, or *clauses* are connected by the conjunction.

**SAMPLE** Either Wanda or Joe will win the science award.
**ANSWERS** either . . . or, two words

### *A Fishy Tale*

1. Not only have I tried live bait when I fish, but I have also used artificial lures.
2. He suggested that I fish at either Lake Jordan or Lake Marian.
3. Before I left for the lake, I packed both my fishing equipment and a good book in case my bad luck followed me to the new lake.
4. Neither my friend Bob nor my buddy Nathan could go with me, so I headed out alone.
5. I remembered the bait shop owner's advice and tried both the live bait and the artificial bait.

## Exercise 74 Distinguishing Between Coordinating and Correlative Conjunctions

Number your paper 1–10. Next to each number, write the *coordinating* or *correlative* conjunction used in each sentence and label the conjunction.

1. If possible, take the application home so you have more time to accomplish both a neat and thoroughly completed document.
2. You may not have very good handwriting, but you must try to print as legibly as possible.
3. Before you start to write, read each section carefully, and look at the position and length of the lines on which you are going to write your responses.
4. Be prepared with the names, telephone numbers, and addresses of past employers.
5. You are going to have to provide your social security number on this application, as well as on hundreds of documents in the future, so it would be wise for you to memorize it.
6. Potential employers not only want neat applications, but they also want clean ones.
7. On most applications, you will be required to list your last job first, for employers want to know what type of work you have been doing most recently.
8. Neither an incomplete nor an unintelligible application will receive much attention.
9. Provide exact dates, including months and days if possible, whether the application requires such precise details or not.
10. A potential employer will not only notice your attention to detail, but he or she will also be impressed with your willingness to take the time to prepare a quality product.

# Subordinating Conjunctions

A **subordinating conjunction** joins two clauses, or ideas, in such a way as to make one grammatically dependent upon the other.

The clause introduced by a subordinating conjunction is considered dependent because it cannot stand by itself as a complete sentence. Notice that introductory adverb clauses are usually set off by commas.

**When** Reggie Jackson played baseball, he was known as Mr. October.

Jackson was given his nickname **because** he excelled during postseason play.

**As soon as** he stepped up to the plate, baseball fans expected a home run.

**Although** he might have had an occasional bad season, Jackson always sparkled in October.

| Common Subordinating Conjunctions | | | |
|---|---|---|---|
| after | as though | provided (that) | until |
| although | because | since | when |
| as | before | as long as | whenever |
| as far as | considering (that) | so that | where |
| as if | if | than | whereas |
| as long as | inasmuch as | though | wherever |
| as soon as | in order that | unless | while |

**Exercise 75** **Identifying Subordinating Conjunctions**

Write the subordinating conjunction that appears in each of the following sentences. Remember that some subordinating conjunctions are made up of more than one word.

*Little-Known Facts About American History*

1. Though the facts remain obscure, Pedro Alonzo Niño, a sailor accompanying Columbus to America, is believed to have been of African descent.
2. As Columbus was, Ponce de León, Balboa, and other explorers were joined on their expeditions by sailors of African descent.
3. In 1526 Africans first set foot in the present-day United States on the Carolina coast, although they soon fled inland to settle with Native Americans.
4. In 1538, soon after Cortés subdued the Aztecs, a man of African heritage, New Mexico Estevanico, led an expedition into present-day Arizona and New Mexico.
5. In 1651 Anthony Johnson received a two-hundred-acre land grant in Virginia, where he established an independent community for himself and other people of African heritage. ➡

6. Lucy Terry, a slave in Massachusetts, became the first known African American poet when in 1746 she wrote *Bars Fight*, a poem about the Deerfield Massacre.
7. No working clocks had been built in America until Benjamin Banneker, a twenty-two-year-old African American, constructed one in 1754.
8. Although Phillis Wheatley arrived in New England as an enslaved worker, she was hailed as a remarkable poet in both Boston and London upon the publication of her book of poems in 1773, at the age of nineteen.
9. Two African Americans, Peter Salem and Salem Poor, fought heroically for the colonies when the Battle of Bunker Hill broke out in 1775.
10. Before the American Revolution ended in 1783, more than ten thousand African Americans had already served the colonies in the cause of independence from Great Britain.

## Exercise 76 Subordinating Conjunctions and Adverb Clauses

Subordinating conjunctions introduce adverb clauses. Number your paper 1–5. Write the subordinating conjunction and the last word of each adverb clause in the following sentences. Then, write what the clause tells: *when, where, how, why, how much, under what condition*. A sentence may have more than one adverb clause.

### *Five Ways to Be the Hit of a Party*

1. As soon as the clown in the group starts to tell a joke, steal his or her thunder by giving away the punch line.
2. Change the subject every chance you get so that you can brag about yourself.
3. While you are busy listing all your shining attributes and describing the major purchases you have recently made, emphasize many uninteresting details.
4. Before you describe rescuing the neighbor's dog from a burning doghouse, make yourself out to be more humane than anyone else in the world.
5. Enjoy yourself as you bulldoze your way through the crowd, because you will probably never be invited again.

## Exercise 77 Subordinating Conjunctions and Prepositions

Several words such as *after, before, since, until,* and *as* may be used as subordinating conjunctions or as prepositions. Read the following five sentences. Number your paper 1–5. Next to each number, write whether the underlined word is being used as a subordinating conjunction or a preposition.

### *Rummy*

1. <u>As</u> rummy became popular in the early twentieth century, it developed into a game for two to six players.
2. <u>After</u> the deal, the player to the left of the dealer begins the game.
3. A player's turn is not complete <u>until</u> he or she discards one card faceup on the discard pile.
4. Cards continue to be retrieved and replaced <u>until</u> the end of the game.
5. I have enjoyed playing rummy <u>as</u> a way to spend an evening with family or friends.

## Conjunctive Adverbs

A **conjunctive adverb** is used to clarify the relationship between clauses of equal weight in a sentence.

Conjunctive adverbs function somewhat like coordinating conjunctions, but they often make the relationship between the clauses stronger and clearer than coordinating conjunctions can.

| | |
|---|---|
| COORDINATING CONJUNCTION | Jan's stereo system is new, **but** it has broken down twice already. |
| CONJUNCTIVE ADVERB | Jan's stereo system is new; **nevertheless,** it has broken down twice already. |

The following examples illustrate the uses of conjunctive adverbs:

| | |
|---|---|
| TO REPLACE *AND* | also, besides, furthermore, moreover |
| TO REPLACE *BUT* | however, nevertheless, still |
| TO STATE A RESULT | consequently, therefore, so, thus |
| TO STATE EQUALITY | equally, likewise, similarly |

### Exercise 78 Using Conjunctive Adverbs

Rewrite each of the following sentences, filling in the blank with a conjunctive adverb that makes the sentence meaningful. In most cases there will be more than one correct answer.

SAMPLE A building's design affects the way people conduct their daily lives; ________, architects must know as much about life as they do about art.

ANSWERS A building's design affects the way people conduct their daily lives; consequently, architects must know as much about life as they do about art.

A building's design affects the way people conduct their daily lives; therefore, architects must know as much about life as they do about art.

*José Luis Sert, Architect*

1. José Luis Sert, born in Barcelona, Spain, in 1902, began a career in architecture there; ________, in 1951 he became a naturalized citizen of the United States.
2. As a designer he tended to think in large terms; ________, he became interested in planning whole communities, towns, and cities.
3. Sert and Pablo Picasso were good friends; ________, their works were exhibited together in the 1937 Paris Exposition.
4. In 1939 the Spanish Republic was overthrown; ________, Sert left his own country for the United States.
5. Sert was now living and working in an unfamiliar setting; ________, his designs continued to reflect a Mediterranean style.
6. This style is from the tradition of southern Spain, where homes have a central open-air patio; ________, the style uses rough concrete, whitewashed walls, and bright colors. ➟

7. Sert's reputation as an exceptional urban planner preceded him across the Atlantic; ________, his new firm gained many commissions to design South American cities.
8. In his designs Sert strove to include a site's natural features, such as a stream or greenery; ________, he tried to create interior spaces that were natural and not dehumanizing.
9. Sert had taught at a university for only one year, in 1944–1945; ________, in 1953 he was named dean of the Graduate School of Design at Harvard.
10. His designs, which may be seen throughout the world, brought Sert wide public notice; ________, his theories about urban planning brought him great respect among his peers.

## Exercise 79 Using Conjunctive Adverbs in Place of Coordinating Conjunctions

Rewrite the following sentences, replacing the underlined conjunctions with conjunctive adverbs and making the relationship between the clauses stronger and clearer. Remember to use a semicolon before each conjunctive adverb and a comma after it.

### *Singin' the Blues*

1. Blues music is a genre of African American folk and popular song, <u>and</u> the music deals with the misfortunes of life and the unpredictable changes of love.
2. In the southern United States during the 1800s, enslaved African Americans sang songs with a distinct lyric and musical form, <u>and</u> blues music was born.
3. W. C. Handy wrote "Memphis Blues" which, in 1912, was widely received, <u>and</u> blues music became popular.
4. Characteristics of blues and jazz overlapped as the two grew in popularity, <u>but</u> blues music was able to develop independently.
5. A blues fan can examine the music written by blues artists, <u>but</u> he or she may not find all the notes played during a performance since much instrumental extemporization is incorporated.

## Exercise 80 Reviewing Conjunctions

For each sentence write the compound construction with its conjunction. If a sentence contains no compound construction, write *no compound.*

**SAMPLE** Kim added fudge and marshmallows to her sundae.
**ANSWERS** fudge and marshmallows

### *Mutual Funds*

1. A mutual fund company manages and invests the combined money of its shareholders.
2. Mutual funds are relatively safe but not guaranteed investments.
3. The mutual fund company invests in both stocks and bonds.
4. The company also invests in so-called money market funds that can include either United States treasury bills or other federal securities.
5. Mutual funds may be considered by the large or small investor.

## Exercise 81 Categorizing Conjunctions

The sentences below contain a variety of conjunctions: coordinating, correlative, subordinating, and conjunctive adverbs. Number your paper 1–5. Locate each conjunction, write it on your paper, and then label it according to the type of conjunction it is.

### *Aaron Copland*

1. Because American Aaron Copland was a great composer, he was a significant contributor to twentieth century music.
2. Copland studied in both New York City and in Paris.
3. Early in his career, Copland was strongly influenced by the French impressionists; nevertheless, he was able to develop his own style.
4. As long as Copland lived, he promoted the music of contemporary composers.
5. Copland fans consider *Lincoln Portrait*, *Billy the Kid*, or *Appalachian Spring* his best work.

## Exercise 82 Creating Sentences with Conjunctions

Think of a recent excursion you have taken to an interesting or unusual place. Write several sentences about getting there and back and about what you saw and did while you were there. Use as many conjunctions as possible.

## Exercise 83 Using Conjunctions

On your paper replace the blank or blanks that appear in each of the following sentences with a conjunction that makes sense. The kind of conjunction to use is stated in parentheses.

### *The Lost Island of Bouvet*

1. __________ people believe it exists and are still searching for it, Atlantis is often called the lost continent. (subordinating conjunction)
2. __________ many tales of rediscovered islands are not likely to be proved true, those about the "lost" island of Bouvet were. (subordinating conjunction)
3. Bouvet Island was first seen in 1739 by sailors __________ they were seeking a southern polar continent. (subordinating conjunction)
4. __________ the sea was too rough for the sailors to land on Bouvet, __________ the coast was too rocky. (correlative conjunction)
5. In 1772 Captain James Cook twice tried to find Bouvet Island __________ failed. (coordinating conjunction
6. __________ the world was concerned, an island that Captain Cook could not find did not exist. (subordinating conjunction)
7. In 1808 Captain James Lindsay __________ saw Bouvet Island __________ sailed around it. (correlative conjunction)
8. People did not believe Captain Lindsay, __________ they thought that Captain Cook could not have failed. (coordinating conjunction)
9. An American seal hunter claimed that he had landed on Bouvet Isand; __________, he was known to be a boastful liar. (conjunctive adverb)
10. On December 1, 1927, a Norwegian whaler rediscovered Bouvet Island; __________, he raised a Norwegian flag there. (conjunctive adverb)

## 10.8 Interjections

**An *interjection* is a word or phrase that expresses emotion or exclamation. An interjection has no grammatical connection to other words.**

**Ha!** I told you so.
**Hey!** I'm over here!
**Oh,** I can't remember all this.
**Eek!** It's slimy!

### Exercise 84 Using Interjections

On your paper fill the blank in each sentence with an appropriate interjection from the following list:

| wow | sh | hey | oops | hi |
|---|---|---|---|---|
| ah | alas | ugh | hurrah | whew |

1. ________, the baby is sleeping.
2. ________! The bundles are falling.
3. ________! The light has turned red.
4. ________, I'm your new teammate.
5. ________! Did you see that triple somersault?
6. ________! It's a good thing we arrived before the downpour.
7. ________! Now I understand what she meant by that cryptic remark.
8. ________, I wish I could hit a serve as hard as Boris Becker does.
9. ________! I'm sure that's one of the ten worst movies ever.
10. ________! Summer is here at last!

### Exercise 85 Review: Identifying the Eight Parts of Speech

Recall the eight parts of speech: noun, pronoun, verb, adjective, adverb, preposition, conjunction, and interjection. Read the following sentences. Number your paper 1–10. Write the part of speech of each italicized word.

***Ansel Easton Adams***

1. Ansel Adams *became* famous for his *photographs* of the American Southwest.
2. *Wow!* His photographs, nearly always in black and white, *really* captured the rawness of those southwestern mountains.
3. Adams's camera seized the *barrenness* of *parched* deserts.
4. *Some* photographs included *only* the enormous clouds of a flatlands sky.
5. *Both* light *and* shadow *dramatized* the sharp detail of Adams's lofty trees.
6. Adams probably did his work at any hour of the day and night; *indeed,* to capture such incredible pictures, *he* must have been willing to try almost anything.
7. *"Fantastic!"* his *admirers* said of Adams's collection of photographs.
8. Adams *nervously* held his first exhibition in *San Francisco* in 1939.
9. *Adams* initiated the first college photography department in the *United States.*
10. *Gee!* I had no *idea* Adams published so many books on his technique.

UNIT 10

Unit Review

# Grammar Review

## Parts of Speech

Joseph Conrad's celebrated short novel *Heart of Darkness* describes the journey of a young seaman up the Congo River in Africa. In this passage the seaman, named Marlow, describes a woman who approaches the boat on which he and a group of ivory seekers (whom Marlow ironically calls pilgrims) are traveling. The passage has been annotated to show Conrad's use of the parts of speech covered in this unit.

*Literature Model*

### *from* HEART OF DARKNESS

***by Joseph Conrad***

"She walked with measured steps, draped in striped and fringed cloths, treading the earth proudly, with a slight jingle and flash of barbarous ornaments. She carried her head high; her hair was done in the shape of a helmet; she had brass leggings to the knee, brass wire gauntlets to the elbow, a crimson spot on her tawny cheek, innumerable necklaces of glass beads on her neck; bizarre things, charms, gifts of witch-men, that hung about her, glittered and trembled at every step. She must have had the value of several elephant tusks upon her. She was savage and superb, wild-eyed and magnificent; there was something ominous and stately in her deliberate progress. And in the hush that had fallen suddenly upon the whole sorrowful land, the immense wilderness, the colossal body of the fecund and mysterious life seemed to look at her, pensive, as though it had been looking at the image of its own tenebrous and passionate soul.

"She came abreast of the steamer, stood still, and faced us. Her long shadow fell to the water's edge. Her face had a tragic and fierce aspect of wild sorrow and of dumb pain mingled with the fear of some struggling, half-shaped resolve. She stood looking at us without a stir, and like the wilderness itself, with an air of brooding over an inscrutable purpose. A whole minute passed, and then she ➡

Adjective: barbarous
Common noun: gauntlets
Relative pronoun: that
Linking verb: was
Adverb: suddenly
Subordinating conjunction: as though
Possessive pronoun: Her
Personal pronoun: She

made a step forward. There was a low jingle, a glint of yellow metal, a sway of fringed draperies, and she stopped as if her heart had failed her. The young fellow by my side growled. The pilgrims murmured at my back. She looked at us as if her life had depended on the unswerving steadiness of her glance. Suddenly she opened her bare arms and threw them up rigid above her head, as though in an uncontrollable desire to touch the sky, and at the same time the swift shadows darted out on the earth, swept around on the river, gathering the steamer into a shadowy embrace. A formidable silence hung over the scene.

"She turned away slowly, walked on, following the bank, and passed into the bushes to the left. Once only her eyes gleamed back at us in the dusk of the thickets before she disappeared."

Coordinating conjunction

Preposition

Verb

## Exercise 1

**Identifying Nouns** On your paper identify each of the nouns in the following sentences, which are based on the passage from *Heart of Darkness.* After each noun write in parentheses *common*, *proper*, or *collective*, depending upon how the noun is used.

1. The group of ivory hunters wondered at her proud demeanor.
2. Her exotic ornaments made her seem a princess of Africa.
3. Her clothing suggested armor.
4. Neighboring tribes had sent her these gaudy necklaces.
5. When she reached the bank of the Congo River, she stopped and stared at the sailors.
6. An ominous silence seized the band of adventurers.
7. To Marlow she represented the soul of the wilderness.
8. He read sorrow in her fierce expression.
9. Her boldness seemed to unnerve the men.
10. She took each step cautiously and slowly.
11. Her decorated neck glistened again in the sun.
12. Had she learned her manner from the tiger or stolen its soul?
13. The ivory seekers grew more frightened of the unusual woman.
14. The woman stood a moment, staring at the group of men.
15. Was she curious about the steamer, the men, or their business?
16. What power the woman exerted when she threw up her arms!
17. Was Marlow frightened, or did he understand her power?
18. Did she signal to warriors crouching in the jungle?
19. The pilgrims' eyes followed her every move.
20. Finally, she left the river bank and slowly retreated into the jungle.

## Exercise 2

**Using Pronouns Effectively** The following sentences describe the scene evoked in *Heart of Darkness.* On your paper write the pronoun that makes sense in the blank. Follow the instructions in parentheses.

**SAMPLE** The woman ________ walked toward the boat seemed to be an African princess. (Use a relative pronoun.)

**ANSWER** The woman who walked toward the boat seemed to be an African princess.

1. The princess carried ________ with great pride. (Use a reflexive pronoun.)
2. Her innumerable necklaces, ________ were made of glass, jingled as she walked. (Use a relative pronoun.)
3. ________ of the men aboard the boat knew what to make of her. (Use an indefinite pronoun.)
4. All of ________ stared at the woman. (Use a third-person plural personal pronoun.)
5. ________ could be her purpose in approaching the steamer? (Use an interrogative pronoun.)
6. ________ was a woman with a menacing air. (Use a demonstrative pronoun.)
7. Marlow ________ wondered at her audacity. (Use an intensive pronoun.)
8. ________ in her behavior hinted that a confrontation was imminent. (Use an indefinite pronoun.)
9. Would she command ________ followers to attack the steamer? (Use a third-person singular possessive pronoun.)
10. The crew members murmured fearfully among ________. (Use a reflexive pronoun.)

## Exercise 3

**Identifying Verbs and Verb Phrases** A list of scrambled verb phrases follows. Unscrambled, they are similar to some of those that appear in the Conrad passage. First, unscramble each verb phrase, and write it on your paper. Then write a sentence, using the verb phrase. Your sentences should describe a proud and exotic person.

**SAMPLE** have been must

**ANSWER** must have been; The man must have been one of the last great hunters.

1. been might have
2. lived have may
3. going have been could
4. have might seen
5. thought would have
6. enjoyed would have
7. attacked have might
8. have should inspected
9. could left have
10. have swum would

## Exercise 4

**Identifying Transitive and Intransitive Verbs** The following sentences contain verbs that appear in the passage from *Heart of Darkness*. For each item write *transitive* or *intransitive* on your paper, depending upon the way the italicized verb is used in the sentence. Then write your own sentence, using the same verb either transitively or intransitively, as it is used in the item.

**SAMPLE** She *watched* the men as a cat watches its prey.
**ANSWER** transitive; Marlow watched the woman with keen interest.

**SAMPLE** The tiger's eyes *gleamed* in the darkness.
**ANSWER** intransitive; The still water gleamed in the moonlight.

1. Stealthily the tiger *carried* its prey up a tree.
2. The tree's limbs *trembled* from the animal's weight.
3. Hours *passed* while the tiger lay silent.
4. Animals *made* soft, rushing noises in the undergrowth.
5. At the approach of another big cat, the tiger *growled* softly.
6. The intruder *opened* its jaws in silence.
7. Tension *hung* in the humid air.
8. Monkeys *threw* leaves and branches toward the intruder.
9. The big cat *darted* abruptly into the thicket.
10. The animal *disappeared* swiftly and silently.

## Exercise 5

**Writing Sentences with Adjectives** The following sentences are adapted from *Heart of Darkness*. First, identify the adjectives in each sentence. Then, for each sentence in this exercise, write a sentence of your own with an identical structure. Place your adjectives in the same position in which they appear in the sentence in this exercise. Each of your sentences may be about a different subject.

**SAMPLE** There was a crimson spot on her tawny cheek.
**ANSWER** crimson, her, tawny
There was a lone wolf on the arctic plain.

1. On her neck sparkled many chains of beads.
2. She was clothed in bizarre charms and exotic ornaments.
3. Savage, superb, and magnificent was her manner.
4. Perhaps she personified the whole sorrowful land.
5. Her eyes, fierce and tragic, startled the men.
6. Inscrutable, she stared at the crew.
7. With a quiet jingle and a glint of yellow metal, she stopped.
8. She thrust her bare arms toward the distant sky.
9. Dusk covered the steamer in a shadowy embrace.
10. A formidable silence fell over the entire scene.

### Exercise 6

**Using Adverbs** The following sentences are inspired by an image from the passage from *Heart of Darkness*. Rewrite each sentence, substituting an appropriate adverb for the phrase in italics. The adverb should express the same idea as the prepositional phrase.

**SAMPLE** The forest loomed *in an ominous way* behind her.
**ANSWER** The forest loomed ominously behind her.

1. The woman walked *with a slow gait* through the forest.
2. Her manner was *in a vague way* menacing.
3. She strode *with an air of deliberation* toward the steamer.
4. The woman gazed at the men *in an unswerving manner.*
5. She turned *with an abrupt movement* and walked away.

### Exercise 7

**Using Prepositions** The following sentences elaborate on a description in the Conrad passage. Rewrite each sentence, filling in the blanks with a preposition that completes the phrase in italics and makes sense in the sentence. In some cases there may be more than one preposition that makes sense.

1. The woman's body swayed ________ *a sinuous motion* as she approached the river.
2. The glass beads ________ *her neck* flashed in the sun.
3. The ivory charms glowed ________ *her dark skin.*
4. She stood ________ *the silent jungle* like a ghost.
5. Marlow saw the woman's shadow ________ *the river bank.*

### Exercise 8

**Using Conjunctions** The following sentences describe the Congo region in Africa, where Conrad's *Heart of Darkness* is set. Rewrite each sentence, filling in the blanks with appropriate conjunctions. Follow the instructions in parentheses.

1. ________ they explored the Congo, Europeans discovered valuable resources. (Add a subordinating conjunction.)
2. In their quest for ivory, the colonial elephant hunters were discouraged by ________ danger ________ physical hardships. (Add a correlative conjunction.)
3. In the late nineteenth century parts of the Congo were controlled by France ________ Belgium. (Add a coordinating conjunction.)
4. The French region became the People's Republic of the Congo, ________ the Belgian sector is now known as Zaire. (Add a subordinating conjunction.)
5. In the Republic of the Congo, most of the people are farmers, ________ only a small percentage of the land is cultivated. (Add a subordinating conjunction.)

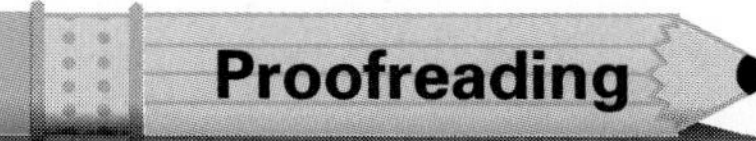


## Exercise 9

The following passage describes the artist Henri Rousseau, whose painting appears on this page. Rewrite the passage, correcting the errors in spelling, capitalization, grammar, and usage. Add any missing punctuation. There are ten errors.

### *Henri Rousseau*

[1]The French painter Henri Julien Félix Rousseau (1844–1910) worked for fifteen years as a goverment clerk before devoting himself to painting. [2]Entirely self-taught, Rousseau does not earn no acclaim for his deliberately naive style until the early years of this century. [3]Then some critics begun to hail him as one of the founders of modern art.

[4]Rousseau, who was famous for his exotic scenes appears to have based them almost entirely on his imagination. [5]Appears never to have traveled outside of France. [6]Critics believe that he modeled his plants on the flora of parisian gardens and based his animals on toys and photographs.

[7]*The Equatorial Jungle* typical of Rousseau's later paintings. [8]It's colors are subtle, the perspective is deliberately distorted, and the vegetation seems animate and menacing. [9]A similar sense of primordial mystery pervades Joseph Conrads' *Heart of Darkness.*

**Henri Rousseau, *The Equatorial Jungle*, 1909**

## Exercise 10

The biography of Joseph Conrad that appears on this page is followed by ten sentences. Rewrite each sentence, filling in the blank with an appropriate word. Use the directions in parentheses as a guide. You will need to consult the biography in order to fill in some of the blanks properly.

### *Joseph Conrad*

One of the great modern masters of English prose, Joseph Conrad did not learn the language until he was twenty years old. He was born in Russia in 1857 of Polish parents, both of whom died when he was young. He was cared for by an uncle until he joined the French merchant marine at the age of sixteen. He spent the next four years sailing on French ships to ports throughout South America and the Caribbean. At the age of twenty, he joined the English merchant marine and for sixteen years traveled to the South Seas. In 1890 he captained a boat traveling up the Congo River in Africa, an experience that inspired *Heart of Darkness.* Conrad ended his seafaring career in 1894, married, and retired to southern England. The Conrads moved about, living in two or three houses not far from London. There, in the various country homes he and his family rented, he wrote sixteen books, including *Lord Jim*, *Nostromo*, and the novella *The Secret Sharer.*

Conrad's life at sea and in foreign ports provided the background for much of his writing. People assumed, because of these tales of foreign places, that Conrad was committed to foreign affairs. The truth was simply that Conrad was concerned with the human condition. He chose his characters out of experience and concern for their situations, not out of an allegiance to some other flag.

*Lord Jim* is Conrad's best-known novel. In this work, a man spends his life trying to make up for an act of cowardice he committed as a young officer during a shipwreck in the East. Conrad's novel studies the man's emotions, the idea of personal honor, and cowardice.

In most of Conrad's writings, his outlook on life is gloomy. *Heart of Darkness* is no exception as Conrad explores the sinister depths to which humans will sink.

1. ________ Conrad did not learn English until he was twenty, he became a master of English prose. (Add a subordinating conjunction.)
2. In his lifetime Joseph Conrad had two careers: he ________ a sailor and a writer. (Add a linking verb.)
3. Conrad had a(n) ________ childhood, for both his parents died when he was young. (Add an adjective.)
4. Conrad was born in Russia to parents who were ethnically________. (Add a proper adjective.)
5. For twenty years he sailed on ________ and ________ ships to Latin America and the South Seas. (Add proper adjectives.)

# Writing Application

**Conjunctions in Writing** In the following paragraph from his novel *The Remains of the Day*, Kazuo Ishiguro uses connectives effectively to link ideas. Read the passage, focusing especially on the italicized connectives.

> The conference of 1923 was the culmination of long planning on the part of Lord Darlington; *indeed*, in retrospect, one can see clearly how his lordship had been moving towards this point for some three years *or* so before. As I recall, he had not been initially so preoccupied with the peace treaty *when* it was drawn up at the end of the Great War, *and* I think it is fair to say that his interest was prompted *not* so much by an analysis of the treaty, *but* by his friendship with Herr Karl-Heinz Bremann.

**Techniques with Conjunctions** Try to apply some of Ishiguro's techniques when you write and revise your own work:

1. When appropriate, use a coordinating conjunction other than *and* to clarify the relationship between ideas.

**Using *And*** some three *and* so years before
**Ishiguro's Version** "... some three *or* so years before."

2. Try to replace some coordinating conjunctions with appropriate conjunctive adverbs.

**Using *And*** Lord Darlington, *and*, in retrospect, one
**Ishiguro's Version** " ... Lord Darlington; *indeed*, in retrospect, one ..."

3. Use appropriate subordinating conjunctions to make the relationships between ideas clear.

**Without** When preoccupied with the peace treaty that was drawn up
**Ishiguro's Version** " ... preoccupied with the peace treaty *when* it was drawn up ..."

4. When appropriate, stress the relationship between ideas by using correlative conjunctions instead of coordinating conjunctions.

**Without *Not... But*** was not prompted by an analysis of the treaty
**Ishiguro's Version** " ... was prompted *not* so much by an analysis of the treaty, *but* by his friendship ..."

**Practice** Practice these techniques by revising the following passage on a separate sheet of paper. Rewrite the entire passage, deleting or changing the italicized words, adding conjunctions in the places marked by carets (^), and making any other appropriate revisions.

> My sister Sally ^ dislikes letting me use her car, *and* she also dislikes driving me anywhere. ^ her schedule may be hectic, *and yet* I find her attitude selfish. She realizes that my summer job is important to the household, *and yet* she offers no assistance in transporting me to work.
>
> ^ she is older than I am, *and so* she has certain privileges, *and yet* with those privileges come certain responsibilities that she is failing to meet.

UNIT

# 11 Parts of the Sentence

Grammar

Lessons

## 11.1 Simple Subjects and Simple Predicates

A **sentence** is a group of words having a subject and predicate and expressing a complete thought.

All sentences have two basic parts, a *subject* and a *predicate.*

The **simple subject** is the key noun or pronoun (or word or group of words acting as a noun) that tells what a sentence is about.

The **simple predicate** is the verb or verb phrase that expresses the essential thought about the subject of the sentence.

| SIMPLE SUBJECT | SIMPLE PREDICATE |
|---|---|
| Rain | will stop. |
| Maya Angelou | was featured. |

To find the simple subject, ask *who?* or *what?* about the verb. For example, in the second sentence above, the noun *Maya Angelou* answers the question *who was featured?*

### Exercise 1 Identifying Simple Subjects

Copy the simple subject in each of the following sentences.

*Early History of San Francisco*

1. In the early 1830s, San Francisco was a small village of about 200 houses and 800 residents.
2. After the discovery of gold at Sutter's Mill, people swarmed to the gold fields northeast of the city.
3. For many years, crime plagued the city of makeshift shacks.
4. After the gold rush, new fortunes brought opera, theater, and the arts to the city.
5. Andrew S. Hallidie designed the first cable car.

### Exercise 2 Identifying Simple Predicates

Copy the simple predicate in each of the following sentences.

*The San Francisco Earthquake*

1. One of the greatest disasters of modern times—the San Francisco earthquake—struck.
2. Many fires erupted.
3. The entire business district and many homes were destroyed.
4. The city recovered from this devastation in time.
5. The need of city residents for protection from the devastating effects of fires and natural disasters grew.

## 11.2 Complete Subjects and Complete Predicates

The addition of other words and phrases to the simple subject and the simple predicate expands or modifies the meaning of a sentence.

The **complete subject** consists of the simple subject and all the words that modify it.

The **complete predicate** consists of the simple predicate and all the words that modify it or complete its meaning.

| COMPLETE SUBJECT | COMPLETE PREDICATE |
|---|---|
| The penguins of Antarctica | dive into ice-cold water. |
| The light rain | will stop within an hour. |
| The gifted Maya Angelou | was featured in a newspaper article about contemporary authors. |

### Exercise 3 Identifying Complete Subjects

Copy the complete subject in each of the following sentences.

*Microscopes*

1. The first simple microscopes were built in the middle of the fifteenth century.
2. Used primarily to study insects, these early models were limited to magnification by single lenses.
3. Impurities in the glass greatly distorted microscope images.
4. In the sixteenth century, the Dutch Zacharias Janssen developed a lens capable of a much higher degree of refinement than earlier lenses.
5. In the middle of the seventeenth century, the experiments of Anton van Leeuwenhoek in grinding glass revolutionized the efficiency of microscopes.
6. With lenses painstakingly ground by hand, this amateur scientist revealed a new world of microscopic life.
7. A major theory of Leeuwenhoek's day, spontaneous generation, was discredited as a result of Leeuwenhoek's studies.
8. According to spontaneous generation, living organisms could originate from nonliving matter.
9. Leeuwenhoek's careful observations of samples of stagnant water, blood cells, and muscle fibers earned him the title of "father of microbiology."
10. About three hundred years after Leeuwenhoek's birth, scientists developed the first electron microscope, an instrument of immense power of magnification.

## Exercise 4 Identifying Complete Predicates

Copy the complete predicate in each of the following sentences.

### *Prehistoric Cave Paintings*

1. A group of explorers in a remote region of France made a startling discovery in 1994.
2. The explorers found four underground chambers with more than three hundred paintings of lions, oxen, mammoths, rhinoceroses, a hyena, and other animals.
3. The paintings, about twenty thousand years old, constitute the most significant discovery of prehistoric art in fifty years.
4. These paintings, in contrast to prehistoric paintings at other sites, depicted different beasts.
5. Prehistoric people adorned the walls of their caves with these paintings for religious or purely decorative reasons, according to some archaeologists.
6. The nature of the animals in the paintings supports the theory of an ancient land bridge between Europe and Africa.
7. Only experts will explore these caverns in the Ardeche region in the foreseeable future.
8. Paintings in the Lascaux cave in France deteriorated after years of tourist visits.
9. Stone Age art at Lascaux has faded substantially.
10. The scientific community in France will protect the archaeological treasures in the Ardeche cave from a similar fate.

## Exercise 5 Review: Identifying Subjects and Predicates

Copy each of the following sentences, and indicate with a vertical line the division between the complete subject and the complete predicate. Then underline the simple subject once and the simple predicate twice.

### *Rosalyn Yalow, Medical Researcher*

1. The second female recipient in the history of the Nobel Prize for medicine was the renowned physicist Dr. Rosalyn Yalow.
2. Dr. Yalow's greatest achievement was the development of radioimmunoassay (RIA).
3. This ingenious application of nuclear physics in the field of clinical medicine allows for the measurement of minute substances in body fluids.
4. Extremely sensitive and precise, RIA can detect the presence of a teaspoon of sugar in a lake.
5. Dr. Yalow's discovery of RIA was made in collaboration with Dr. Solomon Berson, her partner from 1950 to 1972.
6. Dr. Yalow, with the help of her associates at the Bronx Veterans Administration Hospital, measured insulin levels in the blood of diabetics through the use of RIA.
7. This amazing procedure has now been applied in almost every branch of medicine.
8. Scientists in the field of medicine use RIA most often for measuring the hormones, enzymes, vitamins, viruses, and drugs in the human body.
9. The Albert Lasker Prize for Basic Medical Research went to Dr. Yalow in 1976 for her brilliant work with RIA.
10. Her greatest honor, however, was the 1977 Nobel Prize for medicine.

## 11.3 Compound Subjects and Compound Predicates

A **compound subject** is made up of two or more simple subjects that are joined by a conjunction and have the same verb.

**Foxes, wolves,** and **dogs** belong to the Canidae family.
Neither the **fox** nor the **dog** eats only meat.

A **compound predicate** (or **compound verb**) is made up of two or more verbs or verb phrases that are joined by a conjunction and have the same subject.

Everyone **stood** and **cheered.**
The silver dollar **fell** from his pocket and **rolled** away.
Roy **will do** the dishes, **wash** the floor, and **cook** dinner.

Some sentences have both a compound subject and a compound predicate.

S S P P
**Mitsuo** and **Carrie sat** down and **ate** lunch.

### Exercise 6 Identifying Simple and Compound Subjects

Copy the simple subject(s) in each sentence below. Watch for subjects that are compound.

*The Jazz Age*

1. In the period after World War I, American art, music, and literature developed new forms and styles.
2. West African rhythms, African American spirituals and work songs, and European harmonies blended to form jazz, the most uniquely American music.
3. The written melody of a jazz composition is a framework permitting improvisation by musicians.
4. Composer "Jelly Roll" Morton and singer Bessie Smith were among the first great jazz musicians.
5. During the 1920s, new styles of painting gained acceptance among art critics and the public.
6. The cubes, spheres, and other geometric shapes painted by Picasso symbolized the abstract style of modern artists.
7. Edward Hopper's paintings of rural isolation and Georgia O'Keeffe's early urban landscapes captured different aspects of American life in a new, modern age.
8. During the 1920s, many American writers felt alienated from American cultural values and decided to live in Europe.
9. Ernest Hemingway and F. Scott Fitzgerald, two of the most famous expatriate writers, won praise for the depiction of modern life.
10. The term *Jazz Age* still evokes the spirit of this period in American history.

## Exercise 7 Expanding Subjects

(a) Write five sentences. In each sentence use a simple subject and a simple predicate. (b) Then expand each of your sentences by making the subject compound.

**SAMPLE ANSWER** (a) Aeschylus wrote enduring plays.
(b) Aeschylus, Sophocles, Euripides, and Aristophanes wrote enduring plays.

## Exercise 8 Identifying Simple and Compound Predicates

Copy each simple predicate in each sentence below. Watch for compound predicates. A sentence with a compound predicate will have two or more simple predicates.

### *Charles Lindbergh*

1. For several years, a hotel owner in New York City had been offering a prize of $25,000 for the first nonstop flight between New York and Paris.
2. In 1927, a young man named Charles A. Lindbergh flew his plane from California to Roosevelt Field and waited for the weather report.
3. Shortly before eight o'clock in the morning of May 20, Lindbergh climbed into his plane and took off.
4. People in every town across the United States fastened their hopes on Lindbergh and waited anxiously for every report of his progress.
5. Thirty-three and one-half hours after taking off, Lindbergh landed at Le Bourget Field near Paris.
6. More than a hundred thousand people had gathered in the airfield in Paris and greeted Lindbergh with wild enthusiasm.
7. Lindbergh was honored by European rulers and received several medals.
8. Newspapers from one end of the United States to the other proclaimed Lindbergh's feat in huge headlines.
9. Later in his career, Lindbergh became a technical adviser to several airlines and studied the operation of fighter planes during World War II.
10. For many Americans, Lindbergh embodied a spirit of idealism and romance and restored their belief in heroism.

## Exercise 9 Expanding Predicates

(a) Write five sentences. In each sentence use a simple subject and a simple predicate. (b) Then expand each of your sentences by making the predicate compound.

**SAMPLE ANSWER** (a) In the 1800s Susan B. Anthony spoke about women's suffrage.
(b) In the 1800s Susan B. Anthony *spoke and wrote* about women's suffrage.

## Exercise 10 Identifying Simple and Compound Subjects and Predicates

On your paper copy the following sentences. Then for each sentence underline the simple subject(s) once and each simple predicate twice. Then write *CS* to label a compound subject and *CP* to label a compound predicate.

### *Nanye'hi, a Cherokee Leader*

1. The Cherokee leader Nanye'hi was born in the 1730s and lived in Chota, a town on the Little Tennessee River.
2. She married Kingfisher, a Cherokee warrior, and accompanied him to war.
3. After Kingfisher's death in battle, Nanye'hi took his weapon and led the Cherokee to victory.
4. At this time both English agents and American traders were buying and sometimes stealing large tracts of Cherokee land.
5. In May 1776, chiefs, men, and women assembled at a great council.
6. Nanye'hi advocated peace with the Americans but could not convince many of the other council members.
7. During the American Revolution Nanye'hi rescued American prisoners of war and introduced cattle and dairy products to the Cherokee.
8. After the war the Cherokee and the Americans made a peace treaty but soon were at odds again over the question of rights to the land.
9. The Cherokee moved south and became farmers.
10. Sixteen years after Nanye'hi's death, the federal government forced the Cherokee west of the Mississippi.

## Exercise 11: Sentence Writing Using Compound Subjects and Compound Predicates

Read the passages below from Mark Twain's *Autobiography*. Write five sentences that tell about Twain's childhood experiences or his recollection of them. Use a compound subject or a compound predicate in each of your sentences.

### *from Mark Twain's* Autobiography

I can see the farm yet with perfect clearness. I can see all its belongings, all its details: the family room of the house with a "trundle" bed in one corner and a spinning-wheel in another, a wheel whose rising and falling wail, heard from a distance, was the mournfulest of all sounds to me and made me homesick and low-spirited and filled my atmosphere with the wandering spirits of the dead; the vast fireplace, piled high on winter nights with flaming hickory logs from whose ends a sugary sap bubbled out but did not go to waste, for we scraped it off and ate it . . .

The country schoolhouse was three miles from my uncle's farm. It stood in a clearing in the woods and would hold about twenty-five boys and girls. We attended the school with more or less regularity once or twice a week in summer, walking to it in the cool of the morning by the forest paths and back in the gloaming at the end of the day. All the pupils brought their dinners in baskets—corn dodger, buttermilk, and other good things—and sat in the shade of the trees at noon and ate them. . . .

## 11.4 Order of Subject and Predicate

In most sentences in English, the subject precedes the verb. The following are some exceptions to this normal word order:

1. In the case of commands or requests, the subject *you* is understood rather than expressed.

   [You] **Stop!**
   [You] **Stand** up.
   [You] Please **try** again.

2. To add emphasis, a sentence can be written in inverted order, with the predicate coming before the subject.

   | PREDICATE | SUBJECT |
   |---|---|
   | On the plain **are** | two frightened **ostriches.** |
   | Beyond the river **lay** | **freedom.** |

3. The predicate usually comes before the subject when the word *there* or *here* begins a sentence and is followed by a form of the verb *to be.* (The sentence appears in inverted order.) Remember that *there* and *here* are almost never the subject of a sentence.

   | PREDICATE | SUBJECT |
   |---|---|
   | Here **is** | my **opinion.** |
   | There **are** | many **reasons** to go. |

### Exercise 12 Identifying Subjects

Write the subject in each of the following sentences. If the sentence is a command, write the understood subject *you.*

*The Step Pyramid of Djoser*

1. Here is an article about the reconstruction of the Step Pyramid of Pharaoh Djoser.
2. Look at the photograph of this magnificent monument.
3. The monument was designed to impress ancient Egyptians with the strength of their ruler.
4. The construction of the pyramids required a mastery of architecture and art.
5. There was a network of canals off the Nile to transport stone for the pyramids and food for the workers.
6. Imagine the difficulty of transporting thousands of tons of limestone across the Nile to the construction site of Djoser's tomb.
7. Columns resembling bundled reeds guard the only entrance to the pyramid complex.
8. Spaced along the outer walls of the pyramid are thirteen false entrances to structures resembling temples. ➡

9. According to ancient Egyptian beliefs, a work of art or a structure without any use in this world had power in the afterlife.
10. Still eluding scholars are the reasons for the collapse of ancient Egyptian civilization.

## Exercise 13 Recognizing the Order of Subject and Predicate

Copy each sentence, draw a vertical line between the complete subject and the predicate, and label each. Then indicate with the letter *C* or *I* those sentences that are either a command (*C*) or written in inverted order (*I*). (Not all sentences will be labeled *C* or *I*.)

**SAMPLE ANSWER**

P
| Look at the photograph of the astronauts. C

P S
On the next block is | the National Air and Space Museum. I

P S
There are | many requirements for those who want to become astronauts. I

P S
Here is | a summary of the educational and training requirements. I

### *Guion Bluford, Astronaut*

1. Look at this article about Lieutenant Colonel Guion S. Bluford Jr.
2. In 1964 Bluford became a distinguished Air Force ROTC graduate of Pennsylvania State University.
3. Next for Bluford was pilot training at Williams Air Force Base in Arizona.
4. Among his subsequent educational accomplishments are a master's degree and a doctorate in aerospace engineering from the Air Force Institute of Technology, located in Dayton, Ohio.
5. Preceding Bluford's selection as an astronaut candidate were more years of training in aero-mechanics and aerodynamics.
6. Here is the perfect candidate for a successful career in aerospace.
7. Just imagine Bluford's delight at being selected in 1978 as an astronaut candidate!
8. After a period of training and evaluation came Bluford's first assignment in space as mission specialist on a shuttle flight in 1983.
9. Colonel Bluford was the first African American in space.
10. Following this historic flight was Bluford's second mission—a cooperative venture with West Germany.

## Exercise 14 Reversing the Order of Subjects and Predicates

Rewrite sentences 3, 4, 5, 8, and 10 in the preceding set of sentences about Colonel Bluford by reversing the order of the subject and the predicate. You may need to change the wording of some of the sentences.

**SAMPLE SENTENCE** | Following the long, harsh winter came a mild spring.

**ANSWER** | A mild spring followed the long, harsh winter.

## Exercise 15 Recognizing the Order of Subject and Predicate

The passage below is adapted from a letter written by Pliny the Younger, a prominent Roman of the first century A.D. In this letter Pliny gives an eyewitness account of the eruption of Mt. Vesuvius. Copy all the sentences in which the predicate precedes the subject. Underline the subject of each sentence once and the predicate twice.

### *Mt. Vesuvius*

My uncle had gone and I spent the rest of the day in study; for I had stayed at home for this purpose. Then I had a bath and supper and went to bed, but I got little sleep and that only in snatches. There had been earthquakes for several days beforehand, a fairly common occurrence in Campania. But so violent were the shocks that night that the universe seemed to be uprooted. Mother rushed into my bedroom. I was just getting up, meaning to wake her. We sat down in the courtyard of the house. That separated us by a small space from the sea. . . .

Then in came a friend of my uncle's. He had lately arrived from Spain to visit. There were my mother and I sitting and reading. He spoke sharply to me for being so confident and to her for putting up with it. But I took no notice and remained glued to my book.

Illuminating the sky at six o'clock in the morning was a faint and tired-looking light. The buildings around us were already trembling. We stood on open ground, but we should certainly be in danger if they fell. Then we decided to leave the town. Beyond the houses we stopped. There we went through an experience which was wonderful but very terrible. Our carriages could not keep still, though on level ground and wedged with stones. We saw the sea sucked back to its inmost depths and driven back by the shaking of the earth. On the other side yawned a black dreadful cloud of fiery vapor. It burst into weird ribbons of fire, with twisting, forked tongues of flame. They were like the flashes of lightning, only larger.

## Exercise 16 Reversing Subject-Predicate Order for Emphasis

In five of the sentences below, the order of the subject and predicate could be reversed to achieve emphasis. Rewrite those five sentences, labeling the subject and predicate of each.

### *The Battle of Gettysburg*

1. Two years into the Civil War, a battle came to the small Pennsylvania town of Gettysburg.
2. On the fields of Gettysburg 51,000 soldiers fell in the bloodiest battle in American history.
3. General Robert E. Lee had marched the Confederate troops through the Blue Ridge Mountains north into Maryland and Pennsylvania.
4. The Union troops under General Meade were following them.
5. In the first day of fighting, Lee's troops forced the Union troops back through Gettysburg.
6. On the second day, the main portion of both armies assembled on parallel ridges about one mile apart.
7. Up the boulder-strewn ridge Longstreet's troops stormed.
8. Nearly out of ammunition, Union troops from Maine turned back the attack with fixed bayonets.
9. On the third day, fifteen thousand Confederate troops under General George Pickett were turned back in fierce hand-to-hand fighting.
10. After this bloody battle, an end to the war was in sight.

# 11.5 Complements

A **complement** is a word or group of words that completes the meaning of a verb.

The four kinds of complements are *direct objects*, *indirect objects*, *object complements*, and *subject complements*.

## Direct Objects

A **direct object** answers the question *what?* or *whom?* after an action verb.

In general, the subject of a sentence performs the action indicated by the verb. That action may be directed toward or received by someone or something—the direct object. Direct objects are nouns, pronouns, or words acting as nouns. Only transitive verbs have direct objects.

Raymond needs **money.** [Raymond needs *what?*]
Inez saw **us** at the game. [Inez saw *whom?*]
Jerry explained **what you meant.** [Jerry explained *what?*]
Lian invited **Jamal** and **Paula** to the party. [Lian invited *whom?*]

**Exercise 17** **Identifying Direct Objects**

On your paper write the action verb or verbs in each of these sentences. Then list any direct objects.

***Robots***

1. In the 1930s Westinghouse Corporation built two robots for exhibition at the New York World's Fair.
2. Elektro, an automaton with humanlike legs and fingers, could move its limbs and digits by means of eleven internal electric motors.
3. Today industrial robots perform many difficult and dangerous jobs in factories and warehouses.
4. In automobile manufacturing, for example, robots imitate the movement of the human hand.
5. These robots can weld automobile frames faster and better than human beings.
6. Two advanced robots, Viking I and Viking II, conducted an extensive series of scientific tests on Mars.
7. With the guidance of radio messages from Earth, these robots scooped rocks and dirt into receptacles for later chemical analysis.
8. Science-fiction robots have always captured the public's interest because of their amazing capabilities.
9. The android C3P0 in the series of *Star Wars* movies could speak more than one thousand languages.
10. The utility robot R2D2 could send messages and repair complex starships.

# Indirect Objects

An **indirect object** answers the question *to whom? for whom? to what?* or *for what?* after an action verb.

In most cases a sentence must have a direct object in order to have an indirect object. The indirect object always appears between the verb and the direct object.

That noise gives **me** a headache. [That noise gives a headache *to whom?*]

Michael brought **Mary** a gift. [Michael brought a gift *for whom?*]

Tiffany gave the **race** her best effort. [Tiffany gave her best effort *to what?*]

Willie lent his **brother** and **sister** money. [Willie lent money *to whom?*]

## Exercise 18 Identifying Indirect Objects

For each of the following sentences, write the direct object and label it. Then list and label any indirect objects. (There may be more than one indirect object in a sentence, or there may be none at all.)

### *Early Explorers*

1. Long before the time of Christopher Columbus, descendants of immigrants from Asia had settled the continents of North and South America.
2. The historic voyages of Columbus, however, brought Europe new sources of wealth and power.
3. In 1500 the Portuguese navigator Pedro Alvares Cabral sent King Manuel I news of his landing in Brazil.
4. In 1513 friendly Native American guides in Panama offered Vasco Núñez de Balboa and his men a glimpse of a vast new ocean, later called the Pacific.
5. Ferdinand Magellan found an ocean route to the East in 1519.
6. In the same year the Aztec emperor Montezuma gave Hernán Cortés and his soldiers a peaceful welcome.
7. After the conquest of Mexico, the Spaniards brought the territory their language and culture.
8. After finding the Incas of Peru in a state of disorganization and vanquishing them, the Spanish conqueror Francisco Pizarro promised the Inca ruler Atahualpa freedom in exchange for a huge ransom.
9. Despite payment of the ransom, the Spaniards executed Atahualpa and conquered his people.
10. In about 1535 the shipwrecked explorer Alvar Núñez Cabeza de Vaca and his three companions found their way across Texas by foot to the Spanish colony at Culiacán, Mexico.

## Exercise 19 Recognizing Direct and Indirect Objects

The opening paragraphs of *The Rise of Silas Lapham*, by William Dean Howells, are reproduced below. On your paper write whether each underlined word or group of words is a direct object, an indirect object, or neither.

### *from* The Rise of Silas Lapham

When Bartley Hubbard went to interview Silas Lapham for the "Solid Men of Boston" series, which he undertook to finish up in *The Events*, after he replaced their original projector on that newspaper, Lapham received [1]him in his private office by previous appointment.

"Walk right in!" he called out to [2]the journalist, whom he caught sight of through the door of the counting-room.

He did not rise from the desk at which he was writing, but he gave [3]Bartley [4]his left hand for welcome, and he rolled [5]his large head in the direction of a vacant chair. "Sit down! I'll be with you in just half a minute."

"Take your time," said Bartley, with the ease he instantly felt. "I'm in no hurry." He took a note-book from his pocket, laid it on his knee, and he began to sharpen [6]a pencil.

"There!" Lapham pounded with [7]his great hairy fist on the envelope he had been addressing. "William!' he called out, and he handed [8]the letter to [9]a boy who came to get it. "I want that to go right away. Well, sir," he continued, wheeling round in his leather-cushioned swivel-chair, and facing Bartley, seated so near that their knees almost touched, "so you want [10]my life, death, and sufferings, do you, young man?"

## Exercise 20 Rewriting Sentences to Include Direct and Indirect Objects

Rewrite each of the following sentences so that it includes a direct object or indirect object, as indicated in parentheses. You may need to add, delete, or change the order of words in rewriting the sentences. Underline the element you have added.

**SAMPLE** Concert music gives great pleasure. (indirect object)
**ANSWER** Concert music gives its listeners great pleasure.

**SAMPLE** The reputation of the artist was disputed by few people. (direct object)
**ANSWER** Few people disputed the reputation of the artist.

### *Frank Lloyd Wright*

1. The Museum of Modern Art in New York City offered a chance to see the largest retrospective of an architect's work ever assembled. (indirect object)
2. A complete historical overview of Frank Lloyd Wright's work had never been presented before. (direct object)
3. In a career spanning more than sixty years, Wright left a legacy of uniquely personal and distinctly American architecture and influenced architecture and design in generations that followed him. (indirect object)
4. In the early stages of his career, Wright was deeply influenced by the work of Louis Sullivan. (direct object)
5. Wright was one of the first American architects to stress the harmony of a building with its surroundings. (direct object)

## Exercise 21 Identifying Direct and Indirect Objects

List and label the direct objects and indirect objects from the following sentences. (Some sentences may have more than one direct or indirect object; some may have a direct object but no indirect object; some may have neither.)

### *Richard Wetherill*

1. On a bitter cold day in December 1888, Richard Wetherill and his brother-in-law Charlie Mason rode their horses across the top of Mesa Verde in southwestern Colorado.
2. Wetherill and Mason were searching for stray cattle from the family ranch.
3. They stopped at the rim of an enormous canyon and looked across to the cliff opposite them.
4. They noticed a natural cavern sheltered by an overhang in the cliff.
5. Inside the cavern lay the ruins of a city built between one thousand and thirteen hundred years ago.
6. This chance discovery of the two ranchers gave scholars a wealth of information about the history and culture of the Anasazi.
7. Tools and pottery in the two hundred stone and mud rooms were still intact.
8. The village gave the ranchers the impression of a city deserted by its inhabitants.
9. The two men searched for other ruins before the end of daylight.
10. Wetherill headed north and west across the mesa top and discovered the remains of another ancient Anasazi village.
11. An enormous four-story tower dominated a third village discovered in the morning.
12. The discovery of Cliff Palace and the other Anasazi ruins changed Wetherill's life.
13. In the fourteen years after Wetherill's initial discoveries, Wetherill, his brothers, and several other partners discovered and excavated more Anasazi sites than any archaeologist before or since.
14. At first, Wetherill hauled artifacts from the excavation sites to Denver and Durango.
15. Collectors would pay him large amounts for the artifacts.
16. Wetherill realized the value of his collections and sought the advice and support of a patron.
17. A Swedish baron taught Wetherill the importance of proper excavation methods and photographic and written documentation.
18. Some professional archaeologists and scholars still viewed the work of Wetherill with scorn.
19. Today, many scholars honor Wetherill's contributions to the field of archaeology.
20. Each year, Mesa Verde National Park gives about 600,000 visitors a tour through the ruins of Cliff Palace, Spruce Tree House, and Square Tower House.

## Exercise 22 Writing Sentences with Direct Objects and Indirect Objects

On your paper write five sentences describing one of the following:

(a) a person performing in sports or athletics, such as pitching a ball, jumping rope, or running a race
(b) a person or group performing a play or concert before an audience
Use action verbs and a direct and indirect object in each of your sentences. Label the *subject*, *verb*, *direct object*, and *indirect object* in each sentence you write.

## Object Complements

An **object complement** answers the question *what?* after a direct object. That is, it *completes* the meaning of the direct object by identifying or describing it.

Only sentences with direct objects can have object complements. Furthermore, only those sentences with these or similar verbs that have the meaning of "make" or "consider" can have object complements:

| | | | | |
|---|---|---|---|---|
| appoint | consider | make | render | call |
| elect | name | think | choose | find |

An object complement may be an adjective, a noun, or a pronoun. It usually appears in a sentence after the direct object.

The jury found the defendant **innocent** of all charges. [adjective]
Some pet owners consider their dogs **children.** [noun]
The school board made the problem **theirs.** [pronoun]

### Exercise 23 Identifying Object Complements

Write the object complement(s) that appear in the following sentences. (Three sentences have two object complements, and one sentence does not have any.)

*Asian Martial Arts*

1. Many people find martial arts challenging and exciting.
2. Practitioners of judo will use an opponent's strength to their own advantage.
3. With judo a small person can render a larger opponent defenseless.
4. After years of judo lessons, I have made the sport mine.
5. Japanese karate masters make their hands and feet tough and strong.
6. The Chinese call strong, muscular boxing Shaolin kung fu.
7. Many students of tai chi chuan, another Chinese martial art, find the activity a great form of meditation and exercise.
8. Masters of aikido, a nonviolent martial-arts system, consider peace their major goal.
9. For success in all of the martial arts, participants believe timing and discipline essential.
10. Many people consider their favorite martial-arts form both a sport and a means of self-defense.

### Exercise 24 Completing Sentences by Adding Object Complements

Complete the following sentences with an object complement. Write whether your complement is an *adjective* or *noun.*

*Computers*

1. Most people consider computers ___________.
2. Computers make tasks such as writing and organizing information __________.
3. Computer programmers try to make programs __________.
4. Some people fear that computers have rendered many jobs __________.
5. People unfamiliar with computers find them ________.

## Subject Complements

A **subject complement** follows a subject and a linking verb and identifies or describes the subject.

The two kinds of subject complements are *predicate nominatives* and *predicate adjectives.*

A **predicate nominative** is a noun or pronoun that follows a linking verb and points back to the subject to identify it further.

Many doctors are **specialists.**

The surgeon for this operation was **she.**

In general, predicate nominatives appear in sentences with forms of the linking verb *be*. Predicate nominatives may follow a few other linking verbs (for example, *remain* and *become*).

Ethiopia is an African **country.**

Allergies remain a **problem.**

Elizabeth Blackwell, the first woman to graduate from a medical school in the United States, became a **doctor** and a **teacher.**

A **predicate adjective** follows a linking verb and points back to the subject and further describes it.

Pandas are **unique.**

Airline pilots should be **healthy.**

Predicate adjectives may follow any linking verb.

The journey will be **tiring.**
The nation grew more **hopeful.**
The dinner is **delicious** and **nutritious.**
The baby seems **sick.**

**Exercise 25** **Identifying Subject Complements**

On your paper write all the subject complements that appear in the following sentences. Identify each as a *predicate nominative* or a *predicate adjective*. (Three of the sentences have more than one predicate nominative or predicate adjective; one sentence has none.)

*A Performance of African Music*

1. The people on stage were musicians from Africa.
2. At first they remained still and calm.
3. Suddenly they became active.
4. One by one they played their instruments—drums, gongs, rattles, xylophones, flutes, trumpets, harps, and bows. ➡

5. Some of the instruments sounded strange and haunting to my ear.
6. For me the most impressive instrument was the *oding*, a kind of flute from Cameroon.
7. The *ogo*, a large calabash, became the favorite of many in the audience.
8. The *iya-ilu* of Yorubaland is a "talking drum."
9. During his performance the player remained erect and recited *oriki*, praise poetry for important people.
10. All in all the performance was both a musical treat and a great learning experience.

## Exercise 26 Rewriting Sentences to Include Subject Complements

Rewrite each of the following sentences so that it has a subject complement. Underline your complement and label it *predicate adjective* or *predicate nominative*.

**SAMPLE** The soft drizzle soon turned into a downpour.
**ANSWER** The soft drizzle soon became a downpour. (predicate nominative)

### *Earthquakes and Tsunami*

1. Faults, or cracks in the earth's surface, can run through land areas or under the ocean floor.
2. Undersea faults can create powerful ocean waves.
3. Some people call these tidal waves, but the waves have nothing to do with tides.
4. Scientists call these waves *tsunami*, a Japanese word for "harbor waves."
5. Rock can suddenly shift along an undersea fault.
6. Water at the surface of the ocean rises in a huge mound.
7. The mound levels out into a series of broad waves.
8. The waves travel as fast as five hundred miles per hour.
9. Near shore, the waves pile up, forming a towering wall of water.
10. The wall of water crashes on shore, destroying boats, houses, and anything else in its way.
11. A second or third tsunami can follow the first.
12. Small earthquakes can occur almost anywhere on earth.
13. Large earthquakes frequently take place in the rim of the Pacific Ocean, known as the Ring of Fire.
14. Japan lies within the world's most active earthquake region.
15. The Pacific Rim also includes the west coast of North and South America.
16. Large earthquakes also occur in a belt of land running east-west between Indonesia and the Mediterranean.
17. These two regions also have active volcanoes.
18. Lava stirring inside a volcano sometimes causes small earthquakes.
19. For many years, no one could explain the large earthquakes of the Pacific Rim.
20. Scientists have now developed a comprehensive understanding of earthquakes, volcanoes, and the history of the earth.

## Exercise 27 Writing Sentences with Complements

Write four sentences about a favorite outing, such as a picnic, a fair, or a carnival. In each sentence use at least one of the four kinds of complements: direct object, indirect object, object complement, and subject complement. Label the complements in each sentence that you write.

## Exercise 28 Identifying Complements

Identify the underlined word or words in each of the following sentences as a *direct object*, an *indirect object*, an *object complement*, a *predicate nominative*, or a *predicate adjective*.

### *Famous American Houses*

1. Tourists in Virginia can visit the estates of four famous Americans.
2. These estates, lying within sixty miles of one another, are stopping points for visitors.
3. George Washington, Thomas Jefferson, James Monroe, and Robert E. Lee once owned these properties.
4. Washington, Jefferson, and Monroe were the first, third, and fifth presidents of the United States, respectively.
5. Robert E. Lee led the Confederate Army in the Civil War.
6. George Washington's home, enlarged after his marriage, was Mount Vernon.
7. Thomas Jefferson designed his house, Monticello.
8. Jefferson considered classical architecture a model of harmony and proportion.
9. The Temple of Vesta in Rome inspired the columned portico at Monticello.
10. Jefferson selected the site for Monroe's house.
11. General Robert E. Lee's home was Arlington House.
12. Lee's father-in-law gave him Arlington House.
13. Martha Washington's grandson was Lee's father-in-law.
14. A writer in the 1800s considered Arlington House "a noble-looking place."
15. Situated on a high bluff overlooking the Potomac River, George Washington's home and burial place, Mount Vernon, is beautiful.
16. Monticello, Thomas Jefferson's home, contains a copying machine invented by Jefferson.
17. James Monroe raised peacocks on his estate, known as Ash Lawn.
18. Visitors to Mount Vernon see a carefully restored interior and many of the original pieces of furniture.
19. Their location has made the four estates major tourist attractions.
20. These mansions give tourists an idea of life during the 1800s.

## Exercise 29 Identifying Complements

On your paper write the complements that appear in the following paragraph. Next to each complement write the kind of complement it is: *direct object*, *indirect object*, *object complement*, *predicate nominative*, or *predicate adjective*.

### *Castles of Spain*

[1]The castles of Spain play host to many visitors each year. [2]Because of the influence of the Moors, Islamic people from Africa, these castles are unique among all those of Europe. [3]The Moors remained rulers of Spain from 711 to 1492. [4]They gave Spanish architecture a Moorish style. [5]Most people consider the Alhambra in Granada the best example of the Moors' influence on Spanish architecture. [6]The Moorish princes of the Nasrid dynasty made this palace a true architectural wonder. [7]The arches, filigree, and colored tiles in the Alhambra's Court of the Lions are evidence of the Moorish style. [8]These features of the castle are exquisite. [9]Off and on during their rule, the Moors built themselves castles all over Spain. [10]After the surrender of Granada in 1492, however, the Moors left Spain forever.

UNIT 11

Unit Review

# Grammar Review

## Parts of the Sentence

In this scene from Charles Dickens's *Oliver Twist*, Oliver defies the rules of the orphanage where he is living and dares to ask his master for a second helping of gruel, a thin porridge. The gruel is being served from a metal container called a copper. The passage has been annotated to show some of the elements of the sentence covered in this unit.

*Literature Model*

### *from* OLIVER TWIST

***by Charles Dickens***

Subject complement (predicate nominative)

Simple subject

Compound subject

Simple predicate

Direct object

Complete subject

The room in which the boys were fed was a large stone hall, with a copper at one end, out of which the master, dressed in an apron for the purpose, and assisted by one or two women, ladled the gruel at meal-times. Of this festive composition each boy had one porringer, and no more—except on occasions of great public rejoicing, when he had two ounces and a quarter of bread besides. . . . Boys have generally excellent appetites. Oliver Twist and his companions suffered the tortures of slow starvation for three months; at last they got so voracious and wild with hunger that one boy, who was tall for his age, and hadn't been used to that sort of thing (for his father had kept a small cook-shop), hinted darkly to his companions that unless he had another basin of gruel *per diem*, he was afraid he might some night happen to eat the boy who slept next him, who happened to be a weakly youth of tender age. He had a wild, hungry eye, and they implicitly believed him. A council was held; lots were cast who should walk up to the master after supper that evening and ask for more; and it fell to Oliver Twist.

The evening arrived; the boys took their places. The master, in his cook's uniform, stationed himself at the copper; his pauper assistants ranged themselves behind him; the gruel was served out, and a long grace was said over the short commons. The gruel disappeared; the boys whispered each other, and winked at Oliver, while his next ➡

neighbors nudged him. Child as he was, he was desperate with hunger, and reckless with misery. He rose from the table, and advancing to the master, basin and spoon in hand, said, somewhat alarmed at his own temerity:

"Please, sir, I want some more."

The master was a fat, healthy man, but he turned very pale. He gazed in stupified astonishment on the small rebel for some seconds, and then clung for support to the copper. The assistants were paralyzed with wonder, the boys with fear.

"What!" said the master at length, in a faint voice.

"Please, sir," replied Oliver, "I want some more."

The master aimed a blow at Oliver's head with the ladle, pinioned him in his arms, and shrieked aloud for the beadle. . . .

There was a general start. Horror was depicted on every countenance.

Subject complement (predicate adjective)

Compound predicate

Complete predicate

Inverted sentence

## Exercise 1

**Identifying Simple and Compound Subjects and Predicates** The following sentences describe social conditions in England in the time of *Oliver Twist.* Copy each sentence. Then underline and label the simple or compound subject and the simple or compound predicate. Finally, draw a line separating the complete subject from the complete predicate.

**SAMPLE** Prosperous English merchants acquired as much land as possible in the early nineteenth century.

**ANSWER** Prosperous English merchants (SIMPLE SUBJECT) | acquired (SIMPLE PREDICATE) as much land as possible in the early nineteenth century.

1. Technological advancements swept the country and fundamentally altered its society just before and after 1800.
2. New machines accelerated and standardized the production of textiles.
3. The Industrial Revolution's awesome power changed Britain from a mostly rural society to a mostly urban one.
4. Sprawling, dirty cities gradually overtook the English countryside.
5. Such rapidly growing and poorly regulated cities could not maintain adequate housing, fire and police protection, and sanitation.
6. London grew to a city of more than a million people and faced numerous problems as a result of this growth.
7. Impure water, poor law enforcement, and inadequate transportation were a few of the city's many difficulties. ➡

8. Psychological and emotional pressures affected British laborers.
9. The physical working conditions in British factories were generally unhealthful.
10. Poor lighting and little air circulation were typical in mills during these years.
11. Industrial accidents became alarmingly common because of the presence of complex machines in factories and other workplaces.
12. British society endured a difficult struggle between workers and employers.
13. For instance, long working hours in Yorkshire and Lancashire factories caused widespread dissatisfaction among textile workers.
14. The Combination Acts of 1824 and the Poor Law of 1834 limited the rights of workers in England.
15. Gruel, bread, and cheese composed the typical laborer's diet.
16. Unregulated child labor flourished in British factories until the middle of the nineteenth century.
17. The government first concerned itself with reforms and improvements in national education in the 1830s.
18. An 1842 law forbade the employment of young children in underground mines.
19. The Factory Act of 1847 limited a child's workday in a textile mill to ten hours.
20. Authors such as Charles Dickens and Charles Kingsley protested labor conditions.

## Exercise 2

**Writing Sentences with Complete Subjects and Complete Predicates** Each of the following partial sentences elaborates on an idea suggested by the passage from *Oliver Twist.* On your paper rewrite each sentence, making it complete by adding either a complete subject or a complete predicate. Do not repeat the exact wording from the passage, but your sentences should make sense within the context of the passage.

**SAMPLE** The boys of the orphanage ________.
**ANSWER** The boys of the orphanage ate their meals in a large stone hall.

1. Wearing an apron, the master ________.
2. One or two women ________.
3. ________ was all the orphans ordinarily got.
4. ________ drove the boys to extreme measures.
5. One tall boy ________.
6. A council of boys ________.
7. ________ ate the gruel greedily.
8. ________ alarmed Oliver Twist.
9. Oliver ________.
10. The master of the orphanage ________.

## Exercise 3

**Writing Sentences with Compound Subjects and Compound Predicates** Write on your paper a complete sentence answering each of the following questions about *Oliver Twist.* Do not repeat the exact wording from the passage. Begin your sentence with the subject and follow the directions in parentheses. Then underline and label the simple or compound subject and the simple or compound predicate. Finally, draw a line separating the complete subject from the complete predicate.

**SAMPLE** Who are some of the characters in *Oliver Twist?* (Use a compound subject.)

COMPOUND SUBJECT — SIMPLE PREDICATE

**ANSWER** Oliver Twist and the other orphans | are some of the characters in *Oliver Twist.*

1. Who served gruel to the orphans? (Use a compound subject.)
2. What two things were served to the boys on special occasions? (Use a compound subject.)
3. What did the master do the first time Oliver Twist asked for more gruel? (Use a compound predicate.)
4. Who seemed completely paralyzed while they waited for the master's answer? (Use a compound subject.)
5. What did the master do the second time Oliver Twist asked for more gruel? (Use a compound predicate with three verbs.)

## Exercise 4

**Writing Inverted Sentences** The following sentences develop an image or idea suggested by the passage from *Oliver Twist.* On your paper rewrite each sentence in inverted order, following the directions in parentheses.

**SAMPLE** The master of the orphanage stood at one end of the dining hall. (Begin the sentence with *At one end.*)

**ANSWER** At one end of the dining hall stood the master of the orphanage.

1. The orphans walked into the large stone hall. (Begin the sentence with *Into the large stone hall.*)
2. One meager serving of gruel went into each boy's bowl. (Begin the sentence with *Into each boy's bowl.*)
3. Images of delectable feasts danced in their minds. (Begin the sentence with *In their minds.*)
4. No signs of sympathy or compassion were on the master's face. (Begin the sentence with *There were.*)
5. A look of desperation was in Oliver's eyes. (Begin the sentence with *There was.*)

## Exercise 5

**Writing Sentences with Predicate Nominatives and Predicate Adjectives** The pairs of words below are derived from the passage from *Oliver Twist.* For each pair write a sentence using the first word as the subject and the second as a predicate adjective or a predicate nominative. Do not use Dickens's exact words. Add more than a verb to each pair. Then indicate whether the second word of the pair is acting as a *predicate adjective* or a *predicate nominative.*

**SAMPLE** boys, victims

**ANSWER** The boys in the orphanage were victims of a brutal and corrupt system. (predicate nominative)

1. orphans, hungry
2. gruel, food
3. portion, meager
4. bread, treat
5. master, tyrant
6. assistants, paupers
7. boys, desperate
8. Oliver, rebel
9. children, miserable
10. punishment, unfair
11. hall, dining room
12. Oliver, reckless
13. hunger, constant
14. childhood, painful
15. decision, extraordinary
16. appetites, enormous
17. reaction, astonishment
18. orphanage, place
19. master, indifferent
20. boys, fearful

## Exercise 6

**Writing Sentences with Direct and Indirect Objects** Each of the following groups of words relates to an incident in *Oliver Twist.* Each word is labeled *S* (for *subject*), *DO* (for *direct object*), or *IO* (for *indirect object*). Write a sentence using each group of words, but do not use Dickens's exact wording. Add modifiers and prepositional phrases to your sentences.

**SAMPLE** master (S), boys (IO), gruel (DO)

**ANSWER** The master of the orphanage served the boys some gruel.

1. gruel (S), boys (IO), nourishment (DO)
2. master (S), orphans (IO), bread (DO)
3. boys (S), council (DO)
4. council (S), Oliver (IO), responsibility (DO)
5. boys (S), seats (DO)
6. women (S), orphans (IO), bowls (DO)
7. orphans (S), gruel (DO)
8. boys (S), Oliver (IO), encouragement (DO)
9. Oliver (S), master (IO), question (DO)
10. master (S), Oliver (IO), blow (DO)

**Exercise 7** **Proofreading**

The following passage describes the artist John George Brown, whose painting appears on this page. Rewrite the passage, correcting any errors in spelling, grammar, and usage. Add any missing punctuation. There are ten errors.

### *John George Brown*

[1]John George Brown (1831-1913), born in Durham, England, apprenticed himself to a glassworks when he was fourteen, and for a period of several years, he cuts glass by day and studied drawing painting, and design at night. [2]He moved to the United States in 1853 and finded work designing stained-glass windows at a glassworks in Brooklyn, New York. [3]Brown's employer recognized the young mans talent and he encouraged Brown to dedicate himself to painting.

[4]Brown followed his employer's advice and eventually established a sound reputation as a painter holding his first exhibit in 1858. [5]Brown specialized in painting poor children and laborers in precise, highly realistic stile. [6]One of his favorite subjects were street urchins. [7]He often used newsboys and bootblacks as models, posing him to achieve the proper attitudes. [8]The boys who posed for *A Tough Story* might also have pose as the orphans in *Oliver Twist.*

**John George Brown, *A Tough Story*, 1886**

**Exercise 8**

The following sentences describe the life of Charles Dickens. Rewrite each sentence on your paper according to the directions that appear after each item. Make sure your answers are complete sentences.

### *Charles Dickens*

1. Charles Dickens, *of all the great nineteenth-century English novelists,* is perhaps the most beloved by his readers.
   (Rewrite the sentence so that the phrase in italics, which is part of the complete subject, appears in another position.)
2. The ideas for many of the events and people in Charles Dickens's novels grew from his own experiences.
   (Rewrite the sentence so that the subject and the predicate are in inverted order.)
3. Dickens was born in Portsmouth, on the southern coast of England, and grew up in a poor neighborhood of London.
   (Add *and his seven brothers and sisters* to the complete subject.)
4. His father, a clerk, accumulated huge debts.
   (Add *and was eventually thrown into prison* to the complete predicate.)
5. Dickens endured a difficult childhood, for he was forced to work in the factories *from an early age.*
   (Rewrite the sentence so that it begins with the phrase in italics.)
6. His employers were often needlessly cruel.
   (Add *and strict* to create a second predicate adjective.)
7. The painful experiences Dickens endured as a child laborer inspired his acclaimed *Oliver Twist.*
   (Add *and* <u>*David Copperfield*</u> to create a second direct object.)
8. In these two well-known novels appear some of the cruelest characters in English fiction.
   (Rewrite the sentence so that it begins with the complete subject.)
9. Vivid portraits of schoolmasters, criminals, and innocent victims are in many of Dickens's novels.
   (Rewrite the sentence so that it begins with *There are.*)
10. Dickens, who died as a result of continuing poor health at the age of fifty-eight, left an enduring legacy.
    (Add *readers* to the predicate so that it functions as the indirect object.)

# Writing Application

**Varying Sentences in Writing** In the following passage from her short story "The Milk Run," Christina Stead uses a variety of sentence patterns. The sentences in this passage range in length from six to twenty-three words. As you read, discover how Stead varies her sentences to create a pleasing rhythm.

> Matthew...was a little afraid of the new route. He crossed and came along the other side of the Wollongong Road, along a tall apricot-looking fence of new hairy boards. At the farther point of that triangular plot, too, was an interesting wooden post, very old and gray and eaten inside by termites. It had been smoldering for weeks, set alight by the sun, not extinguished by the rain. The sun was on the horizon. Shafts of red touched him across the dairy. He reached the end of the new fence and Lydham Hill could be seen with its great head of trees. He stumbled on a big tussock and fell.

**Techniques for Varying Sentences** Try to apply some of Christina Stead's writing techniques to your own work.

1. Create rhythms in your prose by varying the length of your sentences. You can expand the basic patterns of your sentences by adding modifiers and by compounding.

**Monotonous** Shafts of red touched him.
**Choppy rhythm** He reached the end of the fence. Lydham Hill could be seen.
**Stead's version** Shafts of red touched him across the dairy. He reached the end of the new fence and Lydham Hill could be seen with its great head of trees.

2. Achieve variety by occasionally beginning a sentence with a phrase or a clause or by inverting the order of the subject and predicate.

**Usual word order** An interesting wooden post...was at the farther point of that triangular plot.
**Stead's version** At the farther point of that triangular plot, too, was an interesting wooden post. . . .

**Practice** Practice these techniques by revising the following paragraph on a separate sheet of paper. All of the sentences now have a monotonous, choppy rhythm. To create a pleasing, rhythmic pattern, vary the sentence lengths and add details. To heighten the reader's interest further, avoid starting every sentence with the subject, and put at least one sentence in inverted order.

The plane swooped low. It was on its final approach. It headed for Randall's Airport. The city sparkled below. It looked like a giant sea of tiny jewels. It was night. Rashida eagerly looked out the window. She tried to identify the landmarks of her childhood. The twin red lights glowed in the distance. The lights shone atop the Greenville Water Tower. The ballpark lights glowed beyond. Rashida let out a deep sigh. Then she smiled contentedly, for she was home.

UNIT

# 12 Phrases

Grammar

## Lessons

## 12.1 Prepositional Phrases

A **phrase** is a group of words that acts in a sentence as a single part of speech.

A **prepositional phrase** is a group of words that begins with a preposition and usually ends with a noun or a pronoun, called the **object of the preposition.**

> The bus goes **to the city.** [*The city* is the object of the preposition *to.*]
>
> The bus drove **through the tunnel.** [*Tunnel* is the object of the preposition *through.*]

For lists of common prepositions, turn to page 430.

Adjectives and other modifiers may be placed between the preposition and its object. A preposition may also have more than one object.

> The bus goes **to the distant island city.** [adjectives added]
> The bus goes **to the city and the airport.** [two objects]

Several prepositional phrases may occur sequentially in a sentence.

> The bus goes **to the city on the island in the bay.**

A prepositional phrase normally acts as an adjective or an adverb. When it acts as an adjective, it modifies a noun or a pronoun. When it acts as an adverb, it modifies a verb, an adjective, or another adverb.

> The bus **at the corner** is an express. [adjective phrase modifying the noun *bus*]
>
> Which **of these buses** will leave first? [adjective phrase modifying the pronoun *which*]
>
> **During the day** you should ride this bus **into the city.** [adverb phrases modifying the verb phrase *should ride*]
>
> The bus will be convenient **for you.** [adverb phrase modifying the adjective *convenient*]
>
> You are driving too fast **for your own good.** [adverb phrase modifying the adverb *fast*]

## Exercise 1 Identifying Prepositional Phrases

Write each prepositional phrase that appears in the following sentences. (Most sentences have more than one prepositional phrase.)

### *Native Americans and the Arts*

1. The purpose of Native American artwork stretches beyond mere artistic expression to deeply spiritual concerns.
2. Native American arts express a love for color and symmetry.
3. The Inca, Aztec, and Maya created elaborately carved stone sculptures in South, Central, and North America.
4. The Inca, rulers of the largest empire in the Americas, wrote historical dramas about important events.
5. In addition to beautiful blankets, the Araucanian, a group from South America, also produced pottery and carvings.
6. The Montana group in North America made war bonnets from the feathers of eagles.
7. The Pueblo made sand paintings before festival days.
8. The Navajo used sand paintings in healing ceremonies.
9. The Hidatsa group of upper North Dakota would engage in elaborate ritual dances that lasted until dawn.
10. The Tlingit group have been building totem poles since the time of their migration from northern Russia.

## Exercise 2 Identifying Prepositional Phrases that Act as Adjectives and Adverbs

Write the word that each prepositional phrase in Exercise 1 modifies. Indicate whether each phrase is acting as an *adjective* or an *adverb.*

## Exercise 3 Expanding Sentences with Prepositional Phrases

Expand the following sentences by adding at least two prepositional phrases to each, one functioning as an adjective and one functioning as an adverb phrase.

**SAMPLE** The sound haunted us.
**ANSWER** The sound of the wounded dolphin haunted us during the night.

1. Bodies of water house many creatures.
2. Freshwater fish inhabit rivers and lakes.
3. Ponds are often full.
4. Marshes protect animals.
5. Some swamps nurture alligators.
6. Other swamps protect swans.
7. Ducks also live in swamps.
8. Turtles and frogs swim in creeks.
9. Dolphins swim in oceans.
10. Whales prowl the seas.

## 12.2 Appositives and Appositive Phrases

An **appositive** is a noun or pronoun that is placed next to another noun or pronoun to identify or give additional information about it.

An **appositive phrase** is an appositive plus any words that modify the appositive.

> My cousin **Carol** is studying for a degree in microbiology. [The appositive *Carol* identifies the noun *cousin*.]
>
> Take your application to City Hall, **the large red brick building at 583 San Pablo Avenue.** [The appositive phrase in bold type identifies *City Hall*.]

Commas should be used to set off an appositive that is not essential to the meaning of a sentence, as in the preceding example about City Hall.

### Exercise 4 Appositives and Appositive Phrases

Write the appositives or appositive phrases that appear in the following paragraph. (Three sentences have more than one appositive or appositive phrase.)

***Four Contemporary Directors***

[1]Four contemporary film directors, keen students of their craft, are impressing critics and audiences alike. [2]The director Penny Marshall showed her versatility in the successful comedy *Big* and in the drama *Awakenings*. [3]Marshall, a former television actress, made her directorial debut in 1986 with the Whoopi Goldberg film *Jumpin' Jack Flash*. [4]Another talented director is Emilio Estevez, son of Martin Sheen and brother of Charlie Sheen. [5]In 1986 Estevez directed *Wisdom*, the story of a social crusader turned outlaw. [6]*Wisdom*, Estevez's first film, gave him the distinction of having been the youngest person ever to write, direct, and act in the same Hollywood movie. [7]A year earlier the filmmaker Susan Seidelman released a movie that became a smash hit; the popularity of that film, *Desperately Seeking Susan*, surprised nearly the entire film industry. [8]Po Chih Leong won critical acclaim for directing *Ping Pong*, a film made in 1987. [9]The film features a romance between Mike Wong and Elaine Choi, two Anglo-Chinese characters. [10]It is hoped that these four directors, all talented artists, will continue to produce interesting films.

### Exercise 5 Identifying Appositives

Write the appositive from each of the following sentences. Then write the word that each appositive renames.

1. Ms. Randolph, an attorney, will be away on a business trip to Washington, D.C.
2. My sister T'Aysha is a medical student at the University.
3. Robert Frost wrote the poem "Mending Wall."
4. Rick ate his favorite snack, cold sausage pizza.
5. Greg's car, a restored 1965 convertible, attracts attention everywhere Greg drives it.

## Exercise 6 Writing Sentences with Appositive Phrases

On your paper expand the following sentences by adding an appositive phrase to each one. Be sure to use commas where necessary.

**SAMPLE** Manuel guided the sailboat smoothly into the harbor.
**ANSWER** Manuel, an expert sailor, guided the sailboat smoothly into the harbor.

1. Sylvia attended a computer fair yesterday.
2. My cousins are planning a trip to Tokyo.
3. Michael's grandmother cooked his favorite dish.
4. The television show was nominated for an Emmy Award.
5. Diana Ross sang the song.
6. The tourists eagerly walked to see the ancient ruins.
7. The guide took them to the museum to see the statues.
8. The sculpture in the lobby was famous.
9. The newlyweds went to Washington on their honeymoon.
10. The Iroquois lived in the region now included in central New York State.
11. Our team won the first game at Farley Field.
12. My cousins studied the economic, political, and social structure of the Iroquois.
13. The flowers looked beautiful in the container.
14. She sang at the rallies of Martin Luther King Jr.
15. The supplies will be delivered by Greg.
16. My favorite author has just published a new book.
17. My teacher is planning to visit Jamaica during the winter vacation.
18. The captain of the ship was a quiet man with five years' experience as a skipper.
19. The sailors included Jorge Hernandez and Juan Bolívar.
20. The boat's compass showed that their course was now due west.

## Exercise 7 Writing a Paragraph with Appositive Phrases

On your paper expand the following article by adding appositive phrases. Be sure to use commas where necessary.

### *Hooked on Computers*

TV addicts have been with us almost since the dawn of television. Now there is a new kind of addiction. Some people can't seem to pull themselves away from the computer.

"The computer has a tremendous amount of holding power for many people," says Betsy Sullivan. "Like a slot machine, you put in some money and sometimes get a payback," says Dr. Marcia Littenberg. "I can sit in front of the computer terminal for five hours, and it feels like five minutes," says Carol Lash. The arrest of Kevin Mitnick on charges of computer fraud highlighted the problem of obsessive computer use. Mitnick represents an extreme case of this new kind of screen "addiction." But experts on computer abuse say that even a less obsessive use of the computer can represent a problem. "It would be the same signs as addiction to anything else—sneaking around to do it," says Littenberg. The problem is sure to increase as more people go on-line in the future.

## 12.3 Verbals and Verbal Phrases

A **verbal** is a verb form that functions in a sentence as a noun, an adjective, or an adverb.

A **verbal phrase** is a verbal plus any complements and modifiers.

All verbals—*participles*, *gerunds*, and *infinitives*—can be expanded into phrases.

### Participles and Participial Phrases

A **participle** is a verb form that can function as an adjective.

All *present participles* end in *-ing*. Many *past participles* end in *-ed;* others have different forms, however. Many of the adjectives that you are familiar with are in fact participles.

A **traveling** carnival came to our town.

I took the less **used** path.

A **torn** handkerchief was the only clue to the **puzzling** crime.

When a participle is part of a verb phrase, the participle is not functioning as an adjective.

| | |
|---|---|
| **PARTICIPLE AS ADJECTIVE** | Our **invited** guests are here. |
| **PARTICIPLE IN VERB PHRASE** | The student council **has invited** a guest speaker. |

A **participial phrase** contains a participle plus any complements and modifiers.

Like unmodified participles, participial phrases act as adjectives and appear in various positions.

**Whimpering in his crib,** the baby kept himself awake.

**Picking him up,** I walked back and forth.

The baby, **screaming furiously for two hours,** kept me busy.

**Worn out by the noise,** I was overjoyed to see his parents.

A participial phrase that appears at the beginning of a sentence is usually followed by a comma. A participial phrase in the middle or at the end of a sentence is set off by commas only if it is not essential to the meaning of the sentence.

A past participle may be used with the present participle of the auxiliary verb *have* or *be*. (See Unit 15 for more on the *-ing* form.)

**Having whimpered for hours,** the baby finally fell asleep.
**Being tired,** the child whimpered.

## Exercise 8 Identifying Participles and Participial Phrases

On a separate sheet of paper, write each participle or participial phrase that acts as an adjective in the following sentences. Then identify the word each one modifies.

### *The Plight of the Early Immigrants*

1. Thousands of Irish immigrants, fleeing famine in their own country, came to the United States in the 1840s.
2. Settling in the Eastern cities, the Irish rapidly improved their economic status.
3. Germans disillusioned with political events immigrated here in large numbers after 1848.
4. Struggling European farmers abandoned their rocky soil for the fertile Midwestern prairies of the United States.
5. European countries suffering from overpopulation sent their surplus labor to America.
6. Newly arrived immigrants, ill prepared for America's cities, often found life in this country a bewildering experience.
7. Crowded into urban slums, many immigrants encountered miserable circumstances.
8. The photographs taken by Jacob Riis brought these conditions to the attention of many middle-class people.
9. A social settlement called Hull House, established by Jane Addams, aided poor immigrants in Chicago.
10. A famous poem by Emma Lazarus described the immigrants as "huddled masses yearning to breathe free."

## Exercise 9 Adding Participles and Participial Phrases

On a separate sheet of paper, expand the following sentences by adding participles and participial phrases.

**SAMPLE** The house stays cool in the summer.
**ANSWER** The house, shaded partially by large trees, stays cool in the summer.

1. A sound came from the car's rebuilt engine.
2. The leaves on the tree sounded like ice.
3. The small girl is my sister.
4. The fire department evacuated the building.
5. They ordered hot dogs.

# Gerunds and Gerund Phrases

A **gerund** is a verb form that ends in *-ing* and is used in the same way a noun is used.

**Traveling** can be educational. [gerund as subject]

Yolanda loves **biking.** [gerund as direct object]

Samuel will give **jogging** a try. [gerund as indirect object]

They insult me by **worrying.** [gerund as object of a preposition]

My hobby is **cooking.** [gerund as predicate nominative]

That puppy's habits, **biting** and **whining,** must be modified. [gerunds as appositives]

A **gerund phrase** is a gerund plus any complements and modifiers.

**Very careful driving** is required at night.
He hates **driving a car at night.**

Although the *-ing* ending is common to both the present participle and the gerund, the two verbals act as different parts of speech: the present participle as an adjective and the gerund as a noun.

**Traveling quickly overland,** the Pony Express carried the mail. [participial phrase modifying *Pony Express*]

**Traveling quickly overland** was the goal of the Pony Express. [gerund phrase acting as subject]

## Exercise 10 Identifying Gerunds and Gerund Phrases

List on your paper the gerunds and gerund phrases that appear in the following sentences. (Some of the sentences have more than one gerund or gerund phrase.)

*Native American Languages*

1. Learning the complex Native American languages was an educational experience for some European settlers.
2. Settlers acquired new words for rivers, mountains, animals, and vegetation by listening carefully to Native Americans.
3. Literally translating the Dakota word for hailstones into English produces "seeds of snow."
4. Settlers in Delaware and Iowa gave naming their states with beautiful Native American words great importance.
5. Mastering the local languages led to a keener understanding of the unfamiliar Native American cultures. ➡

6. The Inca wrote messages and kept records by knotting a cord called a *quipu.*
7. Some Native American nations used drawing and painting on bark or animal hides as a way to record and communicate local history.
8. Nonverbal methods of communication, signaling with smoke or drumbeats and signing, were practices of the Plains groups.
9. After acquiring horses, members of the Plains nations met each other much more often and soon developed a useful sigh language, or language made of gestures.
10. An interesting Native American practice is expressing distances in terms of the amount of traveling a person can do in one day.

### *Hobbies and Sports*

11. Ballet dancers learn balance partly by exercising on a wooden barre.
12. Richard's favorite sport is hiking in local nature preserves.
13. Crowds of spectators show their interest in tennis by following the players around the world from tournament to tournament.
14. After running out of water and losing their food to a hungry bear, the Schmidts regretted camping by the isolated lake.
15. Pitching a baseball requires coordination and much practice.
16. Gardening is one of the top three hobbies in America.
17. The basketball team excelled in dribbling and passing.
18. Some surfers wear wet suits for riding the waves.
19. Building a successful kite involves fitting sheets of paper on the kite frame.
20. On hot summer nights, the neighbors enjoy picnicking.

## Exercise 11 — Adding Gerunds and Gerund Phrases

On a separate sheet of paper, expand the following sentences by adding gerunds and gerund phrases. Make sure you use the *-ing* word as a gerund and not as a present participle. You may add other words if necessary.

**SAMPLE** I have a new hobby.
**ANSWER** I have a new hobby, snorkeling.

1. The dog ran into the house.
2. Chris paid the bill.
3. He won the game.
4. I really enjoy jazz.
5. The dieter resisted his weakness.

## Exercise 12 — Creating Sentences with Gerunds

Select five of the gerunds that you identified in Exercise 10, and write an original sentence for each one. Make sure you use the *-ing* word as a gerund and not as a present participle.

## Infinitives and Infinitive Phrases

An **infinitive** is a verb form that is usually preceded by the word *to* and is used as a noun, an adjective, or an adverb.

When *to* precedes the base form of a verb, it is part of an infinitive, not a preposition.

**To succeed** is satisfying. [infinitive as subject]
Everyone needs **to relax.** [infinitive as direct object]
His hope is **to travel.** [infinitive as predicate nominative]

She had the wisdom **to cooperate.** [infinitive as adjective]

We were happy **to arrive.** [infinitive as adverb]

An **infinitive phrase** contains an infinitive plus any complements and modifiers.

They wanted **to eat quickly.**
**To arrive at the theater on time** was their goal.
It was a pleasure **to tell her the good news.**

When an infinitive has its own subject, it is part of a construction called an *infinitive clause.* The subject of an infinitive clause follows the main verb of the sentence and immediately precedes the infinitive. An infinitive clause can appear only after an action verb.

The monitor wanted **Lee to sit down.** [*Lee* is the subject of the infinitive *to sit.* The entire infinitive clause *Lee to sit down* acts as the direct object of the sentence.]

Sometimes the word *to* is dropped before an infinitive.

I saw **a sports car [to] race by.**
Let **me [to] take care of that.**

### Exercise 13 Identifying Infinitive Phrases

Write the infinitive phrases that appear in each of the following sentences. (Several sentences have two infinitive phrases.)

*Building the National Gallery of Art*

1. In 1936 the well-known American financier and philanthropist Andrew W. Mellon provided the funds to build the National Gallery of Art in Washington, D.C.
2. Mellon also had the foresight to acquire nine additional acres for future expansion.
3. The architect I. M. Pei, who had already designed many other public spaces, was hired in 1968 to design a new wing for the National Gallery of Art.
4. The challenge was to work with "a wacky piece of land," according to the gallery's director, and to keep costs down. ➡

5. One day Pei was inspired to draw two triangles.
6. On the basis of the drawing, he designed a wing consisting of two triangular buildings that join to form a trapezoid.
7. The structure seems to move by itself as one walks by it.
8. From almost anywhere inside the new wing, a visitor is able to view the outdoors or the courtyard.
9. To protect the works of art from glare is the function of the slats of aluminum: they reduce the light from the glass ceiling.
10. The sunlight pouring through the glass ceiling made it possible to add trees and other foliage to the lobby.

### *Buying a Car*

11. Before you go out to buy a car, think about performance, optional equipment, price, fuel economy, comfort, repair records, trade-in value, and color.
12. What can you do to learn more about these automobile characteristics?
13. You might want to do some research.
14. You could take a trip to a nearby library to read evaluations of new cars in *Car and Driver* or *Consumer Reports*.
15. You could visit several automobile dealers to look at new or used cars and to drive them yourself.
16. You could call friends to ask them about their car-buying experiences.
17. Of course, you don't have to take anyone's advice.
18. You can make a list to help in your decision.
19. You might want to list advantages and disadvantages.
20. You may want to give more weight to some things than to others.
21. The color of a car, for example, has nothing to do with its performance or comfort.
22. Color, however, is very important to some people who seem to have a personal attachment to their cars.
23. Are white cars easier for other drivers to see at night?
24. Are police more likely to stop red cars for possible traffic violations?
25. Of course, you need to think about price.
26. You must decide how much you can afford to pay for a car.
27. Besides the base price or monthly payment, you will need to budget for gasoline, insurance, and repairs.
28. You might call an automobile insurance agent to get an estimate of insurance premiums.
29. If you are trying to save money, you might ask yourself if you really need a compact-disk player or power windows or even air-conditioning.
30. You could choose a car to please yourself, not to impress others.

## Exercise 14 Using Infinitives

Write down five action verbs. Then make up a sentence using each verb in an infinitive phrase. Underline the infinitive phrases.

## 12.4 Absolute Phrases

An **absolute phrase** consists of a noun or a pronoun that is modified by a participle or a participial phrase. An absolute phrase has no grammatical relation to the rest of the sentence.*

*Absolute phrases are also known as *nominative absolutes*.

Belonging neither to the complete subject nor to the complete predicate, an absolute phrase stands "absolutely" by itself in relation to the rest of the sentence.

**Their throats parched by the searing heat,** the firefighters battled the blaze.

The participle *being* is understood rather than stated in some absolute phrases.

**The fire [being] out,** they coiled their hoses.

### Exercise 15 Identifying Absolute Phrases

Write on your paper the absolute phrase in each of the following sentences.

1. Objects in space give off electromagnetic waves, light waves and radio waves being among them.
2. Visible light revealing much about objects, astronomers generally rely on optical telescopes.
3. Astronomers also use radio telescopes, faint radio waves revealing additional clues.
4. Its "reach" extending about thirteen billion light-years, a radio telescope is considerably more powerful than an optical telescope.
5. Optical telescopes having limitations, astronomers are now using radio telescopes to discover hitherto unknown objects in space.
6. The weary hikers rested for a minute by the camp, their breaths frosty white in the cold, crisp winter air.
7. His teeth chattering, the paper carrier stood shivering in the cold, dark doorway waiting for the family to come home.
8. All things considered, the four main actors were pleased by the reviews in the early-morning newspapers.
9. His dream of glory having been destroyed for good, the boxer left the city and died a bitter man.
10. The work done, the boss called for a big celebration and gave the staff three days' paid vacation time.

## Exercise 16 Review: Verbal Phrases and Absolute Phrases

On your paper write each of the verbal and absolute phrases that appears in the following sentences. (Three of the sentences have more than one verbal or absolute phrase.) Write *participial phrase*, *gerund phrase*, *infinitive phrase*, or *absolute phrase* to identify each phrase. (Remember that an absolute phrase has within it a participle or a participial phrase.)

### *Maya Angelou*

1. Becoming an artist involved great struggle for the author Maya Angelou.
2. After an unhappy childhood Angelou began pursuing careers as a dancer, singer, and writer to express her creativity.
3. Her talents blossoming, she toured Europe in the 1950s, performing in *Porgy and Bess.*
4. Missing her young son, Angelou left the troupe and returned to the United States.
5. Her political awareness deepening, Angelou served as an official of the Southern Christian Leadership Conference in the 1960s.
6. After working with Martin Luther King Jr. to promote racial equality in the United States, Angelou decided to pursue the same goal in South Africa.
7. One of her main pursuits, writing autobiographical volumes, has yielded several significant works.
8. Both her prose and her poetry address the challenge of creating a healthy sense of self amid adverse circumstances.
9. Recognizing her unique achievements, several colleges have awarded her honorary degrees.
10. Through her vibrant works Angelou continues to grow in stature as an author and as a spokesperson for African American women.

## Exercise 17 Expanding Sentences with Absolute Phrases

Read through the sentences quickly to get an idea of the scene, and then rewrite each sentence, making the words in italics into an absolute phrase. Add commas where needed.

**SAMPLE** *Because the threat of war was gone,* the nations of the world no longer spent huge sums on weapons for defense.

**ANSWER** The threat of war being gone, the nations of the world no longer spent huge sums on weapons for defense.

1. Doctors put great effort into research *because disease was a global concern.*
2. *When the world's deserts were turned into farmland,* every family was guaranteed adequate food.
3. *Because the environment had been polluted for decades,* nations agreed on measures to clean up toxic waste.
4. Meanwhile, human rights activists pressed for social reforms *as their followers marched in the streets.*
5. *After every need had been met,* the people renamed their world Utopia.

UNIT
12
Unit Review

# Grammar Review

## Phrases

The dreaded year has come and gone, but George Orwell's *1984* is still a powerful warning against totalitarianism. In the following excerpt from the opening scene of the book, the protagonist, Winston Smith, is about to enter his apartment (or flat, as the British call it) in London. The passage has been annotated to show the types of phrases that have been covered in this unit.

*Literature Model*

### *from* 1984

***by George Orwell***

It was a bright cold day in April, and the clocks were striking thirteen. Winston Smith, his chin nuzzled into his breast in an effort to escape the vile wind, slipped quickly through the glass doors of Victory Mansions, though not quickly enough to prevent a swirl of gritty dust from entering along with him. . . .

Inside the flat a fruity voice was reading out a list of figures which had something to do with the production of pig iron. The voice came from an oblong metal plaque like a dulled mirror which formed part of the surface of the right-hand wall. Winston turned a switch and the voice sank somewhat, though the words were still distinguishable. The instrument (the telescreen, it was called) could be dimmed, but there was no way of shutting it off completely.

❦

Winston kept his back turned to the telescreen. It was safer; though, as he well knew, even a back can be revealing. A kilometer away the Ministry of Truth, his place of work, towered vast and white above the grimy landscape. This, he thought with a sort of vague distaste—this was London, chief city of Airstrip One, itself the third most populous of the provinces of Oceania. He tried to squeeze out some childhood memory that should tell him whether London had always been quite like this. Were there always ➡

Prepositional phrases (adverb phrase) — through the glass doors

Gerund phrase — entering along with him

Prepositional phrases (adjective phrases) — of the surface of the right-hand wall

Participial phrase (past participle) — turned to the telescreen

Appositive phrase — his place of work

Infinitive phrase — to squeeze out some childhood memory

these vistas of rotting nineteenth-century houses, their sides shored up with balks of timber, their windows patched with cardboard and their roofs with corrugated iron, their crazy garden walls sagging in all directions? And the bombed sites where the plaster dust swirled in the air and the willow herb straggled over the heaps of rubble; and the places where the bombs had cleared a larger path and there had sprung up sordid colonies of wooden dwellings like chicken houses? But it was no use, he could not remember: nothing remained of his childhood except a series of bright-lit tableaux, occurring against no background and mostly unintelligible.

Absolute phrase

Participial phrase (present participle)

## Exercise 1

**Expanding Sentences with Prepositional Phrases** The following sentences describe an imaginary totalitarian society. Read the sentences to get an idea of the scene, and then rewrite each sentence, adding at least one prepositional phrase to each. You may imagine any scene.

**SAMPLE** Atlas was a worker.
**ANSWER** Atlas was a worker in an iron foundry.

1. Atlas was walking home.
2. He wore gray overalls and a dirty red kerchief.
3. Soot had blackened his face.
4. It was seven o'clock.
5. The streets were empty.
6. Atlas's fatigue was apparent.
7. Atlas dragged his feet.
8. His mind churned.
9. He vividly recalled the strike.
10. The foundry workers had protested.
11. The foreman had read the informer's message.
12. Atlas, he had discovered, was the ringleader.
13. The workers were sent home.
14. Atlas worried.
15. A loud noise interrupted his thoughts.
16. A black van careered toward Atlas.
17. The headlights blinded him.
18. He covered his face and hid.
19. Two officers jumped out.
20. They handcuffed Atlas and took him away.

## Exercise 2

**Expanding Sentences with Appositives** Rewrite each sentence, incorporating the words in parentheses so that they form an appositive phrase. Use a comma or commas to set off the appositive phrase.

**SAMPLE** Winston Smith went home. (a resident of London)
**ANSWER** Winston Smith, a resident of London, went home.

1. The April wind lashed Winston's face.
   (a harsh reminder of winter)
2. He hurried to his flat.
   (a cheerless room in Victory Mansions)
3. From the telescreen he heard the broadcaster's voice.
   (a falsely sweet drone)
4. Unable to shut off the telescreen, he tried his best to ignore it.
   (a constant presence)
5. He looked out the window at the Ministry of Truth.
   (his workplace)
6. The war had drastically altered London.
   (a nightmare of bomb attacks)
7. Rows of crumbling houses surrounded his flat.
   (ramshackle relics of the past)
8. Had the city always been so gloomy?
   (his lifelong home)
9. Winston tried to recall the former city.
   (a bustling and cheerful place)
10. His childhood memories were incomplete.
    (a series of brightly lighted scenes)

## Exercise 3

**Sentence Building with Appositives** Rewrite each sentence, incorporating the words in parentheses so that they form an appositive phrase. Be sure to set off the appositive phrase with commas if necessary.

1. The band entertained at the party.
   (the Electric Tomato)
2. The family was saved from the flood by climbing to the roof of the shed.
   (a mother and her three children)
3. My brother is in charge of the toxic waste cleanup.
   (a manager for the Environmental Protection Agency)
4. The cat hid in the clothes hamper during thunderstorms.
   (a fearful creature)
5. Christi McGregor taught children how to write different kinds of poems.
   (a famous poet)

## Exercise 4

**Expanding Sentences with Participial Phrases** Combine the sentences, changing the sentence in parentheses into a participial phrase. Be sure to place the participial phrase close to the word it modifies. Remember to add commas where necessary.

1. Winston sought protection from the chill wind.
(He was tucking his chin to his chest.)
2. He finally reached his home.
(He was hurrying through the April cold.)
3. The hallway depressed him.
(The hallway was smelling of boiled cabbage.)
4. A poster bore the caption BIG BROTHER IS WATCHING YOU.
(The poster was hung in the hallway.)
5. The images of Big Brother seemed to watch him.
(The images were posted throughout the building.)
6. Winston climbed the seven flights of stairs to his flat.
(He was pausing several times along the way.)
7. Inside the flat a voice was reciting statistics.
(The voice was emanating from the telescreen.)
8. The telescreen could not be shut off.
(The telescreen was designed to keep track of Winston's actions.)
9. The device made privacy impossible.
(The device was monitored by the Thought Police.)
10. Winston surveyed the view.
(He was walking to the window.)
11. He could see the vast, white Ministry of Truth.
(The Ministry of Truth was towering over the city.)
12. The Ministry of Truth distributed propaganda.
(The Ministry of Truth was cleverly named by Big Brother.)
13. The city he surveyed lay nearly in ruins.
(The city was once hailed as the capital of the British Empire.)
14. Rows of nineteenth-century houses stood in a state of disrepair.
(The houses were once owned by the well-to-do.)
15. The ramshackle houses were a blight on the vicinity.
(The houses were damaged by war and neglect.)
16. Shacks served as homes for many.
(The shacks were made of wood.)
17. Winston was depressed by the gloom.
(The gloom was pervading the streets.)
18. He reflected on the past.
(He was seeking some solace.)
19. His memories were vague and incomplete.
(The memories were blurred with age.)
20. He finally gave up.
(He was exhausted by the mental effort.)

## Exercise 5

**Expanding Sentences with Gerund Phrases** Each of the sentences below describes Newspeak, the official language of the government of Oceania, as described by Orwell in *1984.* Each item consists of a question followed by a phrase in parentheses that answers the question. For each item write a sentence that answers the question, using the words in parentheses as a gerund phrase.

SAMPLE What was one of the triumphs of Big Brother? (inventing Newspeak)
ANSWER Inventing Newspeak was one of the triumphs of Big Brother.

1. What was the goal of Newspeak?
(controlling the thoughts of the people of Oceania)
2. How was this goal accomplished? (by making the language as limited as possible)
3. How was the language limited? (by abolishing all unnecessary words)
4. What was a favorite pastime of Oceania's officials?
(disparaging ordinary English, or Oldspeak)
5. How did Big Brother inject politics into the new language?
(by adding ideological terms such as *goodthink*)
6. What did Big Brother's followers enjoy?
(inventing euphemisms such as *joycamp*, the term for a prison camp)
7. What was forbidden in Newspeak?
(mentioning outdated concepts such as freedom)
8. In Newspeak, what did *thoughtcrime* mean?
(thinking critically about the government)
9. What was *doublespeak*? (expressing two contradictory ideas)
10. What did Winston hate? (hearing the doublespeak slogan "Freedom Is Slavery")

## Exercise 6

**Writing Sentences with Infinitive Phrases** In *1984* George Orwell criticizes the ways in which technology can whittle away at individual freedoms. The sentences that follow describe the positive and negative roles of contemporary computer technology. Each item consists of a question followed by a phrase in parentheses that answers the question. For each item write a sentence that answers the question, using the words in parentheses as an infinitive phrase.

SAMPLE What is a challenge?
(to use technology wisely)
ANSWER To use technology wisely is a challenge.

1. What is a computer's function? (to process masses of information)
2. What is a dangerous misuse of computer technology in contemporary society?
(to invade individual privacy)
3. What may unscrupulous people want? (to gain access to confidential information)
4. Why is security needed? (to prevent misuse of computer data)
5. What is one way to safeguard against theft? (to limit access to sensitive records)

## Exercise 7

**Expanding Sentences Using Participial Phrases** On your own paper combine the sentences and phrases in parentheses by using participial phrases.

**SAMPLE** The children gazed at the monkeys.
(hanging by their tails from the branches)

**ANSWER** The children gazed at the monkeys hanging by their tails from the branches.

1. Sarah told everyone that she would never marry again.
(haunted by the memory of her beloved first husband)
2. I watched the sun set over the fields.
(blazing over the barn, trees, and stable)
3. The third baseman fumbled the line drive.
(distracted by the airplane flying low overhead)
4. The small child waited for the hurricane to pass.
(hiding under the bed with his teddy bear)
5. I took big gulps of the frosty iced tea.
(sitting in a shady corner of the dusty field)

## Exercise 8

**Expanding Sentences** On your own paper combine each pair of sentences by using an appositive, a participial phrase, a gerund phrase, an infinitive phrase, or an absolute phrase.

**SAMPLE** The clown had a big, round red nose.
He was a comic sight.

**ANSWER** The clown, a comic sight, had a big, round red nose.

1. Charlie was a construction worker.
He saved a boy from drowning.
2. The speaker's patience had worn thin.
He shouted at the audience.
3. The woman was last seen at the bus station in Tulsa..
She was wearing a green dress and red shoes.
4. Sondra had one goal in life.
That was to become a veterinarian.
5. There was an accident.
The cause was reckless driving.

## Exercise 9

**Sentence Writing** Select five of the appositives, participial phrases, or gerunds you identified in Exercises 7 and 8, and write an original sentence using each one.

Exercise 10

## Proofreading

**Proofreading** The following passage describes the artist Jean-Michel Folon, whose work appears on this page. Rewrite the passage, correcting the errors in spelling, grammar, and usage. Add any missing punctuation. There are ten errors.

### *Jean-Michel Folon*

[1]Jean-Michel Folon born in 1934 in Brussels, Belgium, studied to become an architect but he turned instead to drawing and painting.

[2]Folon's cartoons throughout his career depicts a dehumanized world of labyrinthine cities and silent forests of fossilized trees. [3]The inhabitants of this world alienated by the very technologies meant to liberate them, wander aimlessly. [4]Automatons with barely human shapes shuffles blindly through the corridors of a concrete city in *The Crowd*. [5]Arrows pointing meaninglessly in various directions.

[6]Folon's work points out the folly of any atempt to institute a utopia driven by technology. [7]Giving his characters a comic look Folon relieves viewers of the darker meaning that his works suggest, although his theme is remarkably similar to that of *1984*. [8]Sounding a warning George Orwell the author of *1984*, wrote about people being manipulated by a Ministry of Truth that towers "vast and white above the grimy landscape."

**Jean-Michel Folon, *The Crowd*, 1979**

**Exercise 11**

**Review** Below is a brief biographical sketch of George Orwell, which is followed by ten sentences. Use the facts in the sketch to expand the ten sentences, following the guidelines that appear in parentheses at the end of each sentence. Be sure to place the phrase you add close to the word it modifies. If you like, you may add other phrases in addition to the one that is required.

### *George Orwell*

George Orwell is the pseudonym of Eric Arthur Blair. He was born in Bengal, India, in 1903. When he was a young boy, Orwell attended a preparatory school in England, and he was later to claim that his experiences at this school forever determined his scathing view of the English class system. Orwell went on to win a scholarship to Eton. Instead of going to college, however, Orwell went to Burma, where he joined the Indian Imperial Police in 1922 at the age of nineteen. He served in Burma until 1927, when, disillusioned with British imperialism, he left Burma to live in Paris and London.

Orwell's first published work, *Down and Out in Paris and London* (1933), vividly portrays the poverty of his existence in Europe at that time. He was unique among the writers of his era in that he deliberately lived in the difficult social conditions he was compelled to chronicle.

In 1935, Orwell went to Spain and fought with the Republican forces in the Spanish civil war. His experiences in that war produced *Homage to Catalonia* (1938), a book in which his anti-communist attitudes are evident.

*Animal Farm*, published in 1945, won Orwell wide acclaim. Considered his best novel, it is a biting satire of Stalinism. He published *1984* four years later. The novel envisions a nightmarish totalitarian world and contains the well-known warning: "Big Brother is watching you."

Orwell suffered from tuberculosis and died in London on January 21, 1950. The final words in his notebooks show his wit and honesty: "At fifty, everyone has the face he deserves." Unfortunately, Orwell, a writer renowned for his defense of individual freedom and praised for his clear, direct prose, never reached that age.

1. Eric Arthur Blair was the real name. (Add a prepositional phrase.)
2. Orwell left Burma. (Add a participial phrase.)
3. He moved to Paris. (Add an infinitive phrase.)
4. Orwell went to Spain. (Add an infinitive phrase.)
5. He nonetheless became a strong critic of communism. (Add an appositive phrase.)
6. He left Spain and returned home. (Add a prepositional phrase.)
7. *Animal Farm* made him famous. (Add an appositive phrase.)
8. Orwell's novel *1984* describes his vision. (Add a prepositional phrase.)
9. He died in 1950. (Add a participial phrase.)
10. Orwell is renowned. (Add the preposition *for* and a gerund phrase.)

# Writing Application

**Phrases in Writing** By adding phrases to expand basic sentence patterns, writers create sentences that are vivid and rhythmically expressive. In this passage from *Lord Jim* by Joseph Conrad, notice how the author uses phrases to add vivid images to the scene:

> It's extraordinary how we go through life with eyes half shut, with dull ears, with dormant thoughts. Perhaps it's just as well; and it may be that it is this very dullness that makes life to the incalculable majority so supportable and so welcome. Nevertheless, there can be but few of us who had never known one of these rare moments of awakening when we see, hear, understand ever so much—everything.
> . . . in a flash—before we fall back again into our agreeable somnolence . . .
> It was a brilliant day; a southerly buster was raging, and we could see the passers-by, men and women, buffeted by the wind of the sidewalk, then sunlit fronts of the houses across the road blurred by the tall whirls of dust.

**Techniques with Phrases** Try to apply some of Joseph Conrad's writing techniques when you write and revise your own work.

1. Conrad's many prepositional phrases tell us *how* ("with eyes half shut, with dull ears, with dormant thoughts"), *where* ("through life"), and to *whom* ("to the incalculable majority").

2. Conrad also uses a participial phrase ("buffeted by the wind of the sidewalk") to describe the people passing by.

3. Use appositive, gerund, and absolute phrases to elaborate on your basic ideas. In this example from the novel *River Song*, the author Craig Lesley expands his sentences with two absolute phrases:

> As the fire moved closer, frightened deer bounded ahead, their gentle brown eyes wide, their tails flared.

Lesley's absolute phrases underscore the idea that the fire has frightened the deer. They also provide more details about the animals' appearance.

**Practice** Practice these techniques by revising the following passage, using a separate sheet of paper. Combine choppy, awkward sentences by turning some of them into phrases that give the final passage a flowing rhythm.

The year was 1943. Gwendolyn Brooks won her first poetry prize. Two years later she published *A Street in Bronzeville*. This was her first full-length poetry volume. She was named one of *Mademoiselle*'s Ten Women of the Year. She soon received many other honors for her works. These included the 1950 Pulitzer Prize. The Pulitzer Prize was for *Annie Allen*. Thereafter, many leading universities hired her. They wanted her to teach creative writing. Brooks is like many of her characters. She is a Midwesterner. She was born in Topeka, Kansas. She soon moved to Illinois and spent several years in a small second-floor apartment. That was on Chicago's East Sixty-third Street.

UNIT

# 13 Clauses and Sentence Structure

Grammar

## Lessons

## 13.1 Main Clauses

A **clause** is a group of words that has a subject and a predicate and that is used as a part of a sentence.

There are two categories of clauses: *main clauses* (also called *independent clauses*) and *subordinate clauses* (also called *dependent clauses*).

A **main clause** has a subject and a predicate and can stand alone as a sentence.

Every sentence must contain at least one main clause. A sentence may also have more than one main clause. Each of the clauses in the following example is a main clause because each one has a subject and verb and can stand alone as a sentence.

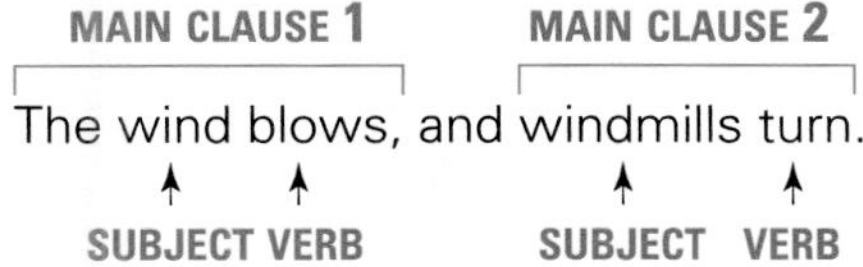


**Exercise 1** **Identifying Subjects and Verbs in Main Clauses**

Each of the following sentences contains one or more main clauses. On your paper write the subject and the verb of each main clause.

*Can the Panther Survive?*

1. The Florida panther is one of America's most critically endangered mammals.
2. Panthers once ranged freely throughout the southeastern United States.
3. The result of agricultural expansion, however, has been steady, relentless pressure on the animal's habitat.
4. According to many experts, the few remaining panthers may be found only in Florida's Everglades and in nearby Big Cypress Swamp.
5. By the early 1990s the population of panthers had declined to about fifty, and the big cat's extinction seemed likely.
6. In early 1991 the U.S. Fish and Wildlife Service supported drastic action to save this species.
7. Wildlife biologists captured six kittens under a year old, and these young panthers formed the nucleus of a captive breeding program.
8. Specially selected zoos supervise this effort to raise a new generation of panthers.
9. Shortly after the year 2000, this new population will be returned to the wild.
10. The captive breeding program is probably the best hope for saving this endangered species.

**Exercise 2** **Sentence Writing Using Main Clauses in Sentences**

Write five original sentences about one of your favorite foods. Be sure that each of your sentences contains at least one main clause. When you have finished, underline the subject of each main clause once and the verb twice.

# 13.2 Subordinate Clauses

A **subordinate clause** has a subject and a predicate, but it cannot stand alone as a sentence.

A subordinate clause is considered dependent because in order for it to make sense, it must be attached to a main clause. Subordinate clauses frequently begin with subordinating conjunctions or relative pronouns.

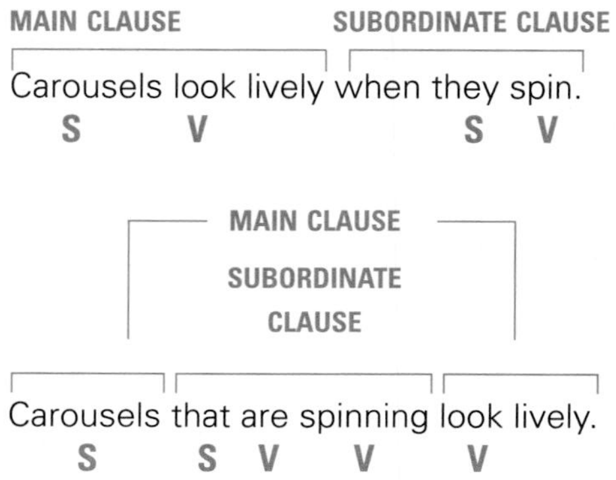


In the first sentence the subordinating conjunction *when* introduces the subordinate clause *when they spin.* This subordinate clause does not express a complete thought, although it has a subject and a predicate.

In the second sentence the relative pronoun *that* introduces the subordinate clause *that are spinning.* This clause appears between the subject and the verb of the main clause, and *that* functions as its subject.

## Exercise 3 Identifying Main and Subordinate Clauses

Each of the following sentences has a clause that appears in italics. On a separate sheet of paper, indicate whether it is a *main clause* or a *subordinate clause.*

1. Although traditional Chinese medicine is an ancient science based on more than two thousand years of accumulated knowledge, *many Westerners are unfamiliar with its principles.*
2. Western medicine differs greatly from Chinese medicine, *which is rooted in Eastern culture and philosophy.*
3. Traditional Chinese doctors view the patient's body, mind, and spirit as inseparable, *whatever the specific illness may be.*
4. Such physicians search for external signs of "disharmony" *so that they can make a diagnosis.*
5. Because one obvious symptom of sickness is lack of vitality, *traditional Chinese doctors attribute illness to a disorder in the flow of qi (bodily energy), caused by an imbalance between the soft, dark, cold, wet yin elements and the hard, light, hot, dry yang elements.*

# 13.3 Simple and Compound Sentences

**A simple sentence has only one main clause and no subordinate clauses.**

Although it has just one main clause, a simple sentence may have a compound subject, a compound predicate, or both. Furthermore, adjectives, adverbs, prepositional phrases, appositives, verbal phrases, and complements can also expand the subject and predicate of a simple sentence.

Carousels spin. [simple sentence]

Carousels and Ferris wheels spin. [simple sentence with compound subject]

Carousels spin and turn. [simple sentence with compound predicate]

Carousels and Ferris wheels spin and turn. [simple sentence with compound subject and compound predicate]

The gilded carousels at the fairgrounds spin their painted wooden horses more and more rapidly. [simple sentence expanded]

**A compound sentence has two or more main clauses.**

Each main clause of a compound sentence has its own subject and its own predicate. The main clauses are usually joined by a comma and a coordinating conjunction (*and*, *but*, *or*, *nor*, *yet*, or *for*).

MAIN CLAUSE 1 | MAIN CLAUSE 2

Carousels spin, and Ferris wheels turn.
S V S V

MAIN CLAUSE 1 | MAIN CLAUSE 2

Jonathan rode the carousel, but Peg preferred the Ferris wheel.
S V S V

MAIN CLAUSE 1 | MAIN CLAUSE 2

The park was crowded, for Monday was a holiday.
S V S V

MAIN CLAUSE 1 | MAIN CLAUSE 2 | MAIN CLAUSE 3

Carousels spin, and Ferris wheels turn, but roller coasters hurtle.
S V S V S V

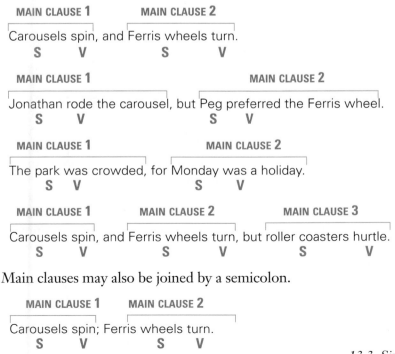

Main clauses may also be joined by a semicolon.

MAIN CLAUSE 1 | MAIN CLAUSE 2

Carousels spin; Ferris wheels turn.
S V S V

## Exercise 4 Identifying Simple and Compound Sentences

Indicate whether each of the following is a *simple* or a *compound sentence*. (Remember that a single main clause can have a compound subject and a compound predicate.)

### *New Energy Sources*

1. The demand for energy in America has been doubling nearly every twenty years.
2. Energy sources have been classified as renewable or nonrenewable; a renewable energy source can never be depleted.
3. The United States is depleting its nonrenewable energy sources: coal, oil, and gas.
4. Coal, oil, and gas are fossil fuels, for they are formed from buried remains of plant and animal life.
5. Fossil fuels were once easy to find and inexpensive but have become increasingly hard to find and expensive.
6. Sun, wind, and water are renewable energy sources, and they do not cause pollution.
7. Energy from the sun is free, but fans, pumps, pipes, and storage tanks may be needed for a solar heating system.
8. In a passive solar heating system, parts of a building absorb the sun's rays and slowly radiate heat to the whole building.
9. Air, plastic, paper, wool, and cork are insulating materials.
10. Insulation can keep a building cool in summer.

## Exercise 5 Combining Sentences

Use a compound subject, a compound predicate, or a compound sentence to combine each pair of sentences below into a single sentence. Make any changes in wording that are necessary.

### *The Revolution Continues*

1. **a.** The information superhighway is an exciting new road to travel for explorers of all ages.
   **b.** As of the mid-1990s, the end of this electronic journey seems nowhere in sight.
2. **a.** Electronic bulletin boards, available through subscriptions to on-line services, are a relatively recent new product in the computer revolution.
   **b.** CD-ROM's, or compact disks storing huge amounts of data, are another new advance.
3. **a.** Subscribers to electronic bulletin boards can shop for products at the best prices.
   **b.** These subscribers can also play electronic games, check local movie listings, or exchange ideas about political issues with other bulletin board users.
4. **a.** Such rapid, wide-ranging communication may seem almost incredible without extensive equipment.
   **b.** The only hardware requirements are a laptop and a modem connecting the computer to phone lines.
5. **a.** Today's CD-ROM technology permits whole libraries to be stored on a single disk.
   **b.** The technology facilitates the job of researchers by offering convenient, cheap, and rapid access to information.

## 13.4 Complex and Compound-Complex Sentences

A **complex sentence** has one main clause and one or more subordinate clauses.

SUBORDINATE CLAUSE

When I asked for lessons in Japanese,
S V

MAIN CLAUSE

my friend Katsuhiro taught me a few basic words.
S V

SUBORDINATE CLAUSE

Since I now can say "hello" in Japanese,
S V

MAIN CLAUSE | SUBORDINATE CLAUSE

I at least can greet someone who knows only that language.
S V S V

A **compound-complex sentence** has more than one main clause and at least one subordinate clause.

MAIN CLAUSE 1

Ocean currents contain a great deal of energy, and
S V

MAIN CLAUSE 2 | SUBORDINATE CLAUSE

they will produce electricity once we learn to harness them.
S V S V

SUBORDINATE CLAUSE

Because they are caused by ocean-atmosphere interaction,
S V

MAIN CLAUSE 1 | MAIN CLAUSE 2

currents can affect the weather; a recent example is the
S V S V

impact on climate of the Pacific current El Niño.

## Exercise 6 Identifying Complex and Compound-Complex Sentences

Write on your paper the one subordinate clause that appears in each of the following sentences. Indicate whether each sentence is a *complex sentence* or a *compound-complex sentence.*

1. Although everyone wonders about the future, no one can predict it with complete accuracy.
2. Overpopulation is one problem that an increasing number of nations will surely face.
3. Unless pollution is controlled, skies will become more smoggy, and cities will be dirtier.
4. Of course, the world's cities may instead become more pleasant and more beautiful, since urban planners are trying to solve these problems.
5. Many adults may work at home, and children may learn at home on computers, which may become as common to households of the future as televisions are today.
6. Since cars and trucks may be banned from designated areas, people may use bicycles with increasing frequency, or perhaps they will travel by moving ramps.
7. If new food products can be developed, no nation will be unable to sustain itself.
8. If people begin to live healthier, longer lives, they may choose to have several different careers in one lifetime.
9. If travelers wish to cross our country, they may have to do so by train, but the trip may last less than a day.
10. As the passenger rides comfortably in a pressurized car, magnetism will propel the train at speeds of more than four hundred miles per hour.

## Exercise 7 Combining Sentences

Combine each pair or group of sentences below into a complex or compound-complex sentence. Be sure to make the necessary changes in wording.

1. **a.** The elephant-headed god Ganesh is one of the best-loved Hindu divinities.
   **b.** Ganesh's origins are probably in ancient animistic religions.
2. **a.** Ganesh has a round belly and an easy-going personality.
   **b.** He is often worshiped with offerings of sweet cakes.
   **c.** He is pictured in a jolly, dancing posture.
3. **a.** Hindus believe that Ganesh will help them to overcome obstacles.
   **b.** This god is called the lord of obstacles and the lord of beginnings.
4. **a.** His father, the god Shiva, beheaded him.
   **b.** Afterwards, Ganesh received his elephant head.
5. **a.** Ganesh's annual festival is celebrated in September.
   **b.** The holiday is celebrated with special devotion in Bombay.
   **c.** Millions of Hindus turn out to honor the god.

## Exercise 8 Creating Sentences with Various Structures

On your paper write a simple sentence. Then rework it, making it a compound sentence. Go back to the simple sentence, and rework it again to make it part of a complex sentence. Finally, rework your compound sentence into a compound-complex sentence.

## 13.5 Adjective Clauses

**An adjective clause is a subordinate clause that modifies a noun or a pronoun.**

An adjective clause normally follows the word it modifies.

A science-fiction novel **that I really enjoyed** is *The Left Hand of Darkness* by Ursula LeGuin.

LeGuin is an author **whose books have won many awards.**

I prefer writers **who add elements of fantasy to a science-fiction framework.**

Adjective clauses are introduced by relative pronouns (*who, whom, whose, that,* and *which*) or by the subordinating conjunctions *when* and *where.*

*The Left Hand of Darkness* takes place in an era **when the inhabited planets of the universe have been united.**

The main character travels to a planet **whose climate is frigid.**

The relative pronoun is sometimes omitted at the beginning of an adjective clause.

LeGuin has created fictional worlds **I would love to visit.** [The relative pronoun *that* has been omitted.]

When an adjective clause makes the meaning of a sentence clear, it is said to be an *essential clause*, or a *restrictive clause*. Without the essential clause, the complete meaning of the sentence would not be clear.

Ursula LeGuin is an author **who combines magic, politics, and philosophy in her novels.** [essential clause]

An adjective clause that is not needed to make the meaning of a sentence clear is said to be a *nonessential clause*, or a *nonrestrictive clause*. Commas are always used to set off a nonessential clause.

Tennessee Williams, **whose real name was Thomas Lanier Williams,** was born in Mississippi in 1914. [nonessential clause]

In general, use the relative pronoun *that* to introduce an essential clause. Use *which* to introduce a nonessential clause.

Williams grew up in a family environment **that was far from happy.** [essential clause]

Williams's favorite pastime as a youth was reading, **which no doubt helped his career as a playwright.** [nonessential clause]

## Exercise 9 Identifying Adjective Clauses

On your paper write the adjective clause in each of the following sentences. Then write the word that the clause modifies. (In one sentence the relative pronoun has been dropped.)

### *Margaret Bourke-White, Photojournalist*

1. Margaret Bourke-White, who was a photojournalist for *Fortune*, *Time*, and *Life* magazines, became the first woman to serve as a war correspondent.
2. Bourke-White, who was born in New York City in 1904, photographed some of the century's momentous events.
3. The photographs she took as a student at Cornell University featured stone buildings and majestic waterfalls.
4. After her graduation from Cornell, she moved to Cleveland, an important industrial center whose vitality captured her imagination.
5. *Fortune*, a business magazine that exhibited her work, commissioned Bourke-White to photograph various industries.
6. The factory was a place where few had found artistic inspiration, but Bourke-White photographed machines as powerful, beautiful objects.
7. During the Great Depression, a time when drought devastated much of the land, she photographed the barren dust bowl described in the fiction of John Steinbeck.
8. Her work documents the sufferings of the sharecroppers, who endured great poverty during this sad era.
9. During World War II Bourke-White took photographs that captured the emotions of both the soldiers and the civilians in war-torn Europe.
10. The photographs that she took of the Nazi prison camp at Buchenwald serve as a grim memorial to the victims of the Holocaust.

## Exercise 10 Combining Sentences

Use one or more adjective clauses to combine the following pairs or groups of sentences.

### *The Great Barrier Reef*

1. **a.** Coral reefs are underwater mounds or ridges at or slightly below sea level.
   **b.** Reefs are most often found in shallow, tropical waters located along the eastern coasts of continents.
2. **a.** Perhaps the world's most famous example is Australia's Great Barrier Reef.
   **b.** This reef was explored by Captain James Cook in his voyage of discovery on the *Endeavour* in 1770.
3. **a.** Over 350 species of coral polyps are the building blocks of the Great Barrier Reef.
   **b.** Coral polyps are actually small animals related to jellyfish.
4. **a.** Other organisms include algae, mollusks, and sponges.
   **b.** These organisms add material to the reef framework.
5. **a.** The Great Barrier Reef is now a major tourist attraction.
   **b.** Visitors enjoy snorkel excursions and admire the strange and beautiful formations.
   **c.** These formations have built up over millions of years.

## Exercise 11 Recognizing Essential and Nonessential Clauses

For each sentence in the pairs below, write the adjective clause, and then identify it as an *essential* or a *nonessential clause.*

### *Native American Ornaments*

1. **a.** Native American ornaments, which have endured for centuries, bear designs varying from group to group.
   **b.** The designs that are worked into centuries-old Native American ornaments are characteristic of the various cultures.
2. **a.** Chilkat women wove bark and wool into blankets that were decorated with abstract figures.
   **b.** Chilkat women, who inhabited the Pacific Coast of North America, wove abstract figures into their blankets of bark and wool.
3. **a.** The artists of some Plains groups used triangular patterns in their beadwork, which often adorned their clothing.
   **b.** The artists of the Plains groups who excelled in beadwork adorned their clothing with triangular patterns.
4. **a.** The Navajo were probably the Native American people who first used a variety of geometric shapes in their rugs and blankets.
   **b.** The Navajo, who often use wool from their own sheep, weave colorful and beautiful textiles.
5. **a.** Zuñi artists, whose silver jewelry is inlaid with turquoise, jet, coral, and shell, often integrate an eagle or a ceremonial dancer into their designs.
   **b.** The silver jewelry that is characteristic of Zuñi artists is inlaid with turquoise, jet, coral, and shell and often depicts an eagle or a ceremonial dancer.

## Exercise 12 Using Commas in Nonessential Clauses

Rewrite the sentences below, correcting errors in the punctuation of essential and nonessential adjective clauses.

### *What's in a Name?*

1. The Native American words, that give many of our states their names, come from a variety of languages.
2. *Oklahoma*, for example, is a word that comes from the Choctaw language.
3. *Nebraska* comes (appropriately) from *nibhdathka* which was the Omaha name for the "flat river," the Platte.
4. *Minnesota* comes from *mnisota* which meant "cloudy water" for the Dakotas.
5. The Seneca word, that means "beautiful river," is the root of the name Ohio.
6. The French who played a major role in the early exploration of America adapted many words from Native American languages.
7. For example, *Illinois* is a French version of an Algonquian name, that meant "men."
8. The Illinois name, that meant "those with dugout canoes," became *Missouri.*
9. *Arizona* whose name refers to a mining camp comes from a Papago word for "little spring."
10. The Mohegans who gave Connecticut its name used a word, that meant "long river."

## 13.6 Adverb Clauses

An **adverb clause** is a subordinate clause that modifies a verb, an adjective, or an adverb. It tells *when, where, how, why, to what extent,* or *under what conditions.*

> **Whenever she trained,** she ran well. [The adverb clause modifies the verb *ran.* It tells *when.*]
>
> She is happy **as long as she is busy.**[The adverb clause modifies the adjective *happy.* It tells *under what condition.*]
>
> They can jump higher **than we can jump.** [The adverb clause modifies the adverb *higher.* It tells *to what extent.*]

Adverb clauses are introduced by subordinating conjunctions, such as those listed on page 436. An adverb clause that modifies a verb can precede or follow a main clause. If the adverb clause comes first, separate it from the main clause with a comma.

*Elliptical adverb clauses* have words left out of them. You can easily supply the omitted words, however, because they are understood, or implied.

> She can work harder **than I [can work].**
> Exercising made Karen thinner **than [it made] me [thin].**

### Exercise 13 Identifying Adverb Clauses

On your paper write the adverb clause that appears in each of the following sentences. (Two sentences have more than one adverb clause.)

#### *Matthew Henson, Polar Explorer*

1. If ever there was anyone with a taste for adventure, it was Matthew Henson.
2. Wherever Henson went, he courted adventure.
3. Henson's mother and father died before he was nine.
4. Because he did not get along with his guardian, he left home at the age of eleven.
5. He signed on to a ship although he knew nothing about sailing.
6. While the ship lay aground in a Russian harbor, Henson learned to speak Russian and to drive a sleigh.
7. When Henson met Robert Peary, Peary was a civil engineer, although he later became a rear admiral.
8. Since they were venturing into unknown territory, Peary and Henson made several expeditions before they finally succeeded in reaching the North Pole.
9. Peary and Henson reached the North Pole after they had driven a sleigh four hundred miles from their camp.
10. Although Henson received little formal education, he wrote a book about his adventure: *A Negro Explorer at the North Pole.*

# 13.7 Noun Clauses

A **noun clause** is a subordinate clause used as a noun.

A noun clause can be used in the same ways as a noun or a pronoun: as a subject, a direct object, an indirect object, an object of a preposition, or a predicate nominative.

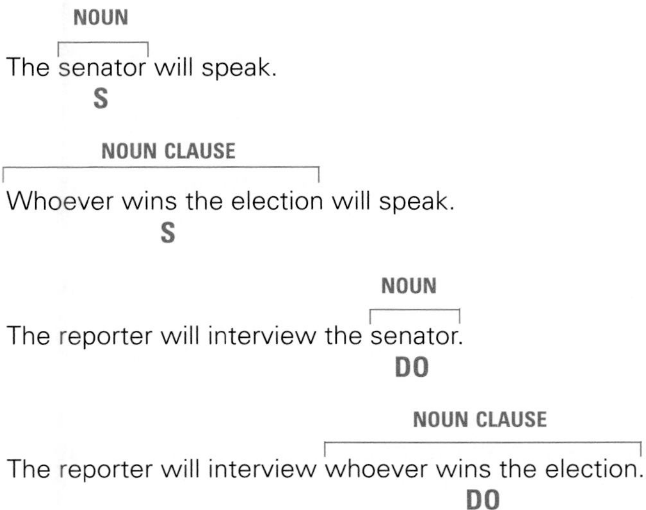

NOUN
The senator will speak.
S
NOUN CLAUSE
Whoever wins the election will speak.
S
NOUN
The reporter will interview the senator.
DO
NOUN CLAUSE
The reporter will interview whoever wins the election.
DO


A noun clause functions as a vital part of a main clause. In the second sentence, for example, the noun clause is the subject of the main clause. In the last sentence the noun clause is the direct object of the main clause.

These are some of the words that can introduce a noun clause:

| | | | |
|---|---|---|---|
| how | whatever | wherever | who, whom |
| if | when | whether | whoever |
| that | whenever | which | whose |
| what | where | whichever | why |

Here are additional examples of sentences with noun clauses.

The senator will give **whoever asks** an interview. [noun clause as an indirect object]

That is **why she included specific data in the article.** [noun clause as a predicate nominative]

A news story should begin with **whatever gets the reader's attention.** [noun clause as an object of a preposition]

The introductory word is sometimes dropped from a noun clause.

I believe **most readers will be confused by this article.** [The relative pronoun *that* has been omitted from the beginning of the clause.]

## Exercise 14 Identifying Noun Clauses

On your paper write the noun clauses that appear in each of the following sentences. (Three of the sentences have two noun clauses each. In one sentence the introductory relative pronoun has been dropped.)

### Women of Achievement, *a Valuable Reference Work*

1. Most people know that women have accomplished a great deal throughout history, but the achievements of many individual women may not be so well known.
2. In their book *Women of Achievement*, Susan Raven and Alison Weir tell what they have learned about many women.
3. Whoever browses through this book will find 475 sketches of notable women from ancient to contemporary times.
4. Readers may marvel at how Raven and Weir assembled such extensive information.
5. That women have excelled in many fields is easily seen from whichever section of the book you choose to read.
6. For example, in the "Travel and Exploration" section you will find whatever you might wish to know about the lives of twenty-three adventurous women.
7. When Hypatia taught and where Florence Nightingale practiced nursing are a few of the book's interesting facts.
8. Whoever is curious about women in war can discover how a young girl in medieval China, Hua Mu-Lan, went to battle dressed as a man and spent twelve years in heavy fighting.
9. The authors believe their book spans the entire range of human achievement.
10. Indeed, the book's comprehensiveness is what makes it a handy reference tool.

## Exercise 15 Identifying the Function of Noun Clauses

On your paper label each of the italicized noun clauses in the sentences below as *subject*, *direct object*, *predicate nominative*, or *object of a preposition*.

### *The Uses of Murals*

1. *How artists through the ages have put mural painting to a variety of uses* is an intriguing subject.
2. A mural, strictly speaking, is *whatever is painted on a wall for decoration.*
3. Historians believe *the earliest examples of murals are the prehistoric cave paintings at Lascaux in France and Altamira in Spain.*
4. In *what experts hailed as a stunning discovery in late 1994*, a cave at Chauvet in southern France yielded fresh prehistoric masterpieces.
5. No one can be certain of *what the Stone Age artists intended.*
6. *Whoever has studied ancient Egyptian, Greek, and Roman art* knows the importance of wall painting in those cultures.
7. *That religious beliefs played a major role in these murals* is not in doubt.
8. Renaissance Europe was *where mural painting, in the form of fresco, may have reached its height.*
9. Some twentieth-century artists and political leaders have believed *that mural painting should serve social aims.*
10. For example, the Mexican muralists Diego Rivera and José Clemente Orozco considered *whatever would promote the good of society* as a fitting subject for their work.

## Exercise 16 Using Noun Clauses to Create Sentences

Write a sentence using each of the following as a noun clause with the function shown in parentheses.

### *Political Concerns*

1. where the election will be held (predicate nominative)
2. whether the senator will win reelection (direct object)
3. whoever participates in the park cleanup (indirect object)
4. why the legislature voted against the pay raise (object of a preposition)
5. that the antipollution measures would be passed by the senate (direct object)
6. what makes the senator so popular (predicate nominative)
7. how the tax debate should be handled (subject)
8. what can be done to stir support for library expansion (subject)
9. whatever will benefit the most people (object of a preposition)
10. whoever is interested in working on the campaign (indirect object)

## Exercise 17 Using Subordinate Clauses in Sentences

Write four original sentences. In the first use an adverb clause. In the second use an adjective clause. In the third use a noun clause as a subject. In the fourth use a noun clause as a direct object.

## Exercise 18 Clauses

On your paper write the subordinate clause that appears in each sentence. Then indicate whether the subordinate clause is (a) an *adverb clause*, (b) an *adjective clause*, or (c) a *noun clause*.

### *Baseball's Sublime and Ridiculous Plays*

[1]Baseball's spectacular defensive plays occur when players catch balls seemingly out of reach. [2]An outfielder may leap and catch a fly ball that looks like a sure home run. [3]Another time an infielder may dive to the ground to snag a ball that everyone in the park expects to be a base hit. [4]Whoever loves baseball is thrilled to watch a sprinting outfielder run down a fly ball four hundred feet from home plate. [5]On the other hand, what looks like an ordinary play sometimes turns truly ridiculous. [6]One afternoon in 1948 when a Boston Red Sox batter hit a ground ball toward Eddie Joost of the Philadelphia Athletics, the ball hit Joost's glove, rolled up his arm, and disappeared into his sleeve. [7]The bewildered shortstop frantically searched everywhere before he found the ball in his shirt. [8]As Joost pulled his shirttail out of his pants, the stubborn ball dropped to the ground and rolled away from him. [9]Ted Williams, who was the runner on third base and could have scored easily, was laughing too hard to run. [10]Fans might well wonder where in all of baseball history they could find a more ludicrous play.

## 13.8 Four Kinds of Sentences

**A declarative sentence makes a statement.**

Spinal injuries are serious.
The human backbone has thirty-three bones.

The declarative sentence is used more frequently than any other kind of sentence. It normally ends with a period.

**An imperative sentence gives a command or makes a request.**

Stand up straight.
Please use your muscles.

In an imperative sentence the subject "you" is understood. Imperative sentences usually end with a period, but if the imperative expresses strong emotion, it will end with an exclamation point.

**An interrogative sentence asks a question.**

Does your back hurt? What is the best exercise?

An interrogative sentence ends with a question mark.

**An exclamatory sentence expresses strong emotion.**

How terrific you look! What an excellent idea that is!

An exclamatory sentence ends with an exclamation point.

### Exercise 19 Identifying Kinds of Sentences

On your paper, identify each of the following sentences as *declarative*, *imperative*, *interrogative*, or *exclamatory*.

1. Think for a moment about cars' latest accessories.
2. Among these options are air bags, which may add $1,000 to the sticker price.
3. Do you know how many cars are now sold with air bags?
4. What life-savers these air bags can be!
5. During an accident an air bag automatically inflates.
6. Air bags protect drivers by surrounding their bodies with a cushion of air.
7. It's too bad an air bag can be used only once!
8. Can car owners install new air bags themsleves?
9. Take your car to an authorized dealer for proper installation of a new air bag.
10. Relax and drive safely!

### Exercise 20 Creating Four Kinds of Sentences

Write four sentences about a recent news event. Use one declarative, one imperative, one interrogative, and one exclamatory sentence.

## 13.9 Sentence Fragments

A **sentence fragment** is an error that occurs when an incomplete sentence is punctuated as though it were complete.

When checking for sentence fragments, look for a group of words without a subject. Then look for a group of words without a complete verb. Look especially for a word group that includes a verbal—a participle, gerund, or infinitive—rather than a complete verb. Finally, be sure you haven't punctuated a subordinate clause as if it were a complete sentence.

| | |
|---|---|
| FRAGMENT | In many families both parents work. **Need two incomes**. [lacks subject] |
| COMPLETE SENTENCE | In many families both parents work because the family needs two incomes. |
| FRAGMENT | **Sometimes two or three generations of one family living together.** [lacks a complete verb] |
| COMPLETE SENTENCE | Sometimes two or three generations of one family live together. |
| FRAGMENT | The simplest family group is the nuclear family. **Which consists of parents and children.** [has subordinate clause only] |
| COMPLETE SENTENCE | The simplest family group is the nuclear family, which consists of parents and children. |

Professional writers sometimes use sentence fragments for special purposes. They might want to create lifelike conversation or make a particular point. Keep in mind that professionals use sentence fragments carefully and intentionally. Generally, you should avoid sentence fragments in most of your writing, including your writing for school.

### Exercise 21 Identifying Sentence Fragments

Read the following paragraph. Then indicate on your paper whether each of the numbered items is a *complete sentence* or a *sentence fragment.*

*Richard Rodriguez, Award-Winning Writer*

[1]When he entered elementary school as a child in California knew only about fifty words of English. [2]Because he was afraid he would be mocked, Richard Rodriguez was reluctant to speak in class. [3]The nuns who taught him asked his parents, who had been born in Mexico, to speak to the child in English rather than in Spanish. [4]Rodriguez developed a deep love of reading. [5]Which became the basis of his later academic success.

## 13.10 Run-on Sentences

Avoid run-on sentences in your writing. A **run-on sentence** is two or more complete sentences written as though they were one sentence.

The following are the three basic kinds of run-on sentences:

1. The most common run-on sentence is a **comma splice.** It occurs when two main clauses are punctuated by a comma rather than a semicolon or a period. To correct a comma splice, add a coordinating conjunction, or replace the comma with an end mark of punctuation, such as a period or a question mark, and begin the new sentence with a capital letter.

| | |
|---|---|
| RUN-ON | Edgar Allan Poe's stories are thrilling, Agatha Christie's mysteries are more realistic. |
| CORRECT | Edgar Allan Poe's stories are thrilling**, but** Agatha Christie's mysteries are more realistic. |
| CORRECT | Edgar Allan Poe's stories are thrilling**.** Agatha Christie's mysteries are more realistic. |

2. A second kind of run-on sentence is created when *no* punctuation separates two main clauses. Correct this kind of run-on by inserting a semicolon or an end mark of punctuation between the main clauses. You can also correct the error by separating the clauses with a comma and a coordinating conjunction.

| | |
|---|---|
| RUN-ON | C. Auguste Dupin is the name of Poe's famous detective he is similar in some ways to Christie's sleuth Hercule Poirot. |
| CORRECT | C. Auguste Dupin is the name of Poe's famous detective**;** he is similar in some ways to Christie's sleuth Hercule Poirot. |
| CORRECT | C. Auguste Dupin is the name of Poe's famous detective**.** He is similar in some ways to Christie's sleuth Hercule Poirot. |
| CORRECT | C. Auguste Dupin is the name of Poe's famous detective**, and** he is similar in some ways to Christie's sleuth Hercule Poirot. |

3. A third kind of run-on sentence is formed when there is no comma before a coordinating conjunction joining two main clauses. Correct the error by inserting the comma before the coordinating conjunction.

| | |
|---|---|
| RUN-ON | Poe's Dupin is the first great amateur detective but Christie's Poirot is probably more widely known. |
| CORRECT | Poe's Dupin is the first great amateur detective**,** but Christie's Poirot is probably more widely known. |

## Exercise 22 Correcting Run-on Sentences

Rewrite each of the following sentences, correcting the run-ons. Watch for the three kinds of run-on errors just shown. You may choose from among the several ways of correcting run-ons that you have learned.

### *Eleanor Roosevelt, First Lady of the World*

1. Eleanor Roosevelt was the wife of President Franklin D. Roosevelt yet she became famous for her own achievements.
2. Mrs. Roosevelt was interested in social reform, no other First Lady had ever been so active in public life.
3. At birth she was named Anne Eleanor but no one called her by her first name.
4. Her husband was crippled by polio in 1921, she became involved in political work on his behalf.
5. During World War II she traveled in Latin America, Europe, and elsewhere and she worked with young people.
6. She was devoted to the underprivileged and fighting for equal rights was one of her central concerns.
7. Mrs. Roosevelt visited places that were inaccessible to her husband for example, she personally inspected working conditions in coal mines.
8. She was appointed the United States delegate to the United Nations by President Harry Truman he called her the First Lady of the World.
9. She wrote over a dozen books among them was an autobiography.
10. Her books include *This Is My Story* (1937) and *On My Own* (1958), she also wrote *Tomorrow Is Now,* which was published after her death.

## Exercise 23 Correcting Run-on Sentences

Rewrite each of the following sentences, correcting any run-ons. You may choose from the several ways of correcting run-ons that you have learned. If a sentence is correct as it stands, write *correct.*

### *Raccoons and Their Relatives*

1. The distribution of the raccoon extends from southern Canada to Central America and these playful, mischievous creatures are familiar to most people.
2. Who has not seen the black, foxlike mask of a raccoon near the garbage barrels at night who has failed to chuckle at the ingenuity with which these animals figure out ways to hoodwink humans?
3. The word *raccoon* is derived from the Algonquian word *aroughcun*, this word can be translated as "one who rubs or scratches with the hands."
4. The animal's manual dexterity clearly impressed Native Americans, and it is striking that more than twenty names for the raccoon have approximately the same meaning.
5. Equally impressive is the animal's adaptability and it is this characteristic of the raccoon that stands out in many Native American legends and folktales.
6. Young raccoons may make charming pets but their curiosity and destructiveness as adults can be extremely irritating. ➡

7. Recently there has been ample cause to be wary of wild raccoons; some of them have been shown to be suffering from rabies.
8. Raccoons are the best-known members of the family of carnivores called Procyonids; this family also includes several other, less familiar species.
9. Experts argue over whether the giant panda is really a member of the raccoon or the bear family but there is no dispute that its much smaller cousin, the red panda, is a true Procyonid.
10. For many years this animal was the only panda known to science after the discovery of the giant panda in 1869, however, it was overshadowed by its larger relative.
11. Confined to a small area of the Himalayas and southern China, red pandas are nocturnal their habits are consequently hard to study.
12. Red pandas, like raccoons, are very good climbers, and they probably do most of their foraging in trees.
13. Another relative of the raccoon is the ringtail, this small Procyonid lives closer to home in the western United States.
14. In the Old West, prospectors and miners often reared ringtails as companions and mousers in their camps; even today, the animal carries the nickname "miner's cat."
15. Two less familiar relatives of the raccoon live in Central and South America these are the olingo and the kinkajou.
16. These animals are quite similar in their appearance and habits for example, both kinkajous and olingos are active at night and eat fruit.
17. Both species have short legs and long, slim bodies, and both weigh anywhere from four to six pounds.
18 These similarities are striking but upon closer inspection the two species also have important differences.
19. For example, the kinkajou has a short-haired, prehensile tail the olingo's tail, on the other hand, is bushy and nonprehensile.
20. Although little is known about these nocturnal animals, kinkajous seem to restrict their diet to fruits and other foods containing sugar, olingos supplement this diet with insects, small mammals, and birds.

## Exercise 24 Punctuating a Passage

Sometimes a writer will ignore the customary rules of usage for special effect. Read the following passage from James Joyce's novel *Ulysses*, with special attention to the second paragraph. In this paragraph, notice that Joyce presents the speaker's words indirectly in one long run-on sentence. Rewrite the second paragraph, inserting punctuation and adding or deleting words to create sentences of reasonable length. Then compare your version with the original. Get together with a small group of classmates and discuss why Joyce might have chosen to write the passage this way. What tone or effect might the author have been trying to create?

No, Mr. Bloom repeated again, I wouldn't personally repose much trust in that boon companion of yours who contributes the humorous element, Dr. Mulligan, as a guide, philosopher and friend if I were in your shoes. He knows which side his bread is buttered ➡

on though in all probability he never realized what it is to be without regular meals. Of course you didn't notice as much as I did. But it wouldn't occasion me the least surprise to learn that a pinch of tobacco or some narcotic was put in your drink for some ulterior object.

He understood however from all he heard that Dr. Mulligan was a versatile all-round man, by no means confined to medicine only, who was rapidly coming to the fore in his line and, if the report was verified, bade fair to enjoy a flourishing practice in the not too distant future as a tony medical practitioner drawing a handsome fee for his services in addition to which professional status his rescue of that man from certain drowning by artificial respiration and what they call first aid at Skerries, or Malahide was it? was, he was bound to admit, an exceedingly plucky deed which he could not too highly praise, so that frankly he was utterly at a loss to fathom what earthly reason could be at the back of it except he put it down to sheer cussedness or jealousy, pure and simple.

## Exercise 25 Sentence Completeness

Rewrite the following paragraphs, correcting all sentence fragments and run-on sentences.

### *Benjamin Banneker, Colonial Mathematician*

[1]Benjamin Banneker, who lived from 1731 to 1806, known to historians as an important African American man of science. [2]The unschooled son of a formerly enslaved person. [3]He was fascinated by mathematical puzzles and games he even built a working clock. [4]Which he made out of carved wood after briefly examining a pocket watch and which kept accurate time for more than forty years. [5]In 1791 Banneker helped survey a ten-square-mile area of land, the Federal Territory, this became the District of Columbia, the site of the nation's capital. [6]Increasingly interested in astronomy, he calculated tables predicting the movements of the stars and this work was published in a 1792 almanac. [7]A remarkable achievement for a self-educated person. [8]Banneker's tables were published in almanacs for six years and they appeared in twenty-nine separate editions during this period. [9]Abolitionists viewing Banneker's achievements as a powerful argument against the institution of slavery. [10]Memorialized when Banneker Circle, in Washington, D.C., was named in his honor.

### *America's Library, the Library of Congress*

[1]Established to serve Congress in Washington, D.C., in 1800. [2]The Library of Congress is now the world's largest library, it holds more than ten million items. [3]Thomas Jefferson's personal library, acquired in 1814, and the Smithsonian collection, acquired in 1866, housed in three buildings near the Capitol. [4]Now the huge collection serves as a public reference library and it is a depository that receives and stores copies of all printed works submitted for copyright. [5]Part of its function, to issue copyrights for the United States under the national copyright laws. [6]Now considered a standard for library cataloging, the Library of Congress classification system used by most large university and municipal libraries. [7]Also issues duplicate catalog cards to subscribing libraries. [8]Exhibition areas offer displays of American literary and historical interest, they are open to the public during regular library hours and often travel to other libraries and museums. [9]Special performances have showcased American music, films, and visual art for the library is more than a storehouse of books. [10]Travelers on the information highway can even visit the Library of Congress by accessing the World Wide Website named after Thomas Jefferson, Users just enter

UNIT 13

Unit Review

# Grammar Review

## Clauses and Sentence Structure

Oscar Wilde's novel tells the story of Dorian Gray, a young English aristocrat whose extraordinary looks are both his pride and his downfall. When an artist paints a picture of Dorian, the portrait entrances the young man. He prays that the picture might age and that he might remain young. In this passage Dorian discovers that his plea has been granted. The passage has been annotated to show some of the kinds of clauses and sentences covered in this unit.

### Literature Model

#### *from* THE PICTURE OF DORIAN GRAY

***by Oscar Wilde***

Complex sentence — As he was turning the handle of the door, his eye fell upon the portrait Basil Hallward had painted of him. He started back as if in surprise. Then he went on into his own room, looking somewhat puzzled. After he had taken the buttonhole [flower] out of his coat, he seemed to hesitate. Finally he came back, went over to the picture, and examined it. In the dim arrested light that struggled through the cream-colored silk blinds, the face appeared to him to be a little changed. The expression looked different. One would have said that there was a touch of cruelty in the mouth. It was certainly strange.

(Adjective clause: that struggled through the cream-colored silk blinds)

(Noun clause: that there was a touch of cruelty in the mouth)

Declarative sentence — He turned round, and, walking to the window, drew up the blind. The bright dawn flooded the room, and swept the fantastic shadows into dusky corners, where they lay shuddering. But the strange expression that he had noticed in the face of the portrait seemed to linger there, to be more intensified even. The quivering, ardent sunlight showed him the lines of cruelty round the mouth as clearly as if he had been looking into a mirror after he had done some dreadful thing. . . .

(Adverb clause: after he had done some dreadful thing)

He rubbed his eyes, and came close to the picture, and examined it again. There were no signs of any change when he looked into the actual painting, and yet there was →

(Compound-complex sentence: There were no signs of any change when he looked into the actual painting, and yet there was) no doubt that the whole expression had altered. It was not a mere fancy of his own. The thing was horribly apparent.

He threw himself into a chair, and began to think. Suddenly there flashed across his mind what he had said in Basil Hallward's studio the day the picture had been finished. Yes, he remembered it perfectly. He had uttered a mad wish that he himself might remain young, and the portrait grow old; that his own beauty might be untarnished, and the face on the canvas bear the burden of his passions and his sins; that the painted image might be seared with the lines of suffering and thought, and that he might keep all the delicate bloom and loveliness of his then just conscious boyhood. Surely his wish had not been fulfilled? Such things were impossible. It seemed monstrous even to think of them. And, yet, there was the picture before him, with the touch of cruelty in the mouth.

❦

He got up from his chair, and drew a large screen right in front of the portrait, shuddering as he glanced at it. "How horrible!" he murmured to himself, and he walked across to the window and opened it.

Simple sentence

Interrogative sentence

Compound sentence

## Exercise 1

**Identifying Main and Subordinate Clauses** The following sentences are based on the passage from *The Picture of Dorian Gray* and on an earlier section of the novel that is not reprinted in this textbook. Each sentence contains a clause that appears in italics. On your paper indicate whether the italicized clause is a *main clause* or a *subordinate clause.*

1. *Dorian Gray*, who was quite wealthy, *did not work.*
2. Instead, he whiled away his days indulging in activities *that brought him pleasure.*
3. Many evenings found him at the theater *because he had fallen in love with a remarkably beautiful actress.*
4. *One morning he arrived home* as dawn was breaking.
5. He passed through the library, *where his portrait hung.*
6. *That night he had rejected the actress*, whom he had been wooing enthusiastically for a period of several months.
7. When he looked at his portrait, *Dorian detected a hint of cruelty around the mouth.*
8. Then he remembered *what he had said to the painter about remaining young and handsome despite the passage of time.*
9. Had the portrait changed *while his face remained the same?*
10. *Although such an occurrence seemed impossible*, it was the only explanation of the portrait's appearance.

## Exercise 2

**Identifying Compound, Complex, and Compound-Complex Sentences** The following sentences are about famous portraits. On your paper indicate whether each is a *compound*, *complex*, or *compound-complex* sentence.

1. Although the picture of Dorian Gray may be the most famous portrait in fiction, many real portraits are better known.
2. The world's most renowned portraits span many centuries, and they reflect many different styles of art.
3. Leonardo da Vinci believed that an artist should reveal his subject's emotions, yet his famed Mona Lisa is best known for her mysterious smile.
4. Hans Holbein, who painted England's Henry VIII, captured the power of his subject rather than his emotions.
5. Some see James Whistler's portrait of his mother as a tribute to motherhood, but the artist was actually more interested in the painting's arrangement of shapes and colors.

## Exercise 3

**Writing Sentences with Adjective Clauses** The sentences that follow elaborate on ideas suggested by the passage from *The Picture of Dorian Gray.* Rewrite each sentence, adding an adjective clause that answers the question in parentheses. Your clause must begin with one of the words listed below, and it must contain a verb. Your sentence should make sense within the context of the passage, but you should not use the exact wording from the passage.

**RELATIVE PRONOUNS** who whom whose which that
**SUBORDINATING CONJUNCTIONS** when where

**SAMPLE** Dorian glanced at the portrait. (What was he doing as he glanced at the portrait?)
**ANSWER** Dorian, who was turning the handle of the door, glanced at the portrait.

1. Dorian carefully studied the painting. (What was Dorian's manner?)
2. Dorian was startled by the expression. (Where did he see the expression?)
3. Dorian opened the blinds. (Where were the blinds?)
4. The change in the portrait was now obvious. (When had the change appeared vague?)
5. The face stared back at Dorian. (What did Dorian notice around the mouth?)
6. Suddenly he remembered his words to Basil Hallward. (What did Basil Hallward have to do with the portrait?)
7. Dorian had voiced a dark and private wish to Hallward on that fateful day. (On what day had Dorian voiced a wish to Hallward?)
8. Dorian wished he would remain young, unlike the portrait. (What would happen to the portrait?)
9. The wish had apparently come true. (Did the wish seem possible?)
10. Dorian placed a screen in front of the portrait. (How did he feel about the portrait?)

## Exercise 4

**Writing Sentences with Adverb Clauses** The sentences that follow elaborate on ideas suggested by the passage from *The Picture of Dorian Gray*. Rewrite each sentence, adding an adverb clause that answers the question in parentheses. Your clause must begin with one of the subordinating conjunctions listed below, and it must contain a verb. The sentence should make sense within the context of the passage, but you should not use the exact wording from the passage. There may be more than one correct answer.

**SUBORDINATING CONJUNCTIONS**

| | | | | | |
|---|---|---|---|---|---|
| after | as | as long as | since | than | when |
| although | as if | because | so that | until | while |

**SAMPLE** Dorian looked surprised. (When?)
**ANSWER** Dorian looked surprised when he saw his portrait.

1. He returned to the portrait. (When?)
2. The light in the room was dim. (Why?)
3. In daylight the expression of the face seemed more intense. (Compared to what?)
4. The face in the portrait looked changed. (In what way?)
5. He recalled the words he had spoken to Basil Hallward. (When?)
6. He had gone to Basil's studio. (Why?)
7. His face would keep its beauty. (When?)
8. Dorian wanted to remain youthful. (Why?)
9. Dorian placed a screen in front of the portrait. (Why?)
10. Dorian shuddered. (When?)

## Exercise 5

**Identifying Noun Clauses** The following sentences describe England's Victorian Age, when *The Picture of Dorian Gray* was written. On your paper write the noun clauses that appear in the sentences. One sentence has two noun clauses.

1. Many people believe that the Victorians embraced a rigid moral code.
2. Whoever reads books about the period will discover that this is only partly true.
3. What the newly emerging middle class valued highly was respect for authority.
4. Queen Victoria condemned whatever did not reflect her strict standards.
5. Victoria's blameless life explains why the prestige of the monarchy increased during her reign.
6. Whatever Victoria and her husband Albert did met with approval.
7. What helped the British monarchy was Victoria's willingness to change.
8. She accepted that the monarchy must reduce its powers and rely on Parliament to govern.
9. During this period Parliament was concerned with how labor conditions could be improved.
10. One new law required that all children attend school.

## Exercise 6

**Writing Four Kinds of Sentences** On your paper identify each of the sentences below as *declarative*, *imperative*, *interrogative*, or *exclamatory*. Then rewrite each sentence in the form noted in parentheses.

**SAMPLE** Dorian Gray saw a change in the portrait. (Rewrite as an interrogative sentence.)
**ANSWER** declarative
Did Dorian Gray see a change in the portrait?

1. Dorian had a puzzled look on his face. (Rewrite as an exclamatory sentence.)
2. Did he raise the blinds? (Rewrite as an imperative sentence.)
3. How strange the face in the portrait seems! (Rewrite as a declarative sentence.)
4. The lines around the mouth seemed cruel. (Rewrite as an interrogative sentence.)
5. Could this change be the result of what Dorian had said to Basil Hallward? (Rewrite as a declarative sentence.)

## Exercise 7

**Correcting Sentence Fragments and Run-Ons** The following paragraph describes a scene from *The Picture of Dorian Gray* not reprinted in this textbook. Revise the paragraph, correcting any sentence fragments or run-ons. The fragments may be corrected by combining sentences, by adding words (such as a subject or a verb), or by changing the form of the verb. The run-ons may be corrected in several ways.

[1]Dorian living in constant fear of the portrait's secret. [2]One day Basil Hallward came to visit Dorian, he wanted to exhibit the portrait in a show. [3]Dorian's threat never to speak to Basil again if Basil insisted on looking at the portrait. [4]The artist wanted to see the portrait again however he valued Dorian's friendship. [5]He yielded to Dorian's wishes he asked Dorian to sit for another portrait. [6]Dorian's answer astonishing. [7]That he would never sit for Basil again. [8]The artist left, Dorian moved the portrait to a locked room. [9]To which he alone had the key. [10]There the portrait unseen while Dorian remained perpetually youthful.

Proofreading

## Exercise 8

**Proofreading** The passage below describes William Merritt Chase, whose work appears on this page. Rewrite the passage, correcting the errors in spelling, grammar, and usage. Add any missing punctuation. There are ten errors.

### *William Merritt Chase*

[1]Born in Indiana, William Merritt Chase (1849–1916) one of America's great realistic painters. [2]After studying at the National Academy of Design which was located in New York City, Chase moved to Missouri. [3]There his carefully rendered pictures impressed local patrons, they provided Chase with the funds to study abroad. [4]Chase settled in Munich in 1872 and studied painting there for five years, then he returned to New York to teach.

[5]Chases paintings are eclectic, spanning a wide range of subjects. [6]Chase, who was influenced by Diego Velázquez was renowned for his dark palette and his brushwork. [7]*Portrait of a Man* illustrates Chase's tecknical skill. [8]The contrasts between light and dark creates a powerful mood. [9]The result a brooding, almost sinister portrait. [10]To readers of Oscar Wilde's novel, might this face suggest the macabre portrait of Dorian Gray

**William Merritt Chase, *Portrait of a Man*, 1873–1876**

**Exercise 9**

## Mixed Review

**Mixed Review** The items that follow describe aspects of Oscar Wilde's life and writings. On a separate sheet of paper, revise each item according to the directions in parentheses.

**SAMPLE** Oscar Wilde came from a comfortable middle-class background. He was born in Dublin in 1854. (Combine the sentences by turning the second sentence into an adjective clause beginning with *who.*)

**ANSWER** Oscar Wilde, who was born in Dublin in 1854, came from a comfortable middle-class background.

1. His father was a well-known surgeon, and his mother was a poet. Her special interest was Irish folklore. (Rewrite as a compound-complex sentence.)
2. While attending Oxford, Wilde decided something. He would devote his life to literature. (Combine the sentences by turning the second sentence into a noun clause beginning with *that.*)
3. Wilde soon became well-known in London society. Many people outraged by his flamboyant comments and behavior. (Eliminate the sentence fragment.)
4. It is true that Wilde was not a humble man. (Rewrite as an interrogative sentence.)
5. When Wilde visited New York in 1882, a customs official asked him something. Did he have anything to declare? (Combine the sentences by turning the second sentence into a noun clause beginning with *whether.*)
6. Wilde replied. He had nothing to declare except his genius. (Rewrite as a complex sentence.)
7. In 1884 Wilde married Constance Lloyd they later had two sons. (Correct the run-on.)
8. Shortly after his first son's birth, Wilde wrote a fairy tale. It was widely praised. (Rewrite as a complex sentence.)
9. Wilde wrote four hilarious social comedies one in particular, *The Importance of Being Earnest*, is considered a work of genius. (Correct the run-on.)
10. There is more to the play than humorous dialogue, however, for it also offers an amusing picture of Victorian society. That picture may be greatly exaggerated. (Rewrite as a compound-complex sentence.)
11. In Victorian times the cult of sincerity or earnestness was often a facade. It concealed materialistic complacency. (Combine the sentences by turning the second sentence into an adjective clause beginning with *that.*)
12. *The Importance of Being Earnest* was first performed in 1895. Audiences were amused by Wilde's witty epigrams. (Combine the sentences by turning the first sentence into an adverb clause beginning with *when.*)
13. Many of the characters in the play spoke nonsense, it was clear that this dialogue was meant to satirize the Victorian upper classes. (Correct the run-on.)
14. In this topical satire many elements from traditional comedies. (Correct this sentence fragment.)
15. Most critics believe this comedy of manners is Wilde's most accomplished play. (Rewrite this sentence adding the word omitted from the beginning of the noun clause.)

# Writing Application

**Sentence Structure in Writing** Carefully study the following paragraph from James Joyce's short story "Araby." In it Joyce uses a variety of sentence structures to develop rhythms that complement the mood.

> When I came home to dinner my uncle had not yet been home. Still it was early. I sat staring at the clock for some time, and when its ticking began to irritate me, I left the room. I mounted the staircase and gained the upper part of the house. The high cold empty rooms liberated me and I went from room to room singing. From the front window I saw my companions playing below in the street. The cries reached me weakened and indistinct and, leaning my forehead against the cool glass, I looked over at the dark house where she lived. I may have stood there for an hour seeing nothing but the brown-clad figure cast by my imagination, touched discreetly by the lamplight at the curved neck, at the hand upon the railings and at the border below the dress.

**Techniques with Sentence Structure** Try to apply some of James Joyce's writing techniques when you write and revise your own work.

1. Avoid using a monotonous series of similar sentence structures. Notice, for example, how Joyce consistently varies simple sentences with other, more complicated sentence structures.

**Monotonous** When I came home to dinner my uncle had not yet been home. Because it was still early, I sat staring at the clock for some time. When its ticking began to irritate me, I left the room.
**Joyce's Version** When I came home to dinner my uncle had not yet been home. Still it was early. I sat staring at the clock for some time, and when its ticking began to irritate me, I left the room.

2. Use sentence structures that create a rhythm appropriate for your content. Notice how Joyce's structure in the first six sentences creates a staccato rhythm that emphasizes the boy's restlessness. By contrast, the last two sentences have an entirely different rhythm—slow and meandering—that evokes the boy's daydreams.

**Practice** Apply these techniques when revising the following series of simple sentences adapted from "Araby." Try to create an alternating rhythm between simple sentences and more complicated sentence structures. Also try to arrange your clauses so that they will create sound clusters conveying a mood of restlessness.

At nine o'clock I heard my uncle's latchkey in the hall door. I heard him talking to himself. I heard the hallstand rocking. It had received the weight of his overcoat. I could interpret these signs. He was midway through his dinner. I asked him to give me the money to go to the bazaar. He had forgotten.

UNIT 14

# Diagraming Sentences

Grammar

## Lessons

# 14.1 Diagraming Simple Sentences

**Diagraming** is a method of showing the relationship of various words and parts of a sentence to the sentence as a whole.

You begin to diagram a sentence by finding the simple subject. Next, find the action or linking verb that goes with the subject. Write the subject and the verb on a horizontal line. Separate them with a vertical line to indicate the division between the subject and the predicate.

Whales swim.

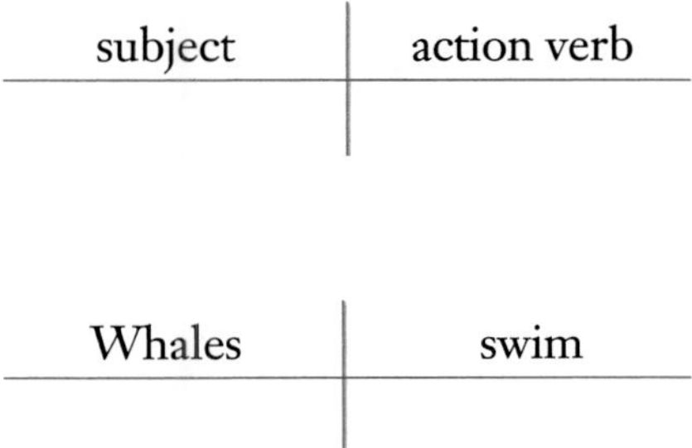


## Adjectives and Adverbs

To diagram a simple sentence with adjectives and adverbs, follow the model diagram below.

The much larger whales swim more slowly.

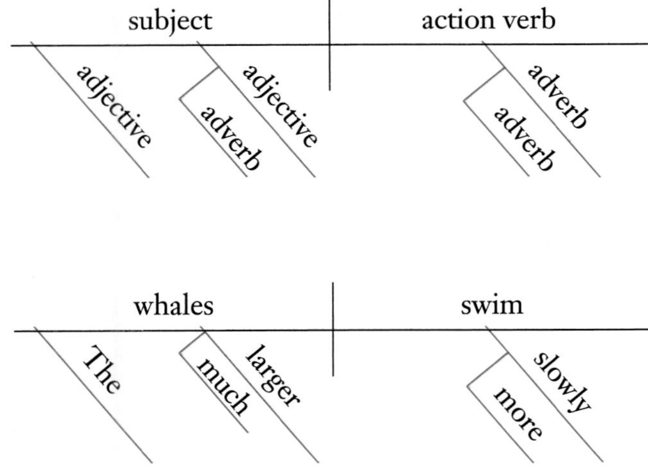

## Direct Objects and Indirect Objects

To diagram a simple sentence with an indirect object and a direct object, follow the model diagram below.

The mother whales feed their infants milk.

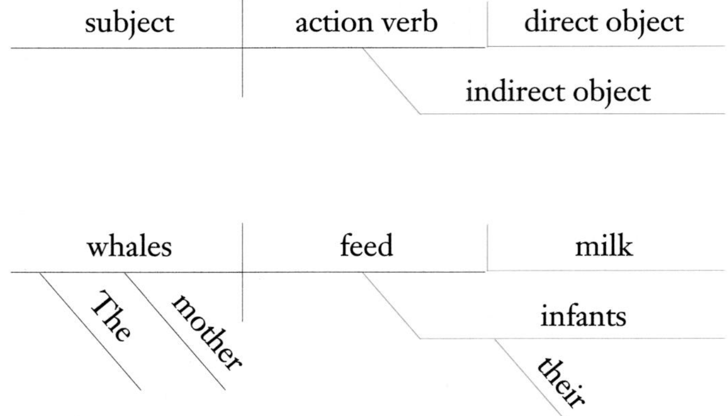


## Object Complements

To diagram a simple sentence with a compound subject, a direct object, and an object complement, follow the model diagram below. If the simple subjects in a compound subject are connected by a coordinating conjunction, place the conjunction on a dotted vertical line between the subjects. If the simple subjects are connected by a correlative conjunction, such as *both . . . and* or *either . . . or*, place the first part of the conjunction on one side of the line and the second part on the other.

Biologists and naturalists consider whales vulnerable.

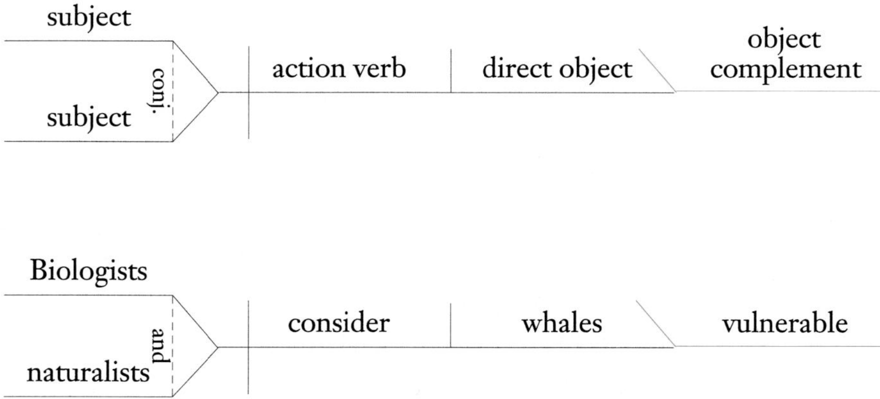

## Subject Complements

To diagram a simple sentence with a subject complement (a predicate nominative or a predicate adjective), follow the model diagrams below.

Whales are the largest mammals.

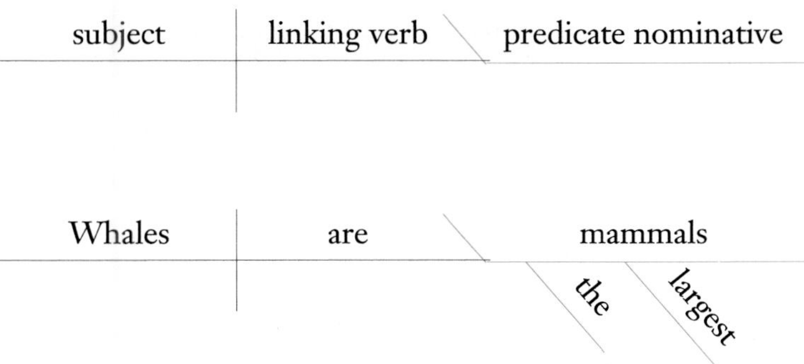


Whales are both friendly and intelligent.

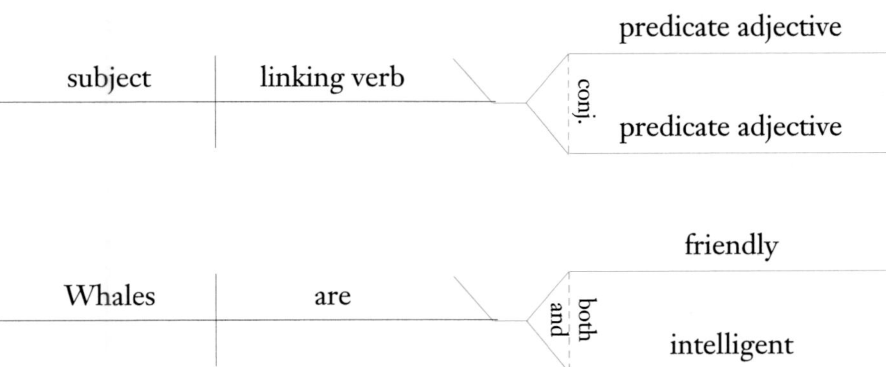


**Exercise 1** **Diagraming Simple Sentences**

Using the preceding models as a guide, diagram the following sentences.

1. The sea prospers.
2. The larger whales certainly have extraordinary appetites.
3. The sea feeds huge whales tiny plankton.
4. The scientists call the whales cetaceans.
5. Some whales seem both inquisitive and playful.

# 14.2 Diagraming Simple Sentences with Phrases

## Prepositional Phrases

Place the preposition on a diagonal line that descends from the word the prepositional phrase modifies. Place the object of the preposition on a horizontal line that extends from the diagonal. The diagonal line on which the preposition is placed should extend somewhat beyond the horizontal on which the object of the preposition is placed, forming a "tail."

Lawyers in criminal cases create sympathy for the defendant in the minds of jurors.

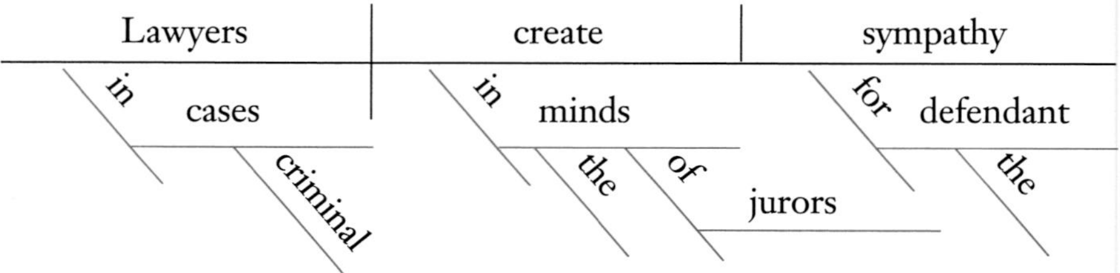


## Appositives and Appositive Phrases

Place an appositive in parentheses after the noun or pronoun it identifies. Beneath it add any words that modify the appositive. Any words that modify the noun or pronoun itself, and not the appositive, should be placed directly beneath the noun or pronoun.

The jury, a group of twelve citizens, must reach a unanimous verdict.

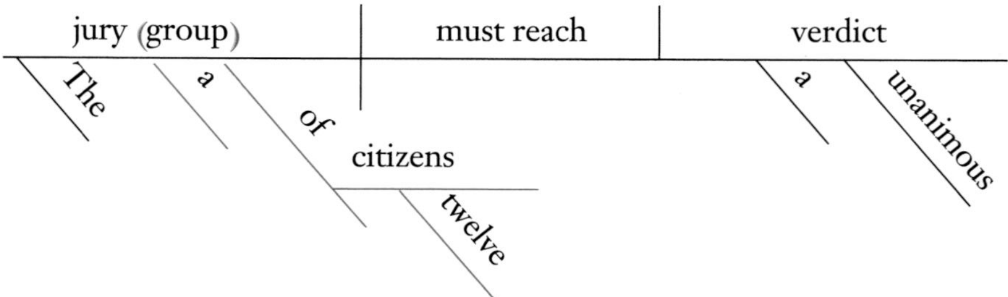

## Participles and Participial Phrases

The line on which the participle is placed descends diagonally from the word the participle modifies and then extends to the right horizontally. The participle is written on the curve, as shown below. Add any modifiers and complements to the horizontal line in the same way that you would show the modifiers and complements of an action verb.

Losing composure, the defendant admitted her guilt.

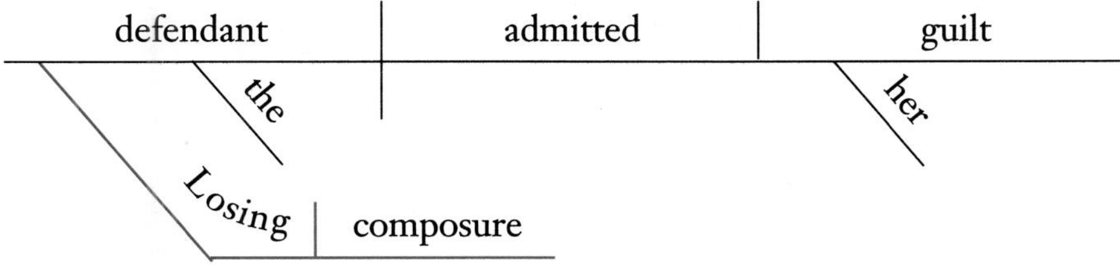


## Gerunds and Gerund Phrases

Place a gerund on a "step," and add objects, complements, and modifiers in the usual way. Then set the gerund or the gerund phrase on a "stilt," and position the stilt in the diagram according to the role of the gerund in the sentence. (Remember that a gerund can be a subject, a complement, an object of a preposition, or an appositive.)

Establishing an alibi is a way of proving innocence.

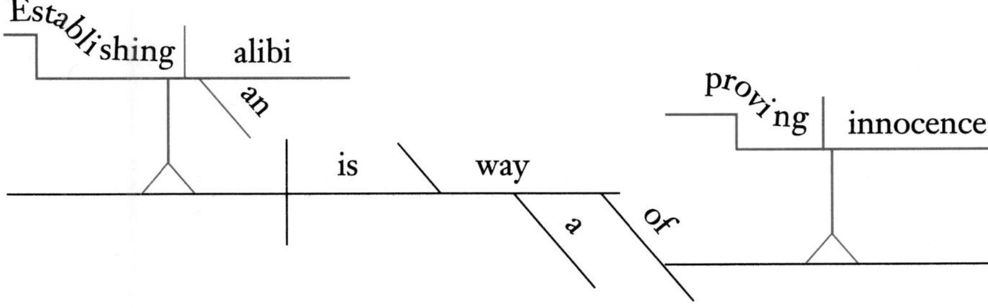


## Infinitives and Infinitive Phrases

When an infinitive or an infinitive phrase is used as an adjective or an adverb, it is diagramed like a prepositional phrase.

When an infinitive or an infinitive phrase is used as a noun, it is diagramed like a prepositional phrase and then placed on a "stilt" in the subject or complement position.

The only way to win the case is to convince the jury.

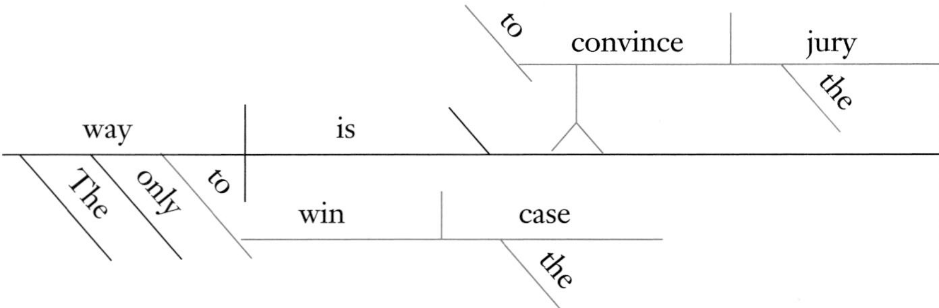


## Absolute Phrases

An absolute phrase is placed above the rest of the sentence and is not connected to it in any way. Place the noun or pronoun on a horizontal line. Place the participle and any modifiers on descending lines.

The trial having been concluded, the witnesses left the courtroom.

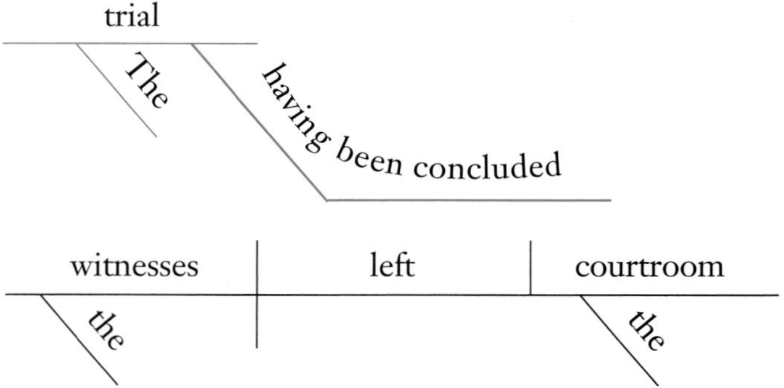


**Exercise 2** **Diagraming Simple Sentences with Phrases**

Using the preceding models as a guide, diagram the following sentences.

1. The world of the open sea is a realm of great dimensions.
2. Classical Latin, the language of Ancient Rome, was a literary language.
3. The sails, flapping idly, suddenly filled.
4. Smoking is an ancient way of preserving meat.
5. Your car parked on shore, you take a boat to reach Venice.

# 14.3 Diagraming Sentences with Clauses

## Compound Sentences

Diagram each main clause separately. If the clauses are connected by a semicolon, use a vertical dotted line to connect the verbs of each main clause. If the main clauses are connected by a conjunction, place the conjunction on a solid horizontal line, and connect it to the verbs of each main clause by vertical dotted lines.

Older senators chair committees, and others make speeches.

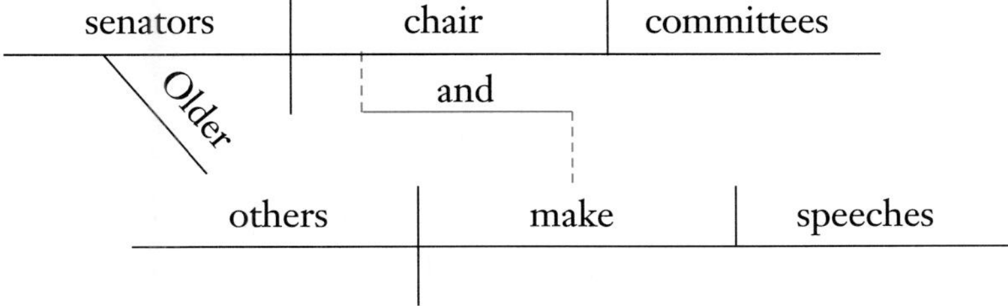


## Complex Sentences with Adjective Clauses

Place the main clause in one diagram and the adjective clause beneath it in another diagram. Use a dotted line to connect the relative pronoun or other introductory word in the adjective clause to the modified noun or pronoun in the main clause.

Senators who make many speeches often address audiences that are already friendly.

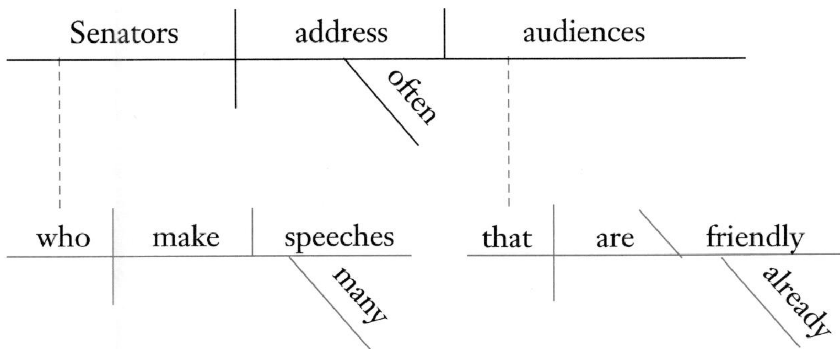

## Complex Sentences with Adverb Clauses

Place the main clause in one diagram and the adverb clause beneath it in another diagram. Place the subordinating conjunction on a diagonal dotted line connecting the verb in the adverb clause to the modified verb, adjective, or adverb in the main clause.

When senators make speeches, journalists take notes.

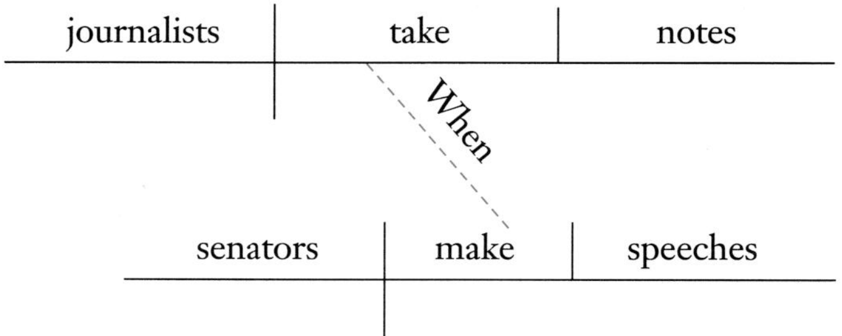


## Complex Sentences with Noun Clauses

First decide what role the noun clause plays within the main clause. Is it the subject, direct object, predicate nominative, or object of a preposition? Then diagram the main clause, placing the noun clause on a "stilt" in the appropriate position. Place the introductory word of the clause in the position of the subject, object, or predicate nominative within the noun clause itself. If the introductory word merely begins the noun clause, place it on a line of its own above the verb in the subordinate clause, connecting it to the verb with a dotted vertical line.

**NOUN CLAUSE AS SUBJECT**

What senators say may become important news.

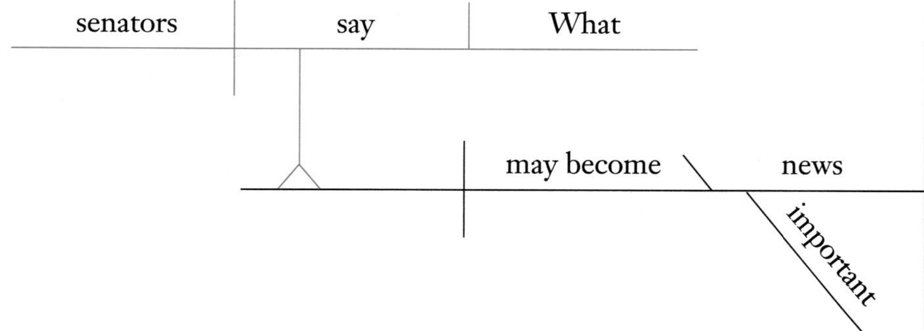

NOUN CLAUSE AS DIRECT OBJECT

Some senators remember that America symbolizes freedom.

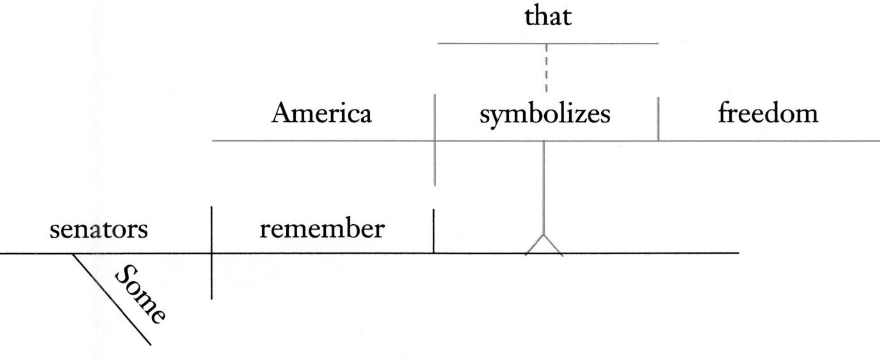


NOUN CLAUSE AS OBJECT OF A PREPOSITION

The Senate assigns positions to whoever merits them.

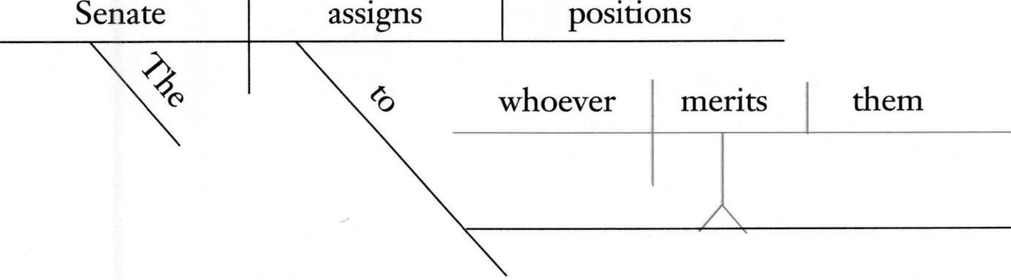


## Exercise 3 Diagraming Sentences with Clauses

Using the preceding models as a guide, diagram the following sentences.

1. Three painters created a new style, and the world loved it.
2. Paul Cézanne, who achieved a unique style, influenced modern painting.
3. The art of van Gogh, because the painter's emotions were intense, is always vivid.
4. That Paul Gauguin was a skilled painter is universally acknowledged.
5. The quality of his drawings is what demonstrates this.

UNIT

# 15 Verb Tenses, Voice, and Mood

Grammar

Lessons

## 15.1 Principal Parts of Verbs

**All verbs have four principal parts—a *base form*, a *present participle*, a *simple past form*, and a *past participle*. All the verb tenses are formed from these principal parts.**

| Base Form | Present Participle | Past Form | Past Participle |
|---|---|---|---|
| talk | talking | talked | talked |
| open | opening | opened | opened |
| wash | washing | washed | washed |
| find | finding | found | found |
| be | being | was, were | been |
| cut | cutting | cut | cut |

You may use the base forms (except for *be*) and the past forms alone as main verbs, but the present and past participles must be accompanied by one or more auxiliary verbs if they are to function as the simple predicate of a sentence.

Actors **rehearse.** [base or present form]
Actors **rehearsed.** [past form]
Actors **are rehearsing.** [present participle with auxiliary verb *are*]
Actors **have rehearsed.** [past participle with auxiliary verb *have*]

### Exercise 1 Identifying Principal Parts

On your paper identify each of the following verbs as *base form*, *present participle*, *simple past form*, or *past participle*. Some sentences have two verbs.

#### *Polar Bears*

1. Many dwellers of the Arctic call the polar bear the King of the North.
2. Polar bears are the largest land predators in the far North.
3. Thanks to its white coat, the polar bear blended perfectly into the Arctic landscape of ice and snow.
4. Thick layers of fat under their skin protect polar bears from the cold.
5. Polar bears have smelled food from fifteen miles away.
6. Once a polar bear dragged a six-hundred-pound seal out of the water and onto the ice.
7. A grown polar bear fears nothing, but predators often have attacked cubs.
8. Polar bears are surviving in spite of the changes that humans have brought to the Arctic.
9. Some bears learned that garbage dumps in Arctic towns contain useful food.
10. Always a symbol of the wild North, the polar bear today also is serving as a tourist attraction.

## 15.2 Regular and Irregular Verbs

**A regular verb forms its past and past participle by adding *-ed* to the base form.**

| Base Form | Past Form | Past Participle |
|---|---|---|
| rehearse | rehearsed | rehearsed |
| perform | performed | performed |
| watch | watched | watched |

Some regular verbs require a spelling change when a suffix beginning with a vowel is added to the base form.

gentrify + **-ed** = gentrif**ied** allot + **-ed** = allot**ted**

**An irregular verb forms its past and past participle in some way other than by adding *-ed* to the base form.**

| Base Form | Past Form | Past Participle |
|---|---|---|
| be | was, were | been |
| bear | bore | borne |
| beat | beat | beaten |
| become | became | become |
| begin | began | begun |
| bite | bit | bitten *or* bit |
| blow | blew | blown |
| break | broke | broken |
| bring | brought | brought |
| burst | burst | burst |
| cast | cast | cast |
| catch | caught | caught |
| choose | chose | chosen |
| come | came | come |
| creep | crept | crept |
| dive | dived *or* dove | dived |
| do | did | done |
| draw | drew | drawn |
| drink | drank | drunk |
| drive | drove | driven |
| eat | ate | eaten |
| fall | fell | fallen |
| feel | felt | felt |
| find | found | found |
| fling | flung | flung |

| Base Form | Past Form | Past Participle |
|---|---|---|
| fly | flew | flown |
| freeze | froze | frozen |
| get | got | got *or* gotten |
| give | gave | given |
| go | went | gone |
| grow | grew | grown |
| hang | hang *or* hanged | hang *or* hanged |
| have | had | had |
| know | knew | known |
| lay* | laid | laid |
| lead | led | led |
| lend | lent | lent |
| lie* | lay | lain |
| lose | lost | lost |
| put | put | put |
| raise* | raised | raised |
| ride | rode | ridden |
| ring | rang | rung |
| rise* | rose | risen |
| run | ran | run |
| say | said | said |
| see | saw | seen |
| set* | set | set |
| shake | shook | shaken |
| shine | shone *or* shined† | shone *or* shined† |
| shrink | shrank *or* shrunk | shrunk *or* shrunken |
| sing | sang | sung |
| sink | sank *or* sunk | sunk |
| sit* | sat | sat |
| speak | spoke | spoken |
| spring | sprang *or* sprung | sprung |
| steal | stole | stolen |
| sting | stung | stung |
| swear | swore | sworn |
| swim | swam | swum |
| swing | swung | swung |
| take | took | taken |
| tear | tore | torn |
| tell | told | told |
| think | thought | thought |
| throw | threw | thrown |
| wear | wore | worn |
| win | won | won |
| write | wrote | written |

*For more detailed instruction on *lay* versus *lie, raise* versus *rise,* and *set* versus *sit,* see Unit 19.

†*Shone* is intransitive. (The sun *shone.*) *Shined* is transitive. (I *shined* my shoes.)

## Exercise 2 Supplying the Correct Principal Part

Complete these sentences with the principal part indicated in parentheses.

### *Cowhand Lore*

1. The era of the American cowhand ________ after the birth of the Republic of Texas. (past form of *begin*)
2. The dangerous life, sad songs, and colorful vocabulary have ________ the cowhand an important part of American folklore. (past participle of *make*)
3. The cowhand had ________ many ideas from the vaquero, a Mexican counterpart. (past participle of *take*)
4. The Mexican chaparejos, or leather leggings, ________ "chaps" to Texas cowhands. (past form of *become*)
5. The Texas saddle with a pommel for the rider's lariat ________ a modification of a Mexican design. (past form of *be*)
6. In the 1860s many cowhands were ________ the Mexican sombrero for the famous hat of John Batterson Stetson. (present participle of *substitute*)
7. Cowhands wore pants made of denim, a material that Levi Strauss had originally ________ west to use in making tents. (past participle of *bring*)
8. The cowhand ________ that a bandanna protected the face during dust and ice storms. (past form of *find*)
9. Carry-all vests, high-heeled boots, and spurs also had ________ part of the cowhand's outfit. (past participle of *become*)
10. The mustang, often the cowhand's most precious possession, ________ its origin on the Arabian Peninsula. (past form of *have*)

## Exercise 3 Changing Principal Parts

Change the italicized verb in each sentence to the form indicated in parentheses.

### *Texas Fights for Independence*

1. It is 1836, and the Mexicans *had* control of the land now called Texas. (base form)
2. Many settlers in Texas, however, *are choosing* independence from Mexico. (past participle)
3. Most of these settlers *come* originally from the United States. (past)
4. Settlers in the Mexican states of Zacatecas and Coahuila y Texas *have risen* in armed revolt. (present participle)
5. Led by General Santa Anna, the Mexican troops easily *have put* down the rebellion in Zacatecas, then *have swung* north into Texas. (base form)
6. Soon a fort called the Alamo *fell* to Santa Anna's forces. (past participle)
7. Sam Houston, the leader of the Texans, and his soldiers *were hearing* the news of the Alamo's fall on March 6. (base form)
8. A little over a month later, on April 21, Houston's troops *have crept* toward the Mexicans in a surprise attack at San Jacinto. (present participle)
9. By the end of the battle, Houston's troops *caught* Santa Anna himself. (past participle)
10. The Mexican government *loses* control of Texas. (past participle)

## 15.3 Tense of Verbs

The **tenses** of a verb are the forms that help to show time.

English has six tenses: the *present*, *past*, and *future* and the *present perfect*, *past perfect*, and *future perfect*.

## Present Tense

The present-tense form of any verb other than *be* is the same as the base form of the verb. When the verb follows a third-person singular subject, however, *-s* or *-es* is added to the base form.

| | Singular | Plural |
|---|---|---|
| FIRST PERSON | I **walk.** | We **walk.** |
| SECOND PERSON | You **walk.** | You **walk.** |
| THIRD PERSON | She, he, or it **walks.** | They **walk.** |
| | Ronnie **walks.** | The children **walk.** |

| | Singular | Plural |
|---|---|---|
| FIRST PERSON | I **am** serious. | We **are** serious. |
| SECOND PERSON | You **are** serious. | You **are** serious. |
| THIRD PERSON | She, he, or it **is** serious. | They **are** serious. |
| | Ivan **is** serious. | The men **are** serious. |

The **present tense** expresses a constant, repeated, or habitual action or condition. It can also express a general truth.

An evergreen **adapts** to almost any climate or location. [not just now but always: a constant action]

All garden flowers and shrubs **need** sunlight. [a condition that is always true]

The **present tense** can also express an action or condition that exists only now.

Sonia **seems** happy about her score on the math test. [not always but just now]

I **nominate** Jesse for treasurer of the Greenville Junior Chamber of Commerce. [at this very moment]

The **present tense** is sometimes used in historical writing to express past events and, more often, in poetry, fiction, and reporting (especially in sports) to convey to the reader a sense of "being there."

> The space shuttle *Columbia* **glides** successfully back to Earth and consequently **becomes** the first reusable spacecraft in the history of the world.
>
> The crowd **cheers** wildly as Jordan **scores** with one second remaining in the third period.
>
> Sunlight **lies** along my table like abandoned pages.
> —Jane Cooper

## Exercise 4 Using the Present Tense

Rewrite each sentence below, changing all verbs to the present tense.

### *The White House*

1. Over a million people came each year to see the White House in Washington, D.C., the home of the presidents of the United States.
2. The White House was almost 200 years old, just a little younger than the United States itself.
3. Some presidents have added a few new touches, but no one has changed the graceful mansion very much.
4. The stately building had over fifty rooms—or 130, if you counted the rooms in the east and west wings.
5. The building contained a priceless collection of historical objects.
6. An army of almost a hundred people cleaned and repaired the house.
7. Both the respectful and the rowdy converged on the presidential mansion.
8. Alarms and guards have kept out unwelcome visitors.
9. Still, the White House had remained one of the few homes of a chief of state that regularly opened its doors to the country's citizens.
10. Many Americans felt that, in a sense, the White House was their home as well as that of the presidents.

## Exercise 5 Expressing the Present Tense in Sentences

Write a sentence using each of the following verb forms. The content of your sentence should express the kind of present time indicated in parentheses.

**SAMPLE** needs (now and always)
**ANSWER** A plant needs sunlight.

1. drives (now and always)
2. look (just now)
3. are (always true)
4. hopes (at this moment)
5. refuse (always)

## Past Tense

**Use the past tense to express an action or condition that was started and completed in the past.**

I **spilled** juice on my shirt.
The juice **stained** my shirt.
I **took** the shirt to the cleaners.
They **removed** the stain.

With the exception of the verb *be*, all regular and irregular verbs have only one past-tense form, such as *struggled* or *spoke*. The verb *be*, however, has two past-tense forms: *was*, used with singular subjects, and *were*, used with plural subjects.

| | Singular | Plural |
|---|---|---|
| FIRST PERSON | I **was** right. | We **were** right. |
| SECOND PERSON | You **were** right. | You **were** right. |
| THIRD PERSON | He, she, or it **was** right.<br>Mr. Chan **was** right. | They **were** right.<br>Meg's parents **were** right. |

**Exercise 6** **Expressing the Past Tense in Sentences**

Write a paragraph using the correct past tense of the following verbs.

1. throw
2. bring
3. give
4. stop
5. walk

## Future Tense

**Use the future tense to express an action or condition that will occur in the future.**

To form the future tense of any verb, use the auxiliary *shall* or *will* with the base form: *I shall succeed; you will understand.*

Donna **will finish** school soon.
I **shall graduate** next year.

The following options allow you to express future time without using *will* or *shall:*

1. Use *going to* along with the present tense of *be* and the base form of a verb.

Donna **is *going to* finish** school soon.
Peter **is *going to* study** calculus this summer.

2. Use *about to* along with the present tense of *be* and the base form of a verb.

Donna **is *about to* finish** school.
Peter **is *about to* study** calculus.

3. Use the present tense with an adverb or an adverb phrase that shows future time.

The countdown **begins *soon.***
The countdown **begins *in one hour.***

## Exercise 7 Using Expressions of Future Time

Change each sentence below so that the verbs are in the future tense. Try to use at least two other ways of expressing future time in addition to *shall* and *will.*

### *Bonsai*

1. An instructor from Japan, Mr. Ikeda, offered a fascinating four-week course in the history and cultivation of bonsai, a potted miniature tree.
2. He showed us living examples of various types of bonsai, including a pine, a maple, and a cherry.
3. Over a period of time, our class observed the proper way to plant and train a bonsai.
4. On the first day of the course, Mr. Ikeda outlined the sometimes difficult procedures for bonsai cultivation.
5. He explained and illustrated the steps in fine detail.
6. During the second week he demonstrated how to cut the deep, main roots of a very young tree.
7. Then he sifted and prepared his potting soil and placed it in a shallow bonsai pot.
8. With great care and patience Mr. Ikeda studied both the tree and the pot to determine the most artistic placement of the tree.
9. After planting the tree in the pot, he added a layer of moss on the soil's surface.
10. According to Mr. Ikeda, the tree needed at least forty-eight more weeks of pruning and training in order for it to take on an elegant and aesthetically pleasing shape.

## Exercise 8 Expressing Future Time in Sentences

Write five sentences in which you describe or predict what you think hair and clothing styles will be like in the future. Your sentences may be as realistic or as imaginary as you wish. Remember to vary the ways in which you express future time.

**SAMPLE ANSWER** In the future people are going to be able to change their hair color several times a day.

## 15.4 Perfect Tenses

### Present Perfect Tense

**Use the present perfect tense to express an action or condition that occurred at some *indefinite* time in the past.**

You form the present perfect tense by using the auxiliary *has* or *have* with the past participle of a verb: *has started, have watched.**

* Do not be confused by the term *present perfect*. This tense expresses *past* time. *Present* refers to the tense of the auxiliary verb *has* or *have*.

Darryl **has washed** his car.
They **have paid** the insurance premium.
I **have driven** far today.

The present perfect tense is used to refer to an action that took place in the indefinite past. You cannot use this tense with adverbs such as *yesterday* that make the time more specific.

I **have started** my report.

To be specific about completed past time, you usually use the simple past tense.

Maribel **started** soccer practice yesterday.
Chandra **swam** six laps this morning.
Ismail **scored** three touchdowns

You can also use the present perfect tense to indicate that an action or a condition that *began* in the past *continues* into the present. When you use the present perfect tense in this way, you should use it with adverbs or phrases expressing time.

I **have kept** an account of my expenses **for three years.**

I **have added** five dollars to my savings **every week for the past seven years.**

The interest on the account **has compounded daily**, so the amount **has increased day by day.**

My bank account **has grown throughout the year.**

**Exercise 9** **Expressing the Present Perfect Tense in Sentences**

Write a paragraph that includes five sentences with verbs in the present perfect tense. Three of the verbs should describe an action that took place in the indefinite past. The other two should describe an action that began in the past and continues into the present. Add adverbs or phrases to show when the action began.

## Past Perfect Tense

**Use the past perfect tense to indicate that one past action or condition began *and* ended before another past action started.**

You form the past perfect tense with *had* and the past participle of a verb: *had found, had put.*

By the time the ticket office **opened,** (PAST) a line of twenty-five people **had formed.** (PAST PERFECT) [The line formed; twenty-five people joined the line; the ticket office opened.]

We **had** already **signed** (PAST PERFECT) the contract when he **arrived.** (PAST) [We signed, and then he showed up.]

Jill **dedicated** (PAST) her book to the teacher who **had encouraged** (PAST PERFECT) her long ago. [First the teacher praised Jill, and years later Jill acknowledged her teacher's help.]

### Exercise 10 Using the Past and Past Perfect Tenses

For each of the following sentences, replace each verb in parentheses with the past or past perfect form of the verb. Use the past perfect form for the verb that describes the action that takes place first.

**SAMPLE** Venki (see) many wild animals in India before he (move) to New York City.
**ANSWER** Venki had seen many wild animals in India before he moved to New York City.

***Nature in the City***

1. By the time anyone (notice) the leak, the plaster in the ceiling (crack) from one corner of the room to the other.
2. When I finally (walk) into the doctor's office, all of the symptoms of my cold already (disappear).
3. If he (visit) Central Park sooner, he would have seen many migrating birds.
4. He (believe) he was hearing an ambulance siren until he (discover) the sound came from a mockingbird.
5. He heard of a man who (live) in a treehouse in a park until park workers (find) him.
6. We (wait) almost an hour when he finally (arrive).
7. Many years later, while looking through an old box of papers, I (realize) how badly I (misunderstand) my first-grade teacher.
8. He (mail) the envelope before realizing that he (address) it incorrectly.
9. Until we heard him sing, we (think) we (cast) the perfect actor.
10. With time-lapse photography, they (see) that the glacier actually (move) several inches over the course of the summer.

## Future Perfect Tense

Use the **future perfect tense** to express one future action or condition that will begin *and* end before another future event starts.

The future perfect tense is formed with *will have* or *shall have* plus the past participle of a verb: *will have written, shall have gone.*

By December Sean **will have lived** here six months. [The six months will be over by the time another future event, the coming of December, occurs.]

By the time Michelle gets to college, tuition **will have increased** substantially.

### Exercise 11 Expressing the Future Perfect Tense in Sentences

Write five sentences showing how you think life will have changed by 2051. Use the future perfect tense in each sentence.

**SAMPLE ANSWER** By 2051, electric cars will have become the most popular form of transportation.

### Exercise 12 Identifying the Perfect Tenses

On your paper write the perfect-tense verb that appears in each of the following sentences. Then identify the verb as *present, past,* or *future perfect.* (One sentence contains two verbs in the perfect tense.)

***Nauvoo, Illinois, a Reclaimed Ghost Town***

1. Before the Mormons built the city of Nauvoo, Illinois, the area had been a swamp.
2. Years later, after the Mormons had left in the greatest wagon train of all time, Nauvoo became a ghost town.
3. Recently, however, the old Mormon city has become a tourist attraction on account of its scenic beauty and historic interest.
4. Since its restoration Mormon Nauvoo has brought large numbers of visitors into the town every year.
5. Of the original twenty-two hundred residences that people had built in Nauvoo, three hundred were brick houses.
6. Before restoration began in earnest, Dr. Leroy Kimball had bought his grandfather's lavish house.
7. To date restorers have completed about a score of houses and other buildings in Nauvoo.
8. By the time its population reaches two thousand citizens, Nauvoo will have earned some renown for its commercial efforts.
9. Restorers have used blocks of limestone from the old Mormon temple to construct a community building.
10. Before much more time has passed, millions of tourists will have visited the restored city.

## Exercise 13 Supplying the Correct Perfect Tenses

Complete these sentences with the form of the verb indicated in parentheses.

### *The Day the Lake Disappeared*

1. Before the day in 1980 when Lake Peigneur disappeared, there __________ a salt mine under the lake for forty years. (past perfect of *be*)
2. Then word spread among people who lived near the lake: "An oil company__________ to drill for oil." (present perfect of *start*)
3. When the oil drill stopped working early on the morning of November 20, no one realized that the drill __________ the ceiling of the mine. (past perfect of *penetrate*)
4. Miners, who __________ with the possibility of catastrophe all their lives, watched in horror as water began pouring into the mine. (present perfect of *live*)
5. People on the shore were shocked to see that the lake _________ a giant whirlpool. (past perfect of *become*)
6. Before long, trees and houses on the shore ___________ boats and fish into the cave-in. (past perfect of *follow*)
7. "By the time this is over, everything around the lake __________," some said. (future perfect of *vanish*)
8. "All the miners __________," a police officer announced happily. (present perfect of *escape*)
9. Late the next night, after the mine __________ up with all the water it could hold, the lake began to refill. (past perfect of *fill*)
10. By 2000, twenty years __________ since the disaster, but the vanishing lake most likely will still haunt residents' dreams. (future perfect of *pass*)

## Exercise 14 Expressing the Present Perfect Tense in Sentences

(a) Rewrite each of the following sentences, changing the tense of the verb from the past to the present perfect. (b) Add appropriate adverbs or adverb phrases to each of your new sentences to communicate the idea that an action or condition began in the past and continues into the present.

**SAMPLE** We looked for a parking space.

**ANSWER** (a) We have looked for a parking space.
(b) We have looked for a parking space for over fifteen minutes.

1. The juniors rehearsed their skit.
2. Our furniture was in storage.
3. Fans criticized the singer's latest recordings.
4. The fire alarm rang.
5. My sister wanted to direct films.

## 15.5 Progressive and Emphatic Forms

Each of the six tenses has a **progressive** form that expresses a continuing action.

You make the progressive forms by using the appropriate tense of the verb *be* plus the present participle of the main verb.

| | |
|---|---|
| PRESENT PROGRESSIVE | They ***are*** **waiting.** |
| PAST PROGRESSIVE | They ***were*** **waiting.** |
| FUTURE PROGRESSIVE | They ***will be*** **waiting.** |
| PRESENT PERFECT PROGRESSIVE | They ***have been*** **waiting.** |
| PAST PERFECT PROGRESSIVE | They ***had been*** **waiting.** |
| FUTURE PERFECT PROGRESSIVE | They ***will have been*** **waiting.** |

The present and past tenses have additional forms, called **emphatic,** that add special force, or emphasis, to the verb.

You make the emphatic forms by using *do* (or *does*) or *did* plus the base form of the verb.

| | |
|---|---|
| PRESENT EMPHATIC | I ***do*** **think** you're right. |
| | **Olga does think** you're right. |
| PAST EMPHATIC | I ***did*** **think** you were right. |

### Exercise 15 Using the Progressive and Emphatic Forms

For each of the following sentences, replace each verb in parentheses with the progressive or the emphatic form of the verb that makes sense in the sentence. (Only one of the sentences requires the emphatic form.)

*Zydeco Music*

1. In southern Louisiana years ago the words *zydeco au soir*—"zydeco tonight"—hollered by a man on horseback meant that the rider (announce) a local dance.
2. He (refer) to an event named for the kind of music that would be played as part of the evening's entertainment.
3. That music was zydeco, a fast dance music with a highly syncopated beat, which (develop) in Louisiana over the past 150 years.
4. Played primarily by members of the region's Creole population, zydeco (deviate) increasingly in recent years from its Cajun, African American, and African Caribbean origins.
5. Today rhythm-and-blues tunes and soul (influence) the musicians who play zydeco.

## Exercise 16 Understanding the Uses of Verb Tenses

Explain the difference in meaning between the sentences in each of the pairs below. Name the tense(s) used in each sentence.

SAMPLE (a) The artisan drills a hole in a clam shell.
(b) The artisan has drilled a hole in a clam shell.

ANSWER In sentence *a* the action is going on now (present tense).
In sentence *b* the action occurred at some indefinite time in the past (present perfect tense).

### *Native American Beadwork*

1. **a.** I saw a demonstration of Native American beadwork.
   **b.** I have seen a demonstration of Native American beadwork.
2. **a.** At the demonstration a friend of mine noticed that one of the workers had drilled holes in a great many turquoise beads.
   **b.** At the demonstration a friend of mine noticed that one of the workers was drilling holes in a great many turquoise beads.
3. **a.** Soon another worker will weave some of the beads into a zigzag pattern.
   **b.** Soon another worker will have woven some of the beads into a zigzag pattern.
4. **a.** A beautiful wampum belt has been evolving at his fingertips.
   **b.** A beautiful wampum belt evolved at his fingertips.
5. **a.** I did applaud the worker's skill.
   **b.** I am applauding the worker's skill.
6. **a.** A third worker had beaded a pair of moccasins before arriving.
   **b.** A third worker was beading a pair of moccasins at the demonstration.
7. **a.** By the time we finish this project, the worker will have spent many hours on it.
   **b.** The worker will spend many hours on this project.
8. **a.** Young apprentices are learning the older masters' skills.
   **b.** Young apprentices have learned the older masters' skills.
9. **a.** Fine examples of beadwork are growing in value.
   **b.** Fine examples of beadwork will be growing in value.
10. **a.** We have been spending a fascinating day at the demonstration.
    **b.** By the end of the demonstration, we will have spent a fascinating day.

## Exercise 17 Expressing Past Time in a Paragraph

Write a paragraph of at least five sentences about an important historical event that you remember or have studied. Underline five verbs or verb phrases that you use in the paragraph. (Remember that the perfect tenses, as well as the past tense, can be used to express past action.)

## 15.6 Compatibility of Tenses

### Do not shift, or change, tenses when two or more events occur at the same time.

INCORRECT The senator **pounded** the podium and **gestures** wildly. [The tense shifts from the past to the present.]

CORRECT The senator **pounded** the podium and **gestured** wildly to make a point. [Now it is clear that both events happened in the past.]

INCORRECT The rain **has poured** down endlessly, and the Kotters' basement **will have flooded**. [The tense shifts from the present perfect to the future perfect.]

CORRECT The rain **has poured** down endlessly, and the Kotters' basement **has flooded**. [Now it is clear that the rain began in the past and is continuing, and at some indefinite time during the rain the Kotters' basement flooded.]

### Shift tenses only to show that one event precedes or follows another.

INCORRECT By the time I **remembered** the roast in the oven, it **burned.** [The two past-tense verbs give the mistaken impression that both events happened at the same time.]

CORRECT By the time I **remembered** the roast in the oven,it **had burned.** [The shift from the past tense (*remembered*) to the past perfect tense (*had burned*) clearly indicates that the burning happened before the remembering.]

INCORRECT By the time I **arrive** at the store, it **will close.** [The future action indicated by the words *by the time I arrive* and the future-tense verb (*will close*) give the mistaken impression that both events will happen simultaneously.]

CORRECT By the time I **arrive** at the store, it **will have closed.** [Here the words *by the time I arrive* indicate a future action. The future perfect tense (*will have closed*) indicates that the second event (the closing of the store) will occur *before* the first event (the arrival at the store).]

## Exercise 18 Making Tenses Compatible

First find the two verbs that appear in each of the following sentences. Then rewrite each sentence, making the second verb compatible with the first verb.

### *W. C. Handy, Father of the Blues*

1. William Christopher Handy was born in 1873 in Florence, Alabama, where he had shown a talent for music very early.
2. Handy did not inherit his musical talent from his mother or his father and was not receiving any encouragement to study music.
3. A schoolteacher of young Handy's, however, understood music and was teaching his students to sing.
4. By the time he had reached his tenth birthday, Handy masters the sol-fa system of ear training.
5. Handy became famous when he writes a campaign song for E. H. Crump, a candidate for mayor of Memphis, Tennessee.
6. The song ridiculed Crump even though the candidate has hired Handy to promote the campaign.
7. Ironically "Mister Crump," later known as the "Memphis Blues," became a hit and helps to elect Crump to office.
8. Handy published his well-known "Memphis Blues" in 1912 and from then on was specializing in blues tunes.
9. The publishing company had cheated Handy out of his profits, but the copyright reverts to him twenty-three years later.
10. "St. Louis Blues," "Beale Street Blues," and other Handy songs became popular in Handy's lifetime, but they were originating long before, in the doleful songs of slavery.

## Exercise 19 Supplying Compatible Verb Tenses

Complete these sentences with a tense of the verb in parentheses that is compatible with the other verb in the sentence.

### *The Mystery of Memory*

1. During the last ten seconds, your brain __________ ten million bits of information. (absorb)
2. You __________ most of this information almost immediately, but you may remember some of it all your life. (forget)
3. You __________ the information that is most important to you—that which helps you deal with your environment. (remember)
4. Some people __________ their memory after head injuries and later have recovered it. (lose)
5. Sometimes many years __________ before they regained their memories. (pass)
6. They never __________ what had happened during those lost years. (recall)
7. As children are growing up, their memories __________ their personalities. (shape)
8. Memories for facts, for skills, and for experiences go to different parts of the brain and, in ways not fully understood, __________ brain cells. (change)
9. Because witnesses __________ memory and imagination, juries sometimes convict people of crimes they have not committed. (confuse)
10. By the time you are old, your brain __________ millions of memories. (store)

## 15.7 Voice of Verbs

**An action verb is in the active voice when the subject of the sentence performs the action.**

The coach **praised** the team.
The team **won** the game.
Melissa Yang **scored** the winning point.

**An action verb is in the passive voice when its action is performed on the subject.**

The team **was praised** by the coach.
The game **was won** by the team.
The winning point **was scored** by Melissa Yang.

The active voice usually creates a stronger impression than the passive. There are times when the passive voice is preferred or even necessary, however. For instance, you should use the passive voice if you do not want to call attention to the performer of an action or if you do not know the identity of the performer.

The glass **was broken.** [You may not want to identify the person who broke the glass.]

The fender **was dented.** [You may not know who dented it.]

Form the passive voice by using the auxiliary verb *be* together with the past participle of the verb. The tense of the passive verb is determined by the tense of the auxiliary verb.

The team **was praised** in the newspapers. [past tense, passive voice.]

The team **is being praised.** [present progressive tense, passive voice]

The team **will have been praised** in the newspapers. [future perfect tense, passive voice]

### Exercise 20 Changing Active Verbs to Passive

Rewrite each active verb below so that it is in the passive voice.

**1.** flung
**2.** explains
**3.** has shattered
**4.** will have flown
**5.** is planting

## Exercise 21 Identifying Active and Passive Voice

Identify the voice of the italicized verb in each sentence below as *active* or *passive*.

### *The Eagle Lady*

1. The bald eagle *was chosen* as the national bird of the United States.
2. As many as forty thousand bald eagles *live* in Alaska—about five times as many as in all the rest of the United States.
3. Seventy-one-year-old Jean Keene *is called* the Eagle Lady by her neighbors in Homer, Alaska.
4. For years, Keene *has been feeding* dozens of eagles in her backyard at dawn each day during winter.
5. She *has tossed* hundreds of pounds of fish each day to the ravenous birds—about two pounds for each eagle.
6. The fish *is being supplied* by a nearby fish packing plant, for which Keene used to work.
7. Each year the plant gives Keene about 45,000 pounds of fish that either cannot feed humans or *has spoiled*.
8. When other food is scarce, the local eagles *have been supported* by Keene's efforts.
9. Along with the eagles, flocks of wildlife photographers *are drawn* to Keene's yard in the hope of photographing the birds.
10. "I *will have shot* a hundred rolls of film by the end of the week," one happy photographer said.

## Exercise 22 Supplying the Correct Voice of Verbs

Complete these sentences with the tense and voice of the verb indicated in parentheses.

### *Baseball Background*

1. Before 1947 African Americans __________ the right to play on major league baseball teams. (past perfect, passive, *deny*)
2. The so-called Negro Leagues __________ players of whom any would have been proud. (past, active, *boast*)
3. Satchel Paige, Smokey Joe Williams, and Cool Papa Bell __________ by many baseball historians. (present perfect, passive, *praise)*
4. These men __________ as some of baseball's top players. (present, passive, *regard*)
5. Nonetheless, they and other African American baseball players seldom __________ decent equipment or salaries. (past, passive, *give*)
6. According to one estimation, during 1906 African American ball players __________ less than a quarter of what white players received. (past perfect, passive, *pay*)
7. Negro League players often regretted that they __________ so much time traveling from town to town. (past perfect progressive, active, *spend*)
8. They often __________ to performing circus tricks, such as juggling and clown acts, to drum up business. (past, passive, *reduce*)
9. After African American Jackie Robinson joined the Brooklyn Dodgers in 1947, it was clear that segregated baseball __________ to an end. (past perfect, passive, *bring*)
10. Today many African Americans __________ their rightful places in the Baseball Hall of Fame. (present perfect, active, *take*)

## Exercise 23 Changing the Voice of Verbs

In each of the following sentences, change the active voice to the passive or the passive voice to the active.

### *Mexico's Pyramids*

1. In the nineteenth century John Lloyd Stephens, a lawyer, and Frederick Catherwood, an artist, investigated rumors of long-lost cities in the Yucatán Peninsula of Mexico.
2. Five lost cities, four of them the work of the Maya people, were discovered by the pair.
3. Many more remarkable structures are uncovered daily by archaeologists in the Yucatán.
4. Most impressively, the Mayas, with neither wheels nor metal tools at their disposal, constructed huge stone pyramids.
5. Large blocks of stone were quarried and shaped by the Maya workers.
6. The pyramids were built by the workers in a layer-upon-layer style.
7. At the very top of the pyramids, the Mayas constructed their temples.
8. By design the exterior of the temples and the pyramids was given far more importance by the builders than was the interior.
9. Sculptures of animals and gods were carved in low relief and in the round by skilled artisans.
10. Today many of the temple sites and the well-planned cities around them are visited by thousands of tourists each year.

## Exercise 24 Judging Appropriateness of Passive Voice

The verbs in all the sentences below are in the passive voice. If you think a sentence would read better in the active voice, rewrite the sentence and change the verb to the active form. If you think a sentence should remain in the passive voice, explain why.

**SAMPLE** Disposal of garbage is considered one of America's worst problems.
**ANSWER** Passive okay. We don't know who is performing the action.

### *The Truth About Garbage*

1. American garbage—over 250,000 pounds of it—has been studied by the Garbage Project at the University of Arizona.
2. Mistakes in many people's beliefs about garbage have been shown by their work.
3. Fast-food containers and Styrofoam packing pellets are often tossed by roadsides.
4. Such materials have been blamed for the American garbage crisis.
5. According to the Garbage Project, however, less than 2 percent of garbage in landfills is made up of these materials.
6. Over 40 percent of landfills is occupied by ordinary paper.
7. That landfill garbage disintegrates has been believed by many people.
8. However, newspapers and even hot dogs have been identified easily after several decades in a landfill.
9. Some changes in the kinds and amount of American garbage have been made by new trends toward recycling.
10. Both recycling and the demand for products using recycled materials will be increased in a garbage-conscious society.

## 15.8 Mood of Verbs

Verbs express mood as well as tense and voice.

**A verb expresses one of three moods: the indicative mood, the imperative mood, or the subjunctive mood.**

You use the indicative mood to make a statement or ask a question. You use the imperative mood to express a command or make a request.

| | |
|---|---|
| INDICATIVE MOOD | He **leaves** the house at 7:00 A.M. |
| IMPERATIVE MOOD | **Leave** the house at 7:00 A.M. |

In informal English the subjunctive mood is frequently replaced by the indicative. The subjunctive does have two important functions in contemporary formal English, however.

1. To express, indirectly, a demand, recommendation, suggestion, or statement of necessity.

   We demand [or recommend or suggest] that he **leave** the house at 7:00 A.M. [The subjunctive mood drops the *-s* from the third-person singular.]

   It is necessary that he **be** here on time. [The subjunctive mood uses *be* instead of *am*, *is*, or *are*.]

2. To state a condition or a wish that is contrary to fact. This use of the subjunctive always requires the past tense.

   If he **were** smart, he would leave the house by 7:00 A.M. [The subjunctive mood uses *were*, not *was*.]

   They spoke to me as if I **were** a child.

   I wish I **were** class president.

### Exercise 25 Expressing the Imperative and Subjunctive Mood in Sentences

The verb in each sentence below is in the indicative mood. Rewrite the sentence to express the mood shown in parentheses.

*Pet Care*

1. Pet cats and dogs are fed every day. (subjunctive—suggestion)
2. She runs to the market to buy cat food. (imperative)
3. The cat is hungry, and it is clawing your leg. (subjunctive—condition contrary to fact)
4. A pet's diet contains all the nutrients needed for good health. (subjunctive—suggestion)
5. He shows responsibility in caring for a pet. (imperative)

## Exercise 26 Using the Indicative Mood and the Subjunctive Mood

For each of the ten sentences that follow, first determine whether the verb should express the indicative mood or the subjunctive mood. Then write each sentence on a separate sheet of paper, supplying the appropriate form of the verb in parentheses.

### *A Lesson About Space*

1. Ms. Cantilana, the director of the planetarium at the science museum, (lecture) to classes from local schools about space facts and fiction.
2. During Ms. Cantilana's visit to our class, my friend Leon wanted to know what would happen if he (be) to fly near a black hole.
3. Ms. Cantilana said that it was important that he (stay) far away from black holes.
4. She explained that black holes are collapsed stars so condensed that nothing, not even light, (escape) from their gravitational fields.
5. Alicia, who wishes she (be) an astronaut, asked where Earth is located in space.
6. Ms. Cantilana explained that Earth (be) situated in one arm of the Milky Way galaxy.
7. Dennis asked whether galaxies really (be) thickest along the walls of the gigantic "bubbles" that stretch out for millions of light years.
8. He requested that Ms. Cantilana (confirm) what he saw on a map of galaxies.
9. Ms. Cantilana said Dennis was correct and suggested that he (bring) the map to class.
10. Since the class seemed interested in the subject of space, Ms. Cantilana recommended that he (join) her at the planetarium.

## Exercise 27 Understanding the Use of Voice and Mood

Explain the difference in meaning between the sentences in each of the pairs below. Then identify the voice and mood used in the main clause in each sentence.

**SAMPLE** (a) When we visited Japan, our group observed a craftsperson making a samurai sword.
(b) A craftsperson making a samurai sword was observed by our group when we visited Japan.

**ANSWER** In sentence *a* attention is called to the group.
Active voice, indicative mood
In sentence *b* attention is called to the craftsperson.
Passive voice, indicative mood

### *Samurai Swords*

1. **a.** A samurai sword is made from two different kinds of steel.
   **b.** Japanese craftspeople make samurai swords from two different kinds of steel.
2. **a.** You do not carelessly run a finger along the edge of the blade.
   **b.** Do not carelessly run a finger along the edge of the blade!
3. **a.** It is well-known that these swords are both hard and flexible.
   **b.** It is important that these swords be both hard and flexible.
4. **a.** That is why they are made by sandwiching together two different kinds of steel.
   **b.** That is why they make them by sandwiching together two different kinds of steel.
5. **a.** It is necessary that the blade be hammered from two red-hot layers of metal.
   **b.** Hammer the blade, as required, from two layers of red-hot metal.

UNIT

15

Unit Review

# Grammar Review

## Verb Tenses, Voice and Mood

*The House of the Spirits* chronicles the fortunes of a Chilean family from the turn of the century until the coup of 1973, when Salvador Allende [ä yen´ dā], Chile's first socialist president and Isabel Allende's uncle, was overthrown. The following passage is narrated by Esteban Trueba, the family patriarch. In it he describes his first encounter with his fiancée, whose long green hair earned her the name Rosa the Beautiful. The passage has been annotated to show some of the verb forms covered in this unit.

*Literature Model*

### *from* THE HOUSE OF THE SPIRITS

***by Isabel Allende***

***translated from the Spanish by Magda Bogin***

More than half a century has passed, but I can still remember the exact moment when Rosa the Beautiful entered my life like a distracted angel who stole my soul as she went by. She was with her Nana and another child, probably one of her younger sisters. I think she was wearing a violet dress, but I'm not sure, because I have no eye for women's clothes and because she was so beautiful that even if she had been wearing an ermine cape all I would have noticed was her face. I don't generally spend my time thinking about women, but only a fool could have failed to spot that apparition, who caused a stir wherever she went, and tied up traffic, with her incredible green hair, which framed her face like a fantastic hat, her fairy-tale manner, and her special way of moving as if she were flying. She crossed right in front of me without seeing me and floated into the pastry shop on the Plaza de Armas. Dumbstruck, I waited in the street while she bought licorice drops, which she selected one by one, with that tinkling laugh of hers, tossing some into her mouth and handing others to her sister. I wasn't the only one to stand there hypnotized, for within a few minutes a whole circle of men had formed, their noses pressed against the window. It was then that I reacted. It didn't cross my mind that since I had no ➡

Present perfect tense (has passed)

Past tense of a regular verb (entered)

Past progressive form (was wearing)

Present form of an irregular verb (have)

Past perfect progressive form (had been wearing)

Subjunctive mood (as if she were flying)

Active voice (waited)

Past perfect tense (had formed)

fortune, was no one's idea of a proper young man, and faced a most uncertain future, I was far from being the ideal suitor for that heavenly girl. I didn't even know her! But I was bewitched and I decided then and there that she was the only woman in the world who was worthy to be my wife, and that if I couldn't have her I would remain a bachelor. I followed her all the way home. I got on the same streetcar and took the seat behind her, unable to take my eyes off her perfect nape, her round neck, and her soft shoulders caressed by the green curls that had escaped from her coiffure. I didn't feel the motion of the car, because I was in a dream. Suddenly she swept down the aisle and as she passed me her astonishing gold eyes rested for a moment on my own. Part of me must have died. I couldn't breathe and my pulse stopped in its tracks. When I recovered my composure, I had to leap onto the sidewalk at the risk of breaking all my bones, and run toward the street down which she had already turned.

Passive voice

Indicative mood

Past tense of an irregular verb

## Exercise 1

**Identifying Principal Parts** The following sentences are based on the passage from *The House of the Spirits.* Each sentence contains a verb in one of four forms: (a) the base form, (b) the past form, (c) the present participle, or (d) the past participle. At the end of the sentence is a second verb in parentheses. First, identify the form of the verb in italics. Then rewrite the sentence, substituting the verb in parentheses for the italicized verb. In the rewritten sentence be sure the new verb is in the same form as the original verb.

**SAMPLE** Rosa has *captured* everyone's interest. (win)
**ANSWER** past participle; Rosa has won everyone's interest.

1. The striking young woman with the incredible green hair had *attracted* every bystander's attention. (catch)
2. Rosa and her sister *select* licorice drops in the pastry shop on the Plaza de Armas. (choose)
3. Rosa was *tossing* licorice drops, one by one, into her mouth. (throw)
4. She generously *handed* some drops to her little sister. (give)
5. Before Rosa left the shop, a circle of admiring men had *formed* close to the window. (draw)
6. By that time Esteban had *realized* that Rosa was the only woman he could ever love. (know)
7. He has *occupied* a seat behind her on the streetcar. (take)
8. When she *got up* from her seat, she looked at him. (rise)
9. Esteban has *jumped* to his feet and hurried down the street after Rosa. (spring)
10. Each night, Esteban's dreams *carry* images of Rosa the Beautiful and her amazing green hair. (bring)

## Exercise 2

**Using the Perfect Tenses** The following sentences are based on passages from *The House of the Spirits* that are not reprinted in this textbook. On your paper rewrite each sentence, adding the appropriate form of the italicized verb in the place indicated by the caret. Write the verb in the tense indicated in parentheses, using the past participle of the main verb and the appropriate form of the helping verb *have*.

**SAMPLE** Because of Rosa's flawless beauty, some people ^ her an angel. (present perfect tense of *think*)

**ANSWER** Because of Rosa's flawless beauty, some people have thought her an angel.

1. Rosa's little sister Clara ^ fame to her family through her gifts of prophecy. (present perfect tense of *bring*)
2. In the past Clara ^ earthquakes before they occurred. (past perfect tense of *foretell*)
3. After tiny Clara ^ aloud rudely in church, the priest called her bewitched. (past perfect tense of *speak*)
4. Old Nana ^ the nurse of these unusual children for many years. (present perfect tense of *be*)
5. By a certain point in the novel, the strange Clara ^ Esteban's bride. (future perfect tense of *become*)

## Exercise 3

**Using the Progressive and Emphatic Forms** The following sentences are based on the passage from *The House of the Spirits*. On your paper rewrite each sentence, adding the appropriate form of the italicized verb in the place indicated by the caret. Write the verb in the form indicated in parentheses. Use the present participle of the main verb with the appropriate form of the auxiliary verb *be* or the base form of the main verb with the appropriate form of *do*.

**SAMPLE** Unaware of the crowd outside, Rosa ^ candy in a pastry shop. (past progressive form of *buy*)

**ANSWER** Unaware of the crowd outside, Rosa was buying candy in a pastry shop.

1. On the day of her first meeting with Esteban, Rosa ^ a violet dress. (past emphatic form of *wear*)
2. Masses of greenish curls ^ Rosa's delicate face and soft shoulders. (past progressive form of *frame*) ➡
3. In a moment the worshipful Esteban ^ upon Rosa's flawless neck. (future progressive form of *gaze*)
4. Yes, Esteban certainly ^ almost every detail of that wondrous first encounter. (past emphatic form of *remember*)
5. In spite of his unworthiness as a suitor of the wealthy girl, the impoverished Esteban ^ an intense courtship. (past progressive form of *begin*)

## Exercise 4

**Voice of Verbs** The following sentences are about *The House of the Spirits.* First, identify each sentence as being in either the *passive voice* or the *active voice.* Then rewrite each sentence, changing the active voice to the passive or the passive voice to the active.

**SAMPLE** Clara was fed licorice drops by Rosa.
**ANSWER** passive voice; Rosa fed Clara licorice drops.

1. Rosa and Clara are chaperoned by Nana.
2. Esteban sends love letters to Rosa.
3. Rosa is courted seriously by no other young men.
4. Many are daunted by her beauty.
5. Rosa's parents will accept Esteban's marriage proposal.

## Exercise 5

**Proofreading**

**Proofreading** The passage below describes Dora Ramirez, whose painting appears on this page. Rewrite the passage, correcting the errors in spelling, grammar, and usage. Add any missing punctuation. There are ten errors.

### *Dora Ramirez*

[1]Dora Ramirez is born in 1923 in Medellín, Colombia. [2]She studied painting in her native city—first at its university and later at it's Institute of Plastic Arts. ➡

**Dora Ramirez, *Self-portrait at an Open Window,* 1977**

[3]The painting on the preceding page captures a personal moment in the artists' life. [4]The feeling that she expresses is one of exultation and exuberant self-possession, and she appeared to embrace life. [5]The outward-reaching gaze in her eyes are echoed in the wing-like billowing of her dress.

[6]Ramirez's style has a graphic simplicity charaterized by bold geometric patches of color. [7]The woman's face is having an unaffected directness; indeed, it is the force of her gesture as she opens the window that establishes the exultant mood.

[8]Isabel Allende has wrote about a beautiful girl who moved as if she were floating or flying. [9]The girl sweeped down the aisle as she passed the narrator. [10]Awed by her beauty the narrator watched her and dreamed.

**Mixed Review**

**Exercise 6**

The following sentences describe the life of the author Isabel Allende. Rewrite each sentence, following the instructions in parentheses.

**SAMPLE** The daughter of a Chilean diplomat, Isabel Allende lives all over the world during her childhood. (Change the verb to the simple past tense.)

**ANSWER** The daughter of a Chilean diplomat, Isabel Allende lived all over the world during her childhood.

***Isabel Allende***

1. Until 1973 Allende worked in Chile as a journalist. (Change the verb to the past progressive form.)
2. Isabel's uncle Salvador Allende becomes the president of Chile, but he died in 1973 during a coup d'état. (Change the first verb to make the tenses compatible.)
3. In 1974 Isabel fled to Venezuela because her opposition to the new regime in Chile jeopardized her safety. (Change the second verb to the past progressive form.)
4. Until the political climate changes in Chile, Allende will write from her current home in California. (Change the second verb to the future progressive form.)
5. Allende started *The House of the Spirits* (1982) as a letter to her sick grandfather. (Rewrite the sentence in the passive voice.)
6. Allende based many of her characters on her family. (Change the verb to the present perfect tense.)
7. When she is a child, the love and violence in Shakespeare's plots fired her vivid imagination. (Correct the error caused by the use of the present tense.)
8. These passions also dominate her novels. (Rewrite the sentence in the passive voice.)
9. Allende's novels combine fantasy with realism. (Change the verb to the present emphatic form.)
10. Journalistic techniques are also employed in her fiction. (Rewrite the sentence in the active voice.)

# Writing Application

**Active Voice in Writing** Junius Edwards uses verbs in the active voice in this passage from his short story "Liars Don't Qualify" to create a feeling of movement and suspense. Examine the passage, focusing especially on the italicized verbs.

> The fat man *swung* his chair around. . . . He *raised* his left arm and *mopped* his face with the handkerchief, his eyes still on Will. The odor from under his sweat-soaked arm *made* Will step back. Will *held* his breath until the fat man *finished* mopping his face. The fat man *put* his handkerchief away. He *pulled* a desk drawer open, and then he *took* his eyes off Will.

Note how the active voice gives the writing a note of liveliness. Although the verbs are in the past tense, they convey a sense of "happening right before your eyes" that helps draw the reader into the story.

**Techniques with Active Voice** Try to apply some of Junius Edward's writing techniques when you write and revise your own work.

1. Whenever possible, use the active rather than the passive voice in your writing to create a feeling of movement. Compare the following:

**Passive** His chair was swung around by the fat man.
**Edward's Version** The fat man swung his chair around.

2. Use the active rather than the passive voice in order to avoid long, awkward, or unclear sentences. Compare the following:

**Passive** His left arm was raised and his face was mopped with the handkerchief, his eyes still on Will.
**Edward's Version** He raised his left arm and mopped his face with the handkerchief, his eyes still on Will.

**Practice** Practice these techniques by revising the following passage, using a separate sheet of paper. Pay particular attention to the underlined words.

> The track portion of the track-and-field events at the Olympics comprises foot races of various distances. The different races <u>are performed</u> by individuals or national teams before cheering crowds. Naturally, the most emotional response from the crowd <u>is</u> usually <u>prompted</u> by an unexpected outcome. Emotions ran especially high in 1964, when the ten-thousand-meter race <u>was won</u> by America's Billy Mills. Mills's victory <u>was anticipated</u> by few onlookers, for an Australian runner <u>had been deemed</u> the likely winner by most experts. As the long race progressed, Mills's unexpected performance <u>was noted</u> with increasing wonder by sportscasters. When the others <u>were outdistanced</u> by Mills and the finish line <u>was crossed</u>, Mills's victory <u>was</u> thunderously <u>applauded</u> by everyone. His brilliant upset <u>is</u> still <u>viewed</u> by sports historians as one of the most exciting events in Olympic history.

UNIT

16

# Subject-Verb Agreement

Grammar

## Lessons

## 16.1 Intervening Prepositional Phrases

Do not mistake a word in a prepositional phrase for the subject of a sentence.

Remember that the subject of a sentence never appears within a prepositional phrase. Be sure that the verb agrees with the actual subject of the sentence and not with the object of a preposition.

> The ***author*** of the stories **uses** a pseudonym. [The subject, *author*, is singular; *of the stories* is a prepositional phrase; therefore, the verb, *uses*, is singular.]

> A **letter** with many mistakes **does** not **make** a good impression. [The subject, *letter*, is singular; *with many mistakes* is a prepositional phrase; therefore, the auxiliary verb, *does*, is singular.]

> The ***books*** on that shelf **are** biographies. [The subject, *books*, is plural; *on that shelf* is a prepositional phrase; therefore, the verb, *are*, is plural.]

> **Beams** of colored light **have passed** through the prism without creating a rainbow pattern. [The subject, *beams*, is plural; *of colored light* is a prepositional phrase; therefore, the auxiliary verb, *have*, is plural.]

A verb must agree with its subject in person and number.

Most verbs change form to indicate agreement only in the present tense: for a third-person singular subject an *-s* (or *-es*) is added to the base verb. The linking verb *be*, however, changes form in both the present and the past tense.

| SINGULAR | PLURAL |
|---|---|
| She **sings.** | They **sing.** |
| He **is** tall. | They **are** tall. |
| It **was** wrong. | They **were** wrong. |

When *be*, *have*, and *do* are used as auxiliaries in verb phrases, their form changes to show agreement with third-person subjects.

| SINGULAR | PLURAL |
|---|---|
| She **is singing**. | They **are singing.** |
| He **has gone** away. | They **have gone** away. |
| He **does work** here. | They **do work** here. |

## Exercise 1 Identifying Verbs and their Subjects

Write the verb in each sentence. Then write the verb's subject along with an *S* if the subject is singular and a *P* if the subject is plural. Do not forget that some verbs occur as verb phrases.

### *When the Forest Goes*

1. The tropical rain forest houses more species of plants and animals than all the remainder of the world's ecosystems combined.
2. Trees comprise approximately seventy percent of all the plants in the tropical rain forest.
3. After being cleared for agriculture, rain forest soils can tolerate only a few crop plantings.
4. The soil then becomes infertile.
5. Rain forests are cleared because of commercial timber cutting and the farming needs of expanding populations.
6. The earth is experiencing the greatest number of animal and plant extinctions ever.
7. The burning and decomposition of the felled trees add to the level of carbon dioxide in the atmosphere.
8. Furthermore, rain forest plants have been removed.
9. They are tremendous users of carbon dioxide during photosynthesis.
10. The negative effects of rain forest destruction are collectively called the Greenhouse Effect.

## Exercise 2 Making Subjects and Verbs Agree When Prepositional Phrases Intervene

First find the simple subject in each of the following sentences. Then write on your paper the verb in parentheses that agrees with the subject of each sentence.

### *The Masai People*

1. The Masai people of East Africa (is/are) nomads who have maintained a distinctive culture throughout many centuries.
2. A typical house within most Masai compounds (has/have) walls of mud.
3. Until they become warriors, the males in this culture (has/have) to postpone marriage.
4. A young Masai man with good hunting skills (gains/gain) the respect of his people.
5. A popular sport among the Masai men (is/are) competitive spear throwing.
6. The pursuit of Western culture and riches (does/do) not really interest the tribe, which values its animals above all else.
7. One belief of these herders (is/are) that they are the rightful custodians of all cattle.
8. Other tribes throughout Africa naturally (remains/remain) wary of the Masai's belief about cattle.
9. Characteristically Masai people near a modern metropolis (has/have) little to do with their big-city neighbors.
10. Sometimes, however, Masai men in financial need (finds/find) employment as night watchmen in Kenya.

## 16.2 Agreement with Linking Verbs

**Do not be confused by a predicate nominative that is different in number from the subject. Only the subject affects the number of the linking verb.**

The first ***act*** **was** jugglers with flaming batons. [The singular verb, *was*, agrees with the singular subject, *act*, not with the predicate nominative, *jugglers*.]

Show ***tickets*** **were** the first prize in the essay contest. [The plural verb, *were*, agrees with the plural subject, *tickets*, not with the predicate nominative, *prize*.]

One **problem** of the circus clowns **was** unexpected attacks from other clowns. [The singular verb, *was*, agrees with the singular subject, *problem*, not with the predicate nominative, *attacks*.]

Traffic **jams** in the parking lot **were** one difficulty for circus attendees. [The plural verb, *were*, agrees with the plural subject, *jams*, not with the predicate nominative, *difficulty*.]

### Exercise 3 Making Linking Verbs Agree with Their Subjects

Find the simple subject or subjects in each of the following sentences. Then write on your paper the form of the verb in parentheses that agrees with the subject of each sentence.

*Visiting Hong Kong*

1. A translation of the name *Hong Kong* (is/are) the words "fragrant harbor."
2. For many visitors the diverse aspects of Hong Kong (has become/have become) its charm.
3. The contrasting examples of ancient and modern architectural design there (seems/seem) a challenge to the senses.
4. The bustling streets of Hong Kong (appears/appear) a blend of nineteenth-century culture and contemporary commerce.
5. On famous Ladder Street a modern thoroughfare (becomes/become) winding steps without warning.
6. Actually, Hong Kong (is/are) three separate districts: Kowloon Peninsula, Hong Kong Island, and the New Territories.
7. The border points between Hong Kong and mainland China (remains/remain) an attraction for both natives and tourists.
8. An interesting sight (is/are) the Chinese junks skimming the harbor.
9. A special feature for gourmet diners (is/are) the foods prepared at the fine restaurants.
10. The galleries in the Museum of Art (is/are) a repository of antiquities, including precious jade, paintings, sculpture, and ceramics.

## 16.3 Agreement in Inverted Sentences

In an **inverted sentence**—a sentence in which the subject follows the verb—take care in locating the simple subject, and make sure that the verb agrees with the subject.

Many inverted sentences begin with a prepositional phrase. Do not mistake the object of the preposition for the subject of the sentence. Remember that the subject of an inverted sentence always follows the verb.

SINGULAR From the pool **leaps** (V) a ***dolphin.*** (S)

PLURAL From the pool **leap** (V) two ***dolphins.*** (S)

### Exercise 4 Subject-Verb Agreement in Inverted Sentences That Begin with Prepositional Phrases

Find the simple subject in each of the following sentences. Then write on your paper the form of the verb in parentheses that agrees with the subject of each sentence.

1. In the forest (burns/burn) three types of fires: ground fires, surface fires, and crown fires.
2. Within the humus layer (blazes/blaze) the ground fire.
3. Amid the surface litter and forest undergrowth (flames/flame) the surface fire.
4. Through the tops of shrubs and trees (reaches/reach) the crown fire.
5. During a common forest fire (rages/rage) two or more types of fires.

When an interrogative sentence contains an auxiliary verb, the auxiliary usually precedes the subject, and the main verb follows the subject.

SINGULAR **Does** (V) that ***dolphin*** (S) **recognize** (V) hand signals?

PLURAL **Do** (V) those ***dolphins*** (S) **recognize** (V) hand signals?

### Exercise 5 Subject-Verb Agreement in Interrogative Sentences

Write five interrogative sentences about forest fires. Make sure that the verb in each sentence agrees with the subject. Underline the verb in each interrogative sentence. After each sentence, write *S* if the subject of the sentence is singular; *P* if it is plural.

SAMPLE have destroyed
ANSWER Have forest fires ever destroyed an entire state park? P

Some inverted sentences begin with the words *there* or *here*. *There* or *here* is almost never the subject of a sentence.

SINGULAR — There **goes** (V) the ***trainer.*** (S)

PLURAL — There **go** (V) the dolphins' ***trainers.*** (S)

**Exercise 6** **Subject-Verb Agreement in Inverted Sentences That Begin with *Here* or *There***

Find the simple subject in each of the following sentences. Then write the form of the verb in parentheses that agrees with the subject of each sentence.

1. Here (is/are) two prevalent causes of forest fires: human negligence and intentional arson.
2. There (is/are) fewer fires ignited by lightning than by humans.
3. Here (is/are) the role that weather plays in influencing the start of a forest fire.
4. There (is/are) factors such as rainfall, temperature, and humidity.
5. There (is/are) means by which the flammability of a forest can be predicted.

**Exercise 7** **Subject-Verb Agreement in Inverted Sentences**

Find the simple subject in each of the following sentences. Then write the form of the verb in parentheses that agrees with the subject of each sentence.

***The Sea, a Subject of Universal Curiosity***

1. Why (does/do) people continue to study and explore the sea?
2. There (is/are) numerous reasons for this persistent interest in the sea.
3. From our oceans (comes/come) information about Earth's climate.
4. From our knowledge of the sea (stems/stem) an ability to increase our food supply.
5. Here (is/are) another compelling reason for the universal curiosity about the sea.
6. In the ocean's depths (lies/lie) great wealth.
7. On the reefs off Bermuda (rests/rest) many sunken ships.
8. There (is/are) often a chest of gold coins waiting to be discovered in an ancient shipwreck.
9. There (is/are) sometimes many problems in the raising of a sunken ship.
10. (Doesn't/Don't) the discoverer of underwater treasure get to keep the treasure?
11. Why (have/has) past explorers been unable to study the luxury liner *Titanic* that sank?
12. There (was/were) numerous changes in rules for passenger ships after the *Titanic* sank.
13. With reforms (come/comes) a measure of safety *Titanic* passengers never had.
14. (Have/Has) recent efforts been made to remove artifacts from the sunken ship?
15. Into the icy waters (plunge/plunges) robot submersibles equipped with television cameras.
16. Behind the robot submersibles (follow/follows) a three-person United States submersible.
17. There (has/have) also been a salvage effort conducted by the French.
18. (Does/Do) the United States and France have to share whatever they find?
19. There (is/are) much power within the sea as well as climate information and a food supply.
20. (Is/Are) we technologically equipped to harness the sea's strength and utilize it for energy?

# 16.4 Agreement with Special Subjects

## Collective Nouns

A **collective noun** names a group. Consider a collective noun singular when it refers to a group as a whole. Consider a collective noun plural when it refers to each member of a group individually.

| | |
|---|---|
| SINGULAR | The ***audience*** **applauds.** |
| PLURAL | The ***audience*** **disagree** on the quality of the performance. |
| SINGULAR | The ***class*** **listens** to the lecture. |
| PLURAL | The ***class*** **go** their separate ways after the bell rings. |

## Special Nouns

Certain nouns that end in *-s*, such as *mathematics*, *measles*, and *mumps*, take singular verbs.

| | |
|---|---|
| SINGULAR | ***Mumps*** **causes** a swelling of the salivary glands below and in front of the ears. |

Certain other nouns that end in *-s*, such as *scissors*, *pants*, *binoculars*, and *eyeglasses*, take plural verbs.

| | |
|---|---|
| PLURAL | The ***binoculars*** **were** powerful. |

Many nouns that end in *-ics* may be singular or plural, depending upon their meaning.

| | |
|---|---|
| SINGULAR | ***Economics*** **is** the science that deals with the production, distribution, and consumption of wealth. [one science] |
| PLURAL | The ***economics*** of her plan **are** not sound. [more than one economic factor] |

**Exercise 8** **Making Verbs Agree with Collective and Special Nouns**

Write ten sentences using the following five collective and special nouns. In your first sentence consider the noun singular and make the verb agree. In your second sentence consider the noun plural and make the verb agree.

| | |
|---|---|
| SAMPLE | fleet |
| ANSWER | The admiral's fleet sails precisely at dawn. |
| | The admiral's fleet transport cargo according to each ship's capacity. |

1. jury 2. faculty 3. swarm 4. days 5. politics

## Nouns of Amount

When a noun of amount refers to a total that is considered as one unit, it is singular. When it refers to a number of individual units, it is plural.

| | |
|---|---|
| SINGULAR | Five ***dollars* is** too much to pay for dues. [one amount] |
| PLURAL | Five ***dollars* are** in my wallet. [five individual one-dollar bills] |
| SINGULAR | Three ***weeks* is** the incubation period. [one unit of time] |
| PLURAL | Three ***weeks* have passed.** [three individual periods of time] |

## Titles

A title is always singular, even if a noun within the title is plural.

| | |
|---|---|
| SINGULAR | ***The Three Musketeers* is** an exciting novel by Alexandre Dumas. |
| SINGULAR | ***Arsenic and Old Lace* was** performed last year by both the local community theater and the high school's drama club. |

### Exercise 9 Making Verbs Agree with Special Subjects

Find the subject in each sentence, and write on your paper the form of the verb in parentheses that agrees with the subject.

| | |
|---|---|
| SAMPLE | Eight days (are, is) the time allotted to build the set for the opera. |
| ANSWER | is |

*Opera*

1. Forty dollars (is/are) not too much to pay for opera tickets.
2. Binoculars in an opera house (enhances/enhance) a viewer's enjoyment of the performance.
3. The orchestra (tunes/tune) their instruments before the opera begins.
4. The *Tales of Hoffmann* (is/are) a famous opera.
5. After a fine performance the audience often (discusses/discuss) the highlights among themselves.
6. Fourteen comic operas (is/are) the legacy of the famous team of Sir William Gilbert and Sir Arthur Sullivan.
7. English politics (was/were) the subject of many Gilbert and Sullivan operas.
8. *The Pirates of Penzance* (is/are) a well-known Gilbert and Sullivan opera.
9. The crew of a ship named H.M.S. *Pinafore* (was/were) the unlikely subject of another Gilbert and Sullivan opera.
10. Twenty-five years (is/are) the length of time during which Gilbert and Sullivan collaborated on their operas.

# 16.5 Agreement with Compound Subjects

## Compound Subjects Joined by *And*

A compound subject that is joined by *and* or *both . . . and* is plural unless its parts belong to one unit or they both refer to the same person or thing.

PLURAL — The ***shark*** *and* the ***porpoise*** **are diving.**
*Both* an ***opera*** *and* an ***operetta*** **are** enjoyable to attend.

SINGULAR — ***Peas*** *and* ***carrots*** **is** a good side dish. [The compound subject is one unit.]
Her ***cousin*** *and* ***tutor*** **helps** him. [One person is both the cousin and the tutor.]

### Exercise 10 Making Verbs Agree with Subjects Joined by *And*

On your paper write the correct form of the verb in parentheses.

***Tsunami***

1. Both *Tsunami* and *seismic sea wave* (refer/refers) to the same thing: a large ocean wave spawned by an undersea earthquake.
2. The tilting of the ocean floor during an earthquake and an undersea landslide (are/is) two theories scientists have purported to describe conditions that trigger the tsunami.
3. Volcanoes and seismic activity (stretch/stretches) 24,000 miles around the Pacific Ocean.
4. Oceanographers and seismologists (suggest/suggests) that tsunamis originate along this alleged Ring of Fire.
5. This colossal wall of water and sometimes lethal enemy (has/have) struck the Hawaiian Islands forty times in the past two hundred years.

## Compound Subjects Joined by *Or* or *Nor*

With compound subjects joined by *or* or *nor* (or by *either . . . or* or *neither . . . nor*), the verb always agrees with the subject nearer the verb.

PLURAL — *Neither* the ***shark*** *nor* the ***porpoises*** **are diving.**

SINGULAR — *Either* the ***shark*** *or* the ***porpoise*** **is diving.**

## *Many a, Every,* and *Each* with Compound Subjects

When *many a*, *every*, or *each* precedes a compound subject, the subject is considered singular.

SINGULAR — *Many a* ***writer, painter,*** and ***musician*** **knows** disappointment.

*Every* ***newspaper*** and ***magazine*** **prints** editorials.

*Each* ***dolphin*** and its ***trainer*** **is** in the pool.

**Exercise 11** — **Subject-Verb Agreement When *Many a, Every,* or *Each* Precedes a Compound Subject**

On your paper, write the correct form of the verb in parentheses.

1. Many a man, woman, and child (has/have) visited the Grand Canyon in Arizona.
2. Not every tourist and local citizen, however, (travels/travel) to the canyon by steam train.
3. Each rider and train worker (is/are) transported from Williams, Arizona, to the canyon by way of a scenic route through a prairie scattered with jack rabbits and ponderosa pines.
4. Many a singer, comedian, and playful bandit (has/have) boarded the steam train in Williams to accompany the passengers.
5. Each child and adult on board the train (enjoys/enjoy) the performances of the entertainers.

**Exercise 12** — **Explaining Why Verbs Agree with Their Subjects**

Look at the underlined verb in each sentence and find its subject. Then write the letter of the explanation that gives the reason for the subject-verb agreement.

**a** A compound subject joined by *and* is plural unless its parts refer to the same person or thing.
**b** With compound subjects joined by *or* or *nor*, the verb agrees with the nearer subject.
**c** A compound subject preceded by *Many a*, *every*, or *each* is considered singular.

1. Juniors and seniors who have participated in spring sports are honored at a banquet.
2. A boy or his parents accept a certificate of participation.
3. Each girl and her mother receives a corsage.
4. As part of the festivities, the choir, the band, and the glee club perform.
5. The secretary and treasurer of the booster club congratulates each student.
6. In this fine group of young people is many a student athlete and scholar.
7. Neither the teachers nor the principal ever misses this outstanding event.
8. Coaches, players, and student managers are recognized during the evening.
9. Ice cream and cake are served for dessert.
10. Every trophy and plaque is treasured by its recipient.

## 16.6 Intervening Expressions

The number of a subject is not affected by expressions such as *accompanied by*, *as well as*, *in addition to*, *plus*, and *together with*. Although expressions such as these have a meaning that is similar to that of the conjunction *and*, they do not create a compound subject.

If a singular subject is linked to another noun by an intervening expression, such as *accompanied by*, the subject is still considered singular.

**SINGULAR** The ***dolphin,*** *along with* its trainer, **is** in the swimming pool.

The ***trainer,*** *as well as* her helper, **is studying** animal behavior.

### Exercise 13 Making Verbs Agree with Their Subjects

On your paper write the appropriate form of the verb in parentheses.

***The Search for Life on Mars***

1. *Viking II* and *Viking I* (was/were) safely landed on Mars in 1976.
2. Careful planning plus good luck (was/were) responsible for the success of the two missions.
3. Advanced technology, together with human resourcefulness, (permits/permit) scientists to speculate about the nature of neighboring planets.
4. Many a human hope and dream (focuses/focus) on finding life on other planets.
5. Mars's desolate landscape, in addition to its freezing temperatures, (makes/make) it an unlikely environment for any form of life.
6. Every scrap of soil and photo scan (was/were) analyzed for signs of past life on Mars.
7. Possibly only a microbe or some other simple organism (is/are) able to survive on Mars.
8. Each new test and experiment (holds/hold) hope of an important discovery.
9. So far neither soil analysis nor photo scans (has/have) provided conclusive evidence for the existence of life on Mars.
10. Both curiosity and optimism (drives/drive) scientists to continue the search for some form of life on one of the other planets.

### Exercise 14 Creating Sentences with Compound Subjects

Write five sentences, each using one of the following items as the compound subject. Make the compound subject agree with a present-tense verb.

1. cream cheese and jelly
2. neither the director nor the actors
3. both *National Wildlife* and *International Wildlife*
4. the owner or a tenant
5. many a singer and dancer

# 16.7 Indefinite Pronouns as Subjects

**A verb must agree in number with an indefinite pronoun subject.**

Some indefinite pronouns are always singular, others are always plural, and still others may be singular or plural, depending upon their usage.

| Indefinite Pronouns | | | |
|---|---|---|---|
| **Always Singular** | | | |
| each<br>either<br>neither<br>one | everyone<br>everybody<br>everything<br>no one | nobody<br>nothing<br>anyone<br>anybody | anything<br>someone<br>somebody<br>something |
| **Always Plural** | | | |
| several | few | both | many |
| **Singular or Plural** | | | |
| some | all | most | none |

SINGULAR ***Everyone* wants** to see that movie.
PLURAL ***Several*** of us **were** at the big game.

If a pronoun can be either singular or plural, make sure that the pronoun agrees with the noun to which it refers.

SINGULAR ***Most*** of the pie **was** eaten. [*Most* refers to *pie*, a singular noun.]
PLURAL ***Most*** of the cookies **were** leftover. [*Most* refers to *cookies*, a plural noun.]

**Exercise 15** **Subject-Verb Agreement with Indefinite Pronouns as Subjects**

Select and write a different indefinite pronoun for each of the following sentences.

*Pro or Con?*

1. Nearly __________ feels compelled at some time or another to support a cause.
2. Practically __________ is able to remain silent about every issue that faces society.
3. __________ has either a pro-constituency or an anti-constituency.
4. __________ of the people involved in causes believe that theirs is the only legitimate aim.
5. __________ of the sides usually have passive and aggressive supporters.

6. __________ dominates the attention of the public more, however, than aggressive behavior on the part of a pro- or anti- group.
7. __________ of the media can resist the temptation to exploit any militant behavior that a group's member or members instigate.
8. To members of the press, __________ that is taken a step beyond acceptable behavior is worthy of news coverage.
9. __________ of the hottest issues in the United States is the environment.
10. __________ of the opposing camps has protesters, vigilantes, and lobbyists.
11. __________ who takes the time to study the issues of both sides carefully is able to weigh the pros and cons of both causes.
12. Likewise, almost __________ has missed the many demonstrations conducted by anti-fur groups opposed to the slaughter of animals for the benefit of the fur industry and vanity.
13. __________ of the victories the United States now holds dear have been the results of strong-willed supporters of a cause.
14. __________ have been supported with the fervor and historical significance of the Civil Rights Movement during the 1960s.
15. __________, such as groups and demonstrations that forced the United States government to delve into the issue of POW's and MIA's, have induced responses in previously inactive areas.
16. In need of a strong leader who can incite powerful feelings, __________ usually leads groups.
17. Not just __________ has the effrontery and courage to be the in the vanguard.
18. Of the two sides, however, __________ wins when violence erupts.
19. If only momentarily, __________ discovers a distaste for the issue when death and destruction come into play.
20. When people organize to support or oppose an issue, __________ have to maintain a respect for human life and property if they expect to maintain positive publicity.

## Exercise 16 Making Verbs Agree with Indefinite Subjects

Write five sentences, each using one of the following indefinite pronouns as the subject. Make each subject agree with a present-tense verb.

1. no one
2. both
3. something
4. everybody
5. few

## Exercise 17 Creating Sentences with Indefinite Pronoun Subjects

For each indefinite pronoun listed below, write two sentences, using the pronoun as the subject of both sentences. In the first sentence of each pair, use a singular present-tense verb. In the second sentence use a plural present-tense verb.

**SAMPLE** Some
**ANSWER** Some of the crop belongs to my neighbor.
Some of the apples fall to the ground every autumn.

1. some
2. all
3. any
4. most
5. none

## 16.8 Agreement in Adjective Clauses

**When the subject of an adjective clause is a relative pronoun, the verb in the clause must agree with the antecedent of the relative pronoun.**

A relative pronoun is often the subject of an adjective clause. The number of the relative pronoun subject depends upon the number of its antecedent in the main clause.

> Opera is one of the entertainment ***forms*** **that combine music, drama, and lavish costumes and stage sets.**

In the preceding example the antecedent of *that* is *forms,* not *one,* because *several* entertainment forms—not just opera—combine music, drama, and lavish costumes and stage sets. Since *forms* is plural, *that* is considered plural, and the verb in the adjective clause, *combine,* must also be plural.

> Opera is the only ***one*** of the entertainment forms **that is unfamiliar to Martha.**

In this example the antecedent of *that* is *one,* not *forms,* because only one kind of entertainment form (opera) is unfamiliar to Martha. Since *one* is singular, *that* is considered singular, and the verb in the adjective clause, *is,* must also be singular.

When you see the expression *one of* in the main clause, you must determine whether the antecedent of the relative pronoun is *one,* as in the second example above, or whether it is the following noun, such as *forms* in the first example. The antecedent of the relative pronoun is *one* when *one of* is modified by *the only,* as in the second example.

### Exercise 18 Making Subjects and Verbs Agree in Adjective Clauses

On your paper complete the following sentences by choosing the correct form of the verb in parentheses.

1. *West Side Story* is the only one of Leonard Bernstein's scores that (comes/come) to mind immediately.
2. The adobe house is one of the ancient Native American dwellings that (is/are) still being used.
3. "The Lady, or the Tiger?" is the only one of the many stories I have read that (has/have) no clear-cut ending.
4. The bamboo pattern is one of the motifs that (decorates/decorate) Chinese pottery and other handicrafts.
5. Emily Dickinson is one of the many nineteenth-century poets who (remains/remain) popular today.

6. The northern oriole is one of the eastern United States birds that (winters/winter) in the warm climates of Latin America.
7. Diana Ross is one of the Supremes who (has adapted/have adapted) her career to the changing styles in contemporary music.
8. Franklin D. Roosevelt was the only one of our presidents who (was/were) a victim of polio.
9. At one time George Washington Carver was the only one of the nation's agricultural chemists who (was fascinated/were fascinated) by the humble peanut.
10. The tango is one of the Latin American dances that (has captured/have captured) the fancy of dancers around the world.
11. Stephen Spielberg is one of those directors who (like/likes) to use unusual special effects.
12. The Kalahari Desert in southern Africa was one of the regions that (were/was) crossed by the nineteenth-century British explorer David Livingstone.
13. E-mail is one of the electronic mail services that (transmit/transmits) documents to other computers or terminals.
14. A library in Iasi, a city in eastern Romania, is the only one of the city's buildings that (house/houses) the chief records of Romanian history.
15. June 6, 1944, when Allied forces landed in Normandy, is the only one of the military's D-days that (have/has) made such a memorable mark in history.
16. U2, an Irish rock band, is one of the many rock groups that (have/has) won Grammy Awards.
17. *Sky Above Clouds* is one of Georgia O' Keeffe's largest works that (hang/hangs) in museums throughout the United States.
18. The British physician Edward Jenner was the only one of many doctors practicing in the eighteenth century who (were/was) willing to administer a smallpox immunization for the first time.
19. The Department of Veteran Affairs, created by the United States Congress in 1988, is the only one of the federal departments that (oversee/oversees) the administration of national benefits to veterans.
20. The fable is the only one of the literary compositions that (convey/conveys) a moral truth while employing the unlikely and impossible.

## Exercise 19 Writing Sentences That Contain Adjective Clauses

Using the information provided on the preceding page as a guide, write three sentences, each containing an adjective clause in which the relative pronoun's antecedent is plural. Then write two sentences, each containing an adjective clause in which the relative pronoun's antecedent is singular. Make sure the verb in each of the adjective clauses agrees with the antecedent of the relative pronoun.

**SAMPLE ANSWER** The red convertible is the only one of the cars that appeals to Mario. (The antecedent of the relative pronoun subject, *that,* is *one*; therefore the singular verb, *appeals*, agrees with the relative pronoun subject.)

**Exercise 20** **Subject-Verb Agreement**

Number your paper 1–10. Read each sentence. If the verb agrees with the subject, write *Correct*. If the verb does not agree with the subject, write the subject and then write a form of the verb that does agree with the subject.

### *China*

1. China, which is one of the world's largest countries, is heavily populated.
2. More than thirty-four hundred offshore islands are a part of China.
3. To the north is the Mongolian Republic and Russia.
4. Within China's borders exists more than one fifth of the world's population.
5. Have the influence of a communist government helped China's economic history?
6. The Chinese public consist of more than a billion people, of which more than seventy million belong to fifty-six national minorities.
7. Two thousand years was the length of time that the Chinese economy operated under a feudal system in which a few landowners rented portions of land to peasant tenants.
8. Chinese economics is currently experiencing rapid growth, but at the cost of high inflation rates in urban areas.
9. Many a Chinese man and woman has heard the adages of K'ung Fu-tzu, the philosopher known in the West as Confucius.
10. China, as well as other Asian countries, provide tourists from the West both a taste of ancient history and a modern culture different from theirs in many ways.

**Exercise 21** **Subject-Verb Agreement**

The following paragraph contains ten errors in subject-verb agreement. Locate the sentences with errors, and rewrite those sentences using the correct verb form. (Not every sentence has an error.)

### *Whales*

[1]The whale is one of the mammals that lives in the ocean. [2]Ten to fifteen whales comes together to form an average family. [3]A family of whales are called a pod. [4]Each of the whale pods lives together for many years. [5]A tiny sea plant, as well as a giant squid, serve as food for whales. [6]In northern oceans thrives the sea life that whales consume. [7]In winter most of the whales migrates to warm waters, where the baby whales are born. [8]The migration of certain whales cover ten thousand miles or more on a round trip. [9]Whales of enormous size successfully migrates. [10]The blubber of these whales permits the animals to go long distances without finding food. [11]Some of the whales' blubber keep the animals warm in chilly waters. [12]There are many characteristics of whales that are similar to human traits. [13]The pods in a way is a support system in which family members care for one another. [14]The conversation of whales has been recorded by scientists. [15]Many an article and book have been written about whales.

UNIT

# 16

## Unit Review

# Grammar Review

## Subject-Verb Agreement

Camara Laye, who was born in Guinea, West Africa, learned French as his first language. He published *The Radiance of the King* in 1956, and it soon became a classic of African literature. In this passage from that work, a poor Frenchman named Clarence comes to offer his services to a young African king. The passage, which shows Laye's mastery of description, has been annotated to show some of the kinds of subject-verb agreement covered in this unit.

*Literature Model*

### *from* THE RADIANCE OF THE KING

***by Camara Laye***

***translated from the French by James Kirkup***

Agreement between a plural pronoun subject and the plural past form of *be*

Agreement between a singular pronoun subject and a singular past form of *be*. The plural predicate nominative does not change the number of the subject.

Agreement between a singular noun subject and a singular past form of *be*. The intervening phrase does not change the number of the subject.

And suddenly the whole crowd . . . began to shout and jump up and down, though what they were shouting and why they were jumping he had no idea at all. But perhaps it was simply the back rows which had begun to jump up and down in the hope, the vain hope, of catching a glimpse of part of the esplanade above the heads of the nearer ranks, and then their agitation had communicated itself to the entire crowd in the end, for it was such a homogeneous gathering and so densely packed that the slightest movement would make itself felt throughout its length and breadth.

"The king!" shouted the beggar, his voice rising over the tumult.

It was then that Clarence saw an adolescent boy dressed in white and gold, mounted on a horse whose caparisonings trailed on the ground—a caparison of green velvet embroidered with silver flowers. An attendant, with a drawn sword in his hand, was leading the horse by a bridle; this seemed quite indispensable, because the horse's head was so laden with flossy plumes and pompoms that it must certainly be able to see nothing at all. A second attendant, walking slightly in the rear, held over the sovereign a huge parasol with deep fringes. Then, at a respectful distance, came a band of pages, or rather dancers, for at ➡

a sign from the attendant with the bared sword, their group unexpectedly spread out in the pattern of a star around the king.

Each of these dancers then began to repeat the same movements as Clarence had seen performed by the boys before the guards drove them away from the track with their lashing whips. But this time all the movements were coordinated: each section of the great star took the lead from the dancer who was at the point. The movements, performed in this fashion, lost much of their barbaric nature, but unfortunately the dancers set up another cloud of red dust on the esplanade, and soon the king was completely hidden from the spectators.

Agreement between the relative pronoun subject of a clause and a singular past form of *be*. The number of the relative pronoun is determined by its antecedent, *dancer*.

## Exercise 1

**Making Subjects and Verbs Agree When Prepositional Phrases Intervene** Each of the following sentences describes the scene in the passage from *The Radiance of the King*. On your paper rewrite each sentence, following the directions in parentheses. In some cases you will need to change the form of the verb to make the sentence correct.

1. Groups of spectators are lined up to see the king. (Change *Groups* to *A group*.)
2. A cloth of green velvet covers the king's horse. (Change *A cloth* to *Cloths*.)
3. Robes with intricate designs adorn the king. (Change *intricate designs* to *an intricate design*.)
4. Behind the king the dancers await the signal. (Move the prepositional phrase so that it comes directly after the subject.)
5. The movement of the dancer kicks up red dust. (Change *dancer* to *dancers*.)

## Exercise 2

**Making Linking Verbs Agree with Their Subjects** Each of the sentences below describes the king's palace in *The Radiance of the King*. On your paper rewrite each sentence, following the directions in parentheses. If necessary, change the number of the linking verb.

1. The palace wall is a defense against invaders. (Change *wall* to *walls*.)
2. The thatched roofs of the structures remain prominent features. (Change *prominent features* to *a prominent feature*.)
3. A feature of particular beauty is the courtyard. (Change *courtyard* to *courtyards*.)
4. A marvelous sight is the staircase of the central tower. (Change *staircase* to *staircases*.)
5. Intriguing attractions are the frescoes on the walls. (Change *Intriguing attractions* to *An intriguing attraction*.)

## Exercise 3

**Making Subjects and Verbs Agree in Inverted Sentences** Each of the following sentences describes the scene in the passage from *The Radiance of the King*. First, write each sentence on your paper, choosing the proper form of the verb in parentheses. Then rewrite each sentence in inverted order.

SAMPLE A loud shout (comes/come) from the crowds.
ANSWER A loud shout comes from the crowds.
From the crowds comes a loud shout.

1. A joyful hope (grows/grow) among the spectators.
2. Many onlookers (stands/stand) in the back row.
3. The beggar's voice (rises/rise) over the cheers.
4. Two attendants (appears/appear) on the esplanade.
5. Several pages (follows/follow) at a respectful distance.

## Exercise 4

**Making Verbs Agree with Subjects** Each of the following sentences describes the scene in the passage from *The Radiance of the King*. On your paper rewrite each sentence, following the directions in parentheses and making any necessary adjustments in the form of the verb.

1. Joy infects the crowd. (Add *and excitement* to the complete subject.)
2. Every man enjoys the spectacle. (Add *and woman* to the complete subject.)
3. An attendant and a page assist the king. (Delete *and a page* from the complete subject.)
4. Many a plume decorates the king's horse. (Add *and pompom* to the complete subject.)
5. The young king and his horse are hidden from view by a cloud of red dust. (Delete *and his horse* from the complete subject.)

## Exercise 5

**Making Verbs Agree with Indefinite Pronoun Subjects** The following sentences describe the nation of Guinea. Rewrite each sentence, replacing the indefinite pronoun in italics with the pronoun in parentheses. If necessary, change the number of the verb.

SAMPLE *Each* of Guinea's groups has a distinct culture. (All)
ANSWER All of Guinea's groups have a distinct culture.

1. *Most* of the Susu people inhabit the coastal areas. (Many)
2. In central Guinea *most* of the people herd cattle. (some)
3. *Many* of the Fulani people are pastoral nomads. (Most)
4. The Malinke and the Toma live in the forests; *both* are interesting to visit. (either)
5. Guinea is poor, and *few* expect a change soon. (no one)

**Exercise 6**

The following passage tells about the Ashanti people and the Ashanti ceremonial stool that appears on this page. Rewrite the passage, correcting any errors in spelling, grammar, and usage. There are ten errors.

### *The Art of the Ashanti*

[1]The Ashanti people live on the west coast of Africa and comprises several tribes, including the Kumasi, Nsuta Daniassi, Juabin, Mampon, Ofinsu, Adansi, and Nkwanta. [2]The Ashanti's tribal organization consist of ruling chieftains and common ownership of land. [3]The Ashanti, skilled craftspeople are renowned for their fine objects made of wood and precious metals many of these objects have spiritual significance.

[4]The Ashanti traditionally venerated the Golden Stool a mythical object believed to have floated down from the sky to unify the Ashanti people. [5]Even today each of the Ashanti village chiefs are given a stool as a symbol of power. [6](One of these elaborate stools, carved in wood and embellished with silver, appear on this page.)

[7]In the passage from Camara Laye's *The Radiance of the King*, a crowd pay hommage to a young West African king and his entourage. [8]Although the ancient empires of West Africa was conquered long ago by European powers, remnants of their proud heritage remain.

**Ashanti people, Ghana, Ashanti stool**

**Exercise 7**

**Review** The following biography of Camara Laye contains a number of examples of subject-verb agreement. Study the underlined verbs. Then complete the ten sentences that follow the biography by writing the appropriate form of the verb in parentheses.

***Camara Laye***

Born January 1, 1928, in a small village in French Guinea (now Guinea), Laye was the son of a goldsmith who, because of his work, was believed by the villagers to possess magical powers. Other ancient African beliefs were also held by the villagers.

Raised a Muslim, Laye first attended school outside his village in Conakry, the capital of Guinea. He was surprised by the modern society of Conakry. It was so different from the society of his village. Laye then attended school in Paris, France. Nearly overwhelmed by the differences between African and European cultures, Laye recorded his memories of Guinea and the countryside. These recollections became his first book, *The Dark Child.* Chiefly, the book poses questions about preserving one's traditions amid the turmoil of change and technology.

Laye wrote four books and contributed to a number of articles and short stories that included information about traditional African culture. *The Radiance of the King* was Laye's second book. First titled *Le Regard du roi,* the book asserts a quandary of Laye's when it takes a white European named Clarence into the African countryside. Clarence is forced to adapt to the traditional culture to survive, just as Laye was compelled to adapt to modern European ways to persevere during his education and subsequent occupations. Mainly, *Radiance of the King* is Laye's explanation of how humankind adjusts to life wherever it may lead. Critics argue whether Laye's work is African literature or French. Many have concluded that it is both. Laye's writing can be considered world literature.

Laye's third book, *A Dream of Africa*, criticized the dictatorial policies of the Guinean leader at the time, and Laye, along with his family, was forced to flee to Senegal. There Laye did research, taught, and wrote his fourth book, *The Guardian of the Word.*

Laye married a Guinean woman named Marie, had four children, and died in 1980.

1. Camara Laye's books (is/are) a literary treasure.
2. Most of Laye's work (focuses/focus) on his homeland.
3. Laye's memories (plays/play) a key role in *The Dark Child.*
4. From the novel *The Radiance of the King* (has/have) emerged many interpretations.
5. A spiritual and intellectual quest (seems/seem) important to Laye's theme.
6. Reviews of Laye's work (has/have) been favorable.
7. In Laye's bitter experiences with the government of Guinea (lies/lie) the germ of his book *A Dream of Africa.*
8. The narrator's opinions in this work (is/are) a veiled expression of Laye's own beliefs.
9. Many an oral tale and traditional story (finds/find) a place in Laye's last book, *The Guardian of the Word.*
10. All of *The Guardian of the Word* (is/are) set in West Africa.

# Writing Application

**Subject-Verb Agreement in Writing** The following quotations contain examples of subject-verb agreement. Examine the quotations, focusing on the italicized words.

Black *reapers* with the sound of steel on
stones
*Are* sharpening scythes.
From "Reapers" by Jean Toomer

From the kitchen *come* the tantalizing *aroma* of beetroot soup and the spirited *sounds* of a cleaver on a chopping board.
From *Heavy Wings* by Zhang Jie

In the United States there is more space where *nobody is* than where *anybody is*.
From *The Geographical History of America* by Gertrude Stein

*Many are* called, but few are chosen.
—Matthew 22:14

In this best of possible worlds . . . *all is* for the best.
From *Candide* by Voltaire

**Techniques with Subject-Verb Agreement** When you are proofreading, keep in mind these guidelines as you check for subject-verb agreement:

1. When a prepositional phrase or another expression falls between a subject and its verb, mentally block out the intervening material as you check for agreement.

Look at the quotation from Jean Toomer's "Reapers" as an example of a sentence.

2. When a sentence is in inverted order, remember that the subject follows the verb.

Study the quotation from Zhang Jie's *Heavy Wings* as an example of a sentence.

3. When the subject is an indefinite pronoun, check to see whether it is one that is always singular, always plural, or sometimes singular and sometimes plural, depending upon the noun to which it refers.

Analyze the final three quotations on this page as examples.

**Practice** Apply the techniques you have just learned as you revise on a separate sheet of paper the following paragraph. Check every instance of subject-verb agreement, and make certain you have used the correct form of every verb.

There is many native languages and dialects in the nation of India. Hindi, the most widely spoken of India's native languages, closely resembles Urdu, the language of neighboring Pakistan. Each descend from Sanskrit, an Indo-European language of ancient times. In the southern part of India lives many Tamil speakers. Tamil, like Kannada and Malayalam, belong to the Dravidian family of languages. Since all of India do not speak one language, many of the non-native Hindi speakers learn Hindi as a second language. Among other popular second languages are English, introduced during India's centuries of British rule. Because of the British presence, there have been much interchange between English and the native languages of India. Several of our common words in English—*shampoo*, for example—is borrowed from Hindi. Not all of the borrowed words comes from Hindi, however; several, such as *curry*, goes back to Tamil.

UNIT

# 17 Using Pronouns Correctly

Grammar

## Lessons

## 17.1 Case of Personal Pronouns

Pronouns that are used to refer to persons or things are called **personal** pronouns.

Personal pronouns have three **cases,** or forms, called **nominative, objective,** and **possessive.** The case of a personal pronoun depends upon the pronoun's function in a sentence (whether it is a subject, a complement, or an object of a preposition).

| Personal Pronouns | | | |
|---|---|---|---|
| **Case** | **Singular Pronouns** | **Plural Pronouns** | **Function in Sentence** |
| NOMINATIVE | I, you,<br>she, he, it | we, you,<br>they | subject or predicate nominative |
| OBJECTIVE | me, you,<br>her, him, it | us, you,<br>them | direct object, indirect object, or object of preposition |
| POSSESSIVE | my, mine,<br>your, yours,<br>her, hers, his, its | our, ours,<br>your, yours,<br>their, theirs | replacement for possessive noun(s) |

The following rules will help you avoid errors in choosing the case of personal pronouns:

**1.** For a personal pronoun in a compound subject, use the nominative case.

> The guitarist and **I** rehearsed a song.
> **He** and the drummer had never met.
> **She** and **I** performed together.

**2.** For a personal pronoun in a compound object, use the objective case.

> Everyone applauded Carmen and **him.**
> The director had given Bob and **her** the lead roles.
> Between you and **me,** I preferred Carmen's performance.
> Is no one but Carlos and **us** going to the second performance?

Hint: When you are choosing the correct pronoun in a sentence that has a compound subject or object, say the sentence to yourself without the conjunction and the other subject or object.

3. After a form of the linking verb *be*, use the nominative case of a personal pronoun to indicate a predicate nominative.

The first one on stage was **she.**
The last to appear was **I.**
The happiest members of the audience were **they.**
The most surprised spectators were **we.**

In recent years this rule has been changing, especially in regard to informal speech. People speaking informally often use the objective case after a form of the linking verb *be;* they say, *It's me*, or *It was him.* There are even some language authorities who recommend the use of the objective case in informal writing to avoid appearing pretentious. In formal writing, however, always use the nominative case after any form of the linking verb *be.*

4. Do not use an apostrophe when spelling possessive pronouns.

The guitar is **hers.**
Are those seats **theirs**?
The tickets I found were **ours.**
Are these gloves **yours**?

Remember that *it's* is a contraction of *it is.* Do not confuse *it's* with the possessive pronoun *its.*

**It's** my violin that she is playing.
One of **its** strings needs to be replaced.

5. Before a gerund (an *-ing* form of a verb used as a noun), use a possessive pronoun.

**Their** being here was a surprise.
We appreciated **his** buying the tickets.

Remember that present participle forms also end in *-ing*. The possessive case is not used for pronouns that come before a participle.

We could see **them** sitting in the audience.
I heard **him** rehearsing his lines.

In some sentences, the form of the pronoun used will depend upon the meaning.

I don't approve of **his** leaping onto the stage.
[possessive pronoun and gerund: emphasizes the action]
I don't approve of **him** leaping onto the stage.
[objective case pronoun and participle: emphasizes the person]

## Exercise 1 Identifying Personal Pronouns

Write all twenty italicized personal pronouns from the following passage taken from "Dream Children: A Reverie" by Charles Lamb. Then identify each pronoun by case (*nominative*, *objective*, or *possessive*) and number (*singular* or *plural*).

Children love to listen to stories about *their* elders, when *they* were children; to stretch *their* imagination to the conception of a traditionally great-uncle, or grandame, whom *they* never saw. *It* was in this spirit that *my* little ones crept about *me* the other evening to hear about *their* great-grandmother Field, who lived in a great house in Norfolk (a hundred times bigger than that in which *they* and Papa lived) which had been the scene (so at least *it* was generally believed in that part of the country) of the tragic incidents which *they* had lately become familiar with from the ballad of "The Children of the Wood." Certain *it* is that the whole story of the children and *their* cruel uncle was to be seen fairly carved out in wood upon the chimney piece of the great hall, the whole story down to the Robin Redbreasts; till a foolish rich person pulled *it* down to set up a marble one of marble invention in *its* stead, with no story upon *it*. Here Alice put out one of *her* dear mother's looks, too tender to be called upbraiding.

Then *I* went on to say how religious and how good *their* great-grandmother Field was, how beloved and respected by everybody, though *she* was not indeed the mistress of this great house . . .

## Exercise 2 Choosing the Correct Case Form

For each sentence, choose the correct personal pronoun from each pair in parentheses.

### *Gabriel García Márquez*

1. After reading a short story by the Colombian author Gabriel García Márquez, Keesha and (I/me) wanted to find out more about him.
2. My brother helped (she/her) and (I/me) with our research about Gabriel García Márquez.
3. (Me/My) reading through several reference books led to (me/my) making some interesting discoveries about García Márquez.
4. It is (he/him) who became a central figure in the Magic Realism movement in Latin American literature.
5. Keesha told my brother and (I/me), "I bet (us/our) learning more about the term *Magic Realism* would be helpful to our research."
6. The best people for that job were my brother and (she/her), and the task was (theirs/their's).
7. Keesha and (he/him) discovered that the term was first used in Germany in the 1920s to describe certain characteristics in the works of German painters of the time; it has since been used to refer to fiction that blends realism with myth, magic, and fantasy.
8. I informed (she/her) and (he/him) that in the late 1950s García Márquez was a reporter in Rome and Paris for a Bogotá newspaper.
9. When I began to read García Márquez's most famous novel, *One Hundred Years of Solitude*, I soon became engrossed in (its/it's) depiction of the village of Maconda.
10. My brother related to Keesha and (I/me) that in his 1982 Nobel Prize acceptance speech, García Márquez acknowledged the influence of William Faulkner on his own prose style.

## 17.2 Pronouns with and as Appositives

**Use the nominative case for a pronoun that is in apposition to a subject or a predicate nominative.**

The yearbook editors, **Geoff** and **I,** appreciate the staff's cooperation. [*Editors* is the subject.]

Representatives of Lynch Brothers Building said that the biggest advertisers, **Coleman Landscaping** and **they**, would support the yearbook generously. [*Advertisers* is the subject of the subordinate clause containing the appositive.]

The illustrators were two art-club members, **Bernice** and **he.** [*Members* is the predicate nominative.]

**Use the objective case for a pronoun that is in apposition to a direct object, an indirect object, or an object of a preposition.**

The class elected the editors, **Geoff** and **me.** [*Editors* is a direct object.]

We offered the photographers, **Cho** and **him,** some suggestions. [*Photographers* is the indirect object.]

Our adviser met with both groups, **them** and **us.** [*Groups* is the object of the preposition *with*.]

**It is customary to place a first-person pronoun last in a pair or series of appositives.**

The editors for the faculty section, **Cho, Ernesto,** and **I,** cooperated effectively. [nominative case]
Ms. Torrance met regularly with the class representatives, **her** and **me**. [objective case]

**When a pronoun is followed by an appositive, choose the case of the pronoun that would be correct if the appositive were omitted.**

**We seniors** support our senior representative's proposal. [*We* is the correct form because *we* is the subject of the sentence.]

The guidance counselor showed a film to **us juniors.** [*Us* is the correct form because *us* is the object of the preposition *to*.]

## Exercise 3 Using Pronouns Correctly with and as Appositives

For each of the following sentences, choose the correct personal pronoun from each pair in parentheses.

### *A Rehearsal*

1. Because it was clear that we needed some extra practice, (we/us) orchestra members had a special rehearsal this afternoon.
2. At Mr. Bautista's request the student conductors, (she/her) and (I/me), arrived a few minutes early for the rehearsal.
3. Mr. Bautista had some suggestions for the violists and (we/us) conductors on how to prepare for tomorrow's concert.
4. Then he gave the two violists, John and (she/ her), advice on playing a difficult passage.
5. It is the viola players, Kim and (he/him), who have struggled so hard to convey the delicacy of this piece.
6. They begin playing right after the flutists, Ellen, Jesse, and (she/her).
7. Mr. Bautista pointed out tactfully that it was the trumpet players, Hiro and (they/them), who had been playing too loudly.
8. He guided (we/us) orchestra members through the entire program.
9. After the rehearsal had finished and we all relaxed for a few minutes, he especially praised the clarinetists, Maria, Richard, and (he/him).
10. By the end of a long but satisfying afternoon, all of (we/us) music enthusiasts were well prepared for the concert.

## Exercise 4 Using Pronouns Correctly with and as Appositives

For each sentence in the following paragraph, choose the correct pronoun from each pair in parentheses.

### *Mohawks on the High Steel*

[1]For Ethnic Awareness Day our Forum Club advisers, Mr. Cheng and (she/her), invited high school students from throughout the school to report on unusual ethnic occupations. [2]Mrs. Williams asked two seniors, Marguerite and (I/me), to talk about the Native Americans who have helped construct steel frames for bridges and skyscrapers throughout North America. [3]It was (we/us) seniors who explained how in 1886 a Canadian engineer trained a crew of Mohawks as riveters after noticing their agility and their lack of fear of heights. [4]The fact that teams of Mohawks were soon riveting steel beams all over Canada and the United States was fascinating to our friends David and (he/him). [5]We told the audience, club members and (they/them), that Mohawks "walked the high steel" on thousands of skyscrapers, including the Secretariat Building at the United Nations and the Empire State Building, both of which are located in New York City.

## Exercise 5 Creating Sentences with Appositives and Pronouns

Write five sentences about a project at school or a vacation or outing. In each of your sentences, use at least one pronoun with or as an appositive.

## 17.3 Pronouns After *Than* and *As*

**In elliptical adverb clauses using *than* and *as*, choose the case of the pronoun if the missing words were fully expressed.**

My brother Brendan bicycles faster than **I.** [The nominative pronoun *I* is the subject of the complete adverb clause *than I bicycle.*]

The news surprised Emily as much as **me.** [The objective pronoun *me* is the direct object of the complete adverb clause *as much as it surprised me.*]

**Sometimes you may choose either the nominative or the objective case for the pronoun in an elliptical construction, depending on the meaning you intend.**

I don't know Darryl as well as **he**. [nominative: I don't know Darryl as well as *he knows Darryl.*]

I don't know Darryl as well as **him**. [objective: I don't know Darryl as well as *I know him.*]

### Exercise 6 Using Pronouns After *Than* and *As*

Expand each of the following expressions into a complex sentence containing an elliptical adverb clause. End each sentence with a personal pronoun other than *you* or *it.*

**SAMPLE** more interested than
**ANSWER** Tod seems more interested in the project than he.

1. faster than
2. as pleased as
3. less friendly than
4. more than
5. as much as
6. more often than
7. less musical than
8. as intelligent as
9. more comic than
10. as timid as

### Exercise 7 Choosing the Correct Pronoun

In each sentence, write the correct personal pronoun from the pair given in parentheses.

***Winners***

1. Gloria won first prize in the vocal competition, and no one deserved it more than (she/her).
2. Oscar is confident that no one will serve more aces in Friday's tennis match than (he/him).
3. The news about Troy's scholarship delighted no one more than (I/me).
4. Although Erika had not expected to win the speaking award, the judges considered that no one was more poised in debate than (she/her).
5. Because I was so fond of Emily, during her long absence I wrote to her much more often than (they/them).

## 17.4 Reflexive and Intensive Pronouns

When using reflexive and intensive pronouns, observe the following rules:

1. Use *himself* and *themselves* instead of the incorrect forms *hisself* and *theirselves.*

   Patrick finished the report **himself.**
   The teachers **themselves** monitored the exam.

2. When a personal pronoun refers to the subject of a sentence, always use a reflexive pronoun.

   INCORRECT Lydia bought her red sneakers.
   CORRECT Lydia bought **herself** red sneakers.

   INCORRECT I found me a true friend.
   CORRECT I found **myself** a true friend.

3. Avoid the unnecessary use of reflexive pronouns. Keep in mind that a reflexive pronoun refers to the subject; it does not take the place of the subject.

   INCORRECT Julia and myself have become close friends.
   CORRECT Julia and **I** have become close friends.

   INCORRECT Floyd and yourself are late.
   CORRECT Floyd and **you** are late.

### Exercise 8 Choosing the Correct Pronoun

In each sentence, choose the correct pronoun from the pair in parentheses.

#### *The New Workplace*

1. Has the relatively recent phenomenon of the virtual office come to the attention of (you/yourself) or your friends?
2. As the information revolution continues, both big and small businesses are wiring (theirselves/themselves) into electronic communications systems.
3. Ten years from now your classmates and (you/yourself) will be part of a virtual office.
4. Between you and (me/myself), having a locker at work rather than a desk seems odd.
5. Workers are accustoming (theirselves/themselves) to using a locker to stow personal stationery and files.
6. Except for these items, paper (it'self/itself) has almost disappeared in the virtual office.
7. Memos sent to (you/yourself) appear on personal computer screens.
8. Entire office staffs operate either from home or on the road, communicating with headquarters and among (them/themselves) by pager, cellular phone, and fax computer.
9. Can the rapidly developing virtual office bring (us/ourselves) closer to an ideal workplace?
10. Although only time will tell, it is already clear that some workers and managers find (them/themselves) needing a considerable period of adjustment to this new working style.

# 17.5 *Who* and *Whom* in Questions and Subordinate Clauses

**In questions use *who* for subjects and *whom* for direct and indirect objects and objects of a preposition.**

**Who** won yesterday's championship game? [*Who* is the subject of the verb *won.*]

**Whom** did you meet this morning? [*Whom* is the direct object of the verb *did meet.*]

When a question includes an interrupting expression, such as *did you say* or *do you think*, try omitting the expression to determine whether to use *who* or *whom.*

**Who** did you say telephoned yesterday? [Ask yourself: *Who* telephoned yesterday? You can then determine that *who* is the subject of the verb *telephoned.*]

**Use the nominative pronouns *who* and *whoever* for subjects and predicate nominatives in subordinate clauses.**

The police knew **who** had done it. [*Who* is the subject of the noun clause *who had done it.*]

Within an hour we realized **who** the perpetrator of the crime was. [*Who* is the predicate nominative of the noun clause *who the perpetrator of the crime was.*]

The detectives will find **whoever** is guilty. [*Whoever* is the subject of the noun clause *whoever is guilty.*]

**Use the objective pronouns *whom* and *whomever* for direct and indirect objects and objects of a preposition in subordinate clauses.**

We wondered **whom** he had called last night. [*Whom* is the direct object of the verb *had called* in the noun clause *whom he had called last night.*]

She is a person for **whom** I have great respect. [*Whom* is the object of the preposition *for* in the adjective clause *for whom I have great respect.*]

The new president will be **whomever** the members of the club elect. [*Whomever* is the direct object of the verb *elect* in the noun clause *whomever the members of the club elect.*]

When speaking informally, people often use *who* in place of *whom* in sentences like this one: *Who did she visit?* In formal writing and speech, however, it is important to make the correct distinction between *who* and *whom.*

## Exercise 9 Using *Who* and *Whom* in Sentences

Complete each sentence by substituting the word *who* or *whom* for each blank.

### *The Harlem Globetrotters*

1. ________ do you suppose basketball fans name as the team that puts on the greatest show?
2. The world-famous clowning basketball team, the Harlem Globetrotters, has excited all ________ have seen it.
3. Die-hard fans probably remember ________ the founder of the Globetrotters was—Abe Saperstein.
4. In Chicago in 1927, Saperstein organized a team of talented African American players ________ toured the Midwest, played local amateur teams, and beat them regularly.
5. At first the Globetrotters were a serious, hard-playing team, as opposing players with ________ they shared the court clearly understood.
6. ________ do you think won the world professional tournament in 1940, beating the Chicago Bruins thirty-one to twenty-nine in overtime?
7. Goose Tatum, ________ early Globetrotter fans knew as the greatest clown, had an astonishingly accurate hook shot, which he could launch without looking at the basket.
8. Marques Haynes, another Globetrotter of ________ fans spoke admiringly, could dribble the ball while running, sitting down, or even lying on his stomach.
9. Meadowlark Lemon, ________ became known as the Clown Prince of Basketball, sometimes directed the Globetrotters' offense to drop-kick the ball rather than shoot it.
10. These great players, ________ Saperstein sent around the world on tour, made the Globetrotters a unique success.

## Exercise 10 Choosing *Whoever* or *Whomever*

For each of the following sentences, choose the correct pronoun from the pair in parentheses.

### *Career Opportunities in the Computer Field*

1. A candidate for a good job in the field of computer science is (whoever/whomever) prospective employers view as a specialist.
2. The increasing use of computers in education, business, industry, science, and government makes opportunities excellent for (whoever/whomever) works with computers.
3. Computer engineering, computer science, and computer operation are the three main areas open to (whoever/whomever) wishes to advance in the field.
4. (Whoever/Whomever) owners call upon for service will be kept busy.
5. Businesses of all kinds will hire (whoever/whomever) they believe excels.
6. A college degree and knowledge of mathematics are important prerequisites for (whoever/whomever) wants a job in the field of computer science.
7. (Whoever/Whomever) has studied mechanical or electrical engineering will probably be able to find a job working with computers.
8. Most colleges offer courses in computer programming and information systems to (whoever/whomever) majors in computer science.
9. Many employers offer apprenticeship programs to (whoever/whomever) they consider a potential specialist.
10. The best jobs may go to (whoever/whomever) employers feel knows the most.

## 17.6 Pronoun-Antecedent Agreement

An **antecedent** is the word or group of words to which a pronoun refers or that a pronoun replaces. All pronouns must agree with their antecedents in number, gender, and person.

### Agreement in Number and Gender

A pronoun must agree with its antecedent in number (singular or plural) and gender (masculine, feminine, or neuter).

A pronoun's antecedent may be a noun, another pronoun, or a phrase or clause acting as a noun. In the examples that follow, the pronouns appear in boldface type and their antecedents in boldface italic type.

> ***Mother Teresa,*** who is internationally famous for her work with the poor in Calcutta, India, won **her** Nobel Peace Prize in 1979. [singular feminine pronoun]
>
> ***Mairead Corrigan*** and ***Betty Williams*** of Northern Ireland won **their** Nobel Peace Prize in 1976. [plural pronoun]
>
> ***Charles Fuller*** won **his** Pulitzer Prize in 1982 for *A Soldier's Play.* [singular masculine pronoun]
>
> ***Frank Loesser*** and ***Abe Burrows*** won **their** Pulitzer Prize in 1962 for *How to Succeed in Business Without Really Trying.* [plural pronoun]
>
> The ***lion,*** despite **its** apparent fierceness and a roar that can carry up to five miles, rests about twenty hours a day. [singular neuter pronoun]
>
> A ***lioness*** and her ***cubs*** spend a good part of **their** day playing. [plural pronoun]

When the gender of an antecedent is unknown or may be either masculine or feminine, a masculine pronoun is traditionally used.

> To make effective presentations in court, a ***lawyer*** must research **his** cases thoroughly.

Today this rule has become controversial. Although some people prefer to use the masculine pronoun, others choose gender-neutral wording. Those who wish to avoid the masculine pronoun can often reword the sentence by (1) using *he or she, his or her,* and so forth, (2) using a plural pronoun, or (3) eliminating the pronoun altogether.

> A ***lawyer*** must research **his or her** cases thoroughly.
> ***Lawyers*** must research **their** cases thoroughly.
> A ***lawyer*** must research cases thoroughly. [no pronoun]

## Agreement with Collective Nouns

When the antecedent of a pronoun is a collective noun, the number of the pronoun depends upon whether the collective noun is meant to be singular or plural.

The ***band*** played **its** last song of the evening. [The collective noun *band* conveys the singular sense of one unit. Therefore, the singular pronoun *its* is used.]

The ***band*** packed **their** instruments and left the stage. [The collective noun *band* conveys the plural sense of several persons performing separate acts. So, the plural pronoun *their* is used.]

The ***jury*** finally reached **its** verdict after two weeks of deliberations. [The collective noun *jury* conveys the sense of a single unit. Therefore, the singular personal pronoun *its* is used.]

The ***jury*** debated among **themselves** for two weeks before finally reaching their verdict. [The collective noun *jury* conveys the plural sense of separate members with different opinions. Therefore, the plural reflexive pronoun *themselves* and the plural personal pronoun *their* are used.]

**Exercise 11** **Making Pronouns and Antecedents Agree**

On your paper complete the following sentences by filling each blank with an appropriate possessive pronoun. Then write the antecedent of each pronoun that you supply.

***The History of Tennis***

1. The game of tennis is thought to have had ________ origins in the East.
2. The ancient Greeks and Romans later adopted the game as ________ own.
3. The rules of lawn tennis were set down by a British major, Walter C. Wingfield, in ________ book *The Major's Game.*
4. The first person to set up a tennis court in the United States seems to have been Mary Outerbridge, who established one right near ________ own home.
5. James Dwight, the Father of American Tennis, played ________ first game in 1875.
6. Bill Tilden and Helen Wills Moody, who dominated the sport in the 1920s, often won ________ matches with great ease.
7. Around the same time four French players, known as the Four Musketeers, kept ________ country in the running in competition for the Davis Cup.
8. In the 1930s Fred Perry of England won at Wimbledon the championship of ________ country three consecutive times.
9. The record stood until Bjorn Borg made ________ mark in tennis history by winning at Wimbledon five consecutive times.
10. Tennis games are known for ________ suspense and fast action.

## Exercise 12 Making Pronouns and Antecedents Agree

In each of the following sentences, find the personal pronoun and its antecedent. Then revise the sentence in one or more ways to correct the error in pronoun-antecedent agreement.

### *Dining Indian-Style*

[1]Ask a waiter in an Indian restaurant what kinds of breads are available, and they will offer a delicious array: whole-wheat *naan*, *paratha* (with or without a vegetable filling), and *poori*, a puffed bread that resembles pastry. [2]A lover of Indian cuisine might consider a curry as one of their favorite dishes. [3]Even people dining on Indian food for the first time will find something to his liking. [4]Fans of spicy foods might try a chicken *vindaloo* and quench his thirst with a cool glass of pomegranate or mango juice. [5]The adventurous diner might complement their meal with chutney, lentils in gravy, and chopped onions.

## Exercise 13 Making Pronouns Agree with Collective Noun Antecedents

On your paper complete the following sentences by filling the blank with an appropriate possessive pronoun. Also write the antecedent of each pronoun that you supply.

### *Animal Tales*

1. The swarm of bees has left ______ hive in search of blossoming clover.
2. The gaggle of geese wings ______ way south each autumn.
3. A litter of pups compete for ______ meals, and the strongest ones are growing rapidly.
4. The flock of sheep graze in spring and peacefully tend ______ newborn lambs.
5. The pack of wolves stalks ______ elusive prey across the frozen timberland.
6. The sounder of wild boar leaves many signs of ______ presence on the sandy ground.
7. The pod of whales are spraying water vapor from ______ air holes.
8. Toward sunset, the murder of crows were returning to ______ trees for the night.
9. A covey of quail betrays ______ presence by the faint call of a young bird.
10. In the pond behind my house, a school of sunfish surfaces from beneath ______ log to eat the bread crumbs I throw into the water each morning.

# Agreement in Person

A pronoun must agree in person with its antecedent.

Confusion regarding the agreement of pronouns with their antecedents may occur with the second-person pronoun *you. You* should not be used to refer to an antecedent in the third person. Instead, use a suitable third-person pronoun or an appropriate noun.

| | |
|---|---|
| POOR | My parents visited Arizona, where **you** can see the reconstructed London Bridge. |
| BETTER | My parents visited Arizona, where **they** saw the reconstructed London Bridge. |
| BETTER | My parents visited Arizona, where **visitors** can see the reconstructed London Bridge. |

When a pronoun has another pronoun as its antecedent, be sure that the two pronouns agree in person. Avoid illogical shifts from *they* to *you, I* to *you*, or *one* to *you.*

POOR On their hike **they** attempted to reach the mountain's summit, where **you** might have a spectacular view of Lake Geneva.

BETTER On their hike **they** attempted to reach the mountain's summit, where **they** might have a spectacular view of Lake Geneva.

POOR Although **one** sometimes might experience work as burdensome, **you** might more often find it very rewarding.

BETTER Although **one** sometimes might experience work as burdensome, **one** might more often find it very rewarding.

**Exercise 14** **Making Pronouns and Antecedents Agree in Person**

Rewrite each of the following items, eliminating the inappropriate use of *you* by substituting a third-person pronoun or a suitable noun.

*The Boston Marathon*

1. Participants in the Boston Marathon must train in all weather, for you cannot predict the weather in Boston in April.
2. Marathon runners may have to contend with days like the one in 1925, when you had to shiver through temperatures in the thirties.
3. Far different conditions can also prevail; you may have to participate when temperatures are in the hundreds, as they were in 1976.
4. Occasionally they encounter a day when the temperature is in the forties, and you are protected from the sun by a cover of clouds.
5. Such days are a blessing for marathoners, and you can run almost all twenty-six miles with a grin.

## Agreement with Indefinite Pronoun Antecedents

In general, use a singular personal pronoun when the antecedent is a singular indefinite pronoun, and use a plural personal pronoun when the antecedent is a plural indefinite pronoun. (See page 575 for a list of singular and plural indefinite pronouns.)

***Each*** of the boys in the play has learned **his** part.
***One*** of the girls is applying **her** own makeup.
***Many*** of the dancers have made **their** own costumes.

Note that the plural nouns in the prepositional phrases—*of the boys*, *of the girls*—do not affect the number of the personal pronouns. *His* and *her* are singular because *each* and *one*, their antecedents, are singular. When speaking informally, however, people often use the plural pronoun *their*.

INFORMAL **_Neither_** of the boys knew **their** lines.

Traditionally, writers use a masculine pronoun with an indefinite antecedent when no gender is specified.

**_Everyone_** on the history project must do **his** share.

This rule also is undergoing a change, because some people now prefer gender-neutral wording. You might substitute a plural indefinite pronoun for the singular one or eliminate the personal pronoun entirely.

**_All_** on the history project must do **their** share.

## Exercise 15 Making Pronouns Agree with Indefinite Pronoun Antecedents

On your paper indicate which sentences are correct. Then revise each incorrect sentence to make it correct. Most can be revised in more than one way. In some cases you will need to change a single word to make a sentence correct; in others, the entire sentence.

### *Nairobi, Capital of Kenya*

1. All of Africa's major cities saw its beginnings in modest settlements, and Nairobi, the capital of Kenya, is no exception.
2. Each of the local landmarks discovered by the Masai tribe was named after their characteristics; for example, a water hole was called Enkare Nairobi (Cold Water).
3. Just as Nairobi derives its name from the Masai language, so most of the African communities derive its name from local languages.
4. It is unlikely that any one of the early residents of Nairobi imagined that their settlement would become a prosperous trading center.
5. After the coming of the railroad in 1899, some of Kenya's rural population began their migration to Nairobi.
6. So many of these migrants found their way to Nairobi that the city soon became one of the largest in sub-Saharan Africa.
7. Few of Kenya's cities, no matter how important their communities, have exerted as much influence on the country as Nairobi has.
8. From the turn of the century to the present, many of Kenya's agricultural products, such as coffee, cotton, coconuts, cashew nuts, and sugarcane, have found its point of distribution in Nairobi.
9. Most of Kenya's industry has their center in Nairobi.
10. In addition, all of the states in eastern Africa paid its respect to Nairobi by making it the headquarters of the East African Community's railroad, harbor, and airline corporation.

## Exercise 16 Choosing the Correct Pronouns

On your paper complete the sentences by filling each blank with an appropriate pronoun.

### *Kangaroos*

1. When visitors to Australia first see a kangaroo, ______ are usually surprised and delighted.
2. A mob of kangaroos hopping ______ way across the arid Australian landscape of thorn bushes and scrub is an amazing sight.
3. These animals, despite ______ apparent awkwardness, are remarkably well adapted to their harsh environment.
4. Kangaroos may live up to thirty years in the wild, and ______ often continue to breed in their twenties.
5. There are over fifty species of kangaroo in Australia and on the island of New Guinea, and each has _____ own distinctive characteristics.
6. One of the largest and most common species is the red kangaroo; ______ is often found on the dry plains of the Australian outback.
7. Male and female red kangaroos look quite different: adult males are rusty brown in color, rather than the females' smoky blue, and may weigh nearly three times as much as ______ adult female counterparts.
8. Red kangaroos have developed several ingenious methods of dealing with the hot, dry conditions of ______ habitat.
9. When a red kangaroo pants to cool off, for example, ______ can adjust the rate of moisture evaporation by varying the air flow through its nostrils.
10. Although kangaroos sweat when exerting themselves, they seem to possess an automatic switch that turns off the sweating mechanism the moment they stop exercising, even though ______ body temperature is still high.
11. A kangaroo can also regulate ______ body temperature through the use of special glands located on the animal's forearms.
12. In very hot weather, kangaroos wipe and lick moisture from ______ mouths and noses onto this area, where the glands and blood vessels are especially active.
13. Any creature living under such extreme conditions of climate must try to adjust ______ behavior in order to reduce heat and conserve water.
14. During the daytime, kangaroos seek shade under a shrub or desert tree, where _____ hunch their bodies to reduce the surface area exposed to the sun.
15. For many periods of the Australian summer, each human in kangaroo territory may need at least ten quarts of water a day; a red kangaroo, on the other hand, will easily satisfy ______ thirst with a drink of a quart or two of water every week.
16. Most observers are surprised when ______ learn that red kangaroos can move at speeds of up to forty miles an hour.
17. It is true that the energy cost of hopping must take ______ toll on kangaroos.
18. Experts think, however, that kangaroos actually expend more energy when walking than when hopping, because of the use of ______ thick tails as an extra leg at slow speeds.
19. How can kangaroos attain so much power and speed when ______ apparently use so little energy?
20. Each researcher has ______ own theory, but one of the leading possibilities is that kangaroos use the principle of the spring in their powerful rear legs, tails, and backs.

## 17.7 Clear Pronoun Reference

**Make sure that the antecedent of a pronoun is clearly stated and that a pronoun cannot possibly refer to more than one antecedent.**

## Vague Pronoun Reference

Never use the pronouns *this, that, which,* and *it* without a clearly stated antecedent. When you check your work for vague pronoun reference, be sure that each time you use the pronouns *this, that, which,* and *it,* you have clearly expressed—usually in a word or two—the object or idea that you mean these words to stand for.

**VAGUE** Many people enjoy the talent of Whoopi Goldberg, and **this** is obvious from the great number of people who go to see her films. [What is obvious from the fact that a great number of people see Goldberg's films? Her popularity is obvious, but *popularity* is not specifically mentioned.]

**CLEAR** Many people enjoy the talent of Whoopi Goldberg, and **her popularity** is obvious from the great number of people who go to see her films.

**VAGUE** Barry and Hector are good friends, **which** began when they were in elementary school. [What began when Barry and Hector were in elementary school? Their friendship began then, but *friendship* does not appear in the sentence.]

**CLEAR** Barry and Hector have a lasting friendship, **which** began when they were in elementary school.

**VAGUE** Since my father enjoyed his years in public office, I also have chosen **it** as my career. [What have I chosen as a career? I have chosen politics, but *politics* has not been specifically mentioned.]

**CLEAR** Since my father enjoyed his years in public office, I also have chosen **politics** as my career.

## Ambiguous Pronoun Reference

If a pronoun seems to refer to more than one antecedent, reword the sentence to make the antecedent clear, or eliminate the pronoun.

**UNCLEAR ANTECEDENT** If you leave the book in your backpack, you will forget **it.** [What is the antecedent of *it?* Will the book or the backpack be forgotten?]

| | |
|---|---|
| CLEAR ANTECEDENT | You will forget the book if you leave **it** in your backpack. |
| NO PRONOUN | If you leave the book in your backpack, you will forget the **book.** |
| NO PRONOUN | Left in your backpack, the book will be forgotten. |

## Indefinite Use of Pronouns

Do not use *you* and *they* as indefinite pronouns. Instead, name the person or group to which you are referring. You may also be able to reword the sentence in such a way that you do not name the person or group and you do not use a pronoun. Usually you would use the passive voice to accomplish this kind of revision.

| | |
|---|---|
| INDEFINITE | In the army **you** must follow orders. |
| CLEAR | In the army **a soldier** must follow orders. |
| INDEFINITE | As part of a basketball team, **they** must learn to work together. |
| CLEAR | As part of a basketball team, the **players** must learn to work together. |

**Exercise 17** **Making Pronoun Reference Clear**

On your paper rewrite each of the following sentences, making sure that all pronoun references are clearly stated. In some cases you may choose to eliminate the pronoun entirely.

### *The Wright Brothers, Aviation Pioneers*

1. In a book I read about the history of aviation, they discussed Orville and Wilbur Wright, pioneers of American aviation.
2. Wilbur Wright learned about Otto Lilienthal's successful gliding experiments in Germany, and this sparked Wright's interest in flying.
3. When the Wrights studied how buzzards keep their balance, they were rewarded.
4. By watching the birds, Wilbur realized that in order to fly successfully, you must operate an airplane on three separate axes.
5. The Wrights constructed a biplane kite in 1899, and that was just the first of their many experiments dealing with aviation.
6. The Wright brothers flew successfully, which occurred on December 17, 1903.
7. Kitty Hawk, North Carolina, was chosen for the flight because it would make history.
8. The Wright brothers flew for fifty-nine seconds, which was aided by the wind.
9. Today they consider Wilbur and Orville Wright's contribution to the development of flight one of the most outstanding engineering achievements in history.
10. Because of the Wright brothers more and more people began to read about aeronautics at the beginning of the twentieth century even though it was relatively new.

## Exercise 18 Review: Choosing the Correct Pronoun

On a separate sheet of paper, write the correct form from the pair of pronouns shown in parentheses in each sentence.

### *A Film Project*

1. In our class multimedia project last spring, the stars were the filmmakers, Alicia and (I/me).
2. The script, in which we were able to create considerable suspense, was written by my friend Jorge and (I/me).
3. I asked my cousin Alicia and (he/him) to do the filming at my house.
4. Alicia is slender and not particularly tall, and the video equipment weighed almost as much as (she/her).
5. The filmmakers (who/whom) I admire, such as Woody Allen, Martin Scorsese, and John Ford, know their audiences.
6. I wonder (who/whom) the audience for our film will be; will the viewers be confined to our classmates, or will our product reach a wider audience?
7. It seems amazing, but the most experienced director in our group of film students made (her/their) fourth film last week.
8. Olivia's friends previewed film, in which (you/they) could see many comic touches.
9. Each of the documentaries made for the project had (its/their) good points, but only one deserved rave reviews.
10. Although the scripting and camera work in Sam's film were clearly weak, Robert argued that (it/they) should win one of the top awards.

## Exercise 19 Review: Pronoun Usage

Rewrite each of the following sentences, eliminating any mistakes in the use of pronouns. Each sentence has one error.

### *The Incas and the Ancient Site of Machu Picchu*

1. The origins of the Incan empire are not entirely clear, but they probably started out during the fourteenth century as a small kingdom in the Andes Mountains.
2. The Quechua word *Inca* refers to the ruler hisself, as well as to the inhabitants of the valley of Cuzco, which was the Incan capital.
3. The territorial expansion of the Inca was remarkable, given the fact that you had neither the wheel nor the horse.
4. Although the Inca did not possess writing as ourselves know it, they had a recording system called quipu, by which numbers were represented in the form of knotted strings.
5. The quipu often had hundreds of strings in different colors, which enabled the Incas to keep accurate records and accounts.
6. Each part of this highly diverse empire developed their own administrative practices and distinctive transportation network of roads, levees, and bridges.
7. The Incan emperors believed that they theirselves were descended from the Sun God, and they were worshipped as divine beings. ➡

8. Perhaps the most remarkable relic of the Incan empire is the city of Machu Picchu, who's spectacular mountain setting has made it a world-famous archaeological monument.
9. Hiram Bingham, an explorer, historian, and statesman whom taught at Yale University, led an expedition to Peru in 1911.
10. High in the Andes, he discovered the remains of an ancient city, although, in fact, the first modern person to see that spot was not him.
11. The local residents theirselves knew of the city's existence long before explorers from the United States arrived on the scene.
12. Bingham's exciting discovery led to further exploration of the ruins by the members of the Yale Expedition in 1912, and they were as enthusiastic as him.
13. The question of whomever actually uncovered this ceremonial site of the Inca has little bearing on the fact that Machu Picchu is an impressive place.
14. The fact that the city walls were constructed so that themselves would maintain comfortable indoor temperatures day and night suggests that the Inca knew at least some of the principles of solar energy.
15. The ancient city was probably abandoned by the Inca rulers when the Spaniards invaded the Urubamba River region, and the two opposing groups, the Inca and them, battled over the territory.
16. The Inca, who the Spaniards ultimately drove from Machu Picchu, probably then settled in the neighboring Vilcabamba region, which was more easily defended and maintained.
17. Recently archaeologists investigating the ruins have discovered aqueducts, warehouses, and ceremonial sites on a cliff face, and they promise to reveal new information about the Inca.
18. Archaeologists also found an important gravesite, where you might be able to uncover a number of ancient mummies.
19. Each of these recent discoveries will make their contribution to the fund of knowledge about a lost culture.
20. The ruins of Machu Picchu tell a great deal about the Inca, which helps us to understand the ways of an ancient civilization.

UNIT

17

Unit Review

# Grammar Review

## Using Pronouns Correctly

In this passage from *The Hound of the Baskervilles*, Sherlock Holmes, along with his assistant, Dr. Watson, and a detective named Lestrade, lies in wait on a foggy night for Sir Henry Baskerville and the strange beast that is pursuing him. The passage, narrated by Watson, has been annotated to show the kinds of pronouns covered in this unit.

*Literature Model*

### *from* THE HOUND OF THE BASKERVILLES

***by Sir Arthur Conan Doyle***

A sound of quick steps broke the silence of the moor. Crouching among the stones we stared intently at the silver-tipped bank in front of us. The steps grew louder, and through the fog, as through a curtain, there stepped the man whom we were awaiting. . . . As he walked he glanced continually over either shoulder, like a man who is ill at ease.

"Hist!" cried Holmes, and I heard the sharp click of a cocking pistol. "Look out! It's coming!"

There was a thin, crisp, continuous patter from somewhere in the heart of that crawling bank. The cloud was within fifty yards of where we lay, and we glared at it, all three, uncertain what horror was about to break from the heart of it. I was at Holmes's elbow, and I glanced for an instant at his face. It was pale and exultant, his eyes shining brightly in the moonlight. But suddenly they started forward in a rigid, fixed stare, and his lips parted in amazement. At the same instant Lestrade gave a yell of terror and threw himself face downward upon the ground. I sprang to my feet, my inert hand grasping my pistol, my mind paralyzed by the dreadful shape which had sprung out upon us from the shadows of the fog. A hound it was, an enormous coal-black hound, but not such a hound as mortal eyes have ever seen. Fire burst from its open mouth, its eyes glowed with a smouldering glare, its muzzle and hackles and dewlap were outlined in flickering flame. Never in ➡

Pronoun in the nominative case used as a subject

The pronoun *whom* in the objective case used as the object of *were awaiting*

The pronoun *who* in the nominative case used as the subject of *is*

Agreement in person and number between the pronoun *it* and its antecedent, *cloud*

Pronoun in the possessive case

the delirious dream of a disordered brain could anything more savage, more appalling, more hellish be conceived than that dark form and savage face which broke upon us out of the wall of fog.

With long bounds the huge black creature was leaping down the track, following hard upon the footsteps of our friend. So paralyzed were we by the apparition that we allowed him to pass before we had recovered our nerve. Then Holmes and I both fired together, and the creature gave a hideous howl, which showed that one at least had hit him. He did not pause, however, but bounded onward. Far away on the path we saw Sir Henry looking back, his face white in the moonlight, his hands raised in horror.

. . . In front of us as we flew up the track we heard scream after scream from Sir Henry and the deep roar of the hound. I was in time to see the beast spring upon its victim, hurl him to the ground, and worry at his throat. But the next instant Holmes had emptied five barrels of his revolver into the creature's flank. With a last howl of agony and a vicious snap in the air, it rolled upon its back, four feet pawing furiously, and then fell limp upon its side. I stooped, panting, and pressed my pistol to the dreadful, shimmering head, but it was useless to press the trigger. The giant hound was dead.

Pronoun in the objective case used as a direct object

Pronoun in the objective case used as the object of a preposition

Agreement in number and gender between the pronoun *him* and its antecedent, *victim*

## Exercise 1

**Choosing the Correct Pronoun Case** Determine whether the italicized pronoun is used correctly. If not, write the pronoun as it should appear. If the pronoun is used properly, write *correct*.

**SAMPLE** The footsteps the men heard were not *their's.*
**ANSWER** theirs

1. Holmes, Lestrade, and *me* crouched down.
2. When Holmes heard the hound coming, he shouted, "Look out! *It's* coming!"
3. Sherlock Holmes and *us* waited and were unsure what horror would appear.
4. As Holmes stared into the mist, it was *him* alone who looked exultant.
5. The hound frightened both Holmes and *we.*
6. The enormous hound had fire bursting from *it's* mouth.
7. The hound was chasing Sir Henry and bounded right past Holmes and *I.*
8. We fired our pistols, but the hound continued to run despite *us* wounding him.
9. A battle between the hound and *him* would have ended Sir Henry's life.
10. The hound was mauling Sir Henry when Sherlock Holmes and *me* arrived and killed it.

## Exercise 2

**Using Pronouns Correctly with and as Appositives** For each sentence determine whether the italicized pronoun appears in the proper form. If it does not, write the pronoun as it should appear. If the pronoun is used properly, write *correct*. Note that the sentences are told from the first-person point of view of Dr. Watson.

1. Hidden by the stones, we, Holmes and *me*, prepared ourselves.
2. Awaiting Sir Henry, we heard the pair of them, the beast and *he*, before we saw them.
3. Lestrade hid his face while Holmes stared expectantly; my two companions, Lestrade and *him*, were a study in contrasts.
4. The beast's size surprised the sleuths, Holmes and *me*.
5. *Us* detectives both fired our pistols.

## Exercise 3

**Pronouns After *Than* and *As*** Each sentence contains an italicized word or group of words. Rewrite each, substituting the correct pronoun for the word or words in italics.

**SAMPLE** No one was more afraid than *Watson*.
**ANSWER** No one was more afraid than he.

1. Watson did not see the hound as quickly as *Lestrade*.
2. The huge black creature leaped down the track more swiftly than *the men*.
3. Lestrade was more terrified than *Holmes and Watson*.
4. On the second round Watson did not shoot as quickly as *Holmes*.
5. The hound had frightened Sir Henry only slightly more than *Holmes and Lestrade*.

## Exercise 4

**Choosing *Who* or *Whom*** The following sentences provide background for *The Hound of the Baskervilles*. For each sentence choose the correct pronoun from the pair in parentheses.

1. Sir Charles Baskerville, (who/whom) was Sir Henry's uncle, died after supposedly being pursued by a monstrous beast.
2. The case was brought to Holmes by Dr. Mortimer, (who/whom) Holmes berated for not coming to him sooner.
3. The Baskervilles' "curse" went back to Hugo Baskerville, (who/whom) a monstrous hound had reportedly killed in the 1700s.
4. The beast that killed Sir Charles had to have been sent by someone; by (who/whom) was the question.
5. Some blamed Sir Charles's death on the Notting Hill murderer, (who/whom) the police had suspected after his escape from prison.

## Exercise 5

**Making Pronouns and Antecedents Agree** The following sentences elaborate on the passage from *The Hound of the Baskervilles.* Each sentence contains an example of pronoun-antecedent agreement. Rewrite each sentence according to the directions in the parentheses, changing the pronouns if necessary. Also change the form of the verb if necessary. (The sentences are told from Dr. Watson's first-person point of view.)

**SAMPLE** Holmes's and my investigation was not as clear-cut as we had thought it would be. (Change *Holmes's and my* to *My.*)

**ANSWER** My investigation was not as clear-cut as I had thought it would be.

1. I looked to see the effect my story had on Sir Henry. (Change *I* to *we.*)
2. My first thought was that I should be by Sir Henry's side. (Change *My* to *Our.*)
3. All of the witnesses are ready to swear that they have seen the creature on the moor. (Change *All* to *Each.*)
4. As I waited, I stared at the fog before me. (Change the first *I* to *Holmes and I.*)
5. We were so paralyzed by the spectacle that we watched helplessly before acting. (Change *We* to *Holmes.*)

## Exercise 6

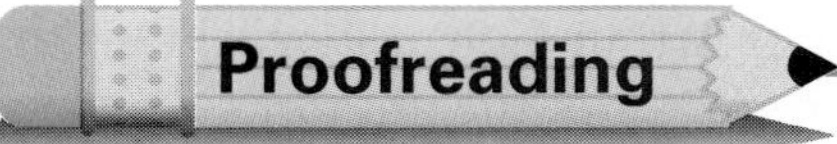


The following passage describes the artist John Constable, whose painting appears on this page. Rewrite the passage, correcting the errors in spelling, grammar, and usage. Add any missing punctuation. There are ten errors.

### *John Constable*

[1]John Constable (1776–1837) was born in the county of Suffolk which is on the eastern coast of England. [2]Moving to London in 1799 to study at the Royal Academy, Suffolk and it's countryside were still missed by Constable. ➡

**John Constable, *Sketch for "Hadleigh Castle,"* c. 1828-1829**

[3]Constable hisself did not reach the height of his powers until the 1820s and the 1830s. [4]Few artists developed as slowly as him. [5]His *Sketch for "Hadleigh Castle"* is tipical of his mature style. [6]In the painting on the preceding page, Constable renders carefully and precisely not only the details of the terrain but also the weather, the quality of light the fauna, and the turbulent sea. [7]Constable, who many overlooked in his day, is now revered both for his naturalism and for his great depth of feeling.

[8]Constable often sketches the same moors Arthur Conan Doyle depicted in *The Hound of the Baskervilles.* [9]Each man used their descriptive skills to capture the moody quality of this dramatic English landscape.

**Exercise 7**

**Review** The sentences that follow describe Sir Arthur Conan Doyle's life and work. For each sentence choose the proper pronoun from the pair in parentheses, and write it on your paper.

### *Sir Arthur Conan Doyle*

1. Most of (we/us) readers of Sir Arthur Conan Doyle know that this most famous of all detective story writers—the creator of the immortal Sherlock Holmes—was born in Edinburgh, Scotland.
2. As a young university student, Doyle originally studied medicine and met a professor, Dr. Joseph Bell, after (who/whom) he later modeled his most famous fictional character.
3. While Doyle was still in his twenties, a lack of patients and the need to make a decent living led to (him/his) taking up short story writing.
4. Sherlock Holmes made his debut in *A Study in Scarlet,* a short novel that Doyle published in Beeton's Christmas Annual in 1887; the gentlemen sleuths, Watson and (he/him), were a huge success.
5. Although *A Study in Scarlet* was published more than a century ago, (its/it's) still a compelling novel to read.
6. The stories about Holmes became popular, but Doyle's earlier tales were not as successful as (they/them).
7. Doyle wrote a total of fifty-six stories about Holmes; every reader has (his or her/their) special favorites.
8. Doyle, for (who/whom) writing proved financially successful, gave up his medical practice in 1890.
9. This decision did not rule out (him/his) serving as a medical officer during the Boer War in South Africa from 1899 to 1902.
10. No writer of the past century has combined detailed observation and shrewd deduction more engagingly than (he/him).

# Writing Application

**Pronouns Usage in Writing** Carefully study the following brief passages from literary works, noting the correct pronoun forms as well as proper case and agreement with antecedents.

1. " 'Three-and-six', he murmured, as old people repeat things to *themselves*."

From "The Train to Rhodesia" by Nadine Gordimer

2. "*Theirs* not to reason why.
*Theirs* but to do and die."

From "The Charge of the Light Brigade" by Alfred, Lord Tennyson

"The rustling of the locust armies was like a big forest in the storm; *their* settling on the roof was like the beating of the rain."

From "A Mild Attack of Locusts" by Doris Lessing

3. "*Whom* they fear they hate."
—Quintus Ennius

**Techniques with Pronoun Usage** When revising your work, check for correct pronoun case and proper noun-antecedent agreement. Also be sure you do not use pronoun forms that do not exist in standard English.

1. Remember that *hisself* and *theirselves* are incorrect forms. Always use *himself* and *themselves*.

2. Remember that no possessive pronoun is ever written with an apostrophe. The correct forms are *yours*, *hers*, *its*, and *theirs*. *It's* is a contraction of *it is* or *it has*. *Whose* is possessive; *who's* is a contraction of *who is* or *who has*.

3. Always check the case of pronouns carefully, especially in phrases with gerunds or in constructions containing the words *who* or *whom*.

**Practice** Apply your knowledge of pronoun usage when checking the following passage, adapted from William Hazlitt's essay "Macbeth." Revise any errors in pronoun usage.

Macbeth hisself appears driven along by the violence of his' fate. . . . His' energy springs from the anxiety and agitation of his' mind. Him blindly rushing forward on the objects of his' ambition and revenge or him recoiling from them equally betrays the harassed state of his' feelings. This part of his' character is admirably set off by being brought in connection with that of Lady Macbeth, who's obdurate strength of will and masculine firmness give her the ascendancy over her husband's faltering virtue. . . . She is a great bad woman, who we hate but whom we fear more than we hate.

UNIT

# 18 Using Modifiers Correctly

Grammar

## Lessons

## 18.1 The Three Degrees of Comparison

**Most adjectives and adverbs have three degrees: the positive, or base, form; the comparative form; and the superlative form.**

**The positive form of a modifier cannot be used to make a comparison. (This form appears as the entry word in a dictionary.)**

**The comparative form of a modifier shows two things being compared.**

**The superlative form of a modifier shows three or more things being compared.**

| | |
|---|---|
| POSITIVE | December can be a **stormy** month. |
| | He always walks **quickly.** |
| COMPARATIVE | December is a **stormier** month than May. |
| | He walks **more quickly** than she does. |
| SUPERLATIVE | February can be the **stormiest** month of all. |
| | Of the three of them, he walks **most quickly.** |

To form comparatives and superlatives, follow some basic rules.

**In general, for one-syllable modifiers add *-er* to form the comparative and *-est* to form the superlative.**

young, young**er,** young**est**
My sister is **younger** than I.
She is the **youngest** in the family.

At times the addition of *-er* and *-est* makes spelling changes necessary.

thin, thin**ner,** thin**nest**
true, tru**er,** tru**est**
happy, happ**ier,** happ**iest**

With certain one-syllable modifiers, using *more* and *most* may sound more natural than adding *-er* and *-est.*

prone, **more** prone, **most** prone
Germaine is **more prone** to accidents than anyone else here.

**For most two-syllable adjectives add *-er* to form the comparative and *-est* to form the superlative.**

heavy, heav**ier,** heav**iest**
That carton is **heavier** than this one.
The atlas is the **heaviest** book on my shelf.

Use *more* and *most* if *-er* and *-est* sound awkward.

famous, **more** famous, **most** famous
She became **more famous** with each new recording.

For adverbs ending in *-ly*, always use *more* and *most* to form the comparative and superlative degrees.

loudly, **more** loudly, **most** loudly
Of all the trumpeters, she played **most loudly.**

For modifiers of three or more syllables, always use *more* and *most* to form the comparative and superlative degrees.

comfortable, **more** comfortable, **most** comfortable
The new furniture made the room **more comfortable.**

*Less* and *least*, the opposite of *more* and *most*, can also be used with most modifiers to show comparison.

The speech was **less interesting** than I expected it to be.
That was the **least interesting** speech I have ever heard.

*Less* and *least* are used before modifiers of any number of syllables.

Certain adjectives describe an absolute condition. These adjectives—such as *unique*, *perfect*, and *final*—have no comparative or superlative form. Something cannot logically be "more unique" or "most dead." Sometimes, though, you can use *more nearly* or *most nearly* with these adjectives.

That copy of my term paper is **more nearly final** than this one.

## Exercise 1 Using Correct Degrees of Adjectives and Adverbs

On a separate sheet of paper, write the correct degree of comparison of the modifier in parentheses to complete each sentence. Then identify the answer as an *adverb* or *adjective* and tell *which* degree of comparison it shows.

SAMPLE Some landmarks are ________ than others. (popular))
ANSWER more popular: comparative adjective

### *Landmarks Around the World*

1. Of all the tourist attractions in Paris, the ________ landmark is probably the Eiffel Tower. (famous)
2. Visitors to New York harbor ________ line up for tours of the Statue of Liberty. (eager)
3. The Sears Tower, located in Chicago, Illinois, is the ______ skyscraper in the world. (tall)
4. Many people in Chicago are even ___________ of the city's many fine museums. (proud)
5. Completed in 1883, the Brooklyn Bridge is ______ than the Queensboro Bridge, which was completed in 1909. (old)
6. The Great Sphinx of Egypt has been one of the ________ discussed structures of the ancient world. (wide)
7. The Taj Mahal in India was built by Shah Jahan as a tomb for his wife and is considered by many to be the _________ building in the world. (beautiful)
8. The Great Wall is perhaps the ________ symbol of China. (well-known)
9. The Tower of London was originally a fortress but was used ______ as a prison. (late)
10. The trip down the Nile, though interesting, was __________ than I had expected. (exciting)

## 18.2 Irregular Comparisons

A few modifiers have irregular comparative and superlative forms.

| Modifiers with Irregular Forms of Comparison | | |
|---|---|---|
| **Positive** | **Comparative** | **Superlative** |
| good | better | (the) best |
| well | better | (the) best |
| bad | worse | (the) worst |
| badly | worse | (the) worst |
| ill | worse | (the) worst |
| far (distance) | farther | (the) farthest |
| far (degree, time) | further | (the) furthest |
| little (amount) | less | (the) least |
| many | more | (the) most |
| much | more | (the) most |

### Exercise 2 Making Correct Comparisons

Complete the following sentences with the correct degree of comparison of the modifier in parentheses. (The positive degree is used in one sentence.)

**SAMPLE** The sky looks ________ today than yesterday. (clear)
**ANSWER** clearer

#### *Perspective in Painting*

1. To achieve the ________ results possible, artists must pay attention to perspective rather than relying totally in shape. (realistic)
2. Those who are skilled in the techniques necessary to represent perspective are able to paint and draw ________ than those who are not skilled in these techniques. (naturalistically)
3. Objects at various points in your field of vision assume a ________ appearance as you continue to study them. (different)
4. An object looks ________ of all when it is standing right next to you. (large)
5. Objects appear ________ as their distance from you increases or as you physically move away from the objects. (small)
6. Furthermore, if you look at two objects in different positions, the object that is ________ will differ from the object that is closer in both color and detail. (distant)
7. The ________ away from it you are, the more an object is obscured by moisture and dust in the air. (far)
8. Thus, the most distant objects seem the most indistinct, standing out the ________. (little)
9. To achieve perspective, the artist uses ________ hues and lines for distant objects than for close ones. (faint)
10. One should not assume that artists who do not use perspective paint ________ than others; they may simply be less concerned with realism. (effectively)

## Exercise 3 Forming Degress of Comparison

On a separate sheet of paper, write the degree of comparison indicated in the parentheses for each adjective and adverb listed.

**SAMPLE** Adverb: happy (superlative)
**ANSWER** most happily

1. Adjective: dreary (comparative)
2. Adverb: well (superlative)
3. Adjective: good (comparative)
4. Adverb: quietly (positive)
5. Adverb: strangely (comparative)
6. Adjective: big (superlative)
7. Adverb: busily (comparative)
8. Adverb: ill (superlative)
9. Adverb: rudely (positive)
10. Adjective: late (comparative)
11. Adverb: slowly (superlative)
12. Adjective: far (positive)
13. Adverb: much (comparative)
14. Adjective: large (comparative)
15. Adjective: strange (comparative)
16. Adverb: loudly (superlative)
17. Adjective: busy (superlative)
18. Adverb: badly (comparative)
19. Adjective: difficult (comparative)
20. Adverb: little (superlative)

## Exercise 4 Making Correct Comparisons

Complete the following sentences with the correct degree of comparison of the modifier in parentheses. (The positive degree is used in two sentences.)

**SAMPLE** I think the medical profession may be ________ to enter than many others. (hard)
**ANSWER** harder

### *Dr. Alexa Canady, Neurosurgeon*

1. Alexa Canady had acheived success in a profession ________ than most. (demanding)
2. She has excelled in neurosurgery, perhaps the ________ medical specialty of all. (prestigious)
3. She reached the top of her profession ________ than anyone could have expected. (soon)
4. Canady's 1984 Teacher of the Year Award acknowledged her as one of the ________ teachers in the country. (good)
5. She became assistant director of neurosurgery at Children's Hospital of Michigan; she was named director a short while ________. (late)
6. In 1989 she was one of seventy-five African American women included in *I Dream a World*, a(n) ________ book of photographs by Brian Lanker. (extraordinary)
7. Among the photographer's subjects are people in every profession who have made some of the ________ contributions to society in recent years. (important)
8. In the book Canady says that her work allows her to make life a little ________ for seriously ill children. (easy)
9. She explains that physicians often get to know their patients' families ________. (intimately)
10. As one of the ________ accomplished neurosurgeons in the nation, Canady can be an inspiration to us all. (highly)

## Exercise 5 Writing Sentences Using Modifiers with Irregular Comparison Forms

On a separate sheet of paper, write a sentence using each word group. Next to each sentence state the degree of comparison for the modifier.

**SAMPLE** a better attitude
**ANSWER** Because he has a better attitude than Horace, Darryl has been selected to play in tonight's basketball game. (comparative)

1. the least likely candidate
2. planned better
3. worse handwriting
4. less appealing
5. best performance
6. walked farthest
7. acted badly
8. the least
9. speaks worse
10. more understanding
11. more qualifications
12. drove farther
13. many reports
14. worst condition
15. furthest into the investigation
16. felt worse
17. bad manners
18. performs best
19. handles more
20. much wisdom

## Exercise 6 Correcting Irregular Forms of Comparison

On a separate sheet of paper, write *correct* if the underlined modifier is used correctly. If it is incorrect, write the correct form.

**SAMPLE** After visiting my friend I could see that her leg was broken <u>bad</u>.
**ANSWER** badly

1. I had to drive <u>further</u> than I had hoped in order to reach the hospital.
2. Of all the problems we had to address, the incompetent ambulance driver was the <u>worse</u>.
3. When asked how she felt after breaking her leg my friend simply answered, "I've felt <u>better</u>."
4. The staff in the emergency room seemed to be <u>least excitable</u> than the paramedics.
5. Going immediately to the hospital was the <u>best</u> decision we made during the emergency.

## Exercise 7 Creating Sentences That Make Comparisons

Select five of the irregular modifiers from the list on page 594. Write a sentence for each, using the positive and comparative degrees of the modifier. Underline each modifier.

**SAMPLE** well
**ANSWER** Yesterday Luisa felt <u>well</u>, and today she feels even <u>better</u>.

## 18.3 Double Comparisons

Do not make a double comparison by using both *-er* or *-est* and *more* or *most.*

| | |
|---|---|
| INCORRECT | The wind is more sharper today than yesterday. |
| CORRECT | The wind is sharper today than yesterday. |
| INCORRECT | Kiichi runs more faster than I. |
| CORRECT | Kiichi runs faster than I. |

### Exercise 8 Correcting Double Comparisons

Rewrite on a separate sheet of paper each of the following sentences, correcting the double comparisons.

*Texas, State of Superlatives*

1. Texas is the second most largest state in the United States; only Alaska covers more area.
2. Texas is about 220 times larger than Rhode Island, the most smallest state in the Union.
3. Texas includes a more greater area than Illinois, Iowa, Michigan, and Wisconsin combined.
4. People travel more farther on Texas highways or railroads than on those of any other state.
5. Texas is more richer in farmland, cattle raising, and oil and natural-gas production than any other state in the United States.

### Exercise 9 Correcting Double Comparisons in a Paragraph

On a separate sheet of paper, correct each sentence in the paragraph below that contains a double comparison.

*Effects of Oil Spills*

Scientists have studied the effects of oil spills on living things. Because the most biggest oil spills have occurred in oceans and seas, a more greater number of studies have been done on saltwater animals and plant life than on those living in freshwater environments. Some effects of oil spills might be considered more worser than death for these animals. For example, fish can lose vision, fail to grow fully, and lose their ability to reproduce from even the most least amount of oil seeping into their environment. An even more lower concentration of oil in the water can harm a fish's ability to smell, rendering it unable to hunt for food.

## 18.4 Incomplete Comparisons

Do not make an incomplete or unclear comparison by omitting *other* or *else* when you compare one member of a group with another.

| | |
|---|---|
| **UNCLEAR** | Basketball players are often taller than any athletes. |
| **CLEAR** | Basketball players are often taller than any **other** athletes. |
| **UNCLEAR** | Chris is smarter than the students. |
| **CLEAR** | Chris is smarter than the **other** students. |
| **UNCLEAR** | Tyrone's voice is usually stronger than everyone's. |
| **CLEAR** | Tyrone's voice is usually stronger than everyone **else's.** |
| **UNCLEAR** | When singing in the chorus, Michelle sings louder than anyone. |
| **CLEAR** | When singing in the chorus, Michelle sings louder than **anyone else.** |

Make certain that you are comparing like things.

| | |
|---|---|
| **UNCLEAR** | A dog's tail wags more than a cat. [The wagging of a dog's tail is being compared illogically to a cat itself.] |
| **CLEAR** | A dog's tail wags more than **that of a cat.** |
| **CLEAR** | A dog's tail wags more than **a cat's.** [The word *tail* is understood after *cat's*.] |
| **UNCLEAR** | The traffic on South Street is heavier than Northern Boulevard. |
| **CLEAR** | The traffic on South Street is heavier than **that on Northern Boulevard.** |
| **CLEAR** | The traffic on South Street is heavier than **Northern Boulevard's.** |
| **UNCLEAR** | My father's pancakes are tastier than my mother. |
| **CLEAR** | My father's pancakes are tastier **than those of my mother.** |
| **CLEAR** | My father's pancakes are tastier than **my mother's.** |
| **UNCLEAR** | The prices at Hector's Sporting Goods are cheaper than Bob's Team Shop. |
| **CLEAR** | The prices at Hector's Sporting Goods are cheaper than **those at Bob's Team Shop.** |
| **CLEAR** | The prices at Hector's Sporting Goods are cheaper than **Bob's Team Shop's.** |

## Exercise 10 Making Complete Comparisons

Rewrite on a separate sheet of paper each of the following sentences to correct the incomplete comparisons.

### *Insect Variety*

1. Insects vary more in form, color, and size than any class of animal.
2. One of the largest insects, the atlas moth, has a wingspread that is one thousand times greater than the smallest insect.
3. The coloring of some insects is as brilliant and beautiful as birds.
4. Other insects have protective camouflaging that enables them to look more like dried twigs than anything.
5. Some mayflies live less than a day, a life span that is shorter than any insect.
6. Insects can survive in more kinds of environments than any creature.
7. There are more insects in areas with tropical climates than anywhere.
8. The fairy fly, which is only about one hundredth of an inch long and can easily crawl through the eye of a needle, is smaller than any insect.
9. Insects' capacity for survival is second only to humanity.
10. Given their weight, the strength of some insects is over fifty times greater than the strongest human.
11. Dragonflies in Central America are larger than the United States.
12. One splendor beetle found in timber from a staircase is believed to be forty-seven years old, which is older than any insect ever found.
13. Large tropical cockroaches can move at a speed of 3.36 miles per hour, which is faster than any insect.
14. In our school, Dr. Laslow has a greater interest in researching insect behavior than anyone.
15. The body of the African stick insect is longer than other insects.
16. No other insect's sound is louder than a male cicada.
17. The long-legged sun spiders that live in dry regions of Africa and the Middle East are faster than any spiders.
18. In 1968 a termite mound larger than any mound was found in Somalia and estimated to be 28.5 feet tall.
19. The poison from the yellow scorpion is more venomous than an emperor scorpion.
20. There seem to be larger insects in Africa than anywhere.
21. The air speed of a dragonfly is faster than a common horsefly.
22. The web of the tropical spider from the genus Nephilia is larger than any spider.
23. The wingspan of a butterfly found in the Canary Islands is less than the pygmy blue butterfly of the U.S.
24. The legs of a millipede can number up to 750, a number that is much greater than a centipede.
25. The study of insects, which is part of our biology course, is more interesting to me than plants.

## 18.5 *Good* or *Well; Bad* or *Badly*

Always use *good* as an adjective. *Well* may be used as an adverb of manner telling how ably something is done or as an adjective meaning "in good health."

Malcolm has a **good** attitude. [adjective]
Malcolm is a **good** actor. [adjective]
Malcolm looks **good** onstage. [adjective after a linking verb]
Malcolm performed his scene **well.** [adverb of manner]
Malcolm works **well** with the other actors. [adverb of manner]
Malcolm is not **well.** [adjective meaning "in good health"]

Always use *bad* as an adjective. Therefore, *bad* is used after a linking verb. Use *badly* as an adverb. *Badly* almost always follows an action verb.

That was a **bad** performance. [adjective]

The clarinets sounded **bad.** [adjective following a linking verb]

We felt **bad** about the poor performance. [adjective following a linking verb]

The mistakes were **badly** handled. [adverb telling *how*]

The chorus sang **badly,** too. [adverb following an action verb]

### Exercise 11 Choosing the Correct Modifier

On your paper complete the sentences correctly by using *good, well, bad,* or *badly.*

*Stage Fright*

1. A performer does not have to be a ________ actor or actress to suffer from stage fright.
2. This malady affects as many ________ performers as it does poor ones.
3. The self-assured actor you see onstage may not have felt ________ before the performance began.
4. No matter how ________ the performer may feel backstage, the problem usually disappears once the curtain rises.
5. An experienced performer will rarely perform ________ because of stage fright.
6. In fact, some actors and actresses believe that stage fright, as uncomfortable as it feels, may actually produce ________ results.
7. They are convinced that the extra tension helps them to perform ________.
8. One singer, for example, claims that when she is not anxious beforehand, she does not reach her peak and therefore sounds ________ in performance.
9. Still, no one enjoys stage fright, for the sufferer not only feels uncomfortable but may look ________ as well.
10. Every professional performer, of course, wants to act as ________ as possible.

## 18.6 Double Negatives

In general, do not use a **double negative,** two negative words in the same clause. Use only one negative word to express a negative idea.

| | |
|---|---|
| INCORRECT | They didn't mail no packages today. |
| CORRECT | They did**n't** mail **any** packages today. |
| INCORRECT | We haven't made no phone calls. |
| CORRECT | We have**n't** made **any** phone calls. |
| CORRECT | We have made **no** phone calls. |
| INCORRECT | He never joins no clubs. |
| CORRECT | He **never** joins **any** clubs. |
| CORRECT | He joins **no** clubs. |
| INCORRECT | I didn't tell no one about the hidden treasure. |
| CORRECT | I did**n't** tell **any** one about the hidden treasure. |
| CORRECT | I told **no** one about the hidden treasure. |
| INCORRECT | Eddie hasn't said nothing about the surprise party. |
| CORRECT | Eddie has**n't** said **anything** about the surprise party. |
| CORRECT | Eddie said **nothing** about the surprise party. |

### Exercise 12 Avoiding Double Negatives

On your paper rewrite the following sentences, eliminating the double negative in each. (Most sentences can be corrected in more than one way.)

*It's About Time*

1. What would life be like if we didn't have no way to measure time?
2. The ability to measure time is fundamental to our way of life, yet no one can't really say what time is.
3. For centuries people tried to fit days and months evenly into years, but they never found no way to accomplish this task.
4. Our months don't bear no relation to the actual cycle of the moon.
5. Furthermore, although one might expect there to be some seven-day celestial phenomenon on which our week is based, there isn't none.
6. It would be strange not to have no calendars, clocks, or watches.
7. For one thing, without the measurement of time, we would not be able to organize nothing.
8. We would not have no idea how long it takes to do things.
9. We couldn't never tell anyone to meet us some place in five minutes.
10. We would not have no sense of the passage of the days except by keeping track of the sunrise and sunset.

## 18.7 Misplaced and Dangling Modifiers

**Place modifiers as close as possible to the words they modify in order to make the meaning of the sentence clear.**

When words or phrases modify the wrong word or seem to modify more than one word in a sentence, they are called **misplaced modifiers.** To correct a sentence with a misplaced modifier, move the modifier as close as possible to the word it modifies.

MISPLACED Leaves floated gently down onto the lawn **with dazzling autumn colors.** [prepositional phrase incorrectly modifying *lawn*]

CLEAR Leaves **with dazzling autumn colors** floated gently down onto the lawn. [prepositional phrase correctly modifying *leaves*]

MISPLACED The big truck just missed a cat **roaring down the road.** [participial phrase incorrectly modifying *cat*]

CLEAR **Roaring down the road,** the big truck just missed a cat. [participial phrase correctly modifying *truck*]

### Exercise 13 Moving Misplaced Modifiers

Rewrite each sentence correctly by moving the underlined modifier to an appropriate position in the sentence.

*Swim Meet*

1. The swimmers on deck <u>with the black and white bathing suits</u> are all on the same swim team.
2. Officials must dress in white uniforms <u>judging the performance of the swimmers</u>.
3. The champion backstroker stormed out of the complex <u>being disqualified</u>.
4. Spectators crowded into the stands <u>carrying lunch bags and portable seats</u>.
5. The authorities requested additional timers <u>making an unusual announcement</u>.
6. The swim team had practiced hard and long for the meet <u>with the best record</u>.
7. Swimmers congregated around the pool <u>with a sense of excitement</u>.
8. Standing on the blocks, the first racers waited for the sound of the starting pistol <u>with intensity on their faces</u>.
9. Medals were given to the winners <u>with the race and time written on the back</u>.
10. One swimmer accidentally pushed an official into the pool <u>paying no attention to where he was going</u>.

## Other Ways to Correct Misplaced Modifiers

Sometimes you can correct a misplaced modifier by creating a subordinate clause or rephrasing the main clause.

MISPLACED **Doing her homework,** the cat distracted Maya. [participial phrase incorrectly modifying *cat*]

CLEAR The cat distracted Maya, **who was doing her homework.** [participial phrase recast as a subordinate clause correctly modifying *Maya*]

CLEAR **Doing her homework,** Maya was distracted by the cat. [by rephrasing the main clause, the participial phrase is correctly modifying *Maya*]

MISPLACED **Replacing the old shingles,** the barking dog frightened the roofer. [participial phrase incorrectly modifying *barking dog*]

CLEAR The barking dog frightened the roofer, **who was replacing the old shingles.** [participial phrase recast as a subordinate clause correctly modifying *roofer*]

CLEAR **Replacing the old shingles,** the roofer was frightened by the barking dog. [by rephrasing the main clause, the participial phrase is correctly modifying *roofer*]

### Exercise 14 Correcting Misplaced Modifiers

On a separate piece of paper, rewrite the sentences. Correct each misplaced modifier by either creating a subordinate clause or moving the main clause.

SAMPLE Rebuilding the motor, the tool box fell on the mechanic.
ANSWER The tool box fell on the mechanic who was rebuilding the motor.

*At the Gas Station*

1. Driving into the gas station, the advertisements for lower gas prices influenced the customers.
2. Pumping the gasoline, the dog in the car licked the attendant.
3. Changing the tires, the customer chatted with the mechanic.
4. Driving into the repair shop, the manager welcomed the new customer.
5. Increasing in price, most drivers conserve gasoline.

## Dangling Modifiers

A **dangling modifier** does not logically modify any word in the sentence in which it appears. Correct a dangling modifier by supplying a word that can be modified by the dangling phrase.

DANGLING **Following the trail closely,** the herd of elephants was located. [participial phrase logically modifying no word]

CLEAR **Following the trail closely,** the naturalists located the herd of elephants. [participial phrase logically modifying the word *naturalists*.]

CLEAR The naturalists located the herd **because they followed the trail closely.** [subordinate clause modifying *located*]

DANGLING **After working so hard,** the test seemed easy. [prepositional phrase logically modifying no word in the sentence]

CLEAR **After working so hard,** I found the test easy. [prepositional phrase modifying *I*]

DANGLING **Relaxing afterward,** my anxieties vanished. [participial phrase logically modifying no word]

CLEAR **Relaxing afterward,** I felt my anxiety vanish. [participial phrase modifying *I*]

## The Adverb *Only*

Place the adverb *only* immediately before the word or group of words it modifies.

A sentence's meaning may be unclear if *only* is positioned incorrectly.

UNCLEAR Michael **only** has chemistry on Friday. [Does Michael have just one class on Friday or no chemistry class on any day but Friday? Or is Michael the only one who has chemistry on Friday?]

CLEAR Michael has **only** chemistry on Friday. [He has no other classes that day.]

CLEAR Michael has chemistry **only** on Friday. [He does not have chemistry on any other day of the week.]

## Exercise 15 Correcting Dangling Modifiers

The following paragraph is about China. Read the paragraph. Then rewrite the sentences that follow, correcting each dangling modifier by adding appropriate information based on the paragraph. Reword the sentences if necessary. If the sentence contains no errors, write *correct.*

For two thousand years China was ruled by emperors. Then, in 1912, the Nationalists, supported by business interests, established a republic. Faced with a vast country, a decayed economy, and popular unrest, the Nationalist government fell to the Communists in 1949. Nevertheless, there persisted some traditional social institutions, especially the family, which continued to arrange marriages. Women, who lacked income and status, were forced to endure these marriages even when their husbands took additional wives.

1. Ruled for two thousand years by emperors, a republican form of government was established in 1912.
2. Burdened with a vast country and a decayed economy, the problems turned out to be insurmountable.
3. Challenged by political upheaval, many traditional social institutions somehow survived the revolution.
4. Ignoring the pleas of unhappy women, arranged marriages persisted after the Communist revolution.
5. Living as only one of many wives and lacking independent power or income, marriage could be a kind of imprisonment for women.

## Exercise 16 Moving the Adverb *Only*

On a separate piece of paper, rewrite each sentence so that it conveys the message indicated in parentheses.

**SAMPLE** Jack rented his home to four tenants for the summer. (Use *only* to show that the home is being rented for no other season except summer.)

**ANSWER** Jack rented his home to four tenants only for the summer.

1. The bungalow has four bedrooms but can comfortably house eight people. (Use *only* to show that no more than eight people will be comfortable.)
2. The condominium has three bedrooms but is limited to four tenants because of stipulations in the lease. (Use *only* to show that there are no more than three bedrooms.)
3. Mr. Kelly put the advertisement in the newspaper on Sunday and received four responses. (Use *only* to show that Mr. Kelly advertised for no more than one day.)
4. The landlord demands that the prospective tenant have a reference from an employer. (Use *only* to show that the reference can come from no one else but the employer.)
5. The new tenant can move in on a weekend after he has paid one month's rent and one month's security. (Use *only* to show that the tenant cannot move in before he has paid one month's rent and one month's security.)

## Exercise 17 Correcting Misplaced and Dangling Modifiers

On a sheet of paper, rewrite each sentence, correcting the misplaced or dangling modifier in each.

**SAMPLE** Taking over a variety of his responsibilities, the ailing Franklin Roosevelt was supported by his wife, Eleanor.

**ANSWER** The ailing Franklin Roosevelt was supported by his wife, Eleanor, who took over a variety of his responsibilities.

### *Women in Government*

1. Appointed in 1922, the state of Georgia was the first to be represented in the United States Senate by a woman, Rebecca Latimer Felton.
2. The governor hoped this gesture would win the support of women voters having a reputation as an opponent of woman suffrage.
3. As Georgia's first congresswoman, many regarded Felton as well qualified for the Senate seat.
4. The eighty-seven-year-old woman was only an active senator for two sessions, however.
5. Senator Felton retired after Georgia elected a permanent senator in her place, having been appointed as a temporary replacement.
6. Similarly, in 1931 Hattie Ophelia Wyatt Caraway was appointed senator by the governor of Arkansas on a temporary basis.
7. Hattie Caraway was appointed to replace her late husband with little political experience of her own.
8. She functioned well in the office using political contacts and instinct.
9. Senator Caraway decided to run for reelection with great difficulty.
10. Having won a decisive victory, the office was hers until 1945.

## Exercise 18 Using Modifiers Correctly in Sentences

On a separate piece of paper, write a sentence using each of the following modifiers. Be sure the modifier correctly modifies the word listed next to it.

**SAMPLE** Modifier: *running for office* Word to modify: *candidate*

**ANSWER** Running for office, the candidate could not accept the tickets to the basketball game.

1. Modifier: *with little confidence* Word to modify: *drove*
2. Modifier: *having lost the key* Word to modify: *banker*
3. Modifier: *declared the winner* Word to modify: *announcer*
4. Modifier: *only* Word to modify: *forty*
5. Modifier: *with no regrets* Word to modify: *left*
6. Modifier: *in the newspaper* Word to modify: *read*
7. Modifier: *that hit the window* Word to modify: *baseball*
8. Modifier: *studying for the exam* Word to modify: *student*
9. Modifier: *laughing at the comedienne* Word to modify: *audience*
10. Modifier: *having no friends* Word to modify: *new student*

## Exercise 19 Correcting Misplaced and Dangling Modifiers

On your paper rewrite the following sentences, correcting the misplaced or dangling modifiers in each.

### *The Craft of Origami*

1. Yesterday we read about origami, the Japanese craft of making images out of folded paper in the encyclopedia.
2. In its Asian homeland we learned that origami has been practiced for a long time.
3. Working in a tradition that is centuries old, origami is treated as a true art form in Japan.
4. It is not true, however, that only origami can be practiced in Japan.
5. With appropriate training, folded figures of animals, fish, insects, birds, people, and flowers are now made all over the world.
6. Symbolizing good fortune and long life in the Japanese origami tradition, I learned that the most popular origami figure is the crane.
7. Our class was treated to an origami demonstration by an expert in traditional crafts after researching the subject.
8. Mrs. Masuzawa made a fantastic paper bird for the class that resembled a peacock with its tail feathers spread.
9. She then created a frog out of green paper that actually hops when its back is tapped.
10. A talented woman, with her guidance most students made several simple figures, although I could only make one of them myself.

## Exercise 20 Explaining Incorrect Modifiers

Identify the modifier in each sentence. Then tell whether the modifier is *misplaced*, *dangling*, or *correct*. For all misplaced and dangling modifiers, explain why they are incorrect.

**SAMPLE** Visiting Egypt, the pyramids are impressive.
**ANSWER** Visiting Egypt, dangling; incorrect becasue there is no word that is modified by this modifier.

### *Traveling in Egypt*

1. Cairo markets attract many tourists with their strange wares.
2. Buying a vase, I learned a few Arabic words.
3. Having so many interesting attractions, thousands of visitors enjoy Egypt.
4. Surrounding the Great Pyramid of Cheops, people explore the mystery.
5. Determined to solve the mystery, the method used to build this structure is baffling.
6. A cubit is a basic measure of ancient Egypt being 18 inches long.
7. Being 365 cubits in length, a year is represented by each side of the pyramid.
8. Claiming that pyramids have unusual powers, experiments have been done.
9. Believing automobiles sell more under pyramids, a pyramid-shaped showroom was built in New Mexico.
10. Some people claim that plants grow faster under pyramids with flowers.

## Exercise 21 Modifiers

The following paragraph contains ten errors in the use of modifiers. Rewrite the paragraph, correcting the errors.

### *Jaime Escalante, Master Teacher*

[1]Jaime Escalante, the hero of the movie *Stand and Deliver*, may have more reason to be proud than any math teacher. [2]Inspiring and cajoling over the years, more than five hundred students at an inner-city high school in Los Angeles have been taught advanced math by Escalante. [3]People may think Escalante only teaches math, but this belief is not true. [4]Handling six classes and an after-school study session each day, as well as Saturday-morning classes at a nearby college, discipline and commitment are really what he teaches. [5]Clearly one of the most dedicated teachers in American education, Escalante is also one of the creativest. [6]From the best sound system money can buy, he energizes each class with booming rock and roll and then changes to more soft music while students take a daily quiz. [7]Because he feels badly when his students don't do well, he constantly tries to encourage them and build their confidence in order that they will perform good. [8]As *Stand and Deliver* shows, Jaime Escalante certainly won't have no reason to doubt his extraordinary success by the time he retires from teaching.

## Exercise 22 Adding Modifiers Correctly to Sentences

On a separate sheet of paper, write two possible modifiers that make sense in each blank in the following sentences.

**SAMPLE** ______, the student registered for three math classes.
**ANSWER** Filling out the application
Sitting at the desk

1. ______, the professor sounded almost like a robot as he lectured the class.
2. The classroom ______ holds a maximum of forty-three students.
3. ______, the undergraduates could not find the science building.
4. The college campus, ______, explodes with life every spring semester.
5. ______, Mitchell lost track of time and was late for class.
6. Biology 101 is ______ taught on Mondays at 10 A.M.
7. ______, the security guard checks the identification of anyone entering the campus through the main entrance.
8. ______, the new student sat in the last row in the back of the lecture hall.
9. The campus bookstore ______ charges tax on hardcover books.
10. ______, the new freshmen were able to see the entire campus.

UNIT
18
Unit Review

# Grammar Review

## Using Modifiers Correctly

In Amy Tan's novel *The Kitchen God's Wife* a Chinese woman, Winnie, and her American-born daughter, Pearl, are forced to share secrets they have long hidden from each other. In this excerpt Winnie relates to Pearl memories of her own mother, who had inexplicably abandoned Winnie as a child. The passage has been annotated to show some of the kinds of modifiers covered in this unit.

*Literature Model*

### *from* THE KITCHEN GOD'S WIFE

***by Amy Tan***

Correct use of *only*

Positive form of the adverb *clearly*

Positive form of the adjective *long*

Correctly placed prepositional phrase modifying *woman*

Correct use of a negative modifier

Of course, I do not remember everything about her. I was only six years old when she disappeared. But some things I can remember very clearly: the heaviness of her hair, the firmness of her hand when she held mine, the way she could peel an apple all in one long curly piece so that it lay in my hand like a flat yellow snake. You remember? That's how I learned to do that for you.

Other things from my memory are confusing. I saw a painting of her once. This was after she was gone. And I did not remember the mouth in that painting, so stiff, so firm. I did not remember those eyes, so sad, so lost. I did not recognize the woman in the painting as my mother. And yet I wanted to believe this painting was my mother, because that was all I had left of her.

I used to hold that painting in my lap, peer at her face from one side to the other. But her face always looked in another direction, never at me. She showed no thoughts. I could not tell what she was thinking before or after her painting was made. I could not ask her all the questions I had before she left: Why she talked so angrily to my father, yet kept a big smile on her face. Why she talked to her mirror at night, as if her own face looking back belonged to someone else. Why she told me that she could no longer ➡

carry me, that I would have to learn to walk everywhere by myself.

One day, when I was perhaps ten—this was after she had already been gone for several years—I was again looking at her painting. I saw a little spot of mold growing on her pale painted cheek. I took a soft cloth and dipped it in water, washed her face. But her cheek grew darker. I washed harder and harder. And soon I saw what I had done: rubbed half her face off completely! I cried, as if I had killed her. And after that, I could not look at that picture without feeling a terrible grief. So you see, I did not even have a painting anymore to call my mother. . . .

So sad! That is the saddest part when you lose someone you love—that person keeps changing. And later you wonder, Is this the same person I lost? Maybe you lost more, maybe less, ten thousand different things that come from your memory or imagination—and you do not know which is which, which was true, which is false.

Correctly placed participial phrase modifying *mold*

Comparative form of the adjective *dark*

Comparative form of the adverb *hard*

Superlative form of the adjective *sad*

## Exercise 1

**Making Correct Comparisons** The following sentences elaborate on ideas suggested by the passage from *The Kitchen God's Wife*. Rewrite each sentence on your paper, substituting the proper comparative or superlative form of the modifier in parentheses for the word or phrase in italics.

**SAMPLE** The story of Winnie's mother was the *strangest* of all. (surprising)
**ANSWER** The story of Winnie's mother was the most surprising of all.

1. Her mother's mysterious departure was one of the *most terrible* events of Winnie's troubled life. (bad)
2. Among the features that Winnie remembered *best* was her mother's thick hair. (vividly)
3. Hardly any memory was *more vivid* than that of the firmness of her mother's hand when Winnie grasped it. (clear)
4. For other memories Winnie had to dig *more deeply.* (far)
5. For a time a painting of her mother was the object Winnie loved *best.* (much)
6. The unfamiliar eyes in the painting were, however, the *most sorrowful* she had ever seen. (sad)
7. She remembered her mother's eyes as being *happier.* (joyful)
8. Still, the painting was all Winnie had left, and looking at it made her feel somewhat *more comforted.* (good)
9. Trying to remove a spot on the painting, Winnie rubbed *harder.* (firmly)
10. She soon found, however, that rubbing made the situation even *more serious.* (bad)

## Exercise 2

**Correcting Incomplete Comparisons** The following sentences are about Shanghai, where parts of *The Kitchen God's Wife* are set. Rewrite the sentences, correcting any incomplete comparisons. If a sentence contains no errors, write *correct.*

1. In the 1920s, when Winnie was a child, Shanghai was more exciting and varied than anyplace else in China.
2. Shanghai was opened to foreign commerce in the 1840s, before any port in the nation.
3. In Shanghai the tempo of economic and cultural change outpaced Peking.
4. The arts flourished there more than anywhere in China.
5. The population of modern Shanghai is greater than other major Chinese cities.

## Exercise 3

**Choosing the Correct Modifier** These sentences are based on passages from *The Kitchen God's Wife*. For each sentence choose the correct form of the modifier in parentheses, and then indicate whether the modifier is an *adjective* or an *adverb.*

**SAMPLE** Winnie's mother always treated her (good/well).
**ANSWER** well—adverb

1. Proud of her beauty, Winnie's mother always looked (good/well).
2. Winnie's wealthy, elderly father may have behaved (bad/badly) toward his young Second Wife.
3. The harsh tones of their voices when they argued sounded (bad/badly) to the young child.
4. Her well-educated mother felt (bad/badly) about having a position as Second Wife among four or five wives.
5. In China during the 1920s, there was no escape for a woman whose marriage was not going (good/well).

## Exercise 4

**Correcting Misplaced Modifiers** The following sentences are based on passages from *The Kitchen God's Wife* that are not reprinted in this textbook. Rewrite the sentences, correcting each misplaced modifier by shifting it or the term it modifies to a position that makes the meaning clearer. If a sentence contains no errors, write *correct.*

1. Bustling with servants, Winnie's wealthy father owned an elegant Shanghai townhouse.
2. Did happy people only live in that splendid house?
3. Winnie took a long tour with her mother of Shanghai.
4. She saw wonderful things, such as high-heeled shoes, crushed pearls, and a rare little fish going out with her mother one day.
5. Despairing and lonely, she would remember that day as her last day with her mother.

**Exercise 5**

The following passage describes the artist William McGregor Paxton, whose drawing appears on this page. Rewrite the passage, correcting the errors in spelling, grammar, and usage. Add any missing punctuation. There are ten errors.

### *William McGregor Paxton*

[1]William McGregor Paxton (1869–1941) growed up in Newton, Massachusetts. [2]Showing a talent for drawing at an early age, his parents encouraged Paxton's interest in art. [3]Paxton travels to Paris in 1889. [4]There he developed what was to become a lifelong intrest in French culture.

[5]Returning to Massachusetts, Paxton begins to refine his gift for portraiture. [6]A careful observer, his portraits managed to capture subtle qualities of character.

[7]In his pastel drawing of the wife of a student at Harvard, Paxton created a more vivider likeness than any he had ever drawn. [8]Like the portrait of Winnie's mother that is described in the passage from *The Kitchen God's Wife*, Paxtons drawing shows a young woman who is neither completely approachable nor completely distant. [9]Because Paxton does not use no bright colors except the touch of red on the lips, he succeeds in depicting the young woman as painfully shy and vulnerable.

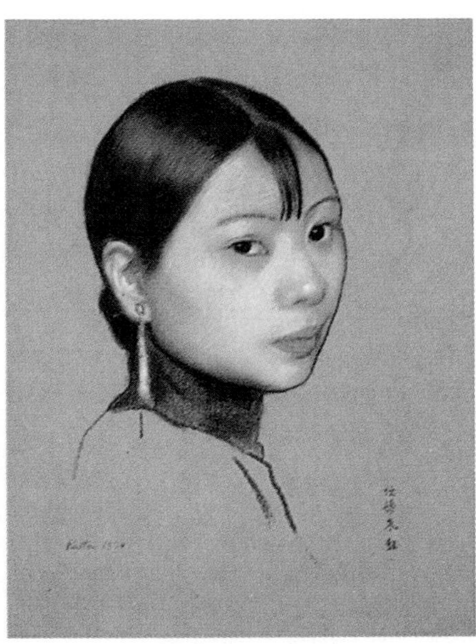

**William McGregor Paxton, *Portrait of Miss Jen Sun-ch'ang*, 1934**

**Exercise 6**

Read this biography of Amy Tan. Then rewrite the sentences below, correcting errors in the use of modifiers. Consult the biography if necessary.

**SAMPLE** Having died in 1967, the family grieved for Amy's brother and father.
**ANSWER** The family grieved for Amy's brother and father, who both died in 1967.

### *Amy Tan*

Amy Tan was born in California in 1952 to parents who had recently emigrated from China. The family lived happily until 1967, when Tan's older brother and father both died. Then the mother revealed to her astonished daughter that she had three other daughters in China from an earlier marriage.

In 1986 her mother fell ill. Stunned by the illness, Tan resolved to learn more about her Chinese background, and she sought out her mother's recollections. Moved and inspired by these memories, she fashioned her own stories, which became *The Joy Luck Club*, published in 1989. This novel about Chinese-born women and their American-born daughters enjoyed vast critical and popular acclaim. In her book Tan movingly described the complex relationships between mothers and daughters from two different worlds. The book eventually was produced as a play on Broadway and then made into a movie. Tan's second book, *The Kitchen God's Wife*, appeared in 1991.

1. Born in 1952, California was where Amy Tan grew up.
2. Emigrating from China in the 1940s, California offered a vast array of opportunities to Tan's parents.
3. As a teen-ager Tan discovered that she had three Chinese half-sisters with astonishment.
4. In 1986 the shock of her mother's illness inspired Tan to delve farther into her Chinese background.
5. Tan felt badly because she knew little about her heritage.
6. Gifted as a storyteller, the reminiscences of Tan's mother have inspired much of Tan's writing.
7. Her first novel, *The Joy Luck Club*, sold so good that it leaped to the top of the best-seller list.
8. In no book can a reader find such a vivid portrait of two generations of Chinese American women.
9. The popularity of Tan's work has spread more widely than most other new writers.
10. Some reviewers think that Tan is the more talented of all Asian American writers.

# Writing Application

**Using Modifiers in Writing** Good writing not only creates vivid images but also presents them clearly and in meaningful order. How to use and place modifiers, especially participial phrases, should be a major concern to writers when they are revising their work. Notice the underlined modifiers, in particular the participial phrases, in this excerpt from Ernest Hemingway's short story, "Big Two Hearted River: Part II."

> Holding the rod in his right hand he let out line against the pull of the grasshopper in the current. He stripped off line from the reel with his left hand and let it run free. He could see the hopper in the little waves of the current. It went out of sight. There was a tug on the line. Nick pulled against the taut line. It was his first strike. Holding the now living rod across the current, he brought in the line with his left hand.

**Techniques with Modifiers** Try to apply some of Hemingway's writing techniques when you write and revise your own work.

1. Avoid misplaced modifiers by placing the modifiers you use as close as possible to the word or phrase being modified.

**Misplaced modifier** "He let out line against the pull of the grasshopper in the current holding the rod in his right hand."
**Hemingway's version** "Holding the rod in his right hand he let out line against the pull of the grasshopper in the current."

2. Avoid dangling modifiers by making sure you include the word or phrase being modified.

**Dangling modifier** "Holding the now living rod across the current, the line was brought in...."
**Hemingway's version** "Holding the now living rod across the current, he brought in the line...."

**Practice** Practice these techniques by revising the following passage that contains dangling and misplaced modifers. Use a separate sheet of paper for your revisions. Pay particular attention to the underlined words.

> Leopold S. Senghor became one of modern Africa's greatest poets, born in Senegal when it was still a colony of France. Writing in French, his poetry is nevertheless strongly African in flavor. A hero in Senegal's independence movement, fellow citizens chose Senghor to be the first president of his homeland. He helped make Senegal one of West Africa's most democratic nations, serving several terms in office.

UNIT 19

# Usage Glossary

Grammar

Lessons

# 19 Usage Glossary

In the following glossary you will find the preferred usage for a number of particularly troublesome expressions. The glossary will help you choose between words that are often confused, and it will also indicate certain words and phrases that you should avoid completely in formal speaking and writing.

**a, an** The article *a* is used when the word that follows begins with a consonant sound, including a sounded *h: a buzzard, a heron.* The article *an* is used when the word that follows begins with a vowel sound or an unsounded *h: an artichoke, an herb.* The article *a* is also used before a word that begins with the "yew" sound: *a euphemism, a unicorn.*

**a lot, alot** This expression is always written as two words and means "a large amount." Some authorities recommend that it be avoided.

> There are **a lot** of tomatoes in the garden.

**a while, awhile** The expression *a while* is made up of two words: an article and a noun. Often the preposition *in* or *for* precedes *a while*, forming a prepositional phrase. The single word *awhile* is used only as an adverb.

> The troops will rest in **a while.**
> The troops will rest for **a while.**
> The troops will rest **awhile.**

**accept, except** *Accept* is a verb meaning "to receive" or "to agree to." *Except* may be a preposition or, less commonly, a verb. As a verb it means "to leave out." As a preposition it means "but."

> Carmen and Brad **accept** your invitation to dinner.
> Tomás is allergic to nuts and must **except** them from his diet.
> They can eat everything **except** the strawberries. [preposition]

**adapt, adopt** *Adapt* means "to adjust" or "to change something so that it can be used for another purpose." *Adopt* means "to take something for one's own."

> Many tropical plants cannot **adapt** to colder climates.
> The author was unable to **adapt** his tale for children.
> The childless couple decided to **adopt** a baby.

**advice, advise** *Advice* is a noun meaning "helpful opinion." *Advise* is a verb meaning "to give advice or offer counsel."

> Jean asked her doctor for **advice** and hoped he would not **advise** her to enter the hospital.

**affect, effect** *Affect* is a verb meaning "to cause a change in; to influence." *Effect* may be a noun or a verb. When used as a noun, it means "result." When used as a verb, it means "to bring about or accomplish."

> How have the dietary changes **affected** her health?
> What **effect** have the dietary changes had on her health?
> She **effected** some important changes in her diet.

**ain't** *Ain't* should not be used in formal speaking or writing unless it is within a quotation. Instead, use *I am not; she is not; he is not;* and so on.

**all ready, already** The two words *all ready* mean "completely ready." The single word *already* is an adverb meaning "before" or "by this time."

> The actors were **all ready** to take another bow, but the applause had **already** died away.

**all right, alright** Always write this expression as two words. Although some dictionaries include the single word *alright,* most authorities prefer that the expression be spelled *all right.*

> Is it **all right** to give the dog a biscuit?

## Exercise 1 Making Usage Choices

For each of the following sentences, choose the correct word or expression from the pair in parentheses.

### *Chien-Shiung Wu, Physicist*

1. Chien-Shiung Wu's father, a school principal in China, encouraged Chien-Shiung to spend (alot/a lot) of time studying.
2. After graduating from National Center College in Nanking, Wu went to California to do graduate work in physics, (a/an) unusual field for women to enter in the 1930s.
3. Wu had (already/all ready) received her doctorate from the University of California at Berkeley when she began to teach at Smith College.
4. Then she taught for (a while/awhile) at Princeton.
5. In 1944 she (accepted/excepted) a position in the Division of War Research at Columbia University; her job was to study radiation detection.
6. On the (advice/advise) of the physicists Tsung-dao Lee and Chen Ning Yang, Wu began a test on subatomic particles.
7. Lee and Yang, later winners of a Nobel Prize in physics, had developed a theory that would have a tremendous (affect/effect) on the way subatomic particles are viewed.
8. In 1957, as the leader of a group of experimenters, Wu confirmed that it was (alright/all right) for physicists to support the Lee-Yang hypothesis.
9. As a result of Wu's work, many physicists have (adapted/adopted) the Lee-Yang hypothesis.
10. It (ain't/isn't) any surprise that Chien-Shiung Wu is considered one of the world's best experimental physicists.

**all together, altogether** Use the two words *all together* to mean "in a group." Use the single word *altogether* as an adverb meaning "completely" or "on the whole."

When the conductor gave the downbeat, the orchestra began **all together.**

The conductor was angry because some players had missed the cue **altogether.**

**allusion, illusion** An *allusion* refers to "an indirect reference." *Illusion* refers to "a false idea or appearance."

In his speech Dr. King made an **allusion** to the Declaration of Independence.

The image in the painting was an **illusion.**

**anywheres, everywheres** It is preferred that these words and others like them be written without a final *-s*: *anywhere*, *everywhere*, *somewhere*.

**bad, badly** See Unit 18.

**being as, being that** Although these expressions are sometimes used informally to mean "because" or "since," in formal speaking and writing you should use only *because* or *since*.

**Since** Sabrina does not like tomato sauce, we are serving the pasta with clam sauce.

**Because** the guests arrived late, the dinner was cold.

**beside, besides** *Beside* means "at the side of" or "next to." *Besides* means "moreover" or "in addition to."

The cattle were grazing **beside** the stream.
**Beside** the barn you will find a pitchfork and a shovel.

No one **besides** Chris wants to play tennis.
**Besides** a stale loaf of bread, the cupboard is bare.

**between, among** *Between* and *among* are prepositions that are used to state a relationship. Use *between* to relate two entities (persons, places, things, or groups) or to compare one entity with another. Use *between* to refer to more than two entities when they are considered equals in a close relationship or are being viewed individually in relation to one another.

The discussion **between** the two senators was heated. [*Between* links the two senators together.]

What are the similarities **between** this poem and the other two? [*Between* is used to compare one poem with a group of others.]

The Triple Entente was an alliance **between** Great Britain, France, and Russia. [*Between* establishes a relationship involving equals.]

*Among* is used to show a relationship in which more than two entities are considered as a group.

The estate was divided **among** the three brothers.
Plant this seedling **among** the other trees.

**borrow, lend, loan** *Borrow* is the opposite of *lend. Borrow* means "to take something with the understanding that it must be returned." *Lend* means "to give something with the understanding that it will be returned." *Loan* is a noun meaning "the act of lending" or referring to "something that is lent." *Loan* may also be used as a verb, but most authorities prefer that *lend* be used instead.

May I **borrow** your history book until next Thursday? [verb]
I can **lend** it to you for only two days. [verb]
Thanks for the **loan** of the book. [noun]

**bring, take** Use *bring* to mean "to carry from a distant place to a closer one." Use *take* to mean the opposite: "to carry from a nearby place to a more distant one."

**Bring** us some Chinese food when you come home tonight.
Don't forget to **take** your umbrella when you go to the movies.

**can, may** *Can* signifies the ability to do something. *May* signifies permission to do something or the possibility of doing it.

I **can** make a pair of jeans in a few hours.
Students **may** wear jeans to class.
"**May** I be excused?" asked the student.

## Exercise 2 Making Usage Choices

On your paper write the correct word or expression from the pair in parentheses to complete each sentence.

### *Children's Literature*

1. Children may choose (among/between) many popular forms of literature.
2. (Beside/Besides) traditional fairy tales, children's literature includes adventure stories, mysteries, and science fiction.
3. Madeleine L'Engle's *A Wrinkle in Time* (brings/takes) the reader through a time warp to another world.
4. Children (everywhere/everywheres) delight in reading Robert Louis Stevenson's *Treasure Island.*
5. Theodor Seuss Geisel, known as Dr. Seuss, wrote (all together/altogether) delightful stories, such as *The Cat in the Hat* and *Bears on Wheels.*

6. E. B. White, an author of sophisticated nonfiction, (lent/ loaned) his talent to children's literature.
7. In E. B. White's *Charlotte's Web* a spider discovers that she (can/may) write messages in her web.
8. Charles Dodgson, a mathematician better known as Lewis Carroll, included many hidden (allusions/illusions) to mathematical ideas in *Alice in Wonderland.*
9. In *Robinson Crusoe* the hero feels (bad/badly) when many of his first attempts at coping with life on a deserted island fail.
10. As Lemuel Gulliver sleeps on a beach in *Gulliver's Travels,* he is a source of wonder to the Lilliputians (being as since) they have never before seen anyone so large.

**can't hardly, can't scarcely** These expressions are regarded as double negatives because *hardly* and *scarcely* by themselves have a negative meaning. Therefore, avoid using *hardly* and *scarcely* with *not* or *-n't.*

David is so hoarse he **can hardly** talk.

The knights **can scarcely** move in their heavy suits of armor.

**continual, continuous** Use *continual* to refer to an action that occurs repeatedly. Use *continuous* to describe an action that proceeds with no interruption or to refer to uninterrupted space.

**Continual** rainstorms make the tropical forest a lush, green place.
Hector's research was **continuous** for ten hours today.
The gray water stretched ahead of him in a **continuous** expanse.

**could of, might of, must of, should of, would of** The auxiliary verb *have,* not the preposition *of,* should follow *could, might, must, should,* or *would.*

If he knew he was going to be late, he **should have** called her.

**different from, different than** In general, the expression *different from* is preferred to *different than.*

Janet is **different from** her sister.
Yodeling is **different from** singing.

**doesn't, don't** *Doesn't* is the contraction of *does not* and is used with *he, she, it,* and all singular nouns. *Don't* is the contraction of *do not* and is used with *I, you, we, they,* and all plural nouns.

She **doesn't** know the answer to your question.
The children **don't** like rainy days.

**emigrate, immigrate** *Emigrate* and *immigrate* are opposites. *Emigrate* means "to leave a country or region." *Immigrate* means "to enter a country to settle there." Use *from* with *emigrate* and *to* or *into* with *immigrate.*

Between 1867 and 1886 nearly 450,000 persons **emigrated** from Sweden.
[These Swedes "left" Sweden.]

Most Swedes who **immigrated** to the United States settled in the Midwest.
[These Swedes "entered" the United States.]

**farther, further** Use *farther* to refer to physical distance. Use *further* to refer to time or degree.

How much **farther** will we have to drive today?
We will not discuss this matter **further.**

**fewer, less** *Fewer* generally refers to nouns that can be counted, whereas *less* refers to nouns that cannot be counted. You should also use *less* to refer to figures used as a single amount or quantity.

There have been **fewer** rainy days this month than last.

This piece of fish has **fewer** calories than that piece of steak.

We've had **less** rain this month than last. [Rain cannot be counted.]

The storm lasted for **less** than three hours. [*Three hours* is treated as a single period of time.]

My new raincoat cost **less** than one hundred dollars. [*One hundred dollars* is treated as a single sum.]

**good, well** See Unit 18.

**Exercise 3** **Making Usage Choices**

On your paper write the correct word or expression from the pair of words in parentheses to complete each sentence.

*Soccer*

1. Someone (emigrating/immigrating) from the United States might be surprised to learn that what is called soccer here is called football in most other countries.
2. This sport is so popular in some countries that fans (can't hardly/can hardly) see enough of the game.
3. Soccer is played on a large rectangular field by no (fewer/ less) than eleven players on each team.
4. A soccer team tries to score by (continually/continuously) kicking the ball toward the opposing goal.
5. Tackling or blocking opponents (doesn't/don't) do a team much good, for the referee will declare a penalty.

6. Players are (further/farther) penalized for pushing or tripping an opponent.
7. Therefore, a soccer player who wants to look (good/well) on the field avoids running into an opponent.
8. Except for the goalkeeper, a soccer player (don't/doesn't) touch the ball with his or her hands.
9. Obviously a soccer game is (different from/different than) an American football game.
10. You (might of/might have) seen a game between the professional North American Soccer League teams.

**had of** Do not use the word *of* between *had* and a past participle.

If she **had** bought the tickets early, we would not have had to wait in line.

If he **had** known, he would have told me.

**hanged, hung** *Hanged* should be used to mean "to put to death by hanging." *Hung* should be used in all other cases.

During the 1800s convicted murderers were **hanged.**
The doctor **hung** her diploma on a wall in her office.

**in, into, in to** Use *in* to mean "inside" or "within a place"; use *into* to indicate movement from outside to a point within or to indicate something pointing inward. The phrase *in to* is made up of an adverb (*in*) followed by a preposition (*to*) and should be carefully distinguished from the preposition *into.*

The sick man was resting **in** bed.
The doctor arrived and immediately went **into** the sickroom.
The doctor arrived and went **in to** the sick man.

**irregardless, regardless** The prefix *ir-* and the suffix *-less* both have negative meanings, and so they form a double negative when used together. Always use *regardless.*

Please call us when you get home, **regardless** of the hour.

**this kind, these kinds** *Kind* is singular, and so it is modified by the singular form *this* or *that.* Similarly, *this* and *that* should be used to modify the singular nouns *sort* and *type* (*this type*, *that type*, *this sort*, *that sort*). *Kinds* is plural, and so it is modified by the plural form *these* or *those.* Similarly, *these* and *those* should be used to modify the plural forms *sorts* and *types.*

**This kind** of mistake is easy to make.
**These kinds** of mistakes are easy to make.

**lay, lie** *Lay* means "to put" or "to place something"; it takes a direct object. *Lie* means "to recline" or "to be positioned"; it never takes an object.

Please **lay** this blanket on the baby's bed.
Most afternoons the baby **lies** quietly in the crib.

To avoid confusion in using the principal parts of *lie* and *lay*, study the following chart. Note that the past tense of *lie* is *lay:*

| | | |
|---|---|---|
| **BASE FORM** | lay | lie |
| **PRESENT PARTICIPLE** | laying | lying |
| **PAST FORM** | laid | lay |
| **PAST PARTICIPLE** | laid | lain |

He **laid** the blanket on the baby's bed last night.
The baby **lay** quietly in the crib yesterday afternoon.

**learn, teach** *Learn* means "to receive knowledge" or "to acquire skill in." *Teach* means "to instruct" or "to give knowledge to."

In this class swimmers will **learn** two new strokes.
This instructor **teaches** the advanced swimming class.

**leave, let** *Leave* means "to go away," and *let* means "to allow" or "to permit."

Dad will **leave** the office in an hour.
**Let** the dog play with the ball.

**like, as** Use *like*, which is a preposition, to introduce a prepositional phrase. Use *as* and *as if*, which are subordinating conjunctions, to introduce subordinate clauses. Many authorities believe that *like* should never be used before a clause.

Debra runs **like** an Olympic track star.
She plans, **as** I do, to run six miles a day.
Rebecca runs **as if** her leg is hurt.

**loose, lose** The adjective *loose* means "free," "not firmly attached," or "not fitting tightly." The verb *lose* means "to have no longer," "to misplace," or "to fail to win."

When I **lose** weight, my belt becomes **loose.**
If we **lose** the match, our school will still win.

## Exercise 4 Making Usage Choices

For each sentence, choose the correct word or expression from the pair in parentheses.

### *Ernest J. Gaines*

1. As a boy in Louisiana, Ernest J. Gaines went (in/into/in to) the fields to work.
2. When he was young, he often felt (like/as if) he had to struggle to bridge the gap between the written and the spoken word.
3. Gaines's roots (lay/laid) in an oral tradition: "We *talked* stories," he said.

4. Because his home parish (had/had of) denied him a high school education and library privileges, he moved to California.
5. There Gaines finished junior college and managed to (loose/lose) himself in a study of books about rural life.
6. His research (learned/taught) him that images of African Americans in American literature were often negative.
7. (Irregardless/Regardless) of this finding, he discovered that he could respond warmly to the accounts of peasant life in Russian literature.
8. Accomplishments such as winning a Wallace Stegner Creative Writing Fellowship must have (laid/lain) to rest any doubts about Gaines's ability to write fiction.
9. He has since written many stories and novels, such as *The Autobiography of Miss Jane Pittman*, and in (this kind/these kinds) of literary works, he has sympathetically portrayed characters of all races.
10. Throughout the years he has also (hanged/hung) on to his interest in scholarship; he is now a professor of English at the University of Southwestern Louisiana.

**passed, past** The word *passed* is always a verb; it is the past tense and the past participle of *to pass.* The word *past* can be an adjective, a preposition, an adverb, or a noun, but it is never a verb.

Many thoughts **passed** through my mind. [verb]

During the **past** year the artist has completed a large sculpture. [adjective]

I drive **past** her office several times a week. [preposition]

The conductor waved to some children as the train chugged **past.** [adverb]

Some people try to forget the **past.** [noun]

**precede, proceed** Use *precede* to mean "to go or come before." Use *proceed* to mean "to continue" or "to move along."

A car carrying Secret Service agents **preceded** the President's limousine.

The President's car **proceeded** slowly up the boulevard.

**raise, rise** *Raise* means "to cause to move upward"; it always takes an object. *Rise* means "to get up"; it is an intransitive verb, and so it never takes an object.

Please do not **raise** your hand unless you know the answer.
The reporters will **rise** when the governor enters the room.

**reason is because** This expression is repetitious since *because* means "for the reason that." Use *because* alone, or use *the reason is that.*

The **reason** Jan stayed home **is that** she is not feeling well.
Jan stayed home **because** she does not feel well.

**respectfully, respectively** Use *respectfully* to mean "with respect." Use *respectively* to mean "in the order named."

> The students greeted their professor **respectfully.**
> Diane **respectfully** requested a vacation.

> *The Bell Jar* and "The Bells" are, **respectively,** a novel and a poem.
> Dale and Pete like golf and tennis **respectively**.

**says, said** *Says* is the third-person singular form of the verb *say. Said* is the past tense of *say*. Do not use *says*, a present form, when you mean *said.*

> A few days ago, you **said** you would organize your closet.
> Then your sister **said** she would be glad to help you.
> She always **says** she is going to help, but she does not.
> Dad **says** you must do the job by yourself.

**sit, set** *Sit* means "to place oneself in a sitting position." It rarely takes an object. *Set* means "to place" or "to put," and it generally takes an object. When *set* is used with *sun* to mean "the sun is going down" or "the sun is sinking out of sight," it is intransitive, however.

> The puppy will **sit** in front of the television set.
> Paula **set** the roses on the mantel.
> Every evening we watch the sun **set** behind the mountains.

**than, then** *Than* is a conjunction that is used in comparisons and to show exception.

> Nina finds trigonometry more difficult **than** geometry.
> The leader of the hike was none other **than** Mrs. Shen, Nina's geometry teacher.

*Then* is an adverb meaning "at that time," "soon afterward," "the time mentioned," "at another time," "for that reason," "in that case," or "besides."

> We were on vacation **then.**
> Pam set the table, and **then** the family sat down to dinner.
> By **then** we had already heard the good news.
> Ernesto works hard; **then** he takes time off.
> If we find a larger apartment, **then** we will move.
> Bicycling is good exercise, and **then** it is fun.

**this here, that there** Avoid using *here* and *there* after *this* and *that.*

> Nancy wants to borrow **this** book.
> **This** is the sort of scarf I want.
> Pass me **that** notebook.
> **That** is what happens when the pasta is undercooked.

**who, whom** See Unit 17.

**Exercise 5** **Making Usage Choices**

Locate and write the incorrect terms used in the dialogue. Next to each incorrect term, write the correct term.

1. "I could of helped you with your math, Johnny, but you didn't ask me," Nelson declared.
   "No problem, Nelson. I got some help from Rick," Johnny responded.
2. "Hey, Joani, did you go in to the haunted house at the carnival?" Blair asked.
   "No way, Blair. I heard they were using live snakes in that attraction," Joani answered.
3. Raoul asked, "Why did you buy a stick-shift car instead of an automatic?"
   Jeremy answered, "The gas mileage in a stick-shift is different than the gas mileage in an automatic. It's better."
4. "You're lucky, Jeff. Your parents will let you drive anywheres you want to. My parents have a short list of places where I can drive, and they're all right around here," Barry complained.
   "Don't be too quick to complain, Barry. My parents let me drive anywhere I want to, but they also give me a long list of things to do for them on the way."
5. Jack said, "I heard that the money Blake and his brothers got for painting their house was not fairly divided."
   Allen responded, "Yeah, I know. Their parents divided the money between the three brothers by giving the oldest brother half, while the other two brothers had to divide the other half."
6. "We will precede with the test at exactly nine o'clock," the teacher announced.
   Ellen questioned, "Do we start with the real test items, or do we do the preceding practice items first, Mrs. Aaron?"
7. Ben's mother asked, "Ben, did you loose your best tie again? What do you plan to wear to your aunt's wedding?"
   "No problem, Mom." Ben responded. "I'll just borrow one of Dad's boring ties. Who cares what I look like? Do you really think that many people will show up?"
8. "Why do you think your mom bought such an ugly vase at the auction?" Sarah asked.
   "She just gets carried away at auctions," Kim answered. "She don't know how to control herself."
9. "Harold," the teacher called. "Would you please rise and go raise the window? It's getting very stuffy in here."
   "Sure, Mrs. Needles." Anthony answered. "I'll raise and go open that window for you."
10. "Why can't I go to the concert, Mom?" Angela pleaded. "Everybody I know will be there."
    "Irregardless of who will be there, Angela, you may not go," Angela's mother answered firmly.

UNIT 19

Unit Review

# Grammar Review

## Usage Glossary

The writers of the following quotations present insights into exploration—of the world, of the intellect, and of the human heart. The quotations, one of which appears in translation, have been annotated to show some of the usage items covered in this unit.

*Literature Model*

### Quotations About Exploration

*May* used to suggest possibility

. . . However ignorant man may be, he still feels within him his immortal spirit yearning after the unknown future.

From *Typee* by Herman Melville

*Like*, a preposition, used to introduce a prepositional phrase

She pulled in her horizon like a great fish net. . . . So much of life in its meshes! She called her soul to come and see.

From *Their Eyes Were Watching God* by Zora Neale Hurston

The transitive verb *raise*

Four hoarse blasts of a ship's whistle still raise the hair on my neck and set my feet to tapping.

From *Travels with Charley* by John Steinbeck

*Would have* rather than *would of*

But surely it would have been a pity
not to have seen the trees along this road,
really exaggerated in their beauty,
not to have seen them gesturing
like noble pantomimists, robed in pink.

From "Questions of Travel" by Elizabeth Bishop

The intransitive verb *lie*

Arriving at each new city, the traveler finds again a past of his that he did not know he had: the foreignness of what you no longer are or no longer possess lies in wait for you in foreign, unpossessed places.

From *Invisible Cities* by Italo Calvino, translated from the Italian by William Weaver

## Exercise 1

**Making Usage Choices** For each of the following sentences, write the correct word or expression from the pair in parentheses.

### *Trickster Characters in Folklore*

1. Traditions, legends, and stories are (passed/past) from generation to generation as folklore.
2. Many cultures' folk tales are so old that their origins (precede/proceed) the development of a writing system.
3. An expert once (says/said) to me that the trickster is a character found in folk tales all over the world.
4. (This here/This) character is always a greedy, lying, boastful cheat.
5. He is also whimsical, clever, and impetuous—an appealing rogue (who/whom) his adversaries can never defeat.
6. In Native American traditions Coyote and Manabohzo are the tricksters of, (respectfully/respectively), Nez Percé and Ojibwa stories.
7. Brer Rabbit, a trickster whose roots are found in West Africa, (raises/rises) delighted chuckles among all who hear stories of his exploits.
8. The reason trickster tales are popular is (because/that) they depict universal struggles between family members, neighbors, friends, or authority figures.
9. Both children and adults can (sit/set) down and listen to trickster tales from Polynesia, Africa, Germany, and Japan.
10. A student of human nature can do worse (than/then) to listen to trickster tales from all over the world.

## Exercise 2

**Usage** For each of the following sentences, write the correct word or expression from the pair in parentheses.

### *Swimming Through the Ages*

1. In the 1924 Olympics, free-style swimmer Johnny Weissmuller set a record by swimming four hundred meters in (fewer/less) than five minutes.
2. Speed swimmers have made (alot/a lot) of progress since the 1924 Olympics.
3. In 1972 (a/an) Argentine woman swam the four hundred meters faster than Weissmuller had, yet she failed to win a medal.
4. One reason speeds have increased so much is (because/ that) water and pool conditions have been improved.
5. The fact that modern coaching methods are (different from/different than) those of Weissmuller's day is another reason for the new records.
6. In ancient times people (might have/might of) learned to swim by imitating the way animals swim.
7. As time (passed/past), swimming became one of the sports in which ancient civilizations held competitions.
8. The popularity of swimming declined for (a while/awhile) during the Middle Ages. ➡

9. The reason for this decline was (because/that) people of the Middle Ages believed that water carries diseases.
10. They mistakenly thought that swimming would make one feel (bad/badly).
11. The nineteenth century saw the popularity of swimming (raise/rise) once more.
12. Swimmers who preferred a controlled environment were probably pleased when the British built pools inside buildings and so (brought/took) the sport indoors.
13. As new strokes were developed, swimmers needed (fewer/less) seconds to cover a given distance.
14. Frederick Cavill (emigrated/immigrated) to Australia and became that country's leading swimming instructor.
15. Cavill's development of a stroke called the Australian crawl had a major (affect/effect) on the sport.
16. Johnny Weissmuller took the Australian crawl a step (farther/further), popularizing the front crawl.
17. Many swimmers improved their time by (adapting/adopting) their style to include the new flip turn.
18. Special parent-child swimming classes today (learn/teach) children to swim before they can walk.
19. Parents should not permit their children to jump (in/into/in to) deep water if the children cannot swim.
20. On their doctor's (advice/advise) many people keep physically fit by swimming.

## Exercise 3

**Usage** For each of the following sentences, write the correct word or expression from the pair in parentheses.

*The Art of Gymnastics*

1. (Between/Among) you and me, I believe that gymnastics is one of the most beautiful sports in the world.
2. A gymnast leaping from the ground (in/into/in to) the air is a figure of grace.
3. (Beside/Besides) grace a gymnast must have considerable strength and muscle control.
4. Some gymnasts would rather take part in the all-around competition (than/then) specialize in one event.
5. (All together/Altogether) there are four events in the women's all-around competition and five in the men's.
6. Men and women compete in different kinds of gymnastic events, (accept/except) for the floor exercise, which has both men's and women's competition.
7. Women gymnasts perform on the balance beam and sidehorse vault, and then they (raise/rise) and swing themselves on the uneven parallel bars.
8. Competitors on the uneven bars try to create a sense of (continual/continuous) motion with no breaks or pauses.
9. (This/This here) event is an important part of the women's gymnastic competition.
10. Without proper concentration gymnasts can (loose/lose) their balance doing flips on the balance beam.
11. Spectators are impressed that gymnasts (can/may) lower themselves into a position called an iron cross. ➡

12. During the floor exercises a graceful gymnast may create the (allusion/illusion) of effortless rolls, leaps, and jumps.For each of the following sentences, write the correct word or expression from the pair in parentheses.
13. During these exercises a gymnast must never (lie/lay) still on the floor.
14. Though gymnasts may move (like/as) dancers, they are performing tremendous muscular feats.
15. (Because/Being that) their sport is so strenuous, gymnasts must be physically fit.
16. A gymnast who is not feeling (all right/alright) will not be able to perform well.
17. As Americans we can feel (good/well) about the performance of American gymnasts in the Olympic competition.
18. The gymnasts (who/whom) fans admire most have been coached by private trainers.
19. When she gave a talk at our school, a local sportswriter (says/said) that many American women have been coached by Bela Karoly.
20. A crowd will often sit quietly and observe a performance and then (respectfully/respectively) burst into thunderous applause when the gymnast's performance is finished.

## Exercise 4

**Usage** For each of the following sentences, write the correct word or expression from the pair in parentheses.

### *About the Olympics*

1. Sports fans (could hardly/couldn't hardly) believe the number of outstanding performances at the World Track and Field Championships in Tokyo in the summer of 1991.
2. A venerable long-jump record was broken by (a/an) American athlete, Mike Powell.
3. If you (had of/had) considered Bob Beamon's 1968 Olympic jump unbeatable, you would have been wrong.
4. In 1991 Powell beat that record by (a lot/alot)—a full two inches.
5. At the same meet, Carl Lewis, called the King of Track and Field, ran the hundred-meter race in no (less/fewer) than 9.86 seconds, another world record.
6. (These kinds/These kind) of records prompted comparisons to those set in Olympic competitions.
7. The World Track and Field Championships are (different from/different than) the Olympic games.
8. The Olympic games, for example, (ain't/aren't) held every year.
9. Since 1896 the Olympics have been held every four years, (accept/except) during the years of World War I and World War II.
10. The original Olympic games (proceeded/preceded) the modern games by about twenty-five hundred years.
11. No women (could of/could have) attended any of the early games, but they held their own games, the Herea.
12. For (a while/awhile) only foot races were run in the Olympics, but later other sports were added.
13. When Greece was conquered by Rome, the Romans copied many Greek practices, including the Olympics, which they (adapted/adopted) as their own. ➡

14. The games of antiquity ended (everywheres/everywhere) in A.D. 394, when Emperor Theodosius discontinued them.
15. In some sports present-day Olympic athletes supposedly (don't/doesn't) have to be amateurs.
16. (Irregardless/Regardless) of this rule, the degree of professionalism among athletes varies from sport to sport and from country to country.
17. When the winter Olympics were instituted in 1924, athletes gathered in Chamonix (all ready/already) to compete for gold, silver, and bronze medals.
18. Track and field events, many of them (borrowed/loaned/ lent) from the ancient Olympics, include a larger variety of sports than any other category.
19. When a gold medal is (hanged/hung) around an Olympian's neck, the athlete's grueling training suddenly seems worth the effort.
20. The city of Atlanta (can/may) take great pride in having been chosen as the site of the 1996 summer Olympic games.

## Exercise 5

**Usage** Write the word from the following list that best completes each sentence.

| | | | | |
|---|---|---|---|---|
| less | leave | adapted | let | then |
| than | passed | fewer | past | adopted |

### *A Vacation in England*

1. During our trip through England, I __________ well to the change in environment.
2. I simply __________ the philosophy that the trip was an adventure, and I was not going to let my old habits get in the way of a wonderful vacation.
3. I decided to __________ my husband choose the towns and cities we would visit.
4. He decided to __________ the choices of restaurants to me.
5. Driving through the English countryside, we __________ a number of herds of sheep.
6. __________ trips we had taken had taught us that staying in a bed and breakfast is cheaper than staying in a hotel, so we chose several bed and breakfast facilities along our route.
7. We toured large cities such as London, and __________ we headed to the countryside to see ancient, small towns such as Chippen Camden.
8. I enjoyed the small towns in England more __________ the large cities.
9. Though our excursion took us through __________ than ten cities and towns, we saw enough of England to know that we want to go back again someday.
10. When I take my next trip, however, I will definitely pack __________ clothing.

## Exercise 6

**Usage** Use your usage glossary to write terms that fit the definitions below.

1. This expression is always written as two words and means "a large amount." Some authorities recommend that this term be avoided ➡

2. This term refers to nouns that cannot be counted, such as *rain*. You should also use this term to refer to figures used as a single amount or quantity.
3. Use this term to describe an action that proceeds with no interruption.
4. This term means "to give something with the understanding that it will be returned." When a verb is needed, authorities prefer that some form of this word be used.
5. Use this single word as an adverb meaning "completely" or "on the whole."

## Exercise 7

**Making Usage Choices** The following sentences describe Arab exploration, especially that by Ibn Battutah. For each sentence choose the correct word or expression in parentheses, and write it on your paper.

1. The Europeans (can't hardly/can hardly) be called the only people to have had a history of exploration.
2. Sandwiched (among/between) Asia and the West were the great capitals of the Muslim world.
3. Every Muslim, (irregardless/regardless) of social class, was obliged to make a pilgrimage to Mecca.
4. The greatest Muslim pilgrim was Ibn Battutah of Tangier, who traveled (further/farther) than Marco Polo.
5. From 1325 to 1349 distant Muslim communities (learned/taught) Ibn Battutah their local customs.

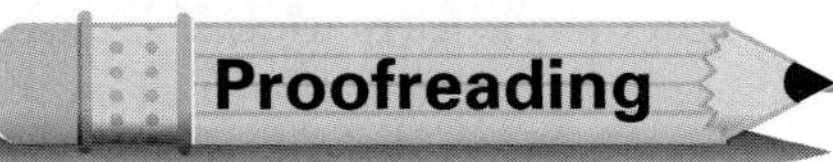


## Exercise 8

**Proofreading** The following passage describes the artist René Magritte, whose painting appears on the next page. Rewrite the passage, correcting the errors in spelling, grammar, and usage. Add any missing punctuation. There are ten errors.

### *René Magritte*

[1]René Magritte (1898–1967) was raised in a middle-class family in Belgium, where he was learned art. [2]He lived for awhile near Paris, where he met the poet André Breton and other surrealist artists.

[3]Magritte was strongly effected by the surrealists, whose work was characterized by fantastic imagery and clever plays on words. [4]Surrealism, in turn, owed a great debt to Sigmund Freud whose writings about the subconscious and it's influence on behavior were just coming into vogue.

[5]Magritte created fantastic images that evoked the mysterius nature of human thought. [6]He painted a single eye reflecting a azure sky in *The False Mirror*. [7]The idea that reality can never be completely captured lays in the title of this work. [8]The writers of the quotations in this unit strove to explore and to understand the world everywheres around them. [9]Similarly, Magritte's painting suggests both vision and introspection—looking out and looking in, respectfully. ➞

**René Magritte, *The False Mirror,* 1928**

## Exercise 9

**Review** The following sentences provide information about the writers of the quotations in this review. For each sentence choose the correct word or expression in parentheses, and write it on your paper.

1. Authors' experiences can (affect/effect) their work.
2. The inspiration for several novels by Herman Melville (lies/lays) in his adventures in the South Seas.
3. Details of nineteenth-century whaling (borrow/lend/loan) Melville's novel *Moby Dick* a ring of authenticity.
4. Zora Neale Hurston's (advice/advise) to African American readers of her novels is to be proud of their roots.
5. In *The Grapes of Wrath* John Steinbeck uses the Joad family to show the (all together/altogether) devastating impact of the Great Depression on people in the Dust Bowl.
6. In *Travels with Charley* Steinbeck recounts a trip he made accompanied by no one (accept/except) his dog.
7. The poet Elizabeth Bishop, (who/whom) many admire for her warm and personal verse, was born in 1911.
8. The reason that home and exile are major themes in Bishop's poems is (because/that) the poet traveled widely.
9. Italo Calvino delved (farther/further) into the realm of the allegorical fantasy than have most contemporary writers.
10. Calvino's work will doubtless have a lasting (affect/effect) on our literary culture.

# Writing Application

**Correct Expressions in Writing** Mary Canrobert, a former English teacher in North Carolina, devoted a unit of study each school year to teaching students how to write résumés and cover letters, two forms of writing that almost every prospective employee must know. Notice the expressions that are in italic.

**The Résumé**

- A résumé is *different from* an application. A résumé offers a degree of flexibility in what you want to include, and you have the option of highlighting your strengths.
- List your most recent employment first, then identify *preceding* employment.
- You *may* list references on a résumé. Choose people *such as* previous employers and teachers.

**The Cover Letter**

- It is essential that you identify your strong points. This is the time to accent your good qualities without sounding *as if* you are egotistical.
- Avoid mediocre expressions such as *all right*. Choose, instead, a variety of complimentary adjectives to describe your skills, accomplishments, and goals.
- In both the cover letter and the résumé, employ formal writing habits at all times. Do not use expressions such as *a lot* and *ain't*, and refrain from contractions such as *don't* and *can't*.

**Techniques with Correct Expressions** Try to apply some of Mary Canrobert's writing techniques when you write and revise your work.

1. Avoid the use of informal terms. Compare the following:

**Informal expression:** Choose *a lot* of complimentary adjectives.
**Canrobert's version:** Choose a *variety* of complimentary adjectives.

2. *Use may*, not *can*, when you want to signify permission to do something or the possibility of doing it.

3. Use *affect*, not *effect*, as a verb meaning "to cause a change in; to influence."

4. Use *as* or *as if*, not *like*, to introduce subordinate clauses. Compare the following:

**Incorrect usage:** Accent your good qualities without sounding *like* you are egotistical.
**Correct usage:** Accent your good qualities without sounding *as if* you are egotistical.

**Practice** Practice these techniques by revising the following passage from a cover letter. Use a separate sheet of paper. Pay particular attention to underlined expressions.

During the past two years, I have been working every afternoon at a local grocery store. During the twenty hours I work each week, I complete <u>a lot</u> of tasks such as stocking shelves and bagging groceries. I <u>don't</u> mean to sound <u>like</u> I am bragging, but I can operate the cash register faster—and with <u>less</u> errors—than any of the store's veteran employees can. Mr. Warren, the store manager, says I <u>effect</u> the other employees' job performances positively by being a good example.

I think my grocery store experience makes me a good candidate for the assistant manager's job at your store. You <u>can</u> call me at 555-3412 any day after 7 P.M.

UNIT

# 20 Capitalization

Grammar

## Lessons

## 20.1 Capitalization of Sentences and the Pronoun *I*

Capitalize the first word of every sentence, including the first word of a direct quotation that is a complete sentence.

> **S**occer, a sport popular throughout the world, has been called the only international language.
>
> **J**ames Baldwin once wrote about his craft, "**T**he artist cannot and must not take anything for granted, but must drive to the heart of every answer and expose the question the answer hides."
>
> **T**he invocation in Shelley's "Ode to the West Wind" begins as follows: "**O** wild West Wind, thou breath of Autumn's being."

Capitalize the first word of a sentence in parentheses that stands by itself. Do not capitalize a parenthetical phrase or a sentence within parentheses that is contained within another sentence.

> The tune to which our national anthem is sung comes from an old English song. (**T**he words are original and were written by Francis Scott Key.)
>
> The national anthem (**so** designated by an executive order of President Woodrow Wilson in 1916) is often judged by musicians to be a difficult piece to sing well.
>
> Francis Scott Key had previously used the same tune in a song called "To Anacreon in Heaven" (**t**he Anacreon of the title was an ancient Greek poet), and that song had become well known in America by 1795.

Do not capitalize the first word of a quotation that cannot stand as a complete sentence.

> Winston Churchill said that he had "**n**othing to offer but blood, toil, tears, and sweat."

Do not capitalize the first word of an indirect quotation. An **indirect quotation,** often introduced by the word *that*, does not repeat a person's exact words.

> In her movies the actress Greta Garbo often said that **s**he wanted to be alone.

Always capitalize the pronoun *I* no matter where it appears in the sentence.

> **I** began to read the encyclopedia when **I** was ten years old because **I** had a great thirst for knowledge.

## Exercise 1 Correcting Errors in Capitalization

Rewrite the following sentences, correcting any errors you find in capitalization. A single sentence may contain more than one error.

### *A Discussion About Socrates*

1. The ancient Greek philosopher Socrates, who lived in the fifth century B.C., said at his trial, "the unexamined life is not worth living."
2. our history teacher began our class discussion of the philosopher by asking us, "do you agree with Socrates' statement?"
3. Paula answered, "before i make up my mind, i'd like to know why Socrates was put on trial."
4. mr. Potozak replied with another question: "can anyone tell Paula the reason?"
5. Sal raised his hand and offered an answer. "i think he was charged with bringing new gods into the city and also with corrupting the youth."
6. Ghisela quickly interrupted, "those charges were really fake, as he said in his speech! the real reason he was tried was that people found his dedication to the truth too upsetting."
7. Clay asked, "How we can be sure that Socrates actually spoke the words Plato (The philosopher's student) gave him in the *Apology*?"
8. our instructor commented, "it's true that Socrates never wrote a word himself. on the other hand, Plato's report of Socrates' speech in his own defense must be fairly accurate, since it was read by many of Plato's contemporaries who were old enough to have witnessed the trial."
9. then he added, "let's get back to the original question. is Socrates' philosophy of life a good one?"
10. Paula told me that She was just about to answer when the bell rang, putting an end to the discussion.

## Exercise 2 Writing Direct Quotations

In each sentence below, identify the indirect quotation. Then rewrite the sentence, presenting the speaker's words as a direct quotation and changing the wording as necessary. Remember to use proper capitalization and punctuation.

**SAMPLE** Our English teacher asked what we students already knew about *Pygmalion.*

**ANSWER** Our English teacher asked, "What do you students already know about *Pygmalion?*"

### *Pygmalion*

1. Olaf commented that the name of Shaw's play comes from a Greek myth.
2. He added that according to this myth the sculptor Pygmalion fell in love with one of his own creations, a statue he had carved of a young woman.
3. Olaf stated that the lovesick artist then begged Aphrodite, the goddess of love, to bring the statue to life.
4. LaKeesha asked if Shaw intended his character Eliza in *Pygmalion* to remind the audience of Galatea, the young woman in the myth.

5. Sam volunteered the opinion that the resemblances between Pygmalion and Professor Higgins were quite striking: for example, both characters try to mold or shape another person.
6. Then Kara objected that at the beginning of the play Higgins doesn't seem to be in love with Eliza.
7. Greg retorted that he thought that was just the point: Higgins falls in love with Eliza only *after* she has been his pupil for some time.
8. Akio said that just the other night he saw on television the movie version of *My Fair Lady*, the musical adapted from *Pygmalion*.
9. Karen wanted to know when the musical had its first performance on Broadway.
10. Garth answered that he thought the first performance was sometime in 1956.

**Exercise 3** **Capitalizing Sentences and the Pronoun *I***

Rewrite correctly any of the following sentences that have one or more errors in capitalization. Write the word *correct* if a sentence has no errors.

***And I Quote . . .***

1. The speaker in Sylvia Plath's poem "Mirror" states, "I am silver and exact. I have no preconceptions."
2. A witty old Japanese proverb says, "the tongue is but three inches long, yet it can kill a man six feet high."
3. The great teacher and religious philosopher Buddha declared that Hatred only ceases when love conquers it.
4. The French author Alexandre Dumas wrote, "We enjoy thoroughly only the pleasure that we give." (his most famous novels are *The Three Musketeers* and *The Count of Monte Cristo*.)
5. Armando Zegri, a Chilean journalist and novelist, made the observation "Joy is a fruit that Americans eat green."
6. In the poem "Nikki-Rosa" (The subject of the poem is the disparity between childhood memories and how biography portrays them), Nikki Giovanni writes that her biographers would "never understand that all the while I was quite happy."
7. The educator Booker T. Washington once wrote that he would never "Stoop so low as to hate any man."
8. One of Confucius's sayings that i particularly like is "the cautious seldom err."
9. Recalling her love of the tales she was told in childhood, Judith Ortiz Cofer writes: "When Mamá told her stories, we sat quietly on our crow's nest because if anyone interrupted her narrative she would stop talking and no amount of begging would persuade her to finish the story that day."
10. Marianne Moore once said that A poem's words should be as pleasing to the ear as the meaning is to the mind.

## 20.2 Capitalization of Proper Nouns

Capitalize a proper noun.

Capitalize a common noun only when it is the first word of a sentence.

When a proper noun is composed of several words, capitalize only the important words. (Articles, coordinating conjunctions, and prepositions of fewer than five letters should not be capitalized.)

**B**oston **T**ea **P**arty
**A**bercrombie and **K**ent
**W**orldwide **F**und for **N**ature
**F**ourth of **J**uly
**A**lfred the **G**reat

1. **Names of individuals**

**G**abriela **M**istral
**M**argaret **B**ourke-**W**hite
**W**illiam the **C**onqueror
**M**ichael **J**ordan
**D**wight **D. E**isenhower
**P**ocahontas

2. **Titles of individuals**

Capitalize titles used before a proper name and titles used in direct address.

**L**ady Ōtomo
**P**resident Taft
**A**rchbishop Tutu
**D**r. Rosalyn Yalow
**G**overnor Rafael Hernández Colón
Thank you, **C**aptain. [direct address]

In general, do not capitalize titles that follow a proper name or are used alone. Most writers, however, do capitalize *president* when referring to the current president of the United States.

The **p**resident of Russia conferred with the **P**resident at the White House yesterday.

In general, capitalize a title that describes a family relationship when it is used with or in place of a proper name.

| | | |
|---|---|---|
| I visited **U**ncle Julius. | *but* | My **u**ncle Julius is a musician. |
| Please call **G**randfather. | | Our **g**randfather is visiting. |
| Where does **C**ousin Fran live? | | My **c**ousin lives in Texas. |
| Will you come, **A**unt? | | Will your **a**unt come to Utah? |

After checking her schedule, **A**unt Enid said she would come.

3. **Names of ethnic groups, national groups, and languages**

**A**sian **A**mericans
**C**herokees
**I**rish
**I**talians
**I**ndo-**E**uropean
**S**anskrit

4. **Names of organizations, institutions, political parties and their members, and firms**

**W**orld **H**ealth **O**rganization
**S**yracuse **U**niversity
the **S**upreme **C**ourt
the **R**epublican party
a **D**emocrat
**A**merican **A**irlines

The word *party* is not capitalized when it follows the name of a political party. Also not capitalized are common nouns such as *court* or *university*, unless they are part of a proper noun.

Great Britain's prime minister is a member of the Tory **p**arty.

Olga had thought she might attend the **s**tate **u**niversity, but it turns out she will be going to **D**uke **U**niversity instead.

5. **Names of monuments, bridges, buildings, and other structures**

**J**efferson **M**emorial
**G**eorge **W**ashington **B**ridge
**M**etropolitan **O**pera **H**ouse
**B**everly **W**ilshire **H**otel
**F**aneuil **H**all
**G**rand **C**oulee **D**am

6. **Trade names**

a **H**onda **A**ccord
**P**urina cat food
**C**ampbell's soup
**W**isk detergent

7. **Names of documents, awards, and laws**

**A**rticles of **C**onfederation
**W**estinghouse **S**cience **A**ward
a **T**ony
**T**aft-**H**artley **A**ct

8. **Geographical terms**

Capitalize the names of continents, countries, states, counties, and cities, as well as the names of specific bodies of water, topographical features, regions, and streets.

**E**urope
**S**pain
**A**labama
**S**helby **C**ounty
**M**emphis
**C**aribbean **S**ea
**L**ake **O**ntario
**A**ndes **M**ountains
**S**an **F**ernando **V**alley
**P**ainted **D**esert
**L**atin **A**merica
**F**ar **E**ast
**N**orthern **H**emisphere
**N**ewbury **S**treet

### 9. Names of planets and other heavenly bodies

| | |
|---|---|
| **N**eptune | **A**lpha **C**entauri |
| **S**aturn | **T**aurus |
| **N**orth **S**tar | **U**rsa **M**ajor |

Do not capitalize the words *sun* and *moon*. *Earth* is capitalized only when it appears in conjunction with the names of the other planets. Never capitalize *earth* when it is preceded by the definite article, *the*.

**M**ercury, the planet closest to the **s**un, and **P**luto, the planet farthest from the **s**un, are both smaller than **E**arth.

Meteors that strike the **e**arth are called meteorites.

### 10. Compass points

Capitalize the words *north*, *east*, *south*, and *west* when they refer to a specific area of the country or the world or when they are part of a proper name. Do not capitalize them when they merely indicate direction.

| | | |
|---|---|---|
| **W**est **A**frica | *but* | the **w**est coast of Greenland |
| the **E**ast | | Travel **e**ast along the coast. |
| the **S**outh Atlantic | | **s**outh of the border |

### 11. Names of ships, planes, trains, and spacecraft

| | |
|---|---|
| U.S.S. ***A**spro* | ***S**outhern **C**rescent* |
| **A**irbus A300 | ***S**kylab 4* |

### 12. Names of most historical events, eras, and calendar items

| | |
|---|---|
| **W**ar of 1812 | **R**oaring **T**wenties |
| **I**ndustrial **R**evolution | **M**other's **D**ay |
| **A**ge of **D**iscovery | **H**ispanic **H**eritage **M**onth |
| **W**ars of the **R**oses | **W**orld **W**omen's **C**ongress |

A historical period that refers to a general span of time should not be capitalized.

| | |
|---|---|
| the **t**wenty-first **c**entury | the **f**orties |
| in **m**edieval **t**imes | the **p**re-**c**olonial **e**ra |

Capitalize the days of the week and the months of the year, but do not capitalize the names of the seasons (*spring*, *summer*, *autumn*, *fall*, *winter*).

Although the season technically began on the previous evening, the first full day of spring in 1995 was **T**uesday, **M**arch 21.

### 13. Religious terms

Capitalize names of deities, religions and their denominations and adherents, words referring to a supreme deity, and religious books and events.

| | | |
|---|---|---|
| **G**od | **R**oman **C**atholic **C**hurch | **D**isciples of **C**hrist |
| **A**llah | the **L**ord | **H**oli |
| **B**uddhism | the **N**ew **T**estament | the **T**almud |
| the **T**orah | **T**aoism | **A**sh **W**ednesday |
| **B**aptists | **P**urim | **I**slam |

### 14. Names of school courses

Capitalize only those school courses that are the name of a language or the title of a specific course. Do not capitalize the name of a subject.

| | | |
|---|---|---|
| **L**atin | *but* | **f**oreign **l**anguage |
| **G**eometry 201 | | I am studying **g**eometry. |

### 15. Titles of works

Always capitalize the first and last word of a title or subtitle. Capitalize all other words except articles, coordinating conjunctions, and prepositions of fewer than five letters.

***T**he **R**ed **B**adge of **C**ourage* [book]
***T**he **W**inter's **T**ale* [play]
***T**he **L**ion **K**ing* [movie]
the ***C**incinnati **E**nquirer* [newspaper]
***S**ports **I**llustrated for **K**ids* [magazine]
the ***M**acNeil/**L**ehrer **N**ewshour* [television series]
***R**ain, **S**team, and **S**peed* [work of art]
Beethoven's ***E**roica **S**ymphony* [long musical composition]
"**T**he **D**oor in the **W**all" [short story]
"**D**ream **V**ariations" [poem]
"**W**e **A**re the **W**orld" [song]

Capitalize articles (*a*, *an*, and *the*) at the beginning of a title only when they are part of the title itself. It is common practice not to capitalize (or italicize) articles preceding the title of a newspaper or a periodical. Do not capitalize (or italicize) the word *magazine* unless it is part of the title of a periodical.

| | | |
|---|---|---|
| ***A** Raisin in the Sun* | *but* | **a** *Smithsonian* **m**agazine article |
| ***T**he Great Gatsby* | | **t**he *Tulsa Tribune* |

## Exercise 4 Capitalizing Proper Nouns

Rewrite the following sentences correctly, adding or dropping capital letters as necessary.

### *The Ivory Coast*

1. The Ivory Coast is the name of a flourishing Republic in west Africa.
2. The portuguese were among the europeans who traded ivory in that region as early as the Sixteenth century.
3. Although the country was considered a Colony of france, its people long resisted foreign domination; still, the french were in control by the end of world war I.
4. In 1946 Félix Houphouet-boigny established the Ivory Coast democratic party and served as the nation's President.
5. Now officially named the republic of the Ivory Coast, the civilian-ruled country became politically independent in 1960, as students in any World History course know.
6. The Ivory Coast was one of the few African States to recognize the independence of the biafrans during the Nigerian civil war (1967–1970).
7. The major religions are christianity, islam, and various African ethnic religions.
8. The largely agricultural country is bordered by Liberia and Guinea on the West and by Ghana on the East.
9. The name of the country's Capital and major port is abidjan, which was made into a deep-water harbor in 1954 following the completion of the vridi canal.
10. Abidjan, the site of a national University, is also known for the famous landmark independence place.

## Exercise 5 Correcting Capitalization Errors

Identify and correct the errors in capitalization. If a sentence is correct, write *correct*.

### *San Francisco*

1. Do you know the song "I left my heart in San Francisco"?
2. This spectacular city in Northern California boasts memorable monuments, restaurants, and neighborhoods.
3. Founded by the Spanish as Yerba Buena in 1776, the city experienced great growth as a result of the California Gold Rush.
4. San Francisco is now the largest port on the west coast.
5. The most interesting areas of the city include Telegraph Hill, North Beach, Pacific Heights, and Chinatown.
6. A favorite tourist destination is Fisherman's wharf right on San Francisco bay.
7. If you travel West along Lombard street, you will come to Golden Gate Park.
8. Visitors who drive across the Golden Gate bridge can get a beautiful view of the city from the small suburb of Sausalito in Marin county.
9. Once across the Bridge, tourists should continue to Muir woods national monument, where they can see the giant redwoods, some of the largest trees in the world.
10. There are many fine Universities in the Bay area, including Stanford and the University of California at Berkeley.

## Exercise 6 Capitalization

Write the letter of the one item that is correctly capitalized in each of the following pairs.

### *Talking History*

1. **a.** During the Winter months of February and March last year, our town Library at Twin Oaks organized a very interesting series of evening programs.
   **b.** During the winter months of February and March last year, our town library at Twin Oaks organized a very interesting series of evening programs.
2. **a.** The title of the series, which consisted of five presentations, was "Talking History: Conversations with Local Residents."
   **b.** The title of the series, which consisted of five presentations, was "Talking history: conversations with local residents."
3. **a.** The sponsors were some of the largest businesses in town, including Johnson's paint and hardware, Phillips department store, and Rescigno brothers landscaping.
   **b.** The sponsors were some of the largest businesses in town, including Johnson's Paint and Hardware, Phillips Department Store, and Rescigno Brothers Landscaping.
4. **a.** The idea was for local residents to tell about their lives and offer insights into the town's diverse historical and cultural traditions.
   **b.** The idea was for local residents to tell about their lives and offer insights into the Town's diverse historical and cultural traditions.
5. **a.** The Library arranged for the programs to be held in a beautifully restored old house that is on the National register of historic places.
   **b.** The library arranged for the programs to be held in a beautifully restored old house that is on the National Register of Historic Places.
6. **a.** One of the guests, who has occupied the post of town historian for many years, gave a talk about the early decades of Twin Oaks in the Seventeenth Century.
   **b.** One of the guests, who has occupied the post of town historian for many years, gave a talk about the early decades of Twin Oaks in the seventeenth century.
7. **a.** I hadn't known that Centre Street was once a wagon track through a cow pasture!
   **b.** I hadn't known that Centre street was once a wagon track through a cow pasture!
8. **a.** Other speakers revealed the town history and cultural traditions of African American and Native American communities.
   **b.** Other speakers revealed the town history and Cultural traditions of African American and native American communities.
9. **a.** My Uncle, who happens to be a weather observer for the National oceanic and atmospheric administration, talked about the storms in our area, which have included some destructive hurricanes.
   **b.** My uncle, who happens to be a weather observer for the National Oceanic and Atmospheric Administration, talked about the storms in our area, which have included some destructive hurricanes.
10. **a.** Another speaker, who holds a degree in agriculture from a well-known university, gave a slide lecture entitled "Farmers, Farming, and Animals."
    **b.** Another speaker, who holds a degree in Agriculture from a well-known University, gave a slide lecture entitled "Farmers, Farming, and Animals."

## 20.3 Capitalization of Proper Adjectives

Capitalize proper adjectives (adjectives formed from proper nouns).

The following are the categories into which most proper adjectives fit:

**1. Adjectives formed from names of people**

**V**ictorian furniture
**E**insteinian theory
**G**regorian chant
**W**agnerian opera

**2. Adjectives formed from place names and names of national, ethnic, and religious groups**

**P**arisian boulevards
**H**awaiian pineapple
**E**gyptian cotton
**N**ear **E**astern artifacts
**C**eltic background
**N**ative **A**merican music
**I**slamic traditions
**B**uddhist shrines

When used as adjectives, many proper nouns do not change form.

**L**ondon fog
**I**daho potatoes
**V**atican policy
**S**ousa marches

### Exercise 7 Capitalizing Proper Adjectives and Proper Nouns

Rewrite the following sentences correctly, adding or dropping capital letters as necessary.

***Greenland, Iceland, and the Faeroe Islands***

1. Greenland, the largest island in the world, lies between the east coast of ellesmere island (the northernmost part of canada) and the northwest coast of norway.
2. The island is neither canadian nor norwegian, however, but danish.
3. First colonized by the norse explorer Eric the red in 982, greenland supported many scandinavian emigrations, but the early european settlements disappeared by 1400.
4. Since 1721, when new explorations took place, greenland has remained under danish control despite norwegian claims to the eastern areas.
5. The native inhabitants, who are called greenlanders, are descendants of the original inuit population and have their own language.
6. The much smaller island of iceland lies Southeast of Greenland.
7. The inhabitants trace their Democratic form of government back to 903.
8. Because fishing is so important to this Island Nation, icelandic ships battled with british ships over fishing rights in a dispute that lasted four years (1972–1976).
9. Southeast of iceland is a group of volcanic islands still under danish control. Warmed by north atlantic currents, the faeroe islands have a mild but rainy climate.
10. The inhabitants of the faeroe islands speak an old norse dialect first brought to the area in the Ninth Century.

| Summary of Capitalization Rules | |
|---|---|
| **Capitalize** | **Do Not Capitalize** |
| We watched the news at a friend's house. (**O**ur television isn't working.) | We watched the news (**o**ur television isn't working) at a friend's house. |
| Aaron Burr wrote, "**T**he rule of my life is to make business a pleasure and pleasure my business." | Aaron Burr wrote that **t**he rule of his life was to make business a pleasure and pleasure his business. |
| **G**overnor Ann W. Richards | the **g**overnor |
| Did you see **G**randfather? | My **g**randfather lives abroad. |
| the **S**upreme **C**ourt | She took her case to **c**ourt. |
| **T**ide detergent; **C**lorox bleach | I need **d**etergent and **b**leach. |
| **P**ulitzer **P**rize | a **p**rize for the best play |
| **L**ake **E**rie; **B**ourbon **S**treet | the **l**ake; the **s**treet |
| **S**aturn; **E**arth | a **p**lanet; the **s**un; the **e**arth |
| **P**ersian **G**ulf **W**ar | the **w**ar |
| **Q**uran; **J**udaism | a **s**acred **b**ook; a **r**eligion |
| **M**usic 201; **H**istory of **A**rt | a **m**usic course; an **a**rt **h**istory class |

## Exercise 8 Revising a Paragraph

Revise the following paragraph, capitalizing words that should be capitalized.

### *Madagascar's Unique History*

[1]The island of Madagascar in the Indian ocean is separated from Africa by the Mozambique channel, which is less than 200 miles wide at its narrowest point. [2]This body of water, however, played a fundamental role in shaping the destiny of madagascan plants and animals. [3]Some experts think that Madagascar was originally joined to the african continent at a point north of its present position, near Tanzania, while others believe the link was farther south. [4]About 65 million years ago madagascar broke free of the supercontinent of Gondwanaland. [5]The separate development of the island's fauna has resulted in such unique animals as the lemurs and the tenrecs.

## Exercise 9 Writing an Oral Report

Imagine that you are delivering an oral report about a recent world news story. Write several sentences describing important aspects of the event.

## Exercise 10 Capitalization I

Write the letter of the one item that is correctly capitalized in each of the following pairs.

1. **a.** My course in Geometry at the University teaches the pythagorean theorem.
   **b.** My course in geometry at the university teaches the Pythagorean theorem.
2. **a.** Do you know the song "O how lovely is the evening"?
   **b.** Do you know the song "O How Lovely Is the Evening"?
3. **a.** Mom and Dad spent a quiet Thanksgiving Day with our grandparents.
   **b.** Mom and dad spent a quiet Thanksgiving day with our grandparents.
4. **a.** Meet us at the Northeast corner of Fifth Avenue.
   **b.** Meet us at the northeast corner of Fifth Avenue.
5. **a.** Gwendolyn Brooks was the first African American writer to win a Pulitzer Prize.
   **b.** Gwendolyn Brooks was the first African american writer to win a Pulitzer prize.
6. **a.** A musical suite by Ferde Grofé celebrates the Grand Canyon.
   **b.** A musical Suite by Ferde Grofé celebrates the grand canyon.
7. **a.** The Island country of Seychelles is in the Indian ocean.
   **b.** The island country of Seychelles is in the Indian Ocean.
8. **a.** In 1980 the winter olympics were held at lake Placid.
   **b.** In 1980 the Winter Olympics were held at Lake Placid.
9. **a.** Freedom of speech and other civil liberties are guaranteed in the Bill of Rights.
   **b.** Freedom of speech and other Civil Liberties are guaranteed in the bill of rights.
10. **a.** Ivan the terrible (His bizarre and cruel behavior won him the nickname) was the first Czar of Russia.
    **b.** Ivan the Terrible (his bizarre and cruel behavior won him the nickname) was the first czar of Russia.
11. **a.** In 1917 Cole Porter (The famous American songwriter) was so depressed about the failure of his first musical (*See America First*) that he briefly joined the Foreign legion.
    **b.** In 1917 Cole Porter (the famous American songwriter) was so depressed about the failure of his first musical (*See America First*) that he briefly joined the Foreign Legion.
12. **a.** William "Refrigerator" Perry of the Chicago Bears is supposed to have received the biggest Superbowl ring ever made—a size 23.
    **b.** William "refrigerator" Perry of the Chicago bears is supposed to have received the biggest superbowl ring ever made—a size 23.
13. **a.** According to the Book of Revelation in the Bible, heaven has twelve pearly gates.
    **b.** According to the book of revelation in the bible, heaven has twelve pearly gates.
14. **a.** According to norse Mythology, the god of snowshoes was named ull.
    **b.** According to Norse mythology, the god of snowshoes was named Ull.
15. **a.** Baseball's hall of fame is located in the small town of Cooperstown, New york.
    **b.** Baseball's Hall of Fame is located in the small town of Cooperstown, New York.

## Exercise 11 Capitalization II

Write the letter of the one item that is correctly capitalized in each of the following pairs.

1. a. The Novel *Jane Eyre* by Charlotte Brontë begins with the words, "there was no possibility of taking a walk that day."
   b. The novel *Jane Eyre* by Charlotte Brontë begins with the words, "There was no possibility of taking a walk that day."
2. a. Camels, or "ships of the desert" (as they are referred to in Arab lore), are fascinating animals.
   b. Camels, or "ships of the Desert" (as they are referred to in arab lore), are fascinating animals.
3. a. The state of Karnataka, whose Capital City is Bangalore, lies in Southwest India.
   b. The state of Karnataka, whose capital city is Bangalore, lies in southwest India.
4. a. Thomas Hardy's later novels devote increasing attention to the reversals that the author collectively referred to as "The persistence of the unforeseen."
   b. Thomas Hardy's later novels devote increasing attention to the reversals that the author collectively referred to as "the persistence of the unforeseen."
5. a. Clara Barton, the principal organizer of the American Red Cross, died in 1912.
   b. Clara Barton, the principal organizer of the American red cross, died in 1912.
6. a. The first stock exchange in America was founded in Philadelphia, Pennsylvania, in 1790, two years before the founding of the more famous New York Stock Exchange.
   b. The first Stock Exchange in America was founded in Philadelphia, Pennsylvania, in 1790, two years before the founding of the more famous New York Stock Exchange.
7. a. During the Eighth Century, while the ummayads ruled in Spain, a brilliant new center of Arab-Muslim Civilization emerged in Baghdad.
   b. During the eighth century, while the Ummayads ruled in Spain, a brilliant new center of Arab-Muslim civilization emerged in Baghdad.
8. a. In 1993 the film *Schindler's List*, a compelling drama about the Holocaust, won a number of Academy Awards.
   b. In 1993 the film *Schindler's List*, a compelling drama about the holocaust, won a number of academy awards.
9. a. Gary and Irene were eager to accompany aunt Paulette to that performance of the New York City ballet.
   b. Gary and Irene were eager to accompany Aunt Paulette to that performance of the New York City Ballet.
10. a. Historians have been unable to verify the popular legend that Betsy Ross first made the stars and stripes in june 1776 at the request of a special Committee that included George Washington.
    b. Historians have been unable to verify the popular legend that Betsy Ross first made the Stars and Stripes in June 1776 at the request of a special committee that included George Washington.

UNIT

# 20

Unit Review

# Grammar Review

## Capitalization

Set in Trinidad, V. S. Naipaul's native country, *A House for Mr. Biswas* tells the story of a Hindu shopkeeper who looks back on the years he spent living with his wife, Shama, at the back of their grocery store in The Chase, a run-down settlement near Port of Spain. The passage has been annotated to show some of the rules of capitalization covered in this unit.

*Literature Model*

### *from* A HOUSE FOR MR. BISWAS

***by V. S. Naipaul***

In all Mr. Biswas lived for six years at The Chase, years so squashed by their own boredom and futility that at the end they could be comprehended in one glance. But he had aged. The lines which he had encouraged at first, to give him an older look, had come; they were not the decisive lines he had hoped for that would give a commanding air to a frown; they were faint, fussy, disappointing. His cheeks began to fall; his cheekbones, in a proper light, jutted slightly; and he developed a double chin of pure skin which he could pull down so that it hung like the stiff beard on an Egyptian statue. The skin loosened over his arms and legs. His stomach was now perpetually distended; not fat: it was his indigestion, for that affliction had come to stay, and bottles of Maclean's Brand Stomach Powder became as much part of Shama's purchases as bags of rice or flour.

Though he never ceased to feel that some nobler purpose awaited him, even in this limiting society, he gave up reading Samuel Smiles. That author depressed him acutely. He turned to religion and philosophy. He read the Hindus; he read the Marcus Aurelius and Epictetus which Mrs. Weir had given him; he earned the gratitude and respect of a stall-keeper at Arwacus by buying an old and stained copy of *The Supersensual Life;* and he began to dabble in Christianity, acquiring a volume, written mostly in capital letters, called *Arise and Walk.*➡

First word of a sentence

Proper adjective formed from a place name

Trade name

Name of a person

Title used directly before a person's name

Title of a book

Name of a religion

He attempted a portrait of Shama. He made her sit on a fat sack of flour—the symbolism pleased him: "Suit your family to a T," he said—and spent so much time on her clothes and the sack of flour that before he could begin on her face Shama abandoned him and refused to sit any more.

He read innumerable novels, particularly those in the Reader's Library; and he even tried to write, encouraged by the appearance in a Port of Spain magazine of a puzzling story by Misir. (This was a story of a starving man who was rescued by a benefactor and after some years rose to wealth. One day, driving along the beach, the man heard someone in the sea shouting for help, and recognized his former benefactor in difficulties; he instantly dived into the water, struck his head on a submerged rock and was drowned. The benefactor survived.)

First word of a sentence in quotation marks

Place name (city)

First word of a sentence that stands by itself in parentheses

**Exercise 1**

The passage below describes Victor Lewis Ferrer, whose painting appears on the next page. Rewrite the passage, correcting the errors in spelling, capitalization, grammar, and usage. Add any missing punctuation. There are ten errors.

*Victor Lewis Ferrer*

[1]Victor Lewis Ferrer was born in 1918 in Colón, which is near the eastern entrance to the Panama canal. [2]A self-taught artist, he earns a living for many years as a sign painter.

[3]Ferrer's favorite subject is Colón and it's people. [4]his street scenes are painted in a simple, direct style. [5]The perspective is deliberately distorted the colors are flat and vivid. [6]Details are rendered with care and presision.

[7]*Walking with Her Blue Umbrella* shows a typical panamanian town with people walking the streets, shopping in bodegas, and gazing from narrow, wooden balconies. [8]Many of the people seem to stare at the Artist as if they are posing for him. [9]V. S. Naipaul's *A House for Mr. Biswas* is set in a caribbean town that resembles the one here. [10]Although the signs in Trinidad would be in english, not Spanish, the gaily painted wooden buildings in Ferrer's painting are similar to those in Port of Spain.

**Victor Lewis Ferrer, *Walking with Her Blue Umbrella*, 1976**

## Exercise 2

Rewrite the following sentences about V. S. Naipaul, correcting all errors in capitalization. If a sentence has no errors, write *correct.*

1. V. S. Naipaul comes from a family of indians who practice the hindu religion.
2. Early in life Naipaul decided to become an author. (his Father and his Brother, Shiva, were also writers.)
3. Feeling "The need to escape" his tiny homeland, Naipaul attended Oxford university in great Britain.
4. After College he worked for the British broadcasting corporation and wrote for the *New statesman* in London.
5. Naipaul felt stifled in England because he believed that The english language was his but that the english tradition was not.

# Writing Application

**Capitalization in Writing** Carefully study the following short passage from Annie Dillard's autobiography, *An American Childhood*, noting the use of capitalization.

> I got a book on birds, took up bird-watching, and saw a Baltimore oriole in an apple orchard. I straddled my bike in amazement, bare feet on the cool morning road, and watched the brilliant thing bounce singing from treetop to treetop in the sun.
>
> I learned to whistle; I whistled "The Wayward Wind." I sang "The Wayward Wind," too, at the top of my lungs for an hour one evening, bored on the porch, hurling myself from chair to chair singing, and wondering when these indulgent grandparents would stop me. At length my grandfather looked up from his paper and said, "That's a sad song you're singing. Do you know that?" And I was amazed he knew that. Did he yearn to wander, my banker grandfather, like the man in "The Wayward Wind"?

**Techniques with Capitalization** When you revise your writing, be sure to check for correct capitalization. Here are some guidelines to keep in mind.

1. Capitalize the first word of every sentence and of each direct quotation that is a complete sentence. Always capitalize the pronoun I.

2. Capitalize proper nouns as well as titles used before proper names and in direct address.

3. Capitalize geographical terms and the names of ethnic and national groups and languages. Also capitalize the names of organizations, monuments and other structures, documents, trade names, heavenly bodies, compass points, calendar items, school courses, and the titles of works.

4. Capitalize proper adjectives formed from the names of people, place names, and the names of national, ethnic, and religious groups.

**Practice** Apply these guidelines to revise the following paragraph. Write your revision on a separate sheet of paper. Remember to check every sentence for correct capitalization.

One line in the song "oh, what a beautiful mornin'!" proclaims, "all the sounds of the earth are like music." (the song is from *Oklahoma!*) The line seems appropriate for Richard Rodgers, who wrote the music for *Oklahoma!* as well as for dozens of other Broadway musicals. Rodgers is perhaps most famous for his collaboration with the great lyricist oscar hammerstein II. Together this team wrote *Oklahoma!*, *South Pacific* (an adaptation of James Michener's *tales of the south pacific*), and *the king and i* (based on *Anna and the King of Siam*). Many of their shows portray american scenes; for example, *State Fair* is set in the midwest, and *Carousel* takes place in new england.

UNIT

# 21 Punctuation, Abbreviations, and Numbers

Grammar

## Lessons

## 21.1 The Period

Use a period at the end of a declarative sentence and at the end of a polite command.

| | |
|---|---|
| **DECLARATIVE SENTENCE** | Camilo José Cela won the Nobel Prize for literature in 1989. |
| **POLITE COMMAND** | Think of another Spanish author who won a Nobel Prize. |

### Exercise 1 Using a Period

Rewrite the following sentences correctly, adding periods where they are needed. Tell whether the sentence is a declarative sentence or a polite command.

| | |
|---|---|
| **INCORRECT** | Joseph Brodsky won the Nobel Prize for literature in 1987 |
| **CORRECT** | Joseph Brodsky won the Nobel Prize for literature in 1987. (declarative) |
| **INCORRECT** | Name three writers from Latin America who have won the Nobel Prize for literature |
| **CORRECT** | Name three writers from Latin America who have won the Nobel Prize for literature. (polite command) |

***Nobel Prizes for Literature***

1. The first Nobel Prize for literature was awarded to Frenchman Sully Prudhomme (pen name of Rene F. A. Prudhomme) in 1901
2. In 1907, Rudyard Kipling of Great Britain won the Nobel Prize for literature
3. Because of the onset of World War I, there was no award given in 1914
4. Name some other years when Nobel Prizes were not awarded
5. Selma O. L. Lagerlof of Sweden was the first woman to receive a Nobel Prize for literature in 1909
6. Choose one winner of the Nobel Prize and write a brief biography of that person
7. The first writer from the United States to win a Nobel Prize for literature was Sinclair Lewis, in 1930
8. I especially like the plays of Luigi Pirandello, the Sicilian who won the prize in 1934
9. Name the 1936 winner, who was also primarily a playwright
10. Many of the short stories of Isaac B. Singer, winner of the Nobel Prize for literature in 1978, were first published in literary magazines
11. Saul Bellow was another United States winner, in 1976
12. Your assignment is to read Bellow's *Seize the Day*
13. In 1953 Sir Winston L. P. Churchill won the Nobel Prize for literature for his contributions to history and biography
14. Sometimes prizes are given to show an author's influence on the style of writing, as was the case with Ernest Hemingway, who won in 1954
15. When a writer seems to speak for the times, the Nobel Prize committee may reward her or him

## 21.2 The Exclamation Point

Use an exclamation point to show strong feeling and indicate a forceful command.

Hurrah**!**
What a beautiful sunset**!**

### Exercise 2 Using End Punctuation

Rewrite the following sentences correctly, adding periods or exclamation points where they are needed. To explain your choice, tell whether the sentence is a declarative sentence, a polite command, a forceful command, or a sentence that shows strong feeling.

**INCORRECT** Hurry up
**CORRECT** Hurry up! (strong feeling)

**INCORRECT** Bring three sharpened number-two pencils to class
**CORRECT** Bring three sharpened number-two pencils to class. (polite command)

*The Academy Awards*

1. The first Oscar given for Best Picture of the Year was awarded in 1928 to *Wings*
2. Luise Rainer won Best Actress two years in a row, in 1936 and 1937
3. After those two awards, Miss Rainer practically disappeared from the movie industry
4. Spencer Tracy also won two years in a row, for *Captains Courageous* in 1937 and for *Boys Town* in 1938
5. Of course, after winning Best Actor twice, Tracy went on to make many more movies
6. I just loved the movie *Gone with the Wind*
7. The movie theater is on fire
8. If I've said it once, I've said it a thousand times: I hate it when people talk in the movies
9. I hope you agree with me
10. *Casablanca*, winner of the Best Picture Oscar for 1943, became a classic film, much to the surprise of the writer and director
11. At the time, they thought they were simply cranking out another film to keep up the country's morale during World War II
12. Little did director Michael Curtiz know that his film would still be watched fifty years later
13. *All the King's Men*, the winner for best picture in 1949, was based on the Pulitzer Prize-winning novel of 1947, by Robert Penn Warren
14. John Ford won Best Director in 1952 for *The Quiet Man*
15. What a passionate performance Maureen O'Hara gave in that splendid film
16. Name the surprise winner of Best Picture for 1955, directed by Delbert Mann and starring Best Actor-winner Ernest Borgnine
17. We're going to miss the seven o'clock show
18. Get me some popcorn while you're up
19. In 1968 Barbra Streisand and Katharine Hepburn shared the Best Actress Oscar
20. Hepburn also won in 1967 for *Guess Who's Coming to Dinner*

## 21.3 The Question Mark

Use a question mark to indicate a direct question.

Are you studying Ancient Greece or the Middle Ages**?**

A declarative sentence containing an indirect question does not take a question mark.

My friend asked whether we were studying Ancient Greece or the Middle Ages**.**

### Exercise 3 Review: Using End Punctuation

Rewrite the following sentences correctly, adding periods, exclamation points, and question marks where they are needed.

INCORRECT Will you be at the bookstore for the reading this afternoon
CORRECT Will you be at the bookstore for the reading this afternoon?

INCORRECT Your assignment for the final paper of the semester is to write a one-thousand-word biography of a person, living or dead, who influenced your life in a positive manner
CORRECT Your assignment for the final paper of the semester is to write a one-thousand-word biography of a person, living or dead, who influenced your life in a positive manner.

### *Military Tales*

**1.** I was wondering whether you have ever read *The Man Who Rode the Thunder*
**2.** What a hair-raising tale it is
**3.** The book is about William H. Rankin, a United States Marine
**4.** Rankin flew missions in Korea and served as a squadron leader
**5.** What would you do if your plane's engine went dead at an altitude of forty-seven thousand feet
**6.** Rankin had to jump from a plane traveling six hundred miles an hour
**7.** How terrified he must have been
**8.** Put yourself in his place
**9.** My friend asked whether she could borrow *The Man Who Rode the Thunder*
**10.** Would you like to read the book when she finishes it
**11.** I enjoy the novels of David Poyer
**12** Poyer, a former member of the military, is now a full-time novelist
**13.** Do you like to read books about the exploits of navy and air force personnel
**14.** Poyer's novels are full of military jargon, and while reading Poyer's latest novel, *The Passage*, I learned a lot about the difficulties of living on and piloting a navy ship
**15.** The novel concerns an enlisted man secretly selling U.S. military information

## 21.4 The Colon

# Colons to Introduce

### 1. Lists

Use a colon to introduce a list, especially after a statement that uses such words as *these*, *the following*, or *as follows*.

> To make my spaghetti sauce, you will need **the following** ingredients**:** celery, onions, tomatoes, ground beef, tomato sauce, olive oil, and seasonings.

> To make pasta, follow **these** instructions**:** (1) boil four quarts of water, (2) add the pasta, (3) stir it until the water begins to boil again, and (4) let it cook for nine to fifteen minutes.

Do not use a colon if a list immediately follows a verb or a preposition.

> Gwendolyn Brooks's volumes of poems **include** *Annie Allen, A Street in Bronzeville,* and *The Bean Eaters.*

> I enjoy many different kinds of music, **such as** jazz, rock, and Tex-Mex.

### 2. Illustrations or restatements

Use a colon to introduce material that illustrates, explains, or restates the preceding material.

> The American presidents John Adams and Thomas Jefferson have something in common**:** they both died on July 4, 1826.

Note that a complete sentence following a colon is generally not capitalized.

# Colons Before Quotations

Use a colon to introduce a long or formal quotation. A formal quotation is often preceded by such words as *this*, *these*, *the following*, or *as follows*.

> Jane Austen's *Pride and Prejudice* opens with **the following** satirical comment**:** "It is a truth universally acknowledged that a single man in possession of a good fortune must be in want of a wife."

Quotations of poetry that are longer than one line and quotations of prose that are longer than four or five lines are generally written below the introductory statement and indented on the page.

"The Rime of the Ancient Mariner" contains **this** stanza:

Water, water, everywhere,
And all the boards did shrink;
Water, water, everywhere,
Nor any drop to drink.

## Other Uses of Colons

Use a colon between the hour and the minute of the precise time, between the chapter and the verse in biblical references, and after the salutation of a business letter.

| | |
|---|---|
| 7:05 A.M. | Dear Sir or Madam: |
| Proverbs 12:2–3 | Members of the committee: |

### Exercise 4 Using the Colon

Rewrite the following sentences correctly, adding colons where they are needed. For the sentences that do not need a colon, write *correct.* Remember that colons are not needed when a list immediately follows a verb or a preposition.

*Tracing Your Family History*

1. Tracing your family history requires at least three things time, patience, and the ability to listen.
2. It is probably best to begin by interviewing members of your family your parents, your aunts and uncles, your grandparents, and your great-grandparents.
3. Your close relatives may have tales about other family members whom you have never met, such as great-uncles, third cousins, and great-great-grandmothers.
4. Try the following ways of locating information about your family history (1) look in attics and cellars, (2) ask about old pictures, and (3) look for old clothing and jewelry.
5. Useful family records include letters, diaries, baby books, and bills.
6. Drawing your family tree can be time-consuming it often requires that you spend many hours conducting research.
7. At 2:15 P.M. Juliana began hunting in her grandparents' attic for books that would help her compile her family tree.
8. She found an old family Bible with this handwritten inscription "To my dear Belinda, who has supported me these fifteen years."
9. Lines in Proverbs 8 22–31 were underlined.
10. In a book of Paul Laurence Dunbar's, Juliana found these lines underlined
    Ah, Douglass, we have fall'n on evil days, / Such days as thou, not even thou didst know, / When thee, the eyes of that harsh long ago / Saw, salient, at the cross of devious ways, / And all the country heard thee with amaze.

## 21.5 The Semicolon

# Semicolons to Separate Main Clauses

Use a semicolon to separate main clauses that are not joined by a coordinating conjunction (*and*, *but*, *or*, *nor*, *yet*, and *for*).

> Claes Oldenburg designs sculptures and monuments of familiar objects; his sculpture *Hamburger with Pickle and Tomato Attached* is one of his best-known works.

Use a semicolon to separate main clauses joined by a conjunctive adverb (such as *however*, *therefore*, *nevertheless*, *moreover*, *furthermore*, and *consequently*) or by an expression such as *for example* or *that is*.

In general, a conjunctive adverb or an expression such as *in fact* or *for example* is followed by a comma.

> Oldenburg once designed a giant pair of scissors as a monument; moreover, he has made sculptures of electric fans and vacuum cleaners.

# Semicolons and Commas

Use a semicolon to separate the items in a series when these items contain commas.

> Three contemporary writers who have helped capture the African American experience are Nikki Giovanni, a poet; Alice Walker, a novelist; and Lorraine Hansberry, a playwright.

Use a semicolon to separate two main clauses joined by a coordinating conjunction when such clauses already contain several commas.

> Langston Hughes, perhaps the most famous figure of the Harlem Renaissance, wrote poetry, fiction, music, and drama; but he is also remembered as a patron of the arts, a man who nurtured the careers of others.

> Maya Angelou, author of the best-selling *I Know Why the Caged Bird Sings*, *Gather Together in My Name*, and *Heart of a Woman*, is a talented actress; and she produced, directed, and starred in *Cabaret for Freedom* at New York's Village Gate and had a role in the movie *Poetic Justice.*

## Exercise 5 Using the Semicolon

Rewrite the following sentences correctly, adding semicolons where they are needed.

### *George Washington and Booker T. Washington*

1. George Washington was born on February 22, 1732 became President on April 30, 1789 and died on December 14, 1799.
2. Many people assume that Washington attended college in fact, his education was probably rather limited.
3. Washington, who was often praised for his striking appearance, was indeed a tall, strong, and commanding figure but he was also known for his honesty, his intelligence, and his high moral principles.
4. Washington was not always a victorious general for example, his first campaign ended in his surrender.
5. George Washington was a gifted politician many consider him one of our best presidents.
6. Washington's cabinet included Jefferson, a Democratic-Republican, Hamilton, a Federalist and Randolph, a Virginia Democrat.
7. Famous likenesses of George Washington were made by Gilbert Stuart, an American painter Jean Antoine Houdon, a French sculptor and John Copley, another American painter.
8. George Washington's retirement from public office in 1796 was partly because of the sting of public abuse nevertheless, upon hearing of his death, John Marshall said that he was "first in war, first in peace, and first in the hearts of his countrymen."
9. Booker Taliaferro Washington, an educator and reformer and the first president of Tuskeegee Institute, did not have a privileged upbringing he was born in a slave hut on a plantation in Franklin County, Virginia.
10. Instead of attending school as a child, Booker T. Washington worked in a salt furnace and a coal mine with his foster father however, his desire for an education was overwhelming.
11. Washington worked as a janitor at the Hampton, Virginia, Normal and Agricultural Institute nothing would stop him from getting an education.
12. After his graduation from the Normal School, Washington went on to establish a school at Tuskeegee, Alabama the flowering of this school would be his life's work and one of his greatest achievements.
13. Of the many books Booker T. Washington wrote are the autobiographies *Up From Slavery*, translated into eighteen languages, and *My Larger Education* in addition, Washington founded several organizations.
14. Booker Taliaferro Washington was given several honorary degrees for example, he received a Master of Arts from Harvard and a Doctor of Laws from Dartmouth.
15. When Booker T. Washington died in 1915, Tuskeegee Institute had more than fifteen hundred students and nearly two hundred faculty in addition, Washington had procured an endowment of approximately two million dollars.

# 21.6 The Comma

## Commas and Compound Sentences

Use commas between the main clauses in a compound sentence.

Place a comma before a coordinating conjunction (*and*, *but*, *or*, *nor*, *yet*, or *for*) that joins two main clauses.

Robert Frost never finished college, but he became a celebrated poet.

Frost lived in Vermont, and his poems contain images of New England.

You may omit the comma between very short main clauses that are connected by a coordinating conjunction, unless the comma is needed to avoid confusion.

I opened the window and I shut the door. [clear]
I opened the window and the door slammed shut. [confusing]
I opened the window, and the door slammed shut. [clear]

## Commas in a Series

Use commas to separate three or more words, phrases, or clauses in a series.

The evenings were cool, calm, and cloudless.

Our campfire smoldered, flickered, and glowed.

We carried canteens, insect repellent, and cameras with us.

Abraham Lincoln believed that government should be "of the people, by the people, and for the people."

The lights dimmed, the conductor came to the podium, and the band began to play.

No commas are necessary when all the items are connected by conjunctions.

The evenings were cool and calm and cloudless.

Do not use commas to separate nouns used in pairs (*thunder and lightning*, *salt and pepper*, *bread and butter*) that are considered single units.

The paired nouns are set off from other nouns or groups of nouns in a series, however.

The menu at the Italian restaurant included spaghetti and meatballs, spaghetti and sausage, baked ziti, and veal and peppers.

## Commas and Coordinate Adjectives

Place a comma between coordinate adjectives that precede a noun.

**Coordinate adjectives** modify a noun equally. To discover whether adjectives are coordinate, reverse their order or put the word *and* between them. If the sentence still sounds natural, the adjectives are coordinate.

A tall, hungry, angry bear stood on the trail.
The weather forecast calls for a hot, dry summer.

If adjectives preceding a noun sound unnatural with their order reversed or with *and* between them, do not use commas. Generally adjectives that describe size, shape, age, and material do not need to be separated by commas.

A big old grizzly bear stood on the trail.
She caught a huge red snapper.

### Exercise 6 Using the Comma (Part 1)

Rewrite the following sentences correctly, adding commas where they are needed. For the four sentences that need no commas, write *correct.*

*Heroes of Many Revolutions*

1. The American Revolution inspired courage in many men women and children.
2. Susan Livingston of New Jersey proved herself to be brave imaginative and intelligent.
3. She was the daughter of the governor of the state and lived in a big white clapboard house.
4. In those days the countryside consisted of dirt roads farmland and small villages.
5. The British held nearby Staten Island and British troops had also captured both Long Island and New York City.
6. One evening British soldiers entered searched and seized Livingston's house.
7. They insisted upon searching the dining room scrutinizing the kitchen and examining the upstairs bedrooms.
8. Livingston faced the British troops coolly calmly and bravely.
9. She prevented them from seeing a stack of secret valuable papers.
10. The papers were saved the British soldiers left and Livingston became famous.
11. Many of the true heroes of any revolution are unknown and unheralded.
12. They do their work quietly secretly and unselfishly.
13. Brief moments of courage go unnoticed yet personal satisfaction remains.
14. Not all wars are fought for freedom from oppressors.
15. There are wars on poverty wars for education and wars for civil rights.
16. The battlefields exist in every nation in every city in every neighborhood.
17. Susan Livingston's name is written in the pages of history.
18. How many other brave true heroes are fighting every day?
19. You can be a revolutionary hero and you can help the causes of freedom and justice.
20. Each of us must simply do what we know is right each and every day and fight the silent ongoing wars against hunger poverty and ignorance.

# Commas and Nonessential Elements

### 1. Participles, infinitives, and their phrases

Use commas to set off participles, infinitives, and their phrases if they are not essential to the meaning of the sentence.

The audience, having risen, applauded wildly.
I remained seated, waiting for the applause to end.
I have never enjoyed opera, to tell the truth.

If participles, infinitives, and their phrases are essential to the meaning of the sentence, do not set them off with commas.

The young lady *selling programs* plans to be an opera singer. [The participial phrase tells *which* young lady plans to be an opera singer.]

She took the job *to learn more about opera*. [The infinitive phrase tells *why* she took the job.]

*To study opera* is her main goal. [The infinitive phrase is the subject of the sentence.]

### 2. Adjective clauses

Use commas to set off a nonessential adjective clause.

Because a nonessential (nonrestrictive) clause provides additional information about a noun, it is considered extra. It is set off by commas because an extra clause adds to the basic meaning of a sentence.

Castroville, which is a city in northern California, is the artichoke capital of the world. [*Which is a city in northern California* is a nonessential clause.]

Do not set off an essential adjective clause. An essential (restrictive) clause provides necessary information about a noun and is therefore needed to convey the precise meaning of the sentence.

People who dislike warm weather should not vacation in Florida. [*Who dislike warm weather* is an essential clause.]

### 3. Appositives

Use commas to set off an appositive if it is not essential to the meaning of a sentence.

A nonessential (nonrestrictive) appositive needs commas because the information it provides is considered *extra.*

Sarojini Naidu**,** an important poet of modern India**,** was an active campaigner for Indian independence.

I am reading *Emma***,** a novel by Jane Austen.

You can sometimes place a nonessential (nonrestrictive) appositive before the word to which it refers.

A doctor**,** William Carlos Williams wrote poetry between office visits.

Do not set off with commas an essential (restrictive) appositive, because the information it provides about a noun is necessary to understand the sentence.

Louisa May Alcott's novel *Little Women* describes incidents from the author's life. [If commas were placed around the essential appositive, *Little Women*, the implication would be that this was Alcott's *only* novel, which is not the case.]

## Commas with Interjections, Parenthetical Expressions, and Conjunctive Adverbs

Use commas to set off interjections (such as *oh* and *well*), parenthetical expressions (such as *on the contrary*, *on the other hand*, *in fact*, *by the way*, *for example*, and *after all*), and adverbs and conjunctive adverbs (such as *however*, *moreover*, and *consequently*).

Well**,** I do plan to visit Europe this summer.

My trip to Paris**,** alas**,** has been canceled.

I intend to visit Rome**,** however.

I also expect to visit Venice; thus**,** I will see two Italian cities.

Florence**,** on the other hand**,** is one city that I will not see.

Oh**,** I didn't see you standing there.

After all**,** you weren't expected until after dinner.

Well**,** I suppose we could fit another place setting at the table.

In fact**,** Father has been saying how much he's missed you.

Mother**,** on the other hand**,** may have a different opinion.

## Exercise 7 Using the Comma (Part 2)

On a separate sheet of paper, rewrite the following sentences correctly, adding commas where they are needed. For the one sentence that needs no commas, write *correct.*

### *African Americans in the Old West*

1. African American cowboys who represented approximately one quarter of all cattle herders in the United States after the Civil War flocked to Texas to work during the cattle boom.
2. James Kelly one of the first famous African American cowboys was a six-foot six-inch bronco buster and horse trainer.
3. Moreover Kelly was a good man to have on your side in a fight.
4. In fact Kelly saved the life of his boss Print Olive by shooting a gambler who wounded Olive in a surprise attack.
5. Cowboy Bill Pickett was known as a fearless steer wrestler who using only his teeth would down an animal.
6. Pickett gaining fame from this feat became a star attraction in a Wild West show during the 1890s.
7. The powerful rodeo star Jesse Stahl would down a steer so skillfully that its horns were actually driven into the ground.
8. Well the rodeo crowds would gasp and cheer as Stahl rode the bucking broncos and threw the steers often taking first prize.
9. Mary Fields a daring woman drove a mail coach through dangerous Montana territory.
10. Fields whose courage and perseverance were astounding would walk miles carrying the mailbag and her shotgun if her wagon became disabled.

## Commas and Introductory Phrases

### 1. Prepositional phrases

You need not use a comma after a short introductory prepositional phrase, but it is not incorrect to do so. Use a comma if the sentence could be misread without a comma.

In the distance we saw Aspen. [comma not needed]

During rush hour**,** traffic is heavy. [comma needed to prevent misreading]

Use a comma after a long prepositional phrase or after two or more successive phrases.

On the left burner of the stove**,** a huge pot of beans simmered.

Do not use a comma if the phrase is immediately followed by a verb.

On the left burner of the stove simmered a huge pot of beans.

**2. Participles and participial phrases**

Use commas to set off introductory participles and participial phrases.

Sparkling, the copper teapot looked like new.

Jogging along the beach one evening, I slipped on a piece of seaweed.

## Commas and Adverb Clauses

Use commas to set off all introductory adverb clauses.

Use commas to set off internal adverb clauses that interrupt the flow of a sentence.

After I hiked to Yosemite, I thought nothing else could impress me as much.

The mountains, because they were formed by glaciers, have spectacular slopes.

Generally do not set off an adverb clause at the end of a sentence unless the clause is parenthetical or it would be misread without the comma.

The slopes are spectacular because they were formed by glaciers.

## Commas and Antithetical Phrases

Use commas to set off an antithetical phrase.

In an **antithetical phrase** a word such as *not* or *unlike* qualifies what precedes or follows it.

Hearts, not bridge, is Janet's favorite card game.

Unlike bridge, hearts is often played without partners.

Lester, not Brad, is my favorite bridge partner.

Unlike Brad, Lester knows what he is doing.

Pizza, not steak, is the food of choice when playing cards.

Unlike a steak, pizza can be eaten with one hand.

**Exercise 8** **Using the Comma (Part 3)**

Rewrite the following sentences correctly, adding commas where they are needed. If a sentence is correct, write *correct*.

***The Debate over Conservation***

1. Some people objected when Congress passed the 1964 Wilderness Act.
2. These people believe that rivers and forests although they are sources of natural beauty are not as important as electricity and wood.
3. While conservationists lobby for more wilderness areas utility companies insist on the need for hydroelectric power.
4. Among the greatest concerns of conservationist groups is the building of dams.
5. Members of the groups feel that wilderness areas not hydroelectric power are more important to society.
6. Many people visiting Yellowstone National Park or the Grand Tetons begin to share the conservationists' views.
7. Because forests unlike rivers can be replenished by replanting lumber companies defend logging.
8. In the Okefenokee Swamp in Florida thousands of trees were cut down before the swamp was made into a wildlife refuge.
9. In the swamp life was not permanently destroyed because trees grow rapidly there.
10. In nationwide debates the differing views of conservationists and industrial groups continue to be expressed.

## Commas with Titles, Addresses, and Numbers

### 1. Titles of people

Use commas to set off titles when they follow a person's name.

John Kerry, senator from Massachusetts, voted in favor of the bill.

### 2. Addresses, geographical terms, and dates

Use commas to separate the various parts of an address, a geographical term, or a date.

My parents have lived at 1870 Hampshire Avenue, Saint Paul, MN 55116, for many years.

Cairo, Egypt, is the setting of the fiction of Naguib Mahfouz.

On Sunday, January 20, 1957, Dwight D. Eisenhower was inaugurated president.

A comma is not used when only the month and the day or the month and the year are given.

In July 1789 the French Revolution began.

The storming of the Bastille on July 14 is celebrated in France to this day.

### 3. References

Use commas to set off the parts of a reference that direct the reader to the exact source.

The theme of the novel is best expressed in Part Four, Chapter Nineteen, page 677.

We performed *Act I, Scene i,* of Shakespeare's *Othello.*

## Commas and Direct Address

Use commas to set off words or names used in direct address.

Donna, please come here.
You, my friend, are not mistaken.
Thank you for the information, Mrs. Sanchez.

## Commas and Tag Questions

Use commas to set off a tag question.

A tag question, such as *shouldn't I?* or *have you?*, emphasizes an implied answer to the statement preceding it.

You answered all the questions, didn't you?
You weren't late today, were you?

## Commas in Letter Writing

Place a comma after the salutation of an informal letter and after the closing of all letters.

Dear Mariko, Sincerely,
Dear Aunt Milly, Love,

Use the following style for the heading of a letter:

239 Dunsmore Road
Denver, CO 80201
January 19, 1996

## Misuse of Commas

A comma should not precede a conjunction that connects the parts of a compound predicate when the predicate has only two parts.

| | |
|---|---|
| INCORRECT | Our team rarely wins the pennant, but every year has the league's most loyal fans. |
| CORRECT | Our team rarely wins the pennant but every year has the league's most loyal fans. |

An error called a *run-on sentence* (or a *comma splice* or a *comma fault*) occurs when only a comma is used to join two main clauses that are not part of a series. To avoid run-on sentences, use a coordinating conjunction with the comma, or use a semicolon.

| | |
|---|---|
| INCORRECT | It was early in the season, every team was still a contender. |
| CORRECT | It was early in the season, **and** every team was still a contender. |
| CORRECT | It was early in the season**;** every team was still a contender. |

A comma should never be used between a subject and its verb or between a verb and its complement.

| | |
|---|---|
| INCORRECT | What she asked me to do, was no easy task. |
| CORRECT | What she asked me to do was no easy task. |
| INCORRECT | Popular holiday gifts include, compact discs, videocassettes, dolls, and home computers. |
| CORRECT | Popular holiday gifts include compact discs, videocassettes, dolls, and home computers. |

### Exercise 9 Using the Comma (Part 4)

Rewrite the following letter, adding commas where they are needed or removing them where they are not needed. (Ten corrections are needed altogether.)

Dear Roberta

I am enclosing a copy of the article we talked about, on the phone. You haven't already obtained a copy of it, have you Roberta? This article appeared in the Sunday March 11 1995 issue of the *New York Times Travel Section* pages 2 to 3. It contains a great deal of information about Scotland and should help you in planning your trip. You're still planning to visit Scotland this summer aren't you?

The *Times* article recommends a number of inexpensive hotels and restaurants. It contains up-to-date information, and should prove useful to you. I hope you enjoy your trip Roberta. You'll send me a postcard from Scotland won't you?

Yours truly,

Jackie

## 21.7 The Dash

When using a keyboard, you may indicate the dash with two hyphens (--). Do not place a comma, semicolon, colon, or period before or after a dash.

### Dashes to Signal Change

Use a dash to indicate an abrupt break or change in thought within a sentence.

> Nanabozho—I believe he was a mythical hero of the Ojibwa culture—is a famous figure in Native American folklore.

### Dashes to Emphasize

Use a dash to set off and emphasize supplemental information or parenthetical comments.

> His baby sister Pao-cheng very likely had been born right here—the site of the future Paoki-Chengtu Railway.
>
> —Tu Peng-cheng

**Exercise 10** **Using the Dash**

Rewrite the following sentences correctly, adding dashes where they are needed.

***The Baseball Hall of Fame***

1. The Baseball Hall of Fame I'm sure you've heard of it was founded in 1936.
2. The building housing the organization in Cooperstown the Cooperstown in New York State, that is didn't open until 1939.
3. To be elected to the Hall of Fame, a baseball player must have played at least ten years in the major leagues, that is.
4. The player also must be retired who knows why? for at least five years before he can be inducted.
5. In the early 1970s a special committee was set up to consider admitting players from the Negro Leagues the Negro Leagues were never part of the major league system.
6. My favorite ballplayer of all time he was the first African American player in the major leagues, you know is Jackie Robinson.
7. I've seen an old newsreel it was in black and white, not color showing him running out onto the Dodger field in 1947.
8. Larry Doby he played for the Cleveland Indians was the first African American player in the American League.
9. Joe DiMaggio remember his 56-game hitting streak? is a favorite of mine.
10. Lou Gehrig a disease was named after him played in 2,130 consecutive games.

## 21.8 Parentheses

Use parentheses to set off supplemental material.

You also use commas and dashes to set off supplemental material; there is a difference between the three marks of punctuation, however. Commas set off material that is closely related to the rest of the sentence. Parentheses set off material that is not meant to be part of the main statement. Dashes set off material that abruptly interrupts the sentence and is added for emphasis.

> The ruins of ancient Troy are located in Turkey, about four miles **(**6.4 kilometers**)** from the mouth of the Dardanelles.

A complete sentence within parentheses that is contained within another sentence is not capitalized and needs no period. Both a capital letter and a period are needed, however, if a sentence in parentheses stands by itself.

> For years archaeologists debated the question of which layer of the excavation **(**nine different cities were built on the site**)** was the Troy of Homer's poem.

> Archaeologist Heinrich Schliemann had studied Homer. **(**In fact, he knew Homer's verses by heart.**)**

# Parentheses with Other Marks of Punctuation

### 1. With a comma, semicolon, or colon

Always place a comma, semicolon, or colon *after* the closing parenthesis.

> The watt was named after James Watt (1736–1819**);** the ohm after George Ohm (1789–1854).

### 2. With a period, question mark, or exclamation point

Place a period, a question mark, or an exclamation point *inside* the parentheses if it is part of the parenthetical expression.

> Many English words are named after people. (Read the book *Word People* for more information**.)**

> The word *zipper* (named for a Mr. Zipper**?)** is of uncertain origin, but there is little doubt that *leotard* comes from the name of the French circus performer who popularized the garment.

Place a period, a question mark, or an exclamation point *outside* the closing parenthesis if it is part of the entire sentence.

> Sylvester Graham gave his name to graham flour (used in graham crackers and graham bread**).**
>
> Did you know that the sandwich was named after John Montagu, the fourth Earl of Sandwich (1718–1792**)?**

## Exercise 11 Using the Dash and Parentheses

Rewrite the following sentences correctly, adding dashes and parentheses where they are needed. Use the marks of punctuation indicated in parentheses at the end of each sentence. Remember that a dash is used to show emphasis or an interruption in thought, whereas parentheses are used to set off supplemental material.

**INCORRECT** Folk songs usually traditional songs with repeated phrases often tell the story of historical events.

**CORRECT** Folk songs (usually traditional songs with repeated phrases) often tell the story of historical events.

### *Folk Singers and Folk Songs*

1. Although Joan Baez's musical career had humble beginnings she sang in coffeehouses, it received a big boost when she performed at the Newport Folk Festival in Rhode Island in 1959 and 1960. (parentheses)
2. Her first record album it was simply titled *Joan Baez* featured traditional folk music, but her earliest national tour 1961 also included songs of social protest. (two sets of parentheses)
3. Other tours and there were many, both in the United States and abroad increased her popularity, and Baez soon was at the forefront of her profession. (dashes)
4. During the 1960s Baez's dedication to social and political causes particularly the civil rights and antiwar movements affected both her music and her personal life. (dashes)
5. Baez a woman I greatly admire has continued to sing in concert and to record, all the time remaining concerned about important issues. She opened the American section of the Live Aid Concert in 1985. (dashes and parentheses)
6. Because Baez sang songs of social protest she's known for that, you know she is typical of many folk singers. (dashes)
7. Great folk songs come into being during times of social change especially wars. (dash)
8. The American Civil War 1860-1865 probably produced more folk songs than any other war in the history of the United States. (parentheses)
9. Other great national changes the building of the railroads is one excellent example also inspired folk songs. (parentheses)
10. "Casey Jones" tells the story of the dangers of railroading "There's many a man been murdered by the railroad, / And laying in a low and lonesome grave." (parentheses)

## 21.9 Brackets

Use brackets to enclose information that you insert into a quotation from someone else's work in order to clarify the quotation.

> Had his **[**Samuel Johnson's**]** friends been as diligent and ardent as I was, he might have been almost entirely preserved.
>
> —James Boswell

Use brackets to enclose a parenthetical phrase that already appears within parentheses.

> The word *tycoon* comes from the Japanese word *taikun,* "mighty lord" **(**which in turn comes from two Chinese words **[***ta,* "great," and *kiun,* "prince"**])**.

### Exercise 12 Using Brackets

Rewrite the following sentences correctly, adding brackets where they are needed.

***The Critics Speak Highly***

1. The critics said, "It *Higher Than the Highest* is a pleasure to read."
2. "I can't say I enjoyed it the film *Climbing.*"
3. "If for no other reason, buy *Soaring the Heights* simply for its exciting description of the failure of the hero's pitons metal spikes at a crucial moment."
4. "The book *Mountain Climbing* is one of my favorites."
5. It sits atop the critic's bookshelf (alongside another popular climbing book, *Soaring the Heights* published 1995).
6. Another critic responded, "I, however, did not enjoy the description of the climb of Mount McKinley the indigenous people call it Denali."
7. "Mount McKinley, the highest peak in North America, is located in Alaska and rises to a height of 20,320 feet 6,194 meters."
8. "It Mount McKinley is located in Mount McKinley National Park."
9. "Denali is a beloved place in Alaska, and the people who live there recently 1994 began a cleanup of the mountain paths."
10. Francis Pratt of the local paper said of the film, "It *Conquering a Fear of Heights* probably will not make a mountain climber out of you."

## 21.10 Ellipsis Points

Use a series of three spaced points, called **ellipsis points,** to indicate the omission of material from a quotation.

If the omission occurs at the beginning of a sentence, use three spaced points. Use the correct punctuation (if any) *plus* three spaced points if the omission occurs in the middle or at the end of a sentence. In using a period plus three spaced points, do not leave any space between the last word before the omission and the first point, the period.

> No man is an island, entire of itself; every man is a piece of the continent, a part of the main. . . . Any man's death diminishes me, because I am involved in mankind. . . .
>
> —John Donne

### Exercise 13 Using Ellipsis Points

Rewrite the following sentences correctly, adding ellipsis points in place of the underlined material.

**SAMPLE** What were we playing? Was it prisoner's base? / I ran with whacking keds / <u>Down the cart-road past Rickard's place</u>, / And where it dropped beside the tractor-sheds ... —Richard Wilbur

**ANSWER** What were we playing? Was it prisoner's base? / I ran with whacking keds/ ... / And where it dropped beside the tractor-sheds ... —Richard Wilbur

*Contemporary American Poets*

1. Everyone thinks I am poisonous. I am not. / Look up and <u>read the authorities on me</u>, ... —Reed Whittemore
2. My seven sons came back from Indonesia. / <u>Each had ruled an atoll twenty years alone.</u> / Twenty years of loneliness, twenty years of craziness, ... —Peter Viereck
3. In this book I see your face and in your face / your eyes <u>holding the world</u> and all else besides ... —May Swenson
4. In a field / I am the absence / of field. / <u>This is / always the case.</u> / Wherever I am / I am what is missing. —Mark Strand
5. I am surprised to see / that the ocean is still going on. / <u>Now I am going back</u> / and I have ripped my hand / from your hand ... —Anne Sexton
6. So much of adolescence is an ill-defined dying, / An intolerable waiting, / A longing for another place and time, / <u>Another condition</u>. —T. Roethke
7. Over the half-finished houses / night comes. / <u>The builders / stand on the roof</u>. —Adrienne Rich
8. This is the light of the mind, <u>cold and planetary</u>. / The trees of the mind are black. The light is blue. —Sylvia Plath
9. What you looking at me for? / <u>I didn't</u> come to stay ... —Maya Angelou
10. I have carried my pillow to the windowsill / <u>And try to sleep, with my damp arms crossed upon it</u> / But no breeze stirs the tepid morning. —Carolyn Kizer

# 21.11 Quotation Marks

## Quotation Marks for Direct Quotations

Use quotation marks to enclose a direct quotation.

Quotation marks should be placed around the quoted material *only*, not around introductory or explanatory remarks. In general, separate such remarks from the quotation with a comma.

> "I only ask of the government to be treated as all other men are treated," said Chief Joseph in a speech he delivered in Washington, D.C.

> Gabriel García Márquez once said, "It's much more important to write than to be written about."

When a quotation is interrupted by explanatory words such as *he said* or *she wrote*, use two sets of quotation marks.

Separate each part of the quotation from the interrupting phrase with marks of punctuation before and after the interrupting phrase. Begin the second part of the quotation with a capital letter if it is a complete sentence.

> "My main reason for adopting literature as a profession," said George Bernard Shaw, "was that, as the author is never seen by his clients, he need not dress respectably."

> "Grammar is a piano I play by ear," declared Joan Didion. "All I know about grammar is its power."

Never use quotation marks in an indirect quotation (a quotation that does not repeat a person's exact words or begins with *that*).

| | |
|---|---|
| **ORIGINAL QUOTATION** | Robert Frost once said, "Writing free verse is like playing tennis with the net down." |
| **INDIRECT QUOTATION** | Robert Frost once said that writing free verse is like playing tennis with the net down. |

Use single quotation marks around a quotation within a quotation.

> During our discussion my friend informed me, "Anaïs Nin once said, 'It is the function of art to renew our perception.' "

In writing dialogue, begin a new paragraph and use a new set of quotation marks every time the speaker changes.

> Musizi first read the telegram in silence, then he looked at Pius and commented, "Well, Sir, I'm afraid it isn't good news."
>
> "Not good news? Has anybody died?"
>
> Musizi smiled. "Well, no. It isn't really as bad as that. The thing is the pools firm say they have discovered that the prize money has to be shared among three hundred other people."
>
> Pius was stunned. Eventually he murmured, "Tell me, how much does it mean I shall get?"
>
> "Three hundred into seventeen thousand pounds won't give you much over a thousand shillings."
>
> To Musizi's amazement, Pius sat back and chuckled. "More than a thousand shillings!" he said. "That is a lot of money!"
>
> —Barbara Kimenye, "The Winner"

## Quotation Marks with Titles of Short Works

Use quotation marks to enclose titles of short works, such as short stories, short poems, essays, newspaper and magazine articles, book chapters, songs, and single episodes of a television series.

"Reynold's Run" [short story]
"Kubla Khan" [poem]
"Dichos" [essay]
"Do You Eat a Balanced Diet?" [article]
"The Missing Glove" [chapter]
"Unforgettable" [song title]
"The Escape" [episode of a television series]

## Quotation Marks with Unusual Expressions

Use quotation marks to enclose unfamiliar slang and other unusual or original expressions.

The voice coming over the CB radio asked whether I had my "ears on."

## Quotation Marks with Definitions

Use quotation marks to enclose a definition that is stated directly.

*Sabbath* comes from the Hebrew *shābath,* meaning "to rest."

# Quotation Marks with Other Marks of Punctuation

### 1. With a comma or a period

Always place a comma or a period *inside* closing quotation marks.

"The frog**,"** states an African proverb, "does not jump without a reason**."**

"Some Enchanted Evening**,"** "Getting to Know You**,"** and "People Will Say We're in Love" are among Rodgers and Hammerstein's greatest songs.

### 2. With a semicolon or a colon

Always place a semicolon or a colon *outside* closing quotation marks.

Baseball French includes the following terms: *circuit,* meaning "home run**";** *programme double,* meaning "double-header**";** and *gaucher,* meaning "left-handed pitcher."

There is at least one good reason for you to read Alice Walker's poem "Women**":** it points out the strength of a generation of women.

### 3. With a question mark or an exclamation point

Place the question mark or exclamation point *inside* the closing quotation marks when it is part of the quotation.

We read Elizabeth Barrett Browning's sonnet "How Do I Love Thee**?"**

Closing the book with a sigh, my friend exclaimed, "I love that poem**!"**

Place the question mark or exclamation point *outside* the closing quotation marks when it is part of the entire sentence.

Have you read Leslie Marmon Silko's short story "Uncle Tony's Goat**"?**

How wonderful that the concert will feature old Beatles' songs like "She Loves You**"!**

If both the sentence and the quotation at the end of the sentence need a question mark (or an exclamation point), use only one punctuation mark, and place it *inside* the closing quotation marks.

Which film star asked, "Tennis, anyone**?"**

## Exercise 14 Using Quotation Marks

Rewrite the following sentences correctly, adding quotation marks where they are needed. For the sentences that need no changes, write *correct.*

**INCORRECT** In his famous essay Compensation Ralph Waldo Emerson comments on the balance of life.

**CORRECT** In his famous essay "Compensation" Ralph Waldo Emerson comments on the balance of life.

### *Writers Speak Out*

1. In her autobiographical essay When the Other Dancer Is the Self Alice Walker writes, Poem after poem comes—which is perhaps how poets pray.
2. Literature, declared the poet Ezra Pound, is language charged with emotion.
3. Remembering an early encounter with writing, Richard Rodriguez relates, When my fourth-grade teacher made our class write about a typical evening at home, it never occurred to me actually to do so. Describe what you do with your family, she told us.
4. The novelist Anne Tyler admits that sometimes the isolation of the writer's life has caused her to miss the friendly conversation enjoyed by co-workers.
5. Maya Angelou writes, Oh, Black known and unknown poets, how often have your auctioned pains sustained us?
6. In the poem O Captain! My Captain! Walt Whitman expresses his sorrow at the death of Abraham Lincoln.
7. According to Ambrose Bierce, the word *novel* means a padded short story.
8. Joan Didion theorizes that keeping a journal connects a person with a series of earlier selves.
9. Thackeray wrote, If a secret history of books could be written, and the author's private thoughts and meanings noted down alongside of his story, how many insipid volumes would become interesting, and dull tales excite the reader!
10. Twenty-three skidoo! might have been the motto of some of F. Scott Fitzgerald's characters, but the author himself saw serious writing as the antidote to a life of frivolity.
11. My favorite line by poet Theodore Roethke is I wake to sleep, and take my waking slow.
12. John Stuart Mill wrote, Ask yourself whether you are happy, and you cease to be so.
13. Wasn't it Groucho Marx who said, Either he's dead or my watch has stopped?
14. Read Washington Irving's short story Rip Van Winkle; it's a classic American tale.
15. Jane Austen is known to have said, Let other pens dwell on guilt and misery.
16. When Lord Charles Beresford was asked to a party, he is quoted as telegraphing this reply: Very sorry can't come. Lie follows by post.
17. Was it Shakespeare who wrote, A rose by any other name would smell as sweet?
18. P. G. Wodehouse once dedicated a book to his daughter, as follows: To my daughter Leonora without whose never-failing sympathy and encouragement this book would have been finished in half the time.
19. Playwright Lillian Hellman is quoted as saying, I cannot and will not cut my conscience to fit this year's fashions.
20. It was Sir Henry Morton Stanley who said these famous words: Dr. Livingston, I presume?

## 21.12 Italics (Underlining)

Italic type is a special slanted type. (*This is printed in italics.*) Italics may be indicated on a computer or with handwriting by underlining.

### Italics for Titles

Italicize (underline) titles of books, lengthy poems, plays, films and television series, paintings and sculptures, long musical compositions, and court cases. Also italicize the names of newspapers and magazines, ships, trains, airplanes, and spacecraft.

*Vanity Fair* [novel]
*Paradise Lost* [long poem]
*Hamlet* [play]
*Glory* [film]
*Great Performances* [television series]
*Guernica* [painting]
*The Age of Bronze* [sculpture]
*Carmen* [long musical composition]
*Plessy v. Ferguson* [court case]
*Chicago Tribune* [newspaper]
*Business Week* [magazine]
H.M.S. *Vanguard* [ship]*
*Silver Meteor* [train]
*Gossamer Albatross* [airplane]
*Telstar* [spacecraft]

*Do not italicize abbreviations such as U.S.S. in the name of a ship.

Italicize (underline) and capitalize articles (*a*, *an*, *the*) written at the beginning of a title only when they are part of the title itself. It is common practice not to italicize (underline) the article preceding the title of a newspaper or a magazine. Do not italicize the word *magazine* unless it is part of the title of a periodical.

| | | |
|---|---|---|
| *The Return of the Native* | *but* | the *Odyssey* |
| *A Midsummer Night's Dream* | | a *Newsweek* magazine cover |
| *An American in Paris* | | an *Atlantic* article |

In forming the possessive of italicized titles, do not italicize the apostrophe and the *-s*.

*Time*'s editorial
*Hamlet*'s plot

## Italics with Foreign Words

Italicize (underline) foreign words and expressions that are not used frequently in English.

If foreign words and expressions are commonly used in English, do not italicize them.

My boss said to do the report ***tout de suite.***
My **fiancé** bought me a bottle of **cologne.**

## Italics with Words and Other Items Used to Represent Themselves

Italicize (underline) words, letters, and numerals used to represent themselves.

Be careful not to confuse ***gorilla*** with ***guerrilla.***
I sometimes make the mistake of typing an ***a*** for a ***w.***
The percent sign (***%***) is on the same typewriter key as the ***5.***

**Exercise 15** **Using Italics**

Rewrite the following sentences correctly, underlining the parts that should be italicized.

***It's a Mystery***

1. The word mystery comes from the Latin word mysterium, meaning "supernatural thing," and from the Greek word mysterion, meaning "a secret rite."
2. Nathaniel Hawthorne's novel of mystery and romance, The Marble Faun, derives its title from an ancient sculpture by Praxiteles known as the Faun.
3. Amelia Earhart disappeared while attempting to pilot her plane, the Friendship, around the world; the book Amelia Earhart: The Final Story (1985) describes the search for the crew and plane that vanished without a trace.
4. The television series Unsolved Mysteries allows viewers to get involved in finding the solutions to crimes and puzzling situations.
5. Agatha Christie used a real train, the Orient Express, as the setting and title of one of her best-known mysteries.
6. In Tony Hillerman's mystery novels The Blessing Way and Coyote Waits, Officer Jim Chee and Detective Lieutenant Joe Leaphorn pursue criminals on a Navajo reservation.
7. The musical City of Angels is a spoof on the hard-boiled detective story.
8. The letters a and f figure prominently in the titles of two mystery novels by Sue Grafton— "A" Is for Alibi (1982) and "F" Is for Fugitive (1989).
9. The most famous American detective periodical is Ellery Queen's Mystery Magazine, first published in 1941.
10. The character of Virgil Tibbs, created by Sidney Poitier in the film In the Heat of the Night, was played by Howard Rollins in the television series of the same name.

# 21.13 The Apostrophe

## Apostrophes with Possessives

### 1. Pronouns

Use an apostrophe and *-s* for the possessive of a singular indefinite pronoun.

Do not use an apostrophe with any other possessive pronouns.

| | | |
|---|---|---|
| one**'s** own room | *but* | whose job |
| everybody**'s** books | | its tail |

### 2. Singular Nouns

Use an apostrophe and *-s* to form the possessive of a singular noun, even one that ends in *-s*.

| | |
|---|---|
| the girl**'s** book | Tokyo**'s** population |
| the glass**'s** design | Gwendolyn Brooks**'s** poetry |
| The lioness**'s** cubs | John Dos Passos**'s** essays |
| the ax**'s** blade | Phoenix**'s** rodeo |

There are a few exceptions to this rule. Add only an apostrophe to form the possessive of ancient proper nouns that end in *-es* or *-is*, the name *Jesus*, and expressions with words such as *appearance* and *conscience*.

| | |
|---|---|
| Achilles' heel | Jesus' sermons |
| Artemis' arrows | the conscience' guide |

### 3. Plural nouns ending in *-s*

Use an apostrophe alone to form the possessive of a plural noun that ends in *-s*.

| | |
|---|---|
| the players' association | the Beatles' albums |
| the skiers' lodge | the Rotarians' meeting |

### 4. Plural nouns not ending in *-s*

Use an apostrophe and *-s* to form the possessive of a plural noun that does not end in *-s*.

| | |
|---|---|
| men**'s** fashion | Women**'s** Medical Association |

### 5. Compound nouns

Put only the last word of a compound noun in the possessive form.

| | |
|---|---|
| my great-grandmother**'s** pearls | the public defender**'s** case |
| his father-in-law**'s** birthday | the court of law**'s** rule |

### 6. Joint possession versus individual possession

If two or more persons (or partners in a company) possess something jointly, use the possessive form for the last person named.

Iris and Steve**'s** new car
Simon and Garfunkel**'s** albums
Strunk and White**'s** book

If two or more persons (or companies) possess an item (or items) individually, put each one's name in the possessive form.

Lorraine Hansberry**'s** and Thornton Wilder**'s** plays
Sony**'s** and Panasonic**'s** television sets

### 7. Expressions of time and money

Use a possessive form to express amounts of money or time that modify a noun.

The modifier can also be expressed as a hyphenated adjective, in which case the possessive form is not used.

| | | |
|---|---|---|
| ten minute**s'** time | *but* | a ten-minute break |
| fifty cent**s'** worth | | a fifty-cent beverage |

## Apostrophes in Contractions

Use an apostrophe in place of letters omitted in contractions.

A **contraction** is a single word made up of two words that have been combined by omitting one or more letters. Most often contractions combine a pronoun and a verb or a verb and an adverb.

| | | |
|---|---|---|
| you're | *formed from* | you are |
| it's | | it is, it has |
| they're | | they are |
| who's | | who is |
| isn't | | is not |
| weren't | | were not |

Use an apostrophe in place of the omitted numerals of a particular year.

the class of '88     the '91 baseball season

## Apostrophes with Special Plurals

Use an apostrophe and *-s* to form the plural of letters, numerals, symbols, and words used to represent themselves.

Italicize (underline) only the letter, numeral, symbol, or word; do not italicize the apostrophe or the *-s*.

His *r*'s looked just like *v*'s.
Some of the *4*'s looked just like *9*'s.
Please be sure to write *and*'s instead of *&*'s.

An apostrophe should not be used to form the plural of a date.

John Steinbeck set many of his novels in the 1930s.

## Exercise 16 Using the Apostrophe

Rewrite the following sentences, using apostrophes correctly. For the one sentence that needs no changes, write *correct.*

| | |
|---|---|
| **INCORRECT** | Sophocles's plays are still performed today. |
| **CORRECT** | Sophocles' plays are still performed today. |
| **INCORRECT** | Lewis's and Clark's expeditions take up an entire chapter in my American history book. |
| **CORRECT** | Lewis and Clark's expeditions take up an entire chapter in my American history book. |

### *Vine Deloria Jr., Spokesperson for Native Americans*

1. While looking under the *d*s in a book about prominent Native Americans, I came across the name Vine Deloria.
2. Delorias status among his people—he is a lawyer and educator—was once described as similar to that of Sitting Bulls leadership of the Sioux a century ago.
3. If people listen to their conscience, they know that Deloria has a valid point when he discusses the stereotyping of his people and the poor treatment they have received.
4. As a professor of political science at the University of Arizona, Deloria educates his Native American students in applying their various cultures traditional customs and beliefs to the solution of contemporary problems.
5. An Episcopal priests son and a former seminary student, Deloria believes that Native American religious practices are really in accord with life in the 1990s.
6. Deloria declares that the Sioux and other Native American groups salvation lies in a return to tribal social organization.
7. Most of all, Deloria wants to preserve his peoples most precious heritage, the group and its land.
8. To no ones surprise, Deloria opposes the idea of Native American integration into the larger society.
9. Deloria hopes to persuade the United States to grant Native Americans quasi-international independence while still acting as their protector.
10. Deloria has worked closely with Clifford Lytle, a colleague; Deloria and Lytles first book is called *American Indians, American Justice*.

## 21.14 The Hyphen

### Hyphens with Prefixes

Ordinarily a hyphen is not used to join a prefix to a word. Exceptions to this rule are as follows:

Use a hyphen after any prefix joined to a proper noun or a proper adjective. Use a hyphen after the prefixes *all-*, *ex-* (meaning "former"), and *self-* joined to any noun or adjective.

pro-American    ex-actor
all-inclusive    self-esteem

Use a hyphen after the prefix *anti-* when it joins a word beginning with *i-*. Also use a hyphen after the prefix *vice-*, except in *vice president.*

anti-intellectual    vice-chancellor

Use a hyphen to avoid confusion between words beginning with *re-* that look alike but are different in meaning and pronunciation.

| | | |
|---|---|---|
| re-creation of a scene | *but* | sports and recreation |
| re-collect the money | | recollect the old saying |

### Hyphens in Compound Adjectives

Use a hyphen in a compound adjective that precedes a noun.

In general, do not hyphenate a compound adjective after a noun.

| | | |
|---|---|---|
| a light-colored balloon | *but* | The balloon is light colored. |

When compound adjectives beginning with *well*, *ill*, or *little* are modified by an adverb, they are usually not hyphenated.

| | | |
|---|---|---|
| an ill-natured child | *but* | a rather ill natured child |
| a well-known actress | | a very well known actress |

An expression made up of an adverb ending in *-ly* and an adjective is not hyphenated.

a brightly colored blouse    a loosely connected wire

## Hyphens in Numbers

### 1. Compound numbers

Hyphenate any spelled-out cardinal or ordinal compound number up to ninety-nine or ninety-ninth.

thirty-four seventy-first

### 2. Fractions used as adjectives

Hyphenate a fraction used as an adjective (but not one used as a noun).

a three-fourths majority *but* three fourths of the voters

### 3. Connected numerals

Hyphenate two numerals to indicate a span.

pages 263-268 1941-1945

When you use the word *from* before a span, use *to* rather than a hyphen. When you use *between* before a span, use *and.*

**from** 1941 **to** 1945 **between** 7:35 **and** 9:15 A.M.

## Hyphens to Divide Words at the End of a Line

In general, divide words between syllables or pronounceable parts. Because deciding where to break a word is often difficult, you might wish to check a dictionary.

In general, if a word contains two consonants occurring between two vowels or if it contains a double consonant, divide the word between the two consonants.

prin-cess pos-sess
pub-lic lad-der
thun-der slip-per

If a suffix has been added to a complete word that ends in two consonants, divide the word after the two consonants.

bill-ing tall-est
fast-er boast-ful

## Exercise 17 Using the Hyphen

Rewrite the following sentences, adding hyphens wherever they are needed. If a sentence is correct, write *correct.* Then make a list of all the italicized words, not including the book title, and show where each would be divided if it had to be broken at the end of a line. (Some words may be divided in more than one place.)

### *Performers of Distinction*

1. It would be fair to say that African American performers like James Earl Jones and Cicely Tyson are "postAldridge actors," since they *follow* in the footsteps of Ira Aldridge.
2. Aldridge, a world famous actor, was born in 1807 in either *Maryland* or New York.
3. While *attending* the African Free School in Manhattan, Aldridge played small parts at the once bustling African Grove Theater.
4. Unfortunately, a group of extremely ill disposed *ruffians* often broke up performances by the African American actors.
5. At the age of twenty one, Aldridge moved to *England.*
6. A *starring* role as Othello led to a long career as the first internationally famous African American star.
7. After Aldridge played Othello in London to wide acclaim, his recreation of the role on tour in Europe was also a huge *success.*
8. Performing in all the major European cities, Aldridge found ample reason for self congratulation, as several kings bestowed medals on him and enthusiastic audiences applauded his *performances.*
9. After a forty year *career* Aldridge died in 1867 while on tour; he was just short of his sixty first birthday.
10. His *marvelous* career is summarized on pages 74 75 of *A Pictorial History of Black Americans* by Langston Hughes, Milton Meltzer, and C. Eric Lincoln.
11. Another great African American *performer* was singer Marian Anderson, born in Philadelphia, Pennsylvania, on February 17, 1902.
12. Even as a young child, Marian was *recognized* as having a remarkably strong singing voice.
13. Her church going parents were too poor to be able to afford lessons for her, and so the *congregation* of the Union Baptist church took up a collection.
14. Marian began to study with Giuseppe Boghetti, who entered her in a contest with the New York Philharmonic *orchestra* when Marian was twenty three years old.
15. Marion took first place honors from among over three hundred *competitors.*
16. Marian did not achieve great success in her race *conscious* homeland.
17. In 1933, at the age of thirty one, Marian went to *Europe* and did not return home for more than two years.
18. Eleanor Roosevelt, well loved First Lady, boosted Anderson's career by asking her to sing in *Washington*, D.C.
19. Anderson *ultimately* achieved great fame, not only because of her immense talent, but also because of her tireless work for other African American people.
20. A well known newsreel shows Marian Anderson singing in front of the Washington Memorial before *thousands* of fans.

## 21.15 Abbreviations

**Abbreviations** are shortened forms of words. They save space and time and prevent unnecessary wordiness. For instance, *B.C.* is more concise and easier to write than *before Christ.* Most abbreviations require periods. If you are unsure of the form of a particular abbreviation, check a dictionary.

Use only one period if an abbreviation occurs at the end of a sentence that would ordinarily take a period of its own.

If an abbreviation occurs at the end of a sentence that ends with a question mark or an exclamation point, use the period *and* the second mark of punctuation.

He left at 8:00 **P.M.**
We visited Washington, **D.C.**

Did she leave at 8:00 **P.M.?**
How we loved Washington, **D.C.!**

# Capitalization of Abbreviations

Capitalize abbreviations of proper nouns.

**Dr.** Ruiz　　**P.O.** Box 331　　**Gov.** Donald F. Gato

Many abbreviations of organizations and government agencies are formed by using the initial letters of the complete name. Such abbreviations, whether pronounced letter by letter or as words, omit periods.

NBA　　NOW　　NFL　　NBC　　FBI　　OSHA

When abbreviating a person's first and middle names, leave a space after each initial.

**J. D.** Salinger　　**W. H.** Auden　　**T. S.** Eliot

The following abbreviations related to historical dates and times should be capitalized:

**A.D.** (*anno Domini*), "in the year of the Lord" (since the birth of Christ); place before the date: **A.D.** 55

**B.C.** (*before Christ*); place after the date: 250 **B.C.**

**B.C.E.** (*before the common era;* equivalent to *B.C.*); place after the date: 2000 **B.C.E.**

**C.E.** (*common era;* equivalent to *A.D.*); place after the date: 50 **C.E.**

**A.M.** (*ante meridiem*), "before noon"; place after exact times: 4:15 **A.M.**

**P.M.** (*post meridiem*), "after noon"; place after exact times: 6:30 **P.M.**

## Abbreviations of Titles of People

Use abbreviations for some personal titles.

For the most part, titles such as *Mrs.*, *Mr.*, *Ms.*, *Sr.*, and *Jr.* and those indicating professions and academic degrees (*Dr.*, *M.D.*, *D.D.S.*, *B.A.*, and so on) are abbreviated.

**Mr.** Vincent Lopez
**Ms.** Vicki Young, **M.S.W.**
Kathleen Peterson, **M.D.**
Henry Yang, **D.D.S.**

## Abbreviations of Units of Measure

Abbreviate units of measure used with numerals in technical or scientific writing but not in ordinary prose.

The following abbreviations stand for plural as well as singular units:

| English System | | Metric System | |
|---|---|---|---|
| **ft.** | foot | **cg** | centigram |
| **gal.** | gallon | **cl** | centiliter |
| **in.** | inch | **cm** | centimeter |
| **lb.** | pound | **g** | gram |
| **mi.** | mile | **kg** | kilogram |
| **mph** | miles per hour | **km** | kilometer |
| **oz.** | ounce | **l** | liter |
| **pt.** | pint | **m** | meter |
| **qt.** | quart | **mg** | milligram |
| **tbsp.** | tablespoon | **ml** | milliliter |
| **tsp.** | teaspoon | **mm** | millimeter |
| **yd.** | yard | **°C** | degrees Celsius or centigrade |
| **°F** | degrees Fahrenheit | | |

### Exercise 18 Using Abbreviations

Write the abbreviations for the italicized words or phrases in the following sentences. Write *correct* if no abbreviation should be used.

1. *Doctor* Ann Pakalnis's speech was received with great enthusiasm.
2. Among the speakers was *Mister* Juan Lopez.
3. The Greek poet Homer is believed to have lived around 800 *before Christ*.
4. The Normans conquered England in *anno Domini* 1066.
5. Gradually add 454 *grams* (that is, 16 *ounces*) of salt to the solution in the beaker until it becomes supersaturated.

## 21.16 Numbers and Numerals

In nontechnical writing some numbers are spelled out and others are expressed in figures. Numbers expressed in figures are called *numerals.*

### Numbers Spelled Out

In general, spell out cardinal and ordinal numbers that can be written in one or two words.

Spell out any number that occurs at the beginning of a sentence.

Saturn is now thought to have **eleven** moons.
We celebrated Aunt Sylvia's **sixty-fifth** birthday.
**Four hundred and seventy-five** people attended the conference.

### Numerals

In general, use numerals to express numbers that would be written in more than two words.

There were **475** people at the conference.
The area of the Irish Republic is **27,137** square miles.

You can often write very large numbers as decimals followed by the word *million* or *billion.*

The population of New York City is roughly **7.1 million.**
That food chain has sold over **9.5 billion** hamburgers.

If related numbers appear in the same sentence and some can be written out while others should appear as numerals, use all numerals.

Of the **125** members of the intercity chorus, only **70** attended the meeting last Monday.

**1. Money, decimals, and percentages**

Use numerals to express amounts of money, decimals, and percentages.

The rent is **$350** a month.
The stock paid a dividend of **13** percent.

Spell out amounts of money that can be expressed in one or two words.

We paid **eighty-six** cents for the onions.
The car costs **seven thousand** dollars.

### 2. Dates and time

Use numerals to express the year and day in a date and to express the precise time with the abbreviations A.M. and P.M.

An earthquake hit San Francisco on October **17, 1989.**
The concert was scheduled to begin at **8:15 P.M.**
I met her at the museum at **11:00 A.M.**

Spell out expressions of time that do not use the abbreviation A.M. or P.M.

The concert was scheduled to begin at **eight** o'clock.

To express a century when the word *century* is used, spell out the number. Likewise, to express a decade when the century is clear from the context, spell out the number.

That vase dates back to the **twelfth century.**
F. Scott Fitzgerald's works describe America in the **twenties.**

When a century and a decade are expressed as a single unit, use numerals followed by an *-s.*

In the **1960s** and **1970s** young Americans were leaders in many movements to promote social justice.

### 3. Addresses

Use numerals for streets and avenues numbered above ten and for all house, apartment, and room numbers. Spell out numbered streets and avenues with numbers of ten or under.

The Apollo Theater is located at **253** West **125th** Street.
We sent the letter to Apartment **4D.**
That bus travels on **Second** Avenue.

**Exercise 19** **Using Numbers and Numerals**

Rewrite the following sentences, making any necessary changes in the use of numbers and numerals. If a sentence is correct as written, write *correct.*

***Sweet Sixteen***

1. Alessandra's 16th birthday is March 25, 1995.
2. 50 people will be attending the party!
3. The rumor is that her parents paid over $375 for the food alone.
4. The party will be at her apartment on 1st Street.
5. That's a lot of money, even for the nineteen nineties.

UNIT

21

Unit Review

# Grammar Review

## Punctuation

Some twenty years ago Paul Theroux boarded a train in Boston and headed south on a journey that took him, over the course of several months and more than twelve thousand miles, to the mountains of Patagonia in southern Argentina. His book *The Old Patagonian Express* documents that journey. In this passage from the book, which has been annotated to show some of the rules of punctuation covered in this unit, Theroux has just reached the sleepy town of Tucumán in northern Argentina.

*Literature Model*

### *from* THE OLD PATAGONIAN EXPRESS

***by Paul Theroux***

Commas to separate items in a series

Period at the end of a declarative sentence

Dashes to indicate a change in thought

Parentheses to set off supplemental material

Semicolons to separate series items already containing commas

Hyphen in a compound adjective preceding a noun

Semicolon to separate two main clauses

Tucumán was older, flatter, cleaner, and a great deal duller than I had expected. It was the ultimate provincial town, self-contained and remote, and being an Argentine town it was thoroughly European in a rather old-fashioned way, from the pinstripe suits and black mustaches of the old men idling in the cafés or having their shoes shined in the plaza, to the baggy shapeless school uniforms of the girls stopping on their way to the convent school to squeeze—it was an expression of piety—the knee of Christ on the cathedral crucifix. Old Europe was evident in the façades of the houses in the center of the city, in all the paperwork at the bank (every transaction recorded in triplicate), in the contrived glamour of the women shopping, and in the vain posturing and haircombing of the young men. The houses were French; the official buildings, Italian baroque; the monuments and statues, pure South American. . . .

After the barrel-chested Indians living among wind-haunted rocks in the high plains, and the farmers in the tumbledown villages near the border, and the yawning, cracked-open river valleys of the north, I was prepared for anything but Tucumán. It was gloomy, but gloom was part of the Argentine temper; it was not a dramatic blackness ➡

but rather a dampness of soul, the hangdog melancholy immigrants feel on rainy afternoons far from home.

❦

The curios in Tucumán were versions of gaucho kitsch—sets of bolas, toy horsewhips, overpriced daggers; and there were also salt shakers, aprons, calendars, and little boxes made out of cactus fiber, all stamped TUCUMÁN. The bookstores were vastly more impressive than any I had seen on this trip, or was this a stubborn bias I had formed after seeing three of my own titles on display in Spanish translation? I made a note of the publisher's address in Buenos Aires: I would look him up when I arrived.

I did little else in Tucumán but buy a pizza—a thick, Neapolitan-style pizza garnished with anchovies. This reminded me of a sad remark I had heard in Peru. "Times are so bad in Peru," a man said," even the anchovy has left our waters and swum away." As the day wore on I became firmer in my resolve to leave Tucumán. . . .

Comma to separate two main clauses joined by a coordinating conjunction

Question mark to indicate a direct question

Colon to introduce a sentence that explains the preceding material

Quotation marks to enclose a direct quotation

## Exercise 1 Using Numbers and Numerals

Write out the following sentences, making any necessary changes in the use of numbers and numerals.

### *The 1936 Olympic Games*

[1]In eighteen ninety-six the Olympic games were reinstated in Athens, Greece, on the site where the ancient games had been held in the 4th century. [2]Of the games held before the 2nd World War, the 1936 Olympics, hosted by Germany, were the most remarkable. [3]Approximately 1,000 male and female athletes representing 28 countries took part in the winter games, which opened on February sixth, 1936. [4]Before the games closed 10 days later, Norway had established its dominance in winter sports, earning eight gold medals. [5]53 nations took part in the summer games, which were held in Berlin from August first through August sixteenth. [6]The games were opened by Adolf Hitler, who viewed them as a public relations bonanza for the Nazi party; indeed, thousands of spectators saw the Germans win thirty-one of a possible 120 gold medals. [7]But Hitler's theory of Aryan racial superiority was debunked when Jesse Owens, an African American, took 4 gold medals in track-and-field events. [8]Owens won the 200-meter race and the gold medal for the long jump with a leap of twenty-six feet five point thirty-one inches. [9]He ran one leg of the 400-meter relay and tied the world record for the 100-meter race at ten point three seconds. [10]You can find out more about the 1936 Olympics in *The Olympic Games: Complete Track and Field Results 1896–1988* by Barry J. Hugman and Peter Arnold, which costs forty dollars and is published by Facts on File Inc., Four Hundred Sixty Park Avenue South, New York, NY 10016.

## Exercise 2 Using Punctuation, Abbreviations, and Numbers

Rewrite the following sentences, adding marks of punctuation and italicizing (underlining) where necessary, using abbreviations where appropriate, and making any needed changes in the use of numbers and numerals.

**INCORRECT** Albert Einstein german 1879 1955 is quoted as saying The most incomprehensible thing about the world is that it is comprehensible.

**CORRECT** Albert Einstein (German, 1879–1955) is quoted as saying, "The most incomprehensible thing about the world is that it is comprehensible."

### *Earth: The View from Afar*

1. Photographs of the planet Earth taken from the moon have become very familiar
2. What a sight that must have been for the astronauts who took the pictures
3. Have you ever thought about how you would have felt in that situation
4. Anyone seeing the Earth as a small, distant sphere might have experienced feelings such as these awe, triumph, humility, homesickness, and fear.
5. Earth was no longer a vast homeland it was too remote too tiny and too vulnerable.
6. We were used to seeing the moon as a small luminous silvery disk floating in the sky but we were shocked to see the Earth as a tiny mottled blue sphere suspended in the void.
7. This new view of Earth which made its fragility suddenly vivid may persuade us to value it.
8. If you gaze across an extensive landscape from a mountaintop however you may form a different impression of our planet
9. Your perspective from downtown Los Angeles California would also be quite different.
10. From such vantage points—mountaintops and city streets the world seems like a permanent home, not just our cosmic pied-à-terre meaning temporary lodging.
11. A striking feature of the photographs of Earth (those taken from lunar orbit is the complete absence of any sign of human presence.
12. What seems to be a massive human impact here on Earth, said one scientist, becomes invisible from any point beyond its atmosphere.
13. Writers of stories and songs may accurately use expressions like deep blue sea our oceans viewed from space are very blue indeed.
14. On the other hand, though Robert Heinlein wrote a novel called The Green Hills of Earth, the planets landmasses appear rather brownish from space.
15. Some features of Earths geological history are obvious from the moon. (This is true despite the planets great distance from that body
16. Viewing North and South America, Europe, and Africa, its clear that these continents Atlantic coasts were once joined.
17. The all encompassing, self contained, islandlike supercontinent that existed before the landmass broke apart into separate continents was given the name Pangaea in 1912.
18. Doctor A. L. Wegener, a German geologist, coined the name hypothesizing that the split took place 200 million years before the common era.
19. 200 million years ago may seem like the very distant past the mountains of New England however were formed about two hundred fifty million years before that time.
20. Gaia, is the name of Earth personified as a goddess, but J. E. Lovelock's book Gaia: A New Look at Natural History was not published until nineteen hundred seventy nine.

## Exercise 3 Using Punctuation, Abbreviations, and Numbers

Rewrite the following sentences, adding marks of punctuation and italicizing (underlining) where necessary, using abbreviations where appropriate, and making any needed changes in the use of numbers and numerals.

**INCORRECT** In 130 *before Christ*, Hipparchus of Nicea calculated the correct distance to the moon.

**CORRECT** In 130 B.C., Hipparchus of Nicea calculated the correct distance to the moon.

### *Astronomy's Greatest Hits*

1. In *anno Domini* 1543 Nicholas Copernicus published De Revolutionibus which presented the controversial theory that the Earth revolves around the Sun.
2. In this book Copernicus is quoted as saying So the sun sits as upon a royal throne, ruling his children the planets, which circle around him
3. Galileo supported Copernicus theory, but in sixteen thirty three was forced by church leaders to recant
4. Edmond Halley discovered the comet that bears his name and in 1682 predicted its return in 1758 76 years later.
5. George Gamow Russian American 1904 68, Ralph Alpher American and Robert Herman American published the Big Bang theory of the origin of the universe.

## Exercise 4

The following passage describes the artist Joaquin Sorolla y Bastida, whose painting appears on the next page. Rewrite the passage, correcting the errors in spelling, grammar, and usage. Add any missing punctuation. There are ten errors.

### *Joaquin Sorolla y Bastida*

[1]Born in Valencia Joaquin Sorolla y Bastida (1863–1923) was among the most successful Spanish painters of his day. [2]At the age of 15, he entered an art school in Valencia and shortly thereafter made trips to France and Italy. [3]After he had spent four years in Rome he returned to Valencia in 1888. [4]There he worked as an illustrater and refined his painting skills.

[5]An indefatigable worker Sorolla y Bastida applied his bravura technique to subjects that included the following landscapes, historical events, and portraits. [6]He prefers to paint outdoors, focusing on light and atmosphere more than on actual forms. [7]Bold brush strokes, strong compositions and dramatic tonal contrasts are hallmarks of his work.

[8]Like the city of Tucumán the town in Argentina described by Paul Theroux, Plasencia seems "self-contained and remote." [9]The mood of the painting, like the mood of the passage from *The Old Patagonian Express*, is melancholy

**Joaquin Sorolla y Bastida, *Plasencia*, 1917**

**Exercise 5**

The following items describe the life and achievements of Paul Theroux. Rewrite each numbered item, correcting all errors in punctuation. Underline any words that should be in italics.

### *Paul Theroux*

1. Author, Paul Theroux, was born on April 10 1941 in Medford Massachusetts.
2. Reading, writing and art were stressed in the Theroux home, in fact the five sons put out competing family newspapers.
3. Pauls siblings include: Alexander a novelist, Mary a nurse, and Eugene a lawyer.
4. Planning to study medicine in college Theroux excelled in science. (he twice won his high schools' science fair)
5. Later he went to Africa with the Peace Corps, and wrote for a newspaper, the "Christian Science Monitor."
6. There he met a West Indian author V. S. Naipaul who took an interest in the aspiring young author.
7. Naipaul told Theroux, "A book needs a reason for being written;" Theroux later said of Naipaul "With me he was a generous, rational teacher.
8. From 1968 to 1971 Theroux taught seventeenth-century English literature.
9. Theroux—he loves to travel abroad lives in a London home filled with mementos.
10. "Waldo" Theroux' first novel was published in 1967!

# Writing Application

**Punctuation, Abbreviations, And Numbers In Writing** The correct use of punctuation, abbreviations, and numbers in writing is essential. Notice, for example, the use of these elements in the following passage from Charles Dickens's novel *Bleak House*.

Thus, in the midst of the mud and at the heart of the fog, sits the Lord High Chancellor in his High Court of Chancery.

"Mr. Tangle," says the Lord High Chancellor, latterly something restless under the eloquence of that learned gentleman.

"Mlud," says Mr. Tangle. Mr. Tangle knows more of Jarndyce and Jarndyce than anybody. He is famous for it—supposed never to have read anything else since he left school.

"Have you nearly concluded your argument?"

"Mlud, no—variety of points—feel it my duty tsubmit—ludship," is the reply that slides out of Mr. Tangle.

"Several members of the bar are still to be heard, I believe?" says the Chancellor, with a slight smile.

**Techniques With Punctuation, Abbreviations, And Numbers** Keep these guidelines in mind as you write and revise your own work:

1. Use a comma between the main clauses in a compound sentence. Place a comma before a coordinating conjunction (*and, but, or, nor, yet,* or *for*) that joins two main clauses.

2. Use a semicolon to separate main clauses that are not joined by a coordinating conjunction (*and, but, or, nor, yet,* or *for*).

3. In general, spell out cardinal and ordinal numbers that can be written in one or two words.

4. Use an apostrophe in place of letters omitted in contractions.

5. Use an exclamation point to show strong feeling.

6. Use a dash to indicate an abrupt break or change in thought within a sentence.

**Practice** Practice these techniques by revising the following passage, also taken from Charles Dickens's *Bleak House*. Use a separate sheet of paper.

Eighteen of Mr. Tangle's learned friends, each armed with a little summary of eighteen hundred sheets, bob up like eighteen hammers in a pianoforte, make eighteen bows, and drop into their eighteen places of obscurity.

"We will proceed with the hearing on Wednesday fortnight," says the Chancellor. For the question at issue is only a question of costs, a mere bud on the forest tree of the parent suit, and really will come to a settlement one of these days.

The Chancellor rises; the bar rises; the prisoner is brought forward in a hurry; the man from Shropshire cries, "My lord!"

# Inside Resources

*The lessons in this unit give you the skills necessary to prepare and deliver a speech, take a test, use a dictionary, and find books in the library. Each lesson is complete, concise, and easy to use.*

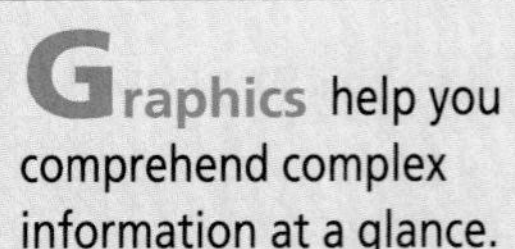

**Graphics** help you comprehend complex information at a glance.

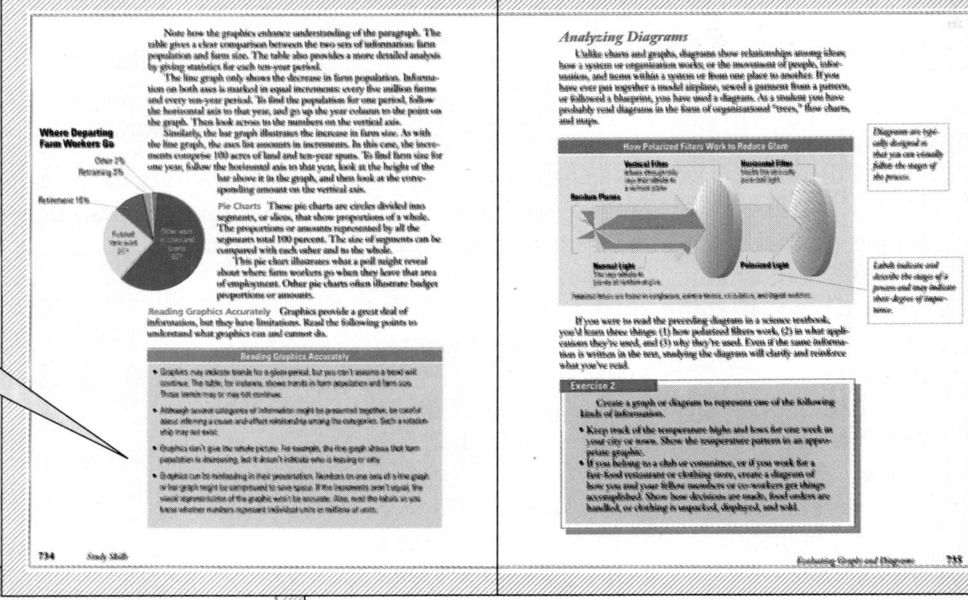

Note how the graphics enhance understanding of the paragraph. The table gives a clear comparison between the two sets of information: farm population and farm size. The table also provides a more detailed analysis by giving statistics for each ten-year period.

The line graph only shows the decrease in farm population. Information on both axes is marked in equal increments: every five million farms and every ten-year period. To find the population for one period, follow the horizontal axis to that year, and go up the year column to the point on the graph. Then look across to the numbers on the vertical axis.

Similarly, the bar graph illustrates the increase in farm size. As with the line graph, the axes list amounts in increments. In this case, the increments comprise 100 acres of land and ten-year spans. To find farm size for one year, follow the horizontal axis to that year, look at the height of the bar above it in the graph, and then look at the corresponding amount on the vertical axis.



Pie Charts These pie charts are circles divided into segments, or slices, that show proportions of a whole. The proportions or amounts represented by all the segments total 100 percent. The size of segments can be compared with each other and to the whole.

This pie chart illustrates what a poll might reveal about where farm workers go when they leave that area of employment. Other pie charts often illustrate budget proportions or amounts.

Reading Graphics Accurately Graphics provide a great deal of information, but they have limitations. Read the following points to understand what graphics can and cannot do.

Reading Graphics Accurately

734 Study Skills

*Analyzing Diagrams*

Unlike charts and graphs, diagrams show relationships among ideas, how a system or organization works, or the movement of people, information, and items within a system or from one place to another. If you have ever put together a model airplane, sewed a garment from a pattern, or followed a blueprint, you have used a diagram. As a student you have probably read diagrams in the form of organizational "trees," flow charts, and maps.



*Diagrams are typically designed so that you can visually follow the stages of the process.*

*Labels indicate and describe the stages of a process and may indicate their degree of importance.*

If you were to read the preceding diagram in a science textbook, you'd learn three things: (1) how polarized filters work, (2) in what applications they're used, and (3) why they're used. Even if the same information is written in the text, studying the diagram will clarify and reinforce what you've read.

Exercise 2

Create a graph or diagram to represent one of the following kinds of information.

- Keep track of the temperature highs and lows for one week in your city or town. Show the temperature pattern in an appropriate graphic.
- If you belong to a club or committee, or if you work for a fast-food restaurant or clothing store, create a diagram of how you and your fellow members or co-workers get things accomplished. Show how decisions are made, food orders are handled, or clothing is unpacked, displayed, and sold.

Evaluating Graphs and Diagrams 735

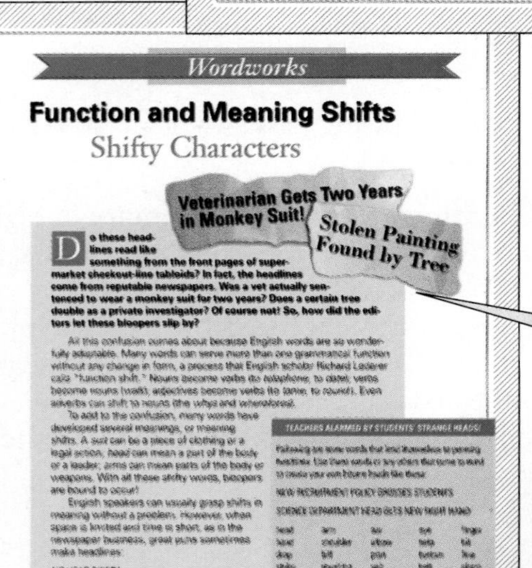

*Wordworks*

**Function and Meaning Shifts**

Shifty Characters



**Do these headlines read like something from the front pages of supermarket checkout-line tabloids? In fact, the headlines come from reputable newspapers. Was a vet actually sentenced to wear a monkey suit for two years? Does a certain tree double as a private investigator? Of course not! So, how did the editors let these bloopers slip by?**

TEACHERS ALARMED BY STUDENTS' STRANGE HEADS!

Language Differences: Syntax and Grammar 697

**Wordworks** pages like this one provide a humorous look at how we use and misuse our language. These features appear in the first unit in Resources, which puts you in command of basic facts about the English language.

# Part 3

# Resources and Skills

# Part 3 Resources and Skills

UNIT

# 22 The English Language

## 22.1 Language Universals

What's your native language? Is it English, Vietnamese, Spanish, Korean, Hindi, Latvian? Linguists estimate about 3,000 languages are in use worldwide today, not including the thousands of spoken dialects.

Yet, despite this diversity of human speech, language scholars know that all languages share important characteristics. These common aspects are called language universals.

Language universals number in the hundreds. Some of the most important ones are listed in the chart below and on the following page.

**1. Wherever there are people, there is language.**

All people communicate orally, whether they are part of large social groups or members of small, isolated communities. Some groups of people have no writing system for their language, but scholars have never encountered any group that did not have a spoken language.

**2. All languages use sound to express meaning.**

Certain languages have more sounds than others. Some languages have sounds that are nonexistent in other languages. But all languages use sounds to communicate thoughts and ideas.

**3. Most languages are equally complex.**

There is no such thing as a primitive language. Most ideas that can be expressed in one language can be expressed in other languages, although the means of expression (the grammar and the vocabulary) may differ.

**4. No language remains static.**

Languages grow and change over time, often drastically. Most native speakers of Modern English, for example, cannot read, speak, or understand Old English, the language from which Modern English evolved over many centuries.

**5. Similar grammatical categories and concepts are found in all languages.**

All languages have words (nouns) that name people, places, things, and ideas, and all languages have words (verbs) that express actions. Similarly, all languages can express relationships in time through the use of tense or other means.

**6. Any normal child will learn whatever language he or she is exposed to in infancy.**

Imagine a girl, just born to Russian parents working in Somalia in eastern Africa. The parents are lost in a devastating flood, and the child is raised in a Somalian family where Swahili is spoken. The girl will grow up speaking perfect Swahili, even though she has a different ethnic and racial heritage than her Somalian foster family. Had she been raised in China, she would speak Chinese; in France, she would speak French.

Despite the universality of language, individual languages have many unique aspects. In the next two lessons, you will learn how English differs from other languages throughout the world.

## Exercise 1

In 1799 a young boy was found in the Aveyron forest in France. The boy had apparently grown up with the animals of the forest; he moved as they moved, ate the food they ate, and showed no ability for human speech. He was called "the wild boy of Aveyron."

Do some research on this wild boy. How did he learn to speak a human language? Two books you might consult are *The Wild Boy of Aveyron* by Jean-Marc-Gaspard Itard, and *The Forbidden Experiment: The Story of the Wild Boy of Aveyron* by Roger Shattuck. You may also want to view a French film of the boy's story, *L'Enfant Sauvage* (*The Wild Child*) by François Truffaut (1969). Share your findings with your classmates.

## Wordworks

# Clips

## Trimming the Edges

**What common English word comes from *pantaloons*? If you guessed *pants,* you're correct. What words come from *cabriolet, reputation,* and *percolate*?**

*Pants, cab, rep,* and *perk* are clips—shortened forms of words. Clips are considered new words, especially when they have completely replaced their longer versions, such as *pantaloons* or *omnibus* (the clipped form of which is, of course, *bus*).

English speakers have been clipping words for a long time, but not everyone has approved of the practice. In 1711 the English author and politician Joseph Addison complained that "It is perhaps this humour of speaking no more than we needs must which has so miserably curtailed some of our words, as in *mob, rep,* . . . and the like."

However, most English speakers usually speak "no more than [they] needs must" and continue to clip, such as in *fan* (*fanatic*), *copter* (*helicopter*), *pop* (*popular*), *rehab* (*rehabilitate*), *bio* (*biography*), and *high tech* (*high technology*).

Another form of clipping is back-formation, in which a shortened verb is made from a noun: to *burgle,* from *burglar,* or to *edit,* from *editor.* You might wonder, following such logic, whether an usher "ushes" or a butler "buttles"!

A second type of back-formation is a singular form of a word made from a supposed plural. For instance, during the seventeenth century the word *pease* was mistaken for a plural, even though it was the singular form for the green vegetable that grows in pods (just as *cheese* is a singular form). As a result, *pease* was clipped to a more traditional-sounding singular form, and now we have one *pea* and two *peas.* However, we do not as yet have one *chee* and two *cheese.*

### Clip Along with the Clippers

Try your skill at word-making. Develop a list of nouns ending in *-er, -ar,* or *-or.* Then use back-formation to create new verbs. For example, if an editor edits, what does a doctor do? How about a pastor, undertaker, or minister? Don't be shy. Remember, there were once no such verbs as *baby-sit* or *bargain-hunt.* You might just make linguistic history!

# 22.2 Language Differences: Phonology

When babies first begin communicating with the world around them, their "speech" is limited to sounds: coos, murmurs, cries, giggles, and so on. Even though these sounds are not words, they nevertheless communicate a great deal about what the baby is trying to say. Coos and soft murmurs are signs of contentment; giggles indicate happiness or pleasure; cries tell us of hunger, pain, or frustration.

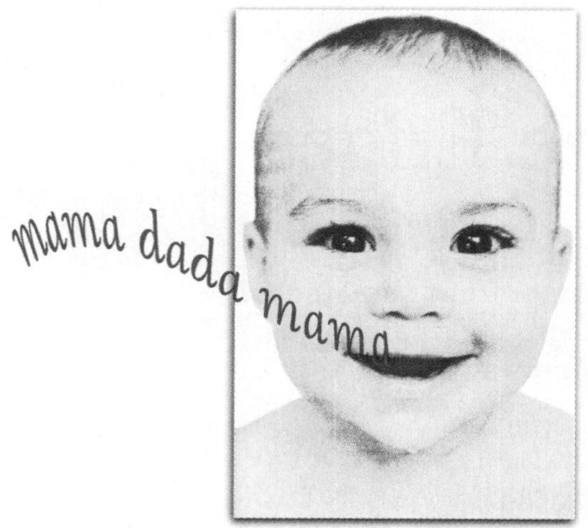


Eventually, a baby learns to make specific sounds in order to say specific words. For example, a baby growing up in an English-speaking family learns to put its lips together to make the *m* sound in *mama;* it learns to touch its tongue to the roof of its mouth to make the *d* sound in *dada.* Such basic sounds that make up a language are called phonemes. The study of such sounds in language is called phonology. The field of phonology emerged in India about 2,300 years ago. Indian scholars studied the early pronunciations of Sanskrit to preserve the traditional pronunciations in holy works.

## Sounds, More or Less

According to phonetic experts, there are about ninety sounds that human beings make to create language. Many sounds are common to a large number of languages. For instance, languages in most of western Europe and in Central and South America use many sounds that are also used in English. This means that even though German uses a different sequence of sounds—*wasser,* pronounced "vä-sāre" in English—to name the substance that in English is called *water,* most English speakers do not have trouble pronouncing the sounds used in the German sequence.

Nevertheless, languages do not all have the same sounds or the same number of sounds. Some have sounds that occur in no other language. For example, a baby learning to speak Twi, the language spoken by the Ashanti people in the West African country of Ghana, will learn to make sounds that a baby learning to speak English will never encounter.

English and Twi share many of the same consonants (including *p, t, k, b,* and *d*) and the same vowels (including *a, e, i,* and *u*). However, Twi has no sounds equivalent to the English sounds *z, v,* and *l.* At the same time, Twi includes sounds that do not occur in English.

Try to say *ch* (as in *church*) with your lips rounded. Now, try to say *j* (as in *judge*), again with your lips rounded. These sounds are common in Twi but nonexistent in English.

## Clicks, Drums, Chirps, and Repetitions

Sound differences can be fascinating. In some African and Asian languages called click languages, a clicking sound is made in the speaker's mouth as some words are pronounced. These clicks attach certain meaning to the words; if the speaker changes the click, the meaning of the word also changes.

Think of the sound represented by "tsk-tsk" in English. Now, think of the sound made to encourage a horse to move faster. These are two kinds of clicks that are used regularly in the Zulu language in South Africa.

Anyone who watches old movies has probably viewed more than one scene in which a European adventuring in Africa wonders what message the natives' distant drumbeats convey. In fact, the indigenous peoples of sub-Saharan Africa did communicate over distances with drumbeats. The drumbeats imitated the pronunciation of their spoken language and could be understood by the drummers.

Sounds that resemble bird chirps can also be a regular feature of language. In the Turkish village of Cuskoy, townspeople often communicate with a system of chirps. Cuskoy is located in a ravine, and the river that passes through the town frequently creates a fog that prevents people from seeing each other across the river. The chirps allow their voices to carry across the river despite the foggy conditions.

In still other languages, the number of repetitions of a sound can affect the meaning of an expression. For example, in Chinese, the sound *ma* repeated four times with different tones means "Mother scolds the horse." If *ma* is repeated five times, however, the sentence becomes a question: "Is Mother scolding the horse?"

Notice that languages throughout the world use sounds and repetitions of sounds to create meanings in ways English does not. No one system of language is superior to another; languages are merely sound differences that vary across time and cultures.

### Exercise 2

With your teacher's help, locate a musical recording of a singer whose songs include clicking sounds as described in this lesson. One such singer is Miriam Makeba of Africa; other songs of this type are included on Paul Simon's *Graceland* recording.

In a small group, listen carefully to several songs on the recording. Try to duplicate the words that incorporate clicks, and coach each other on your pronunciation. Then, try to devise a way to write down the words, using a symbol or other documentation to represent the clicking sounds. Share your group's written representations with the class.

*Wordworks*

# Mixed Metaphors
## Barking Snakes

rrr bark bark bark

**When Senator Blather tells the press that his opponent, Representative Dither, is "barking up the wrong tree," what is he actually saying? And when Representative Dither replies that Senator Blather is a "snake in the grass," what is *his* point?**

Neither Blather nor Dither is suggesting that his opponent is really a dog or a snake. They are both using metaphors–figures of speech that make implied comparisons between two unlike things. Used correctly, metaphors add color and emphasis to spoken and written language.

Sometimes, however, speakers and writers mix their metaphors. That is, they unintentionally combine one metaphor with another, or they misspeak the metaphor they want to use. The results can be both funny and confusing, as in this Blather bluster: "Dither is nothing but a snake in the grass barking up the wrong tree!"

Imagine the startled expression on the face of the doctor whose exhausted interns protested, "We've been working our brains to the bone!" What was the talk show host to make of this comment by an argumentative guest: "That's a horse of a different feather"? Surely the people of Wisconsin were surprised to hear that "Milwaukee is the golden egg that the rest of the state wants to milk." And perhaps only Jacques Cousteau could empathize with the Hollywood actor who complained of her lack of privacy, "It's difficult living in a bowl of fish."

### Murdered Metaphors

Unscramble the following mixed metaphors. What is the speaker actually trying to say?

1. It's time to take the bull by the teeth!
2. Clearly this issue is a double-barreled sword.
3. Let dead dogs sleep.
4. The police went over the crime scene with a fine-tuned comb.
5. The cows have come home to roost.

## 22.3 Language Differences: Syntax and Grammar

Can you read this sentence?

Boy the shuffled street tired the down.

This sentence makes no sense because it's not really a sentence. It violates the rules of English syntax and grammar. Syntax and grammar refer to conventions for combining words into acceptable sentences. English syntax and grammar do not allow for a "sentence" such as the one above. However, when these same words are recombined according to the rules, the meaning becomes quite clear.

The tired boy shuffled down the street.

Languages have different syntactic rules. Let's take a look at three ways in which English syntax differs from that of other languages.

### Word Order

In English the preferred word order for declarative sentences is S-V-O (subject-verb-object), as in the following sentences.

(S)**Carolyn**, calm and collected, (V)**sank** the winning (O)**basket.**

A (S)**detonation** (V)**rocked** the (O)**neighborhood.**

This same word order is also preferred in Spanish and in French. But notice the preferred word orders in these languages.

| | |
|---|---|
| Japanese and Korean | S-O-V |
| Classical Hebrew and Welsh | V-S-O |
| Malagasy (Madagascar) | V-O-S |

Linguists have found no languages that have an O-V-S or an O-S-V pattern. In other words, in no language does the preferred word order begin with an object.

### Modifiers

In English, adjectives usually precede the noun they modify: **blue** sky. The same is true in Russian: ***interesnaya*** *gazeta* **(interesting** newspaper).

In French and Spanish, however, adjectives generally *follow* the nouns they modify: French—*le livre* ***rouge*** (the book **red**); Spanish—*el hombre* ***viejo*** (the man **old**).

## Gender

Originally, Old English words had gender. Some words were masculine, some were feminine, and some were neuter, or neither. The gender of a word was usually indicated by special endings and influenced the form of words that were used with it.

Gradually, gender disappeared from the English language, but it is a prominent part of the grammars of other languages. For example, notice the definite article that precedes the following words in English.

| | |
|---|---|
| **the** boy | **the** girl |
| **the** library | **the** book |

Because English has no gender, the same article, *the*, can precede all nouns. Spanish words, however, do have gender: masculine and feminine forms. A Spanish speaker must know the gender of each noun and the correct article to go with it. Generally, masculine nouns end in *-o* and feminine nouns end in *-a*.

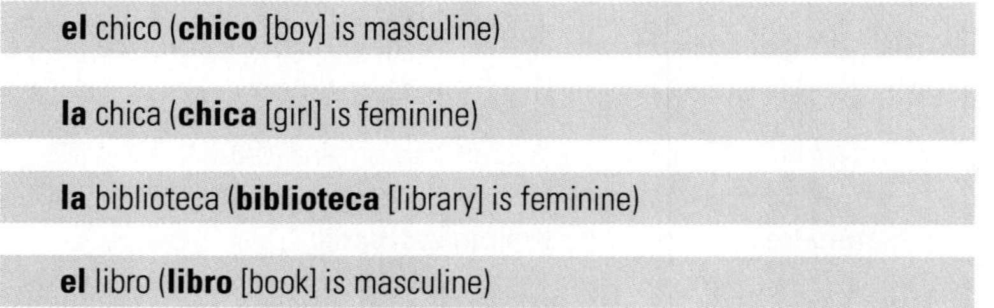

**el** chico (**chico** [boy] is masculine)

**la** chica (**chica** [girl] is feminine)

**la** biblioteca (**biblioteca** [library] is feminine)

**el** libro (**libro** [book] is masculine)

It is important to note that a word is not masculine, feminine, or neuter because of any inherent characteristics of the object or idea it represents. That is, to Spanish speakers a library is not necessarily a "feminine" structure, nor is a book inherently "masculine." The gender of a word is merely a grammatical label that signals speakers to use the correct form of words, such as articles and adjectives, that accompany the gendered words.

### Exercise 3

English sentences have a fixed word order. That is, nearly every declarative sentence follows the S-V-O pattern. In some languages, however, the order is not fixed. Try your hand at writing some declarative sentences in English that follow the preferred word order of other languages. Try S-O-V, V-S-O, and V-O-S. Which of these orders can produce an intelligible English sentence? Do the sentences sound natural? What does this tell you about the similarities and differences in languages?

*Wordworks*

# Function and Meaning Shifts

## Shifty Characters

**Veterinarian Gets Two Years in Monkey Suit!**

**Stolen Painting Found by Tree**

**Do these headlines read like something from the front pages of supermarket checkout-line tabloids? In fact, the headlines come from reputable newspapers. Was a vet actually sentenced to wear a monkey suit for two years? Does a certain tree double as a private investigator? Of course not! So, how did the editors let these bloopers slip by?**

All this confusion comes about because English words are so wonderfully adaptable. Many words can serve more than one grammatical function without any change in form, a process that English scholar Richard Lederer calls "function shift." Nouns become verbs (to *telephone,* to *date*); verbs become nouns (*walk*); adjectives become verbs (to *tame,* to *round*). Even adverbs can shift to nouns (the *whys* and *wherefores*).

To add to the confusion, many words have developed several meanings, or meaning shifts. A *suit* can be a piece of clothing or a legal action; *head* can mean a part of the body or a leader; *arms* can mean parts of the body or weapons. With all these shifty words, bloopers are bound to occur!

English speakers can usually grasp shifts in meaning without a problem. However, when space is limited and time is short, as in the newspaper business, great puns sometimes make headlines:

AIR HEAD FIRED!
SCHOOL BOARD DEMANDS
BUS PASSENGERS BE BELTED

### TEACHERS ALARMED BY STUDENTS' STRANGE HEADS!

Following are some words that lend themselves to punning headlines. Use these words or any others that come to mind to create your own bizarre heads like these:

NEW RECRUITMENT POLICY GROSSES STUDENTS

SCIENCE DEPARTMENT HEAD GETS NEW RIGHT HAND

| | | | | |
|---|---|---|---|---|
| head | arm | ear | eye | finger |
| hand | shoulder | elbow | help | hit |
| drop | bill | plan | bottom | fine |
| strike | revolting | suit | belt | alarm |
| hearing | swell | turning | attack | gross |

# 22.4 English Throughout the World

In Alan Lerner and Frederick Loewe's musical *My Fair Lady*, adapted from George Bernard Shaw's play *Pygmalion*, Professor Henry Higgins attempts to transform a poor cockney woman, Eliza Doolittle, into a refined lady. At one point the exasperated professor sings a song entitled "Why Can't the English Teach Their Children How to Speak?" The professor laments the fact that so many people in his country do not speak the same proper, standard English that he speaks.

Were Professor Higgins alive today, he would be dismayed to discover that Britons still speak a variety of English dialects. In fact, wherever English is spoken around the world, variations in vocabulary, spelling, and pronunciation abound. Let's compare some differences between American English and English as it is spoken in Great Britain, Canada, and Australia.

| **American word** | French fries | gas | truck | railroad | can (of soup) |
|---|---|---|---|---|---|
| British word | chips | petrol | lorry | railway | tin (of soup) |
| Canadian word | chips | gas | truck | railway | tin (of soup) |

## Vocabulary

One obvious difference in the English of these four countries is vocabulary. Notice in the chart above that sometimes Canadian vocabulary follows the British terminology, but at other times it follows the American terminology.

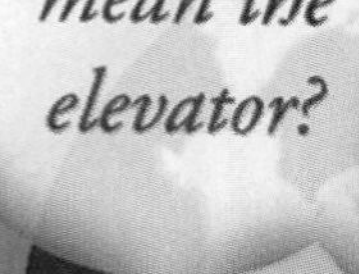

Excuse me, could you direct me to the lift?
Do you mean the elevator?


When Australia was initially settled by the British, the land was so different from anything the settlers had ever experienced that their vocabulary was inadequate to describe it. Thus, they borrowed many words from the languages of the original people of Australia. Some of these words have become part of English around the world: *kangaroo*, *koala*, and *boomerang*. However, many Australian English words are foreign to other English speakers: *currawong* (a type of bird), *boobialla* (a type of tree), and *woomera* (a type of weapon).

In addition, some common English words have highly modified meanings when used in Australia. For example, *forest land* has nothing to do with trees; it describes an expanse of grassland. A *mob* is a flock or herd, as in "a mob of geese."

Australians also abbreviate many nouns by shortening the word and ending it in *-ie* or *-o*. They call themselves *Aussies;* a letter carrier is a *postie;* someone who works on the docks is a *wharfie;* an Australian who is enlisted in the National Service is a *nasho;* swimming suits, which the Australians call *bathing costumes*, are abbreviated to *cossies;* and Australians enjoy their shrimp grilled on a *barbie.*

English undergoes similar changes in other countries where it is used. So, on a trip around the world, if you were to converse with English speakers in other countries, you would soon notice words in their vocabulary that are unfamiliar to you.

## Spelling

Generally, English words follow either the American spelling or the British spelling. Canadians and Australians tend to follow the British style. Notice the different spellings of the following words in the chart below.

| **American spelling** | labor | program | draft | tire | traveling |
|---|---|---|---|---|---|
| **British spelling** | labour | programme | draught | tyre | travelling |

## Pronunciation

Some English words receive different pronunciations around the world. Here too the American pronunciation tends to differ from the British pronunciation. Australians usually follow the British style, while Canadians adopt the American style.

In American English the word *lieutenant* is pronounced loo•**ten**•ant. The British, however, pronounce the same word lef•**ten**•ant. In the United States the pronunciation of *lever* rhymes with *ever;* in Britain it rhymes with *weaver.* Americans pronounce *figure* as **fig**•yer; the British pronounce it **fig**•er. And anyone who enjoys the Hollywood horror classic *Frankenstein*, starring British actor Boris Karloff, knows that the mad doctor always works in his la•**bore**•a•tree; were he an American, he would have created his monster in a **la**•bra•to•ry.

### Exercise 4

Do some research on the vocabulary, spelling, and pronunciation of American, British, Canadian, and Australian English. One source you might consult is *International English Usage* by Loreto Todd and Ian Hancock. What new words, spellings, and pronunciations can you add to those given in this lesson? Share your findings with the class.

## Wordworks

# Empty Language
## Doublespeak

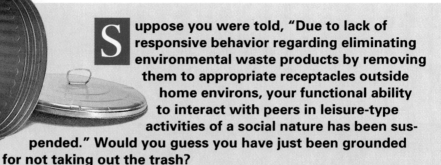

**Suppose you were told, "Due to lack of responsive behavior regarding eliminating environmental waste products by removing them to appropriate receptacles outside home environs, your functional ability to interact with peers in leisure-type activities of a social nature has been suspended." Would you guess you have just been grounded for not taking out the trash?**

The language of empty words and puffed-up phrases is called doublespeak. It is often used to mislead, disguise meaning, or make something seem more (or less) important than it is.

Doublespeak can seem humorous. For example, a report by one federal agency talked about "small faunal species" (rats), "aircraft with lower noise emission characteristics" (quieter planes), and areas "overlain by impervious surfaces" (paved). In the food industry, "food technologists" (people who develop food) create "food systems" (fake food) such as "cheese analogs" (fake cheese).

Sometimes doublespeak is not amusing. Politicians pass "revenue enhancers" (tax increases), and hospitals experience "negative patient-care outcomes" (deaths). Doublespeak can even be deadly. Bombing is called "air-to-ground activity," and civilian deaths and destruction of nonmilitary targets are called "collateral damage."

Doublespeak is used to mask reality and to limit thought—something to think about if you hear, "Nothing is certain but negative patient-care outcomes and revenue enhancers."

### Name Your Game—or, How to Doublespeak Without Trying

Here's a game one government official developed to create instant doublespeak phrases. Just choose any three numbers from 0 to 9, say 6-5-3 (no fair peeking at the list of words). Then read the corresponding words from each column: "optional logistical mobility." *Sounds* impressive, right? How might your phrase be rendered in simpler terms?

| | | |
|---|---|---|
| **0.** integrated | **0.** management | **0.** options |
| **1.** total | **1.** organizational | **1.** flexibility |
| **2.** systematized | **2.** monitored | **2.** software |
| **3.** parallel | **3.** reciprocal | **3.** mobility |
| **4.** functional | **4.** digital | **4.** programing |
| **5.** responsive | **5.** logistical | **5.** concept |
| **6.** optional | **6.** transitional | **6.** time-phase |
| **7.** synchronized | **7.** incremental | **7.** projection |
| **8.** compatable | **8.** third-generation | **8.** hardware |
| **9.** balanced | **9.** policy | **9.** contingency |

# 22.5 A Lingua Franca

When a German Lufthansa pilot requests clearance for takeoff at Rome's Leonardo da Vinci Airport and a Finnish Finnair copilot radios the tower at O'Hare International Airport in Chicago for landing instructions, the pilot, the copilot, and the tower personnel all have something in common. No matter what their native languages may be, on the job they all speak English, the official language of civil air transportation.

For international civil aviation, English has become a lingua franca, a language that facilitates communication among people with different native languages. Throughout history many languages have been used as lingua francas. Today, partly because of European colonial expansion during the eighteenth and nineteenth centuries, English has become a lingua franca—and sometimes even the official language—in some unlikely places around the world, including India, East Africa, the Republic of Fiji, Jamaica, and Nigeria, the most populous nation on the African continent.

## Nigerian English

An estimated four hundred languages are spoken within Nigeria's territorial borders. English, however, is both the official language of the country and the lingua franca of educated Nigerians.

English has a long history in Nigeria. British seafarers began visiting this part of West Africa during the fifteenth century. Modern Nigerian English reflects the growth and change of a transplanted language.

## Vocabulary

Just as American English has borrowed words from Native American languages, many words in contemporary Nigerian English have been borrowed from native Nigerian languages: *akara* ("bean cake," from Hausa) and *chichi* ("fritter," from Igbo).

Nigerian vocabulary also includes a number of calques. A calque is a word-for-word translation of a phrase from one language to another, with both the original phrase and the translated phrase having the same meaning. *Smell pepper* is a calque meaning "to suffer" in both its native language and in Nigerian English. Two other calques in Nigerian English are *spray money*, which means to attach money to dancers as an expression of appreciation, and *wash an event*, which means to celebrate an event by "washing it down" with beverages.

## Grammar

Nigerian English also has several grammatical features that distinguish it from American English.

1. *Could* and *would* are used where American English uses *can* and *will.*

   I **could** remember that she called last night.

   We **would** arrive at noon next Saturday.

2. Nouns that in American English are uncountable form their plurals like countable nouns.

   The class appreciates your **advices.**

   The new **machineries** will arrive next month.

3. Sometimes the definite article is omitted where it occurs in American English, and sometimes it is inserted where American English would omit it.

   She is in **hospital.**

   **The** freedom is a cherished human right.

4. Nigerians whose native language is Hausa will use *no* and *any* to mean "no" when speaking English.

   Unfortunately, I have **no any** money.

Nigeria isn't the only African nation where English has a strong presence. Kenya, Ghana, Egypt, Libya, and Malawi all have large English-speaking populations. It may be that English in Africa, as well as in other parts of the world, will become a dominant lingua franca as we enter the twenty-first century.

**Exercise 5**

Esperanto is a language created specifically to be a lingua franca, a universal language that would enable people throughout the world to communicate with one another. Find out more about Esperanto by researching books and encyclopedias. When was it created? By whom? Is it based on any existing languages? Discuss your findings in class, comparing your knowledge of English (and any other languages you may know) with Esperanto. Would a new language like Esperanto make a better worldwide lingua franca than an established language such as English? Why or why not?

## Wordworks

# Secret Languages

## Cracking the Code

**When you were younger did you ever "alktay ikelay isthay"? Or maybe "likemay thismay"? Or "likehay thishay"?**

As you may know, these odd-looking mishmashes of letters represent different dialects of "Pig Latin," one of the many "secret languages" that people have invented. Children are big fans of secret languages; using them makes children feel mysterious and keeps outsiders from eavesdropping on their secrets.

People all over the world use secret languages. In The Cat's Elbow, a German secret language, the vowel *o* is added after each consonant, and then the consonant is repeated. Gog-e-tot i-tot?

In China, children speak Sa-La, in which each syllable is repeated twice. The first repetition of the syllable begins with the letter *l*, and the second repetition begins with *s*. Ea-lea-sea-sy-ly-sy, right-light-sight?

One of the most complex secret languages—"upside-down talk," used by the Walbiri of Australia—distorts meaning rather than pronunciation. The sounds and order of the words remain the same, but all nouns, verbs, pronouns, and adjectives are replaced by their opposites. *These things are small* means, in English, *That one is big. Another is standing on the sky* means *I am sitting on the ground.* And *They are just beginning* means *We have come to the end.*

### Dodecocododode Tothohisos!

How "secret" are secret languages? Usually a code follows one or two simple rules which, when learned, make it easy to translate the language. See if you can figure out the rules for each of the following secret languages, and translate both passages. Then write a sentence or two using the secret languages.

### B Language

Tombom tombom thebe pibiperber's sonbon
Stolebole aba pigbig andband abawaybay hebe didbid runbun.
Thebe pigbig wasbas eatbeat andband tombom wasbas beatbeat
Andband tombom ranban crybyingbing downbown thebe streetbeet.

### Iggity

There was a young girl from New York
Who ate only soup with a fork.
To her mother's chagrin,
She grew terribly thin.
Moriggityaliggity: Eatiggityingiggity soupiggity withiggity aiggity forkiggity doesiggi-tyntiggity workiggity.

UNIT 23

# Library Resources

## 23.1 Locating a Book

Using a library efficiently means learning its layout and knowing its resources. Most libraries contain the same basic elements: books of fiction and nonfiction, reference works, periodicals, and various audio-visual materials. Some also have special collections of books on particular subjects, historical documents, or donated materials. Before using these, patrons must usually prove the legitimacy of their research.

If you're looking for specialized information, you might want to use a library that specializes in that subject area. Many universities, for example, have specialized libraries devoted entirely to law or music or art. If you want to use a university library's resources, ask the library staff to grant you special user's privileges.

### Classification Systems

Most libraries organize their materials by using either the Library of Congress classification system or the Dewey decimal system. The Library of Congress system, or LC, is more popular. In the LC, books are divided into twenty general categories, each represented by a letter. Each general category also has subcategories, which are identified by additional letters and a certain combination of numbers. For example, science, the category signified by the letter *Q*, is further broken down into *QA* for mathematics, *QB* for astronomy, *QC* for physics, and so on to *QR* for bacteriology.

| Library of Congress Classification System | | | |
|---|---|---|---|
| **Letters** | **Major Category** | **Letters** | **Major Category** |
| A | General works | N | Fine arts |
| B | Philosophy and religion | P | Language and literature |
| C–F | History | Q | Science |
| G | Geography and anthropology | R | Medicine |
| | | S | Agriculture |
| H | Social sciences | T | Technology |
| J | Political science | U | Military science |
| K | Law | V | Naval science |
| L | Education | Z | Bibliography and library science |
| M | Music | | |

The Dewey decimal system organizes books numerically into ten broad categories that also contain subcategories. The more specific the topic, the more specific the classification number. Books are shelved numerically by Dewey decimal number and then alphabetically by author. Fiction works are usually organized alphabetically on the shelves by authors' last names. If a library has more than one book by the same author, those books are also alphabetized by title. Look at the Dewey decimal chart and the example subject card that follows the chart.

| Dewey Decimal System | | |
|---|---|---|
| **Category Numbers** | **Major Category** | **Examples of Subcategories** |
| 000–099 | General works | Encyclopedias, bibliographies |
| 100–199 | Philosophy | Ethics, psychology |
| 200–299 | Religion | Theology, mythology |
| 300–399 | Social sciences | Law, political science, education |
| 400–499 | Language | Dictionaries, foreign languages |
| 500–599 | Sciences | Chemistry, astronomy, mathematics |
| 600–699 | Technology | Medicine, engineering, agriculture |
| 700–799 | Arts | Painting, music, theater, sports |
| 800–899 | Literature | Poetry, plays, essays |
| 900–999 | History and geography | Ancient history, biography |

## Card Catalogs and Computer Catalogs

Both paper and electronic catalogs contain the same information. You can locate fiction books by author or title; you can locate nonfiction books by author, title, or subject. The cards in a card catalog each have a call number—the book's classification number, printed in the upper left-hand corner. The same call number is printed on the spine of the book.

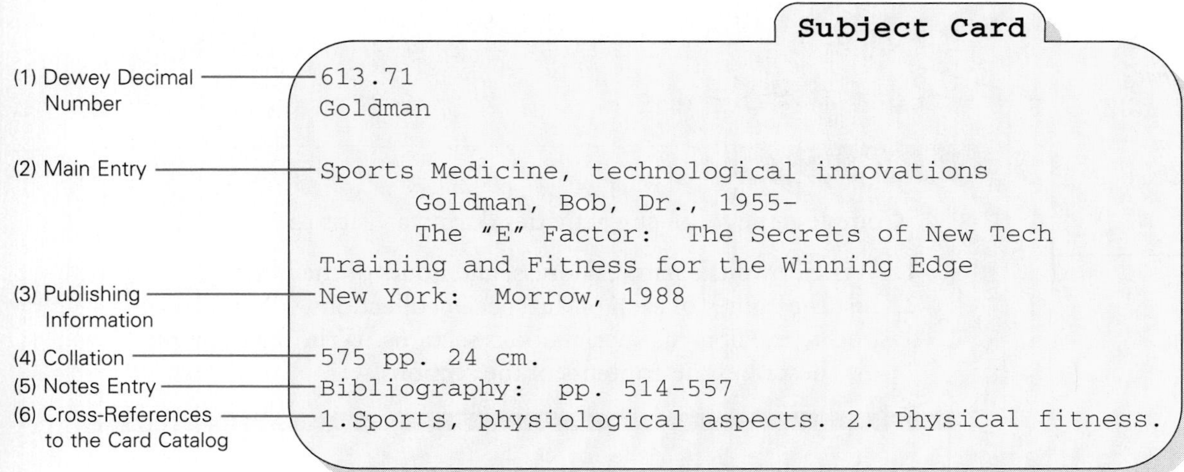

Subject Card
(1) Dewey Decimal Number
613.71
Goldman
(2) Main Entry
Sports Medicine, technological innovations
Goldman, Bob, Dr., 1955-
The "E" Factor: The Secrets of New Tech Training and Fitness for the Winning Edge
(3) Publishing Information
New York: Morrow, 1988
(4) Collation
575 pp. 24 cm.
(5) Notes Entry
Bibliography: pp. 514-557
(6) Cross-References to the Card Catalog
1.Sports, physiological aspects. 2. Physical fitness.

To search through alphabetical lists of authors, titles, and subjects:

Press key F5 (Author)
F6 (Title)
F7 (Subject)

Search for: sports medi

SPORTS MEDICINE
To select an entry, press the ↓ or ↑ key.
To see that entry, press ENTER.

| | Titles |
|---|---|
| Sports Medicine – Bibliographies | 4 |
| Sports Medicine – Congresses | 3 |
| Sports Medicine – Dictionaries | 1 |
| Sports Medicine – Handbooks and Manuals | 14 |
| Sports Medicine – Technological Innovations | 3 |
| Sports Medicine – Vocational Guidance | 2 |

To return to the opening screen, press F1
To return to the previous screen, press F2

SPORTS MEDICINE:
TECHNOLOGICAL INNOVATIONS
To view other titles, press PG UP or PG DN

| | |
|---|---|
| AUTHOR | Goldman, Bob 1955- |
| TITLE | The "E" Factor: The Secrets of New Tech Training and Fitness for the Winning Edge |
| PUB/DATE | New York: Morrow, 1988 |
| DESCRIPTION | CIP reported |
| LOCATION | 613.71 Goldman |
| NOTE | Bibliography |

To return to the opening screen, press F1
To return to the previous screen, press F2

*On-screen prompts tell you how to operate the computer catalog to search for resources. These screens show the progress of a computer catalog search.*

*A computer catalog electronically searches for authors, titles, and subjects.*

Some books, such as biographies, autobiographies, oversize books, and special references, are often shelved in separate sections. Letters above the call number will denote such a book and its section.

*ART and RARE designations in the first two lines indicate that this book can be found in the Rare Book Collection of the Art Library.*

```
ART
RARE      O'Keeffe, Georgia, 1887-1986
ND 237       Georgia O'Keeffe. New York
0  5         Viking Press, 1976. ca. 200 p.:
A 46         col. ill; 42 cm. (A Studio book)
1976
4•
```

*Patrons of this library are informed in the Guide to Book Stacks: "Call numbers that end in '4 •' are OVERSIZE and are shelved in a separate section on each floor."*

## Exercise 7

Complete the following activities during a visit to a library.

1. Write down the name, address, and hours of the library.
2. List the names of each of the special collections.
3. Locate the library's special books sections. Write a paragraph that describes the contents of the sections.

# 23.2 Locating Periodicals

Newspapers, magazines, and journals are the best sources of up-to-date information on current events or specialized fields of rapid change, such as the sciences. Special indexes make locating information in periodicals quick and easy.

## Using Indexes

Like book catalogs, indexes for periodicals can be printed on paper or computerized. Indexes can also be stored as microforms—small photographs of printed pages. Microforms include microfilm (filmstrips) and microfiche (film cards). Periodical indexes are most commonly reproduced on microfilm. Both microfilm and microfiche are viewed on special machines with screens that magnify the text. A librarian can give you instructions about their operation.

Unlike book catalogs, there are many periodical indexes. Some indexes are specialized and cover only one publication, such as the *New York Times Index*, which may be available on paper or on microfilm. Other indexes, such as the *Business Periodicals Index*, cover one field. Still other periodical indexes are general and cover many subjects. General indexes include the *Magazine Index*, a microfilm index, and the *Readers' Guide to Periodical Literature*, a paper index.

## *Readers' Guide to Periodical Literature*

The most popular paper index for magazine articles is the *Readers' Guide to Periodical Literature*. Articles from over 175 magazines are indexed by author and by subject. The *Readers' Guide* is updated by special paperback supplements every two weeks. Larger paperback editions covering a three-month period are published quarterly. Hardbound volumes of all the entries for an entire year are issued at the end of each year. The *Readers' Guide* also indexes book reviews in a separate book review section. Sometimes titles for fiction works are indexed as well.

Subjects are organized alphabetically under subject headings, which may be further subdivided. Under each heading, articles are listed alphabetically by title. For example, in the excerpt that follows, the subject heading is OIL FIRES; one of the subdivisions is "Kuwait." Articles about oil fires in Kuwait are listed alphabetically by title under "Kuwait."

If you are writing a research paper or are seeking information about a specific subject, cast a wide net. Check several issues of the *Readers' Guide* for relevant articles. For a historical perspective, check older issues. Cross-references in the *Readers' Guide* will help you to find related information. The annotated excerpt from the *Readers' Guide* on the next page shows you the format of *Readers' Guide* listings.

*Subject headings are in boldfaced capital letters. Subdivision titles are centered and arranged alphabetically under the subject.*

*Explanations of article titles are in brackets. The abbreviation "il" means "illustrated." "137:50–1 My 27 '91" means "volume 137, pages 50–51 in the May 27, 1991, issue."*

*Author entries include works written by an author or about an author.*

**OIL FIRES**

**Kuwait**

Clouds over Kuwait. il *World Press Review* 38:55 My '91

Death in the Gulf. T. A. Roberts. il map *Buzzworm* 3:52–9 My/Je '91

Getting blacker every day [Kuwaiti oil fire fallout]. E. Linden. il map *Time* 137:50–1 My 27, '91

The Kuwait cleanup: who's in charge here? R. Buderi. il *Business Week* p. 54+ My 27 '91

Satellite depicts Kuwaiti oil-well fires. il *Science News* 139:197 Mr 30 '91

**OIL POLLUTION**

Trouble below [leaking underground storage tanks]. C. Tevis. il *Successful Farming* 90:16 Ap '91

**Alaska**

*See also* Exxon Valdez (Ship) oil spill, 1989

**Persian Gulf**

Death in the Gulf. T. A. Roberts. il map *Buzzworm* 3:52–9 My/Je '91

The Kuwait cleanup: who's in charge here? R. Buderi. il *Business Week* p. 54+ My 27 '91

**O'LAUGHLIN, MICHAEL**

To die in New Orleans. il por *Commonweal* 118:321–3 My 17 '91

## Other Indexes

More specialized indexes covering individual fields include the *General Science Index*, the *Applied Science and Technology Index*, and the *Social Science Index*. The *Wall Street Journal Index* covers a single publication. In addition, the *CBS News Index* offers microfilm and microfiche transcripts of its daily television news broadcasts and programs, such as *60 Minutes* and *CBS Reports*.

### Exercise 2

Use the preceding excerpt from the *Readers' Guide* to answer the following questions.

1. What are the subdivisions of OIL POLLUTION?
2. If you wanted to see a map of the damage done by the Kuwaiti oil fires, in which articles would you look?
3. Which article about the Kuwaiti oil fires was published first? ➟

4. If you wanted to read articles with a business slant about the Kuwaiti oil fires, which articles would you choose?
5. If you wanted to read an article about leaking underground storage tanks, in which article would you look?
6. In what issue of *Commonweal* was the article about Michael O'Laughlin published?

## 23.3 Additional Sources of Information

Many libraries have an overwhelming number of resources. To find the answer to a particular question, you won't want to wade through countless volumes. Reference works provide a shortcut for your search.

### General Reference Works

You are already familiar with many general reference works, including encyclopedias, yearbooks, and atlases. The chart below reviews some of these valuable resources.

| General Reference Works | |
|---|---|
| **Type of Source** | **Examples of Sources** |
| **Encyclopedias** contain alphabetically arranged articles about a broad range of subjects. | *World Book Encyclopedia, Encyclopædia Britannica, Encyclopedia Americana, Columbia Encyclopedia* |
| **Biographies** contain brief histories for persons living and deceased. Biographies are usually organized by the subject area or field in which the person is best known. | *Contemporary Authors, Current Biography, Everyman's Dictionary of Literary Biography, Who's Who in America, Dictionary of American Biography* |
| **Yearbooks and Almanacs** are published annually. They contain information and statistics for the past year. | *Americana Annual, Britannica Book of the Year, Europa Year Book, The World Almanac and Book of Facts, World Book Yearbook* |
| **Atlases** contain maps, charts, plates, or tables illustrating the world or a region. | *Hammond Ambassador World Atlas, National Atlas of the United States of America, Times Atlas of the World* |
| **Gazetteers** are geographical dictionaries. | *Chambers World Gazetteer, Webster's New Geographical Dictionary* |

## Specialized Reference Works

Many fields have their own specialized resources. For example, the *Encyclopedia of Dance and Ballet*, the *Encyclopedia of World History*, the *McGraw-Hill Encyclopedia of Science and Technology*, and the *Encyclopedia of World Art* are invaluable to students in those fields. The following chart lists additional resources specific to the study of literature.

| Using Literature Reference Works to Answer Questions | |
|---|---|
| **Questions** | **Sources for Answers** |
| **1.** Why was Tess, in Thomas Hardy's novel *Tess of the d'Urbervilles,* considered bathetic? Where is this novel set? | **1.** *Oxford Companion to English Literature, A Literary Gazetteer of England, A Mapbook of English Literature* |
| **2.** How did Mark Twain's writing style change during his lifetime? | **2.** *Oxford Companion to American Literature, Critical Dictionary of English Literature and British and American Authors* |
| **3.** What is the outstanding characteristic of Cyrano de Bergerac, the main character in the French play of the same name? | **3.** *Columbia Dictionary of Modern European Literature, Penguin Companion to European Literature, Cassell's Encyclopedia of World Literature* |
| **4.** Which Greek dramatist wrote a trilogy of tragedies about a son who unknowingly murders his father and marries his mother? What is the plot of each play? | **4.** *Oxford Companion to Classical Literature; Penguin Companion to Classical, Oriental, and African Literature* |
| **5.** Who was the Egyptian author who won the Nobel Prize for literature in 1988? | **5.** *MLA International Bibliography, The New York Public Library Desk Reference* |

## Electronic Sources of Information

Many libraries use computer databases to store information about both their holdings and those of other libraries. Some databases are easy to access. The computer catalog search-in-progress on page 738 is an example of such a database. Other databases require a library staff member to run them.

You begin a computer search by typing in key words. The computer searches its database for those key words and lists corresponding information sources. If key words are general, such as *ecology,* many titles will be displayed; if key words are specific, such as *stream ecology,* fewer titles will be displayed. Use specific words to target your needs.

Some libraries have databases that include only books; others have databases for periodical articles, unpublished materials, and government documents. A few libraries are electronically linked to a central database that pools the titles of the books and periodicals in all libraries in the network. If a local library does not own what a researcher requires, one of the libraries in the network may be able to provide it. Some search services provide on-line information about all titles on a given subject. These searches are usually available only on a fee-for-use basis. Your research librarian can suggest the most useful electronic sources.

## Using Parts of a Book

Using all parts of a book can help you to determine whether a book has useful information. The title page contains the complete book title, edition number, and author's name. The copyright page tells when the book was first published and how recently it was updated, which can help you to determine whether the book is outdated. The table of contents identifies the topics covered. The introduction, if it is written by the author, may indicate the author's purpose. If the introduction is written by another person, it may provide you with a larger context in which to view the author's work.

In the back of a book, the appendix may contain additional information, such as maps, charts, tables, illustrations, or graphs. The glossary alphabetically lists special terms used in the book or field. For example, some computer books list acronyms. The bibliography lists other sources of information for material covered in the book. If you are preparing a research paper, use the bibliography to locate other sources of information. The index alphabetically lists all people, places, events, and significant topics covered in the book. The index pinpoints the specific page on which this information appears.

### Exercise 3

Use the charts and information found in this unit to name possible reference sources that could be used to answer each of the following questions.

1. What cities are currently located near the sites of Shakespeare's play *Macbeth*?
2. When it is 2:00 A.M. in Paris, what time is it in Sao Paolo?
3. What are South Africa's chief crops?
4. Which American author wrote *Moby Dick*?
5. Which French author is primarily responsible for instituting the Theater of the Absurd?
6. Is there a library nearby with *The Story of English*?
7. What is Draconian law?
8. What was Mikhail Gorbachev's first occupation?
9. Which city hosted the 1992 winter Olympics?
10. Where would you look in a world history book to find out whether it covers the Peloponnesian War?

UNIT

# 24 Using Dictionaries

## 24.1 Varieties of Dictionaries

Dr. Samuel Johnson, with only six assistants, published the first major English dictionary (with more than 40,000 entries) in 1755. He had accomplished in only nine years what forty Frenchmen needed forty years to produce: the first national dictionary.

### General Dictionaries

Two types of general dictionaries are available—abridged and unabridged. You should be familiar with the components and advantages of each.

**Types of General Dictionaries** You're probably most familiar with college dictionaries, often called abridged dictionaries. Although abridged means "shortened," these dictionaries contain more than 150,000 entries and provide detailed definitions that are sufficient for most college students and general users. College dictionaries also contain separate lists of abbreviations, biographical and geographical names, foreign words and phrases, and tables of measures. *Webster's II New Riverside University Dictionary* and the *American Heritage Dictionary of the English Language* are college dictionaries.

Unabridged dictionaries contain as many as 500,000 entries and provide detailed definitions and extensive word histories (etymologies). These dictionaries, possibly in several volumes and mostly found in libraries, are excellent sources for scholarly inquiries. Unabridged dictionaries include the *Oxford English Dictionary* and the *Random House Dictionary of the English Language.*

**Dictionary Main Entries** A dictionary entry has many elements: multiple definitions, syllabication, preferred spelling and pronunciation (some words have more than one acceptable spelling and pronunciation), and part-of-speech labels. Some entries also include plurals and capitalized forms, synonyms, antonyms, and derivatives. Americanisms and etymologies may be provided along with usage notes, cross-references, and idioms. The dictionary entries for *feat* illustrate some of these features.

The two entries for *feat* indicate they are homographs—words that are spelled the same but have different etymologies and meanings. The label *archaic* indicates a meaning no longer in common usage. You may encounter archaic meanings in classic literature.

[1]**feat** \'fēt\ *n* [ME *fait,* fr. MF, fr. L *factum,* fr. neut. of *factus,* pp. of *facere* to make, do — more at DO] (14c) **1 :** ACT, DEED **2 a :** a deed notable esp. for courage **b :** an act or product of skill, endurance, or ingenuity

***syn*** FEAT, EXPLOIT, ACHIEVEMENT mean a remarkable deed. FEAT implies strength or dexterity or daring; EXPLOIT suggests an adventurous or heroic act; ACHIEVEMENT implies hard-won success in the face of difficulty or opposition.

[2]**feat** *adj* [ME *fete, fayt,* fr. MF, *fait* pp. of *faire* ] (15c) **1** *archaic* : BECOMING, NEAT **2** *archaic* : SMART, DEXTEROUS

*The etymology appears in brackets;* [1]feat *came from Middle English* fait, *which came from Middle French, which came from the Latin word* facere, *meaning "to make" or "to do."*

*Synonym notes differentiate words that have close meanings.*

*Homographs are words that are spelled the same but that have different etymologies and meanings. Homographs are marked by small raised numbers immediately before or after the entry word.*

## Using Specialized Dictionaries

Specialized dictionaries provide in-depth information about a particular field. For example, there are dictionaries for the specialized vocabularies of law, computer technology, and medicine. In addition, there are dictionaries of synonyms, clichés, slang, and even regional expressions, such as the *Dictionary of American Regional English (DARE).* There are also dictionaries of foreign languages, famous people's names, literary characters' names, and place names. Other examples of specialized dictionaries are in the following chart.

**Specialized Dictionaries**

| Question | Sources for Answers |
|---|---|
| • Was Pancho Gonzales born in Mexico? | *Dictionary of Mexican American History* |
| • When were the United Arab Emirates formed? | *Political Dictionary of the Arab World; Dictionary of Dates* |
| • What was the significance of the Civil War campaign at Antietam? | *The Civil War Dictionary; Dictionary of American History* |
| • Where is James Joyce buried? | *A Dictionary of Irish Biography; Dictionary of Irish Literature* |
| • What does a television director mean if he or she writes "Z1" on notes to a camera operator? | *NTC's Mass Media Dictionary* |
| • Was Zora Neale Hurston's early life difficult? | *Dictionary of American Negro Biography* |
| • What has Costa Rica's standard of living been in the last fifty years? | *Dictionary of Development; Dictionary of Modern Economics* |

**Exercise 1**

List which sources in the chart of specialized dictionaries might be consulted to answer the following questions.

1. What is the international banking zone?
2. What is meant if an actress gives a "Macbeth"?
3. What happened at Goliad, Texas, during the Texas Revolt?
4. What was Yevgeny Yevgenevich Yeney's function at the Leningrad film studios?
5. What are African American author Richard Wright's famous works?
6. When did Francis Joy found the *Belfast News Letter*?
7. What were the effects of World War II on the Mexican economy and the political climate?
8. How can you find out what the UNEF was in the Middle East?
9. Who was the "Angel of Cairo" in the Civil War?
10. How have interest rates in the United States changed in the past five years?

## 24.2 Kinds of Thesauruses

A thesaurus lists synonyms. The best known thesaurus is *Roget's Thesaurus*, named for the British doctor, Peter Mark Roget. Words in a thesaurus may be arranged in traditional style or dictionary style.

### Traditional Style

A traditional-style thesaurus groups words by category. Using a traditional *Roget's* is a two-step process: first you must look up a word in the index. Each entry has a number next to it. Then look up the number from the index in the body of the thesaurus. If you want a synonym for the word "intelligent," this is what you will find.

*This is the twelfth entry in the category INTELLIGENCE, WISDOM. "ADJ" indicates these words are adjectives. Notice that "intellectual" is an archaic synonym and "not so dumb" is an informal synonym.*

.12 ADJ **intelligent**, intellectual [archaic]; ideational, conceptual, conceptive, discursive, sophic, noetic; knowing, understanding, reasonable, rational, sensible, bright; sane 472.4; not so dumb [informal], strong-minded

*Notice that the synonym "sane" refers you to another entry.*

## Dictionary Style

Thesauruses in dictionary style present words in alphabetical order. Each word is followed by several synonyms and cross-references to any related major category. A major category includes nouns, verbs, adjectives, and adverbs all related to one main idea. Antonyms are not listed, but they may be indicated by a cross-reference at the end of an entry. See the thesaurus entry for OCCASION that follows.

*Major categories, such as OCCASION, appear in capital letters. For additional synonyms for "occasion," see CIRCUMSTANCE, EVENT, and LEISURE.*

**OCCASION**

*Nouns*——occasion, opportunity, room; CIRCUMSTANCE, EVENT; opportuneness; crisis, turn, juncture, psychological moment, conjuncture; turning point; given time; nick of time; chance of a lifetime; golden opportunity; clear field; spare time; LEISURE.

*Verbs*——seize an opportunity; suit the occasion; strike while the iron is hot; make hay while the sun shines, take time by the forelock; take the bull by the horns. *Slang*, get the jump on, jump the gun.

*Adjectives*——opportune, timely, well-timed, seasonable; providential, lucky, fortunate, happy, favorable, propitious, auspicious, critical; apropos, suitable (see AGREEMENT)

*Synonyms are listed by part of speech. They may be labeled by level of usage. In this example, "get the jump on" and "jump the gun" are labeled as "Slang."*

*Sometimes you will be referred to a particularly helpful entry by a cross-reference. If you are looking for a word that means* suitable, *"see AGREEMENT" tells you to look under "agreement" for more synonyms.*

When you use words from a thesaurus, make sure they express the meaning you intend. For example, you may be at a *juncture* but not in a *crisis* or in a *chance of a lifetime* situation.

### Exercise 2

Use a thesaurus to find two synonyms for each word below. Then, on a separate sheet of paper, write an original sentence to illustrate the meaning of each synonym. You may wish to check the exact meaning of each word in a dictionary before you use it in a sentence.

1. obstinacy
2. incredulity
3. hindrance
4. fashion
5. perpetuity
6. undertaking
7. unskillfulness
8. copy
9. cooperation
10. clothing

UNIT 25

# Vocabulary

## 25.1 Analyzing Words in Context

A large vocabulary allows you to choose words that exactly express what you mean. For example, many words express shades of conscientiousness: *exacting*, *punctilious*, *fussy*, *finicky*, and *particular*. If you want to tell your coach that he's conscientious, you won't want to use the word *fussy*.

### Learning Words from Context

New words usually appear in a setting with familiar words. You can often determine a word's meaning by examining its setting, or context.

**Specific Context Clues** Sometimes the context in which a word is used provides obvious clues to its meaning. If you watch for the clues, you can often figure out the meaning of a new word. Even if you think that you can guess a word's meaning from its context, always use a dictionary to verify its meaning. In addition to providing multiple definitions of a word, a dictionary will also provide a word's pronunciation and, in some cases, even a guide to correct usage. In the following examples, use the clue word to glean the meanings of the unfamiliar words.

| Learning Words from Context | | |
|---|---|---|
| | **Clue Words** | **Example** |
| **Examples as Clues** | for example, such as, for instance, like, including, especially | Feelings *such as* tiredness, sluggishness, and indifference often create a *lethargic* state. |
| When examples are used, the meaning of the unfamiliar word is gleaned through other illustrations. You can figure out that *lethargic* means "sluggish" from the examples. | | |
| **Comparisons as Clues** | also, likewise, similarly, in the same way, like, as | *Like harbingers*, robins and daffodils indicated that spring was imminent. |
| When comparisons are made, you can liken an unfamiliar word to a familiar word. Because you know that robins "announce" that spring is on its way, you can figure out that a *harbinger* is a herald that announces the approach of something. | | |

| Learning Words from Context | | |
|---|---|---|
| | **Clue Words** | **Example** |
| **Contrasts as Clues** | but, on the contrary, unlike, however, although, in contrast to, whereas | *Unlike* his laughing, victorious rival, the defeated player looked *despondent.* |
| A contrast shows the unfamiliar word as the opposite of a familiar word or phrase. You can figure out that *despondent* means the opposite of *laughing. Despondent* means "feeling extreme discouragement or depression." | | |
| **Causes and Effects as Clues** | because, since, therefore, when | The first test-review session was voluntary, and no one came; *since* we all failed the test, the next test-review session will be *mandatory.* |
| An action's unfamiliar cause can be understood by a familiar effect, or a familiar cause can explain an unfamiliar effect. You can figure out that a *mandatory* session is not voluntary; *mandatory* means "obligatory." | | |
| **Definitions as Clues** | which means, that is, which is, who is | Rita loves to examine fossils and wants to become a *paleontologist,* a scientist who studies forms of life existing in former geologic periods. |
| A definition provides an explanation of the unfamiliar word. You know, therefore, that a *paleontologist* is a scientist who studies fossils. | | |
| **Restatements as Clues** | or, also known as, in other words, also called | A person who receives a *writ,* or court order, must legally obey it. |
| Restatements of unfamiliar words simply reword them in more familiar ways. You can easily understand that a *writ* is a court order. | | |

Punctuation marks can also supply clues; for example, restatements and definitions might be set off with commas or dashes: "The Vatican is an enclave—an independent country—surrounded by Italy." Semicolons are often used before clue words, which is the case in the Causes and Effects as Clues example.

**General Context Clues** Even without clue words, you can often guess the meaning of an unfamiliar word from the larger context in which it appears. In the next example, you can guess the general meaning of *habitation* from supporting details. For instance, the *habitation* mentioned was "large enough for many guests" and "without a household fire."

My heart was a habitation large enough for many guests, but lonely and chill, and without a household fire. I longed to kindle one! It seemed not so wild a dream.

—Nathaniel Hawthorne, *The Scarlet Letter*

Since the context indicates that *habitation* is some sort of living quarters, you might also try to substitute familiar words, such as *residence* or *dwelling*, in the place of the unfamiliar word. You might want to think of related words, such as the word *inhabit*. *Inhabit* means "to live in." A *habitation* is a dwelling place. Look at the next example.

Our simple life and peaceful, healthy routine were violently interrupted, and we were precipitated into the midst of a series of events which caused the utmost excitement not only in Cornwall but throughout the whole west of England.

—Sir Arthur Conan Doyle, "The Adventure of the Devil's Foot"

Even if you do not know what *precipitated* means, you probably know the meaning of *precipitation* from listening to weather reports. You might guess that *precipitated* means something like "rained into" or "brought into." You can guess that *precipitate* involves sudden or abrupt movement because the sentence speaks of being "violently interrupted." In fact, this is correct.

## Enhancing Your Word Power

Having an extensive vocabulary helps you to figure out the meaning of new words more quickly. Even if you think you have correctly guessed the meaning of a new word from its context, however, always use a dictionary to check the pronunciation as well as the word's multiple meanings. Maintain a list of new words on which to study and quiz yourself.

### Exercise 1

For each of the following sentences, use context clues to determine the meaning of the word in italic type. On a separate sheet of paper, write the word and what you think it means. Verify the accuracy of your guess by looking up the word in a dictionary.

1. Copper is far more *malleable* than steel; it can easily be shaped by hammering or pressing.
2. In contrast to the modern scientific theories he expresses, his lab procedures seem *antediluvian*.
3. The ending of Mendelssohn's *Scherzo* has to be played *pianissimo*—very softly. ➡

4. The hockey player and puck *caromed* off the sideboards just as the referee gave the sign for high-sticking.
5. The captain sent a *reconnaissance* patrol out at the beginning of the evening, but by morning they had learned nothing about the location of the enemy's army.
6. The prices in that store run the *gamut* from being extraordinarily inexpensive to requiring an outrageous outlay of money.
7. Proctors are not allowed to *iterate* the directions; test-takers are expected to understand them after hearing them once.
8. Whereas learning should be a joyful task, many groups make it an *onerous* one.

## 25.2 Analyzing Word Parts

In addition to context clues, an analysis of a word's parts may also provide clues to its meaning. Many common word parts have their origins in Latin and Greek words. If you know what some of those word parts mean, you can often guess the meaning of an unfamiliar word. A word may contain three parts, as shown below.

**Prefix** *A prefix comes before the main part of a word; this prefix,* trans-, *is a Latin prefix meaning "across" or "through."*

**Root** *A root is the core of a word; this root,* fer, *is a Latin root meaning "to carry."*

**Suffix** *A suffix is attached to the ending of a word; this suffix,* -able, *means "able to do" and changes the verb "transfer" into an adjective meaning "able to be transferred."*

## Word Roots

While prefixes and suffixes can give you hints about a word's meaning, the word's root provides the real clue. In the word *transferable*, the prefix *trans-* and the suffix *-able* have been attached to the root *fer* and modify its meaning.

In the list on the next page, the roots suggest the meaning of the words in the Examples column. Sometimes, however, you'll encounter words that do not mean what their roots suggest. For example, *fervent* means "exhibiting a great intensity of feeling." Whenever necessary, check a word's meaning in a dictionary.

| Word Roots | | |
|---|---|---|
| **Root** | **Meaning** | **Examples** |
| *ag, ac* | do | agenda, action |
| *agr* | farm | agriculture, agribusiness |
| *am* | love, friend | amorous, amicable |
| *audi* | hear | auditorium, audience |
| *ben, bene* | good, well | benign, benevolent |
| *bio* | life | biopsy, biochemistry |
| *cide* | killing, killer | germicide, homicide |
| *corp* | body | corps, corpse, corpulent |
| *cred, credit* | believe | incredulity, accredit |
| *cur, curs* | run | concur, cursory |
| *dict* | speak | dictator, diction |
| *duc, duct* | lead, draw | deduce, conduct, viaduct |
| *ferous* | bearing, producing | coniferous, somniferous |
| *fid* | faith, trust | confidant, fidelity |
| *grat* | pleasant, thank, favor | congratulate, gratuity |
| *gress, grad* | step, walk, go | egress, transgress, gradation |
| *ject* | throw | conjecture, eject, inject |
| *jur, jus* | law | jury, justice |
| *leg, lect* | read | legible, intellectual |
| *locut* | speak, talk | circumlocution, interlocutor |
| *logy* | science, study | bacteriology, genealogy |
| *mis, mit* | send | emissary, remit |
| *mon, monit* | warn | admonish, premonition |
| *mor, mort* | death | mordant, mortal, mortician |
| *path, pathy* | feeling, suffering | pathetic, empathy |
| *phil, phile* | loving, fond of | philanthropist, Anglophile |
| *phon* | sound | telephone, phonics |
| *phys* | body, nature | physical, physics |
| *prehend* | seize, grasp | apprehend, comprehend |
| *scrib, script* | write | scribble, manuscript |
| *secut, sequ* | follow | consecutive, sequel |
| *tact, tang* | touch | contact, tangible |
| *terr* | earth | territory, extraterrestrial |
| *tomy* | cutting, operation of | anatomy, lobotomy |
| *vac* | empty | vacuum, vacuous, evacuation |
| *vert, vers* | turn | avert, perverse |

# Word Prefixes

Prefixes are attached to the beginning of words. Prefixes can modify, change, or completely reverse the meaning of a root. Prefixes commonly show quantity, time, direction, or position. Notice that some prefixes in the following chart have more than one meaning.

**Word Prefixes**

| | Prefix | Meaning | Prefixes in Words |
|---|---|---|---|
| **Prefixes Showing Quantity or Size** | *semi-, hemi-* | half | semiannual, hemisphere |
| | *uni-, mon-, mono-* | one | unicycle, monarchy, monorail |
| | *bi-, di-, dich-* | two | bimonthly, dilemma, dichotomy |
| | *macro-* | large, long | macrocosm, macrostructure |
| | *micro-* | small | microscopic, microbe |
| | *omni-* | all, every, everywhere | omnipotent, omniscient |
| | *poly-* | many | polyglot, polysyllabic |
| | *quadr-, quar-* | four | quadruple, quartet |
| | *tri-* | three | tripod, triangle |
| **Prefixes Showing Negation** | *a-, an-* | not, without | abacterial, atypical |
| | *ant-, anti-* | against | antacid, antipathy |
| | *counter-* | opposite to | counterclockwise, counterweight |
| | *de-* | remove, reduce | devalue, dehorn |
| | *dis-* | deprive of, do the opposite of | disbelieve, disillusion, disinterest |
| | *im-, in-, un-* | without, not | immoral, invalid, unsold |
| | *mis-* | hate, bad | misanthrope, misfortune |
| | *pseudo-* | false | pseudonym, pseudoscience |
| **Prefixes Showing Direction or Position** | *circum-* | around | circumnavigate, circumspect |
| | *eu-* | good, well, advantageous | eulogize, euphemism, euphoria |
| | *exo-, extra-* | out of, outside | exotic, extraordinary |
| | *hetero-* | different | heterogeneous, heteronym |
| | *hom-, homo-* | same | homogenized, homograph |
| | *inter-* | between, among | international, interdependent |
| | *intra-* | within | intrastate, intramural |
| | *mid-* | in the middle of | midlife, midweek |
| | *peri-* | around, about, near, enclosing | periscope, periphery, peripatetic |
| | *pro-, pre-* | in front of | proceed, precede, prefix |
| | *sub-* | below, outside of | submarine, suburban |
| | *super-* | above, over | supervise, supercharge |
| | *trans-* | across, over | transporter, transgress |

# Word Suffixes

Suffixes can be added to the ends of words to create new words with new meanings. Besides having specific meanings, suffixes also have grammatical functions. Notice that the spelling of a root may change when a suffix is added. The following chart lists some common suffixes, their meanings, and the parts of speech that they may signify.

| Word Suffixes | | | | |
|---|---|---|---|---|
| | **Suffix** | **Meanings** | **Original Word** | **New Word** |
| **Suffixes That Form Nouns** | *-acy* | state, act, quality of | democrat | democracy |
| | *-age* | result, process | lever | leverage |
| | *-al* | state, act, quality of | commit | committal |
| | *-ance* | state, quality | relevant | relevance |
| | *-ant, -ent* | agent, doer | reside | resident |
| | *-ce* | state, act, quality of | independent | independence |
| | *-dom* | condition, state | king | kingdom |
| | *-er, -or* | doer, maker, resident | bake, island | baker, islander |
| | *-hood* | state, act, quality of | adult | adulthood |
| | *-ism* | system, practice | commune | communism |
| | *-ment* | action, result | astonish | astonishment |
| | *-ness* | quality, state | light | lightness |
| | *-ship* | state, act, quality of | partner | partnership |
| | *-th* | state, act, quality of | warm | warmth |
| | *-tion, -sion* | action, state, result | prosecute | prosecution |
| | *-tude* | quality, state | sole | solitude |
| | *-ty* | state, act, quality of | secure | security |
| **Suffixes That Form Adjectives** | *-able* | capable of | read | readable |
| | *-al* | characteristic of | nation | national |
| | *-en* | made of, like | trod | trodden |
| | *-fold* | to a certain degree | five | fivefold |
| | *-ful* | full of, having | wonder | wonderful |
| | *-ile* | capable, like | infant | infantile |
| | *-ish* | like | self | selfish |
| | *-ive* | capable, able to | adapt | adaptive |
| | *-less* | lacking, without | care | careless |
| | *-ous* | full of | space | spacious |
| | *-some* | apt to, tending to | burden | burdensome |
| | *-ward* | in the direction of | home | homeward |
| | *-y* | resembling, full of | bone | bony |
| **Suffixes That Form Verbs** | *-ate* | become, form | fluoride | fluoridate |
| | *-en* | make, cause to be | length | lengthen |
| | *-fy, -ify* | cause, make | verity | verify |
| | *-ize* | make, cause to be | modern | modernize |

## Exercise 2

Analyze the following words for their roots, prefixes, and suffixes. (Most of the words won't have all three parts.) Write what you think each word means, but be aware that not all words mean what their word parts indicate. Use a dictionary to check your accuracy.

1. autocratic
2. biophysics
3. monograph
4. herbivorous
5. pedestrian
6. aggressive
7. immortality
8. ingrate
9. credentials
10. tenacious
11. astringent
12. insectivorous
13. homicide
14. incorruptible
15. philanthropist
16. impediment
17. retrogression
18. concurrent
19. consecutive
20. coniferous
21. missile
22. amorphous
23. anonymous
24. atheism
25. symbiosis
26. ductile
27. psychology
28. odoriferous
29. intermittent
30. precursor

## Exercise 3

Create a list of 20 words, using in each word at least one word part from the following list of roots, prefixes, and suffixes; for example, tran*script*, *circum*stance, standard*ize*. Check the spelling of each word in a dictionary.

| Roots | Prefixes | Suffixes |
|---|---|---|
| *ac, ag* | *exo-, extra-* | *-ance* |
| *audi* | *anti-* | *-er, -or* |
| *am* | *omni-* | *-ness* |
| *capit* | *a-, an-* | *-ship* |
| *cide* | *counter-* | *-tion, -sion* |
| *corp* | *dys-* | *-able* |
| *dic, dict* | *im-, in-, un-* | *-en* |
| *ject* | *circum-* | *-ive* |
| *leg, lect* | *inter-* | *-less* |
| *locut, loqu* | *sub-* | *-ous* |
| *mor, mort* | *micro-* | *-less* |
| *phone* | *tri-* | *-hood* |
| *scrib, script* | *pre-, pro-* | *-ate* |
| *ter, terr* | *uni-, mon-, mono-* | *-en* |
| *vac* | *mid-* | *-fy, -ify* |
| *vert, vers* | *mis-* | *-ize* |

UNIT 26

# Spelling

## 26.1 Spelling Rules

If you have problems spelling words correctly, try this method: First, check the spelling in a dictionary. Then say the word aloud. Say it again, pronouncing each syllable. Visualize the word. Write it several times. Use this method in conjunction with the rules in this lesson.

### Mastering the Basics

Since most words follow spelling rules, learning the rules will help you to spell words correctly. However, because not all words follow the rules, you should check the spelling of difficult words in a dictionary.

**Adding Prefixes** You are probably already familiar with prefixes such as *co-*, *dis-*, *ex-*, *infra-*, *ir-*, *macro-*, *mid-*, *mis-*, *multi-*, *pre-*, *pro-*, *re-*, *sub-*, *ultra-*, and *un-*. Here are the two rules for spelling words with prefixes.

**Adding Prefixes**

When adding a prefix to a word, retain the spelling of the original word.

*ir-* + rational = irrational
*non-* + nuclear = nonnuclear

When adding a prefix to a lowercase word, do not use a hyphen in most cases. When adding a prefix to a capitalized word, use a hyphen. Always use a hyphen with the prefix *ex-* meaning "previous" or "former."

*co-* + author = coauthor
*un-* + American = un-American
*mid-* + ocean = midocean
*ex-* + archer = ex-archer

Many different suffixes can be added to words, too. You're probably already familiar with common suffixes such as *-able*, *-ism*, and *-ize*. Most words that contain suffixes are spelled in a straightforward way. You'll have to memorize exceptions to the rules.

**Adding Suffix *-ly*** When adding *-ly* to a word that ends in a single *l*, keep the *l*. When the word ends in double *l*, drop one *l*. When the word ends in a consonant + *le*, drop the *le*.

accidental + *-ly* = accidentally
dull + *-ly* = dully
able + *-ly* = ably
lateral + *-ly* = laterally
smell + *-ly* = smelly
horrible + *-ly* = horribly

**Adding Suffix *-ness*** When adding *-ness* to a word that ends in *n*, keep the *n*.

| | |
|---|---|
| sudden + *-ness* = suddenness | lean + *-ness* = leanness |
| mean + *-ness* = meanness | plain + *-ness* = plainness |

**Adding Suffixes to Words Ending in a Silent *e*** There are many exceptions to rules for words ending in silent *e*. Generally, however, drop the final silent *e* before a suffix that begins with a vowel.

desire + *-able* = desirable  judge + *-ing* = judging

Keep the final silent *e* in words ending in *ce* or *ge* that have suffixes that begin in *a* or *o*.

peace + *-able* = peaceable  courage + *-ous* = courageous

Keep the final silent *e* before a suffix that begins with a consonant.

complete + *-ly* = completely  grace + *-ful* = graceful

**Adding Suffixes to Words Ending in a Consonant** The following chart contains rules and examples for doubling the final consonant when adding a suffix to a word.

| When adding a suffix... | |
|---|---|
| **Double the final consonant . . .** | **Examples** |
| • if the original word is one syllable. | spin, spinner |
| • if the original word has its accent on the last syllable and the accent remains there after the suffix is added. | dispel, dispelling<br>occur, occurrence |
| • if the original word is a prefixed word based on a one-syllable word. | reset, resetting |
| ***Do not* double the final consonant . . .** | |
| • if the accent is not on the last syllable or if the accent shifts when the suffix is added. | murmur, murmured<br>refer, reference |
| • if the final consonants are *x* or *w*. | wax, waxing |
| • when adding a suffix that begins with a consonant to a word that ends in a consonant. | daunt, dauntless<br>equip, equipment |

**Forming Compound Words** When joining a word that ends in a consonant to a word that begins with a consonant, keep both consonants.

*lamp* + *post* = lamppost  *break* + *through* = breakthrough

**Forming Plurals** There are many rules for forming plurals. Study the list on the next page to review some of them.

| Rules for Regular Plurals | Examples |
|---|---|
| To form the plural of most nouns, including proper nouns, add *-s.* If the noun ends in *-ch, -s, -sh, -x,* or *-z,* add *-es.* | box, boxes<br>Jones, Joneses<br>ranch, ranches |
| To form the plural of common nouns ending in a consonant + *-y,* change the *y* to *i* and add *-es.* | library, libraries<br>sky, skies |
| To form the plural of most nouns ending in *-f,* including all nouns ending in *-ff,* add *-s.* For some nouns ending in *-f,* especially those ending in *-lf,* change the *f* to *v* and add *-es.* | brief, briefs<br>skiff, skiffs<br>calf, calves<br>wolf, wolves |

| Rules for Irregular Plurals | Examples |
|---|---|
| Some nouns become plural by adding *-en, -ren,* or by substituting letters. | ox, oxen<br>man, men |
| Some nouns are the same in the singular and the plural. | deer, deer<br>series, series |

**Unstressed Vowels** To decide which vowel to use for the "schwa" sound, think of another form of the word in which the syllable containing the vowel sound is stressed, and then use the same vowel.

me*di*cine, me-DIC-i-nal hypo*cri*sy, hyp-o-CRIT-i-cal

***ie* and *ei*** Write *i* before *e* except after *c,* or when sounded like *a* as in *neighbor* and *weigh.*

belief ceiling beige

Exceptions to the rule include *weird, height, foreign, leisure, neither, seize, forfeit,* and *either.*

***-cede, -ceed,* and *-sede*** Because of the relatively few words with these constructions, these words are probably best memorized. Use *-sede* in only one word: *supersede.* Use *-ceed* in only three words: *exceed, proceed,* and *succeed.* Use *-cede* in all other cases: *concede, intercede,* and so on.

## Using a Computer Spelling Checker

Although spelling checkers are handy, you can't rely solely on one to find spelling errors. When a spelling checker highlights a misspelled word and suggests a replacement, it searches for words spelled similarly, but it can't determine the exact word that you want. For example, if you type "rase," the spelling checker may suggest "erase," "rise," or "raise."

Moreover, a spelling checker can't check for sense. Therefore, the words in a sentence such as "The bogs threw the window threw the rock" won't be noted as incorrect because all the individual words are correctly spelled. Even grammar checkers that check for usage errors are not infallible. Always proofread your writing to find errors, such as transposed words and incorrect usage, that the computer software didn't catch.

You might use a spelling checker to target your spelling or typing problems. You can list words that the spelling checker highlights, and then quiz yourself on those words until you master them.

**Exercise 1**

Each of the following sentences contains one, two, or no misspelled words. Write the misspelled words in each sentence correctly. Check your answers in a dictionary.

1. Self-confidence and great team play propeled the soccer team to an unforgettable victory.
2. Was it a courageous deed or an irresponsible act?
3. The dayly newspaper's editorial policy seems changable.
4. The zoos transfered a total of five deer and twelve wolfes.
5. Policies implemented this year seem unAmerican.
6. Choose an authority who is truely knowledgeable.
7. The greenness of the grass is receeding by the shore.
8. What is managment's commitment to the plan?
9. Lavinia gaily announced that her gas mileage exseeded mine.
10. They succeeded in a peaceable disarmament.

## 26.2 Spelling Challenges

As you know, not all words follow spelling rules. To simplify spelling, some people have proposed changing the spelling of words so that every word would be spelled as it is pronounced. Since there are regional differences in pronunciation, however, that solution could cause more problems than it would solve. Your best strategy for spelling difficult words is to develop a list of words that you frequently misspell and study them often.

### Commonly Misspelled Words

A list of words that people often misspell appears on the next page. You can master the spelling of these words by writing and rewriting the words. You might also try to develop memory aids. For example, you might say to yourself, "There's pap*er* in station*ery*."

Some words have more than one correct spelling, such as "acknowledgment"/ "acknowledgement."

Some words are correctly spelled with or without accent marks, such as "naive"/"naïve."

| Commonly Misspelled Words | | | |
|---|---|---|---|
| academically | descendant | legitimate | prophesy (v.) |
| accessible | detrimental | leisurely | psychoanalysis |
| acclimated | devise | luxurious | questionnaire |
| accompaniment | diligence | magnificence | receive |
| acknowledgment | disciple | malicious | reference |
| acquaintance | diseased | maneuver | rehearsal |
| admission | division | martyrdom | reminiscent |
| adolescent | efficiency | mathematics | representative |
| aerial | embarrassed | melancholy | responsibility |
| against | emperor | metaphor | seize |
| allegiance | endeavor | mischievous | sergeant |
| allotting | entertainment | mortgage | significance |
| anonymous | entrance | municipal | specimen |
| apparatus | espionage | naive | statistics |
| arousing | exhibition | neurotic | stubbornness |
| atheistic | expensive | nucleus | succession |
| bankruptcy | familiarize | nutritious | superintendent |
| behavior | fascism | occasionally | suppress |
| bibliography | financier | omitting | susceptible |
| blasphemy | forfeit | orchestra | symmetrical |
| boulevard | fundamentally | pageant | synonymous |
| bureaucrat | galaxy | parallel | temperament |
| camouflage | grammatically | paralysis | tendency |
| carburetor | harassment | pastime | tolerance |
| catastrophe | hindrance | pedestal | tortoise |
| cemetery | hospital | perceive | tragedy |
| chassis | hypocrisy | permissible | transparent |
| circumstantial | idiomatic | perspiration | twelfth |
| conceivable | independent | physician | undoubtedly |
| connoisseur | inevitable | playwright | unmistakable |
| conscientious | ingenious | politician | unnecessary |
| consistency | innocent | presence | vaccine |
| controversy | inoculate | presumption | valedictory |
| curriculum | institution | privilege | vehicle |
| decadent | interference | propaganda | versatile |
| deference | irresistible | prophecy | villain |

# Frequently Confused Words

Some words are easily confused because they contain the same or similar sounds but have different meanings and spellings. Study the list of easily confused words on the next page. For additional words see Unit 19.

| Frequently Confused Words | | |
|---|---|---|
| **Word** | **Meaning** | **Example of Usage** |
| accede | to comply with | I acceded to Mom's wishes. |
| exceed | to go beyond | Don't exceed the speed limit. |
| access | admittance | He gained access with a key. |
| excess | surplus | We invested excess profits. |
| a lot | much | They invested a lot of money. |
| allot | allow | I can allot an hour for study. |
| council | panel of people | Who is on the city council? |
| counsel | advice; lawyer | I would counsel you to wait. |
| cite | to quote or name | I cited my research sources. |
| sight | a view | The canyon is quite a sight. |
| site | a location | That's the site of the fair. |
| loath | reluctant | I am loath to wait for you. |
| loathe | to hate | Juan loathes baked fish. |
| miner | worker in mines | The miners work in shifts. |
| minor | small; not of age | The actor has a minor role. |
| moral | lesson in virtue | What's the moral of the story? |
| morale | mental state | Morale was low when we lost. |
| ordinance | law | An ordinance prohibits noise. |
| ordnance | weapons | The ordnance was guarded. |
| personal | private | Voting is a personal choice. |
| personnel | employees | All personnel leave at 5 P.M. |
| persecute | to torment | The refugees were persecuted. |
| prosecute | to sue | All criminals were prosecuted. |

## Exercise 2

Rewrite the paragraph to correct misspelled words.

When you apply for a job, ocassionally a business or a personell office may ask you to fill out an aplication or a questionnaire. It may seem like unecessary work, but it is a legitamate request. Some employers like to receive information formatted in a certain manor. Before begining, glance over the form to see what the questions are like, so you don't make alot of mistakes. When filing out the form, be concientious. Proofread your answers to make sure their factually and gramatically correct.

UNIT

# 27 Study Skills

## 27.1 Improving Your Study Habits

Cultivating good study habits will benefit you long after you've left high school or college. For example, you may need to study the performance requirements for a job. Your employer may require you to take night classes. Making major purchases, such as a home or a car or a VCR, will require you to "study up."

### Listening and Taking Notes

Most people take notes because they can't remember everything that is said during a class lecture or a business meeting. How can you get more out of lectures and your notes? Try the following.

**Overcoming Barriers to Taking Good Notes**

- **How can anyone write fast enough to keep up with what the speaker is saying?** Take notes in a modified outline form, and write only the main ideas and key points. Also, if you read the material before the speaker goes over it, the topic will be more familiar. You can anticipate where the discussion is headed.
- **What's the best way to identify key points and concepts?** You'll know an idea is important if the speaker (1) dwells on it or mentions it more than once, (2) writes it on a chalkboard, or (3) uses visual aids to illustrate it. As you take notes, think about the sense of what you hear. Organize your notes to set off main ideas.
- **How can an audience anticipate when a speaker is moving on to another point?** Listen for transitional words such as *on the other hand, next,* and *another point.* Body language can also be a clue. Some speakers employ arm gestures to indicate a shift in thought or tick off enumerated points on their fingers.
- **What is the best way to take meaningful notes?** Take notes in a modified outline so that ideas will be logically organized. Also try filling in gaps in your notes soon after the lecture ends. Your notes will be more complete, and you'll have an excellent review of the material.

### Managing Your Study Time

Try to establish a regular time and place for study. If you set reasonable goals for short- and long-term assignments, you'll spend less time trying to "fit in" studying and more time actually getting the job done.

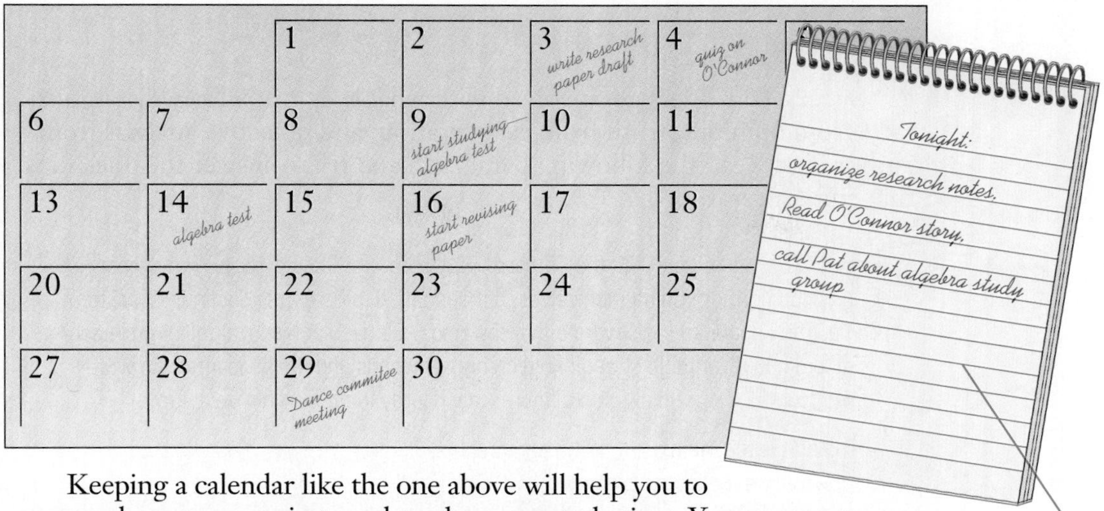

Keeping a calendar like the one above will help you to manage long-term projects and to plan your study time. You can see at a glance what needs to be accomplished and when.

*Set priorities for short-term assignments. Longer assignments take more planning. Break up the work into manageable segments.*

For an individual study session, set attainable goals before you begin to study. Try to divide assignments so that they can be completed in a reasonable block of time, such as an hour. Then, when you finish an assignment block, take a short break. You'll avoid fatigue if you pace yourself.

The place where you study should be free from distractions and offer you enough room to spread out your materials comfortably. If you study in the same place each day, you can keep materials, like dictionaries, paper and pens, and even your computer, conveniently at hand. You won't waste time getting settled. If study groups work well for you, try scheduling a weekly study session with classmates.

## Reading to Remember

Unlike the reading that you do for pleasure, reading for a class requires you not only to read the material but also to analyze it and remember it. Fortunately, there's a way to get the most out of your reading time. Suppose, for example, that you're going to read a chapter in your history book. First, skim the chapter, noting titles, headings, boldface terms, photographs, and illustration captions. Read chapter or section review questions. This overview will give you an idea of the significant concepts.

Next, read the chapter in depth. Find the answers to the review questions as you read. Take notes and jot down any questions you have. You may find the answers as you continue to read or in class discussion. Also review what you've read. Note key ideas in your textbook and notes. Reread the textbook's review questions and your own questions; study the answers you've found. The review will help you remember what you've read and will provide a useful context in which to learn new material as you continue to study.

## Evaluating What You Read

Successful readers get involved with what they read. They distinguish facts from opinions, truth from exaggeration, and objective analysis from author bias. Read the following paragraph and try to answer the questions that come after it.

> From 1122 B.C. until A.D. 256, the Chinese lived under the Chou dynasty. The dynasty kings ruled northern China themselves, but appointed lords to rule sections of eastern China. The appointed lords were either the king's relatives or his loyal followers. Each local lord had a veritable stranglehold on his own lands and the peasants who were forced to work them. To enforce authority, each lord maintained his own army.
>
> - What is the main point of the paragraph?
> - What are the facts? Exaggerations? Opinions?
> - What implications does the author make?
> - What additional information do you need to evaluate the system of government?

The main point of the paragraph is that the Chou kings ruled the eastern part of their realm through appointed lords.

Fact, exaggeration, and opinion are tangled. The facts: (1) the Chou ruled China from 1122 B.C. until A.D. 256, (2) they used a system of appointed lords to rule eastern China, and (3) the appointed lords were relatives or followers. It is the author's exaggeration that the lords had a "veritable stranglehold" on their lands and peasants. The word *veritable* means "actual"; a *stranglehold* is an illegal wrestling move used to choke an opponent. It is the author's opinion that peasants were "forced" to work the lands. *Forced* means "compelled against one's will." Another historian might point out that peasants were traditionally farmers and that in exchange for their labor, the peasants received the lord's armed protection against invaders.

The information is incomplete and misleading because readers might infer that the lords used their armies against the peasants rather than against outside invaders. Readers might also infer that the lords were not qualified to rule, since appointments were based on a family connection or favoritism. You would need more information before judging the rulers and their system of rule.

### Exercise 1

Find editorials or other writings that you feel are opinionated. Pick out unsupported opinions and exaggerations. Also look for information that seems incomplete and misleading. Share your examples in class, and explain your evaluations.

## 27.2 Evaluating Graphs and Diagrams

When you read textbooks, don't overlook the charts, graphs, and diagrams. These graphics will help you to clarify complex relationships among lists of numbers, geographic locations, groups of people or things, and time spans. In addition, graphics may be used to emphasize important points or to summarize key ideas in the text.

# Reading Tables, Graphs, and Charts

Some of the most common graphics are tables, line graphs, bar graphs, and pie charts. Most graphics have purposes to which they are best suited. Tables, for example, are best used to present detailed, specific information in a variety of categories. Line graphs, however, show trends or changes in data over a period of time. Bar graphs compare amounts. Pie charts segment a "pie" into "slices" to illustrate the proportional relationship of parts to each other and to a whole.

**Reading Tables and Graphs** When you read a graphic, ask yourself: What does the graphic show? Does it illustrate increases or decreases? Does it describe a trend?

The following paragraph discusses United States farms during a specific time. The graphics that follow it visually represent some aspects of the data in the paragraph.

> The United States farm population declined steadily from 15.6 million farms in 1960 to 5.2 million farms in 1990. The average size of farms, however, increased from an average of 297 acres in 1960 to 435 acres in 1990.

*Notice that the amounts on the graphs are not as exact as the data in the table.*

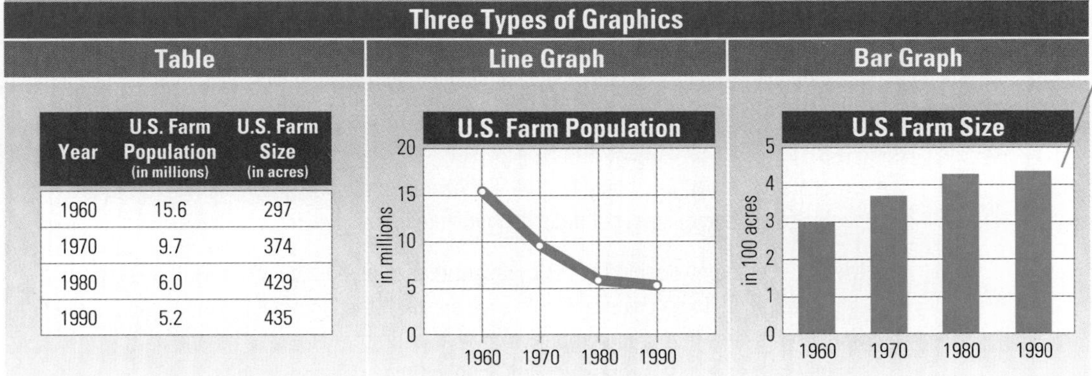

Three Types of Graphics

Table

| Year | U.S. Farm Population (in millions) | U.S. Farm Size (in acres) |
|---|---|---|
| 1960 | 15.6 | 297 |
| 1970 | 9.7 | 374 |
| 1980 | 6.0 | 429 |
| 1990 | 5.2 | 435 |

Note how the graphics enhance understanding of the paragraph. The table gives a clear comparison between the two sets of information: farm population and farm size. The table also provides a more detailed analysis by giving statistics for each ten-year period.

The line graph only shows the decrease in farm population. Information on both axes is marked in equal increments: every five million farms and every ten-year period. To find the population for one period, follow the horizontal axis to that year, and go up the year column to the point on the graph. Then look across to the numbers on the vertical axis.

Similarly, the bar graph illustrates the increase in farm size. As with the line graph, the axes list amounts in increments. In this case, the increments comprise 100 acres of land and ten-year spans. To find farm size for one year, follow the horizontal axis to that year, look at the height of the bar above it in the graph, and then look at the corresponding amount on the vertical axis.

**Where Departing Farm Workers Go**

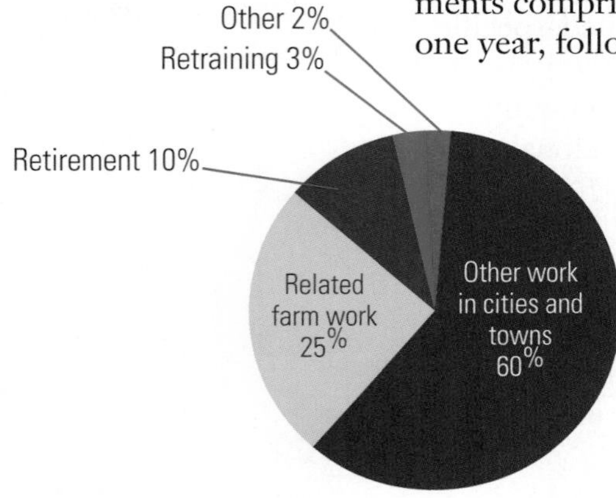


**Pie Charts** These pie charts are circles divided into segments, or slices, that show proportions of a whole. The proportions or amounts represented by all the segments total 100 percent. The size of segments can be compared with each other and to the whole.

This pie chart illustrates what a poll might reveal about where farm workers go when they leave that area of employment. Other pie charts often illustrate budget proportions or amounts.

**Reading Graphics Accurately** Graphics provide a great deal of information, but they have limitations. Read the following points to understand what graphics can and cannot do.

**Reading Graphics Accurately**

- Graphics may indicate trends for a given period, but you can't assume a trend will continue. The table, for instance, shows trends in farm population and farm size. Those trends may or may not continue.
- Although several categories of information might be presented together, be careful about inferring a cause-and-effect relationship among the categories. Such a relationship may not exist.
- Graphics don't give the whole picture. For example, the line graph shows that farm population is decreasing, but it doesn't indicate who is leaving or why.
- Graphics can be misleading in their presentation. Numbers on one axis of a line graph or bar graph might be compressed to save space. If the increments aren't equal, the visual representation of the graphic won't be accurate. Also, read the labels so you know whether numbers represent individual units or millions of units.

# Analyzing Diagrams

Unlike charts and graphs, diagrams show relationships among ideas; how a system or organization works; or the movement of people, information, and items within a system or from one place to another. If you have ever put together a model airplane, sewed a garment from a pattern, or followed a blueprint, you have used a diagram. As a student you have probably read diagrams in the form of organizational "trees," flow charts, and maps.

*Diagrams are typically designed so that you can visually follow the stages of the process.*

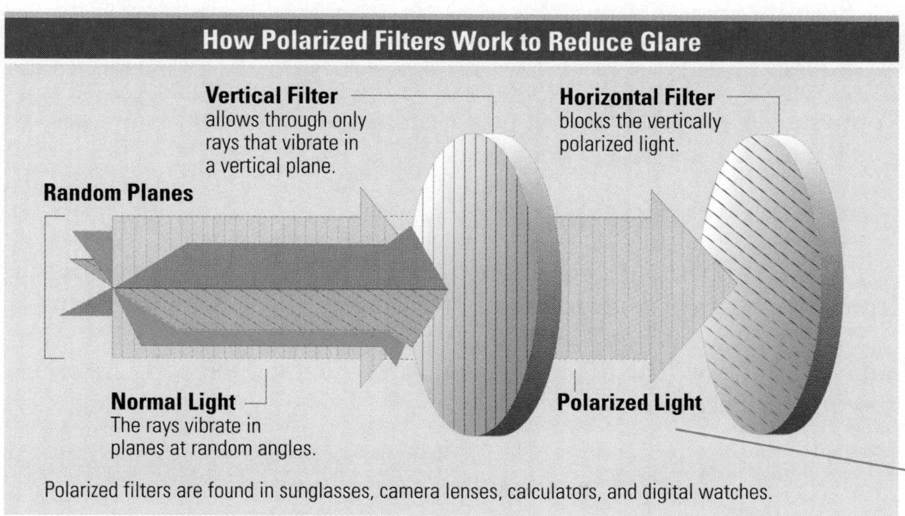

How Polarized Filters Work to Reduce Glare
Vertical Filter
allows through only rays that vibrate in a vertical plane.
Horizontal Filter
blocks the vertically polarized light.
Random Planes
Normal Light
The rays vibrate in planes at random angles.
Polarized Light

Polarized filters are found in sunglasses, camera lenses, calculators, and digital watches.

*Labels indicate and describe the stages of a process and may indicate their degree of importance.*

If you were to read the preceding diagram in a science textbook, you'd learn three things: (1) how polarized filters work, (2) in what applications they're used, and (3) why they're used. Even if the same information is written in the text, studying the diagram will clarify and reinforce what you've read.

## Exercise 2

Create a graph or diagram to represent one of the following kinds of information.

- Keep track of the temperature highs and lows for one week in your city or town. Show the temperature pattern in an appropriate graphic.
- If you belong to a club or committee, or if you work for a fast-food restaurant or clothing store, create a diagram of how you and your fellow members or coworkers get things accomplished. Show how decisions are made, food orders are handled, or clothing is unpacked, displayed, and sold.

UNIT 28

# Essay Tests and Standardized Tests

## 28.1 Writing Essay Tests

For out-of-class writing, you probably spend a great deal of time planning, drafting, revising, and editing. When you write an in-class essay test, however, you usually have only one class period in which to create your essay. If you know how to prepare for and take in-class essay tests, you'll make the best use of your time.

### Preparing for Essay Tests

The key to writing a good essay test is to plan ahead. Allow yourself at least several days of study to prepare for the test. If you cram the night before the test, you won't remember as much as if you spend several days studying, and you'll be tired when you write the test. Following are other tips that may help you.

**Preparing for In-Class Essays**

1. Learn what your textbook indicates is most important. Main ideas are expressed in chapter titles, headings, boldface terms, visual aid captions, and chapter summaries. Exercises and questions emphasize the points that the author thinks that you should remember.
2. Study your class notes and handouts. The amount of time that your teacher takes to cover certain ideas indicates their importance.
3. Anticipate essay questions and write out possible answers. This thinking exercise will help you to gauge how well you know the material. Also review homework assignments: one of the questions might be rephrased as a test question.

### Taking Essay Tests

Once the test is before you, be sure to read the question or questions all the way through before you begin. Make sure that you know what you're being asked to do. Key words such as *compare*, *contrast*, *analyze*, *explain*, *trace*, *prove*, *describe*, and *summarize* tell you how to present your answer. For example, if you summarize, you'll discuss main ideas; if you explain, you'll discuss main ideas and use details as supporting evidence for your reasoning.

The clock below suggests how to allot your time if you are writing one essay in fifty-five minutes. Your time is limited, so say a few things well rather than writing everything you know.

**Allotting Your Time**

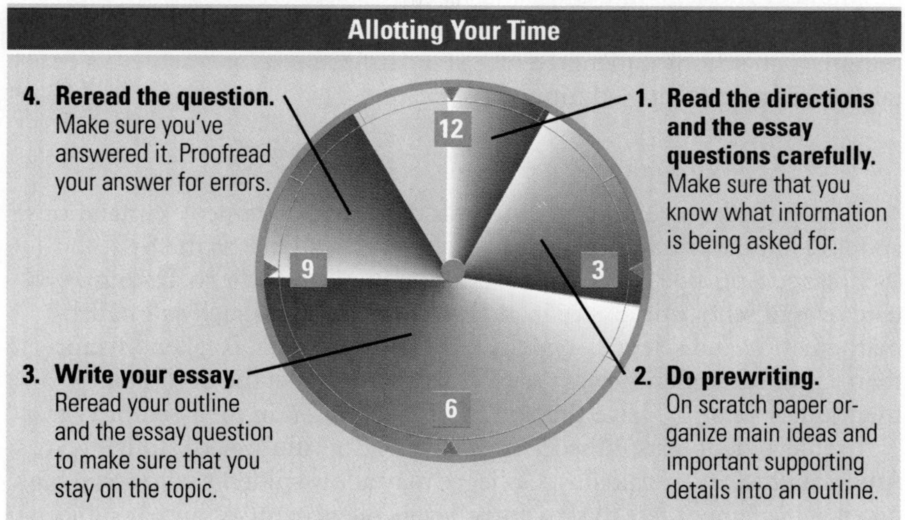

12
3
6
9
**4. Reread the question.** Make sure you've answered it. Proofread your answer for errors.
**1. Read the directions and the essay questions carefully.** Make sure that you know what information is being asked for.
**3. Write your essay.** Reread your outline and the essay question to make sure that you stay on the topic.
**2. Do prewriting.** On scratch paper organize main ideas and important supporting details into an outline.


As you can see, you'll need to compress the writing process. Prewriting should consist of organizing main ideas and listing supporting details and statistics. The success of your essay depends on cogent prewriting.

When you draft, state your thesis clearly in the first paragraph. Your thesis statement should be specific and limited to one idea that you will develop in your essay. Refer to your thesis statement as you write in order to guide your writing. To develop the body of your essay, use transitions to move smoothly from idea to idea. Since you won't have time for revision, carefully proofread your draft. Make corrections neatly.

## Exercise 1

Create prewriting for one of the following two questions. Spend no more than fifteen minutes on prewriting. Decide which main ideas and supporting details to use and how best to organize them. At the end of the fifteen minutes, compose a brief first paragraph that includes a thesis statement.

1. Compare and contrast the advantages and disadvantages of growing up in "the age of mass media."
2. Support or dispute the notion that people who are exposed to cultures and ethnic groups different from their own are better able to understand and solve world problems such as hunger, war, and pollution.

## 28.2 Standardized Tests

Standardized tests are designed to be given to many people, administered under similar conditions, and scored objectively (usually by computer). Test scores are compared and thus "standardized." Many colleges require high school students to take standardized tests and achieve a certain score before being admitted.

### Purpose of Standardized Tests

You can take several different kinds of college-entrance examinations, and each kind has a different purpose. Some tests, such as the SAT (Scholastic Aptitude Test) and the ACT (American College Testing), evaluate overall scholastic ability in general areas of study, such as English, mathematics, and science. The SAT, the most popular, is taken by more than a million students each year. Most students take the SAT during their junior year and have the option of repeating it in their senior year.

Achievement tests measure strength in a specific area of study, such as American history or calculus. Colleges may allow students who score high on an achievement test to skip entry-level college courses in that subject.

Aptitude tests help people to explore their talents and interests. If you're unsure of your career goals, try taking an aptitude test to help steer you toward the kinds of jobs best suited to your interests and abilities.

### Preparing for Standardized Tests

Unlike classroom tests, most standardized tests are difficult to study for because they measure years of acquired knowledge. Although you won't be able to study for the specific questions on a standardized test, you can prepare yourself to take the test. Ideas for preparing for standardized tests follow.

**Before You Take a Standardized Test**

1. See your high school counselor for registration details.
2. Verify that the colleges to which you're going to apply accept the results of the tests you're taking; some colleges accept the results of only one test, such as the SAT.
3. Take practice tests such as the PSAT (Preliminary SAT), which is a shorter version of the SAT. You can also buy practice books at bookstores. Practice exams will familiarize you with the test format, will give you an idea of how to pace yourself, and will help eliminate some of your anxiety.
4. Find out if the test you're taking is designed to be completed; many standardized tests aren't. You'll lose points if you try to rush through to complete such a test.

Just as you can make some general preparations before taking a test, you can also use some strategies that will help you during the test.

**Tips for Taking a Standardized Test**

1. Find out if there is a penalty for incorrect answers. The SAT, for instance, penalizes incorrect answers, so you're better off not guessing if you can't narrow the choices.
2. Read the directions before you begin each section of the test. Directions may change from section to section.
3. First, answer the questions that you're sure of. Then, if there's time, go back and answer the rest. When you skip a question, be sure to skip the corresponding space on the answer form.
4. To record your answers, you'll use a pencil to fill in circles on a computer-readable form. Make sure your marks are heavy and within the circle, or they may be misread.
5. For multiple-choice items, read all the answers before marking your choice. One choice may seem correct, but another choice may be more correct.
6. Pay attention to answers that contain qualifying words such as *mainly, most important, only,* and *least.* They can guide you to the right answer.

**Exercise 2**

In small groups of four or five students, share your experiences in taking standardized tests. Discuss strategies that worked and those that didn't. Also exchange information about sources of practice test books, mock exams, and test preparation groups. If you can, invite as a classroom guest someone who has recently taken the same standardized test that you plan to take.

## 28.3 Standardized Test Items

Standardized test questions measure your knowledge or abilities in specific areas. Colleges will review your scores to determine your status for admission and, once you are accepted, your placement in certain courses, such as composition or mathematics.

### Antonym Questions

Antonym test items require you to choose a word from a list of possible choices that has a meaning opposite, or most *nearly* opposite, a given word. (Not all words have direct opposites.) Look at the following given word and try to think of an antonym for it before reading the answer choices. Anticipating possible answers will clarify your thinking so you will not be distracted or confused by the choices given.

| **SCANTY:** | (A) adept | (B) latent | (C) inelastic | (D) copious |
|---|---|---|---|---|

If you can't find your antonym among the choices, think about other possible meanings. *Scanty* can mean "barely adequate," and the choice that is the opposite of that meaning is (D), *copious.*

## Analogy Questions

Analogy questions ask you to determine what the relationship between two words is in a given word pair and then to find that same relationship in another word pair. The key to answering these questions is to determine the relationship in the given word pair before you read the choices. Some common analogy relationships follow.

| Analogy Relationships | |
|---|---|
| Synonym—thin : diluted | Antonym—sour : sweet |
| Cause/Effect—deluge : flood | Time—prologue : epilogue |
| Part/Whole—suit : wardrobe | Objects/Class—rubies : gems |
| Object/Action—trowel : levels | Object/User—hammer : carpenter |

To clarify a given relationship, formulate a sentence that explains it. For example, using the above Cause/Effect word pair, you could say that "A *deluge* can cause a *flood.*" Determine the relationship between the two given words before reading the answer choices. Now try this analogy.

**KNIFE : INCISION ::**
(A) sharp : unhappiness
(B) tool : surgery
(C) combine : farming
(D) journalist : editor
(E) backhoe : excavation

You might think that the relationship of the given pair is "Knives are used for incisions." By substituting each word pair in the relationship sentence, you'll see that answers (A) and (B) don't work. Answer (C) seems right. Answer (D) is wrong. Answer (E), however, also seems right. If two answers seem right, you need to narrow the meaning of the relationship sentence. For example, "A knife is used to cut into something to make an incision." Since a combine threshes grain and makes no incisions, you know that choice (C) cannot be correct. The correct answer is (E): "A backhoe is used to cut into the earth to make an excavation."

## Sentence-Completion Questions

These test problems present sentences with one or two missing words. You need to recognize the logical and grammatical relationships among parts of the sentence and then fill in the blanks with the answer choice that makes the sentence correct.

In the following problem, the sentence itself provides clues. The words *although* and *never* point to a particular thought pattern: a person who acts in a characteristic or expected manner. Try all of the choices in the blanks until you find the one that fits the pattern and that makes sense in the context.

Although Tyrone had never considered himself a ______, he found himself ______ the committee's self-serving findings.

(A) cynic . . . doubting (B) skeptic . . . believing (C) politician . . . maligning
(D) investigator . . . ignoring (E) perfectionist . . . questioning

Answer (A) is correct.

## Reading-Comprehension Questions

Reading-comprehension test items are designed to test how well you understand what you read. Since these items don't test understanding of a specific subject, no outside knowledge is required. Before reading a passage, read the questions that follow it so you will know what information is sought. Read the following passage and questions.

Under the rule of the Han dynasty of ancient China, Confucian values governed all aspects of personal and social life. "With harmony at home, there will be order in the nation," Confucius had said. "With order in the nation, there will be peace in the world." And indeed, the family was supreme in Chinese society. It was the focus of life, bound together strongly by mutual love, loyalty, and dependence.

1. The best title for the passage would be: (A) The Han dynasty (B) Confucianism (C) Family Life in Han China (D) China (E) The Influence of Confucian Values in Han China
2. According to Confucianism, world peace is related to (A) family harmony (B) the Han dynasty (C) dependence (D) love, loyalty, and dependence (E) all of the above

The answer to question 1 is (E) because it most nearly summarizes the passage. Question 2 asks for a specific detail, and the answer is (A). Reading the questions before reading the passage will alert you to important details as you read. If a passage is a half page or more, you won't have time to reread it to find an answer.

## English-Composition Questions

These items test your basic knowledge of standard written English. You will be asked to identify problems in grammar, such as errors in subject-verb agreement and agreement of pronouns and their antecedents. You will also need to recognize sentence structures that are incomplete or unclear and word choices that violate accepted standards of written English.

**Usage Questions** Usage questions test your ability to spot language that is unclear or grammatically incorrect. Each sentence contains several underlined parts, labeled A through D. An error may exist in an underlined part, or the sentence may be correct, in which case answer choice E is correct.

Read the following sentence. Is an error obvious? If not, examine each underlined section for an error in grammar, usage, diction, or idiom.

> In *A Tale of Two Cities* (A), Sydney Carton, which is a pitiable misanthrope (B), sacrifices his own life to save Charles Evremonde (C) from the guillotine (D). no error (E)

The error occurs in section (B); "which" should be "who."

**Sentence-Correction Questions** Unlike usage questions, sentence-correction questions ask you not only to identify an error but also to choose the best correction from a list of possible choices. Errors to watch for include wordy phrases, illogical reasoning, and faulty structures. The first choice, (A), will always be identical to the underlined section of the sentence and indicates "no error."

Now read the sentence-correction test item below. Remember, an error can occur only in the underlined portion of the sentence.

> I have always loved animals and been interested in veterinary medicine, so I've finally decided to become one.
>
> (A) so I've finally decided to become one.
> (B) so I have finally decided to become one.
> (C) so finally I've decided to be one.
> (D) so I've finally decided to become a veterinarian.
> (E) so I've finally decided to do it.

Again, reading the sentence all the way through will help you to decide if there's an error. In the example above, the problem is a faulty reference. Even though you can guess at the author's meaning, a clearer construction is represented by choice (D).

## Exercise 3

On a separate sheet of paper, write the correct answer choice for each of the questions that follow. Use the strategies you've learned in this lesson.

### Antonym

1. SOLEMN: (A) sad (B) frivolous (C) murky (D) plain (E) easy

### Analogy

2. ABHOR : AVOID:: (A) history : event (B) love : condemn (C) explain : clarify (D) savor : devour (E) think : wait
3. BIRD : CARDINAL:: (A) feathers : tickle (B) fly : arachnid (C) novel : *War and Peace* (D) swift : red (E) collie : dog

### Sentence Completion

4. The scientist's findings were _______ by later experiments. (A) reviewed (B) confiscated (C) revised (D) substantiated (E) forewarned

### Reading Comprehension

The ancient Greeks believed that Zeus had nine daughters who were known as the Muses. Each one governed a field of study. The daughters are said to have inspired some of the greatest works of literature. Calliope, the muse of epic poetry, was thought to have influenced Homer as he wrote his masterpieces *The Iliad* and *The Odyssey*.

5. According to the passage, these statements are true except:
   (A) The Muses were daughters of Zeus.
   (B) Calliope helped Homer to write his great epic poems.
   (C) Calliope was the muse of epic poetry.
   (D) The Muses inspired great works of art and science.
   (E) Homer wrote *The Iliad* and *The Odyssey*.

### Usage

6. The drought had a bad (A) effect on the corn (B) crop, but it (C) didn't seem to harm the wheat crop (D). no error (E)

### Sentence Correction

7. She was going to attend the dinner with a man who owned a pickup truck named Ralph.
   (A) who owned a pickup truck named Ralph.
   (B) named Ralph, who owned a pickup truck.
   (C) that owned a pickup truck named Ralph.
   (D) whom owned a pickup truck named Ralph.
   (E) which owned a pickup truck named Ralph.

## 28.4 College Applications

As you prepare for and take standardized tests, you should also be applying to colleges for admission. You should apply to more than one school as "insurance" in case your first choice doesn't accept you.

## Application Forms

Most college application forms are somewhat similar. They usually consist of a page or two of fill-in questions about your personal life and scholastic achievements plus one or more essay questions. After you complete a fill-in form, photocopy it for your records. The following checklist is designed to help you with the fill-in forms.

**College Application Procedure Checklist**

1. After you receive your application, note the deadline for returning it and the fee that must accompany it.
2. Photocopy the application. If you fill out the copy first, you can submit a neat original.
3. Read the entire application, and gather the required information. You may be asked to supply any or all of the following: high school transcripts, class rank, standardized test scores, minority status, financial status, and written recommendations from teachers.
4. Be thorough in describing your nonacademic accomplishments, such as your participation in school clubs and sports, your jobs, and your community service. Colleges look for well-rounded, committed students.
5. After completing the photocopied form, have your parents or teachers critique it for content, grammar, and accuracy. Then transfer the information to the original form.

If you require financial aid, investigate possible scholarships, grants, loans, and work-study programs as part of your application process. Your school guidance counselor can supply information.

## College Application Essays

In addition to filling out an application form, many colleges also ask you to answer an essay question. Sometimes the topic is personal, and sometimes it has a more academic focus. The purpose of the essay is to give the admissions board the kind of subjective information that test scores and grades don't convey. (Refer to Unit 1, Lesson 4, pages 22–25 for more information.) Some sample essay topics follow.

### Sample Essay Topics

Cite and discuss a literary quotation or brief passage that has special meaning for you.

What do you consider your most important achievement in life?

Explain why you feel a college education is important, beyond preparing one for a career. Please be specific.

As you can see from the examples, the essay topics are rather general. You must therefore focus your response, be specific, and provide concrete details to support your opinions. The chart below contains other tips.

### Tips for Writing College Application Essays

Take your time. This may be the most important essay that you'll ever write; your acceptance or rejection may hinge on the quality of your writing. Do thorough prewriting, write several drafts, and have teachers or others whom you trust critique your essay. Consider their comments as you revise your essay.

Make sure that you stay on the given topic. If there's a limit on length, stay within this limit.

Be complete. If the essay question asks for a certain number of reasons or examples, be sure that you provide them.

Make your essay interesting and original. The judges read thousands of essays, and you'll want yours to stand out. Also, try to be yourself; you're an original, and that's what you want to convey.

Type your essay, and proofread it until it's perfect.

### Exercise 4

Choose one of the following topics and write a 200- to 500-word essay. Then, working in peer groups, critique each other's writing for both strengths and weaknesses.

1. What has been the most significant discovery or event in the past twenty years? Explain your response.
2. What single event from your childhood contributed to your maturity in an important way?
3. What makes you special?
4. Why do you want to attend this university?
5. What work of literature most influenced your thinking? Why?

UNIT 29

# Listening and Speaking

## 29.1 Listening Effectively

Composer Igor Stravinsky once commented, "To listen is an effort, and just to hear is no merit. A duck hears also." Listening is an effort, but it's an effort that pays off.

### Active Listening

Effective listening is an activity, not a passive state of being. To be an active listener, you must concentrate on hearing and understanding the message, analyzing the message, and then remembering the message. Here are some solutions for overcoming barriers to active listening.

**Problems and Solutions**

**I always understand what I hear, but I can't remember it.**
If you're in class, take notes in an informal outline format. Making an outline will help you to create a "mental map" of what's being said. Note main ideas as you write, and fill in the details later. If you can, ask questions. Your questions will force you to "replay" what you think you heard.

**How can I best follow a speaker's line of reasoning?**
Concentrate on doing three things: (1) Determine the speaker's purpose so you can frame what you hear in a larger context. (2) Pick out the main ideas, which should follow a logical pattern. (3) Listen for transition words that show direction, such as *next, secondly, on the other hand, as a result,* and *however.*

**How can I avoid confusing the details of what I hear?**
First, make sure that you don't have a hearing problem. Then practice building your accuracy. If you can, get videotaped documentaries with written transcripts. Listen to and watch a portion of the program, and then write what you think you heard—details and main ideas. Play the tape again, listening for the points that you wrote. Correct what you wrote. Then read the transcript to check your accuracy.

### Critical Listening

In addition to being an active listener, you need to be a thinking listener. If you don't critically evaluate what you hear, you accept it as being true. When you hear political candidates' speeches, for example, you know that you're hearing a mix of fact and opinion. To evaluate the candidates, you need to evaluate their speeches by first separating their opinions from the facts. Then you might evaluate the facts by asking yourself if the facts can be interpreted in more than one way.

Similarly, when you hear a commercial, you know that much of what you hear is not factual. In fact, advertisers often count on product sales that are based on the emotional appeal of the advertisement rather than on the merit of the product. In using celebrity endorsements for example, the advertiser hopes that if you like the celebrity, you'll transfer those positive feelings to the product without critical evaluation.

## Listening with Your Eyes

Watching speakers can often provide clues to their opinions and feelings. Obviously, facial expressions are a cue to a speaker's feelings, but you should watch what the speaker does with the rest of his or her body. Hand and arm gestures, for example, can signal important ideas. Similarly, if a speaker leans forward, it's often an indication of enthusiasm. Hand-wringing and fidgeting usually signal anxiety.

As you look at a speaker, also be aware of how you're reacting to his or her physical appearance. A terrific suit and an engaging smile have nothing to do with the quality of the message.

### Exercise 1

Work in groups of five. As a group listen to the lyrics of a folk song that not one of you has heard before, or watch a short videotape. Each person should then write a summary of what was heard. Compare your papers, and choose the paper that the group thinks most closely captures the meaning of what you heard. Listen to the recording again, and evaluate the accuracy of the paper that you selected.

As an alternative make two columns, "facts" and "nonfacts," on your paper. Then watch five recorded television commercials. For each commercial, list the facts and the nonfacts (for example, opinions and unsupported claims, such as "makes you feel like a winner") that you hear. Compare your list with those in your group. Replay the tape to check your accuracy.

# 29.2 Speaking Effectively

Why does giving a speech frighten people? In a survey, the majority of Americans rated speaking in public as more terrifying than perilous heights, insects, financial problems, or illness. This lesson focuses on making public speaking less fearsome.

# 29.2 Effective Speaking

A public relations official for a manufacturer was to address a union meeting; the union was threatening to strike. The official prepared a speech, hoping to win the union over with statistics. Listening to the speeches that preceded hers, she realized that she had miscalculated her audience's expectations. The official made rapid notes. Her new speech pointed out areas of common ground that both the management and the union shared. This proved effective and her speech was well received.

Not all speakers can adapt so appropriately to audience response, but the story illustrates two key rules for good public speaking: be prepared and be responsive to audience needs.

## Informal Speeches

People frequently make informal speeches. These speeches can be as brief as an introduction of one friend to another and as casual as telling a group of friends what you did during your family's vacation. You may not realize it, but even informal speeches follow commonly accepted patterns of organization and delivery. Because of their brief, informal nature, however, these speeches rarely require advance preparation.

## Making a Formal Speech

Unlike informal speeches, formal speeches are rehearsed and are delivered in more formal settings. In some ways, giving a formal speech is more like writing a research paper because it, too, is more easily managed when divided into stages, such as those that follow.

**Consider Your Topic, Purpose, and Audience** Once you have chosen or been assigned a topic, focus on your purpose for making the speech. Do you want to inform your audience, persuade them, or move them to action? Next, evaluate what your audience already knows and believes about your topic. What terms do you need to define? What misconceptions do you need to dispel?

**Research Your Topic** Gather facts, examples, and experts' opinions to explain and support your speech. You may gather information through library research, polls, and interviews. The amount of information that you need will depend on the complexity of your topic and the length of time you have been allotted to speak. Include explanations of terms and concepts that will be unfamiliar to your audience.

**Organize Your Speech into an Outline** Choose a pattern of organization that effectively presents your information. (See pages 80–81 and 208–228 for methods of organization.) Create a stimulating introduction that grabs your audience's attention. The chart on the next page lists several ideas for beginning your speech.

## Getting Your Audience's Attention

**Use humor**
How much string does it take to reach the moon? Just one piece—but it's a very long piece!

**Tell a story**
When my grandmother came to this country, she expected that the roads would be paved with gold. . . .

**Ask a question**
If you could spend 60 cents a day to save a child's life, would you do it?

**State an amazing fact or statistic**
Every minute of every day, 60 acres of rain forest are destroyed.

**Create Note Cards** Transfer the main points of your speech to note cards. You will sound more natural and make eye contact with your audience more often if you speak from note cards rather than read from a script. After deciding on the most effective order in which to present your ideas, prepare note cards that contain main ideas, important details, quotations, and statistics. Remember to number your note cards to keep them in order.

**Practice Your Speech** If possible, practice before an audience of parents or close friends who will be supportive and honest. Ask them to time your delivery and to offer suggestions. Rehearse several times, but don't rehearse to the point of memorization. If you do memorize your speech, your final delivery will probably sound "canned," or you will be tempted to talk too fast.

**Deliver Your Speech** Strive for a natural stance, and use gestures to accentuate your meaning. Make an effort to speak clearly and at a normal pace so that the audience will understand you. If you feel strongly about your topic, let some of that emotion show; it will create empathy in the audience. Be sure to vary your gaze around the room so that everyone in the audience feels included.

### Exercise 2

Many local television stations present editorials as a public service. Editorials are short speeches in which the speaker voices an opinion about an issue or expresses pleasure or displeasure with the outcome of a current event. Prepare a three-minute editorial to present to your class. Choose a topic that you feel strongly about and that relates to your school or community.

### Stage 4: Practicing

1. *For one practice session, use a live audience and ask for criticism.* Ask your audience to critique both the content of your speech and your delivery of it.
2. *Have someone time you.* If you are allotted a certain length of time in which to speak, your speech should last approximately that length of time.
3. *Don't overrehearse.* If you memorize your speech, you'll be bored with it by the time of your actual delivery, and you'll be tempted to rush through your speech to get it over with.

Ask your practice-session audience to critique your speech's content for its strengths and weaknesses. Ask them to note information that is difficult to understand, incomplete, or boring. Your audience should also tell you whether you use any mannerisms that are annoying, distracting, or inappropriate.

### Stage 5: Delivery

1. *Stand up straight.* Maintain normal but not rigid posture.
2. *Use natural gestures.*
3. *Speak clearly and at a normal pace.* Also remember that enthusiasm is contagious, so let your enthusiasm show.
4. *Vary your gaze around the audience.* You'll want everyone to feel included.

If you feel nervous about getting up in front of people, you're not alone. Even speakers who are famous for their oratory say they always "get butterflies" before they speak. Try to remember that you have worthwhile information to share with your audience. If someone giggles or the equipment breaks down, take it in stride, and don't become unnerved.

### Exercise 2

Imagine you're going to give a fifteen-minute orientation talk to a group of new students. Think of the practical information they'll need to know, and what tips you could give them as a "veteran" of your school. Prepare the note cards that you would use if you were to give such a speech.

As an alternative, imagine that you've been given the opportunity for a free one-minute radio commercial in which you can advertise any product or public service that you choose. Prepare your talk and deliver it to the class.

# 29.3 Formal Debates

A debate, in its simplest form, is the presentation of two sides of an issue before a panel of judges or an audience. The democratic process is based on the ideas of open discussion and respect for differing view points.

## The Structure of a Debate

You're probably familiar with congressional debates. Debates can also be academic exercises, however, such as the debates in which many high school and college students participate.

Most academic debates are structured in the same way. The issue being debated, called the proposition, is expressed as either a statement or a question and contains only one idea, for example, "Should students at our high school be required to follow a dress code?" or, "Any student who wishes to play high school football should be required to maintain a C average or better in all classes." The affirmative side of a debate supports the proposition; the negative side opposes it.

During the debate itself, each side is timed and speaks twice. First, each side presents its argument in what are called constructive speeches. Then, in what are called rebuttal speeches, each side refutes the opposition's arguments. The judges determine the winning side.

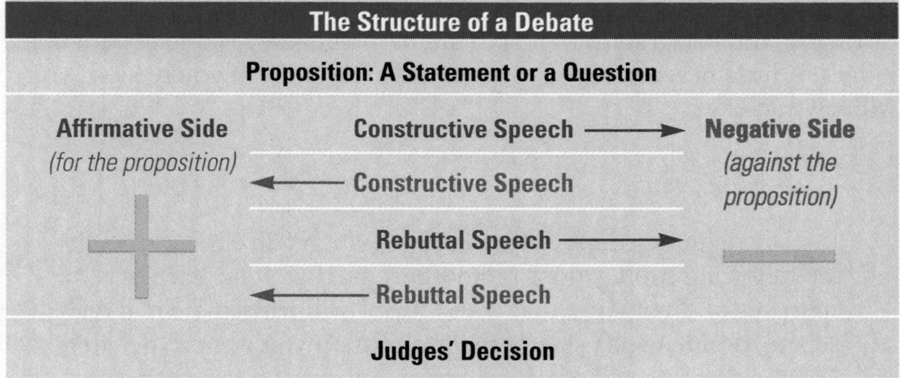


## Gathering Information for a Debate

In many ways, preparing for a debate is much the same as preparing to write a persuasive essay. (See pages 270–274.) You'll gather facts and experts' opinions to support your case and examine your arguments for errors in logic. You'll also want to anticipate the opposition's arguments and to look for facts with which to disprove them, as illustrated in the graphic organizer on the next page. Some high schools don't assign sides of a proposition until it's time for the actual debate, so participants must prepare to debate either side.

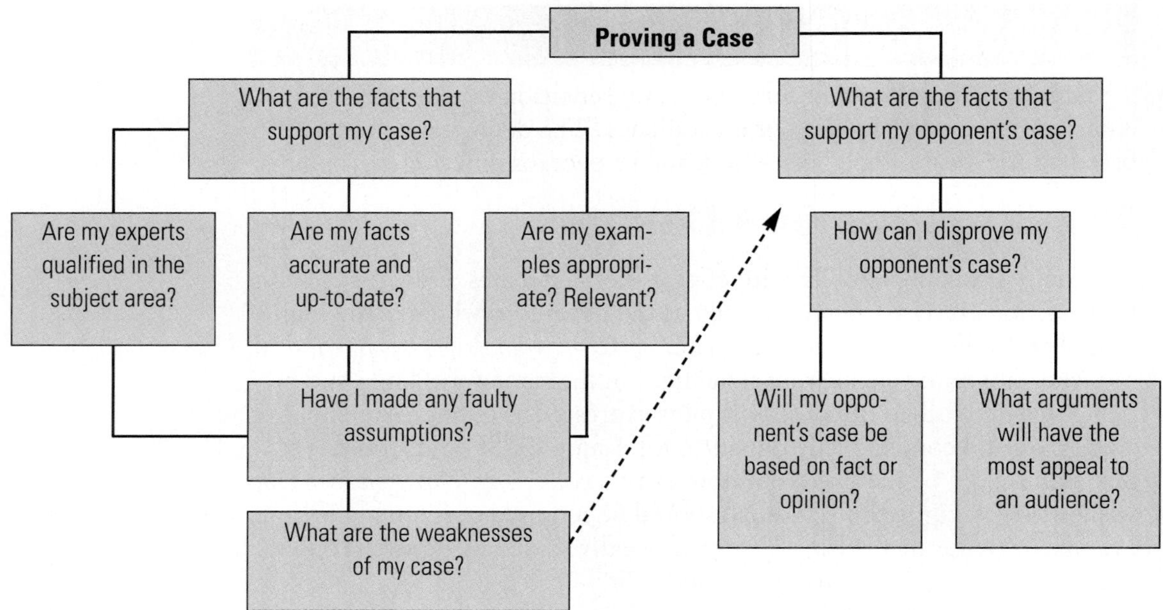
Proving a Case
What are the facts that support my case?
Are my experts qualified in the subject area?
Are my facts accurate and up-to-date?
Are my examples appropriate? Relevant?
Have I made any faulty assumptions?
What are the weaknesses of my case?
What are the facts that support my opponent's case?
How can I disprove my opponent's case?
Will my opponent's case be based on fact or opinion?
What arguments will have the most appeal to an audience?

## Participating in a Debate

Participating in a debate is like giving a formal speech: you practice before an audience, speak from note cards, and strive to speak clearly and distinctly. You'll also want to make sure to maintain eye contact with the judges. A little nervousness is natural, and even good. If you're alert, you will have an edge.

### Exercise 3

Divide into groups of four or five. As a group choose one of the following propositions or another one that your teacher approves of. Imagining that your "team" will participate in a real debate, decide which side of the proposition you want to debate. Assume that you will speak for fifteen minutes on your constructive speech and for five minutes on your rebuttal speech. As a group decide what issues to consider for each speech and what sources of information to consult. Prepare outlines of your constructive speech and your rebuttal speech.

Propositions:

- The school year should be twelve months long.
- Should record lyrics be censored?
- Should there be legal penalties for unpatriotic acts?
- The minimum wage should be increased.
- College education should be free.

## 29.4 Formal Meetings

How are stockholders' meetings, congressional committee meetings, and student body meetings alike? They're all highly structured, formal proceedings. Formal meetings help groups to discuss complex issues and to reach decisions efficiently.

## Roles in Group Meetings

In formal groups, certain people are assigned specific duties to maintain order, to keep the group on track, and to see that the goals of the group are reached as quickly as possible.

| Roles in Group Meetings | | |
|---|---|---|
| **Chairperson: leads all meetings** | **Recorder: keeps a written record of topics discussed** | **Treasurer: maintains finances in groups that generate money** |
| • decides who will speak and when<br>• makes sure that everyone gets a chance to be heard<br>• supervises others as they work to achieve goals | • notes proposals and decisions<br>• notifies members about scheduled meetings<br>• handles the group's correspondence | • collects and deposits money<br>• keeps financial records<br>• helps prepare the budget |

## Participating in a Formal Meeting

If you take part in a formal meeting, you need to understand and follow a set of rules known as "parliamentary procedure." These rules, developed from the procedures of the British Parliament, help groups to focus on the goals of discussion, to discuss issues in an orderly manner, and to give consideration to all speakers. The book most commonly used as a guide to parliamentary procedure is *Robert's Rules of Order.*

Parliamentary procedure uses proposals for action called "motions" to conduct business. For example, if a member wants the group to consider a certain proposal or take a vote, the member must make a motion for that action. Note, however, that not all meetings culminate in happy agreements. Often, parliamentary procedure is a way of managing disagreement. When you watch a televised congressional debate or attend a town council meeting, you're watching parliamentary procedure in action. The chart on the next page shows you some of the different motions used in parliamentary procedure.

| Motions in Parliamentary Procedure | |
|---|---|
| **Kinds of Motions** | **Examples** |
| **Main Motions:** Introduce new business or reconsider old business | A member of the prom committee may make a motion to discuss decorations: "I move that . . ." |
| **Subsidiary Motions:** Provide ways to modify or eliminate main motions | A member of your French club may make a motion to table, or postpone, discussion of a trip to Paris until a study is done to establish the cost of the trip. |
| **Incidental Motions:** Interrupt the meeting to consider errors in parliamentary procedure, to raise an objection, or to request information | A member of the student council may identify an error in parliamentary procedure by saying, "Point of order: Alexis can't speak yet; she doesn't have the floor." |
| **Privileged Motions:** Concern the well-being of the group itself | These motions include adjourning or recessing a meeting as well as requests to move to a less noisy or warmer room before continuing with the meeting. |

Most meetings follow this format: The meeting opens with the recorder reading the minutes of the last meeting. Then any special committees give their reports. Next, the group discusses unfinished business from the previous meeting. Finally, new business is considered and discussed, votes are taken, and the meeting is adjourned.

## Exercise 4

Using the preceding chart, identify each of the following motions as a main, subsidiary, incidental, or privileged motion.

1. "I move that we refer the issue of assigned parking places to a committee for study."
2. "I move that we reconsider the issue of recycling."
3. "Point of order: we cannot consider that issue until the issue on the table is resolved."
4. "I move that we recess until after lunch."
5. "I move that we open for debate the question: Should we have a fund-raising dance?"
6. "I move that debate on the issue of a fund-raising dance be limited to twenty minutes."
7. "I move that we adjourn the meeting."

# Part 4

# Strunk and White

## The Elements of Style

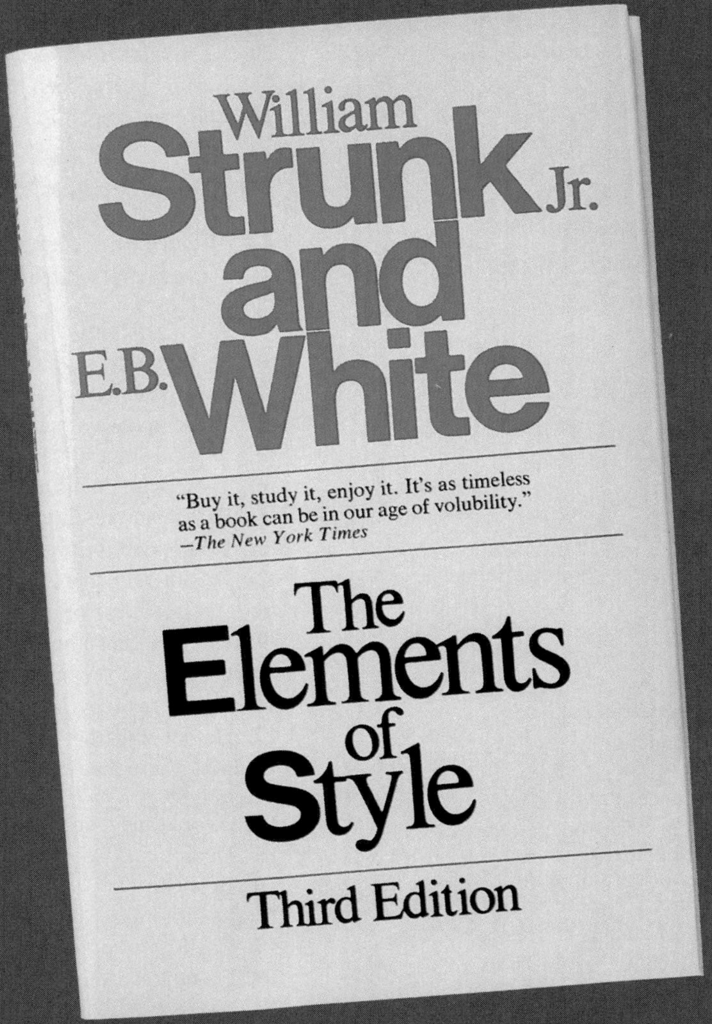

William Strunk Jr. and E.B. White

"Buy it, study it, enjoy it. It's as timeless as a book can be in our age of volubility."
—*The New York Times*

The Elements of Style

Third Edition

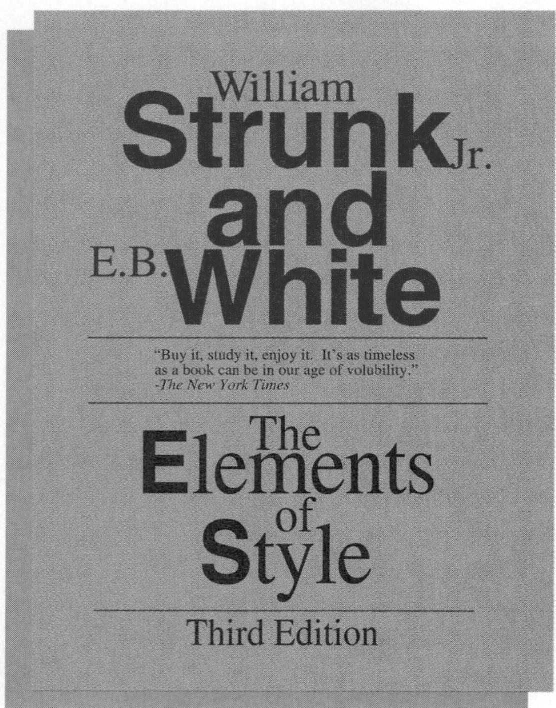
William
Strunk Jr.
and
E.B. White
"Buy it, study it, enjoy it. It's as timeless as a book can be in our age of volubility."
-The New York Times
The
Elements
of
Style
Third Edition

# Contents

# I
# *Elementary Rules of Usage*

## *1. Form the possessive singular of nouns by adding 's.*

Follow this rule whatever the final consonant. Thus write,

Charles's friend
Burns's poems
the witch's malice

Exceptions are the possessives of ancient proper names in *-es* and *-is,* the possessive *Jesus',* and such forms as *for conscience' sake, for righteousness' sake*. But such forms as *Moses' Laws, Isis' temple* are commonly replaced by

the laws of Moses
the temple of Isis

The pronominal possessives *hers, its, theirs, yours,* and *ours* have no apostrophe. Indefinite pronouns, however, use the apostrophe to show possession.

one's rights
somebody else's umbrella

A common error is to write *it's* for *its,* or vice versa. The first is a contraction, meaning "it is." The second is a possessive.

It's a wise dog that scratches its own fleas.

## *2. In a series of three or more terms with a single conjunction, use a comma after each term except the last.*

Thus write,

red, white, and blue
gold, silver, or copper
He opened the letter, read it, and made a note of its contents.

This comma is often referred to as the "serial" comma.

In the names of business firms the last comma is usually omitted. Follow the usage of the individual firm.

Brown, Shipley and Co.
Merrill Lynch, Pierce, Fenner & Smith Incorporated

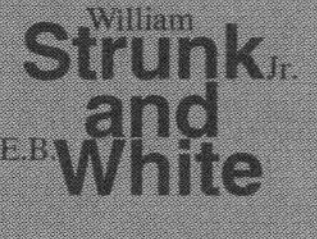

### 3. *Enclose parenthetic expressions between commas.*

The best way to see a country, unless you are pressed for time, is to travel on foot.

This rule is difficult to apply; it is frequently hard to decide whether a single word, such as *however,* or a brief phrase is or is not parenthetic. If the interruption to the flow of the sentence is but slight, the writer may safely omit the commas. But whether the interruption is slight or considerable, he must never omit one comma and leave the other. There is no defense for such punctuation as

Marjorie's husband, Colonel Nelson paid us a visit yesterday.

or

My brother you will be pleased to hear, is now in perfect health.

Dates usually contain parenthetic words or figures. Punctuate as follows:

February to July, 1972
April 6, 1956
Wednesday, November 13, 1929

Note that it is customary to omit the comma in

6 April 1958

The last form is an excellent way to write a date; the figures are separated by a word and are, for that reason, quickly grasped.

A name or a title in direct address is parenthetic.

If, Sir, you refuse, I cannot predict what will happen.
Well, Susan, this is a fine mess you are in.

The abbreviations *etc., i.e.,* and *e.g.,* the abbreviations for academic degrees, and titles that follow a name are parenthetic and should be punctuated accordingly.

Letters, packages, etc., should go here.
Horace Fulsome, Ph.D., presided.
Rachel Simonds, Attorney
The Reverend Harry Lang, S.J.

No comma, however, should separate a noun from a restrictive term of identification.

Billy the Kid
The novelist John Fowles
William the Conqueror
Pliny the Younger

Although *Junior,* with its abbreviation *Jr.,* has commonly been regarded as

parenthetic, logic suggests that it is, in fact, restrictive and therefore not in need of a comma.

> James Wright Jr.

Nonrestrictive relative clauses are parenthetic, as are similar clauses introduced by conjunctions indicating time or place. Commas are therefore needed.
A nonrestrictive clause is one that does not serve to identify or define the antecedent noun.

> The audience, which had at first been indifferent, became more and more interested.
>
> In 1769, when Napoleon was born, Corsica had but recently been acquired by France.
>
> Nether Stowey, where Coleridge wrote *The Rime of the Ancient Mariner,* is a few miles from Bridgewater.

In these sentences, the clauses introduced by *which, when,* and *where* are nonrestrictive; they do not limit or define, they merely add something. In the first example, the clause introduced by *which* does not serve to tell which of several possible audiences is meant; the reader presumably knows that already. The clause adds, parenthetically, a statement supplementing that in the main clause. Each of the three sentences is a combination of two statements that might have been made independently.

> The audience was at first indifferent. Later it became more and more interested.
>
> Napoleon was born in 1769. At that time Corsica had but recently been acquired by France.
>
> Coleridge wrote *The Rime of the Ancient Mariner* at Nether Stowey. Nether Stowey is a few miles from Bridgewater.

Restrictive clauses, by contrast, are not parenthetic and are not set off by commas. Thus,

> People who live in glass houses shouldn't throw stones.

Here the clause introduced by *who* does serve to tell which people are meant; the sentence, unlike the sentences above, cannot be split into two independent statements. The same principle of comma use applies to participial phrases and to appositives.

> People sitting in the rear couldn't hear. (*restrictive*)
>
> Uncle Bert, being slightly deaf, moved forward. (*nonrestrictive*)
>
> My cousin Bob is a talented harpist. (*restrictive*)
>
> Our oldest daughter, Mary, sings. (*nonrestrictive*)

When the main clause of a sentence is preceded by a phrase or a subordinate clause, use a comma to set off these elements.

> Partly by hard fighting, partly by diplomatic skill, they enlarged their dominions to the east and rose to royal rank with the possession of Sicily.

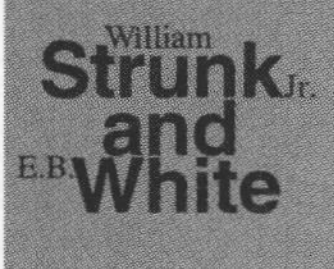


## 4. *Place a comma before a conjunction introducing an independent clause.*

> The early records of the city have disappeared, and the story of its first years can no longer be reconstructed.
>
> The situation is perilous, but there is still one chance of escape.

Two-part sentences of which the second member is introduced by *as* (in the sense of "because"), *for, or, nor,* or *while* (in the sense of "and at the same time") likewise require a comma before the conjunction.

If a dependent clause, or an introductory phrase requiring to be set off by a comma, precedes the second independent clause, no comma is needed after the conjunction.

> The situation is perilous, but if we are prepared to act promptly, there is still one chance of escape.

When the subject is the same for both clauses and is expressed only once, a comma is useful if the connective is *but.* When the connective is *and,* the comma should be omitted if the relation between the two statements is close or immediate.

> I have heard his arguments, but am still unconvinced.
>
> He has had several years' experience and is thoroughly competent.

## 5. *Do not join independent clauses by a comma.*

If two or more clauses grammatically complete and not joined by a conjunction are to form a single compound sentence, the proper mark of punctuation is a semicolon.

> Stevenson's romances are entertaining; they are full of exciting adventures.
>
> It is nearly half past five; we cannot reach town before dark.

It is, of course, equally correct to write each of these as two sentences, replacing the semicolons with periods.

> Stevenson's romances are entertaining. They are full of exciting adventures.
>
> It is nearly half past five. We cannot reach town before dark.

If a conjunction is inserted, the proper mark is a comma. (Rule 4.)

> Stevenson's romances are entertaining, for they are full of exciting adventures.
>
> It is nearly half past five, and we cannot reach town before dark.

A comparison of the three forms given above will show clearly the advantage of the first. It is, at least in the examples given, better than the second form because it suggests the close relationship between the two statements in a way that the second does not attempt, and better than the third because it is briefer and therefore more forcible. Indeed, this simple method of indicating relationship

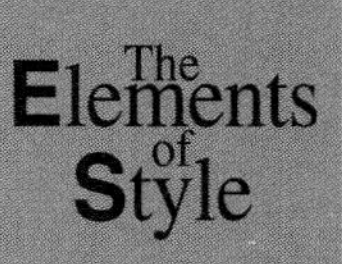


between statements is one of the most useful devices of composition. The relationship, as above, is commonly one of cause and consequence.

Note that if the second clause is preceded by an adverb, such as *accordingly, besides, then, therefore,* or *thus,* and not by a conjunction, the semicolon is still required.

> I had never been in the place before; besides, it was dark as a tomb.

An exception to the semicolon rule is worth noting here. A comma is preferable when the clauses are very short and alike in form, or when the tone of the sentence is easy and conversational.

> Man proposes, God disposes.
>
> The gates swung apart, the bridge fell, the portcullis was drawn up.
>
> I hardly knew him, he was so changed.
>
> Here today, gone tomorrow.

## 6. *Do not break sentences in two.*

In other words, do not use periods for commas.

> I met them on a Cunard liner many years ago. Coming home from Liverpool to New York.
>
> He was an interesting talker. A man who had traveled all over the world and lived in half a dozen countries.

In both these examples, the first period should be replaced by a comma and the following word begun with a small letter.

It is permissible to make an emphatic word or expression serve the purpose of a sentence and to punctuate it accordingly:

> Again and again he called out. No reply.

The writer must, however, be certain that the emphasis is warranted, lest his clipped sentence seem merely a blunder in syntax or in punctuation. Generally speaking, the place for broken sentences is in dialogue, when a character happens to speak in a clipped or fragmentary way.

Rules 3, 4, 5, and 6 cover the most important principles that govern punctuation. They should be so thoroughly mastered that their application becomes second nature.

## 7. *Use a colon after an independent clause to introduce a list of particulars, an appositive, an amplification, or an illustrative quotation.*

A colon tells the reader that what follows is closely related to the preceding clause. The colon has more effect than the comma, less power to separate than the semicolon, and more formality than the dash. It usually follows an independent clause and should not separate a verb from its complement or a preposition from

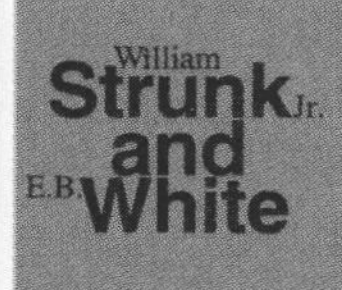


its object. The examples in the left-hand column, below, are wrong; they should be rewritten as in the right-hand column.

| | |
|---|---|
| Your dedicated whittler requires: a knife, a piece of wood, and a back porch. | Your dedicated whittler requires three props: a knife, a piece of wood, and a back porch. |
| Understanding is that penetrating quality of knowledge that grows from: theory, practice, conviction, assertion, error, and humiliation. | Understanding is that penetrating quality of knowledge that grows from theory, practice, conviction, assertion, error, and humiliation. |

Join two independent clauses with a colon if the second interprets or amplifies the first.

> But even so, there was a directness and dispatch about animal burial: there was no stopover in the undertaker's foul parlor, no wreath or spray.

A colon may introduce a quotation that supports or contributes to the preceding clause.

> The squalor of the streets reminded him of a line from Oscar Wilde: "We are all in the gutter, but some of us are looking at the stars."

The colon also has certain functions of form: to follow the salutation of a formal letter, to separate hour from minute in a notation of time, and to separate the title of a work from its subtitle or a Bible chapter from a verse.

> Dear Mr. Montague:
>
> *Practical Calligraphy: An Introduction to Italic Script*
>
> departs at 10:48 P.M.
>
> Nehemiah 11:7

## 8. *Use a dash to set off an abrupt break or interruption, and to announce a long appositive or summary.*

A dash is a mark of separation stronger than a comma, less formal than a colon, and more relaxed than parentheses.

> His first thought on getting out of bed—if he had any thought at all—was to get back in again.
>
> The rear axle began to make a noise—a grinding, chattering, teeth-gritting rasp.
>
> The increasing reluctance of the sun to rise, the extra nip in the breeze, the patter of shed leaves dropping— all the evidences of fall drifting into winter were clearer each day.

Use a dash only when a more common mark of punctuation seems inadequate.

| | |
|---|---|
| Her father's suspicions proved well-founded—it was not Edward she cared for—it was San Francisco. | Her father's suspicions proved well-founded. It was not Edward she cared for, it was San Francisco. |
| Violence—the kind you see on television—is not honestly violent—there lies its harm. | Violence, the kind you see on television, is not honestly violent. There lies its harm. |

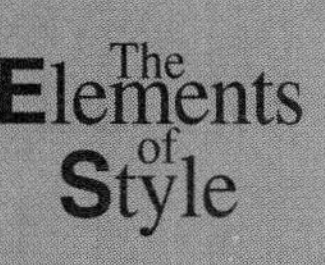

## *9. The number of the subject determines the number of the verb.*

Words that intervene between subject and verb do not affect the number of the verb.

| | |
|---|---|
| The bittersweet flavor of youth—its trials, its joys, its adventures, its challenges—are not soon forgotten. | The bittersweet flavor of youth—its trials, its joys, its adventures, its challenges—is not soon forgotten. |

A common blunder is the use of a singular verb form in a relative clause following "one of . . ." or a similar expression when the relative is the subject.

| | |
|---|---|
| One of the ablest men who has attacked this problem | One of the ablest men who have attacked this problem |
| One of those people who is never ready on time | One of those people who are never ready on time |

Use a singular verb form after *each, either, everyone, everybody, neither, nobody, someone*.

Everybody thinks he has a sense of humor.

Although both clocks strike cheerfully, neither keeps good time.

With *none,* use the singular verb when the word means "no one" or "not one."

| | |
|---|---|
| None of us are perfect. | None of us is perfect. |

A plural verb is commonly used when *none* suggests more than one thing or person.

None are so fallible as those who are sure they're right.

A compound subject formed of two or more nouns joined by *and* almost always requires a plural verb.

The walrus and the carpenter were walking close at hand.

But certain compounds, often clichés, are so inseparable they are considered a unit and so take a singular verb, as do compound subjects qualified by *each* or *every.*

The long and the short of it is . . .

Bread and butter was all she served.

Give and take is essential to a happy household.

Every window, picture, and mirror was smashed.

A singular subject remains singular even if other nouns are connected to it by *with, as well as, in addition to, except, together with,* and *no less than.*

His speech as well as his manner is objectionable.

A linking verb agrees with the number of its subject.

What is wanted is a few more pairs of hands.

The trouble with truth is its many varieties.

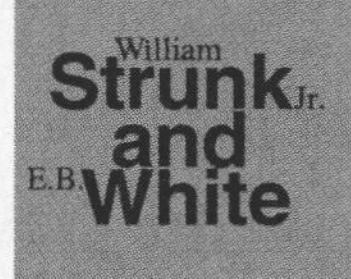


Some nouns that appear to be plural are usually construed as singular and given a singular verb.

> Politics is an art, not a science.
>
> The Republican Headquarters is on this side of the tracks.

But

> The general's quarters are over the river.

In these cases the writer must simply learn the idioms. The contents of a book is singular. The contents of a jar may be either singular or plural, depending on what's in the jar—jam or marbles.

### *10. Use the proper case of pronoun.*

The personal pronouns, as well as the pronoun *who,* change form as they function as subject or object.

> Will Jane or he be hired, do you think?
> The culprit, it turned out, was he.
> We heavy eaters would rather walk than ride.
> Who knocks?
> Give this work to whoever looks idle.

In the last example, *whoever* is the subject of *looks idle;* the object of the preposition *to* is the entire clause *whoever looks idle.* When *who* introduces a subordinate clause, its case depends on its function in that clause.

| | |
|---|---|
| Virgil Soames is the candidate whom we think will win. | Virgil Soames is the candidate who we think will win. |
| Virgil Soames is the candidate who we hope to elect. | Virgil Soames is the candidate whom we hope to elect. |

A pronoun in a comparison is nominative if it is the subject of a stated or understood verb.

> Sandy writes better than I. (Than I write.)

In general, avoid "understood" verbs by supplying them.

| | |
|---|---|
| I think Horace admires Jessica more than I. | I think Horace admires Jessica more than I do. |
| Polly loves cake more than me. | Polly loves cake more than she loves me. |

The objective case is correct in the following examples.

> The ranger offered Shirley and him some advice on campsites.
> They came to meet the Baldwins and us.
> Let's talk it over between us, then, you and me.
> Whom should I ask?
> A group of us taxpayers protested.

*Us* in the last example is in apposition to taxpayers, the object of the preposition *of.* The wording, although grammatically defensible, is rarely apt. "A group of us protested as taxpayers" is better, if not exactly equivalent.

Use the simple personal pronoun as a subject.

| | |
|---|---|
| Blake and myself stayed home. | Blake and I stayed home. |
| Howard and yourself brought the lunch, I thought. | Howard and you brought the lunch, I thought. |

The possessive case of pronouns is used to show ownership. It has two forms: the adjectival modifier, *your* hat, and the noun form, a hat of *yours.*

> The dog has buried one of your gloves and one of mine in the flower bed.

Gerunds usually require the possessive case.

> Mother objected to our driving on the icy roads.

A present participle as a verbal, on the other hand, takes the objective case.

> They heard him singing in the shower.

The difference between a verbal participle and a gerund is not always obvious, but note what is really said in each of the following.

> Do you mind me asking a question?
>
> Do you mind my asking a question?

In the first sentence, the queried objection is to *me,* as opposed to other members of the group, putting one of the questions. In the second example, the issue is whether a question may be asked at all.

## *11. A participial phrase at the beginning of a sentence must refer to the grammatical subject.*

> Walking slowly down the road, he saw a woman accompanied by two children.

The word *walking* refers to the subject of the sentence, not to the woman. If the writer wishes to make it refer to the woman, he must recast the sentence.

> He saw a woman, accompanied by two children, walking slowly down the road.

Participial phrases preceded by a conjunction or by a preposition, nouns in apposition, adjectives, and adjective phrases come under the same rule if they begin the sentence.

| | |
|---|---|
| On arriving in Chicago, his friends met him at the station. | On arriving in Chicago, he was met at the station by his friends. |
| A soldier of proved valor, they entrusted him with the defense of the city. | A soldier of proved valor, he was entrusted with the defense of the city. |

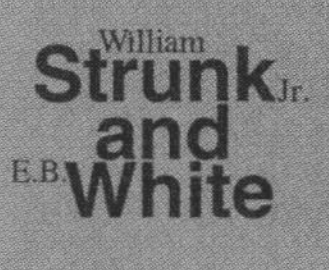

| | |
|---|---|
| Young and inexperienced, the task seemed easy to me. | Young and inexperienced, I thought the task easy. |
| Without a friend to counsel him, the temptation proved irresistible. | Without a friend to counsel him, he found the temptation irresistible. |

Sentences violating Rule 11 are often ludicrous:

> Being in a dilapidated condition, I was able to buy the house very cheap.
>
> Wondering irresolutely what to do next, the clock struck twelve.
>
> As a mother of five, with another on the way, my ironing board is always up.

# II
# *Elementary Principles of Composition*

## *12. Choose a suitable design and hold to it.*

A basic structural design underlies every kind of writing. The writer will in part follow this design, in part deviate from it, according to his skill, his needs, and the unexpected events that accompany the act of composition. Writing, to be effective, must follow closely the thoughts of the writer, but not necessarily in the order in which those thoughts occur. This calls for a scheme of procedure. In some cases the best design is no design, as with a love letter, which is simply an outpouring, or with a casual essay, which is a ramble. But in most cases planning must be a deliberate prelude to writing. The first principle of composition, therefore, is to foresee or determine the shape of what is to come and pursue that shape.

A sonnet is built on a fourteen-line frame, each line containing five feet. Hence, the sonneteer knows exactly where he is headed, although he may not know how to get there. Most forms of composition are less clearly defined, more flexible, but all have skeletons to which the writer will bring the flesh and the blood. The more clearly he perceives the shape, the better are his chances of success.

## *13. Make the paragraph the unit of composition.*

The paragraph is a convenient unit; it serves all forms of literary work. As long as it holds together, a paragraph may be of any length—a single, short sentence or a passage of great duration.

If the subject on which you are writing is of slight extent, or if you intend to treat it briefly, there may be no need to divide it into topics. Thus, a brief description, a brief book review, a brief account of a single incident, a narrative merely outlining an action, the setting forth of a single idea—any one of these is best written in a single paragraph. After the paragraph has been written, examine it to see whether division will improve it.

Ordinarily, however, a subject requires division into topics, each of which should be dealt with in a paragraph. The object of treating each topic in a paragraph by itself is, of course, to aid the reader. The beginning of each paragraph is a signal to him that a new step in the development of the subject has been reached.

As a rule, single sentences should not be written or printed as paragraphs. An exception may be made of sentences of transition, indicating the relation between the parts of an exposition or argument.

In dialogue, each speech, even if only a single word, is usually a paragraph by itself; that is, a new paragraph begins with each change of speaker. The application of this rule when dialogue and narrative are combined is best learned from

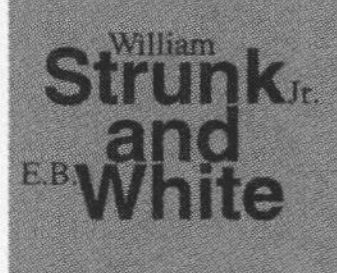


examples in well-edited works of fiction. Sometimes a writer, seeking to create an effect of rapid talk or for some other reason, will elect not to set off each speech in a separate paragraph and instead will run speeches together. The common practice, however, and the one that serves best in most instances, is to give each speech a paragraph of its own.

As a rule, begin each paragraph either with a sentence that suggests the topic or with a sentence that helps the transition. If a paragraph forms part of a larger composition, its relation to what precedes, or its function as a part of the whole, may need to be expressed. This can sometimes be done by a mere word or phrase (*again; therefore; for the same reason*) in the first sentence. Sometimes, however, it is expedient to get into the topic slowly, by way of a sentence or two of introduction or transition.

In narration and description, the paragraph sometimes begins with a concise, comprehensive statement serving to hold together the details that follow.

> The breeze served us admirably.
>
> The campaign opened with a series of reverses.
>
> The next ten or twelve pages were filled with a curious set of entries.

But when this device, or any device, is too often used, it becomes a mannerism. More commonly the opening sentence simply indicates by its subject the direction the paragraph is to take.

> At length I thought I might return toward the stockade.
>
> He picked up the heavy lamp from the table and began to explore.
>
> Another flight of steps, and they emerged on the roof.

In animated narrative, the paragraphs are likely to be short and without any semblance of a topic sentence, the writer rushing headlong, event following event in rapid succession. The break between such paragraphs merely serves the purpose of a rhetorical pause, throwing into prominence some detail of the action.

In general, remember that paragraphing calls for a good eye as well as a logical mind. Enormous blocks of print look formidable to a reader. He has a certain reluctance to tackle them; he can lose his way in them. Therefore, breaking long paragraphs in two, even if it is not necessary to do so for sense, meaning, or logical development, is often a visual help. But remember, too, that firing off many short paragraphs in quick succession can be distracting. Paragraph breaks used only for show read like the writing of commerce or of display advertising. Moderation and a sense of order should be the main considerations in paragraphing.

### *14. Use the active voice.*

The active voice is usually more direct and vigorous than the passive:

> I shall always remember my first visit to Boston.

This is much better than

> My first visit to Boston will always be remembered by me.

The latter sentence is less direct, less bold, and less concise. If the writer tries to make it more concise by omitting "by me,"

> My first visit to Boston will always be remembered,

it becomes indefinite: is it the writer or some person undisclosed or the world at large that will always remember this visit?

This rule does not, of course, mean that the writer should entirely discard the passive voice, which is frequently convenient and sometimes necessary.

> The dramatists of the Restoration are little esteemed today.
>
> Modern readers have little esteem for the dramatists of the Restoration.

The first would be the preferred form in a paragraph on the dramatists of the Restoration, the second in a paragraph on the tastes of modern readers. The need of making a particular word the subject of the sentence will often, as in these examples, determine which voice is to be used.

The habitual use of the active voice, however, makes for forcible writing. This is true not only in narrative concerned principally with action but in writing of any kind. Many a tame sentence of description or exposition can be made lively and emphatic by substituting a transitive in the active voice for some such perfunctory expression as *there is* or *could be heard.*

| | |
|---|---|
| There were a great number of dead leaves lying on the ground. | Dead leaves covered the ground. |
| At dawn the crowing of a rooster could be heard. | The cock's crow came with dawn. |
| The reason he left college was that his health became impaired. | Failing health compelled him to leave college. |
| It was not long before he was very sorry that he had said what he had. | He soon repented his words. |

Note, in the examples above, that when a sentence is made stronger, it usually becomes shorter. Thus, brevity is a by-product of vigor.

## *15. Put statements in positive form.*

Make definite assertions. Avoid tame, colorless, hesitating, noncommittal language. Use the word *not* as a means of denial or in antithesis, never as a means of evasion.

| | |
|---|---|
| He was not very often on time. | He usually came late. |
| He did not think that studying Latin was a sensible way to use one's time. | He thought the study of Latin a waste of time. |
| *The Taming of the Shrew* is rather weak in spots. Shakespeare does not portray Katharine as a very admirable character, nor does Bianca remain long in memory as an important character in Shakespeare's works. | The women in *The Taming of the Shrew* are unattractive. Katharine is disagreeable, Bianca insignificant. |

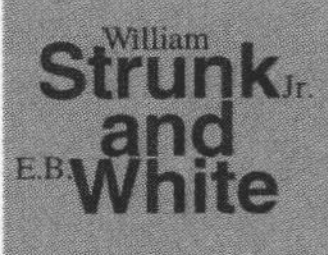


The last example, before correction, is indefinite as well as negative. The corrected version, consequently, is simply a guess at the writer's intention.

All three examples show the weakness inherent in the word *not.* Consciously or unconsciously, the reader is dissatisfied with being told only what is not; he wishes to be told what is. Hence, as a rule, it is better to express even a negative in positive form.

| | |
|---|---|
| not honest | dishonest |
| not important | trifling |
| did not remember | forgot |
| did not pay any attention to | ignored |
| did not have much confidence in | distrusted |

Placing negative and positive in opposition makes for a stronger structure.

> Not charity, but simple justice.
>
> Not that I loved Caesar less, but that I loved Rome more.
>
> Ask not what your country can do for you—ask what you can do for your country.

Negative words other than *not* are usually strong.

> Her loveliness I never knew/Until she smiled on me.

Statements qualified with unnecessary auxiliaries or conditionals sound irresolute.

| | |
|---|---|
| If you would let us know the time of your arrival, we would be happy to arrange your transportation from the airport. | If you will let us know the time of your arrival, we shall be happy to arrange your transportation from the airport. |
| The applicant can make a good impression by being neat and punctual. | The applicant will make a good impression if he is neat and punctual. |
| Keats may be ranked among those romantic poets who died young. | Keats was one of those romantic poets who died young. |

If your every sentence admits a doubt, your writing will lack authority. Save the auxiliaries *would, should, could, may, might,* and *can* for situations involving real uncertainty.

## *16. Use definite, specific, concrete language.*

Prefer the specific to the general, the definite to the vague, the concrete to the abstract.

| | |
|---|---|
| A period of unfavorable weather set in. | It rained every day for a week. |
| He showed satisfaction as he took possession of his well-earned reward. | He grinned as he pocketed the coin. |

If those who have studied the art of writing are in accord on any one point, it is on this: the surest way to arouse and hold the attention of the reader is by being

specific, definite, and concrete. The greatest writers—Homer, Dante, Shakespeare—are effective largely because they deal in particulars and report the details that matter. Their words call up pictures.

Jean Stafford, to cite a modern author, demonstrates in her short story "In the Zoo" how prose is made vivid by the use of words that evoke images and sensations:

> . . . Daisy and I in time found asylum in a small menagerie down by the railroad tracks. It belonged to a gentle alcoholic ne'er-do-well, who did nothing all day long but drink bathtub gin in rickeys and play solitaire and smile to himself and talk to his animals. He had a little, stunted red vixen and a deodorized skunk, a parrot from Tahiti that spoke Parisian French, a woebegone coyote, and two capuchin monkeys, so serious and humanized, so small and sad and sweet, and so religious-looking with their tonsured heads that it was impossible not to think their gibberish was really an ordered language with a grammar that someday some philologist would understand.
>
> Gran knew about our visits to Mr. Murphy and she did not object, for it gave her keen pleasure to excoriate him when we came home. His vice was not a matter of guesswork; it was an established fact that he was half-seas over from dawn till midnight. "With the black Irish," said Gran, "the taste for drink is taken in with the mother's milk and is never mastered. Oh, I know all about those promises to join the temperance movement and not to touch another drop. The way to Hell is paved with good intentions."
>
> We were still little girls when we discovered Mr. Murphy, before the shattering disease of adolescence was to make our bones and brains ache even more painfully than before, and we loved him and we hoped to marry him when we grew up. We loved him, and we loved his monkeys to exactly the same degree and in exactly the same way; they were husbands and fathers and brothers, these little, ugly, dark, secret men who minded their own business and let us mind ours. If we stuck our fingers through the bars of the cage, the monkeys would sometimes take them in their tight, tiny hands and look into our faces with a tentative, somehow absent-minded sorrow, as if they terribly regretted that they could not place us but were glad to see us all the same. Mr. Murphy, playing a solitaire game of cards called "once in a blue moon" on a kitchen table in his back yard beside the pens, would occasionally look up and blink his beautiful blue eyes and say, "You're peaches to make over my wee friends. I love you for it." There was nothing demanding in his voice, and nothing sticky; on his lips the word "love" was jocose and forthright, it had no strings attached. We would sit on either side of him and watch him regiment his ranks of cards and stop to drink as deeply as if he were dying of thirst and wave to his animals and say to them, "Yes, lads, you're dandies."*

If the experiences of Walter Mitty, of Dick Diver, of Rabbit Angstrom have seemed for the moment real to countless readers, if in reading Faulkner we have almost the sense of inhabiting Yoknapatawpha County during the decline of the South, it is because the details used are definite, the terms concrete. It is not that every detail is given—that would be impossible, as well as to no purpose—but that all the significant details are given, and with such accuracy and vigor that the reader, in imagination, can project himself into the scene.

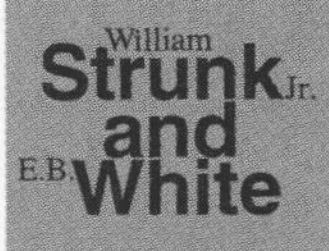


In exposition and in argument, the writer must likewise never lose his hold upon the concrete; and even when he is dealing with general principles, he must furnish particular instances of their application.

In his *Philosophy of Style*, Herbert Spencer gives two sentences to illustrate how the vague and general can be turned into the vivid and particular:

> In proportion as the manners, customs, and amusements of a nation are cruel and barbarous, the regulations of its penal code will be severe.

> In proportion as men delight in battles, bullfights, and combats of gladiators, will they punish by hanging, burning, and the rack.

To show what happens when strong writing is deprived of its vigor, George Orwell once took a passage from the Bible and drained it of its blood. On the left, below, is Orwell's translation; on the right, the verse from Ecclesiastes (King James Version).

> Objective consideration of contemporary phenomena compels the conclusion that success or failure in competitive activities exhibits no tendency to be commensurate with innate capacity, but that a considerable element of the unpredictable must inevitably be taken into account.

> I returned, and saw under the sun, that the race is not to the swift, nor the battle to the strong, neither yet bread to the wise, nor yet riches to men of understanding, nor yet favor to men of skill; but time and chance happeneth to them all.

## *17. Omit needless words.*

Vigorous writing is concise. A sentence should contain no unnecessary words, a paragraph no unnecessary sentences, for the same reason that a drawing should have no unnecessary lines and a machine no unnecessary parts. This requires not that the writer make all his sentences short, or that he avoid all detail and treat his subjects only in outline, but that every word tell.

Many expressions in common use violate this principle.

| | |
|---|---|
| the question as to whether | whether (the question whether) |
| there is no doubt but that | no doubt (doubtless) |
| used for fuel purposes | used for fuel |
| he is a man who | he |
| in a hasty manner | hastily |
| this is a subject that | this subject |
| His story is a strange one. | His story is strange. |
| the reason why is that | because |

An expression that is especially debilitating is *the fact that*. It should be revised out of every sentence in which it occurs.

| | |
|---|---|
| owing to the fact that | since (because) |
| in spite of the fact that | though (although) |
| call your attention to the fact that | remind you (notify you) |
| I was unaware of the fact that | I was unaware that (did not know) |
| the fact that he had not succeeded | his failure |
| the fact that I had arrived | my arrival |

See also the words *case, character, nature* in Chapter IV.

*Who is, which was,* and the like are often superfluous.

| | |
|---|---|
| His brother, who is a member of the same firm | His brother, a member of the same firm |
| Trafalgar, which was Nelson's last battle | Trafalgar, Nelson's last battle |

As a positive statement is more concise than a negative one, and the active voice more concise than the passive, many of the examples given under Rules 14 and 15 illustrate this rule as well.

A common way to fall into wordiness is to present a single complex idea, step by step, in a series of sentences that might to advantage be combined into one.

| | |
|---|---|
| Macbeth was very ambitious. This led him to wish to become king of Scotland. The witches told him that this wish of his would come true. The king of Scotland at this time was Duncan. Encouraged by his wife, Macbeth murdered Duncan. He was thus enabled to succeed Duncan as king. (51 words ) | Encouraged by his wife, Macbeth achieved his ambition and realized the prediction of the witches by murdering Duncan and becoming king of Scotland in his place. (26 words) |

## *18. Avoid a succession of loose sentences.*

This rule refers especially to loose sentences of a particular type: those consisting of two clauses, the second introduced by a conjunction or relative. A writer may err by making his sentences too compact and periodic. An occasional loose sentence prevents the style from becoming too formal and gives the reader a certain relief. Consequently, loose sentences are common in easy, unstudied writing. The danger is that there may be too many of them.

An unskilled writer will sometimes construct a whole paragraph of sentences of this kind, using as connectives *and, but,* and, less frequently, *who, which, when, where,* and *while,* these last in nonrestrictive senses. (See Rule 3.)

> The third concert of the subscription series was given last evening, and a large audience was in attendance. Mr. Edward Appleton was the soloist, and the Boston Symphony Orchestra furnished the instrumental music. The former showed himself to be an artist of the first rank, while the latter proved itself fully deserving of its high reputation. The interest aroused by the series has been very gratifying to the Committee, and it is planned to give a similar series annually hereafter. The fourth concert will be given on Tuesday, May 10, when an equally attractive program will be presented.

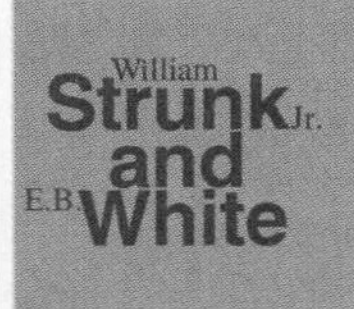

Apart from its triteness and emptiness, the paragraph above is bad because of the structure of its sentences, with their mechanical symmetry and singsong. Compare these sentences from the chapter "What I Believe" in E. M. Forster's *Two Cheers for Democracy:*

> I believe in aristocracy, though—if that is the right word, and if a democrat may use it. Not an aristocracy of power, based upon rank and influence, but an aristocracy of the sensitive, the considerate and the plucky. Its members are to be found in all nations and classes, and all through the ages, and there is a secret understanding between them when they meet. They represent the true human tradition, the one permanent victory of our queer race over cruelty and chaos. Thousands of them perish in obscurity, a few are great names. They are sensitive for others as well as for themselves, they are considerate without being fussy, their pluck is not swankiness but the power to endure, and they can take a joke.*

If the writer finds that he has written a series of loose sentences, he should recast enough of them to remove the monotony, replacing them by simple sentences, by sentences of two clauses joined by a semicolon, by periodic sentences of two clauses, by sentences (loose or periodic) of three clauses—whichever best represent the real relations of the thought.

## *19. Express coordinate ideas in similar form.*

This principle, that of parallel construction, requires that expressions similar in content and function be outwardly similar. The likeness of form enables the reader to recognize more readily the likeness of content and function. The familiar Beatitudes exemplify the virtue of parallel construction.

> Blessed are the poor in spirit: for theirs is the kingdom of heaven.
>
> Blessed are they that mourn: for they shall be comforted.
>
> Blessed are the meek: for they shall inherit the earth.
>
> Blessed are they which do hunger and thirst after righteousness: for they shall be filled.

The unskillful writer often violates this principle, from a mistaken belief that he should constantly vary the form of his expressions. When repeating a statement to emphasize it, the writer may need to vary its form. But apart from this he should follow the principle of parallel construction.

| | |
|---|---|
| Formerly, science was taught by the textbook method, while now the laboratory method is employed. | Formerly, science was taught by the textbook method; now it is taught by the laboratory method. |

The left-hand version gives the impression that the writer is undecided or timid; he seems unable or afraid to choose one form of expression and hold to it. The right-hand version shows that the writer has at least made his choice and abided by it.

* From *Two Cheers for Democracy,* copyright, 1951, by E. M. Forster. Published by Harcourt, Brace and Company, Inc.

By this principle, an article or a preposition applying to all the members of a series must either be used only before the first term or else be repeated before each term.

| | |
|---|---|
| the French, the Italians, Spanish, and Portuguese | the French, the Italians, the Spanish, and the Portuguese |
| in spring, summer, or in winter | in spring, summer, or winter (in spring, in summer, or in winter) |

Some words require a particular preposition in certain idiomatic uses. When such words are joined in a compound construction, all the appropriate prepositions must be included, unless they are the same.

| | |
|---|---|
| His speech was marked by disagreement and scorn for his opponent's position. | His speech was marked by disagreement with and scorn for his opponent's position. |

Correlative expressions (*both, and; not, but; not only, but also; either, or; first, second, third;* and the like) should be followed by the same grammatical construction. Many violations of this rule can be corrected by rearranging the sentence.

| | |
|---|---|
| It was both a long ceremony and very tedious. | The ceremony was both long and tedious. |
| A time not for words but action. | A time not for words but for action. |
| Either you must grant his request or incur his ill will. | You must either grant his request or incur his ill will. |
| My objections are, first, the injustice of the measure; second, that it is unconstitutional. | My objections are, first, that the measure is unjust; second, that it is unconstitutional. |

It may be asked, what if a writer needs to express a rather large number of similar ideas—say, twenty? Must he write twenty consecutive sentences of the same pattern? On closer examination he will probably find that the difficulty is imaginary—that his twenty ideas can be classified in groups, and that he need apply the principle only within each group. Otherwise he had best avoid the difficulty by putting his statements in the form of a table.

## *20. Keep related words together.*

The position of the words in a sentence is the principal means of showing their relationship. Confusion and ambiguity result when words are badly placed. The writer must, therefore, bring together the words and groups of words that are related in thought and keep apart those that are not so related.

| | |
|---|---|
| He noticed a large stain in the rug that was right in the center. | He noticed a large stain right in the center of the rug. |
| You can call your mother in London and tell her all about George's taking you out to dinner for just sixty cents. | For just sixty cents you can call your mother in London and tell her all about George's taking you out to dinner. |

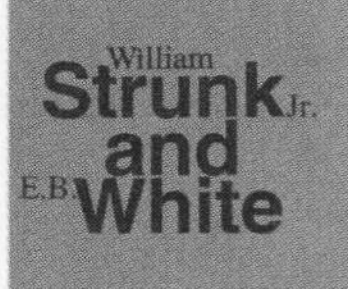

New York's first commercial human-sperm bank opened Friday with semen samples from 18 men frozen in a stainless steel tank.

New York's first commercial human-sperm bank opened Friday when semen samples were taken from 18 men. The samples were then frozen and stored in a stainless steel tank.

In the left-hand version of the first example, the reader has no way of knowing whether the stain was in the center of the rug or the rug was in the center of the room. In the left-hand version of the second example, the reader may well wonder which cost sixty cents—the phone call or the dinner. In the left-hand version of the third example, the reader's heart goes out to those eighteen poor fellows frozen in a steel tank.

The subject of a sentence and the principal verb should not, as a rule, be separated by a phrase or clause that can be transferred to the beginning.

Wordsworth, in the fifth book of *The Excursion,* gives a minute description of this church.

In the fifth book of *The Excursion,* Wordsworth gives a minute description of this church.

A dog, if you fail to discipline him, becomes a household pest.

Unless disciplined, a dog becomes a household pest.

Interposing a phrase or a clause, as in the left-hand examples above, interrupts the flow of the main clause. This interruption, however, is not usually bothersome when the flow is checked only by a relative clause or by an expression in apposition. Sometimes, in periodic sentences, the interruption is a deliberate device for creating suspense. (See examples under Rule 22.)

The relative pronoun should come, in most instances, immediately after its antecedent.

There was a stir in the audience that suggested disapproval.

A stir that suggested disapproval swept the audience.

He wrote three articles about his adventures in Spain, which were published in *Harper's Magazine*

He published three articles in *Harper's Magazine* about his adventures in Spain.

This is a portrait of Benjamin Harrison, grandson of William Henry Harrison, who became President in 1889.

This is a portrait of Benjamin Harrison, who became President in 1889. He was the grandson of William Henry Harrison.

If the antecedent consists of a group of words, the relative comes at the end of the group, unless this would cause ambiguity.

The Superintendent of the Chicago Division, who

No ambiguity results from the above. But

A proposal to amend the Sherman Act, which has been variously judged

leaves the reader wondering whether it is the proposal or the Act that has been variously judged. The relative clause must be moved forward, to read, "A proposal, which has been variously judged, to amend the Sherman Act. . . ."

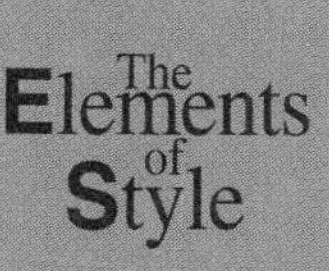


Similarly

| | |
|---|---|
| The grandson of William Henry Harrison, who | William Henry Harrison's grandson, Benjamin Harrison, who |

A noun in apposition may come between antecedent and relative, because in such a combination no real ambiguity can arise.

> The Duke of York, his brother, who was regarded with hostility by the Whigs

Modifiers should come, if possible, next to the word they modify. If several expressions modify the same word, they should be so arranged that no wrong relation is suggested.

| | |
|---|---|
| All the members were not present. | Not all the members were present. |
| He only found two mistakes. | He found only two mistakes. |
| The chairman said he hoped all members would give generously to the Fund at a meeting of the committee yesterday. | At a meeting of the committee yesterday, the chairman said he hoped all members would give generously to the Fund. |
| Major R. E. Joyce will give a lecture on Tuesday evening in Bailey Hall, to which the public is invited on "My Experiences in Mesopotamia" at eight P.M. | On Tuesday evening at eight, Major R. E. Joyce will give a lecture in Bailey Hall on his experiences in Mesopotamia. The public is invited. |

Note, in the last left-hand example, how swiftly meaning departs when words are wrongly juxtaposed.

## *21. In summaries, keep to one tense.*

In summarizing the action of a drama, the writer should use the present tense. In summarizing a poem, story, or novel, he should also use the present, though he may use the past if it seems more natural to do so. If the summary is in the present tense, antecedent action should be expressed by the perfect; if in the past, by the past perfect.

> Chance prevents Friar John from delivering Friar Lawrence's letter to Romeo. Meanwhile, owing to her father's arbitrary change of the day set for her wedding, Juliet has been compelled to drink the potion on Tuesday night, with the result that Balthasar informs Romeo of her supposed death before Friar Lawrence learns of the nondelivery of the letter.

But whichever tense is used in the summary, a past tense in indirect discourse or in indirect question remains unchanged.

> The Friar confesses that it was he who married them.

Apart from the exceptions noted, whichever tense the writer chooses he should use throughout. Shifting from one tense to another gives the appearance of uncertainty and irresolution.

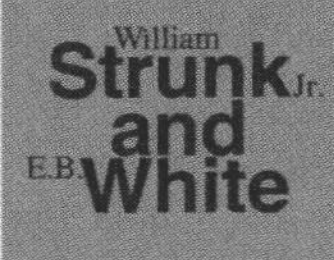

In presenting the statements or the thought of someone else, as in summarizing an essay or reporting a speech, the writer should not overwork such expressions as "he said," "he stated," "the speaker added," "the speaker then went on to say," "the author also thinks." He should indicate clearly at the outset, once for all, that what follows is summary, and then waste no words in repeating the notification.

In notebooks, in newspapers, in handbooks of literature, summaries of one kind or another may be indispensable, and for children in primary schools retelling a story in their own words is a useful exercise. But in the criticism or interpretation of literature the writer should be careful to avoid dropping into summary. He may find it necessary to devote one or two sentences to indicating the subject, or the opening situation, of the work he is discussing; he may cite numerous details to illustrate its qualities. But he should aim at writing an orderly discussion supported by evidence, not a summary with occasional comment. Similarly, if the scope of his discussion includes a number of works, he will as a rule do better not to take them up singly in chronological order but to aim from the beginning at establishing general conclusions.

## *22. Place the emphatic words of a sentence at the end.*

The proper place in the sentence for the word or group of words that the writer desires to make most prominent is usually the end.

| | |
|---|---|
| Humanity has hardly advanced in fortitude since that time, though it has advanced in many other ways. | Since that time, humanity has advanced in many ways, but it has hardly advanced in fortitude. |
| This steel is principally used for making razors, because of its hardness. | Because of its hardness, this steel is used principally for making razors. |

The word or group of words entitled to this position of prominence is usually the logical predicate—that is, the *new* element in the sentence, as it is in the second example.

The effectiveness of the periodic sentence arises from the prominence it gives to the main statement.

> Four centuries ago, Christopher Columbus, one of the Italian mariners whom the decline of their own republics had put at the service of the world and of adventure, seeking for Spain a westward passage to the Indies to offset the achievement of Portuguese discoverers, lighted on America.
>
> With these hopes and in this belief I would urge you, laying aside all hindrance, thrusting away all private aims, to devote yourself unswervingly and unflinchingly to the vigorous and successful prosecution of this war.

The other prominent position in the sentence is the beginning. Any element in the sentence other than the subject becomes emphatic when placed first.

> Deceit or treachery he could never forgive.

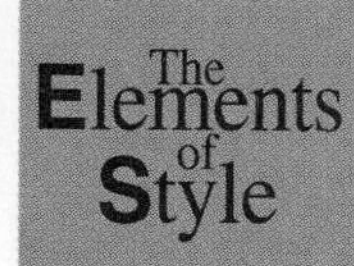

> Vast and rude, fretted by the action of nearly three thousand years, the fragments of this architecture may often seem, at first sight, like works of nature.
>
> Home is the sailor.

A subject coming first in its sentence may be emphatic, but hardly by its position alone. In the sentence

> Great kings worshiped at his shrine

the emphasis upon *kings* arises largely from its meaning and from the context. To receive special emphasis, the subject of a sentence must take the position of the predicate.

> Through the middle of the valley flowed a winding stream.

The principle that the proper place for what is to be made most prominent is the end applies equally to the words of a sentence, to the sentences of a paragraph, and to the paragraphs of a composition.

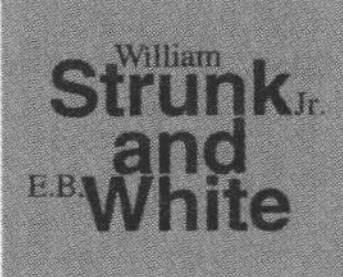


# III
# *A Few Matters of Form*

## *Colloquialisms.*

If you use a colloquialism or a slang word or phrase, simply use it; do not draw attention to it by enclosing it in quotation marks. To do so is to put on airs, as though you were inviting the reader to join you in a select society of those who know better.

## *Exclamations.*

Do not attempt to emphasize simple statements by using a mark of exclamation.

| | |
|---|---|
| It was a wonderful show! | It was a wonderful show. |

The exclamation mark is to be reserved for use after true exclamations or commands.

> What a wonderful show!
> Halt!

## *Headings.*

If a manuscript is to be submitted for publication, leave plenty of space at the top of page 1. The editor will need this space for his penciled directions to the compositor. Place the heading, or title, at least a fourth of the way down the page. Leave a blank line, or its equivalent in space, after the heading. On succeeding pages, begin near the top, but not so near as to give a crowded appearance. Omit the period after a title or heading. A question mark or an exclamation point may be used if the heading calls for it.

## *Hyphen.*

When two or more words are combined to form a compound adjective, a hyphen is usually required. "He belonged to the leisure class and enjoyed leisure-class pursuits." "He entered his boat in the round-the-island race."

Do not use a hyphen between words that can better be written as one word: *water-fowl, waterfowl*. Your common sense will aid you in the decision, but a dictionary is more reliable. The steady evolution of the language seems to favor union: two words eventually become one, usually after a period of hyphenation.

| | | |
|---|---|---|
| bed chamber | bed-chamber | bedchamber |
| wild life | wild-life | wildlife |
| bell boy | bell-boy | bellboy |

The hyphen can play tricks on the unwary, as it did in Chattanooga when two newspapers merged—the *News* and the *Free Press*. Someone introduced a hyphen into the merger, and the paper became *The Chattanooga News-Free Press*, which sounds as though the paper were news-free, or devoid of news. Obviously, we ask too much of a hyphen when we ask it to cast its spell over words it does not adjoin.

### *Margins.*

Keep right-hand and left-hand margins roughly the same width. Exception: If a great deal of annotating or editing is anticipated, the left-hand margin should be roomy enough to accommodate this work.

### *Numerals.*

Do not spell out dates or other serial numbers. Write them in figures or in Roman notation, as may be appropriate.

| | |
|---|---|
| August 9, 1968 | Chapter XII |
| Rule 3 | 352d Infantry |

Exception: When they occur in dialogue, most dates and numbers are best spelled out.

"I arrived home on August ninth."
"In the year 1970, I turned twenty-one."
"I shall read Chapter Twelve."

### *Parentheses.*

A sentence containing an expression in parentheses is punctuated outside the marks of parenthesis exactly as if the parenthetical expression were absent. The expression within the marks is punctuated as if it stood by itself, except that the final stop is omitted unless it is a question mark or an exclamation point.

> I went to his house yesterday (my third attempt to see him), but he had left town.
>
> He declares (and why should we doubt his good faith?) that he is now certain of success.

(When a wholly detached expression or sentence is parenthesized, the final stop comes before the last mark of parenthesis.)

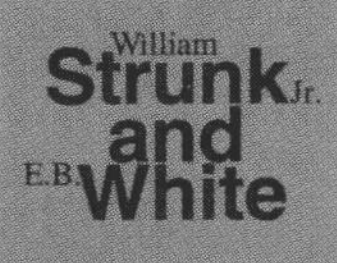


## *Quotations.*

Formal quotations cited as documentary evidence are introduced by a colon and enclosed in quotation marks.

> The United States Coast Pilot has this to say of the place: "Bracy Cove, 0.5 mile eastward of Bear Island, is exposed to southeast winds, has a rocky and uneven bottom, and is unfit for anchorage."

A quotation grammatically in apposition or the direct object of a verb is preceded by a comma and enclosed in quotation marks.

> I am reminded of the advice of my neighbor, "Never worry about your heart till it stops beating."
>
> Mark Twain says, "A classic is something that everybody wants to have read and nobody wants to read."

When a quotation is followed by an attributive phrase, the comma is enclosed within the quotation marks.

> "I can't attend," she said.

Typographical usage dictates that the comma be inside the marks, though logically it often seems not to belong there.

> "The Clerks," "Luke Havergal," and "Richard Cory" are in Robinson's *Children of the Night.*

When quotations of an entire line, or more, of either verse or prose are to be distinguished typographically from text matter, as are the quotations in this book, begin on a fresh line and indent. Quotation marks should not be used unless they appear in the original, as in dialogue.

> Wordsworth's enthusiasm for the French Revolution was at first unbounded:
>
> > Bliss was it in that dawn to be alive,
> > But to be young was very heaven!

Quotations introduced by *that* are indirect discourse and not enclosed in quotation marks.

> Keats declares that beauty is truth, truth beauty.

Proverbial expressions and familiar phrases of literary origin require no quotation marks.

> These are the times that try men's souls.
>
> He lives far from the madding crowd.

## *References.*

In scholarly work requiring exact references, abbreviate titles that occur frequently, giving the full forms in an alphabetical list at the end. As a general practice, give the references in parentheses or in footnotes, not in the body of the

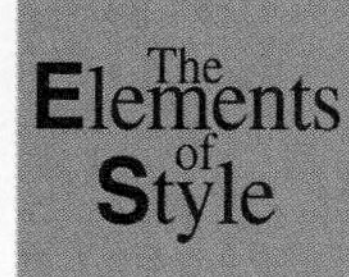

sentence. Omit the words *act, scene, line, book, volume, page,* except when referring by only one of them. Punctuate as indicated below.

| | |
|---|---|
| in the second scene of the third act | in III.ii (Still better, simply insert III.ii in parentheses at the proper place in the sentence.) |

After the killing of Polonius, Hamlet is placed under guard (IV.ii. 14) .

2 Samuel i:17–27

*Othello* II.iii. 264–267, III.iii. 155–161

## *Syllabication.*

When a word must be divided at the end of a line, consult a dictionary to learn the syllables between which division should be made. The student will do well to examine the syllable division in a number of pages of any carefully printed book.

## *Titles.*

For the titles of literary works, scholarly usage prefers italics with capitalized initials. The usage of editors and publishers varies, some using italics with capitalized initials, others using Roman with capitalized initials and with or without quotation marks. Use italics (indicated in manuscript by underscoring) except in writing for a periodical that follows a different practice. Omit initial *A* or *The* from titles when you place the possessive before them.

*A Tale of Two Cities*; Dickens's *Tale of Two Cities.*

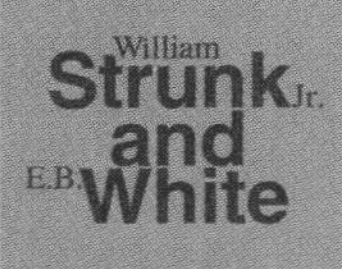


# IV
# *Words and Expressions Commonly Misused*

Many of the words and expressions here listed are not so much bad English as bad style, the commonplaces of careless writing. As is illustrated under *Feature,* the proper correction is likely to be not the replacement of one word or set of words by another but the replacement of vague generality by definite statement.

The shape of our language is not rigid; in questions of usage we have no lawgiver whose word is final. Students whose curiosity is aroused by the interpretations that follow, or whose doubts are raised, will wish to pursue their investigations further. Books useful in such pursuits are *Webster's New Collegiate Dictionary,* Revised Edition; *The Random House College Dictionary; The American Heritage Dictionary of the English Language; Webster's New International Dictionary of the English Language,* Second Edition; H. W. Fowler's *Dictionary of Modern English Usage,* Second Edition; *Watch Your Language,* by Theodore M. Bernstein; and Roy H. Copperud's *American Usage: The Consensus.*

### *Aggravate. Irritate.*

The first means "to add to" an already troublesome or vexing matter or condition. The second means "to vex" or "to annoy" or "to chafe."

### *All right.*

Idiomatic in familiar speech as a detached phrase in the sense "Agreed," or "Go ahead," or "O.K." Properly written as two words—*all right.*

### *Allude.*

Do not confuse with *elude.* You *allude* to a book; you *elude* a pursuer. Note, too, that *allude* is not synonymous with *refer.* An allusion is an indirect mention, a reference is a specific one.

### *Allusion.*

Easily confused with *illusion.* The first means "an indirect reference"; the second means "an unreal image" or "a false impression."

### *Alternate. Alternative.*

The words are not always interchangeable as nouns or adjectives. The first

means every other one in a series; the second, one of two possibilities. As the other one of a series of two, an *alternate* may stand for "a substitute," but an *alternative*, although used in a similar sense, connotes a matter of choice that is never present with *alternate*.

> As the flooded road left them no alternative, they took the alternate route.

### *Among. Between.*

When more than two things or persons are involved, *among* is usually called for: "The money was divided among the four players." When, however, more than two are involved but each is considered individually, *between* is preferred: "an agreement between the six heirs."

### *And/or.*

A device, or shortcut, that damages a sentence and often leads to confusion or ambiguity.

| | |
|---|---|
| First of all, would an honor system successfully cut down on the amount of stealing and/or cheating? | First of all, would an honor system reduce the incidence of stealing or cheating or both? |

### *Anticipate.*

Use *expect* in the sense of simple expectation.

| | |
|---|---|
| I anticipated that she would look older. | I expected that she would look older. |
| My brother anticipated the upturn in the market. | My brother expected the upturn in the market. |

In the second example, the word *anticipated* is ambiguous. It could mean simply that the brother believed the upturn would occur, or it could mean that he acted in advance of the expected upturn—by buying stock, perhaps.

### *Anybody.*

In the sense of "any person" not to be written as two words. *Any body* means "any corpse," or "any human form," or "any group." The rule holds equally for *everybody, nobody,* and *somebody*.

### *Anyone.*

In the sense of "anybody," written as one word. *Any one* means "any single person" or "any single thing."

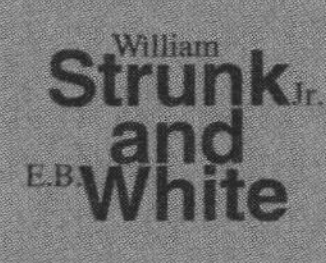


## *As good or better than.*

Expressions of this type should be corrected by rearranging the sentences.

| | |
|---|---|
| My opinion is as good or better than his. | My opinion is as good as his, or better (if not better) . |

## *As to whether.*

*Whether* is sufficient.

## *As yet.*

*Yet* nearly always is as good, if not better.

| | |
|---|---|
| No agreement has been reached as yet. | No agreement has yet been reached. |

The chief exception is at the beginning of a sentence, where *yet* means something different.

Yet (*or* despite everything) he has not succeeded.

As yet (*or* so far) he has not succeeded.

## *Being.*

Not appropriate after *regard . . . as*.

| | |
|---|---|
| He is regarded as being the best dancer in the club. | He is regarded as the best dancer in the club. |

## *But.*

Unnecessary after *doubt* and *help*.

| | |
|---|---|
| I have no doubt but that | I have no doubt that |
| He could not help but see that | He could not help seeing that |

The too-frequent use of *but* as a conjunction leads to the fault discussed under Rule 18. A loose sentence formed with *but* can usually be converted into a periodic sentence formed with *although,* as illustrated under Rule 4.

Particularly awkward is one *but* closely following another, thus making a contrast to a contrast, or a reservation to a reservation. This is easily corrected by rearrangement.

| | |
|---|---|
| America had vast resources, but she seemed almost wholly unprepared for war. But within a year she had created an army of four million men. | America seemed almost wholly unprepared for war, but she had vast resources. Within a year she had created an army of four million men. |

### *Can.*

Means "am (is, are) able." Not to be used as a substitute for *may.*

### *Case.*

Often unnecessary.

| | |
|---|---|
| In many cases, the rooms were poorly ventilated. | Many of the rooms were poorly ventilated. |
| It has rarely been the case that any mistake has been made. | Few mistakes have been made. |

### *Certainly.*

Used indiscriminately by some speakers, much as others use *very,* in an attempt to intensify any and every statement. A mannerism of this kind, bad in speech, is even worse in writing.

### *Character.*

Often simply redundant, used from a mere habit of wordiness.

| | |
|---|---|
| acts of a hostile character | hostile acts |

### *Claim (verb).*

With object-noun, means "lay claim to." May be used with a dependent clause if this sense is clearly intended: "He claimed that he was the sole heir." (But even here *claimed to be* would be better.) Not to be used as a substitute for *declare, maintain,* or *charge*.

| | |
|---|---|
| He claimed he knew how. | He declared he knew how. |

### *Clever.*

Note that the word means one thing when applied to men, another when applied to horses. A clever horse is a good-natured one, not an ingenious one.

### *Compare.*

To *compare to* is to point out or imply resemblances between objects regarded as essentially of a different order; to *compare with* is mainly to point out differences between objects regarded as essentially of the same order. Thus, life has been *compared to* a pilgrimage, *to* a drama, *to* a battle; Congress may be

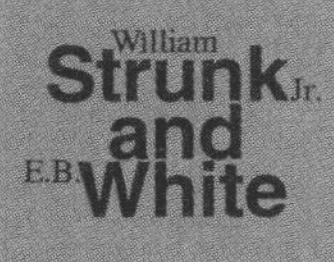

*compared with* the British Parliament. Paris has been *compared to* ancient Athens; it may be *compared with* modern London.

### *Comprise.*

Literally, "embrace": A zoo comprises mammals, reptiles, and birds (because it "embraces," or "includes," them). But animals do not comprise ("embrace") a zoo—they constitute a zoo.

### *Consider.*

Not followed by *as* when it means "believe to be."

| | |
|---|---|
| I consider him as competent. | I consider him competent. |

When *considered* means "examined" or "discussed," it is followed by *as:*

The lecturer considered Eisenhower first as soldier and second as administrator.

### *Contact.*

As a transitive verb, the word is vague and self-important. Do not *contact* anybody; get in touch with him, or look him up, or phone him, or find him, or meet him.

### *Cope.*

An intransitive verb used with *with.* In formal writing, one doesn't "cope," one "copes with" something or somebody.

| | |
|---|---|
| I knew she'd cope. (jocular) | I knew she would cope with the situation. |

### *Currently.*

In the sense of *now* with a verb in the present tense, *currently* is usually redundant; emphasis is better achieved through a more precise reference to time.

| | |
|---|---|
| We are currently reviewing your application. | We are at this moment reviewing your application. |

### *Data.*

Like *strata, phenomena,* and *media, data* is a plural and is best used with a plural verb. The word, however, is slowly gaining acceptance as a singular.

| | |
|---|---|
| The data is misleading. | These data are misleading. |

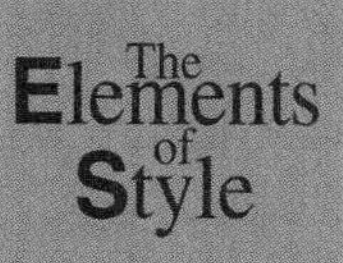


### *Different than.*

Here logic supports established usage: one thing differs *from* another, hence, *different from.* Or, *other than, unlike.*

### *Disinterested.*

Means "impartial." Do not confuse it with *uninterested*, which means "not interested in."

> Let a disinterested person judge our dispute. (an impartial person)
>
> This man is obviously uninterested in our dispute. (couldn't care less)

### *Divided into.*

Not to be misused for *composed of.* The line is sometimes difficult to draw; doubtless plays are divided into acts, but poems are composed of stanzas. An apple, halved, is divided into sections, but an apple is composed of seeds, flesh, and skin.

### *Due to.*

Loosely used for *through, because of,* or *owing to,* in adverbial phrases.

| | |
|---|---|
| He lost the first game due to carelessness. | He lost the first game because of carelessness. |

In correct use synonymous with *attributable to:* "The accident was due to bad weather"; "losses due to preventable fires."

### *Each and every one.*

Pitchman's jargon. Avoid, except in dialogue.

| | |
|---|---|
| It should be a lesson to each and every one of us. | It should be a lesson to every one of us (to us all). |

### *Effect.*

As a noun, means "result"; as a verb, means "to bring about," "to accomplish" (not to be confused with *affect,* which means "to influence").

As a noun, often loosely used in perfunctory writing about fashions, music, painting, and other arts: "an Oriental effect"; "effects in pale green"; "very delicate effects"; "subtle effects"; "a charming effect was produced." The writer who has a definite meaning to express will not take refuge in such vagueness.

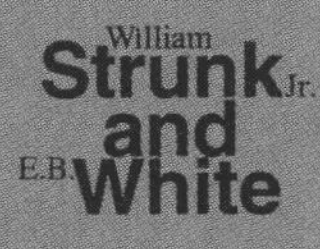


### *Enormity.*

Use only in the sense "monstrous wickedness." Misleading, if not wrong, when used to express bigness.

### *Enthuse.*

An annoying verb growing out of the noun *enthusiasm.* Not recommended.

| | |
|---|---|
| She was enthused about her new car. | She was enthusiastic about her new car. |
| She enthused about her new car. (expressed enthusiasm) | She talked enthusiastically about her new car. |

### *Etc.*

Literally, "and other things"; sometimes loosely used to mean "and other persons." The phrase is equivalent to *and the rest, and so forth,* and hence is not to be used if one of these would be insufficient—that is, if the reader would be left in doubt as to any important particulars. Least open to objection when it represents the last terms of a list already given almost in full, or immaterial words at the end of a quotation.

At the end of a list introduced by *such as, for example,* or any similar expression, *etc.* is incorrect. In formal writing, *etc.* is a misfit. An item important enough to call for *etc.* is probably important enough to be named.

### *Fact.*

Use this word only of matter capable of direct verification, not of matters of judgment. That a particular event happened on a given date, that lead melts at a certain temperature are facts. But such conclusions as that Napoleon was the greatest of modern generals or that the climate of California is delightful, however defensible they may be, are not properly called facts.

### *Facility.*

Why must jails, hospitals, schools suddenly become "facilities"?

| | |
|---|---|
| Parents complained bitterly about the fire hazard in the wooden facility. | Parents complained bitterly about the fire hazard in the wooden schoolhouse. |
| He has been appointed warden of the new facility. | He has been appointed warden of the new prison. |

### *Factor.*

A hackneyed word; the expressions of which it forms part can usually be replaced by something more direct and idiomatic.

| | |
|---|---|
| His superior training was the great factor in his winning the match. | He won the match by being better trained. |
| Air power is becoming an increasingly important factor in deciding battles. | Air power is playing a larger and larger part in deciding battles. |

### *Farther. Further.*

The two words are commonly interchanged, but there is a distinction worth observing: *farther* serves best as a distance word, *further* as a time or quantity word. You chase a ball *farther* than the other fellow; you pursue a subject *further*.

### *Feature.*

Another hackneyed word; like *factor,* it usually adds nothing to the sentence in which it occurs.

| | |
|---|---|
| A feature of the entertainment especially worthy of mention was the singing of Miss A. | (Better use the same number of words to tell what Miss A. sang and how she sang it.) |

As a verb, in the sense of "offer as a special attraction," to be avoided.

### *Finalize.*

A pompous, ambiguous verb. (See Chapter V, Reminder 21.)

### *Fix.*

Colloquial in America for *arrange, prepare, mend.* The usage is well established. But bear in mind that this verb is from *figere:* "to make firm," "to place definitely." These are the preferred meanings of the word.

### *Flammable.*

An oddity, chiefly useful in saving lives. The common word meaning "combustible" is *inflammable*. But some people are thrown off by the *in-* and think *inflammable* means "not combustible." For this reason, trucks carrying gasoline or explosives are now marked FLAMMABLE. Unless you are operating such a truck and hence are concerned with the safety of children and illiterates, use *inflammable.*

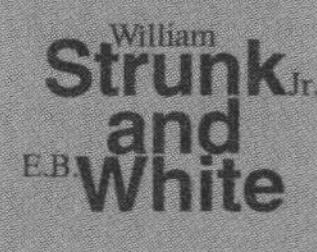


## *Folk.*

A collective noun, equivalent to *people*. Use the singular form only. *Folks,* in the sense of "parents," "family," "those present," is colloquial and too folksy for formal writing.

| | |
|---|---|
| Her folks arrived by the afternoon train. | Her father and mother arrived by the afternoon train. |

## *Fortuitous.*

Limited to what happens by chance. Not to be used for *fortunate* or *lucky.*

## *Get.*

The colloquial *have got* for *have* should not be used in writing. The preferable form of the participle is *got,* not *gotten.*

| | |
|---|---|
| He has not got any sense. | He has no sense. |
| They returned without having gotten any. | They returned without having got any. |

## *Gratuitous.*

Means "unearned," or "unwarranted."

The insult seemed gratuitous. (undeserved)

## *He is a man who.*

A common type of redundant expression; see Rule 17.

| | |
|---|---|
| He is a man who is very ambitious. | He is very ambitious. |
| Vermont is a state that attracts visitors because of its winter sports. | Vermont attracts visitors because of its winter sports. |

## *Hopefully.*

This once-useful adverb meaning "with hope" has been distorted and is now widely used to mean "I hope" or "it is to be hoped." Such use is not merely wrong, it is silly. To say, "Hopefully I'll leave on the noon plane" is to talk nonsense. Do you mean you'll leave on the noon plane in a hopeful frame of mind? Or do you mean you hope you'll leave on the noon plane? Whichever you mean, you haven't said it clearly. Although the word in its new, free-floating capacity may be pleasurable and even useful to many, it offends the ear of many others, who do not like to see words dulled or eroded, particularly when the erosion leads to ambiguity, softness, or nonsense.

## *However.*

Avoid starting a sentence with *however* when the meaning is "nevertheless." The word usually serves better when not in first position.

| | |
|---|---|
| The roads were almost impassable. However, we at last succeeded in reaching camp. | The roads were almost impassable. At last, however, we succeeded in reaching camp. |

When *however* comes first, it means "in whatever way" or "to whatever extent."

> However you advise him, he will probably do as he thinks best.
>
> However discouraging the prospect, he never lost heart.

## *Illusion.*

See *allusion.*

## *Imply. Infer.*

Not interchangeable. Something implied is something suggested or indicated, though not expressed. Something inferred is something deduced from evidence at hand.

> Farming implies early rising.
>
> Since he was a farmer, we inferred that he got up early.

## *Importantly.*

Avoid by rephrasing.

| | |
|---|---|
| More importantly, he paid for the damages. | What's more, he paid for the damages. |
| With the breeze freshening, he altered course to pass inside the island. More importantly, as things turned out, he tucked in a reef. | With the breeze freshening, he altered course to pass inside the island. More important, as things turned out, he tucked in a reef. |

## *In regard to.*

Often wrongly written *in regards to*. But *as regards* is correct, and means the same thing.

## *In the last analysis.*

A bankrupt expression.

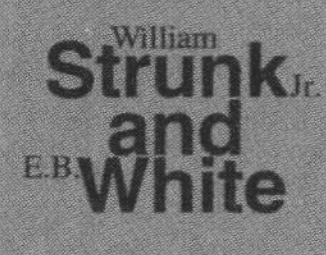

## *Inside of. Inside.*

The *of* following *inside* is correct in the adverbial meaning "in less than." In other meanings *of* is unnecessary.

> Inside of five minutes I'll be inside the bank.

## *Insightful.*

The word is a suspicious overstatement for "perceptive." If it is to be used at all, it should be used for instances of remarkably penetrating vision. Usually, it crops up merely to inflate the commonplace.

| | |
|---|---|
| That was an insightful remark you made. | That was a perceptive remark you made. |

## *In terms of*

A piece of padding usually best omitted.

| | |
|---|---|
| The job was unattractive in terms of salary. | The salary made the job unattractive. |

## *Interesting.*

An unconvincing word; avoid it as a means of introduction. Instead of announcing that what you are about to tell is interesting, make it so.

| | |
|---|---|
| An interesting story is told of | (Tell the story without preamble.) |
| In connection with the forthcoming visit of Mr. B. to America, it is interesting to recall that he | Mr. B., who will soon visit America |

Also to be avoided in introduction is the word *funny*. Nothing becomes funny by being labeled so.

## *Irregardless.*

Should be *regardless*. The error results from failure to see the negative in *-less* and from a desire to get it in as a prefix, suggested by such words as *irregular, irresponsible,* and, perhaps especially, *irrespective*.

## *-ize.*

Do not coin verbs by adding this tempting suffix. Many good and useful verbs do end in *-ize: summarize, temporize, fraternize, harmonize, fertilize.* But there is a growing list of abominations: *containerize, customize, prioritize, finalize,* to name four. Be suspicious of *-ize;* let your ear and your eye guide you. Never tack *-ize* on-

to a noun to create a verb. Usually you will discover that a useful verb already exists. Why say "moisturize" when there is the simple, unpretentious word *moisten*?

### *Kind of.*

Except in familiar style, not to be used as a substitute for *rather* or *something like*. Restrict it to its literal sense: "Amber is a kind of fossil resin"; "I dislike that kind of publicity." The same holds true of *sort of.*

### *Lay.*

A transitive verb. Except in slang ("Let it lay"), do not misuse it for the intransitive verb *lie.* The hen, or the play, *lays* an egg; the llama *lies* down. The playwright went home and *lay* down.

lie; lay; lain; lying
lay; laid; laid; laying

### *Leave.*

Not to be misused for *let.*

| | |
|---|---|
| Leave it stand the way it is. | Let it stand the way it is. |
| Leave go of that rope! | Let go of that rope! |

### *Less.*

Should not be misused for *fewer.*

| | |
|---|---|
| He had less men than in the previous campaign. | He had fewer men than in the previous campaign. |

*Less* refers to quantity, *fewer* to number. "His troubles are less than mine" means "His troubles are not so great as mine." "His troubles are fewer than mine" means "His troubles are not so numerous as mine."

### *Like.*

Not to be used for the conjunction *as. Like* governs nouns and pronouns; before phrases and clauses the equivalent word is *as*.

| | |
|---|---|
| We spent the evening like in the old days. | We spent the evening as in the old days. |
| Chloë smells good, like a pretty girl should. | Chloë smells good, as a pretty girl should. |

The use of *like* for *as* has its defenders; they argue that any usage that achieves currency becomes valid automatically. This, they say, is the way the language is

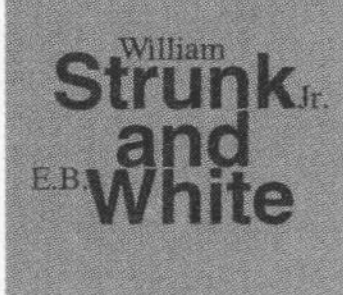


formed. It is and it isn't. An expression sometimes merely enjoys a vogue, much as an article of apparel does. *Like* has long been widely misused by the illiterate; lately it has been taken up by the knowing and the well-informed, who find it catchy, or liberating, and who use it as though they were slumming. If every word or device that achieved currency were immediately authenticated, simply on the ground of popularity, the language would be as chaotic as a ball game with no foul lines. For the student, perhaps the most useful thing to know about *like* is that most carefully edited publications regard its use before phrases and clauses as simple error.

### *Line. Along these lines.*

*Line* in the sense of "course of procedure, conduct, thought" is allowable, but has been so overworked, particularly in the phrase *along these lines,* that a writer who aims at freshness or originality had better discard it entirely.

| | |
|---|---|
| Mr. B. also spoke along the same lines. | Mr. B. also spoke to the same effect. |
| He is studying along the line of French literature. | He is studying French literature. |

### *Literal. Literally.*

Often incorrectly used in support of exaggeration or violent metaphor.

| | |
|---|---|
| a literal flood of abuse | a flood of abuse |
| literally dead with fatigue | almost dead with fatigue (dead tired) |

### *Loan.*

A noun. As a verb, prefer *lend.*

Lend me your ears.

the loan of your ears

### *Meaningful.*

A bankrupt adjective. Choose another, or rephrase.

| | |
|---|---|
| His was a meaningful contribution. | His contribution counted heavily. |
| We are instituting many meaningful changes in the curriculum. | We are improving the curriculum in many ways. |

### *Memento.*

Often incorrectly written *momento*.

### *Most.*

Not to be used for *almost* in formal composition.

| | |
|---|---|
| most everybody | almost everybody |
| most all the time | almost all the time |

### *Nature.*

Often simply redundant, used like *character.*

| | |
|---|---|
| acts of a hostile nature | hostile acts |

*Nature* should be avoided in such vague expressions as "a lover of nature," "poems about nature." Unless more specific statements follow, the reader cannot tell whether the poems have to do with natural scenery, rural life, the sunset, the untracked wilderness, or the habits of squirrels.

### *Nauseous. Nauseated.*

The first means "sickening to contemplate"; the second means "sick at the stomach." Do not, therefore, say "I feel nauseous," unless you are sure you have that effect on others.

### *Nice.*

A shaggy, all-purpose word, to be used sparingly in formal composition. "I had a nice time." "It was nice weather." "She was so nice to her mother." The meanings are indistinct. *Nice* is most useful in the sense of "precise" or "delicate": "a nice distinction."

### *Nor.*

Often used wrongly for *or* after negative expressions.

| | |
|---|---|
| He cannot eat nor sleep. | He cannot eat or sleep.<br>He can neither eat nor sleep.<br>He cannot eat nor can he sleep. |

### *Noun used as verb.*

Many nouns have lately been pressed into service as verbs. Not all are bad, but all are suspect.

| | |
|---|---|
| Be prepared for kisses when you gift your girl with this merry scent. | Be prepared for kisses when you give your girl this merry scent. |

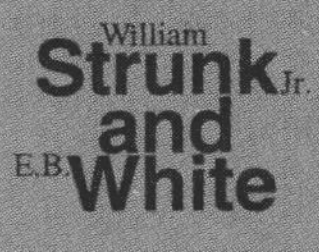


The candidate hosted a dinner for fifty of his workers. | The candidate gave a dinner for fifty of his workers.

The meeting was chaired by Mr. Oglethorp. | Mr. Oglethorp was chairman of the meeting.

He headquarters in Newark. | He has headquarters in Newark.

She debuted last fall. | She made her debut last fall.

## *Offputting. Ongoing.*

Newfound adjectives, to be avoided because they are inexact and clumsy. *Ongoing* is a mix of "continuing" and "active" and is usually superfluous.

She devoted all her spare time to the ongoing program for aid to the elderly. | She devoted all her spare time to the program for aid to the elderly.

*Offputting* might mean "objectionable," "disconcerting," "distasteful." Select instead a word whose meaning is clear. As a simple test, transform the participles to verbs. It is possible to *upset* something. But to *offput?* To *ongo?*

## *One.*

In the sense of "a person," not to be followed by *his.*

One must watch his step. | One must watch one's step. (You must watch your step.)

## *One of the most.*

Avoid this feeble formula. "One of the most exciting developments of modern science is . . ."; "Switzerland is one of the most beautiful countries of Europe." There is nothing wrong with the grammar; the formula is simply threadbare.

## *-oriented.*

A clumsy, pretentious device, much in vogue. Find a better way of indicating orientation or alignment or direction.

His was a manufacturing-oriented company. | His was a company chiefly concerned with manufacturing.

Many of the skits are situation-oriented. | Many of the skits rely on situation.

## *Partially.*

Not always interchangeable with *partly*. Best used in the sense of "to a certain degree," when speaking of a condition or state: "I'm partially resigned to it." *Part-*

*ly* carries the idea of a part as distinct from the whole—usually a physical object.

| | |
|---|---|
| The log was partially submerged. | The log was partly submerged. |
| He was partially in and partially out. | He was partly in and partly out. |
| | He was part in, part out. |

### *Participle for verbal noun.*

| | |
|---|---|
| There was little prospect of the Senate accepting even this compromise. | There was little prospect of the Senate's accepting even this compromise. |

In the left-hand column, *accepting* is a present participle; in the right-hand column, it is a verbal noun (gerund). The construction shown in the left-hand column is occasionally found, and has its defenders. Yet it is easy to see that the second sentence has to do not with a prospect of the Senate but with a prospect of accepting.

Any sentence in which the use of the possessive is awkward or impossible should of course be recast.

| | |
|---|---|
| In the event of a reconsideration of the whole matter's becoming necessary | If it should become necessary to reconsider the whole matter |
| There was great dissatisfaction with the decision of the arbitrators being favorable to the company. | There was great dissatisfaction with the arbitrators'decision in favor of the company. |

### *People.*

A word with many meanings. (*The American Heritage Dictionary* gives ten.) *The people* is a political term, not to be confused with *the public*. From the people comes political support or opposition; from the public comes artistic appreciation or commercial patronage.

The word *people* is best not used with words of number, in place of *persons*. If of "six people" five went away, how many people would be left? Answer: one people.

### *Personalize.*

A pretentious word, often carrying bad advice. Do not *personalize* your prose; simply make it good and keep it clean. See Chapter V, Reminder 1.

| | |
|---|---|
| a highly personalized affair | a highly personal affair |
| Personalize your stationery. | Get up a letterhead. |

### *Personally.*

Often unnecessary.

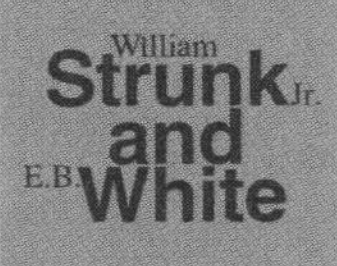


| | |
|---|---|
| Personally, I thought it was a good book. | I thought it a good book. |

### *Possess.*

Often used because to the writer it sounds more impressive than *have* or *own*. Such usage is not incorrect but is to be guarded against.

| | |
|---|---|
| He possessed great courage. | He had great courage (was very brave). |
| He was the fortunate possessor of | He was lucky enough to own |

### *Presently.*

Has two meanings: "in a short while" and "currently." Because of this ambiguity it is best restricted to the first meaning: "He'll be here presently" ("soon," or "in a short time").

### *Prestigious.*

Often an adjective of last resort. It's in the dictionary, but that doesn't mean you have to use it.

### *Refer.*

See *allude*.

### *Regretful.*

Sometimes carelessly used for *regrettable:* "The mixup was due to a regretful breakdown in communications."

### *Relate.*

Not to be used intransitively to suggest rapport.

| | |
|---|---|
| I relate well to Janet. | Janet and I see things the same way. |
| | Janet and I have a lot in common. |

### *Respective. Respectively.*

These words may usually be omitted with advantage.

| | |
|---|---|
| Works of fiction are listed under the names of their respective authors. | Works of fiction are listed under the names of their authors. |

| | |
|---|---|
| The mile run and the two-mile run were won by Jones and Cummings respectively. | The mile run was won by Jones, the two-mile run by Cummings. |

### *Secondly, thirdly, etc.*

Unless you are prepared to begin with *firstly* and defend it (which will be difficult), do not prettify numbers with *-ly*. Modern usage prefers *second, third,* and so on.

### *Shall. Will.*

In formal writing, the future tense requires *shall* for the first person, *will* for the second and third. The formula to express the speaker's belief regarding his future action or state is *I shall; I will* expresses his determination or his consent. A swimmer in distress cries, "I shall drown; no one will save me!" A suicide puts it the other way: "I will drown; no one shall save me!" In relaxed speech, however, the words *shall* and *will* are seldom used precisely; our ear guides us or fails to guide us, as the case may be, and we are quite likely to drown when we want to survive and survive when we want to drown.

### *So.*

Avoid, in writing, the use of *so* as an intensifier: "so good"; "so warm"; "so delightful."

### *Sort of.*

See *kind of.*

### *Split infinitive.*

There is precedent from the fourteenth century down for interposing an adverb between *to* and the infinitive it governs, but the construction should be avoided unless the writer wishes to place unusual stress on the adverb.

| | |
|---|---|
| to diligently inquire | to inquire diligently |

For another side to the split infinitive, see Chapter V, Reminder 14.

### *State.*

Not to be used as a mere substitute for *say, remark.* Restrict it to the sense of "express fully or clearly": "He refused to state his objections."

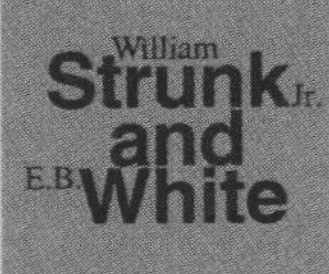


## *Student body.*

Nine times out of ten a needless and awkward expression, meaning no more than the simple word *students.*

| | |
|---|---|
| a member of the student body | a student |
| popular with the student body | liked by the students |

## *Than.*

Any sentence with *than* (to express comparison) should be examined to make sure no essential words are missing.

| | |
|---|---|
| I'm probably closer to my mother than my father. (Ambiguous.) | I'm probably closer to my mother than to my father. |
| | I'm probably closer to my mother than my father is. |
| It looked more like a cormorant than a heron. | It looked more like a cormorant than like a heron. |

## *Thanking you in advance.*

This sounds as if the writer meant, "It will not be worth my while to write to you again." In making your request, write, "Will you please," or "I shall be obliged." Then, later, if you feel moved to do so, or if the circumstances call for it, write a letter of acknowledgment.

## *That. Which.*

*That* is the defining, or restrictive pronoun, *which* the nondefining, or nonrestrictive. See Rule 3.

> The lawn mower that is broken is in the garage. (Tells which one)
>
> The lawn mower, which is broken, is in the garage. (Adds a fact about the only mower in question)

The use of *which* for *that* is common in written and spoken language ("Let us now go even unto Bethlehem, and see this thing which is come to pass.") Occasionally *which* seems preferable to *that,* as in the sentence from the Bible. But it would be a convenience to all if these two pronouns were used with precision. The careful writer, watchful for small conveniences, goes *which*-hunting, removes the defining *whiches,* and by so doing improves his work.

## *The foreseeable future.*

A cliché, and a fuzzy one. How much of the future is foreseeable? Ten minutes? Ten years? Any of it? By whom is it foreseeable? Seers? Experts? Everybody?

## *The truth is. . . . The fact is. . . .*

A bad beginning for a sentence. If you feel you are possessed of the truth, or of the fact, simply state it. Do not give it advance billing.

## *They.*

Not to be used when the antecedent is a distributive expression such as *each, each one, everybody, every one, many a man*. Use the singular pronoun.

| | |
|---|---|
| Every one of us knows they are fallible. | Every one of us knows he is fallible. |
| Everyone in the community, whether they are a member of the Association or not, is invited to attend. | Everyone in the community, whether he is a member of the Association or not, is invited to attend. |

A similar fault is the use of the plural pronoun with the antecedent *anybody, anyone, somebody, someone,* the intention being either to avoid the awkward "he or she" or to avoid committing oneself to one or the other. Some bashful speakers even say, "A friend of mine told me that they. . . ."

The use of *he* as pronoun for nouns embracing both genders is a simple, practical convention rooted in the beginnings of the English language. *He* has lost all suggestion of maleness in these circumstances. The word was unquestionably biased to begin with (the dominant male), but after hundreds of years it has become seemingly indispensable. It has no pejorative connotation; it is never incorrect. Substituting *he or she* in its place is the logical thing to do if it works. But it often doesn't work, if only because repetition makes it sound boring or silly. Consider the following unexceptional sentences from *The Summing Up,* by W. Somerset Maugham:

> Another cause of obscurity is that the writer is himself not quite sure of his meaning. He has a vague impression of what he wants to say, but has not, either from lack of mental power or from laziness, exactly formulated it in his mind, and it is natural enough that he should not find a precise expression for a confused idea.

Rewritten to affirm equality of the sexes, the same statement verges on nonsense:

> Another cause of obscurity is that the writer is herself or himself not quite sure of her or his meaning. He or she has a vague impression of what he or she wants to say, but has not, either from lack of mental power or from laziness, exactly formulated it in her or his mind, and it is natural enough that he or she should not find a precise expression for a confused idea.

No one need fear to use *he* if common sense supports it. The furor recently raised about *he* would be more impressive if there were a handy substitute for the word. Unfortunately, there isn't—or, at least, no one has come up with one yet. If you think *she* is a handy substitute for *he,* try it and see what happens. Alternatively, put all controversial nouns in the plural and avoid the choice of sex alto-

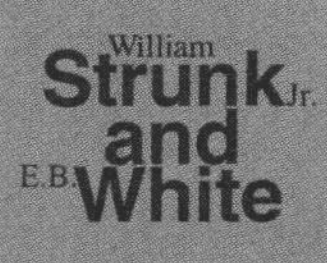


gether, and you may find your prose sounding general and diffuse as a result.

### *This.*

The pronoun *this*, referring to the complete sense of a preceding sentence or clause, can't always carry the load and so may produce an imprecise statement.

| | |
|---|---|
| Visiting dignitaries watched yesterday as ground was broken for the new high-energy physics laboratory with a blowout safety wall. This is the first visible evidence of the university's plans for modernization and expansion. | Visiting dignitaries watched yesterday as ground was broken for the new high-energy physics laboratory with a blowout safety wall. The ceremony afforded the first visible evidence of the university's plans for modernization and expansion. |

In the left-hand example above, *this* does not immediately make clear what the first visible evidence is.

### *Thrust.*

This showy noun, suggestive of power, hinting of sex, is the darling of executives, politicos, and speech-writers. Use it sparingly. Save it for specific application.

| | |
|---|---|
| Our reorganization plan has a tremendous thrust. | The piston has a five-inch thrust. |
| The thrust of his letter was that he was working more hours than he'd bargained for. | The point he made in his letter was that he was working more hours than he'd bargained for. |

### *Tortuous. Torturous.*

A winding road is *tortuous,* a painful ordeal is *torturous*. Both words carry the idea of "twist," the twist having been a form of torture.

### *Transpire.*

Not to be used in the sense of "happen," "come to pass." Many writers so use it (usually when groping toward imagined elegance), but their usage finds little support in the Latin "breathe across or through." It is correct, however, in the sense of "become known." "Eventually, the grim account of his villainy transpired" (literally, "leaked through or out").

### *Try.*

Takes the infinitive: "try to mend it," not "try *and* mend it." Students of the language will argue that *try and* has won through and become idiom. Indeed it has, and it is relaxed and acceptable. But *try to* is precise, and when you are writing formal prose, try and write *try to*.

### *Type.*

Not a synonym for *kind of*. The examples below are common vulgarisms.

| | |
|---|---|
| that type employee | that kind of employee |
| I dislike that type publicity. | I dislike that kind of publicity. |
| small, home-type hotels | small, homelike hotels |
| a new type plane | a plane of a new design (new kind) |

### *Unique.*

Means "without like or equal." Hence, there can be no degrees of uniqueness.

| | |
|---|---|
| It was the most unique egg beater on the market. | It was a unique egg beater. |
| The balancing act was very unique. | The balancing act was unique. |
| Of all the spiders, the one that lives in a bubble under water is the most unique. | Among spiders, the one that lives in a bubble under water is unique. |

### *Utilize.*

Prefer *use*.

| | |
|---|---|
| I utilized the facilities. | I used the toilet. |
| She utilized the dishwasher. | She used the dishwasher. |

### *Verbal.*

Sometimes means "word for word" and in this sense may refer to something expressed in writing. *Oral* (from Latin *ōs,* "mouth") limits the meaning to what is transmitted by speech. *Oral agreement* is more precise than *verbal agreement*.

### *Very.*

Use this word sparingly. Where emphasis is necessary, use words strong in themselves.

### *While.*

Avoid the indiscriminate use of this word for *and, but,* and *although.* Many writers use it frequently as a substitute for *and* or *but,* either from a mere desire to

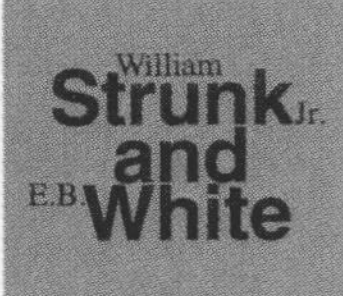

vary the connective or from doubt about which of the two connectives is the more appropriate. In this use it is best replaced by a semicolon.

| | |
|---|---|
| The office and salesrooms are on the ground foor, while the rest of the building is used for manufacturing. | The office and salesrooms are on the ground floor; the rest of the building is used for manufacturing. |

Its use as a virtual equivalent of *although* is allowable in sentences where this leads to no ambiguity or absurdity.

> While I admire his energy, I wish it were employed in a better cause.

This is entirely correct, as is shown by the paraphrase

> I admire his energy; at the same time, I wish it were employed in a better cause.

Compare:

> While the temperature reaches 90 or 95 degrees in the daytime, the nights are often chilly.

The paraphrase shows why the use of *while* is incorrect:

> The temperature reaches 90 or 95 degrees in the daytime; at the same time the nights are often chilly.

In general, the writer will do well to use *while* only with strict literalness, in the sense of "during the time that."

## *-wise.*

Not to be used indiscriminately as a pseudosuffix: *taxwise, pricewise, marriagewise, prosewise, saltwater taffywise*. Chiefly useful when it means "in the manner of": *clockwise.* There is not a noun in the language to which *-wise* cannot be added if the spirit moves one to add it. The sober writer will abstain from the use of this wild additive.

## *Worth while.*

Overworked as a term of vague approval and (with *not*) of disapproval. Strictly applicable only to actions: "Is it worth while to telegraph?"

| | |
|---|---|
| His books are not worth while. | His books are not worth reading (are not worth one's while to read; do not repay reading). |

The adjective *worthwhile* (one word) is acceptable but emaciated. Use a stronger word.

| | |
|---|---|
| a worthwhile project | a promising (useful, valuable, exciting) project |

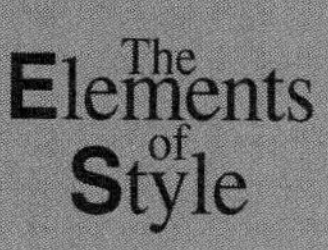

### *Would.*

Commonly used to express habitual or repeated action. ("He would get up early and prepare his own breakfast before he went to work.") But when the idea of habit or repetition is expressed, in such phrases as *once a year, every day, each Sunday,* the past tense, without *would,* is usually sufficient, and, from its brevity, more emphatic.

| | |
|---|---|
| Once a year, he would visit the old mansion. | Once a year he visited the old mansion. |

In narrative writing, always indicate the transition from the general to the particular—that is, from sentences that merely state a general habit to those that express the action of a specific day or period. Failure to indicate the change will cause confusion.

> Townsend would get up early and prepare his own breakfast. If the day was cold, he filled the stove and had a warm fire burning before he left the house. On his way out to the garage, he noticed that there were footprints in the new-fallen snow on the porch.

The reader is lost, having received no signal that Townsend has changed from a mere man of habit to a man who has seen a particular thing on a particular day.

> Townsend would get up early and prepare his own breakfast. If the day was cold, he filled the stove and had a warm fire burning before he left the house. One morning in January on his way out to the garage, he noticed footprints in the new-fallen snow on the porch.

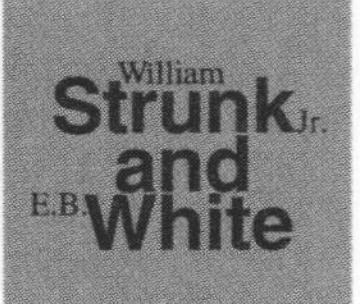


# V
# *An Approach to Style*
## (With a List of Reminders)

Up to this point, the book has been concerned with what is correct, or acceptable, in the use of English. In this final chapter, we approach style in its broader meaning: style in the sense of what is distinguished and distinguishing. Here we leave solid ground. Who can confidently say what ignites a certain combination of words, causing them to explode in the mind? Who knows why certain notes in music are capable of stirring the listener deeply, though the same notes slightly rearranged are impotent? These are high mysteries, and this chapter is a mystery story, thinly disguised. There is no satisfactory explanation of style, no infallible guide to good writing, no assurance that a person who thinks clearly will be able to write clearly, no key that unlocks the door, no inflexible rule by which the young writer may shape his course. He will often find himself steering by stars that are disturbingly in motion.

The preceding chapters contain instructions drawn from established English usage; this one contains advice drawn from a writer's experience of writing. Since the book is a rule book, these cautionary remarks, these subtly dangerous hints, are presented in the form of rules, but they are, in essence, mere gentle reminders: they state what most of us know and at times forget.

Style is an increment in writing. When we speak of Fitzgerald's style, we don't mean his command of the relative pronoun, we mean the sound his words make on paper. Every writer, by the way he uses the language, reveals something of his spirit, his habits, his capacities, his bias. This is inevitable as well as enjoyable. All writing is communication; creative writing is communication through revelation—it is the Self escaping into the open. No writer long remains incognito.

If the student doubts that style is something of a mystery, let him try rewriting a familiar sentence and see what happens. Any much-quoted sentence will do. Suppose we take "These are the times that try men's souls." Here we have eight short, easy words, forming a simple declarative sentence. The sentence contains no flashy ingredient such as "Damn the torpedoes!" and the words, as you see, are ordinary. Yet in that arrangement they have shown great durability; the sentence is almost into its third century. Now compare a few variations:

> Times like these try men's souls.
> How trying it is to live in these times!
> These are trying times for men's souls.
> Soulwise, these are trying times.

It seems unlikely that Thomas Paine could have made his sentiment stick if he had couched it in any of these forms. But why not? No fault of grammar can be detected in them, and in every case the meaning is clear. Each version is correct, and each, for some reason that we can't readily put our finger on, is marked for oblivion. We could, of course, talk about "rhythm" and "cadence," but the talk would be vague and unconvincing. We could declare *soulwise* to be a silly word, inappropriate to the occasion; but even that won't do—it does not answer the main question. Are we even sure *soulwise* is silly? If *otherwise* is a serviceable word, what's the matter with *soulwise*?

Here is another sentence, this one by a later Tom. It is not a famous sentence, although its author (Thomas Wolfe) is well known. "Quick are the mouths of earth, and quick the teeth that fed upon this loveliness." The sentence would not take a prize for clarity, and rhetorically it is at the opposite pole from "These are the times." Try it in a different form, without the inversions:

> The mouths of earth are quick, and the teeth that fed upon this loveliness are quick, too.

The author's meaning is still intact, but not his overpowering emotion. What was poetical and sensuous has become prosy and wooden; instead of the secret sounds of beauty, we are left with the simple crunch of mastication. (Whether Mr. Wolfe was guilty of overwriting is, of course, another question—one that is not pertinent here. )

With some writers, style not only reveals the spirit of the man but reveals his identity, as surely as would his fingerprints. Here, following, are two brief passages from the works of two American novelists. The subject in each case is languor. In both, the words used are ordinary, and there is nothing eccentric about the construction.

> He did not still feel weak, he was merely luxuriating in that supremely gutful lassitude of convalescence in which time, hurry, doing, did not exist, the accumulating seconds and minutes and hours to which in its well state the body is slave both waking and sleeping, now reversed and time now the lip-server and mendicant to the body's pleasure instead of the body thrall to time's headlong course.
>
> Manuel drank his brandy. He felt sleepy himself. It was too hot to go out into the town. Besides there was nothing to do. He wanted to see Zurito. He would go to sleep while he waited.

Anyone acquainted with Faulkner and Hemingway will have recognized them in these passages and perceived which was which. How different are their languors!

Or take two American poets, stopping at evening. One stops by woods, the other by laughing flesh.

> My little horse must think it queer
> To stop without a farmhouse near
> Between the woods and frozen lake
> The darkest evening of the year.*
>
> I have perceived that to be with those I like is enough,
> To stop in company with the rest at evening is enough,
> To be surrounded by beautiful, curious, breathing,
> laughing flesh is enough . . .

*From "Stopping by Woods on a Snowy Evening" from *The Poetry of Robert Frost,* edited by Edward Connery Latham. Copyright 1923, © 1969 by Holt, Rinehart, and Winston, Inc. Copyright 1951 by Robert Frost. Reprinted by permission of Holt, Rinehart, and Winston, Inc., and Jonathan Cape Ltd.

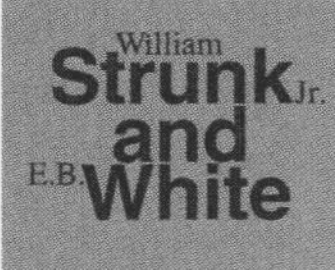

Because of the characteristic styles, there is little question about identity here, and if the situations were reversed, with Whitman stopping by woods and Frost by laughing flesh (not one of his regularly scheduled stops), the reader would still know who was who.

Young writers often suppose that style is a garnish for the meat of prose, a sauce by which a dull dish is made palatable. Style has no such separate entity; it is nondetachable, unfilterable. The beginner should approach style warily, realizing that it is himself he is approaching, no other; and he should begin by turning resolutely away from all devices that are popularly believed to indicate style—all mannerisms, tricks, adornments. The approach to style is by way of plainness, simplicity, orderliness, sincerity.

Writing is, for most, laborious and slow. The mind travels faster than the pen; consequently, writing becomes a question of learning to make occasional wing shots, bringing down the bird of thought as it flashes by. A writer is a gunner, sometimes waiting in his blind for something to come in, sometimes roaming the countryside hoping to scare something up. Like other gunners, he must cultivate patience; he may have to work many covers to bring down one partridge. Here, following, are some suggestions and cautionary hints that may help the beginner find his way to a satisfactory style.

## 1. *Place yourself in the background.*

Write in a way that draws the reader's attention to the sense and substance of the writing, rather than to the mood and temper of the author. If the writing is solid and good, the mood and temper of the writer will eventually be revealed, and not at the expense of the work. Therefore, the first piece of advice is this: to achieve style, begin by affecting none—that is, place yourself in the background. A careful and honest writer does not need to worry about style. As he becomes proficient in the use of the language, his style will emerge, because he himself will emerge, and when this happens he will find it increasingly easy to break through the barriers that separate him from other minds, other hearts—which is, of course, the purpose of writing, as well as its principal reward. Fortunately, the act of composition, or creation, disciplines the mind; writing is one way to go about thinking, and the practice and habit of writing not only drain the mind but supply it, too.

## 2. *Write in a way that comes naturally.*

Write in a way that comes easily and naturally to you, using words and phrases that come readily to hand. But do not assume that because you have acted naturally your product is without flaw.

The use of language begins with imitation. The infant imitates the sounds made by its parents; the child imitates first the spoken language, then the stuff of books. The imitative life continues long after the writer is on his own in the language, for it is almost impossible to avoid imitating what one admires. Never imi-

tate consciously, but do not worry about being an imitator; take pains instead to admire what is good. Then when you write in a way that comes naturally, you will echo the halloos that bear repeating.

### 3. *Work from a suitable design.*

Before beginning to compose something, gauge the nature and extent of the enterprise and work from a suitable design. (See Chapter II, Rule 12.) Design informs even the simplest structure, whether of brick and steel or of prose. You raise a pup tent from one sort of vision, a cathedral from another. This does not mean that you must sit with a blueprint always in front of you, merely that you had best anticipate what you are getting into. To compose a laundry list, a writer can work directly from the pile of soiled garments, ticking them off one by one. But to write a biography the writer will need at least a rough scheme; he cannot plunge in blindly and start ticking off fact after fact about his man, lest he miss the forest for the trees and there be no end to his labors.

Sometimes, of course, impulse and emotion are more compelling than design. A deeply troubled person, composing a letter appealing for mercy or for love, had best not attempt to organize his emotions; his prose will have a better chance if he leaves his emotions in disarray—which he'll probably have to do anyway, since one's feelings do not usually lend themselves to rearrangement. But even the kind of writing that is essentially adventurous and impetuous will on examination be found to have a secret plan: Columbus didn't just sail, he sailed west, and the New World took shape from this simple and, we now think, sensible design.

### 4. *Write with nouns and verbs.*

Write with nouns and verbs, not with adjectives and adverbs. The adjective hasn't been built that can pull a weak or inaccurate noun out of a tight place. This is not to disparage adjectives and adverbs; they are indispensable parts of speech. Occasionally they surprise us with their power, as in

> Up the airy mountain,<br>
>     Down the rushy glen,<br>
> We daren't go a-hunting<br>
>     For fear of little men . . .

The nouns *mountain* and *glen* are accurate enough, but had the mountain not become airy, the glen rushy, William Allingham might never have got off the ground with his poem. In general, however, it is nouns and verbs, not their assistants, that give to good writing its toughness and color.

### 5. *Revise and rewrite.*

Revising is part of writing. Few writers are so expert that they can produce what they are after on the first try. Quite often the writer will discover, on

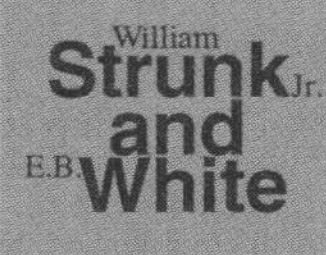


examining the completed work, that there are serious flaws in the arrangement of the material, calling for transpositions. When this is the case, he can save himself much labor and time by using scissors on his manuscript, cutting it to pieces and fitting the pieces together in a better order. If the work merely needs shortening, a pencil is the most useful tool; but if it needs rearranging, or stirring up, scissors should be brought into play. Do not be afraid to seize whatever you have written and cut it to ribbons; it can always be restored to its original condition in the morning, if that course seems best. Remember, it is no sign of weakness or defeat that your manuscript ends up in need of major surgery. This is a common occurrence in all writing, and among the best writers.

### *6. Do not overwrite.*

Rich, ornate prose is hard to digest, generally unwholesome, and sometimes nauseating. If the sickly-sweet word, the overblown phrase are a writer's natural form of expression, as is sometimes the case, he will have to compensate for it by a show of vigor, and by writing something as meritorious as the Song of Songs, which is Solomon's.

### *7. Do not overstate.*

When you overstate, the reader will be instantly on guard, and everything that has preceded your overstatement as well as everything that follows it will be suspect in his mind because he has lost confidence in your judgment or your poise. Overstatement is one of the common faults. A single overstatement, wherever or however it occurs, diminishes the whole, and a single carefree superlative has the power to destroy, for the reader, the object of the writer's enthusiasm.

### *8. Avoid the use of qualifiers.*

*Rather, very, little, pretty*—these are the leeches that infest the pond of prose, sucking the blood of words. The constant use of the adjective *little* (except to indicate size) is particularly debilitating; we should all try to do a little better, we should all be very watchful of this rule, for it is a rather important one and we are pretty sure to violate it now and then.

### *9. Do not affect a breezy manner.*

The volume of writing is enormous, these days, and much of it has a sort of windiness about it, almost as though the author were in a state of euphoria. "Spontaneous me," sang Whitman, and, in his innocence, let loose the hordes of uninspired scribblers who would one day confuse spontaneity with genius.

The breezy style is often the work of an egocentric, the person who imagines that everything that pops into his head is of general interest and that uninhibited prose creates high spirits and carries the day. Open any alumni magazine, turn to the class notes, and you are quite likely to encounter old Spontaneous Me at work —an aging collegian who writes something like this:

> Well, chums, here I am again with my bagful of dirt about your disorderly classmates, after spending a helluva weekend in N'Yawk trying to view the Columbia game from behind two bumbershoots and a glazed cornea. And speaking of news, howzabout tossing a few chirce nuggets my way?

This is an extreme example, but the same wind blows, at lesser velocities, across vast expanses of journalistic prose. The author in this case has managed in two sentences to commit most of the unpardonable sins: he obviously has nothing to say, he is showing off and directing the attention of the reader to himself, he is using slang with neither provocation nor ingenuity, he adopts a patronizing air by throwing in the word *chirce,* he is tasteless, humorless (though full of fun), dull, and empty. He has not done his work. Compare his opening remarks with the following—a plunge directly into the news:

> Clyde Crawford, who stroked the varsity shell in 1928, is swinging an oar again after a lapse of forty years. Clyde resigned last spring as executive sales manager of the Indiana Flotex Company and is now a gondolier in Venice.

This, although conventional, is compact, informative, unpretentious. The writer has dug up an item of news and presented it in a straightforward manner. What the first writer tried to accomplish by cutting rhetorical capers and by breeziness, the second writer managed to achieve by good reporting, by keeping a tight rein on his material, and by staying out of the act.

## *10. Use orthodox spelling.*

In ordinary composition, use orthodox spelling. Do not write *nite* for *night, thru* for *through, pleez* for *please,* unless you plan to introduce a complete system of simplified spelling and are prepared to take the consequences.

In the original edition of *The Elements of Style,* there was a chapter on spelling. In it, the author had this to say:

> The spelling of English words is not fixed and invariable, nor does it depend on any other authority than general agreement. At the present day there is practically unanimous agreement as to the spelling of most words. . . . At any given moment, however, a relatively small number of words may be spelled in more than one way. Gradually, as a rule, one of these forms comes to be generally preferred, and the less customary form comes to look obsolete and is discarded. From time to time new forms, mostly simplifications, are introduced by innovators, and either win their place or die of neglect.
>
> The practical objection to unaccepted and oversimplified spellings is the disfavor with which they are received by the reader. They distract his attention and exhaust his patience. He reads the form *though* automatically, without thought of its needless complexity; he reads the

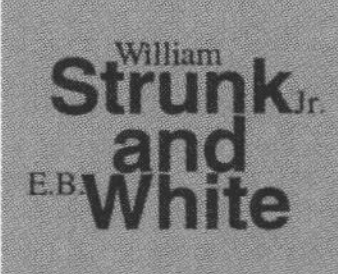


abbreviation *tho* and mentally supplies the missing letters, at the cost of a fraction of his attention. The writer has defeated his own purpose.

The language manages somehow to keep pace with events. A word that has taken hold in our century is *thruway;* it was born of necessity and is apparently here to stay. In combination with *way, thru* is more serviceable than *through;* it is a high-speed word for readers who are going sixty. *Throughway* would be too long to fit on a road sign, too slow to serve the speeding eye. It is conceivable that because of our thruways, *through* will eventually become *thru*—after many more thousands of miles of travel.

### *11. Do not explain too much.*

It is seldom advisable to tell all. Be sparing, for instance, in the use of adverbs after "he said," "she replied," and the like: "he said consolingly"; "she replied grumblingly." Let the conversation itself disclose the speaker's manner or condition. Dialogue heavily weighted with adverbs after the attributive verb is cluttery and annoying. Inexperienced writers not only overwork their adverbs but load their attributives with explanatory verbs: "he consoled," "she congratulated." They do this, apparently, in the belief that the word said is always in need of support, or because they have been told to do it by experts in the art of bad writing.

### *12. Do not construct awkward adverbs.*

Adverbs are easy to build. Take an adjective or a participle, add *-ly,* and behold! you have an adverb. But you'd probably be better off without it. Do not write *tangledly*. The word itself is a tangle. Do not even write *tiredly*. Nobody says *tangledly* and not many people say *tiredly*. Words that are not used orally are seldom the ones to put on paper.

| | |
|---|---|
| He climbed tiredly to bed. | He climbed wearily to bed. |
| The lamp cord lay tangledly beneath his chair. | The lamp cord lay in tangles beneath his chair. |

Do not dress words up by adding *ly* to them, as though putting a hat on a horse.

| | |
|---|---|
| overly | over |
| muchly | much |
| thusly | thus |

### *13. Make sure the reader knows who is speaking.*

Dialogue is a total loss unless you indicate who the speaker is. In long dialogue passages containing no attributives, the reader may become lost and be compelled to go back and reread in order to puzzle the thing out. Obscurity is an imposition on the reader, to say nothing of its damage to the work.

In dialogue, make sure that your attributives do not awkwardly interrupt a spoken sentence. Place them where the break would come naturally in speech—

that is, where the speaker would pause for emphasis, or take a breath. The best test for locating an attributive is to speak the sentence aloud.

| | |
|---|---|
| "Now, my boy, we shall see," he said, "how well you have learned your lesson." | "Now, my boy," he said, "we shall see how well you have learned your lesson." |
| "What's more, they would never," he added, "consent to the plan." | "What's more," he added, "they would never consent to the plan." |

## *14. Avoid fancy words.*

Avoid the elaborate, the pretentious, the coy, and the cute. Do not be tempted by a twenty-dollar word when there is a ten-center handy, ready and able. Anglo-Saxon is a livelier tongue than Latin, so use Anglo-Saxon words. In this, as in so many matters pertaining to style, one's ear must be one's guide: *gut* is a lustier noun than *intestine*, but the two words are not interchangeable, because *gut* is often inappropriate, being too coarse for the context. Never call a stomach a tummy without good reason.

If you admire fancy words, if every sky is *beauteous,* every blonde *curvaceous,* if you are tickled by *discombobulate,* you will have a bad time with Reminder 14. What is wrong, you ask, with *beauteous*? No one knows, for sure. There is nothing wrong, really, with any word—all are good, but some are better than others. A matter of ear, a matter of reading the books that sharpen the ear.

The line between the fancy and the plain, between the atrocious and the felicitous, is sometimes alarmingly fine. The opening phrase of the Gettysburg address is close to the line, at least by our standards today, and Mr. Lincoln, knowingly or unknowingly, was flirting with disaster when he wrote "Four score and seven years ago." The President could have got into his sentence with plain "Eighty-seven"—a saving of two words and less of a strain on the listeners' powers of multiplication. But Lincoln's ear must have told him to go ahead with four score and seven. By doing so, he achieved cadence while skirting the edge of fanciness. Suppose he had blundered over the line and written, "In the year of our Lord seventeen hundred and seventy-six." His speech would have sustained a heavy blow. Or suppose he had settled for "Eighty-seven." In that case he would have got into his introductory sentence too quickly; the timing would have been bad.

The question of ear is vital. Only the writer whose ear is reliable is in a position to use bad grammar deliberately; only he knows for sure when a colloquialism is better than formal phrasing; only he is able to sustain his work at the level of good taste. So cock your ear. Years ago, students were warned not to end a sentence with a preposition; time, of course, has softened that rigid decree. Not only is the preposition acceptable at the end, sometimes it is more effective in that spot than anywhere else. "A claw hammer, not an ax, was the tool he murdered her with." This is preferable to "A claw hammer, not an ax, was the tool with which he murdered her." Why? Because it sounds more violent, more like murder. A matter of ear.

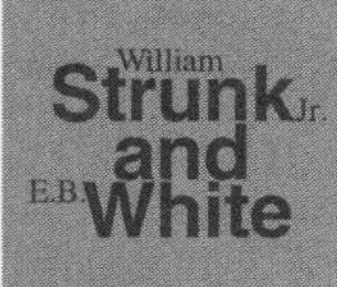

And would you write "The worst tennis player around here is I" or "The worst tennis player around here is me"? The first is good grammar, the second is good judgment—although the *me* might not do in all contexts.

The split infinitive is another trick of rhetoric in which the ear must be quicker than the handbook. Some infinitives seem to improve on being split, just as a stick of round stovewood does. "I cannot bring myself to really like the fellow." The sentence is relaxed, the meaning is clear, the violation is harmless and scarcely perceptible. Put the other way, the sentence becomes stiff, needlessly formal. A matter of ear.

There are times when the ear not only guides us through difficult situations but also saves us from minor or major embarrassments of prose. The ear, for example must decide when to omit *that* from a sentence, when to retain it. "He knew he could do it" is preferable to "He knew that he could do it"—simpler and just as clear. But in many cases the *that* is needed. "He felt that his big nose, which was sunburned, made him look ridiculous." Omit the *that* and you have "He felt his big nose. . . ."

## *15. Do not use dialect unless your ear is good.*

Do not attempt to use dialect unless you are a devoted student of the tongue you hope to reproduce. If you use dialect, be consistent. The reader will become impatient or confused if he finds two or more versions of the same word or expression. In dialect it is necessary to spell phonetically, or at least ingeniously, to capture unusual inflections. Take, for example, the word *once.* It often appears in dialect writing as *oncet,* but *oncet* looks as though it should be pronounced "onset." A better spelling would be *wunst.* But if you write it *oncet* once, write it that way throughout. The best dialect writers, by and large, are economical of their talents, they use the minimum, not the maximum, of deviation from the norm, thus sparing the reader as well as convincing him.

## *16. Be clear.*

Clarity is not the prize in writing, nor is it always the principal mark of a good style. There are occasions when obscurity serves a literary yearning, if not a literary purpose, and there are writers whose mien is more overcast than clear. But since writing is communication, clarity can only be a virtue. And although there is no substitute for merit in writing, clarity comes closest to being one. Even to a writer who is being intentionally obscure or wild of tongue we can say, "Be obscure clearly! Be wild of tongue in a way we can understand!" Even to writers of market letters, telling us (but not telling us) which securities are promising, we can say, "Be cagey plainly! Be elliptical in a straightforward fashion!"

Clarity, clarity, clarity. When you become hopelessly mired in a sentence, it is best to start fresh; do not try to fight your way through against the terrible odds of syntax. Usually what is wrong is that the construction has become too involved at some point; the sentence needs to be broken apart and replaced by two or more shorter sentences.

Muddiness is not merely a disturber of prose, it is also a destroyer of life, of hope: death on the highway caused by a badly worded road sign, heartbreak among lovers caused by a misplaced phrase in a well-intentioned letter, anguish of a traveler expecting to be met at a railroad station and not being met because of a slipshod telegram. Usually we think only of the ludicrous aspect of ambiguity; we enjoy it when the *Times* tells us that Nelson Rockefeller is "chairman of the Museum of Modern Art, which he entered in a fireman's raincoat during a recent fire, and founded the Museum of Primitive Art." This we all love. But think of the tragedies that are rooted in ambiguity; think of that side, and be clear! When you say something, make sure you have said it. The chances of your having said it are only fair.

### *17. Do not inject opinion.*

Unless there is a good reason for its being there, do not inject opinion into a piece of writing. We all have opinions about almost everything, and the temptation to toss them in is great. To air one's views gratuitously, however, is to imply that the demand for them is brisk, which may not be the case, and which, in any event, may not be relevant to the discussion. Opinions scattered indiscriminately about leave the mark of egotism on a work. Similarly, to air one's views at an improper time may be in bad taste. If you have received a letter inviting you to speak at the dedication of a new cat hospital, and you hate cats, your reply, declining the invitation, does not necessarily have to cover the full range of your emotions. You must make it clear that you will not attend, but you do not have to let fly at cats. The writer of the letter asked a civil question; attack cats, then, only if you can do so with good humor, good taste, and in such a way that your answer will be courteous as well as responsive. Since you are out of sympathy with cats, you may quite properly give this as a reason for not appearing at the dedicatory ceremonies of a cat hospital. But bear in mind that your opinion of cats was not sought, only your services as a speaker. Try to keep things straight.

### *18. Use figures of speech sparingly.*

The simile is a common device and a useful one, but similes coming in rapid fire, one right on top of another, are more distracting than illuminating. The reader needs time to catch his breath; he can't be expected to compare everything with something else, and no relief in sight.

When you use metaphor, do not mix it up. That is, don't start by calling something a swordfish and end by calling it an hourglass.

### *19. Do not take shortcuts at the cost of clarity.*

Do not use initials for the names of organizations or movements unless you are certain the initials will be readily understood. Write things out. Not everyone

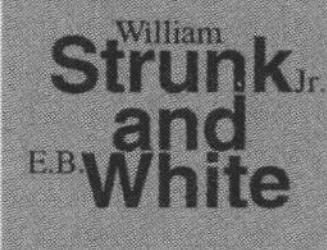


knows that SALT means Strategic Arms Limitation Talks, and even if everyone did, there are babies being born every minute who will someday encounter the name for the first time. They deserve to see the words, not simply the initials. A good rule is to start your article by writing out names in full, and then, later, when the reader has got his bearings, to shorten them.

Many shortcuts are self-defeating; they waste the reader's time instead of conserving it. There are all sorts of rhetorical stratagems and devices that attract writers who hope to be pithy, but most of them are simply bothersome. The longest way round is usually the shortest way home, and the one truly reliable shortcut in writing is to choose words that are strong and sure-footed to carry the reader on his way.

### *20. Avoid foreign languages.*

The writer will occasionally find it convenient or necessary to borrow from other languages. Some writers, however, from sheer exuberance or a desire to show off, sprinkle their work liberally with foreign expressions, with no regard for the reader's comfort. It is a bad habit. Write in English.

### *21. Prefer the standard to the offbeat.*

The young writer will be drawn at every turn toward eccentricities in language. He will hear the beat of new vocabularies, the exciting rhythms of special segments of his society, each speaking a language of its own. All of us come under the spell of these unsettling drums; the problem for the beginner is to listen to them, learn the words, feel the vibrations, and not be carried away.

Youth invariably speaks to youth in a tongue of his own devising: he renovates the language with a wild vigor, as he would a basement apartment. By the time this paragraph sees print, *uptight, ripoff, rap, dude, vibes, copout,* and *funky* will be the words of yesteryear, and we will be fielding more recent ones that have come bouncing into our speech—some of them into our dictionary as well. A new word is always up for survival. Many do survive. Others grow stale and disappear. Most are, at least in their infancy, more appropriate to conversation than to composition.

Today, the language of advertising enjoys an enormous circulation. With its deliberate infractions of grammatical rules and its crossbreeding of the parts of speech, it profoundly influences the tongues and pens of children and adults. Your new kitchen range is so revolutionary it *obsoletes* all other ranges. Your counter top is beautiful because it is *accessorized* with gold-plated faucets. Your cigarette tastes good *like* a cigarette should. And, *like the man says,* you will want to try one. You will also, in all probability, want to try writing that way, using that language. You do so at your peril, for it is the language of mutilation.

Advertisers are quite understandably interested in what they call "attention getting." The man photographed must have lost an eye or grown a pink beard, or he must have three arms or be sitting wrong-end-to on a horse. This technique is proper in its place, which is the world of selling, but the young writer had best not adopt the device of mutilation in ordinary composition, whose purpose is to engage, not paralyze, the reader's senses. Buy the gold-plated faucets if you will, but do not accessorize your prose. To use the language well, do not begin by hacking it to bits; accept the whole body of it, cherish its classic form, its variety, and its richness.

Another segment of society that has constructed a language of its own is business. The businessman says that ink erasers are in *short supply,* that he has *updated* the next shipment of these erasers, and that he will *finalize* his recommendations at the next meeting of the board. He is speaking a language that is familiar to him and dear to him. Its portentous nouns and verbs invest ordinary events with high adventure; the executive walks among ink erasers, caparisoned like a knight. We should tolerate him—every man of spirit wants to ride a white horse. The only question is whether his vocabulary is helpful to ordinary prose. Usually, the same ideas can be expressed less formidably, if one makes the effort. A good many of the special words of business seem designed more to express the user's dreams than to express his precise meaning. Not all such words, of course, can be dismissed summarily; indeed, no word in the language can be dismissed offhand by anyone who has a healthy curiosity. *Update* isn't a bad word; in the right setting it is useful. In the wrong setting, though, it is destructive, and the trouble with adopting coinages too quickly is that they will bedevil one by insinuating themselves where they do not belong. This may sound like rhetorical snobbery, or plain stuffiness; but the writer will discover, in the course of his work, that the setting of a word is just as restrictive as the setting of a jewel. The general rule here is to prefer the standard. *Finalize,* for instance, is not standard; it is special, and it is a peculiarly fuzzy and silly word. Does it mean "terminate," or does it mean "put into final form"? One can't be sure, really, what it means, and one gets the impression that the person using it doesn't know, either, and doesn't want to know.

The special vocabularies of the law, of the military, of government are familiar to most of us. Even the world of criticism has a modest pouch of private words (*luminous, taut*), whose only virtue is that they are exceptionally nimble and can escape from the garden of meaning over the wall. Of these Critical words, Wolcott Gibbs once wrote, ". . . they are detached from the language and inflated like little balloons." The young writer should learn to spot them—words that at first glance seem freighted with delicious meaning but that soon burst in air, leaving nothing but a memory of bright sound.

The language is perpetually in flux: it is a living stream, shifting, changing, receiving new strength from a thousand tributaries, losing old forms in the backwaters of time. To suggest that a young writer not swim in the main stream of this turbulence would be foolish indeed, and such is not the intent of these cautionary remarks. The intent is to suggest that in choosing between the formal and the informal, the regular and the offbeat, the general and the special, the orthodox and the heretical, the beginner err on the side of conservatism, on the side of established usage. No idiom is taboo, no accent forbidden; there is simply a better

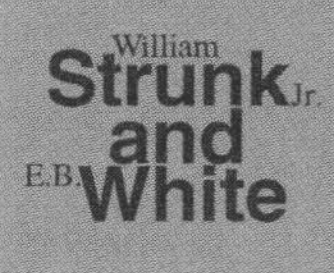


chance of doing well if the writer holds a steady course, enters the stream of English quietly, and does not thrash about.

"But," the student may ask, "what if it comes natural to me to experiment rather than conform? What if I am a pioneer, or even a genius?" Answer: then be one. But do not forget that what may seem like pioneering may be merely evasion, or laziness—the disinclination to submit to discipline. Writing good standard English is no cinch, and before you have managed it you will have encountered enough rough country to satisfy even the most adventurous spirit.

Style takes its final shape more from attitudes of mind than from principles of composition, for, as an elderly practitioner once remarked, "Writing is an act of faith, not a trick of grammar." This moral observation would have no place in a rule book were it not that style *is* the writer, and therefore what a man is, rather than what he knows, will at last determine his style. If one is to write, one must believe—in the truth and worth of the scrawl, in the ability of the reader to receive and decode the message. No one can write decently who is distrustful of the reader's intelligence, or whose attitude is patronizing.

Many references have been made in this book to "the reader"—he has been much in the news. It is now necessary to warn the writer that his concern for the reader must be pure: he must sympathize with the reader's plight (most readers are in trouble about half the time) but never seek to know his wants. The whole duty of a writer is to please and satisfy himself, and the true writer always plays to an audience of one. Let him start sniffing the air, or glancing at the Trend Machine, and he is as good as dead, although he may make a nice living.

Full of his beliefs, sustained and elevated by the power of his purpose, armed with the rules of grammar, the writer is ready for exposure. At this point, he may well pattern himself on the fully exposed cow of Robert Louis Stevenson's rhyme. This friendly and commendable animal, you may recall, was "blown by all the winds that pass/And wet with all the showers." And so must the young writer be. In our modern idiom, we would say that he must get wet all over. Mr. Stevenson, working in a plainer style, said it with felicity, and suddenly one cow, out of so many, received the gift of immortality. Like the steadfast writer, she is at home in the wind and the rain; and, thanks to one moment of felicity, she will live on and on and on.

# Index

## A

## B



## C

## D

## E

## F



## G

## N



## O

## P

## S

## T



## U



## V

## W



## Y

## Acknowledgments

(continued from page v)

### Text

**10** From "They Dance Alone" on *Nothing Like the Sun* by Sting. Copyright © by Unichappel, Inc. Published by Magnetic Publishing Ltd. **14** From *Portrait in Motion* by Arthur Ashe with Frank Deford. Copyright © 1975 by Arthur Ashe and Frank Deford. Published by Houghton Mifflin Company. **24** From *100 Successful College Applications*, edited by Christopher J. Georges and Gigi E. Georges with members of the staff of the *Harvard Independent*. Copyright © 1988 by Harvard Independent. Published by Penguin U.S.A. **33** From *Time Magazine*, January 25, 1963. **34** From *The Brand X Anthology of Poetry* edited by William Zaranka. Copyright © 1981 by Apple-wood Books, Inc. Published by Apple-wood Books, Inc. **40, 42** "My Face" by Gail Godwin from *The Bread Loaf Anthology* edited by Robert Pack and Jay Parini. Copyright © 1982 by Gail Godwin. Published by University Press of New England. **62** From *Black Women Writers at Work* edited by Claudia Tate. Copyright © 1983 by Claudia Tate. Published by The Continuum Publishing Company. **69** From "Is Our Democracy at Risk?" by Barbara Jordan. Copyright © 1988 by Barbara Jordan. Published by Houghton Mifflin Company. **72** From *Green Thoughts* by Eleanor Perényi. Copyright © 1981 by Eleanor Perényi. Published by Random House, Inc. **74, 75, 76** From "Science Can't Give Us Everything" by Sydney J. Harris from *The Best of Sydney J. Harris*. Copyright © 1975 by Sydney J. Harris. Published by Houghton Mifflin Company. **78** From *Unbuilding* by David Macaulay. Copyright © 1980 by David Macaulay. Published by Houghton Mifflin Company. **80** Excerpt from *Lucy* by Jamaica Kincaid. Copyright © 1990 by Jamaica Kincaid. Reprinted by permission of Farrar, Straus & Giroux, Inc. **83** Edited manuscript by Eudora Welty from *Women Writers at Work: The* Paris Review *Interviews* edited by George Plimpton. Copyright © 1989 The Paris Review, Inc. Published by the Penguin Group. **87** From *On Writing Well* by William Zinsser. Copyright © 1988 by William Zinsser. Published by Harper & Row, Publishers. **88** From "Woolgathering, Ventriloquism, and the Double Life" by Diana Chang from *The Third Woman: Minority Women Writers of the United States* edited by Dexter Fisher. Copyright © 1970 by Diana Chang. Published by Houghton Mifflin Company. **96** From "Mr. Mistoffelees" by T. S. Eliot from *Old Possum's Book of Cats* by T. S. Eliot. Copyright © 1967 by Esme Valerie Eliot. Published by Harcourt Brace Jovanovich, Publishers (t); from *A Brief History of Time* by Stephen W. Hawking. Copyright © 1988 by Stephen W. Hawking. Published by Bantam Books (b). **98** "Wind and Silver" by Amy Lowell. Copyright © 1983 by Houghton Mifflin Company. Published by Houghton Mifflin Company (l); from "Moons" by John Haines from *The Stone Sharp* by John Haines. Copyright © 1967 by John Haines. Published by Holt, Rinehart, and Winston, Inc. (r). **99** From *Dombey and Son* by Charles Dickens. Copyright © 1848 by Charles Dickens. Published by Oxford University Press. **104, 106** "Georgia O'Keeffe" from *The White Album* by Joan Didion. Copyright © 1979 by Joan Didion. Published by Simon and Schuster. **120** From *Things Fall Apart* by Chinua Achebe. Copyright © 1959 Chinua Achebe. Published by McDowell, Oblensky. **122** From *The Remains of the Day* by Kazuo Ishiguro. Copyright © 1989 by Kazuo Ishiguro. Published by Alfred A. Knopf. **122-23** From "The Hornet's Nest" by Feng Jicai from *Chrysanthemums and Other Stories* by Feng Jicai. Copyright © 1983 by Susan Wilf Chen. Published by Harcourt Brace Jovanovich, Publishers (t); from "Phantom Place" by Isabel Allende from *The Stories of Eva Luna* by Isabel Allende. English translation copyright © 1991 by Macmillan Publishing Company. Published by Macmillan Inc. (b). **126** From *West with the Night* by Beryl Markham. Copyright © 1983 by Beryl Markham. Published by Houghton Mifflin Company. **130** From *The Harder They Fall* by Budd Schulberg. Copyright © 1947 by Budd Schulberg. Published by Random House. **135** From *Stephen Crane: Prose and Poetry* arranged by J. C. Levenson. Copyright © 1984 by Literary Classics of the United States, Inc. Published by the Press Syndicate of the University of Cambridge. **138** From *Tar Baby* by Toni Morrison. Copyright © 1981 by Toni Morrison. Published by Alfred A. Knopf. **143, 146** From *The Road from Coorain* by Jill Ker Conway. Copyright © 1989 by Jill Conway. Published by Vintage Books. **160** Excerpt from *Lucy* by Jamaica Kincaid. Copyright © 1990 by Jamaica Kincaid. Reprinted by permission of Farrar, Straus & Giroux, Inc. **163** From *The Women of Brewster Place* by Gloria Naylor. Copyright © 1982 by Gloria Naylor. Published by Penguin Books. **164** From *Giants in the Earth* by O. E. Rölvaag. Copyright © 1955 by Jennie Marie Rölvaag. Published by Harper & Row. **166** From *Shoeless Joe* by W. P. Kinsella. Copyright © 1982 by W. P. Kinsella. Published by Houghton Mifflin Company. **170** From "The Rocking-Horse Winner" by D. H. Lawrence from *The Portable D. H. Lawrence*. Copyright © 1933 by the estate of D. H. Lawrence. Published by The Viking Press. **174** From "Maud Martha Spares the Mouse" by Gwendolyn Brooks from *Blacks* by Gwendolyn Brooks. Copyright © 1987 by Gwendolyn Brooks. **178** From *The Joy Luck Club* by Amy Tan. Copyright © 1989 by Amy Tan. Published by Ballantine Books. **182** From "Dialogue on Film: Steven Spielberg" from *American Film: Magazine of the Film and Television Arts*. Copyright © June 1988 by *American Film*. Reprinted by permission. **183** From *The Treasure of the Sierra Madre* by B. Traven. Copyright 1935 by Alfred A. Knopf, Inc. and B. Traven, renewed 1963 by B. Traven (l); from *The Treasure of the Sierra Madre*, edited by James Naremore. Copyright 1979 by The Board of Regents of the University of Wisconsin System (r). **187, 190** From *My Left Foot* by Christy Brown. Copyright © 1954 by Christy Brown. Reprinted by permission of Martin Secker and Warburg Limited. **208** From "New Hairdo, No Angst" by Anne-Marie Schiro. Copyright © July 16, 1981 by *New York Times*. **216** From *Since Yesterday: The 1930s in America* by Frederick Lewis Allen. Copyright © 1968 by Agnes Rogers Allen. Published by Harper & Row, Publishers. **217** From "The Great American Cooling Machine" by Frank Trippet from *The Riverside Reader: Second Edition*. Copyright © 1987 by Houghton Mifflin Company. Published by Houghton Mifflin. **218-19** From *1941: Our Lives in a World on the Edge* by William Klingaman. Copyright © 1977 by Lady Spencer Churchill, the Honorable Lady Sarah Audley, the Honorable Lady Soames. Published by Houghton Mifflin Company. **223** From *The Fatal Shore* by Robert Hughes. Copyright © 1986 by Robert Hughes. Published by Alfred A. Knopf. **224** From "The Uses of Sidewalks: Safety" by Jane Jacobs from *The Death and Life of Great American Cities* by Jane Jacobs. Copyright © 1961 by Jane Jacobs. Published by Random House (t); from *Heart of Darkness* by Joseph Conrad. Copyright © 1970 by G. P. Putnam's Sons. Published by J. M. Dent & Sons (b). **230** From *Buckminster Fuller's Universe: An Appreciation* by Lloyd Steven Sieden. Copyright © 1989 by Lloyd Steven Sieden. Published by Plenum Publishing Corp. **234** From "I'm innocent, pal" by Brock Yates from *Car and Driver*. Copyright © 1990 by *Car and Driver*. Published by Car and Driver Inc. **235** From "Are America's carmakers headed for the junkyard?" from *The Economist*, April 14, 1990. **236** From "Good Country People" by Flannery O'Connor from *A Good Man Is Hard to Find* by Flannery O'Connor. Copyright © 1983 Regina O'Connor. Published by Harcourt Brace Jovanovich. **244** From "The Myth of the Welfare Rancher" by Sharman Apt Russell from *New York Times*. Copyright © July 19, 1991 by *New York Times*. **245** From "The Price Is Wrong" by George Wuerthner from *Sierra Club Magazine*. Copyright © 1990 by *Sierra Club Magazine*. **247** From "Columbus as Well as Western Civilization Should Be Honored," by Michael S. Berliner, in *The Boston Herald*, January 5, 1992 (t); from *Bill Moyers: A World of Ideas*, edited by Betty Sue Flowers. Copyright 1989 by Public Affairs Television, Inc. Published by Doubleday (b). **249** From *Morgan the Magnificent: the Life of J. Pierpont Morgan (1837-1913)* by John K. Winkler. Copyright © 1930 by John K. Winkler. Published by The Vanguard Press, New York (t); from *Corsair: The Life of J. Pierpont Morgan* by Andrew Sinclair. Copyright © 1981 by Andrew Sinclair. Published by Little, Brown and Company (b). **254,**

**256** Excerpt from "What's That Pig Outdoors?" by Henry Kisor. Copyright © 1990 Henry Kisor. Reprinted by permission of Farrar, Straus & Giroux, Inc. **268** Excerpt from *The Miami Herald* article by Dave Barry May 14, 1989. **270** From *Dr. Kookie, You're Right* by Mike Royko. Copyright © 1989 by Mike Royko. Published by E. P. Dutton. **273** © 1985, The Boston Globe Newspaper Company/Washington Post Writers Group. Reprinted with permission. **287** From "Letter from Birmingham Jail" by Martin Luther King Jr. from *Patterns of Exposition 8* by Randall E. Decker. Copyright © 1980 by Randall E. Decker. Published by Little, Brown and Company. **292** From "Learn with BOOK" by R. J. Heathorn from *Adventures in Appreciation* Pegasus edition. Copyright © 1985 by Harcourt Brace Jovanovich. Published by Harcourt Brace Jovanovich. **298** From "*Breaking Away: A Review*" by Roger Ebert from *Roger Ebert's Movie Home Companion: 1989 Edition.* Copyright © 1988 by Roger Ebert. Published by Andrews and McMeel. **304, 306** "Mother Tongue" by Amy Tan. Copyright © 1990 by Amy Tan. First published by *The Threepenny Review.* **330** Quote from Malcom X, Oxford Union Society Debate, 1964. **336** From "In a Station of the Metro" by Ezra Pound from *Ezra Pound Selected Poems.* Copyright © 1957 by Ezra Pound. Published by New Directions Publishing Company. **342-47** From *The Concord Review*, Summer 1990, Volume Two, Number Four, © 1990, by The Concord Review, Inc., P. O. Box 661, Concord, MA, 01742. Reprinted by permission. **397** Excerpt from *Singing Softly/Cantando Bajito* by Carmen de Monteflores. Copyright © 1989 by Carmen Monteflores. Reprinted by permission of Aunt Lute books (415) 558-8116. **410** "Constantinople's Church" from *World History, The Human Experience.* Copyright © 1992. Published by Glencoe/McGraw-Hill. **419** Excerpt from "The Tambourine Lady" from *Fever, Twelve Stories* by John Edgar Wideman. Copyright © 1989 by John Edgar Wideman. Reprinted by permission of Henry Holt and Company, Inc. **442** From *Heart of Darkness* by Joseph Conrad. Copyright © 1984. Published by Viking Penguin. **449** Excerpt from *The Remains of the Day* by Kazuo Ishiguro. Reprinted by permission of Random House, Inc. **456** From *Mark Twain's Own Autobiography* by Mark Twain. Copyright © 1990. Published by the University of Wisconsin Press. **462** From *The Rise of Silas Lapham* by William Dean Howells. Copyright © 1983. Published by Viking Penguin. **468** From *Oliver Twist* by Charles Dickens. Copyright © 1982. Published by Bantam. **475** Excerpt from "The Milk Run" from *Ocean of Story* by Christina Stead. Copyright © 1985, the estate of Christina Stead. Reprinted by permission of Penguin Books Australia, Ltd. **489** Excerpt from *1984* by George Orwell. Copyright 1949 by Harcourt Brace Jovanovich, Inc. Copyright renewed 1977 by Sonia Brownell Orwell. Reprinted by permission of Harcourt Brace Jovanovich, Inc. **497** From *Lord Jim* by Joseph Conrad. Copyright © 1981. Published by Bantam. **516** From *Ulysses* by James Joyce. Copyright © 1992. Published by Random House. **518** From *The Picture of Dorian Gray* by Oscar Wilde. Copyright © 1985. Published by Random House. **525** Excerpt from "Araby" from *Dubliners* by James Joyce. Copyright 1916 by B. W. Heubsch. Definitive text copyright © 1967 by the Estate of James Joyce. Used by permission of Viking Penguin, a division of Penguin Books USA Inc. **558** Excerpt from *The House of the Spirits* by Isabel Allende. Reprinted by permission of Random House, Inc. **563** Excerpt from "Liars Don't Qualify" by Junius Edwards from *Urbanite* Vol. 1, No. 4, June 1961. Reprinted by permission of the author. **580** Excerpt from *The Radiance of the King* by Camara Laye, translated from the French by James Kirkup. Copyright © 1956 Librairie Plon. English translation copyright © 1965 Wm. Collins Sons & Co., Ltd. Copyright © 1971 by Macmillan Publishing Company. Reprinted with the permission of Macmillan Publishing Company. **585** Excerpt from "Reapers" from *Cane* by Jean Toomer. Copyright © 1923 by Boni & Liveright, Inc. Copyright © 1951 by Liveright Publishing Company. Reprinted by permission of W. W. Norton & Co. From *Heavy Wings* by Zhang Jie. Copyright © 1989. Published by Grove-Atlantic Monthly Press; from *The Geographical History of America* by Gertrude Stein. Copyright © 1936. Published by Random House. Matthew 22:14 from the Bible; from *Candide* by Voltaire. Copyright © 1950. Published by Viking Penguin. **589** From "Dream Children: A Reverie" by Charles Lamb from *Essays of Elia.* Copyright © 1962. Published by New American Library - Dutton. **606** From *The Hound of the Baskervilles* by Sir Arthur Conan Doyle. Copyright © 1981. Published by Viking Penguin. **611** From "The Train from Rhodesia" by Nadine Gordimer from *Soft Voice of the Serpent, and Other Stories.* Copyright © 1952. Published by Simon & Schuster; from "The Charge of the Light Brigade" by Alfred, Lord Tennyson from *The New Oxford Book of Victorian Verse.* Copyright © 1987. Published by Oxford University Press; from "A Mild Attack of Locusts" by Doris Lessing from *African Stories.* Copyright © 1965. Published by Simon & Schuster; Fragment from a work by Quintus Ennius from *The Tragedies of Ennius: The Fragments.* Copyright © 1969. Published by Books on Demand; from "Macbeth" by William Hazlitt. Copyright © 1921. Published by Charles Scribner's Sons. **630** Excerpt from *The Kitchen God's Wife* by Amy Tan. Copyright © 1991 by Amy Tan. Reprinted by permission of The Putnam Publishing Group. **635** From "Big Two Hearted River: Part II." by Ernest Hemingway from *The Complete Short Stories of Ernest Hemingway: The Finca Vigia Edition.* Copyright © 1991. Published by Macmillian. **648** From *Typee* by Herman Melville. Copyright © 1964. Published by New American Library - Dutton; from *Their Eyes Were Watching God* by Zora Neale Hurston. Copyright © 1990. Published by Harper Collins; from *Travels with Charley in Search of America* by John Steinbeck. Copyright © 1980. Published by Viking Penguin; from "Questions of Travel" by Elizabeth Bishop from *Elizabeth Bishop–The Complete Poems, 1927–1979.* Copyright 1984. Published by F S & G; from *Invisible Cities* by Italo Calvino. Copyright © 1978. Published by Harcourt Brace. **670** Excerpt from *A House for Mr. Biswas* by V. S. Naipaul. Copyright © 1961, 1969, 1983 by V. S. Naipaul. Reprinted by permission of Alfred A. Knopf. **673** From *An American Childhood* by Annie Dillard. Copyright © 1988. Published by Harper Collins. **697** From "The Winner" by Barbara Kimenye from *Looking for a Rain God; an Anthology of Contemporary African Short Stories.* Copyright © 1990. Published by Simon & Schuster. **712** Excerpt from *The Old Patagonian Express* by Paul Theroux. Copyright © 1979 by Cape Cod Scriveners Company. Reprinted by permission of Houghton Mifflin Company. All rights reserved. **717** From *Bleak House* by Charles Dickens. Copyright © 1985. Published by Bantam. **740** From *Readers' Guide to Periodical Literature*, July 1991, Volume 91, Number Seven. Copyright © 1991 by The H.W. Wilson Company. **745** From *Webster's Ninth New Collegiate Dictionary.* Copyright © 1991 by Merriam-Webster, Inc. Published by Merriam-Webster, Inc. **746** From *Roget's International Thesaurus*, revised by Robert L. Chapman. Copyright © 1977 by Harper & Row, Publishers, Inc. **747** From *The New American Roget's Thesaurus*, revised by Philip D. Morehead. Copyright © 1958, 1962 by Albert H. Morehead; copyright © 1978 by Andrew T. Morehead and Philip D. Morehead. **750** From *The Scarlet Letter* by Nathaniel Hawthorne. Copyright © 1981. Published by Bantam; from "The Adventure of the Devil's Foot" by Sir Arthur Conan Coyle from *Sherlock Holmes Through Time and Space.* Copyright © 1984. Published by Bluejay Books. **787-852** *Elements of Style* (Third Edition), by William Strunk Jr. and E. B. White, Copyright © 1979, Macmillan Publishing Co., Inc. Earlier editions © 1959 and © copyright 1972 by Macmillan Publishing Co., Inc. Reprinted by permission of Macmillan Publishing Co.

## Photos

AR=Art Resource, New York; EF=Eric Futran; RJB=Ralph J. Brunke; SB=Stock Boston, Inc.; SK=Stephen Kennedy; TIB=The Image Bank, Chicago, Schlowsky=Schlowsky Photography.

**Front Cover** **ii** EF (bottom half of the page). **iii** North Carolina Museum of Art, Raleigh, Purchased with funds from the State of North Carolina. **xxiv** Betsy Bassette (tl); Gwendolyn Cates (tc); Joe Willis (tr); John Soares (cr); RJB (c); **1** Wassily Kandinsky, *Improvisation with Green Center*, No. 176, oil on canvas, 109.9-by-120.6 cm, Arthur Jerome Eddy Memorial Collection, © 1992 The Art Institute of Chicago. **4** RJB. **5** RJB. **6** RJB. **7, 8** RJB. **9** Norman Owen Tomalin/Bruce Coleman, Inc. **10** Robert Frerck/Odyssey Productions. **11** Robert Llewellyn/Superstock. **13** Courtesy of The City of Oakland, The Oakland Museum, 1991. **14** Schlowsky. **15** © 1977 by Webb & Bower Ltd./photo by Schlowsky Photography. **16** Schlowsky. **17** Private collection (br). **18** David M. Barron/Earthwatch. **20** Schlowsky. **22** Schlowsky. **30** Schlowsky. **32** ©Touchstone/Archive Photo. **33** Kenzo Okada, 1902–1958. 131.7-by-104.4 cm. The Brooklyn Museum of Art. 59.87 Gift of Joseph Cantor. **34** Movie Still Archives. **37** The Metropolitan Museum of Art, The Alfred Stieglitz Collection, 1949. **47** Superstock. **51** EF (both). **54** Gwendolen Cates. **55** Schlowsky. **56** Gwendolen Cates. **57** Gwendolen Cates. **58** Chicago Tribune/photo by Schlowsky. **59** Schlowsky. **60** Spencer Grant/Stock Boston, Inc. **63** Firenze Accademia Nimatallah/AR, NY. **67** '52-61-58: Philadelphia Museum of Art:The A. E. Gallatin Collection. **68** Stuart Cohen/COMSTOCK, Inc. (tl); P.R. Productions/Superstock (bl); Cliff Feulner/TIB (cl). **72** Dave Forbert/Superstock. **78** Yagy Studio I/Superstock; **81** Tate Gallery/The Bridgeman Art Library. **82** Clive Barda Photography/London. **85** Worcester Art Museum, Worcester, MA. Gift of Mr. and Mrs. Albert W. Rice. **86** Drawing by Frascino; ©1978. The New Yorker Magazine, Inc. **88** Drawing by Handelsman: © 1978 The New Yorker Magazine, Inc. **93** Giraudon/AR, NY. **98** ©The Phillips Collection, Washington, D.C. **101** North Carolina Museum of Art, Raleigh, Purchased with funds from the Sarah Graham Kenan Foundation and the North Carolina Art Society (Robert F. Phifer Bequest). **108** The Metropolitan Museum of Art, The Alfred Stieglitz Collection, 1952 (52.203). **111** EF (both). **114** Gwendolen Cates. **115** The Art Institute of Chicago. **116** The Art Institute of Chicago/photo by Schlowsky (tr); The Art Institute of Chicago (tl). **117** The Art Institute of Chicago. **118** The Art Institute of Chicago (t); The Art Institute of Chicago (b). **119** Schlowsky. **120** Peabody Museum of Salem, Photo by Mark Sexton. **121** Michael Thompson/COMSTOCK, Inc. **125** Christie's, London/Bridgeman Art Library. **126** UPI/Bettmann (tl); M. Kahl/FPG International Corp. (c). **130** Guido Alberto Rossi/TIB. **132** Steve Vidler/Superstock. **133** Joan Miró, *Landscape (The Hare)*. Autumn 1927; Solomon R. Guggenheim Museum, NY; Photo by David Heald; "Photograph © Solomon R. Guggenheim Foundation." **134** David Madison/Bruce Coleman, Inc. (tr); Bob Wickley/Superstock (tl). **138** Wadsworth Atheneum, Hartford. Ella Gallup Sumner and Mary Catlin Sumner Collection. **141** © Charly Herscovici/AR, NY. **148** Edward Officer, *On the Plains of the Darling*, oil on canvas 44-by-78 cm purchased 1907 Art Gallery of New South Wales. **151** EF (both). **154** John Soares. **155** William McMahon/Gamma Liaison. **156** John Soares. **157** John Soares. **158** John Soares (both). **159** Schlowsky. **160** Gwen Fidler/COMSTOCK, Inc. **165** OK Harris Works of Art, NY/Photo by D. James Dee. **166** National Museum of American Art, Smithsonian Institution, Museum Purchase/AR, NY. **168** Movie Still Archives. **170** Courtesy Ralph Gibson. **173** North Carolina Museum of Art, Raleigh, Purchased with funds from the State of North Carolina. **180** UPI/Bettmann (tl); Drawing reproduced by special arrangement with Hirschfeld's exclusive representative, The Margo Feldon Galeries, New York (tr). **181** Staaliche Kunstsammlungen, Dresden/Bridgeman Art Library. **182** ©1985 Warner Brothers, Inc. **183** Wisconsin Center for Film and Theater Research. **195** Collection of Pembroke Herbert. **199** EF (both). **202** Betsy Bassette. **203** Schlowsky. **204** Garden Source Furnishings, Inc. (br); National Survey of Fishing, Hunting, and Wildlife-Associated Recreation. © 1982 U.S. Government Printing Office, Washington, D.C./photo by Schlowsky (bl). **205** Betsy Bassette. **206** Gone Birding! ©1990 by Rupicola VCR Games, Inc./photo by Schlowsky. **207** Schlowsky. **208** Lisa Johnstone, New Images Industries, Inc. (both). **211** *Parson Weems' Fable* by Grant Wood (1939), oil on canvas, #1970.43 Amon Carter Museum, Fort Worth. **212** Schlowsky. **216** UPI/Bettmann. **221** © Curtis Publishing Co. **222** Schlowsky. **225** Mondrian, Piet. *Broadway Boogie-Woogie*. 1942-43. Oil on Canvas, 50-by-50 inches (127-by-127 cm). Collection, The Museum of Modern Art, NY. Given anonymously. **226** Designer's Guide to Creating Charts and Diagrams by Nigel Holmes. **230** © 1960, The Estate of Buckminster Fuller. Courtesy, Buckminster Fuller Institute, Los Angeles. **234** Drawing by William Hamilton; © 1975 The New Yorker Magazine, Inc. **239** AR, NY. **240** Schlowsky. **244** Cows, Jaime Villaseca/TIB; toll booth, D. Blank/FPG International Corp. **248** FPG International Corp. **251** National Gallery London, Reproduced by courtesy of the Trustees (bl); Kenwood House, London/The Bridgeman Art Library (br). **259** Courtesy Sydney Janis Gallery, NY. **261** EF (both). **264** Joe Willis. **265** American Red Cross/Schlowsky. **266** Joe Willis. **267** Archive Photo (c); American Red Cross/Schlowsky (tr); Schlowsky (b). **269** Erma Bombeck ©1978 Erma Bombeck (l), Ambrose Bierce ©1988 University of Nebraska Press (c), E.B. White © 1954 E.B.White (r)/photo by Schlowsky. **270** Art Director/Designer George Lois, Photographer Carl Fischer. **275** Giraudon/AR. **279** National Museum of American Art, Washington, DC/AR, NY. **280** Dilbert reprinted by permission of United Feature Syndicate, Inc. **284** Collier's Cover 9/26/1903 by Frederick Dorr Steele. **290** Schlowsky. **293** Duane Hanson's "Tourists" 1970, Scottish National Gallery of Modern Art. **294** Drawing by Mort Gerberg; © 1975. The New Yorker Magazine, Inc. (t); Cathy © 1977 Cathy Guisewite, Universal Press Syndicate, Inc. All Rights Reserved (b). **295** Carraro/Gamma Liaison (l); painting by Philip Burke (r). **296** Reprinted with permission of the Philadelphia Business Journal, Inc. **298** Courtesy Andrews and McMeel. **301** ©1992 Richard Serra/ARS, NY photo courtesy of Leo Castelli Gallery, NY. **310** Musee Guimet, Giraudon/AR, NY. **313** EF (both). **315** Daniel J. Terra Collection, Terra Museum of American Art, Chicago. **316** Schlowsky. **318** Schlowsky. **322** Collection of Charles Cowles, NY (tl); Rosenthal Art Slides (br). **326** The Boston Public Library Archives, photo by Schlowsky. **330** Schmid/Langsfeld/TIB. **336** Schlowsky. **340** Schlowsky. **473** North Carolina Museum of Art, Raleigh, Purchased with funds from the State of North Carolina. **496** The Metropolitan Museum of Art, Gift of the Artist, 1990. **523** Albright-Knox Art Gallery, Buffalo, NY. Fellows for Life Fund, 1926. **561** Museum of Modern Art of Latin America, Washington, D.C. **583** British Museum, Museum of Mankind, photo by Michael Holford. **609** Tate Gallery, London/The Bridgeman Art Library. **633** Private collection/Schlowsky. **654** Magritte, René. *The False Mirror*. (1928). Oil on canvas, 21 1/4-by-31 7/8 inches. Collection, The Museum of Modern Art, NY. Purchase. **672** Museum of Modern Art of Latin America, Washington D.C. **687** RJB. **716** Mary-Anne Martin Fine Art, NY; **721** Bob Daemmrich/SB. **723** Schlowsky. **732** Schlowsky. **787** © Macmillan Publishing Co./photo by RJB. **Back Cover** Aaron Haupt.

Picture Research by Ligature, Inc.